Life in a Multi-Cultural Society: Egypt from Cambyses to Constantine and Beyond

Studies in Ancient Oriental Civilization • Volume 51

ERRATA SHEET

Chapter 7: "A Cult Function for the So-Called Faiyum Mummy Portraits?" by Lorelei H. Corcoran

1) The final two lines (following the word "between") are missing from the second paragraph on page 57:

   the use of a triptych of panel portraits in a domestic context and the veneration of Roman ancestor busts.

2) Footnote # 3, page 57 is missing:

   3. See also his comments (1982, pp. 24–27) on "other paintings" that he describes as being produced for veneration or commemoration.

Chapter 9: "The *Kbn.wt* Vessels of the Late Period" by John Coleman Darnell

1) The final four lines of page 69 are repeated at the top of page 70.
2) The middle portion of the sentence which straddles pages 70–71 has been deleted, and footnote 12 is missing; the sentence in full, with the footnotes, is:

   The rushed operations of Antigonos occurred in November,[12] Antigonos attempting to take advantage of the height of the Nile and press on to Memphis with his fleet.[13]

   12. According to Seibert 1969, p. 221, Antigonos left Egypt at the end of November.

   13. D. Bonneau (1964, pp. 77-8) misunderstood Antigonos' strategy, and assumed that the inundation prevented the naval operations of Demetrios. These were hampered by Ptolemy and his small vessels. The operations which the officers decline to carry out due to the inundation (Diodorus XX.76, cited by Bonneau, p. 78 note 1) are land operations, proposed as a last hope of invasion after the failure of the primary, naval plan.

Chapter 34: "Implicit Models of Cross-Cultural Interaction: A Question of Noses, Soap, and Prejudice" by Robert K. Ritner

1) Page 287 should be as follows (*Please see the reverse*):

"Cultures in Conflict," yet the question of cultural animosity was ignored by all speakers.[16] Old concepts of cultural synthesis or subjugation are giving way to theories of cultural separation.[17] While this separation should perhaps please everyone, allowing Greek and Egyptian culture to be "vital" independently, I fear that it can be taken too far, and am suspicious of the underlying motives in *overstressing* the absence of interaction, and wonder whether cultural "vitality" is again confused with cultural "purity."

Consider the 1989 discussion by Heinrich von Staden on the question of the influence of Egyptian medicine on the Alexandrian physician Hierophilus.[18] Von Staden admits certain similarities in terms of pulse taking, drugs, and disease theory, but his arguments are often carried by adjectives, not evidence: Egyptian pulse theory is dismissed as "struggling but insistent,"[19] Egyptian disease theory is "not alien" to the Greek (von Staden 1989, p. 5), the Egyptian physician's touch is "aggressive," the Greek's is "restrained" (von Staden 1989, p. 15). Egyptian enema treatments are said to represent "a pathological preoccupation with the anus ... bound to elicit an ethno-psychological study of Pharaonic Egypt sooner or later" (!!!)[20] It should be added that one Egyptian enema specialist is known to have had enough Greek patients to require the services of a well-paid interpreter; here at least there is cross-cultural preoccupation![21] Having accused the Egyptians of neurotic cleanliness,[22] von Staden then faults them as dirty, for not knowing soap (von Staden 1989, p. 15). Soap, as we know it, was invented in 1787 by the French surgeon Nicolas Leblanc, prompted by an earlier offer of a state prize by Louis XVI.[23] Until then, "soap" had been imported from the Arabs, and had consisted of fats *and natron from the Wadi Natrun*. This was the "soap" that had been available to the Greeks — and before them to the Egyptians. Von Staden's arguments show the survival of the old notion of the low class, cultureless Egyptian, whose influence on superior culture is *unthinkable*.

Old feelings of cultural superiority die hard, but what is important is that such prejudices are often the feelings of *scholars*, not those of the people they study. A good case in point is the famous quotation of Polybius on the Alexandrian population as excerpted by Strabo (XXIV. 14). According to Polybius, the mercenary troops are numerous, rough, and uncivilized, the Alexandrians are mongrels, but the native Egyptians are acute and civilized (οχυ και πολιτικον). This favorable characterization of the Egyptians has generally confounded Classicists, whose models of Egyptian culture were determined by contemporary stereotypes of natives as cultureless, rude, second-class citizens.

16. "Ptolemaic Egypt: Cultures in Conflict" held December 2–3, 1988 at the Brooklyn Museum. Lecturers instead emphasized cooperation and cross-influence between cultures. A direct question posed by this author regarding the validity of the notion of "cultures in conflict" generated complete disavowal.

17. See A. Samuel 1989, passim; idem 1983, especially pp. 105–17 ; and Bagnall 1988, pp. 21–27.

18. Reviewed by myself 1989, pp. 39–40.

19. Von Staden 1989, p. 10. Egyptian influence here is said to be "not inconceivable."

20. Von Staden 1989, p. 12. This hyperbolic bombast derives from the author's distortion of Egyptian disease theory, which prescribed enemas and emetics for internal complaints in preference to bleeding. A reasoned analysis is found in Steuer 1948 and Steuer and Saunders 1959.

21. Admitted grudgingly in von Staden 1989, p. 26. The author insists that this must be an isolated case in Alexandria since "evidence of this kind is very rare"; in fact, evidence *of any kind* from Alexandria is "very rare" and generalizations about medical interactions are mere speculation. Bagnall 1981, p. 18, attempts to find in this transaction "deeper and darker aspects" of the Greek "exploitative attitude" since it involves mercenary motives. Bagnall is unaware of the theoretical basis of the Egyptian treatment, which is dismissed as "primitive" and "a toy" (in contrast to "Hellenistic science"): "I forbear to offer modern parallels to exotic practices like this becoming fashionable." Smirking remarks aside, the supposed "toy" of suppository and enema treatment remains a basic adjunct to modern medical practice; it is in no sense "exotic." Where, however, is the "Hellenistic science" of bleeding?

22. Von Staden 1989, p. 12: "legendary obsession with personal cleanliness."

23. A good, popular account of the tragi-comic development of modern soap is found in Bodanis 1986, pp. 206–09.

STUDIES IN ANCIENT ORIENTAL CIVILIZATION • No. 51

THE ORIENTAL INSTITUTE OF THE UNIVERSITY OF CHICAGO

THOMAS A. HOLLAND, Editor

Richard M. Schoen, Assistant Editor

LIFE IN A MULTI-CULTURAL SOCIETY: EGYPT FROM CAMBYSES TO CONSTANTINE AND BEYOND

Edited by

JANET H. JOHNSON

THE ORIENTAL INSTITUTE OF THE UNIVERSITY OF CHICAGO

STUDIES IN ANCIENT ORIENTAL CIVILIZATION • No. 51

CHICAGO • ILLINOIS

Library of Congress Catalog Card Number 92-60741

ISBN: 0-918986-84-2

The Oriental Institute, Chicago

Published 1992. Printed in the United States of America.

Cover Illustration: Facsimile Drawing of the Central Portion of the Rosetta Stone. After Stephen Quirke and Carol Andrews, *The Rosetta Stone, facsimile drawing with Introduction and Translations* (London: The Trustees of the British Museum, 1988).

TABLE OF CONTENTS

LIFE IN A MULTI-CULTURAL SOCIETY: EGYPT FROM CAMBYSES TO CONSTANTINE (AND BEYOND)

in conjunction with the

Fourth International Congress of Demotists

The Oriental Institute, The University of Chicago
September 4–8, 1990

Tuesday, September 4
James Henry Breasted Hall, The Oriental Institute

1:00–1:15 *OPENING REMARKS*
JANET H. JOHNSON, The Oriental Institute, The University of Chicago
WELCOME
WILLIAM M. SUMNER, Director, The Oriental Institute, The University of Chicago

1:15–6:00 *EGYPTIAN SOCIETY FROM CAMBYSES TO CHRISTIANITY*
Chair: WILLY CLARYSSE, Katholieke Universiteit Leuven

KARL-THEODOR ZAUZICH, The University of Würzburg*
Ein Zug nach Nubien unter Amasis

LISA HEIDORN, The Oriental Institute, The University of Chicago* and § (1991)
The Persian Claim to Kush in Light of Evidence from Lower Nubia

H. S. SMITH, University College London*
Foreigners in the Documents from the Sacred Animal Necropolis at Saqqara, an Interim Report

J. D. RAY, Cambridge University*
The Jews in Late Period Egypt

BREAK

JAN QUAEGEBEUR, Katholieke Universiteit Leuven*
Greco-Egyptian Double Names as a Feature of a Bi-Cultural Society, The Case Ψοσνεῦς ὁ καὶ Τριάδελφος

ROBERT S. BIANCHI, Brooklyn Museum*
A Group of Seated Male Figures from the Faiyum

SHARON HERBERT, Kelsey Museum of Archaeology, The University of Michigan
Excavations at Coptos: Reflections of Ethnicity in the Archaeological Record

THELMA K. THOMAS, Kelsey Museum of Archaeology, The University of Michigan*
Greeks or Copts?: Documentary and Other Evidence for Artistic Patronage during the Late Roman and Early Byzantine Period at Heracleopolis Magna and Oxyrhynchus

---

* after the name and affiliation of the participant indicates inclusion of the paper in this volume.

§ and a year after the name and affiliation of the participant indicates the publication of the paper elsewhere. Please consult the *Bibliography* for the complete reference.

BREAK

MARILINA BETRÒ, The University of Pisa
Aspects of Cultural Interactions in Greco-Roman Egypt: The Medical-Botanic Culture

JOHN DARNELL, The Oriental Institute, The University of Chicago*
Kbn - triremes

DOMINIC MONTSERRAT, University College London§ (1991)
Puberty Rituals in Roman Egypt

ALAN K. BOWMAN, Oxford University
Property, Status, and Ethnicity in Early Roman Egypt

Wednesday, September 5
James Henry Breasted Hall, The Oriental Institute

9:00–12:00 *LITERATURE & LITERACY*
Chair: LUDWIG KOENEN, The University of Michigan

ALESSANDRO ROCCATI, The University of Rome*
Writing Egyptian: Scripts and Speeches at the End of Pharaonic Civilization

DOROTHY THOMPSON, Cambridge University*
Literacy in Ptolemaic Egypt

JAN MERTENS, Katholieke Universiteit Leuven*
Bibliography and Description of Demotic Literary Texts: A Progress Report

W. J. TAIT, University College London*
Demotic Literature and Egyptian Society

BREAK

HEINZ-JOSEF THISSEN, The University of Marburg
Das demotische Gedicht vom Harfner als Produkt der Begegnung mit griechischer Literatur

PETER PICCIONE, The Oriental Institute, The University of Chicago
Did Setne play Senet?

STANLEY BURSTEIN, California State University, Los Angeles*
The Egyptian History of Hecataeus of Abdera

1:30–5:00 *BILINGUAL TEXTS*
Chair: JOHN D. RAY, Cambridge University

RICHARD STEINER, Yeshiva University
Was the Scribe of P. Amherst 63 Bilingual?

BEZALEL PORTEN, Hebrew University*
Aramaic-Demotic Equivalents: Who is the Borrower and Who the Lender?

WILLIAM BRASHEAR, Staatliche Museen, Berlin*
Egyptians and Greeks in an Early Laographia Account (P. Berol. 25161)

ANN ELLIS HANSON, The University of Michigan*
The Agricultural Accounts of Lucius (P. Mich. inv. 880, P. Princ. *3.152)*

JAMES MIDGELY, Macquarie University*
P. Macquarie inv. 499: A Bilingual Text from the Macquarie University Collection

BREAK

EMMANUEL TASSIER, Katholieke Universiteit Leuven*
Greek and Demotic School-Exercises

E. VAN'T DACK, Katholieke Universiteit Leuven/Koninklijke Academie van België*
L'armée, microcosme d'un monde multiculturel?

S. HÉRAL, Katholieke Universiteit Leuven/Sorbonne*
Archives bilingues de nomarques dans les papyrus de Ghôran

LUDWIG KOENEN, The University of Michigan*
Early Roman Texts from Oxyrhynchus

5:15–7:00 *BYZANTINE EGYPT*
Chair: BEZALEL PORTEN, Hebrew University

TERRY WILFONG, The Oriental Institute, The University of Chicago§ (1990)
The Archive of a Family of Moneylenders at Jême

JAMES KEENAN, Loyola University, Chicago§ (1990)
Evidence for the Byzantine Army in the Syene Papyri

J. JOEL FARBER, Franklin & Marshall College§ (1990)
Legal and Financial Problems of People in the Patermouthis Archive

G. HUSSON, The University of Rouen§ (1990)
Les maisons de Syène dans les archives de Patermouthis

LESLIE MACCOULL, The Society for Coptic Archaeology§ (1990)
Christianity at Elephantine/Syene/Aswan

Thursday, September 6
James Henry Breasted Hall, The Oriental Institute

8:30–1:15 *CHURCH & STATE*
Chair: ROBERT K. RITNER, The Oriental Institute, The University of Chicago

WERNER HUSS, The University of Bamberg*
Gedanken zum Thema "Staat" und "Kirche" im ptolemäischen Ägypten

JOHN F. OATES, Duke University*
The Basilikos Grammateus in the Ptolemaic Administration

LINDA RICKETTS,† The University of North Dakota*
The Administration of Late Ptolemaic Egypt

SCHAFIK ALLAM, The University of Tübingen*
Observations on Egyptian Law Courts

CARY J. MARTIN, University College London*
Demotic Contracts as Evidence in a Court Case

BREAK

LANNY BELL, The Oriental Institute, The University of Chicago
Alexander as an Egyptian God-King

E. LANCIERS, Katholieke Universiteit Leuven*
Die ägyptischen Priester des ptolemäischen Königskultes

HERWIG MAEHLER, University College London*
Visitors to the Temple of Khnûm on Elephantine: Who Were They?

BREAK

J. K. WINNICKI, The University of Warsaw
Pkalasiris—a Libyan or a Syrian God in Roman Egypt?

ROGER V. MCCLEARY, Kelsey Museum of Archaeology, The University of Michigan*
Ancestor Cults at Terenouthis in Lower Egypt: A Case for Greco-Roman Oecumenism

LORELEI CORCORAN, Memphis State University*
A Cult Function for the So-Called "Faiyum Mummy Portraits"?

J. VAN HAELST, Centre National de la Recherche Scientifique
Les débuts du christianisme dans la province égyptienne à la lumière des découvertes papyrologiques

3:00–6:00 *ROUND TABLE/CLOSING REMARKS*
Chair: RICHARD SALLER, The University of Chicago

WILLY CLARYSSE, Katholieke Universiteit Leuven*
Some Greeks in Demotic Documents

ROGER BAGNALL, Columbia University§ (forthcoming)
Languages, Literacy, and Ethnicity in Late Roman Egypt

ROBERT K. RITNER, The Oriental Institute, The University of Chicago*
Implicit Models of Cross-Cultural Interaction: A Question of Noses, Soap, and Prejudice

BREAK

EVERYONE, *Round Table*

Friday, September 7
Pick Hall, Room 218

8:30–11:15 *QUESTIONS FROM DEMOTIC TEXTS*
Chair: A.-H. NUR-EL-DIN, The University of Cairo

MARK SMITH, Oxford University§ (1991)
Did Psammetichus I Die Abroad?

OLA EL-AGUIZY, The University of Cairo*
Is Demotic a New Script?

SVEN VLEEMING, The University of Leiden*
The Tithe of the Scribes (and) Representatives

EUGENE D. CRUZ-URIBE, Northern Arizona University*
The Lake of Moeris: A Reprise

BREAK

URSULA KAPLONY-HECKEL, The University of Marburg*
Thebanische Feldermessung nach enchorischen Dokumente

RENATE MÜLLER-WOLLERMANN, The University of Tübingen*
Demotische Termini zur Landesgliederung Ägyptens

JOSEPH MANNING, The Oriental Institute, The University of Chicago
On the Status Designation "Occupation Title + B3k + Divine Name" in Ptolemaic Demotic Texts

The Oriental Institute, Rooms 212, 216, and 220

11:30–1:00 GEORGE R. HUGHES, JANET H. JOHNSON, ROBERT K. RITNER, & STAFF
Chicago Demotic Dictionary Project

Saturday, September 8
Pick Hall, Room 218

9:00–12:30 *PROJECTS*

Chair: GEORGE R. HUGHES, The Oriental Institute, The University of Chicago

MARILINA BETRÒ and SERGIO VOLPI, The University of Pisa
Computerized Analysis of the Determinatives in the Archive of Medinet Madi

URSULA KAPLONY-HECKEL, The University of Marburg*
The Medinet Habu Ostraca

BREAK

MICHEL CHAUVEAU, Institut Français d'Archéologie Orientale du Cairo
Copenhagen Project

JAN MERTENS, Katholieke Universiteit Leuven*
Bibliography and Description of Demotic Literary Texts: A Progress Report

HEINZ-JOSEF THISSEN, The University of Marburg
Einführung in die Demotistik

2:00–5:45 *TEXTS*

Chair: KARL-THEODOR ZAUZICH, The University of Würzburg

CAROL A. R. ANDREWS, The British Museum*
Unpublished Demotic Texts

WILLY CLARYSSE, Katholieke Universiteit Leuven
A Demotic Census List in the Petrie Papyri

PAOLO GALLO, The University of Pisa*
Toponyms in the Demotic-Greek Ostraca from Medinet Madi

RICHARD JASNOW, The Oriental Institute, The University of Chicago
A Demotic Wisdom Text in the Ashmolean Museum (P. Ashm. 1984.77)

BRIAN MUHS, The University of Pennsylvania*
Demotic Ostraca from the 3rd Century B.C.

BREAK

A.-H. NUR-EL-DIN, The University of Cairo*
Report on New Texts from Tuna-el-Gebel

JAN QUAEGEBEUR, Katholieke Universiteit Leuven
Demotic Ostraca Excavated at ElKab

W. J. TAIT, University College London
Aspects of the Orthography of the Saqqara Demotic Papyri

BREAK

J. K. WINNICKI, The University of Warsaw*
Demotic Graffiti from Terenouthis

LIST OF FIGURES AND ACKNOWLEDGMENTS

LIST OF PLATES AND ACKNOWLEDGMENTS

CHAPTER 3. THE CULTURAL TRANSFORMATION OF EGYPT AS SUGGESTED BY A GROUP OF ENTHRONED MALE FIGURES FROM THE FAIYUM

Photographs of Documents A-1, B-4, C-1, and D-2 courtesy of The Egyptian Museum, Cairo.

Photographs of Documents B-1, B-2, B-3, C-2, C-3, C-4, and E-1 courtesy of The Graeco-Roman Museum, Alexandria.

Photograph of Document D-1 courtesy of The Kelsey Museum of Archaeology, The University of Michigan, Ann Arbor.

CHAPTER 7. A CULT FUNCTION FOR THE SO-CALLED FAIYUM MUMMY PORTRAITS?

Photographs courtesy of the Board of Directors of the Egyptian Museum, Cairo.

CHAPTER 10. ABOUT THE ORIGINS OF EARLY DEMOTIC IN LOWER EGYPT

Hand copy of Stele C 101 and photographs courtesy of Ola el-Aguizy.

CHAPTER 11. THREE MIRRORS WITH DEMOTIC INSCRIPTIONS

Photograph of Mirror Inv. Nr. E 1856 courtesy of Les Musées Royaux d'Art et d'Histoire, Brussels.
Photographs of Mirrors Nr. 292 and JE 46375 courtesy of the Egyptian Museum, Cairo.

CHAPTER 19. A FIRST CENTURY ARCHIVE FROM OXYRHYNCHOS OR OXYRHYNCHITE LOAN CONTRACTS AND EGYPTIAN MARRIAGE

Photograph courtesy of the Special Collections Library, The University of Michigan, Ann Arbor.

CHAPTER 21. VISITORS TO ELEPHANTINE: WHO WERE THEY?

Photographs by H. Maehler; courtesy of the German Archaeological Institute, Cairo.

CHAPTER 23. ANCESTOR CULTS AT TERENOUTHIS IN LOWER EGYPT: A CASE FOR GRECO-EGYPTIAN OECUMENISM

Photographs courtesy of The Kelsey Museum of Archaeology, The University of Michigan, Ann Arbor.

CHAPTER 25. A BILINGUAL ACCOUNT OF MONIES RECEIVED

Photograph courtesy of Professor E. A. Judge, Macquarie University, Sydney, Australia.

CHAPTER 39. GREEKS AND COPTS?: DOCUMENTARY AND OTHER EVIDENCE FOR ARTISTIC PATRONAGE DURING THE LATE ROMAN AND EARLY BYZANTINE PERIODS AT HERACLEOPOLIS MAGNA AND OXYRHYNCHUS, EGYPT

Photograph of Brooklyn Museum 41.1226 courtesy of the Brooklyn Museum.
Photograph of Fragment of Niche Decoration after G. Duthuit (1931).

CHAPTER 43. DEMOTISCHE STELEN AUS TERENUTHIS

Photographs courtesy of J. K. Winnicki.

LIST OF TABLES

PREFACE

Egypt from its incorporation into the Persian Empire in 525 B.C. was home to a multi-cultural society with several strong cultural traditions. An Egyptian majority population lived in contact (sometimes closer, sometimes more distant; sometimes more frequent, sometimes less frequent) with non-Egyptian populations who had come to reside in Egypt. By the Hellenistic period these non-Egyptian populations included large numbers of Greeks and Macedonians who had settled in Egypt after its conquest by Alexander the Great as well as Jews and other semitic-speaking people from Syria-Palestine; after Egypt's incorporation into the Roman Empire, Roman citizens and Roman soldiers from around the Empire appear more and more frequently. Integrated study of the period from Cambyses to Constantine (a period of almost 1000 years), therefore, requires knowledge and appreciation of the material remains (documentary, artistic, architectural, and archaeological) and cultural antecedents of several cultures. The rich documentary and "archaeological" resources preserved from this period would allow it to serve as a model for analysis of other multi-cultural societies.

One serious problem in the study of Egypt during this period is that the Egyptian element in this multi-cultural society has often been undervalued. Classicists, Greek papyrologists, and ancient historians base their studies overwhelmingly on the extensive Greek materials which come primarily from a limited geographical area (the Faiyum) or reflect concerns of the literate, ruling class (in Alexandria). Egyptologists tend to ignore these "late" periods and Egyptian texts, especially those written in Demotic, are notoriously difficult to read; the majority of such texts remain unpublished and the richness of literary and religious texts, the wealth of low- and middle-level administrative documents, and the vast number of private documents (legal and otherwise) remain underutilized in our analyses.

In recent years the field of Demotic studies has attracted more and better prepared scholars who are preparing basic resource tools, cataloguing and publishing major text collections, and incorporating Egyptian materials into historical analyses. As this has happened, scholars in related fields have become aware of the potential information contained in the Egyptian sources and serious discussions have begun about the nature and extent of interaction between individuals and groups with different ethnic or cultural backgrounds.

For this reason, people working on late period Egyptian hieroglyphic and hieratic texts, Aramaicists, Greek papyrologists, classicists and ancient historians, religious and legal historians, archaeologists and art historians working on Egypt during the "late" period were invited to a symposium entitled "Life in a Multi-Cultural Society: Egypt from Cambyses to Constantine (and Beyond)" held in association with the 4th International Congress of Demotists. Over eighty scholars participated in this symposium, which took place at the Oriental Institute, the University of Chicago, in September, 1990. Those whose main scholarly activity involves deciphering, translating, and interpreting written sources interacted with archaeologists and art historians who themselves were tying their artifacts to the literate culture which produced them. Specialists in the various linguistic stages and scripts of the Egyptian language had the opportunity to talk in depth with scholars working on the massive collections of non-Egyptian papyri, especially Greek, which have been found in Egypt.

Major focuses of current research in the various fields represented were discussed; how much each of the "separate" disciplines has to offer to an adequate solution of the problems being tackled by any of us dominated conversations. Everyone talked about interaction — how much interaction was there between Egyptians, Greeks, speakers of various semitic languages, and the like; what did this interaction consist of — among the culturally or politically elite, among the bureaucracy, among the varied inhabitants of a provincial capital, and so on; what is the significance of the amount and type of interaction which did occur? Many people stayed for the more specialized Demotic meetings of the 4th International Congress of Demotists, where more detailed studies of individual Demotic texts or text categories, reports on major projects, and discussions of work in progress were presented.

Most of the papers presented at the Symposium are included in *Life in a Multi-Cultural Society*; the published version has been revised taking into account the formal and informal discussions which took place there. Each individual paper makes a significant contribution to our understanding of an important period in world history, but the volume as a whole is more than the sum of its parts. It shows what a wide range of material and approaches must be considered in the study of complex societies, especially societies preserving several cultural or ethnic traditions. As such, it may serve as inspiration for further studies of multi-cultural societies; with the increasing attention being paid to the multi-cultural aspects of modern societies, this volume has relevance far beyond the apparently narrow confines of Late Antiquity.

The institutions represented at the Symposium underscore the range and diversity of the participants:

Australia	Macquarie University
Belgium	Katholieke Universiteit Leuven; Koninklijke Academie van België
Canada	The University of Toronto
Egypt	Ain Shams University; The Egyptian Museum, Cairo; L'Institut Français d'Archéologie Orientale, Cairo; The University of Cairo
England	The British Museum; Cambridge University; Oxford University; University College London
France	Centre National de la Recherche Scientifique; Sorbonne; The University of Rouen
Germany	Staatliche Museen, Berlin; The University of Bamberg; The University of Marburg; The University of Tübingen; The University of Würzburg
Israel	The Hebrew University
Italy	The University of Pisa; The University of Rome
The Netherlands	The University of Leiden
Poland	Warsaw University

United States	The American Research Center in Egypt; The Brooklyn Museum; California State University, Los Angeles; Columbia University; Duke University; Franklin & Marshall College; The Kelsey Museum of the University of Michigan; Loyola University of Chicago; Memphis State University; The Oriental Institute of the University of Chicago; The Society for Coptic Archaeology; Texas A & M University; The University Museum of the University of Pennsylvania; The University of Chicago; The University of Michigan; The University of Northern Arizona; The University of North Dakota; Yeshiva University

Janet H. Johnson
Chicago, Illinois

July 1992

ACKNOWLEDGMENTS

With the exception of updated bibliographic references, the articles for this volume were written in early 1991. In order to meet our publication schedule, we were unable to accept substantive additions to the content of these articles after September 1991. We would like to thank the contributors for their forbearance in this regard.

Two of the fonts used in this volume — CuneiformOriental and JudeoArabicGan — were provided by Lloyd Anderson (Ecological Linguistics, P. O. Box 15156, Washington, D.C. 20003). The hieroglyphic font was provided by Cleo Huggins (196 Castro Street, Mountain View, CA 94041) and we are especially grateful to Cleo for the three additional signs added to the font for this book. The Greek font, Kadmos, was provided by Marc Cogan (Allotype Typographics, 1600 Packard Road, Suite 5, Ann Arbor, MI 48104). The Coptic font was kindly provided by Professor Ludwig Koenen of The University of Michigan.

The camera-ready screen shots for the plates were made by Lynn Michaels of Color Concept Company, Chicago, IL. We would also like to thank Professor Janet Johnson for the use of her equipment to scan the many Demotic hand copies included in this volume.

The compilation of the *Bibliography* was greatly facilitated by the assistance of Charles Jones, Research Archivist of The Oriental Institute, and his assistants, Terry Wilfong and Paul Cobb. We were also able to use the NCSA Telnet 2.3 -MacTCP- software (National Center of Supercomputing Applications, The University of Illinois, Urbana-Champaign) to access the electronic card catalogs of several university libraries around the country.

The *Index of Authors Cited* and the *Objects Index* were compiled by the Assistant Editor who takes full responsibility for their accuracy and completeness. The Assistant Editor compiled the personal names, place names, and foreign words and phrases for the *General Index*, to which were added subject entries submitted by the authors for their own chapters. We would like to thank the authors for their assistance with the *General Index*. We hope that we have included neither too much nor too little in the indices. We would also like to thank Jim Willis for his careful checking of the final proofs of this book.

Thomas A. Holland, Series Editor
Richard M. Schoen, Assistant Editor

July 1992

CHAPTER 1

OBSERVATIONS ON CIVIL JURISDICTION IN LATE BYZANTINE AND EARLY ARABIC EGYPT*

SCHAFIK ALLAM
University of Tübingen

For our concern it seems opportune to consider a legal conflict between Egyptians, which is made known to us by a number of Coptic and Greek papyri closely connected with each other and extending, as they do, over twenty-five years (for the Coptic Papyrus Budge, see Schiller 1968, pp. 79ff.; for the Greek Papyri BM 2017 and 2018, see Zilliacus 1940, pp. 79ff.; cf. Schiller 1961, pp. 193ff. and 1964, pp. 107ff.; and Allam 1991). All of these documents originally formed part of the private archive of a certain Philēmōn, who lived in Apollonopolis Magna (Edfu) during the first half of the 7th century of our era (for such archives, see Schiller 1953, pp. 368ff. and 1957, pp. 200f.). The story began in the year 622, in the time of the incursion of the Persians into Egypt; the story came to its end in 647, shortly after the Arab conquest of Egypt. It affords invaluable insight into civil jurisdiction in late Byzantine and early Arabic Egypt.

Its subject matter is civil strife over the ownership of a parcel of house-property in Edfu, this real property being given in security for a loan. About this struggle ample information can particularly be derived from the Coptic papyrus which the Library of Columbia University acquired from Sir Wallis Budge in 1932. This lengthy yet outstanding papyrus (of some 286 lines) is a verbatim report of hearings before a board of adjudicators with respect to the disputed house-property. A brief sequence of the events as disclosed in the protracted pleas of the disputants may be given before we endeavor to give any commentary.

The story starts with the mortgage by a woman, named Thekla, of her portion in a house to Philēmōn and his wife in 622 (Schiller 1964, pp. 114f.).[1] The loan (of one holocot) secured by the mortgage was for a fixed term. This security transaction gave to the mortgagees, Philēmōn and his wife, the right of rent-free dwelling in lieu of interest, with the title vesting in the couple upon default in repayment.

Around the time of the Persian incursion, roughly before 629, Thekla left the city to settle down as far as Heracleopolis Magna, in the northern neighborhood of Oxyrhynchos; she had failed, however, to repay the loan. The couple Philēmōn then entered into full title and ownership. In order to secure written evidence of their title, they journeyed north to obtain a title-deed from Thekla. But she refused, and the couple returned empty-handed.

* An outline of this paper was delivered on 6 September 1990 at the interdisciplinary Symposium "Life in a Multi-Cultural Society: Egypt from Cambyses to Constantine (and Beyond)" held at The Oriental Institute of The University of Chicago.

1. The terms employed in the Coptic hearings to designate the pledging of the property in question give no definite clue to the nature of the transaction involved, for the various expressions are loosely used.

We are told that she and her son subsequently addressed several letters to her nephew Iohannes and to her ex-husband Tsoker. Accordingly Iohannes was to repay the amount of the loan and take the house for himself in return for the offerings to be given for Thekla upon her death. Thekla and her son died sometime later.

Thereafter the controversy flared up, as Iohannes laid claim to the portion of the said house and sought to deprive the couple Philēmōn of their possession. The Arab invasion of Egypt apparently caused little stir in the local happenings, for the couple Philēmōn moved down the Nile again to Oxyrhynchos apparently with no intervention by public authorities; and there they obtained a deed of property-transfer (πρᾶσις) from the heirs of Thekla, sometime in the year 644/645. This deed has fortunately come down to us in a Greek papyrus now preserved in the British Museum (no. 2018; Schiller 1964, pp. 116ff.).[2]

Upon their return to Edfu, Iohannes still maintained his claim and refused to surrender possession to the couple. But after a good deal of controversy the two parties agreed to submit their case to mediation by some persons; and the trial probably took place in 646.

As to the duration of the proceedings, which came to pass in Edfu before the mediators, a reference in the address of one party hints at the span of five months. Within this period each party repeatedly set forth the statement of facts favorable to his cause, while trying to categorically discredit the arguments of his adversary. Papyrus Budge makes clear that the complaint (*narratio*) of the plaintiff Iohannes was followed by a rebuttal (*contradictio*) of the defendant Philēmōn. In fact, Iohannes had to present his claim on three successive occasions, and every time he was strongly countered by his adversary, Philēmōn. The record of the hearings, which were a long drawn-out affair, closes with a confirmation of pleas and counterpleas by the parties, the renunciation of further proceedings being assured by the signatures of both parties.

The conclusion to the controversy is disclosed by the final document in the series; this is another Greek papyrus which is also kept in the British Museum (no. 2017). It is a deed of settlement after adjudication (Ἀκυλιανὴ ἀμεριμνεία/διάλυσις),[3] which was issued at the outcome of the hearings. In this deed Iohannes explicitly renounces all his claims and acknowledges the full rights of the couple Philēmōn to the property in dispute. And anticipating that he would be adjudged to pay heavy damages (costs) if he continued to press his claims, he was obligated to sign this deed of settlement on the 16th July 647.

From the standpoint of legal scholars, the matter of major concern in this story might be the recourse of the litigants to a council of mediators in order to bring about an equable and fair ending of their litigation. Through the final document we come to know namely that the mediation was effected by the two parties upon selecting two notables of the city, precisely "two illustrious town councillors" (τοῖς περιβλέπτοις πολιτευομένοις ταύτης τῆς πόλεως, apparently not magistrates). These have to act as judges (δικασταί); evidently they not only have to hear the pleas of the litigants, but they also have to examine the proof set out by them and to adjudicate irrevocably on the disputed house-property.

A crucial point is the total absence of any State trial. Instead, mediation was resorted to for the determination of the controversy. As a matter of fact, settlement of civil controversies by means other than State adjudication was current in Greco-Roman and Byzantine Egypt. The evidence in

2. This deed, which apparently proved conclusive later in the trial, was executed in Oxyrhynchos. It contains the usual enumeration of the rights to be conveyed in such a deed to the addressee, together with the formulae to ensure full enjoyment of ownership by the addressee and his successors. This deed also divests the heirs of any claim to the property which had been mortgaged. It results from the supplemental payment of three holocots for the portion of the house, in addition to the one holocot earlier advanced as a loan. It was drawn up by a notary. The full transaction thus resembles the deeds of cession of late Byzantine times.

3. Schiller 1957, p. 207, thought a settlement agreement was to be called *dialysis*, where the division of property took place; otherwise it was termed ἀμεριμνεία.

the documents clearly illustrates that arbitration as well as settlement after mediation or negotiation were commonly employed as alternatives to State adjudication; these simple means of settling disputes had apparently deep roots in the people's mind.

Some criteria can be provided for identifying the various means of ending disputes instead of State trial. Three methods can be readily discerned:[4] 1) When the disputants voluntarily get together and succeed themselves in terminating their dispute without the intervention of a third person and embody then the terms of their own settlement in a deed, we may call this negotiation. 2) If, however, one or more outsiders without any official authority are called upon to lend their good offices in order to get the disputants to come to terms, this is said to be mediation or conciliation; the suggestion of the mediator is not necessarily binding upon the disputants, since his task is merely to reconcile them. 3) Where the parties choose an arbiter, who agrees to serve, and a decision is reached by him upon inquiry and investigation, there is arbitration (see Steinwenter 1920, pp. 19ff., 52ff.; Schiller 1935, p. 20; Schiller 1953, pp. 370 ff.; and Schiller 1957, pp. 205ff.).[5] His decision is supported by the authority vested in him either by the parties who elected him or because of compulsory arbitration.[6]

Settlement of civil controversies by way of negotiation cannot fairly be considered as a substitute for State adjudication. But the frequency of the other two devices, arbitration and mediation, in our documentation warrants the conclusion that the inhabitants of Egypt took advantage of these methods to end their civil differences without recourse to law-courts.

As far as private arbitration in the late Byzantine period is concerned, there is a close similarity to the familiar device provided by the Roman law for the determination of civil controversies (*arbiter ex compromisso*), which reached its full diffusion at that period (see Modrzejewski 1952, pp. 239ff.; cf. Seidl 1962, pp. 83f.). In our material there are indeed agreements (termed *compromissum* or *pactum compromissi*) concluded before a notary, between the parties in conflict, by which they jointly sought out an arbiter (or arbiters) and further promise to conform to his judgement to the substance; they secure this promise by oath or/and penalty clauses (for damages).[7] The subsequent step of the arbitration process was the agreement between the parties and the arbiter, in which the charge is accepted by the arbiter himself (*receptum arbitri*). Such undertaking is frequently met with in our material as well.[8]

As to the mediation/conciliation, its identification in the documents is much less evident. After a good deal of quarreling, we are often told, the concerned disputants selected an esteemed and trustworthy personality within the community and petitioned him to aid them in finding a way out of their dispute. Although it is difficult to distinguish this rather vague procedure from private arbitration (in the proper sense of the terms *pactum compromissi* and *receptum arbitri*), it seems safe, for the sake of a better understanding of their precise meaning, not to classify them as being

4. In the following demonstration I am generally following the classification of Schiller 1971a, pp. 493ff. There is some lack of precision, however, when he sees arbitration even in cases where no allusion is made to the relative procedure (selection of an arbiter, etc.); in such cases there is, to my mind, mediation rather than arbitration.

5. This private arbitration is not to be confused with the public one. In many Coptic documents from the Arabic times (till the eighth century) some local magistrates (such as *dioikētēs* and *lashane*) in a given village could sometimes participate in arbitrations.

6. One can reasonably see in the local court dispensing justice in a given locality, such as Deir el-Medineh during the Ramesside period, a kind of public/compulsory arbitration/mediation, the persons (e.g. chief workmen, scribes, etc.) being State functionaries and not magistrates. The point requires a fresh analysis of our texts. For an instance of possible mediation in the times of the Old Kingdom; see *Urk.* I, p. 13.

7. For the effects of penal clauses, without which the agreement would not be binding upon the parties concerned; see Berger 1911, pp. 212ff.

8. For a treatment of the relevant documents coming from Egypt and dating from the 6th–7th centuries A.D.; see K.-H. Ziegler 1971, pp. 263 ff. and cf. Seidl 1973, p. 112.

one and the same device, as some scholars hold (cf. Schiller 1971b). It is noteworthy, however, that in the course of time mediation/conciliation seems to supplant private arbitration, if we may judge from the increasing reliance on that procedure by the Copts as revealed in many deeds of settlements from the 8th century (Schiller 1971a, p. 497). It would appear that the rigid system of private arbitration according to the principles of Roman law had but little effect upon the practice of out-of-court adjudication in Egypt (cf. Schiller 1971b). It was namely the paramount device of mediation which continued to prevail, and persisted well into Arabic times.[9] Such is also the situation in our litigation, the relevant texts, Coptic and Greek, implying neither *compromissum* nor *receptum arbitri.*

To round off the picture of the practice for extra-judicial settlement of civil disputes, we may draw a sketch of ecclesiastical adjudication (*audientia episcopalis*).[10] It undoubtedly originated in the concept that Christians should not resolve their legal differences before the pagan State institutions. The State, on the other hand, seems initially to have taken no notice of such ecclesiastical adjudication. A turning point came about, however, after Constantine had converted to the Christian faith. As a matter of fact, Constantine and many emperors following him promulgated several imperial enactments in favor of the ecclesiastical adjudication over civil litigations (see Thür and Pieler 1978, pp. 467ff.).

At all events, the Coptic documentation discloses that pious Christians, instead of appealing to State institutions, set their litigious affairs first before the clergy/bishop. Accordingly in late Byzantine and early Arabic times the clergy, who also used to play a great part in the local administration of the secular affairs of the people,[11] were frequently called upon by the laity to help in settling civil disputes,[12] the more so in Byzantine times, since the central government became less efficient and local officials were liable to be corrupt so that the population looked up to the clerics as the most faithful and equitable persons in society. Yet much litigation was brought directly to State judicial institutions (e.g. Papyrus Princeton 55 [A.D. 481]: Ensslin 1926, pp. 422ff.; see also Steinwenter 1929–30, pp. 665f.) or to the attention of arbitrators or mediators. In our litigation too, we do not chance upon any intervention by the church authorities. The contestants apparently preferred to submit their conflict to secular mediation, though one of them, namely Iohannes, was regularly called "deacon" and might have been of some clerical connection. At any rate, we are not told whether the contestants had already approached any local magistrates who would have formally directed them to settle their controversy before a council of mediators (cf. Steinwenter 1920, pp. 21, 23, and 56 and Schiller 1935, p. 20).

A final matter of general concern in our discussion is the fact that our dispute was seemingly terminated without any award rendered by the mediators, though the position of the claimant, Iohannes, was wholly unyielding throughout the hearings. Instead, the last Greek papyrus

9. In late Byzantine Egypt, after 500 A.D., namely during the century and a half before Arab rule, the resolution of litigations by means of arbitration and mediation became very widespread. For this reason, combined with the total absence of positive evidence of trials in civil justice (even after the Arab conquest), Schiller (1971a, pp. 469ff.) ventured the suggestion that there were no more State courts available for the trial of civil controversies at that period. However, Simon (1971, pp. 623ff. and 1974, p. 389) has ably demonstrated that a State judicial structure was in reality extant, but for some reason the indigenous population apparently preferred to resolve their conflicts extra-judicially. One might well expect that the population would submit disputes to fellow-townsmen and co-religionists rather than trust themselves to the foreign ruling class; cf. K.-H. Ziegler 1971, pp. 201, 272f., and 386.

10. For the *audientia episcopalis* over civil litigations in general and in Egypt in particular; see Lammeyer 1933, pp. 193ff. For further literature; see Modrzejewski 1952, p. 256, n. 172.

11. For the position of the bishop in society and administration; see the remarks of Schiller 1935, p. 45 and Steinwenter 1956, pp. 77ff.

12. It is to be noted that the resolution of civil disputes by way of arbitration occurred also as an extra-judicial device within the ecclesiastical adjudication; cf. Krause 1972, pp. 101ff. and Seidl 1973, p. 109.

amazingly recounts that it was Iohannes who voluntarily agreed to abstain from any claims and spontaneously acknowledged the property rights of the adverse party. This change of mind on the part of the obstinate claimant is totally unexpected, so that not much trust can be placed in the text at this point. I have hence no hesitation in assuming that it was only upon a negative outcome of the trial that the claimant was made to sign the deed of settlement in favor of his adversary.

We do know that the prevalent idea among ancient Egyptians, while sitting at court to judge, was to refrain generally from the strict utterance of formal judgements. They would rather obligate the defeated party to give up his point and admit the rightful position of his adversary (see Allam 1973b, pp. 49f. [especially note 90], 67ff., 85, 95; and Seidl 1973, p. 112). This does not mean, however, that in such a situation no judicial decision whatsoever was to be taken; the defeated party had to be informed somehow of the judicial determination regarding his trial. It appears plausible then that in our dispute an award of some kind was made known by the mediators, so that the losing party should take notice of the consequences of his dealings.[13] Our assumption (see below notes 25–26) is in accordance with other scholars' opinion that the judicial decision was often made effective by making the losing party execute a deed of settlement in favor of his adversary. Such a deed essentially reflects the judicial decision, the terms of which are to be incorporated definitively in the deed (cf. Steinwenter 1920, p. 25 and K.-H. Ziegler 1971, pp. 269f.). Such would seem to be the nature of the Greek papyrus which was drawn up by the claimant, Iohannes, as the result of the proceedings before the council of mediators.

This deed, by which our dispute is settled out-of-court, is expressly termed *dialysis* (Vergleichsurkunde). Taking upon itself a strict form, it contains the generic elements common to a category[14] well attested by a good number of texts, not only of Byzantine but also of Arabic date (8th century; see Steinwenter 1920, pp. 17 and 20). This instrument which played a prominent part in common judicial practice merits a special attention in our discussion.

It commences with the invocation of the Holy Trinity; following the indiction date there appears a clause with the names of the parties. A statement of the facts, namely the history of the dispute (*narratio*), occupies the major portion of the σῶμα of the document; thereafter comes the complex and long-winded renunciation clause whereby the defeated Iohannes agrees not to litigate any more the controverted matters; this clause is strengthened by an oath; the body of the document closes with a stipulation and sanction clause in which a considerable sum of money (12 holocots) is fixed beforehand that shall be the penalty for not refraining from further litigation. The instrument ends with the subscription of Iohannes himself, the attestations of five witnesses and the concluding words (*completio*) of a public notary.

Now, it has been observed by scholars that the dialysis-instrument finds parallels in other civilizations and legal systems (cf. Steinwenter 1920, p. 18; Schiller 1927, p. 439; and Seidl 1964,

13. Steinwenter (1935, p. 86) is of the opinion, however, that in cases resulting in dialysis-agreement the arbitrators/mediators were but to suggest a way out of the litigation in question; their suggestion became then the basis of the dialysis-agreement between the parties involved. For the opinion that before a dialysis was agreed upon ordinary legal proceedings might have already taken place; see Simon 1971, pp. 651f.

14. For the division of a Coptic dialysis-document (of Arabic date) into component elements; see Schiller 1927, pp. 443ff. and 1931, pp. 226ff. His division can generally be applied to our Greek document. In his comment (1927, pp. 440f.), he emphasizes the likeness of the Coptic dialysis-document to the late Byzantine *tabellio*-document (written by a particular type of scribe, the *tabellio*), which was publicly approved in the time of Justinian and persisted through late imperial and Byzantine times; cf. *idem* 1932, pp. 6f. and Steinwenter 1935, pp. 77f. and 87. An intriguing fact to note is, however, that our document is qualified by its notary as διάλυσις / ἀμεριμνεία Ἀκυλιανή as though it contained besides the *stipulatio Aquiliana* an appertaining *acceptilatio*. This stipulation embraces all conceivable civil claims which could ever be set up by the stipulating person; in declaring the *acceptilatio* he then renounces the plurality of all his claims at one time; see Kaser 1971, p. 649 and 1975, pp. 446f. Nevertheless, Steinwenter (1935, pp. 88f.) admits its application in our instance, the *acceptilatio* being indicated by, or reshaped in, the form of a renunciation clause.

pp. 38f.). It has also been noticed that the Byzantine dialysis in Egypt has, regarding form and phraseology, a striking similarity to what the legal literature informs us about the dialysis as known elsewhere in the eastern Byzantine Empire, so that one might speak of a standardized pattern for the dialysis throughout the East, including Egypt, already before the time of Justinian. It has therefore been suggested that such a very common pattern for the dialysis could have originally evolved somewhere in the East (Constantinople) where the Roman legal concepts prevailed, and thence it was introduced later into the Egyptian documentary practice (Steinwenter 1935, pp. 90ff. and 1951, p. 29)[15] In the end, one would be tempted to postulate the Byzantine dialysis in Egypt as a direct outgrowth of Roman law (Schiller 1927, p. 440; cf. Steinwenter 1951, p. 32 and Springer 1885, pp. 132ff.). All these problems are much too complex to enter into within the scope of the present paper. We would rather trace the idea and development of the dialysis-instrument back to its earliest occurrences in the Egyptian materials, i.e. from the Hellenistic period back into the Pharaonic period.

In an analysis of the formulae used in Coptic and Demotic documents E. Lüddeckens (1972, pp. 24ff.)[16] has succinctly treated, *inter alia*, the relationship between the Coptic dialysis (Streitbeilegungsurkunde) and the Demotic instrument for settlement of legal disputes (Prozeßurkunde/Prozeßvertrag). He has consequently come to the conclusion that both types reveal a fundamental likeness, not only in that either employs a similar formulaic wording, but also the same sequence of formulae. I essentially agree with his view, with the reservation that the Coptic dialysis, like its Byzantine precursor in Greek, contains some more component elements such as the oath of the party issuing the document and the penalty (πρόστιμον) for eventually breaching the agreement.[17] The fact remains, however, that the clause of renunciation, which is the vital issue in the Coptic dialysis,[18] is equally common to the Byzantine deeds in Greek and to the Hellenistic ones in Demotic, so that there can be no doubt about the Demotic clause of renunciation as the forerunner of the Byzantine one.[19]

As to the use of the renunciation clause in Demotic texts, our vast material provides innumerable examples, mostly in connection with business affairs. Yet, some papyri have bearing in particular on legal proceedings. It emerges from the contexts of these proceedings that such an instrument was to be drawn up after a lawsuit had been terminated; the defeated party had then to

15. In fact, Steinwenter hesitated first as to whether it was the Egyptian practice being adopted in other parts of the Empire, or the other way around. He finally took a definitive position, with the argument that the Egyptian notaries in the Byzantine period cannot have had a higher legal level than others, hence they rather have taken over the foreign practice; see further Steinwenter 1955, pp. 55f. For his previous view; see 1920, pp. 24 and 59.

16. In fact, Lüddeckens is developing an old opinion of Steinwenter who, in the literature mentioned above (note 15), has taken thereafter a totally different position; see further M. Green (1983, pp. 120f.) discussing the preservation of the Demotic legal formulae in Coptic legal texts.

17. These elements are by no means new to the Egyptian legal practice in general (see notes 21–22, below). But the requisite to consistently include them in the dialysis was possibly the result of a formal development of the Roman-Byzantine period.

18. Without this clause the dialysis-instrument would be meaningless.

19. Lüddeckens (1972, pp. 24ff.) has further established the Demotic origin of another clause recurring in the Coptic dialysis-document, namely enumerating the possible judicial institutions before which the party issuing the document might bring an action.

extinguish for all times his claims against his adversary.[20] However, all extant examples of this instrument go as far back as the Hellenistic period, so that one could argue that the Demotic instrument might simply have been the offshoot of a comparable Greek one used during the Ptolemaic and early Empire periods, namely the συγχώρησις, which obviously has an extraordinary affinity (cf. Gradenwitz, Preisigke, and Spiegelberg 1912, pp. 6ff.; Steinwenter 1920, pp. 24, 59; Seidl 1962, p. 62; Wolff 1970, p. 224; and Wolff 1978, pp. 91ff.). We have therefore to turn to the texts from the Pharaonic era.

In the hieratic material we can indeed trace the renunciation clause back to the Ramesside period. At that period the clause already had a wide range of usage. It could be employed in various situations of everyday undertakings (such as sale, division of property rights arising from succession, and the like).[21] What is significant for our investigation is its frequent application for judicial purposes, whether the procedure was ultimately conducted by the court personnel or by way of divine judgement.[22] In court minutes, we currently encounter the defeated party giving up his position while spelling out this particular clause, thus renouncing all claims to the disputed matter and acknowledging the rights of the adverse party.[23] In some cases his declaration was separately written down in a detached record.[24] Such a record is basically similar to the dialysis-instrument as known from later periods.

20. Papyrus Berlin 3113 (Thebes, 141 B.C.; Erichsen 1942, pp. 92ff.) yields an informative example. Three men, as a party who had been defeated before an Egyptian court (*nꜣ wpti.w* = the judges) in a controversy over the rights to a one-seventh share in a plot of land, had to draw up a papyrus, which was then written down by a priest (notary) and attested to by sixteen witnesses. They had expressly to relinquish their claims in favor of their adversary, saying, amongst other things, the following: "We have no word/contest on earth against you regarding it (the land) from today onwards; he who will come unto you on account of it in our name, we shall make him abandon you ..." (*mn m-tw=n md nb n pꜣ tꜣ i.ir-n=k n rn=f n ṯꜣi n pꜣ hrw r-ḥri; pꜣ nti iw=f y r.r=k r-ḏbꜣ.ti=f n rn=n, iw=n r di.t wi=f r.r=k* ...). At present there exist two other examples of this instrument in our Demotic material: Papyrus Elephantine 12 (= Berlin 13554, 245/44 B.C., with sixteen witness names verso: Sethe and Partsch 1920, pp. 752ff.; cf. Nims 1948, p. 249 and *LÄ* IV, col. 771) and Papyrus BM 10446 (Thebes, 230 B.C., with sixteen witness names verso: Revillout 1885, p. 15 and pls. 3–4; Andrews 1990, pp. 66f.). Two other Demotic papyri disclose a similar context and seem to belong to this category: Papyrus dem. Wiss. Ges. 16 (Gebelen, 135 B.C., with sixteen witness names verso: Gradenwitz, Preisigke, and Spiegelberg 1912, pp. 39ff.; cf. *LÄ* IV, col. 885) and Papyrus dem. Wiss. Ges. 18 (Gebelen, 133 B.C.: Gradenwitz, Preisigke, and Spiegelberg 1912, pp. 49ff.; cf. *LÄ* IV, col. 885).

21. For the sale of animals (the vendor renounces his rights); see Ostracon DeM 56 and Ostracon Turin 6672 (Allam 1973a, pp. 82f., 249f.). For division of property rights in immovables (daughters and sons relinquish their claims and mutually recognize each other's rights); see Papyrus Cairo 58092 (Boulaq 10) verso and Papyrus Turin 2070 verso, col. II (Allam 1973a, pp. 290f., 327f.; Allam 1985, p. 5). See further Ostracon Florence 2620 (Allam 1973a, p. 147) concerning the right to a house bestowed on two men. An interesting fact is that the persons concerned in these cases (except that in Papyrus Cairo) declared their renunciation while swearing an oath. Furthermore, all persons (except in Ostracon DeM) promised to pay a penalty in case of breaching their agreement. The party (in Ostracon DeM) affirmed moreover that no other person would violate the agreement.

22. For proceedings by divine judgements (oracles) over disputed rights in immovables; see Ostracon Gardiner 23 and Ostracon Geneva 12550 (Allam 1973a, pp. 153, 193f.). For ordinary proceedings over a donkey; see Ostracon Gardiner 182 (ibid., p. 186f.). For making a last will before court, whereby the disinherited person had to relinquish his claims; see Papyrus Ashmolean Museum 1945.97, col. 5, 12 (will of Naunakhte: ibid., p. 270). It is pertinent to note that in these cases (except the last but one) the renunciation was asserted under oath. Besides, in Papyrus Ashmolean Museum a penalty would be paid in case of breaching the settlement, and in Ostracon Geneva, the involved party ascertained that no third person (relatives) would raise any claim.

23. It is characteristic of this clause that it is constructed by means of the verb *mdw* "speak/contest" (or the infinitive/noun thereof), the person involved saying *bn mdw=i* ... "I shall not contest ..." or *m-tw=i mdw/pn ꜥ-r-mdwt* ... "If I contest/reverse-(my-understanding-as)-to-contest (it again, I shall be liable to) ... ." Identical constructions are also found in cursive hieratic (*mn m-di=i mdt nbt* ... "I have no contest whatsoever ...") and Demotic (see above note 20). Note furthermore that μηδένα λόγον ἔχειν was the corresponding expression in the Byzantine documents; Steinwenter 1935, p. 88.

24. See my remarks on Ostracon Gardiner 104 (1967, pp. 47ff.). For a similar situation in the Demotic Papyrus Loeb 43; see Nims 1948, pp. 247f.

We are moreover in a favorable position to establish that such a declaration given at court by the defeated party became in the course of centuries rich in details and its phraseology grew considerably. This development is manifest in two papyri successively published by M. Malinine some years ago. Both papyri, which are written in cursive hieratic, come from Thebes and date to the 7th century B.C.[25] As far as the formulae in general and the renunciation clause in particular are concerned, both papyri disclose a remarkable similarity not only in relation to each other, but also to their Demotic counterparts (Prozeßurkunde/Prozeßvertrag).

Hence there can be definitively no uncertainty that the species *dialysis* as known from later periods (in Greek, then in Coptic) stemmed from an age-old indigenous practice.[26] Under Roman/Byzantine rule, however, its structure might have undergone a novel development so that it came to have more elaborate formulae, intermingled with other new elements (such as the *stipulatio Aquiliana* and the penalty)[27] in order to produce more effects.[28]

As a final point, our study demonstrates, on the one hand, the interrelation of Greek and Coptic documents; the juxtaposition of Greek and Coptic documents dealing with a single case is far from common. Our study shows, on the other hand, that in Greek texts the enchoric law may actually be present, either resuscitated in later periods or latent since Pharaonic times, but undetected as yet. This gives support to the idea that customary rules of Pharaonic law persisted into later periods; a cursory reading of Coptic documents even dating from the 8th century of our era would indeed illustrate this idea.

As to the particular problems posed by the Coptic Papyrus Budge and the related Greek documents, they warrant the cooperation of scholars from various fields. Their ultimate objective is not only to specify the formal heritage, but also to determine its component parts whether Greco-Roman or native Egyptian. Lastly, the question of the tie between legal institutions of Pharaonic Egypt and those reflected in the texts of the following ten centuries squarely places the study of common law, as indicated in these texts, in the context of a greater problem, namely the evolution of legal systems within a multi-cultural environment.

25. Papyrus Louvre E 3228c (Thebes, 685 B.C., with copies of six witnesses: Malinine 1951, pp. 157ff.) and Papyrus Vienna D 12003 (Thebes, 648 B.C., with copies of eight witnesses: Malinine 1973, pp. 192ff.). It is worthy of note that in both lawsuits the losing party gave his declaration not of his own free will, but by order of the judges. He had then to affirm his renunciation on oath and further to promise that there will be no claim arising from any third person or successor in interest.

26. Note finally that the instrument *sẖ-n-wy* "writing for withdrawal/abandonment" is not wholly identical with the one under discussion. That instrument, the wording of which is characterized by the use of the verb *wi* "be far," did not come into general use at court for renouncing one's claim on disputed matters, so far as I can see; the documents determinating lawsuits (referred to in note 20, above) do not employ any formula with the verb *wy*. Yet in the law book of Hermopolis (early Hellenistic period) we are told in a section about disputed property rights to a house that the judges should make the defendant draft a writing of withdrawal from the house in question (Mattha and Hughes 1975, p. 133, s.v. *sẖ-n-wy*, particularly col. VII, 10). Also in the well-known trial at Siut (170 B.C.) the lady Chratiankh, who lost her case, is said to have been compelled to draw up such a written withdrawal in favor of her brother-in-law (H. Thompson 1934, pp. 54f.; Papyrus BM 10591 verso, col. IV, 7); regarding the text recto col. X, 15; see ibid., p. 33; Seidl 1973, p. 303 and 1968, p. 117.

27. This conforms in principle to the Justinian law. Yet it appears superfluous to provide the dialysis with the formula of Aquilian stipulation, the written settlement of the dispute in question bringing about the same legal effect. But such was characteristic of the Byzantine legal style (Modrzejewski 1952, pp. 254f.).

28. A crucial point is that in dialysis agreements, if the clause not to sue was breached, besides incurring the stipulated monetary fine, the covenantor still remained bound by the settlement, namely by its so-called *salvatorische Klausel* (Schiller 1927, p. 450; Steinwenter 1935, p. 92; and K.-H. Ziegler 1971, pp. 240f., 270, and 276f.).

CHAPTER 2

UNPUBLISHED DEMOTIC TEXTS IN THE BRITISH MUSEUM

CAROL A. R. ANDREWS
The British Museum

The Department of Egyptian Antiquities at the British Museum contains perhaps the greatest collection of Demotic papyri and ostraca in the world but the vast bulk of them are still, for the most part, unpublished. By the end of 1990 my *Catalogue of Demotic Papyri in the British Museum IV: Ptolemaic Legal Documents from the Theban Area* will be available. It comprises forty-eight entries incorporating fifty-five texts, all written on papyri, except for one on a pottery ostracon. From internal evidence they are known to originate from the Theban area, including Hermonthis but excluding Gebelein which will be the subject of future publications. The earliest text dates to year 6 of Alexander IV (311 B.C.), the remainder are Ptolemaic, ranging in date from 265 B.C. to 119 B.C. Only ten of the texts were known previously outside the Department and even then only from selective hand copies or translations into French made by E. Revillout or from references to specific clauses or named persons. The bulk of the texts in the *Catalogue* comprises sales and cessions, donations, divisions, transfers and leases of property, whether buildings, land, or tombs, with a single loan, one acknowledgment of debt, one oath, one receipt and one definite withdrawal after judgement. As will be appreciated, they provide a wealth of prosopographical, topographical, linguistic, legal, social, religious, and historical information. This paper will be restricted to those texts which were previously unknown outside the Department and will not constitute a complete survey of the contents of the *Catalogue*.

Papyrus BM 10390 (*Cat.* no. 33), dated to 136 B.C., is a cession and much of its corresponding sale, reconstituted from variously accessioned and stored fragments. The property in question is a room and its adjoining workshop in the southern quarter of Djeme; its location is defined further by the words *ẖn Pa-ḳs* 'in Pakesy'. In Papyrus Berlin 3101 (118 B.C.) published in S. Grunert's *Thebanisches Kaufverträge* (1981) the land concerned is described in the Greek subscription as being situated ἐν Πακένει. A. Bataille in *Les Memnonia*, 32 (1952), locates Πάκενις and Πάκεις close together at Djeme. Presumably, then, *Pa-ḳs* is the only Demotic writing thus far noted of that part of Djeme called by the Greeks Pakeis.

Of further interest is the fact that the property measures fifty-seven square cubits. The difficulty for the Egyptians of expressing 0.57 land cubits has led to this example, unique so far as can be ascertained, of less than one land cubit being expressed as a recognized fraction of a land cubit plus the odd remaining number of square cubits, i. e. half a land cubit plus seven square cubits.

The contractors in this papyrus are both embalmers, using the extremely rare word *ḳs* which has been rendered in some Greek texts by the term σκυτεύς suggesting that this branch of the profession was concerned with the cutting open of the corpse and the removal of the internal organs and so was particularly antisocial. Certainly, by this time embalming was just another job; indeed, there is every likelihood that by now it was such a lowly and despised profession that it was mainly foreigners who worked in it. This is suggested because Papyrus BM 10390 is one of those extremely rare Demotic texts which records the age and physical characteristics of one of the contractors, a feature far more common in Greek texts. Panekhati is said to be 'a black man' (*rmt ḳm*) surely pointing out that he is a foreigner. Exactly the same term with the same unexpected spelling is found in Papyrus Berlin 3090/1, dated to 140 B.C. and published in S. Grunert's *Thebanisches Kaufverträge*. The feeling that he is an exotic is further heightened by the reference to his having one ear pierced (his right) — *ỉw p3y⸗f msḏ wnm wtf*. Panekhati's full description is '25 years old, average size, narrow-headed (only in the sale); there is a scar on his left temple' (*ỉw⸗f tn rnp.t 25 ḏnf slm ḏ3ḏ3 r t3 ꜥḏn.t ḥr p3y⸗f sme ỉ3by*) — a remarkable thumbnail portrait of a man born in 161 B.C.

Papyrus BM 10721/10727/10679A (*Cat.* no. 9) dated to 182 B.C. are the sale, cession and abstract for a ruined house in Thebes sold by the man Damon (*Tm3n*), who is termed 'a Greek born in Egypt' (*Wynn ms Kmy*) who receives pay among the infantrymen (*ỉw⸗f šp ḥbs ẖn n3 rmt.w rd.wy.ṯ⸗f*), of *Glwbwls*, *Pṯlwmys*, and *3ntrtrs*, i.e. Kleoboulos, Ptolemaios, and Andrytos. These three men were brothers, the sons of Ptolemaios, and proxenoi at Delphi in 188–87 B.C. Indeed, until this papyrus was read, that was the only record of them but here they are high-ranking military officers at Thebes. The first thing to ask is was the house ruined as a result of the disturbances which accompanied the end of the reign of the local native pharaoh Ankhwennefer in 186 B.C.? The fact that Damon purchased the house at the public auction (*ḥr p3 ꜥyš n (pr- ꜥ3)*|) perhaps confirms these circumstances for it is difficult otherwise to explain how a ruined, ownerless house came to be standing in the middle of ancient Thebes where land was at a premium.

The text of the sale (Papyrus BM 10721) contains a thus far unique clause: when specifying the property which now belongs to the purchaser the words used are 'your house which is ruined and everything which appertains to it *and the deposited agreement which has been drawn up for me in respect of it*' (*ḥnꜥ t3 gtbwl3 r.ỉr⸗w n⸗y r.r⸗f*). *T3 gtbwl3* can only be the Demotic rendering of the Greek, καταβολή, the noun from καταβάλλω, the verb used for 'depositing' agreements in the public archives. This, then, would presumably be the archival registration made when Damon first acquired the property. Thus a word has had to be adopted in Egyptian for a purely Greek practice imposed upon them in matters of buying and selling property.

The sale also has a Demotic subscription recording the payment of the five percent sales tax; this in itself would be rare enough for comment, although there are two other examples in the *Catalogue*. However, this one may well be unique for a house sale in Demotic since it allows the purchase price to be reconstructed. The amount in question is four deben of silver, i. e. twenty staters in bronze calculated at a rate of twenty-four obols per kite. Thus the value of a ruined house at Thebes in 182 B.C. was 100 staters.

An indication of the richness of the British Museum's collection of Demotic papyri and of the unplumbed nature of its contents is provided by this and the next *Catalogue* entry (no. 10, Papyrus BM 10722/3). Each is a sale and cession and both now have an abstract — a rare occurrence — which would have been attached originally to the right-hand edge of the sale. Both abstracts (Papyrus BM 10679A/B) entered the collection in 1933, five years before the main documents and from a different source. They were not identified until this catalogue was being compiled.

Five papyri are concerned with property located in the northwest quarter of Hermonthis (Papyrus BM 10386/10387/10407/10410 and 10437, *Cat.* nos. 35–39) which range in date from 224 to 210 B.C. In all but one (Papyrus BM 10410, which is damaged, and even there restoration is possible), the location is further defined as being *ẖn n3 ptr.w*, i. e. 'in the peteru'. The word appears to be derived from hieroglyphic *ptr.t* (*Wb.*1, 565) but it is difficult to be sure of its interpretation here. In Papyrus BM 10407, however, it is further defined as being situated 'on the southern highland' which suggests that a meaning of 'vantage point' or 'observation place' as advocated by E. Drioton (1944, p. 134) is probably preferable.

Of further interest is the fact that both Papyrus BM 10407 (*Cat.* no. 35) dated to 224 B.C. and Papyrus BM 10386 (*Cat.* no 39) dated to 210 B.C. cite as a neighbor of the house which is the subject of the transactions the pyramid of Theodoros (*pꜣ mr Twtrs*). Moreover, by the time Papyrus BM 10386 was drawn up, another house had been built on what was earlier open ground (*wrḥ*) to be yet another neighbor to the pyramid. The reference is clearly to a pyramid-capped tomb chapel of the type still being built during the Greco-Roman period. However, the fact that not only is the pyramid situated in what is rapidly becoming a residential area but its owner has a Greek name is surprising. To judge by a further reference in a related papyrus (Papyrus BM 10387) to *nꜣ mr.w* there is, as might be expected, more than one pyramid in the vicinity. The only other instance which comes to mind of tombs and dwellings cheek by jowl is at the workmen's village at Deir el-Medineh but that example, for a number of reasons, is not truly analogous. Is perhaps the foreign nationality of the pyramid-owner of some relevance?

Papyrus BM 10464 (*Cat.* no. 26) is a cession corresponding to a sale recorded in Papyrus BM 10463 which was published by F. Ll. Griffith (1901). The subject is land in the temple estate of Amun in the district of western Thebes called Pestenemenophis, the date is 210 B.C. and, of course, both texts were written by the same scribe, Khensthotes. However, there are some rather startling discrepancies between the two documents in the listing of the neighbors of the land in question. In Papyrus BM 10463 the only southern neighbor recorded is a Greek called Ammonios, son of Kallikrates; in Papyrus BM 10464, however, there is a second southern native Egyptian neighbor. A similar omission occurs regarding the eastern neighboring property when Papyrus BM 10463 cites only the village called The Migdol whereas Papyrus BM 10464 lists a second eastern neighbor — the land of Philon, son of Antipatros, which is held by his brother Theodoros. It is not unknown for a scribe inadvertently to reverse the specified neighbors of a property but these discrepancies between a sale and cession are unique so far as can be ascertained and caused D. Devauchelle (1987a) insurmountable problems when he published Papyrus Louvre E 9416. Although it is dated only four years earlier and deals with contiguous land, Greek-held property alone is its eastern neighbor and the village appeared to have disappeared completely. It was tempting at first to wonder if the fact that the vendor was a Greek had any relevance and whether the text concentrated for his benefit solely on Greek-held neighboring land but that theory cannot be maintained. Incidentally, the vendor is Nikon, also called Petekhonsis, and so is yet another example of a Greek with a Greek father (in this case Athenion) bearing a second name which is Egyptian.

Papyrus BM 10829 (*Cat.* no. 18) is a division of tombs as a share of an inheritance dated to 209 B.C. with two Demotic subscriptions. The end of the second, which was published out of context (Zauzich 1986) appears to translate as 'the agent of Agathinos (son of) Sostratos who is in charge of the *aggryn* of the nome of Pathyris' (*pꜣ rd n ꜣgtynws Sstrtws nty ḥr pꜣ ꜣggryn n pꜣ tš n Pr-Ḥw.t-Ḥr*). If the end of line 2 (Agathinos [son of] Sostratos) is indeed to be read as suggested, not only is the filiation missing but the beginning of the father's name is written, most unusually, with two different forms of *s*. However, perhaps the initial *s* of *Sstrtws* is actually the less common sign for filiation. If the name is thus to be read *Strtws* rather than *Sstrtws* it could still be a Demotic rendering of Sostratos through haplography. In fact, even the reading of the signs is open to dispute: perhaps *strḳws* should be read rather than *strtws*, in which case a writing of 'strategos' becomes a possibility. Then the first sign is not an *s* but the possessive article *pa* and the whole phrase *pa strḳws*, 'he who belongs to the strategos,' is a Demotic rendering of the Greek expression beginning ὁ παρά used to designate a subordinate. Equally, *ꜣggryn* would appear to be the Demotic rendering of (τὸ) ἀγγαρηΐον, 'posting system,' or 'requisition for public service'. Yet the Greek group γγ is normally treated in Demotic as a sequence *-ng*. It is thus rather tempting to see *ȝggryn* as the Demotic rendering of ἀρχεῖον by a process of metathesis, although the reduplication of *g* for χ is still a problem. The arkheion or town hall was the office of the agoranomos, the official before whom sales were drawn up. The usual Greek expression ἐπὶ τοῦ ἐν Παθύρει ἀρχείου would normally be rendered in Demotic by *n pȝ ȝrgn n Pr-Ḥw.t-Ḥr*, not by *nty ḥr pȝ ȝrgn*. Perhaps the scribe misunderstood ἐπί as meaning 'in charge of' rather than 'in' which would certainly tend to confirm P. W. Pestman's (1978) view that some agoranomoi at least were Egyptian in origin and so not completely fluent in Greek. This papyrus sheds some light on the bilingual situation in the administration of Ptolemaic Egypt. This text also provides a new earliest date, January 13, 209 B.C., for the joint rule of Ptolemy IV and his son Ptolemy V.

Papyrus BM 10380 (*Cat.* no. 45) dated to year 16 of Ptolemy III, i. e. 231 B.C., is a cession after judgment as the text makes clear. What makes this papyrus of peculiar interest is that attached to the right hand edge is 25 cm of text, the central part of six lines from another document, now upside-down to the main text and attached to it in such a way that only about 4.5 cm of the last sheet at the right is visible. An attempt was made to erase what was on it but it is still possible to ascertain that it was concerned with matrimonial property, dated to year 23 of Ptolemy III, i. e. August 225–24 B.C., six years after the main document was drawn up. This fragment can only have been attached to strengthen the exposed edge of the main document although why so much papyrus was necessary to do so is not clear. One must also assume that the marriage to which it appertains had broken down irretrievably.

Papyrus BM 10372 (*Cat.* no. 43) is a damaged cession datable to the late 4th to mid 3rd centuries B.C. — the beginning of the papyrus is lost — in which a man of Aswan (*rmt Swn*) cedes 20 arourae of land on the highland of Hermonthis to a like-titled man. It was long ago suggested, though not universally accepted, that this epithet represents not a geographical designation but a military title based on the long-standing position of Syene as a military enclave. If this is correct, the appearance of men of Aswan so far away from Egypt's southern frontier should cause no surprise. However, what makes this text so important is that the plot is specifically stated to be 'your land (held) as a man of Aswan (*pȝy=k ȝḥ n rmt Swn*), strongly suggesting an office is intended by this term. Moreover, all the holders of the neighboring land are also men of Aswan and, in one instance, a man of Afneti which was probably another military post near Aswan. The same 20 arourae is the subject of the transaction recorded in Papyrus BM 10389 (*Cat.* no. 44) dated to 243 B.C. and although the holders of the continuous plots have moved on a generation (they are the sons of the land holders cited in the earlier papyrus) they are still all men of Aswan and of Afneti suggesting that this was some sort of military veterans' colony established in Hermonthite territory. The scribe of this papyrus, Neshor, son of Khapokhrates, is other wise unknown.

Papyrus BM 10831 (*Cat.* no. 19) is a complete Doppelurkunde, still sealed, dated to year 7 of the rebel native pharaoh Ankhwennefer, i. e. 194 B.C., which provides a thus far unique example in a Demotic legal document of a word far better known in hieroglyphs, Coptic, and Greek. The sealed section was unrolled by the Conservation Department of the British Museum so that the scriptura interior could be examined; it was then returned to its original appearance. As expected, the sealed text contained a précis of the main document which records a loan of $1\frac{1}{2}$ artabae of wheat and $3\frac{1}{3}$ artabae of barley. However, the form of its recording was totally unexpected: the scriptura interior begins with the words *wʿ.t ʿrb* which can only be translated as 'a surety' or 'a pledge'.

Some of the material in the *Catalogue* at first sight might appear unrewarding but a single example will serve to give an indication of the information to be gleaned from what might look to be an unpromising source. Papyrus BM 10512 (*Cat.* no. 48) is a rather damaged and apparently run-of-the-mill sale of a half-share of a house in Hermonthis. The beginning of the text is lost and the whole of one line deliberately erased but it can be dated from the names and titulary of the eponymous priests to year 5 or 6 of Ptolemy VI, i. e. 177–75 B.C. Thus when mention is made in line 4 to year 26 of an unspecified pharaoh the reference must be to the preceding ruler Ptolemy V who is usually credited with twenty-five years of reign, May 20 being the last recorded date. Sometimes, especially in the case of Upper Egyptian documents, the death of the ruler was not noted immediately: that of Ptolemy VIII took five months to reach the Theban scribes. Or was the precedent set by the death of Ptolemy V's own father which probably occurred around November 28, 205 B.C. but was kept secret until the summer of 204 B.C.

This is only a small sample of the contents of the *Catalogue* but even its fifty-five texts are just the tip of the iceberg so far as the Demotic collection of the British Museum is concerned. The following examples will give some slight indication of what can emerge in a totally unexpected fashion when registering previously unaccessioned Demotic papyrus fragments.

First of all three fragments which belong to the Rylands Papyri were identified. There is no information on when or whence they were obtained but the Manchester collection was acquired in Egypt during 1898–99. The most interesting of these is now numbered Papyrus BM 10991 and joins with Papyrus Rylands 19 to reveal that the vendors, known to be more than one in number, are actually two and one of them a Greek born in Egypt. Papyrus BM 10995 belongs with Papyrus Rylands 23, a sale of unbuilt land. It does not really provide much more information but it does make the text more complete than it was, as does Papyrus BM 10999, which is part of Papyrus Rylands 27, a marriage contract.

However, something far more startling emerged from the fragments released when a made-up roll of papyrus was relaxed as an exercise by the British Museum's Department of Conservation in 1978. Again there is no record of how or when the roll was obtained but it seems to have languished for some time in the Departmental Fakes Cupboard. The larger fragments obtained remained unaccessioned until last year when registration of them began. It was at once clear that the text on them was of a mathematical nature but it was a total surprise to discover that they actually joined with Papyrus BM 10399 published by Parker (1972). This part of the text, which had entered the collection in 1868, concerns the mathematical problem of ascertaining the volume of a ship's mast of a given height and diameter through water displacement. The section which Parker worked on contained the solutions for masts of 100 and 90 cubits with only a fragment of those for 80 and 70 cubits. Thanks to the new fragments the latter two problems are now completed and most of those for 60 and 50 cubits are supplied.

The *British Museum Quarterly* for 1931–32 recorded that an important collection of Demotic papyri had recently been purchased of which most came from Tebtunis, including a series of documents relating to self-dedication. It concluded tersely that 'two of the documents appear to contain literary texts of considerable interest.' Although the bulk of this accession was registered in 1931, for some reason the two literary texts were not. They were only identified and registered as Papyrus BM 10660 and 10661 earlier this year. They are of extraordinary interest.

A preliminary examination of the contents suggested a consultation of Hughes' (1951) publication of Papyrus Cairo 31222 and then further of Parker's (1959). There is no doubt that Papyri BM 10660 and 10661 belong to the same genre as those texts and, what is more, appear to be Ptolemaic in date. There is the same method of forecasting events, usually pessimistic. 'There will be mourning,' 'misfortune will come,' 'discord will happen in the entire land and among the children of pharaoh' if certain omina or events are noted. Less often 'good things will happen in the year in question' and 'weapons of war will be destroyed.' Reference is made in Papyrus BM 10661 to the land of Syria (*pꜣ tš ꜣIšwr*) and more unusually to the ruler of Pelem (*pꜣ wr Plm*) — perhaps the same country or people referred to in H. S. Smith's Saqqara lists, reading there *rmt Prm* rather than *Srm*. However, what the published texts do not have is the mention made in Papyrus BM

10661 in two separate places of the death of the ruler of Persia (*pꜣ wr Mty mwt*) if certain events occur. Papyrus BM 10660, however, is even more surprising for it contains two clauses beginning respectively *ỉw=w ḏd pꜣ ỉḳd* and *mtw ḏd pꜣ ỉḳd*. What can this mean but that here is a fragment of the original Demotic version of the Potter's Oracle?

All these texts, which are not part of the *Catalogue*, will be published individually at a later date.

CHAPTER 3

THE CULTURAL TRANSFORMATION OF EGYPT AS SUGGESTED BY A GROUP OF ENTHRONED MALE FIGURES FROM THE FAIYUM

ROBERT STEVEN BIANCHI
*Brooklyn Museum**

My recent investigations into the nature of the art — both pharaonic and Hellenistic — created in Egypt during the Ptolemaic period suggested that pharaonic art remained impervious to fundamentally Greek stylistic tenets whereas contemporary Greek art was much more receptive to incorporating into its stylistic repertoire formal elements derived from pharaonic, visual traditions (Bianchi 1988, pp. 55–81). This analysis of the visual arts suggests a slight emendation to the papyrologists' consensus that the culture of Ptolemaic period Egypt is characterized by two social groups, the native Egyptian and the immigrant Greek, who more often than not conducted their lives in separate and unequal spheres of endeavor.[1] It is clear that the Greeks, but not the Egyptians, were the borrowers of culture and that more often than not their borrowing of the pharaonic visual legacy was accompanied by concomitant written epitomes. This phenomenon adequately explains the commonplace occurrence in Ptolemaic Egypt of large numbers of objects, the figural decorations of which are clearly pharaonic but whose accompanying inscriptions are in Greek. The stela of Pasos dedicated to Apollonios in the mid-third century B.C. is both a fitting and early exemplar of this phenomenon (Cairo JE 44048: Muszynski 1980, pp. 275ff.). To my knowledge no corresponding object, that is one decorated with a classical scene but accompanied by a hieroglyphic inscription, has been identified. The same phenomenon appears to be operative in the Faiyum during the early first century A.D. to judge from a group of statues representing enthroned male figures which are the subject of this paper. These statues stand at the very end of this tradition, and must be briefly presented before one engages in a more detailed discussion about their importance for a clearer understanding of a significant, and heretofore unnoticed, cultural transformation in Roman Egypt.

DOCUMENT A-1 — A STATUE FOR HERODES, SON OF ASKLEPIOS

Cairo JE 49370
Black Basalt — 24 cm in height
From Kom Ouchim — Figure 3.1

* Dr. Bianchi now holds a position with the Metopolitan Museum of Art, New York.

1. For a recent assessment of this phenomenon, see now A. E. Samuel 1989.

The statue is headless and represents an enthroned male figure, clothed in the so-called Persian wrap-around costume (Bothmer, de Meulenaere, and Müller 1960, pp. 74ff.)[2] and holding an unrolled papyrus scroll on his lap. The front of the plinth and the back of the throne are inscribed in Greek:

> [An image] of Herodes, son of Asklepios. Peteesis [has dedicated this image of] Herodes, his savior. Year XI, 16 Epiphi (E. Bernand 1975, pp. 194–95).

DOCUMENT B-1 — AN ENTHRONED FIGURE DEDICATED ON BEHALF OF HERGEUS

Alexandria 3199
Basalt — 30 cm in height
From Dime — Figure 3.2

The seated statue, recalling Document A-1, lacks its head and upper torso. The nature of the costume cannot be determined with the exception of the skirt which is scored with a noticeable double incision, representing its hem, just above the ankles. The open scroll across the lap has been partially unrolled so that each hand holds a portion of the rolled up papyrus. One assumes that this statue was inscribed at some interval after its creation because the Greek inscription on the front of the base continues to the left with its letters accommodating themselves to the damaged area of the block. A second inscription, also in Greek, has been scratched into the left side of the throne. These translate:

> For Hergeus, Pnepheros, his wife, and children have dedicated this statue (E. Bernand 1975, pp. 160–61); and
>
> The work of Peteesis, son of Papos [or, Papes] (E. Bernand 1979, p. 76, note 9).

DOCUMENT B-2 — THE LOWER PART OF AN ENTHRONED MALE FIGURE

Alexandria 3201
Basalt — 43 cm in height
From Dime — Figure 3.3

The enthroned figure wears a long skirt and is shown with each hand on each thigh, with the palm down, the left fisted. The piece is not inscribed.

DOCUMENT B-3 — AN UNINSCRIBED, ENTHRONED MALE FIGURE

Alexandria 3197
Basalt (?) — 48 cm in height
Dime — Figure 3.4

Each of the fisted hands rests on the thighs, but the remaining details are difficult to describe inasmuch as the statue is covered in parts with linen which adheres to a covering of "pitch." Although the exact findspot of this statue is not known, these "bandages" need not be regarded as evidence that this is a tomb, as opposed to a temple, statue. Temple statues, particularly those of Osiris, might be so wrapped during the festival of Khoiak.[3]

2. This wrap-around garment is attested on pharaonic monuments of Dynasty XXVI (de Meulenaere 1987, p. 139; Bothmer 1988, p. 56). In my view this skirt may be regarded as a typically native Egyptian garment and one which was certainly considered to be indigenous by the Egyptians themselves (Russman and Finn 1989, p. 190).

3. C. Ziegler (1979, p. 253) cites the ritual of the cloth in *Denderah IV* (pp. 109 [7]–10 [3]). Furthermore, one knows that the temple statues of both ibises and falcons were wrapped in linen (see Smelik 1979, p. 232) based on the evidence of Papyrus Strassb. 91.4ff.

DOCUMENT B-4 — AN ENTHRONED STATUE IN A TRIPARTITE COSTUME DEDICATED TO THE DEITY PRAMENIS

Cairo CG 1190
Basalt — 54 cm in height
Dime — Figure 3.5

The statue is well preserved, including its inlaid eyes, and represents a male figure in the tripartite costume which is Egyptian in origin and was first represented in the round in stone sculpture of officials of the Ptolemaic period (Bianchi 1988, pp. 125–27, cat. nos. 30–32). It is significant to note that this is the only example known to me of a seated stone statue in the round of a private individual shown wearing this costume.[4] The Greek inscription on the base translates:

> Tesenouphis made [me as an offering] for the god Pramenis (E. Bernand 1975, pp. 158–60, no. 79).

DOCUMENT C-1 — AN ENTHRONED MALE FIGURE OFFERED AS A PRAYER TO THE EMPEROR TIBERIUS

Cairo CG 1191
Basalt (?) — 52 cm in height
Dime — Figures 3.6–3.7

The statue is exceptionally well preserved, including its inlaid eyes. The costume, a variant of the tripartite costume worn by Document B-4, consists of a long skirt which reaches to just above the ankles. The "cuffs" of a long sleeved, round necked tunic appear at both wrists and this is worn under a cape of sorts which is apparently fastened by a round clasp at the neck. The front of the base and the left side of the throne are inscribed with Demotic inscriptions which were added to the statue by a copyist who was himself not intimate with this script, as Zauzich has observed (1987a, pp. 215–17). These texts translate:

> Year 19, 16 Parmuthe. [A prayer (?)] for Tiberius Caesar Sebastos, before Pakysis, the god, by Horus, the son of Harpagathes, his wife and children, forever; and
>
> Psais and his brother and his [their?] wife and his [their?] children.

On the left side of the throne is a representation of a quadruped, which can only be interpreted as a camel[5] with what has been identified as both a saddle on its back and a bell around its neck.[6]

4. Representations are known, of course, in relief, such as those from the Tomb of Petosiris at Tuna-el-Gebel where officials wearing this costume are shown both standing and seated (Lefebvre 1923, pls. XII [lower register, far left] and XVI [top left and bottom right]) as well as from temple relief where the king is likewise shown either standing (Quaegebeur 1988, p. 51, fig. 22; p. 52, fig. 23) or seated (Sauneron 1963, no. 141 = Wessel 1964, fig. 51) in this costume.

5. Bagnall (1985, pp. 1–6) demonstrates that the camel, already well established in the mid third century B.C., did not go out of use. Its "disappearance" is dependent upon one's use, or rather misuse, of the evidence.

6. The identification of this beast as a camel is certain by comparing it to other, contemporary representations of the camel, such as those in terracotta (Berlin 10333: Philipp 1972, pp. 21–22, no. 13, with both bell and saddle, from the Faiyum, dated to the second century A.D.). This example, listed as no. 24 but identified as inv.nr. 1003, has been discussed together with other examples by Nachtergael (1989, pp. 287–336). To these examples one should add yet another from the Sudan: Dunham 1957, p. 127, no. 63 (= excavation number 21-12-63), a bronze figure of a kneeling camel with similar saddle from the pyramid of Queen Amanitere, wife of Natakamani, who S. Wenig (1967, p. 43, no. 50,1) dates to the period between A.D. 1–20.

DOCUMENT C-2 AN ENTHRONED MALE FIGURE

Alexandria 3193
Basalt (?) 53 cm in height
Dime Figure 3.8

This uninscribed statue, although damaged and now missing a major portion of its right shoulder and upper arm, is so close in material, size, coiffure, inlaid eyes, and details of the costume to Document C-1 that one can reasonably conclude that both are the products of one and the same atelier (see Bothmer, de Meulenaere, and Müller 1960, p. 182).

DOCUMENT C-3 AN ENTHRONED MALE FIGURE

Alexandria 3198
Basalt (?) 51 cm in height
Dime Figure 3.9

This uninscribed statue is virtually identical to Documents C-1 and C-2, and is to be assigned to the same workshop. It is interesting to see how this atelier, working within a formula for the enthroned male figure, could incorporate elective details into the design. Here the eyes are not inlaid, but the features of the face have not been significantly altered with the result that they still bear a striking resemblance to those of Documents C-1 and C-2.

DOCUMENT C-4 AN ENTHRONED MALE FIGURE

Alexandria 3203
Basalt 57 cm in height
Dime Figure 3.10

This uninscribed statue, although lacking inlaid eyes, appears to be incomplete because of the blocky nature of the forms, particularly the arms and legs, and the lack of linear adjuncts for the articulation of the costume which gives the false impression that the individual is wearing a broad collar. The statue is stylistically close in spirit to Documents C-1, C-2, and C-3, and, although not a replica, may nevertheless be considered the product of the same or closely related atelier. The treatment of the hair and of the eyes and mouth, in particular, are stylistically similar to these same features on Document C-3 (see Bothmer, de Meulenaere, and Müller 1960, p. 182).

DOCUMENT D-1 AN ENTHRONED MALE FIGURE

Ann Arbor 8281
Basalt 50 cm in height
Kom Ouchim Figure 3.11

Uninscribed, this image represents an official with a shaven pate wearing both a kilt and a curious, asymmetrical upper garment which exposes the right side of the chest and shoulder. It may be possible that this costume is a very late version of the fashion worn by Narmer on his palette in Cairo (Cairo CG 14716: Saleh and Sourouzian 1987, p. 42, fig. 8a; see Gazda et al. 1978, pp. 41–42, no. 35 and Bianchi 1988, pp. 244–45, no. 133).

DOCUMENT D-2 AN ENTHRONED MALE FIGURE

Cairo CG 1192
Schist (?) 49.3 cm in height
Dime Figure 3.12

Despite its condition, this uninscribed statue bears a striking resemblance to Document D-1, particularly in the profile views which reveal exact correspondences in the contours of the heads, the positioning and details of the large ears, and in the configuration of the kilt. One suggests that both are the products of the same atelier, created either by different hands or at somewhat different times. This observation then explains why the statues differ in other respects, particularly in the shape of the throne and the absence of a back pillar on this example. Of particular note on this statue are the traces of what can only be regarded as an *ankh* sign in the left hand (Fischer 1973, p. 27, note 59; see Borchardt 1930, pp. 94–95).

DOCUMENT E-1 — AN ENTHRONED MALE FIGURE

Alexandria 3196
Quartzite (?) — 35 cm in height
Dime — Figure 3.13

This uninscribed example is complete together with its inlaid eyes. The costume, somewhat maladroitly rendered, is perhaps intended to replicate that worn by Document D-1, although admittedly here the kilt is not indicated, and there was some confusion about the rendering of the back pillar at its intersection with the throne at the rear of the piece. Nevertheless the craftsmen have paid particular attention to the details of the coiffure, the right nipple, and the toes and fingers, those on the right hand even have their nails indicated. The extreme disintegration of the whole and the insistence on observing a rigid frontality, particularly in the rendering of the face, suggest that this statue is in fact among the most recent in the series. Because it is atypical, this image ought to be called to the attention of a wider audience but it will not figure prominently in the discussions which follow (Bothmer, de Meulenaere, and Müller 1960, p. 182).

THE QUESTION OF PROVENANCE

Ten of the twelve statues (Documents B-1, B-2, B-3, B-4, C-1, C-2, C-3, C-4, D-2, and E-1) are said to have come from Dime, Soknopaiou Nesos, although the literature does not record any archaeological mission responsible for their recovery (see, for example, Zucker 1910, cols. 244ff.; Boak 1935; *LÄ* I, col. 1094; and E. Bernand 1975, pp. 212–63). The statues seem to have been collected by Grébaut at some time prior to the publication in 1900 of the catalogue of the Graeco-Roman Museum in Alexandria by Botti because there he credits Grébaut with the discovery of about a dozen Dime statues which were then divided up between the collections in Cairo, Alexandria and Berlin.[7] One wonders, then, how much weight can be placed on this statement of their provenance. The same remark can be directed against the two statues, Documents A-1 and D-1, said to have come from Kom Ouchim, Karanis. Of these only Document D-1, the male figure in Ann Arbor, has a documented provenance.[8] The second, Document A-1, is assigned to Karanis, but is, like the statements made regarding the findspots of the Dime statues, unsubstantiated.[9] It would, therefore, appear that with the exception of Document D-1, a provenance in the Faiyum for this group of statues is entirely possible, but any insistence on the exact provenance of either Dime or Karanis is open to question.

7. Botti (1900, p. 467) relates: "Les numéros 5, 24, 28, 29, 30, 31, 33, 34, 38 et 40 appartiennent à une série de statuettes d'époque romaine, partagée entre Berlin, Alexandrie et Le Caire. De cette heureuse trouvaille faite par M. Grébaut, la Direction Générale des Antiquités de l'Egypte a bien voulu nous céder une douzaine des plus remarquables statues qui en faisaient partie." The registers in the Graeco-Roman Museum which I was permitted to consult in 1990 do not add any additional information to Botti's text.

8. Gazda et al. (1978, p. 41) report "8218 (28-SG-Q III) from the area west of South Temple; lowest occupation level."

9. Bernand (1975, p. 194) writes: "Provenance: Kom Ouchim, fouilles de l'Université du Michigan," despite the fact that I could discover no record of this piece in the excavation records at Michigan when I investigated the issue in 1979.

However imprecise the data on the findspots of this group of statues may be, it is interesting to note that the two groups are associated only with northern Faiyumic sites. Furthermore, one seems to be unable to document any Faiyum portrait panels for mummies (see Parlasca 1966, p. 36, note 138 for Dime; and pp. 36, 54 [note 263], 69, 212, and 287–88 for Kom Ouchim/Karanis) or cartonnage ensembles[10] with either Dime or Karanis. This observation may be significant inasmuch as Dendera, which also produced a number of contemporary stone examples of the striding, draped male figure[11] has, to date, not yielded any panels (Parlasca 1966, p. 38, map b) or cartonnages (Grimm 1974, p. 194). Whereas both types of funerary items have been found at Tebtunis with its elaborate archaeological ensemble (Grimm 1974 p. 54 and Parlasca 1966, pp. 35 and 144), one must explore this architectural phenomenon further in order to determine whether the presence of stone statuary together with the absence of such funerary items is either causal or coincidental.

The Dating

Document C-1, dated to the Year 19 of the Roman Emperor Tiberius according to its Demotic inscription, is the key piece in the series. It is contemporary with Documents C-2 and C-3 because of their identical, shared correspondences. Taken together, these three statues provide the criteria with which to suggest that Document C-4 is their near contemporary. These four statues form a unified typology, here labeled Group C, all of the examples of which can be broadly datable to the first half of the first century A.D.

Document D-1, from Karanis, has long been recognized as standing at or near the end of the sequence of pharaonic sculpture (Bothmer, de Meulenaere, and Müller 1960, no. 140 and Bianchi 1988, no. 133). Its findspot, the area west of the South Temple in the lowest occupation level, suggest not only its dating, shortly before or after the turn of the millennium, but also its function. There is no reason to assume that a statue from the Late period, found in what appears to be a mudbrick habitation context, has been removed from its original archaeological context. Zivie, in treating the hieroglyphic texts on the statue of Pa-en-merit (Cairo JE 67094), concludes that this statue was erected in a *pr*, or house, within a *wbꜣ*,[12] or temenos, in order to partake of the services of the daily cult offered to the deities of the sanctuary (Zivie-Coche 1987, pp. 179–80). One might, therefore, cautiously suggest that Document D-1, the Ann Arbor statue from Karanis, was erected in a similar chapel. In light of this new evidence the archaeological context of the draped, striding male figure in London (BM 22750; see Taylor 1988, no. 62), inscribed in Demotic for an official named Askaikhet,[13] could be profitably reinvestigated as well (see Nachtergael 1985, p. 227, although again misreading the name as "Bakakhuiu"). The close correspondences between Documents D-1 and D-2 can be taken as evidence that these two also form a typological set, Group D, which can be more narrowly assigned to the Faiyum and are roughly contemporary with those of Group C, datable as well to the first half of the first century A.D.

Of the remaining statues, three, Documents A-1, B-4, and E-1, are sufficiently well preserved to warrant a stylistic analysis. An examination of the wrap-around costume worn by the figure Document A-1 suggests a dating for the statue. Because the treatment of the tuck has been shown to become more stylized and rudimentary in form as time passed (Bianchi 1988, p. 128), its form on

10. See Grimm 1974, p. 21 for the *mention* of a mask in a papyrus from Dime; and p. 124, note 219 for a wall painting from Karanis.

11. Although this group of statues requires further investigation, two of its members have been recently published, see Bianchi 1988, no. 32 [Detroit 51.83]; and A. Farid 1980, pp. 155–68 [Cairo 6/6/22/5].

12. The objections and alternative interpretation of Wallet-Lebrun (1985, pp. 67–88) do not appear very cogent in this context.

13. Already read correctly by Stricker (1959, p. 5, fig. 6) but repeatedly cited as "Bakakhuiu," *inter alia* Kaplony-Heckel (1974, pp. 242–43) following the initial incorrect rendering of Petrie (1885, pp. 41–42).

this statue suggests a dating no later than the fourth century B.C. Statues of this type were apparently the models upon which later enthroned male figures might be based. One can, therefore, cogently suggest that this particular statue was usurped at some later time when the Greek inscriptions were added. Consequently these Greek inscriptions on Document A-1 are contemporary with the statues of Groups C and D, whereas the statue is much earlier.

Although insufficiently preserved to warrant an extended discussion of their details Document B-1 is stylistically sufficiently close enough both to Document B-2 and to Document B-3 to suggest that all three are roughly contemporary with one another. These shared characteristics approximate to greater or lesser degrees the formal characteristics of Groups C and D and, thereby, invite the suggestion that they too ought to be considered members of a third, although admittedly less homogeneous, typology, Group B, which likewise dates to the same general period. Document B-1 is, however, somewhat enigmatic because it would appear that its Greek inscription, datable as well to the first century A.D., was a later addition, although how much later is a matter of speculation. The statue was apparently sculpted and inscribed only after it was subsequently damaged, as an examination of how the Greek letters of its inscription were accommodated into the breaks of the front and left-hand side of the base clearly reveals.

The configuration of the head and the treatment of both the hair and inlaid eyes of Document B-4 are so analogous to these same features in Documents C-1 and C-2 as to suggest a dating in the early first century A.D. for this piece as well. One should note that the cutting of its accompanying Greek inscription, datable to this same period within the first half of the first century A.D. (E. Bernand 1975, p. 159, note 291a), is somewhat maladroitly rendered when compared to the infinitely superior quality of the statue's formal, linear adjuncts.

Document E-1, in Alexandria, is so different in its material and in the treatment of its details from the remaining statues discussed in this essay to warrant its exclusion from those ateliers. While the comparanda are far from certain, the treatment of the features of the face as well as of the hair do in fact bear a striking, initial resemblance to Egyptian works attributed to the Emperor Caracalla (Bianchi 1988, no. 140 [University Museum E. 976] and J. Hermann 1988, no. 73 [Brooklyn 36.161]) and incline one to suggest, however tentatively, a date in the first quarter of the third century A.D. If this suggestion is accepted, this statue would be among the very last ancient Egyptian statues ever sculpted in a pharaonic idiom.

THE DONORS

Of the twelve statues, three (Documents A-1, B-1, and B-4) are inscribed in Greek and only one, Document C-1, which is admittedly the finest of the series,[14] is inscribed in Demotic. All are dedicated to individuals other than the named donors; Documents A-1 and B-1 are dedicated to private citizens bearing non-native names, whereas Document C-1 is dedicated to the reigning emperor and Document B-4 to a deity. Nevertheless, in each case, the individual claiming responsibility for either the creation of the statue and/or the dedication itself bears an Egyptian name: Document A-1 Peteesis, as donor; Document B-1 Pnepheros, as donor, with Peteesis as "artist"; Document B-4 Tesenouphis, as donor and "artist"; and Document C-1 Horus and Psais as donors.[15]

14. I concur with Zauzich's (1987a, p. 217) aesthetic appraisal of the piece.

15. The distinct possibility remains that the piece was a simultaneous dedication on behalf of all parties inasmuch as Zauzich (1987a, pp. 215–17) has suggested that the parties named in the inscription on the side were perhaps relatives of Horus, the donor. Moreover, the individual responsible for cutting the inscription was himself unfamiliar with the script and was probably working from a copy. Such a set of circumstances inclines one to believe that the two inscriptions originally may have been part of one which here suffered from an ellipsis on the part of the stonecutter.

THE SIGNIFICANCE OF THE ENTHRONED MALE FIGURE

Within the history of Egyptian art, the throne was a sign of rank, originally reserved for pharaohs and deities but was soon appropriated for private dedications as well. Nevertheless the throne was used sparingly in statuary of private individuals in the Late period, restricted in time, it appears, to the Twenty-fifth and Twenty-sixth Dynasties, after which the image of an enthroned official virtually disappears from the repertoire of types of Egyptian private statuary (Aldred et al. 1980, p. 121), being only rarely encountered thereafter (Bothmer, de Meulenaere, and Müller 1960, p. 182). Furthermore, it appears that for the Ptolemaic period there is only one known example of a seated royal statue, that of a group including Arsinoe II now on view in the sculpture garden at Pompey's Pillar in Alexandria (Sauneron 1960, p. 84, note 1 [Alexandria 11261]). It is somewhat surprising, therefore, to discover such an inordinately large concentration of statues of male figures, seated on thrones, not chairs, within the narrow geographic confines of the Faiyum at the very beginning of the Roman occupation of Egypt.

Since this is the case, one can forcefully suggest that the choice of a male figure seated on a throne by these native Egyptians as a fitting image for their dedications was both conscious and purposeful. Von Bissing (1914, text to plate 111:5 [Cairo CG 1191]), early on, perceptively compared the significance of these thrones to that of the image of Chephren in Cairo (CG 14). I would further his observation by suggesting that each of these enthroned dedications are, to a greater or lesser degree, indebted to earlier images of intercessors — divine, royal, and human — traditionally depicted enthroned in an attempt to emphasis their status, i. e. distinct and separate from that of mortals. Among these enthroned intercessors of the Late period, Imhotep is the most prominent (Wildung 1977 pp. 37–38, no. 15 [Louvre N. 4541, dated to the Twenty-seventh–Twenty-eighth Dynasties]; pp. 86–87, no. 55 [Brooklyn 37.1356E, dated to the Twenty-sixth–Thirtieth Dynasties]; and pp. 195–96, no. 139 [Amsterdam 7876, dated to the first century A.D.]; cf. note 19). Indeed, this general impression gains support from the fact that Document A-1 is so close to that statue inscribed for Imhotep in Amsterdam as to suggest a common source as the model for both,[16] a model which is evoked as well by the papyrus scroll held by Document B-1. To this observation must be added a second, namely that the donor of Document A-1, Peteesis, erected his statue to Herodes, whom he calls his savior (see Quaegebeur 1971b, p. 200, note 2 for the Egyptian equivalent). In such a context, then, the appearance of the *ankh* sign in the hand of Document D-2 is a fitting attribute for an intercessor (Christensen 1983, p. 22). Finally, one can regard the dedications on both Documents B-1 and C-1, to an individual and the emperor respectively, as offerings for either anticipated or received benefactions shared in common by members of large families in much the same way in which Tesenouphis (Document B-4) wishes to benefit from his dedication to Pramenis. These texts uniformly imply beneficial intervention by the honoree on behalf of the donor.

It would appear, therefore, that individuals, both living in the Faiyum in the century following the Roman occupation of Egypt and bearing native Egyptian names, consciously elected to usurp and recreate a statue type, that of the enthroned male intercessor, which in three (Documents A-1, B-1, and C-1) of the four inscribed cases studied, honored individuals with non-native names. The motivation for this archaizing phenomenon at this time must be regarded in terms of the intellectual concerns of the native priesthoods who could and did survey their cultural past in an effort to select a model appropriate to their current circumstances. So, for example, they could convincingly integrate Augustus into the pharaonic program at Dendur (Winter 1981, pp. 373–82) or select from the

16. Wildung 1977, pp. 195–96. I would, however, question the dating of the piece because the cutting of the hieroglyphs appear to have more in common with a date in the late Ptolemaic period than with those from the Roman Imperial period at which time the hieroglyphs, if the examples from Dendera are taken as representative (see note 11 above), appear to be scratched onto the surface of the stone, rather than cut as here.

sculptural repertoire the image of the enthroned male figure. The former integration does not rely on any glosses for its message, which is entirely pharaonic in form and content. The latter, on the other hand, is symptomatic of a tendency begun already in the Ptolemaic period and earlier, whereby a pharaonic image is provided with a non-hieroglyphic legend, more frequently in either Greek or Demotic, by which the meaning of the image is rendered comprehensible to a wider audience.[17] This phenomenon has already been identified in the Ptolemaic period and commented upon by Bingen (1970, pp. 35–36) in his discussion of the stela of Pasos, cited earlier (see p. 15 above), and by Yoyotte (1969, pp. 127–41) in his treatment of certain funerary stelae from Edfu. From these discussions it appears that there was a need to provide portable pharaonic images with accompanying inscriptions in the vernacular so that the images depicted thereon might become intelligible to those members of the community who were unable to understand the hieroglyphs. In the case of the twelve statues discussed here, the same process appears to have been operative. Individuals with non-native names elected to honor others with non-native names with a pharaonic statue type, that of the enthroned male figure, and elected to accompany this form of dedication with non-hieroglyphic glosses, in these cases either Greek or Demotic. By so doing, the theme of the intercessor became meaningful to both native and non-native named inhabitants of this region of the Faiyum.

THE GROUP OF STATUES AS A REFLECTION OF CONTINUED SOCIETAL CHANGE

As visual, pharaonic images made meaningful, by the addition of a Greek or Demotic inscription, to those members of society not conversant in the hieroglyphs in the Faiyum during the early first century of the Roman occupation of Egypt, these images of enthroned intercessors can be regarded as the latest expressions of a process which began earlier in the Ptolemaic period, as the discussions of the stelae studied by Bingen and Yoyotte, above, reveal.

Such a process must, however, never be considered in isolation because it intricately relates to a parallel phenomenon in which pharaonic elements, both visual and thematic, are completely veiled in the classical mantle. The earliest and most significant manifestation of this tendency is, of course, the cult of Serapis, whose images and rituals completely concealed any of their pharaonic components. This situation is entirely analogous to that discussed by Quaegebeur (1983b, pp. 41–54) in his treatment of Nemesis as a griffin where the fundamentally pharaonic theological statement is presented to a wider audience as a series of classical, not pharaonic, images. I am certain that other examples of this tendency can be adduced as well. The popularization, for want of a better term, of pharaonic religious tenets by presenting them clothed in either the vernacular of classical motifs or pharaonic images with the addition of glosses in either Greek or Demotic cannot be accepted as evidence for the ascendancy of things classical and the eclipse of things pharaonic. To do so fails to take into account the strength of an admittedly numerically small but nevertheless intellectually vigorous native priesthood, whose members throughout the Ptolemaic period kept the ancient Egyptian hieroglyphs alive and built on that foundation in such a way that the profound theological speculation at Esna in the Roman Imperial period was couched in a hieroglyphic expression which only a handful could understand and appreciate (Sauneron 1982). The kind of collaboration, about which both Bingen and Yoyotte speculate, between Greek and native Egyptian intellectuals in the Ptolemaic period continued unabated into the Roman period, as the discussions about Nemesis reveal. That such putative collaboration did in fact take place can be graphically supported by examining the historical aspects of the Egyptian titularies of the Roman emperors (Grenier 1987, pp. 81–104) and the accuracy with which hieroglyphic inscriptions, some attributed

17. See John D. Ray (p. 273, below), who has identified forty-nine scripts used by various individuals living in Egypt during this time period.

to specific Egyptian priests (Fowden 1987, pp. 51–57 and 1986, pp. 54–56, 64–65), on Roman monuments are cut (Derchain 1987; Grenier and Coarelli 1986, pp. 217–29). Far from retrenching, the native pharaonic priesthood in Roman period Egypt, content to remain within the confines of their temples, nevertheless welcomed the opportunity for continued collaboration with non-natives, thereby spreading aspects of ancient Egyptian culture beyond the boundaries of Egypt herself.

In my view, then, these seemingly irreconcilable tendencies, the one intent on popularizing, the other on obfuscating pharaonic religious tenets, must be regarded as the product of one and the same theological impetus. The native priests were simultaneously content to develop profound theological formulations which might be expressed in the complex subtleties of the hieroglyphs and to collaborate with non-natives with a view toward making other pharaonic speculations comprehensible to an audience unlettered in the pictograms.

In the process primacy of place was denied to pharaonic sculpture in stone which, after this period of transition in the early first century A.D., was progressively replaced and virtually supplanted by two-dimensional relief representations in temples. These flat surfaces may have been deemed the more appropriate medium for such messages, which were primarily intended to be "read," like scrolls, rather than "interpreted," in the traditional manner in which pharaonic sculpture was intended to be understood because Egyptian sculpture in the round was invariably integral to the larger cultic complex of which it was only part. Indeed, realizing that I may be overstating my case, I will nevertheless suggest that the primacy of the two-dimensional representation is coincident with the primacy of the two-dimensional nature of the hieroglyphs in which the profound theological speculations of the selected priesthoods continued to be made manifest. The implications of this suggestion must now be explored.

Art Historical Assessment

Two of the enthroned images, Documents A-1 and B-1, appear to be the works of individuals named Peteesis according to their accompanying Greek inscriptions.[18] Since Document A-1 appears to be a usurped statue, one questions whether it was sculpted by Peteesis, inasmuch as this "signature" is so maladroitly cut in comparison to the careful details exhibited in the sculpting of the statue itself. One is tempted to regard this Peteesis as the same individual responsible for the acquisition of Document B-1, itself a statue with an inscription added subsequent to its manufacture. I would welcome an epigrapher's comments on a comparative study of the letter forms of both inscriptions. Be that as it may, I think it highly unlikely that an individual named Peteesis did sculpt Document B-1. I am, rather, inclined to regard Documents A-1 and B-1 as statues procured and erected by the agency of one or more individuals named Peteesis, neither of whom can be regarded as the artist responsible for the actual sculpting of the statue bearing his name. I am of the same opinion as well for Document B-4, ostensibly signed by Tesenouphis, despite the fact that the statue and the inscription are contemporary. Here again, there is a great disparity between the quality of the letter forms of the inscription and the linear adjuncts of the statue proper. I wonder, therefore, whether the Greek verbs *epoi(ei)* and *epoe* in these inscriptions might be taken figuratively, in the sense of the Egyptian *irj*, to encompass all of the processes involved in erecting such a dedication.

One is, nevertheless, justified in speaking of schools of pharaonic sculpture in the Faiyum at the beginning of the Roman domination. Assuredly, the similarities noted above among the statues assigned to Group C, on the one hand, and those placed in Group D, on the other, indicate that native Egyptian craftsmen were still capable of developing and adhering to sculptural tenets, derived from earlier models, for at least two different formulations of the enthroned male figure. The relatively small size of each of these images and their strict adherence to the contours of the

18. E. Bernand (1975, pp. 160–61) accepts both inscriptions at face value as evidence that they represent artists' signatures.

blocks of stone from which they were cut may have contributed to the noticeable lack of axial asymmetry in their designs (Bianchi 1988, p. 71), but the bichromatic effect of their surfaces, particularly noticeable in the unfinished surfaces of Document C-3, are to be expected (ibid., pp. 71–72).[19] The geometric simplification of their planes is in keeping with the general stylistic development of pharaonic sculpture at the end of the Ptolemaic period (Bowman 1986, pp. 141–42; Kiss 1984, p. 25) as is the practice of inlaying the eyes (Braemer 1984, p. 423, note 10). The appearance of so many statues in hard stone from the Faiyum during the first half of the first century A.D. represents a considerable outlay of capital, indicative of the status of an advantaged class. Their individual financial circumstances, like that of others in the Faiyum in this period (Hanson 1989b, pp. 429–40), must not mask the fact that the temples of the Faiyum, to judge from their relatively modest dimensions and from the fact that their walls are almost never covered with Egyptian relief decoration and accompanying hieroglyph inscriptions, were already disadvantaged when compared to the thriving religious communities of Upper Egypt. And because customs and individuals do not automatically expire when political realities are altered, it stands to reason that the production of temple statuary would continue, however haltingly, into the beginning of the first century A.D. at which time it virtually disappeared. It is, therefore, interesting to note that after this period of transition, pharaonic visual expression tends to confine itself to relief decoration, Document E-1 ranking among the known exceptions. Taken as a whole, this group of statues, in its own quaint, almost folk art approach to sculpture, is a fitting conclusion to the final chapter of ancient pharaonic sculpture from Egypt.

This virtual disappearance of pharaonic sculpture for private dedications about A.D. 50 in the Faiyum is symptomatic of a greater cultural dislocation, namely the progressive distancing of the native Egyptians themselves from their pharaonic traditions. In addition to the disappearance of their sculpture, private relief dedications made during the first and following centuries A.D. tend to cloak pharaonic religious tenets in classical garb; the dedications to Nemesis discussed above are a case in point. Furthermore, as Thelma Thomas (see pp. 317–22 below) has suggested, the sculptural decoration of private tombs, in some regions of the country, appears to have relied exclusively upon the classical, and not a pharaonic, visual vocabulary. The virtual denial, then, of traditional Egyptian art forms, sculpture in the round and in relief embellished with pharaonic motifs and hieroglyphs, to the native Egyptians occurs at precisely the same point in time at which they are denied the use of their language as a written vernacular. That the episode of illiteracy, which Roger Bagnall (forthcoming) has suggested, did in fact exist accords well with my observation about a concomitant visual illiteracy as well. The native Egyptians appear, then, to have been denied visual and literal links with their past.

If we are, therefore, correct in our consensus, which this symposium has brought into sharper focus, that the native Egyptians, from the time of the first century A.D. onward, were progressively divorced from their language and art, we must not neglect an overview of the native priesthood during this very same period. These prelates appear to belong to a small, elite group who apparently confined their activities to select temples throughout the land. Their members were, nevertheless, permitted an as yet undefined, but admittedly unfettered, degree of intellectual freedom which enabled them to promulgate profound religious expressions which they were then able to translate into the most complex hieroglyphic expressions known from ancient Egypt. These expressions were then given visual expression on the walls of their temples which continued to be designed, constructed, and adorned according to millennia-old pharaonic traditions. Moreover, members of this same elite priesthood then participated in formulating genuine Egyptian expressions employed by various Roman emperors both in Egypt and abroad in accordance with the specific ideology for

19. This feature does not automatically indicate that the statue on which it was found is unfinished, as suggested *inter alia*, by Bowman 1986, p. 126, fig. 75.

which they were commissioned. The discussions earlier about these titularies and Italian obelisks are sufficient demonstration of this set of circumstances, however ill-defined their actual mechanisms may currently be. Some of these priests seem to have been active as well in certain funerary preparations because of the continued use of both the hieroglyphs and of an internally consistent repertoire of traditional motifs encountered on the types of cartonnage ensembles presented by L. Corcoran (see pp. 57–61, below).[20] This much is certain.

It remains, perhaps as the subject of one or more future congresses, to inquire about the hows and the whys. Just what were the forces — societal, cultural, political, religious, and the like — and their natures which could so fragment a society in such a way that its prelates, safe within their living traditions, could seemingly conspire with the officials of the foreign forces of occupation while their congregations of impoverished native Egyptians were simultaneously denied access to their own traditional visual and written truths?

20. This paper is a further development of the points she raised earlier in her Ph.D. dissertation (1988).

Photograph of Document A-1 (Cairo JE 49370)

PLATE 3.2

Photograph of Document B-1 (Alexandria 3199)

Photograph of Document B-2 (Alexandria 3201)

PLATE 3.4

Photograph of Document B-3 (Alexandria 3197)

PLATE 3.5

Photograph of Document B-4 (Cairo CG 1190)

PLATE 3.6

Photograph of Document C-1 (Cairo CG 1191)

Photograph of Document C-1 (Cairo CG 1191)

PLATE 3.8

Photograph of Document C-2 (Alexandria 3193)

Photograph of Document C-3 (Alexandria 3198)

PLATE 3.10

Photograph of Document C-4 (Alexandria 3203)

Photograph of Document D-1 (Ann Arbor 8281)

PLATE 3.12

Photograph of Document D-2 (Cairo CG 1192)

Photograph of Document E-1 (Alexandria 3196)

CHAPTER 4

EGYPTIANS AND GREEKS IN AN EARLY LAOGRAPHIA ACCOUNT (P. BEROL. 25161)

WILLIAM BRASHEAR
Ägyptisches Museum

The document under discussion was assembled from fragments evidently extracted from cartonnage at the beginning of this century and deposited with other unedited cartonnage material in boxes for safe keeping. The boxes survived the vicissitudes of World War II and eventually landed in the Ägyptisches Museum und Papyrussammlung (Staatliche Museen zu Berlin Preussischer Kulturbesitz) in the western part of the city, where they were rediscovered in the early 1980s during a research project financed by the Deutsche Forschungsgemeinschaft. (Out of these unedited cartonnage papyri derived a large part of the Ptolemaic documents making up BGU XIV. The early Augustan era documents out of the same cache will be published in BGU XVI due to go to press in 1992. The present document = BGU XVI 2577.)

PROVENANCE

The only concrete internal evidence for the provenance is a tally involving the gymnasiarchs of an unnamed metropolis. The external evidence is circumstantial. Since most of the late Ptolemaic and early Roman papyri in the Berlin collection (extricated from cartonnage coffins found by the German excavators at the beginning of this century in Abusir el Melek, site of the ancient Busiris) come from the Herakleopolite nome, this can be posited with reasonable assurance as provenance of this text. While it surprisingly turned out that some of the papyri were written in Alexandria (BGU IV 1050–1060, 1098–1184—*synchoreseis* contracts, for the most part), most of the documents from the Abusir el Melek find derive from closer to home. Furthermore, possible internal supporting evidence are two putative *Herkunftsbezeichungen* in the text itself: line 72: Κρηκίτης; line 80: Οννίτης for citizens of Krekis (BGU XIV 2437.44; 2439.20, 62) and Onne (BGU XIV 2370.82.86, 2440.44) respectively, both villages in the Herakleopolite nome. The presence of these indications of origin in a list otherwise devoid of such designations implies that these men were registered as inhabitants of their respective home villages while they were residing temporarily for one reason or another presumably in the metropolis, Herakleopolis.

DATING

The document commences with a heading of several lines undoubtedly once indicating the function and purpose of the ensuing listing. Καίσαρος, obviously referring to Augustus, appears in this heading. However, the papyrus is broken off on the left, and the heading is otherwise so lacunose that the exact year and date as well as any title which once might have indicated the nature of the ensuing list are lost and forever irretrievable. Since most of the cartonnage documents from Augustan era Herakleopolis date from the 20s B.C., one can tentatively place this list in that period. A further criterion for the dating is the paleography. The writing shows striking similarities to the *Laterculi Alexandrini* (Diels 1904, with facsimile) but is somewhat more crude and cursive, befitting its documentary character. The same person who was responsible for this roll may have also penned another tax list in the Berlin collection (P. Berol. 25185–25186, 16948A–B).

Five non-contiguous fragments 14–19 cm high and 25–52 cm wide constituting the upper part of a papyrus roll are extant. All told, the remaining portion of the roll measures ca. 160 cm in length. Since only the uppermost portion of the roll is preserved, its exact height must remain a matter for speculation; the same is true for its original length. Altogether there are twenty-nine columns and 526 lines.

The order of the major fragments A–C results from various internal chronological data. Fragment A preserves portions of the descriptive heading for the whole document. Phaophi in the first line there is undoubtedly the first month for which tallies are recorded in the ensuing lines up to line 117. The first entries on Fragment B (lines 118–94) must obviously be for the month Hathyr, since Choiak (line 199) heads the subsequent listing extending to the end of the fragment. Since Tybi appears in the first line of Fragment C (= line 214), this fragment must obviously follow immediately after Fragment B. The two remaining fragments cannot be assigned with certainty to any place in the role. However, since Fragment D includes mostly amounts of four drachmas it might originally have belonged to Fragment A. Fragment E recording amounts of two drachmas probably belonged to Fragment C.

Since the beginning of this account with its heading is so lacunose and the end (which might have contained itemized summaries) is entirely missing, it is difficult to posit any but the most general statement about its character and purpose. In all likelihood the list once constituted a month-by-month, day-by-day and even morning-to-evening, κατ' ἄνδρα list of (exclusively male) taxpayers for probably the nome capital Herakleopolis. Each taxpayer is identified by name and (sometimes) father's name, or failing that, his profession (for cross reference in a list of taxpayers according to occupation?) and the amount he has paid (or is expected to pay?) on an unknown tax. (See most recently Bogaert 1989, pp. 207–26, on the *status quaestionis* on the function of tax lists in Roman Egypt.) The multifarious occupations and professions standing in lieu of the father's name reflect all levels of society: line 14 τέκτων, 30 σιτομέτρης, 43 ἱπποκόμος, 47 λίνυφος, 48 γναφεύς, 49 λαχαωοπώλης, 51 αὐλητής, 57 παστοφόρος, 58 ἡπητής, 59 ὀνηλάτης, 71 οἰκοδόμος, 77 ποιμήν, 83 γέρδις, 84 χρυσοχοῦς, 110 ταριχευταί, 161, 427 χαλκεύς, 293 γρ(αφεύς?), 313 ἰατρός, 323 κεραμεύς, and 370 σκυτεύς (see H. Harrauer 1987, pp. 49–173 for these trades and occupations).

While the criteria are most tenuous and any thesis built upon them highly susceptible to collapsing, I would like to suggest that the present tax list might record payments on the poll tax in Herakleopolis in the early years of Augustus' reign. It is particularly regrettable that the date is lost, since this list might have been one of the earliest attestations to the capitation tax. Although not a single word in the whole document gives the slightest clue as to which tax is involved here, the fact that the names are all masculine and the fact that so many occupations are indicated remind one of the capitation tax lists in the Princeton and Columbia collections.

The sole reference to the laographia in the Heracleopolite nome during the entire Roman occupation of Egypt has heretofore been another Abusir el Melek cartonnage document, BGU IV 1198 (Busiris, 5/4 A.D.), wherein four priests complain that they have been charged sixteen drachmas apiece for the laographia. Hence, our knowledge of the capitation tax in this area is just about nil.

The ethnic interest of this tax list lies in lines 214–16. This subheading for the subsequent roster divides the civil population of the political entity involved into catoecs, Greeks, and Egyptians: Τῦβι ἄλλης λογηας (l. -ίας) (δρ.) ι / κατοίκων καὶ Ἑλλήνων / καὶ Αἰγυπτίων. The indication of ten drachmas is obscure, since none of the succeeding payments in the ensuing sixty-some lines ever exceeds one or two drachmas. One possibility is to assume that the ten drachmas represent the total sum assessed upon each individual for that year. Another is to associate this amount with the following word and assume the presence of ten-drachma catoecs in the early Augustan era Herakleopolite nome. However, in that case, one would expect ι (δρ.) κατοίκων and not (δρ.) ι κατοίκων (ten-drachma catoecs are otherwise attested only once in BGU I 118 [Arsinoe, 189 A.D.], regarding which Wallace [1938, 409.40] says, "There is certainly no indication of a 10 dr. rate of capitation tax in the Arsinoite nome").

According to Montevecchi (1970, p. 23) catoecs in Roman period Egypt are, by and large, an Arsinoite phenomenon, with relatively few coming from the Hermupolite nome (P. Sarap.) where the designation seems to be more general and equivalent with γεοῦχος (Méautis, 1918, p. 65.1; Schwartz, P. Sarap. 24.12n.). So far only one catoec is attested in the Heracleopolite nome (P. Oslo 98: 131/132 A.D.) where the designation seems to have a connotation similar to that of the Arsinoite occurrences. According to the entries in lines 214–16, the catoecs in the Heracleopolite nome of the early Augustan era are clearly distinguished from the rest of the population consisting of Greeks and Egyptians. However, in the ensuing list of names no attempt is otherwise made at designating who is catoec and who is not. Neither does there seem to be any distinguishing feature between the people paying one and those paying two drachma installments on their taxes.

While Wallace (1938a) argues for the catoecs' poll tax liability, Nelson (1979, p. 38) argues for their exemption. Since, however, the overwhelming majority of the pitifully few documents shedding any light on the issue derive from the Arsinoite nome and date, generally speaking, several centuries later, they afford no help at all in deciding the status of the catoecs here in the early Augustan era Herakleopolite nome and whether or not they were totally or partially exempt from the poll tax—provided that this is a poll tax list at all.

Hence, the questions and issues this new tax list raises are for the most part *imponderabilia*: what is the status of these early Roman catoecs? Is it the same as the Ptolemaic catoecs or has Augustus already changed it by this time? What is the difference between the catoecs and the Greeks? Why are all these three lumped here together in one category? (If there is no difference among the three in the end, why bother to make the distinction at all unless they are all lumped together here as payers of the poll tax regardless of the rate?) A point which evokes even such further questions, impossible to answer, as: What was the poll tax in the early Augustan era? Were there privileged classes either partially or entirely exempt from paying the laographia? (cf. *CPR* VIII 20, a letter of unknown provenance from the 3rd century A.D., which mentions Alexandrians, Romans, and catoecs.)

In closing and in passing—onomasticians will have a heyday with this tax list, for alongside its intriguing, but unfortunately all too fragmentary mention of catoecs, Greeks, and Egyptians in Herakleopolis, this list presents us with some seventy names heretofore unattested, thus providing a rich, new source of material on nomenclature in the early Augustan era Heracleopolite nome. It is amusing to see alongside such obviously Egyptian, and for the accountant indeclinable, names as Otokulis (line 45) or Tualis (line 128) quite stolid and venerable Greek names—hallowed by centuries of tradition—such as Polydeukes (line 53), Kastor, son of Dionysos (line 222), Orpheus (line 232), Diomedes (line 137), Poliantes (line 418), and even an Achilleus, son of Atreus (line 518). In line 419 one furthermore finds an Ammenneus, son of Pindar — Pindar in the tax rolls!

Literature on the laographia includes: Wallace 1938a, pp. 116–34; Wallace 1938a, pp. 418–42; Préaux 1939a, pp. 381f.; Préaux 1935, pp. 28–33; Bell 1947, pp. 12–23; Braunert 1956, pp. 302–05; Tcherikover 1950, pp. 187.19–20; D. Samuel 1977, pp. 129f.; Tsiparis, 1979; Hobson 1984, p. 855; Papyrus Harris 199; Goudriaan 1988, p. 14; Gallazzi 1979, pp. 4–7; Samuel 1981, pp. 389–403; Omar 1988, p. 288.

CHAPTER 5

HECATAEUS OF ABDERA'S HISTORY OF EGYPT

STANLEY M. BURSTEIN
California State University, Los Angeles

From the Mycenaean period to the end of antiquity contact with Egypt and its civilization was one of the constants of Greek history. Not surprisingly, therefore, the attempt to understand Egypt was one of the central themes of Greek historiography as is revealed by the fact that the largest single section in Felix Jacoby's great *Die Fragmente der griechischen Historiker* (1958, nos. 608a–665) is that devoted to the historians of Egypt. Although most of these works survive only in fragments, it is clear that the historiographical tradition to which they belonged was dominated by two works, the second book of Herodotus' *History of the Persian Wars* and the *Aegyptiaca* of Hecataeus of Abdera, a work now lost in its original form but of which an extensive epitome survives in the first book of the *Library of History* of the first century B.C. universal historian Diodorus Siculus.[1] Despite their joint responsibility for the formation of the Greek tradition on Egypt, however, modern scholarly assessments of Herodotus' and Hecataeus' works differ significantly.

Assessments of Herodotus' achievement in his Egyptian *logos* tend to be generous, perhaps because book two is generally agreed to be the earliest portion of Herodotus' *History of the Persian Wars*, and, therefore, the account of the kings of Egypt in chapters 99–182 of that book may represent the first substantial attempt by a Greek historian to reconstruct a portion of the past (cf. Fornara 1971, pp. 1–23). Thus, after a thorough analysis of these chapters, Lloyd clearly demonstrated that Herodotus' history of the kings of Egypt "shows no genuine understanding of Egyptian history," but still concluded that "it is extremely doubtful whether any historian before modern times could have significantly improved on Herodotus' performance ... " (1988b, pp. 52–53). Considerably less sympathetic, however, have been the evaluations of Hecataeus' *Aegyptiaca*, the work that superseded it as the standard Greek account of Egypt. In contrast to Herodotus' book, Hecataeus' *Aegyptiaca* has been dismissed as an "edifying novel" intended "to establish the superiority of the kingdom ruled over by [sc. Ptolemy] Soter" (Fraser 1972, vol. 1, p. 504) while his account of Egyptian history, much of which is preserved in chapters 44 to 68 of Diodorus' work, is "taken with only the smallest alterations from Herodotus" and is of "no importance, for it is clear that Hecataeus was not particularly interested in history" (Murray 1970, p. 152).

In part, the denunciation of Hecataeus' work as little more than "warmed over Herodotus" is probably the result of frustration over a great opportunity wasted, and it cannot be denied that there

1. For the few attested fragments see Jacoby, 3A, 264 Ff 1–6. For Hecataeus as the principal source of Diodorus' first book see Jacoby, *FGrH*, 3a, pp. 75-87; and Murray 1970, pp. 144–50. The arguments for the use of multiple sources in Diodorus' first book by Anne Burton 1972, pp. 1–34, are unconvincing in view of the evidence for Diodorus' consistent tendency to rely on a single source for each of his major topics assembled by Hornblower 1981, pp. 22–39.

is some justification for such a feeling. Hecataeus denounced Herodotus as one of those writers who told "marvelous tales" and invented "myths for the pleasures of their readers" (Diodorus 1.69.7). His work, Hecataeus claimed, however, was based on Egyptian priestly records and personal observations made during his stay in Egypt in the early years of the reign of Ptolemy I whom he served as a diplomat.[2] These claims, moreover, are given some credibility by the remarkable accuracy of his description of the Ramesseum (Diodorus 1.47–49 with the analysis of Leblanc 1985, pp. 70–82) with its allusions to the reliefs accompanying Ramses II's Kadesh inscription (cf. Burton 1972, pp. 150–51) and partially correct interpretation of Ramses' titulary (Leblanc 1985, pp. 76–77). Equally clear, unfortunately, is the fact that the bulk of Hecataeus' Egyptian history is obviously derived from Herodotus and includes many of his great predecessor's most notorious errors including his dating of the pyramid kings to the late second millennium B.C. (Diodorus 1.63–64) and ascription of extensive conquests in Europe and Asia to a king Herodotus called Sesostris and Hecataeus Sesoosis.[3] Understandably, therefore, scholars have generally dismissed Hecataeus' claim that his work was based on Egyptian sources merely as "window dressing" intended to lend credibility to his idealized depiction of Egypt, its culture, and its ties to Greece. Closer analysis, however, suggests that, to reverse a familiar cliche, this may be a case of scholars not being able to see the trees because of the forest.

Faced with new evidence, the first reaction of scholars is to attempt to integrate that evidence into existing historical frameworks with as little disruption as possible as can be seen from the early attempts to reconcile the new evidence made available by Champollion's decipherment of Egyptian hieroglyphic writing with the traditional Biblical and classically-based version of Egyptian history (e.g. Heeren 1838, pp. 439–51). Similarly, ancient critics tended to fault the details of Herodotus' history, not its general outlines. Thus, Egyptian evidence was adduced to correct factual errors, not to offer an alternative reconstruction of Egyptian history. Even Manetho, probably Herodotus' best qualified ancient critic and, in fact, the author of a critique of his work (Manetho, *FGrH*, 3C, 609 F 13), did not wholly escape this tendency. Accordingly, while he rejected Herodotus' dates for the pyramid kings and Sesostris, Manetho did accept his stories about Khufu's tyranny (Manetho, *FGrH*, 3C, 609 Ff 2–3a, p. 20) and Sesostris' world conquests (Manetho, *FGrH*, 3C, 609, Ff 2–3a, pp. 30–31). The possibility that Hecataeus' treatment of Herodotus was similar was raised almost a century ago by Fr. W. von Bissing. In a detailed analysis of Diodorus', that is, Hecataeus', account of the pyramid kings von Bissing (1901) showed that, although he preserved the main outlines of Herodotus' account, Hecataeus made numerous changes in detail.[4] Some of these changes, such as the correction of Herodotus' measurements of the pyramids, could have been the results of his own observations. Others, however, such as the use of more accurate transcriptions of the pyramid king's names, his identification of the smaller pyramids at Gizeh as queens' tombs (Diodorus 1.64.10) and his reference to an alternative dating of the pyramids similar to that adopted later by Manetho (Diodorus 1.63.5), can only be explained by assuming that Hecataeus used Egyptian sources just as he claimed. A similar analysis of the whole of Hecataeus' history of Egypt would exceed the space allotted me. Here I can only make a beginning on that project by considering Hecataeus' revision of Herodotus' Egyptian kinglist so far as his changes can be recovered from Diodorus and other sources that drew on his work.

The deficiencies of Herodotus' Egyptian history are well known as are the reasons for them. In book two, chapter 154, Herodotus discounted the accuracy of his account of Egyptian history prior

2. Hecataeus of Abdera, *FGrH*, 264 T 5 with Jacoby's comment in *FGrH*, 3a, pp. 33-4. For Hecataeus' claim to have used priestly sources see Murray 1970, p. 151.

3. Diodorus 1.53–58. For the development of the Sesostris legend see Braun 1938, pp. 13–18.

4. For a similar analysis of Diodorus' account of Sesostris/Sesoosis see Obsomer 1989, pp. 41–43.

to the Twenty-sixth Dynasty by noting that it was only with the settlement of Greeks in Egypt under Amasis that reliable evidence became available. The results of this distinction between the two parts of Herodotus' account of the kings of Egypt are apparent in the uneven distribution of royal names in his kinglist. Thus, his treatment of the first millennium B.C. kings is comparatively full with seven or more than a third of Herodotus' twenty purported Egyptian royal names being those of kings of the Twenty-fifth and Twenty-sixth Dynasties while the remainder of Egyptian history is represented by only thirteen names, three of which belong to the pyramid kings and two of which, Pheros and Proteus, are fictitious, the former being the result of an obvious misunderstanding of the title Pharaoh and the latter an import from Homer. The same disparity is evident in Herodotus' omission of reports of the lengths of reign for kings prior to the Twenty-fifth dynasty except for the pyramid kings and his failure to construct an overall chronology of Egyptian history, offering instead only the observation that, as there had been 341 kings of Egypt prior to the Persian conquest and as there were three generations to a century, the period of human rule in Egypt had lasted 11,340 years (Herodotus 2.142; cf. Lloyd 1988b, pp. 31–33).

As was true of his account of the pyramid kings, Hecataeus retained the broad outlines of Herodotus' kinglist, emphasizing the same kings and repeating many of the same stories about them, but he made numerous changes in detail including offering historical explanations for events mentioned by Herodotus but left unaccounted for by him such as, for example, the emergence of Memphis and Sais as important political centers.[5] The most important of Hecataeus' modifications of Herodotus' account, however, was the creation of a precise chronology of Egyptian history to replace Herodotus' crude estimate of the length of human rule in Egypt, a chronology whose dependence on Egyptian sources is clear from its close similarity in structure and detail to that of Manetho with Hecataeus reckoning that between Menes and Alexander 480 plus kings ruled for a period of slightly more than 4,700 years and Manetho listing 500 plus kings for something between 5,271 and 5,471 years.[6] Possible additional evidence of Hecataeus' use of Egyptian sources may be found in a passage of the Roman historian Tacitus that suggests that he used the Sothic cycle to articulate the main divisions of his kinglist if, as is likely, the *Aegyptiaca* was the ultimate source of Tacitus' antiquarian information about Egypt.[7] Less obvious but equally significant are the changes in the number and distribution of royal names in Hecataeus' kinglist.

Twenty-nine supposedly royal names,[8] an increase of nine over Herodotus' kinglist, can be recovered from Diodorus and other works dependent on Hecataeus. Of these twenty-three are identifiable as the names of actual Egyptian kings; one, Ketes, is problematic although its position prior to a king named Remphis, that is, Ramses, suggests Seti I (Diodorus 1.62); another, Actisanes, is actually the name of a fourth century B.C. Napatan king (Priese 1977, pp. 343–67); and four, Busiris I and II, Aegyptus and Nileus are fictitious. Even more remarkable than the increase in the number of names in Hecataeus' kinglist, and it is clear that our knowledge of his

5. In both cases Hecataeus emphasized the commercial advantages of these cities to account for their rise to prominence (cf. Diodorus 1.50.3 [Memphis] and 1.66.8–10 [Sais]).

6. Diodorus 1.44. It is impossible to exactly determine Manetho's overall chronology of Egyptian history because of textual variants in the dynastic summaries that closed each of the three books of Manetho's history (cf. Manetho, *FGrH*, 609 Ff 2–3c, pp. 28–29, 44–45, 54–55). It is clear from Diodorus that Hecataeus also attempted to firm up his chronicle of Egyptian history by specifying the intervals between kings in terms of generations as was pointed out already by Heeren 1838, p. 403.

7. Tacitus, *Annales* 6.28; cf. Jacobson 1981, pp. 260–61, for discussion. Hecataeus is unlikely to have been Tacitus' immediate source but two facts strongly suggest that he was the ultimate source, namely, the use of forms Sesosis and Amasis for Sesostris and Ahmose and the reference to the appearance of the Phoenix during the reign of Ptolemy, the third Macedonian to rule Egypt, who, contra Tacitus, should be Ptolemy I and not Ptolemy III.

8. Omitted in this count are Armaeus and Inaros (Diodorus 1.64.13) because of the uncertainty that the former was included in Hecataeus' kinglist and the post-Twenty-sixth Dynasty date of the latter (cf. Burton 1972, p. 191).

kinglist is incomplete,[9] is their chronological distribution. Particularly noticeable is the fact that only three of the twenty-nine recoverable Hecataean royal names are those of rulers of the Twenty-sixth dynasty while twenty-six are those of rulers of earlier periods of Egyptian history for which as, Herodotus noted, only Egyptian sources were available. Further, the expansion of Hecataeus' kinglist was not limited to the Third Intermediate Period as might be expected but extended over the whole of Egyptian history. Thus, included among the Hecataean names are two new Old Kingdom royal names, Chabryes, possibly the Horus name of Ra-djed-ef,[10] and Uchoreus,[11] usually explained as an alternative name for Menes; three additional Middle Kingdom names, Nencoreus,[12] that is, Nubkaure, the praenomen of Amenemhet II; and Marrus and Mendes (Vergote 1962, pp. 66–76), abbreviated forms of Nemare, the praenomen of Amenemhet III; four further New Kingdom names, Amasis, that is, Ahmose; Ketes, perhaps, as suggested above, Seti I; Remphis, Ramses II; and, of course, Osymandias, long recognized as a rendering of Usimare, part of the praenomen of Ramses II (Leblanc 1985, p. 76); and, finally, three Third Intermediate Period names, Tnephacthus and Bocchoris, that is, Tephnacht and Bakenrenef of the Twenty-fourth dynasty and Tearco, Taharqa,[13] of the Twenty-fifth dynasty. Finally, and most important, not only did Hecataeus expand Herodotus' kinglist; he also corrected it in ways that clearly presuppose Egyptian sources.

Most of Hecataeus' corrections are relatively straightforward, involving either matters of fact such as assigning the famous Egyptian Labyrinth, most probably to be identified with the mortuary temple of Amenemhet III, a Middle Kingdom date and a funerary function (Diodorus 1.61.2) instead of the Third Intermediate Period date and political function suggested by Herodotus (Herodotus 2.148); or the replacement of Herodotean forms of royal names with more accurate transcriptions such as: Menas for Min; Chemmis for Cheops, reflecting Knomkhufwey, the full form of Khufu's nomen (Burton 1972, p. 187); Mencherinus for Mycerinus; Sasychis for Asychis, probably Shepseskaf (Kitchen 1988, pp. 148–51); Sesoosis for Sesostris, reflecting a more accurate rendering of the actual pronunciation of Senwosre (Malaise 1966, pp. 247–49); and Remphis for Rhampsinitus. One correction, however, the alteration of the name of Sesostris' son and successor from Pheros to Nencoreus, that is, as noted above, Nubkaure, the praenomen of Amenemhet II, is more revealing of the extent of Hecataeus' knowledge of things Egyptian for two reasons: first, it presupposes his recognition of the true character of the supposed royal name Pheros, which he seems to have treated as an "epithet" assumed at a king's accession; and, second, and even more remarkable,[14] it clearly reflects an attempt to identify Sesostris/Sesoosis with a specific king of the Twelfth dynasty, albeit, Sesostris I instead of Sesostris III who was to be Manetho's candidate.

9. E.g. Hecataeus referred to five ruling queens, none of whom are mentioned by Diodorus, and four Ethiopian kings, only two of which can be identified. Hecataeus' reference to five ruling queens is particularly striking in view of the fact that modern scholars also increasingly recognize the same number, namely, Nitocris, Sobekneferu, Hatshepsut, Tewosret and Nefertiti (cf. Harris 1973, pp. 5–13 and 1974, pp. 11–21).

10. Diodorus 1.64.1–2; cf. Burton (1972, p. 188) who notes that Chabryes might represent the Horus name of Ra-djed-ef, Kheper. Her objection to the identification, namely, that the other Fourth Dynasty kings are represented by the nomen, is unconvincing.

11. Diodorus 1.50.3; cf. Burton (1972, p. 158) for the suggestion that it is a corruption of Ὀχυρεύς and represents a translation of Egyptian *Mn*, "He who endures." Also possible would be an identification with Userkaf, the founder of the Fifth Dynasty (cf. Manetho, *FGrH*, 3C, 609 F 2, p. 24, who renders his name as Ousercheres).

12. Pliny, *Naturalis Historiae* 36.74. Ultimate derivation from Hecataeus is likely in view of the use of the form Sesosis for the name of Nencoreus' father.

13. Reference to Tearco occurs in the fragments of the *Indica* of Megasthenes (*FGrH*, 3C, 715 F 11) but it is likely that Megasthenes was dependent on Hecataeus for his knowledge of Egyptian history in view of his clear use of the *Aegyptiaca* as a model for his own book on India (cf. Murray 1970, pp. 207–08).

14. Diodorus 1.59.1–3. Comparison with Herodotus 2.111 indicates that the king in question is "Pheros."

There is no need to pursue this analysis further. Lloyd's assertion that no historian "before modern times could have significantly improved on Herodotus' performance" is clearly wrong. Hecataeus did so, and he did so, as he claimed, on the basis of Egyptian sources. The extent of his success, of course, was limited. Ignorant of Egyptian, Hecataeus did not always understand his Egyptian informants as can be seen from the inclusion in his kinglist of alternative transcriptions of the same royal name as the names of different kings or his ascription of vast conquests in Asia to Ramses II on the basis of a misunderstanding of the Ramesseum version of Ramses' Kadesh inscription.[15] Equally important, Hecataeus used his Egyptian sources to revise, not replace Herodotus' account of Egyptian history so that his vision of the Egyptian past remains essentially the same as that of his great predecessor, and, therefore, equally unhistorical. Nevertheless, his revised kinglist was a considerable achievement, an achievement which suggests that a similar analysis of the fragments of those portions of Hecataeus' work that dealt with Egypt in his own time would also be worthwhile. That such a study might be rewarding is suggested by Georges Posener's (1953, p. 107) recognition of a possible bit of the lost conclusion of the story of the *Doomed Prince* in Diodorus 1.89.3.

15. Diodorus 1.47.6; cf. the similar extension of the geographical scope of Ramses II's campaigns by Manetho (*FGrH*, 3C, 609, F 9.99). For a plausible explanation of how Ramses' campaign against the Hittites might have been interpreted as referring to Bactria see Spalinger 1977b, pp. 11–18.

CHAPTER 6

SOME GREEKS IN EGYPT

WILLY CLARYSSE
Katholieke Universiteit, Leuven

When the Greeks arrived in Egypt in the footsteps of Alexander, they came there to stay. Only some mercenaries returned to their homeland after the end of their service (e.g. Skopas), but most Greeks were closely bound to their new land by means of land tenure (the cleruchs were paid in land by the Ptolemies), investment of capital in immovables (e.g. the misthophoroi) and all kinds of economic activities (e.g. Zenon) and new family ties.

Such a situation almost of necessity calls for a twofold reaction: on the one hand the colonists will defend their cultural identity by grouping together, on the other they will gradually adapt themselves to their new environment. Both tendencies are active at the same time with the same people, on the conscious as well as on the subconscious level.

The Greeks in Egypt have defended their cultural identity mainly by the continued use of their language through education at home, in the schools (cf. Maehler 1983a, pp. 191–202), and in the gymnasion. This national reflex is evident, for instance, in the names of the cleruchic population until far into the Roman period. Originally the names even reflect the onomastic particularism of the Greek world at large (Panakestor, Agreophon from Caria, Druton from Crete), in the Roman period the models may be taken from Greek literature or history (names such as Achilleus, Orestes, Priamos, Leonidas, Spartiates, and Helladios).

But I do not want to dwell now on the preservation of Greek identity, but rather on the opposite phenomenon, that of Greek integration in Egyptian society. I want to do this on the basis of three case studies, each of which can be shown to be typical of larger sections of the population. In fact I will discuss three individuals or individual families which assimilated themselves respectively on the sociological, the religious, and the economic level.

1. For Greeks arriving in Egypt the most likely way to become involved with the local population was through marriage. If some immigrants had married before arriving or could find a girl in the Greek community within Egypt (e.g. Druton's first marriage), many others no doubt lived with native girls and married native women. Lists have been made of what scholars call "mixed marriages" and "abnormal filiations," where the husband or the father has a Greek name and the mother an Egyptian name (Peremans 1981, pp. 273–81). Apparently they were not very numerous in the third century B.C. I can now add one more mixed family to the list, a family about which we know something more than just plain names of father, mother, and children.

In Papyrus Petrie[2] I 1 (= Papyrus Petrie III 1), dated to 238/237 B.C. Maron, an eighty-year-old Libyan of the epigone (i.e. born in Egypt before 317 B.C.) bequeaths some real estate, among which is a shrine of Aphrodite Arsinoe and Berenike, mother of the gods, to two Alexandrian ladies, Musta and Menneia. Both women are accompanied by their respective κύριοι, also Alexandrian citizens. The guardian of Menneia is Kleandros son of Monimos, of the Alexandrian deme Andromacheios. He is about seventy years old (and thus born before 300 B.C.), of reddish complexion, and he has a scar on the right side of his nose. The will is drawn up at Krokodilonpolis and the context is purely Greek, as is the case with all Petrie wills. Egyptians are only mentioned among the neighbors of some of the real estate in the order East-South-West-North, which is completely un-Egyptian (in Egyptian documents the South always comes first and this custom is found also in the overwhelming majority of Greek documents from Egypt [Posener 1965, pp. 69–78; Luckhardt 1914, pp. 3–8]).

It came therefore as a surprise to find a certain Monimos, son of Kleandros, certainly a member of the same family, in a Demotic census list of the later third century as the head of a mixed household (Papyrus dém. Lille III 101 column 3 lines 1–4). The patronymic reads *Ql꜠ntrs* in Demotic and was rendered by the editor as Kleinodoros, but there can be no doubt we should change this into Kleandros (Clarysse 1988, pp. 137–40). Monimos, son of Kleandros, is, I think, a son of the Alexandrian kyrios in the preceding will. He is married to *Is.t-wr.t* (Esoeris), who is called his *rmt.t.* His daughter has a good Greek name, Demetria (Demeter is one of the few Greek goddesses who have no Egyptian counterpart) and so does his slave girl Sostrate. Monimos is, as far as I know, the first Alexandrian (or descendant of an Alexandrian) of whom we know that he married an Egyptian woman. Fraser's suggestion that Alexandrian immigrants in the chora "are unlikely to have contracted marriages with Egyptian women" (because this would endanger the civil status of their offspring [Fraser 1972, pp. 71–72]) is here for the first time disproved. And I doubt if Alexandrians living in the chora really behaved differently from other Greeks at all.

Monimos was certainly not the only Greek in the village or the town to marry an Egyptian girl; the same census document substantially augments the number of mixed families known for the third century B.C.: Stephanos, son of *ꜣmyꜣ.t*, Protarchos, son of *Pa-n-Is.t*, Peisikles, brother of *Pꜣ-dj.w*, and Diodoros, brother of another *Pꜣ-dj.w*. Protarchos and Diodoros are moreover married to Egyptian women themselves. Perhaps the scarcity of mixed marriages in our third century documentation is for a large part due to the types of documents on which modern surveyance is based (in the Zenon archive for instance "irregular" filiations are totally absent from the 1700 Greek documents, but two are found in the twenty-odd Demotic texts).

One last point should be stressed in this text; though he belongs to an Alexandrian family, Monimos has to pay the poll tax (salt tax) at the rate of one drachma just like the other Greeks. Egyptians had to pay an extra obol (the one obol tax) as is clear both from the Demotic Papyrus Lille III 101 and from CPR XIII 1 and 2, recently published by Harrauer (1987). This is an important new element, as we have here for the first time clear proof of official discrimination against the Egyptian part of the population. Such a discrimination, even if the payment involved was very small, necessitated separate official registers of Greeks and Egyptians. Thus being a Greek or an Egyptian was not just a matter of personal and community feeling ("ethnicity"), but also official policy: being Greek involved some privileges that an Egyptian could not claim (*pace* Goudriaan 1988).

2. Among the numerous cleruchs mentioned in the Zenon archive few are better known than Stratippos and his son Neoptolemos. Stratippos was a Macedonian cavalryman belonging to the company of Antigonos and stationed in the Heracleopolite nome (PSI VIII 976). He owned several vineyards in the Aphroditopolite nome, one of which was brought into cultivation about 260 B.C., i.e. a few years before the dioiketes Apollonios received his famous dorea in Philadelphia. His son Neoptolemos is already an adult man in 254 B.C., when he styles himself Μακεδὼν τῶν ἐν Φιλαδελφείαι κληρούχων (Papyrus Cairo Zenon II 59236). He owns a vineyard near Philadelphia,

which is exploited by Zenon, and he helps his father growing vines in the Aphroditopolites. All by all a very typical family of Macedonian military settlers interested in the typically Greek agricultural activity of growing vines.

In 1986, Thissen published four fragmentary Demotic self-dedications, contracts of individuals with the god Anubis, in which the people dedicate themselves (and often their children as well) to the god for the rest of their lives and promise to pay him a monthly sum of five drachmas, in exchange for his protection against all kinds of evil forces, ghosts and *afrits*. One of these texts was written for a certain Neoptolemos (Papyrus Freib. IV Add. 1 = Papyrus Berl. inv. 15791). During a study-visit in Freiburg-im-Breisgau I found the missing lower half of that text, which gives us the name of Neoptolemos' father: Stratippos (Clarysse 1988, pp. 7–10).

Thissen located the texts in Memphis because of the cult of Anubis, but we know that an Anubis cult existed also in Philadelphia. In fact the only Greek inscription from that site is a dedication stele for Zenon and Apollonios in honor of Anubis (I. Fayoum I 98 = Pap. Lugd.-Bat. XX text F). Thissen dated the texts to 270/269 because of the dating formula "Ptolemy son of Ptolemy," usually attributed to Ptolemy II. If this would be true the Macedonian cleruch of the Zenon archive would be identical with the man dedicating himself to the Egyptian god of the dead. I have however very strong arguments to prefer a date after 210 B.C. and to consider Onnophris alias Neoptolemos as a grandson of the homonymous cleruch. If I am right, the family tree below clearly shows the gradual integration of the Macedonian settlers into the Egyptian environment:

Stratippos I
|
Neoptolemos I
|
Stratippos II × *Ḥr-ʿnḫ*
|
Wn-nfr alias Neoptolemos II

The last scion of the family has a Greco-Egyptian double name, well illustrating his assimilation into the native society.

Again Neoptolemos is not an isolated case. We now know some fifty similar Demotic self-dedications ("Hierodulieurkunden"). Among those in the British Museum, most still unpublished, at least two are written for people with Greek backgrounds: Tanebtunis, alias Sarapias, daughter of Sosipolis and Teuxon, and NN, alias Petesouchos, son of Nikanor and Artemidora.

It is difficult to say what were the practical consequences of these self-dedications. Herbert Thompson (1965, pp. 497-504; 1940, pp. 68–78) pointed out that often the father's name is replaced by the formula "I know not his name" and he draws the conclusion that there was a link with temple prostitution. But some people, among them those with Greek names, do mention the name of both parents. What did the self-dedication mean to them? My hypothesis is that this was a kind of insurance against all kinds of illnesses (illnesses were of course caused by demons!); by paying a small monthly sum to the temple the dedicants received the protection of the god. In practice this may very well have meant that they received medical treatment in the temple. We know that temples were often at the same time medical centers (cf. the Greek Asklepieia and modern Lourdes). If this is true, it shows that some of the Greek immigrants adopted not only native religious practices, but also took a kind of insurance policy with the Egyptian temples. This did not prevent the cleruchs among them from paying the ἰατρικόν and calling upon a Greek doctor as well. In this respect the Egyptian temples may have played the role of alternative medicine in our times.

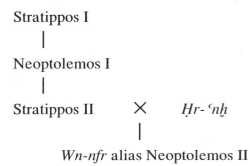

3. In 1973 Fr. de Cenival published some sixty Demotic surety documents, dated, with few exceptions, between 230 and 220 B.C. (de Cenival 1973 = Papyrus dém. Lille II). In them surety is offered, usually for small sums of money (five to ten drachmas) by several people in favour of local artisans (oil producers, washers, but most often brewers), who received the raw materials of their trade (sesame seeds, natron, barley) from the government storehouses. As is to be expected, the people involved, both the guarantors and the guarantees, are usually Egyptians. But it is surprising to find even here a few Greeks, not only among the guarantors, but even among the guarantees.

If we take the guarantees as a starting point, we find twenty-eight Egyptians versus four Greeks. The picture is confirmed by Papyrus Petrie III 58e, a list of sureties in which several times the same people are found as in the Lille cautionnements. Here we find fourteen Egyptians versus three Greeks and one Hellenized Persian (Perses son of Mithridates).

Both the Greek Petrie papyrus and the Demotic surety contracts show us Greek families of artisans and merchants living among the Egyptian population in the villages, making contracts with the Greek government of the Ptolemies by means of *Demotic* surety documents.

Thus Artemidoros son of Agathon is a washerman at Philoteris and caution is given for him by the Egyptian farmers Aspheus (Papyrus dém. Lille II 76), Phanesis (Papyrus dém. Lille II 77), and Marres junior (Papyrus dém. Lille II 84). He is known also from a Greek Petrie papyrus (Papyrus Petrie III 117a lines 7–8), where he pays the *nitrike* tax together with an Egyptian colleague Semtheus, son of Teos.

Another washerman in the same village is Zenodoros, son of *Bḏ*. He is called in the text (Papyrus dém. Lille II 95) a "Greek washerman," whatever this may mean, and his patronymic (de Cenival reads *Qḏꜣ*) does not sound Greek, but it is followed nevertheless by the foreigner determinative.

Hermaiskos, son of Dionusios appears as a brewer at Theadelphia in Papyrus dém. Lille II 46[1] and in Papyrus Petrie III 58e col. 4 lines 14–15, where I now read: Πᾶσις Στοτοήτιος εἰς [ὃ ἐνεγύ(ησεν) Ἑρμαί]σκον Διονυσίου Θε[αδελφείας]. But the same Hermaiskos reappears as an oil merchant in Papyrus Petrie III 66 *passim*. Apparently he was the owner of the local village store. In this case we can even see how the family kept alive a Greek onomastical tradition; the sequence Dionusios, son of Hermaiskos, turns up again more than a century later in a list of witnesses in the village Kerkeosiris, some twenty miles south of Theadelphia (Papyrus Teb. I 104 line 39).

The newest addition to this dossier is particularly interesting. It is a small fragment of a surety contract of the usual type, not more than five cm long, but preserving the essential data of both the Demotic on the recto and of the Greek on the verso (P. Sorb. inv. 567). Surety is given for an Egyptian Pasis, son of Teos, by a *Wynn ms n Kmj Slwqs pꜣ ntj ḏd n≠f Sbk-Ḥꜥpj*, son of *Priꜣ*, his mother being *ꜣsytrꜣ*. The names of the surety correspond in Greek to Σέλευκος ὃς καὶ Σοκόνωπις Πυρρίου. The man is a farmer (γεωργός) and both his parents have Greek names. This is one of the few clear instances of a Greco-Egyptian double name in a purely Greek family. The text is dated to February–March 223 B.C.

Papyrus Sorb. inv. 567

1 *[Ḥꜣ.t-sp 23 nty ir ḥꜣt-sp 24, ibd-1 pr.t]*
2 *[pr-ꜥꜣ Ptlwmys sꜣ Ptlwmys irm]*
3 *ꜣrsynꜣ nꜣ ntr.w sn.w nꜣ ntr.w*
4 *mnḫ.w, ḏd Wynn ms*

1. The village name should be read as *Pꜣ-ꜥ-sn(.t)* instead of *Pꜣ-ꜥ-Itm* (so edit. on p. 125 and p. 261). The word *sn(.t)* "sister" (or "brother") is written with the divine determinative: "the village of the divine sister" corresponds exactly to Θεαδέλφια.

n Kmy Slwqs nty iw(=w) ḏd n.f Sbk-
Ḥ ʿpy sꜣ Pryꜣt mw.t =f ꜣ sytrꜣ
[n NN pꜣ ꜣ yqwnms] n tꜣ dny.t
[n Thmsts - -

[Year 23 also called year 24 month, day,] (=
[of king Ptolemy son of Ptolemy and of]
Arsinoe the brother gods, the gods
Euergetai, has said the Greek born
in Egypt Seleukos, whom they call Sobek-
Hapi son of Purrias and Isidora
to NN the oikonomos of the meris [of Themistes etc.]

(Ἔτους) κδ Τῦβι. Σελεύκο[υ]
ὃς καὶ Σοκονώπιος
Πυρρίου γε(ωργοῦ) ἐγγυω-
[μένου Π]ᾶσιν Τεῶτος.

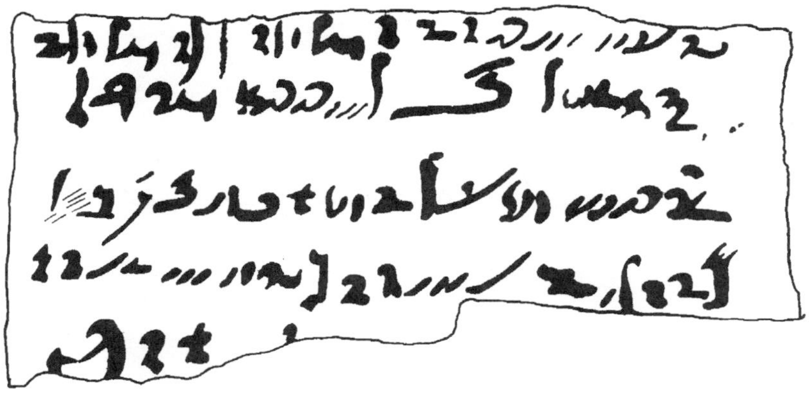

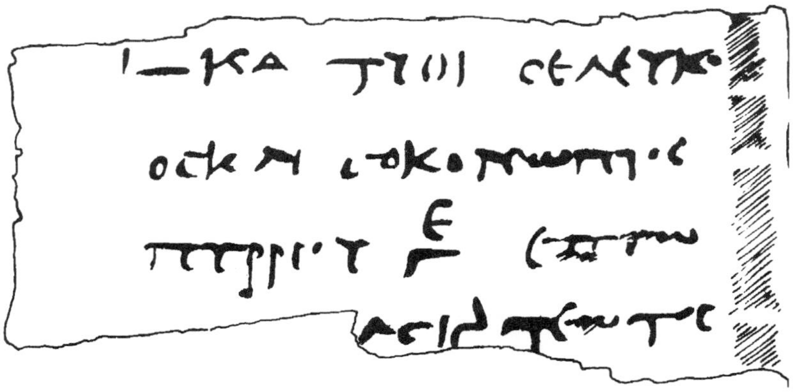

The three cases discussed above are all based on a combination of Greek and Demotic sources. Maybe the most important conclusion we can draw from them is the fact that, as long as we base ourselves on one kind of source material, either Greek or Demotic, we will always get a one-sided and preprogrammed picture of the people involved: cleruchs will always appear as Greek land owners, while on the other hand Demotic documents may give an impression of almost total assimilation within Egyptian society. It is only when the two types of sources can be combined (as happens only from time to time) that we can exceed this one-sidedness and see how both integration and self-consciousness existed side by side.

For that reason the increase of Demotic papyri from the Faiyum, a region where many Greeks lived in the villages, provides a very promising field of study, on condition that these new Demotic texts are studied in combination with the Greek papyri. Because this intertwining of Greek and Demotic documentation is essential for any historical study of the society of Ptolemaic Egypt, it is to be regretted that the combination of Egyptologist and classical scholar, which was still self-evident two generations ago, is steadily giving way to an early specialization; not only are very few classicists studying Egyptology (they always were a tiny minority), but nowadays we get more and more students in Egyptology without any knowledge of Greek. The disadvantages of this can only partially be made up for through interdisciplinary research.

CHAPTER 7

A CULT FUNCTION FOR THE SO-CALLED FAIYUM MUMMY PORTRAITS?*

LORELEI H. CORCORAN
Memphis State University

The discovery at Hawara by Sir Flinders Petrie of a portrait painting still within a wooden, Oxford-type frame (Petrie 1889, p. 10 and pl. 12) confirmed the suspicions of certain scholars[1] that the panel portraits in encaustic and tempera found on Roman period (1st to 4th centuries A.D.) mummies were used prior to their inclusion in funerary wrappings. A prior use for some of the portraits had been inferred from other facts: the earliest examples of the panels had all been cut down at the upper corners from an original, squared shape; painted borders are preserved on some panels; and some panels show signs of wear in areas covered by the mummy wrappings but that previously must have been exposed (Parlasca 1966, pp. 61–62 and 64–65). If, therefore, the portraits were used for some purpose prior to their funerary use, what was it? Petrie and others have speculated that the portraits were examples of domestic art hung on the walls of houses for aesthetic or decorative purposes (D. L. Thompson 1982, p. 8). I should like to propose a cultic, rather than a decorative, function for these portraits.

In many cases, particularly in the earlier examples of the series, wealthy patrons sat for their portraits (D. L. Thompson 1982, p. 14, fig. 20 and p. 15, fig. 22). Although Parlasca (1966, p. 66) acknowledged that posthumous paintings could depict the individual in the guise of the goddess Isis, he denied the possibility of a "heroization" of the individuals depicted in portraits painted from life because he did not consider the possibility of an individual undergoing apotheosis while still alive.[2] The only suggestion put forth until now, therefore, for a cultic use for the portraits has been that by David Thompson (1978–79, p. 185, note 3)[3] who tentatively offered a comparison between

* This is a revised version of a paper delivered at the symposium "Life in a Multi-Cultural Society: Egypt from Cambyses to Constantine (and Beyond)," and is based upon material and conclusions presented in my doctoral dissertation, *Portrait Mummies from Roman Egypt*. Research for the dissertation (1984–85) was supported by a Ryerson Travel Grant, administered by the University of Chicago, and a fellowship administered by the American Research Center in Egypt. For permission to research these materials at the Egyptian Museum, Cairo, in 1984–85, I thank Dr. Mohamed Saleh and Mme. Elhan Montasser. I am especially grateful to Dr. Mohamed Mohsen, Director, and the Board of Directors of the Egyptian Museum, Cairo, for permission to publish photographs of Inv. CG 6839.

1. Although Parlasca (1966, pp. 66–67) speculates as to whether framed examples such as this were not made especially for inclusion in the burial.
2. See Berger, Parlasca, and Pintaudi 1985, p. 128. Parlasca (1969, p. 41) also discusses this question in regard to the case of an individual who appears unclothed due to damage to the panel. However, there are other examples (ibid., pp. 67 and 71) where individuals were intentionally depicted in the nude.

In my doctoral dissertation, *Portrait Mummies from Roman Egypt* (1988), I proposed that the manufacture of portrait mummies adhered to a coherent program of design. Like the disposition of scenes on a monumental wall (Gaballa 1976, pp. 102, 104, and 140), the iconographic elements that decorate these mummies can be "read" in a logical and coherent sequence from bottom to top. The overall iconographic theme of the mummies embodies traditional pharaonic concepts about the afterlife. The goal of the iconography is the transformation of the deceased into a cosmic deity with celestial, principally solar, attributes.

The representation of the feet becomes very important on Ptolemaic and Roman mummies. A boot-like piece of cartonnage was commonly added to mummies of this period. Feet, shod in sandals, were drawn or modeled in relief on the upper sides of these casings. The feet were either painted pink or gilded, like the flesh of the sun-god. The purpose of representing the feet in a permanent material can perhaps be traced to an attempt to ensure the deceased the ability to stand upright and to come and go in the netherworld as expressed in Spell 188 of the Book of the Dead:

> I ask that I may come and go and that I may have power in my feet
> (Faulkner 1972, p. 185).

On the upper side of a previously unpublished late Ptolemaic or early Roman footcase (figure 7.1) in the collection of the Egyptian Museum, Cairo (Inv. CG 6839), in a vertical band that runs between a drawing of two, sandaled feet with gilded toenails, is a somewhat carelessly rendered hieroglyphic text that emphasizes the solar implications of the representation of the feet:

> *ꜥḥꜥ sp sn ḥr rdwy·f* [sic *ṯ*] *ꜥḥꜥ Wsỉr ꜣst n Ḫbt m ꜥꜣ-ḫrw ḥr rdwy* [*·ṯ*] *ḥnꜥ Rꜥ m wỉꜣ·f m ẖrt hrw nty rꜥk* [sic *nb*]
>
> Rise up, rise up upon your feet. Rise up, O Isis-of-Chemmis (deceased), upon your feet to be with Reꜥ in his bark in the course of every day (author's transliteration and translation).

The goal of mobility as here stated is to join the sun-god, a goal expressed in ancient Egypt from the Pyramid Texts on. The fortuitous survival of this footcase and its text allows us to place the motif of the representation of feet in a permanent material within a long tradition of ancient Egyptian beliefs that survived into the Ptolemaic and Roman periods. Other motifs with solar connotations are depicted on the sides of these footcases — lotus blossoms, *wadjet* eyes, and the two Wepwawet jackals (figure 7.2) at either side of the feet — and help in determining the precise goal of the motif: that the deceased should have the facility to stand up among the gods who travel in the solar boat.

Additional elements in the design of portrait mummies strengthen the overall solar theme. One of the most popular scenes to be included within the horizontal registers that decorate the body fields of portrait mummies is the "baptism of pharaoh."[4] Used in a royal context since the Middle Kingdom, this scene depicts the transfiguration of the king's bodily limbs into the heavenly body of a god through the agency of the waters of Nun. The appearance of this scene on the body field of non-royal mummies probably indicates a desire on the part of the deceased to experience a similar transfiguration.

From temple walls, we know that the baptism scene preceded coronation and also imparted legitimacy and justification. At the top of portrait mummies is the crowning touch to the visual statement that the deceased has become transformed and justified. Gilded crowns were painted on the heads of individuals in some portraits.

In a tale of metamorphosis, contemporary with the mummy portraits, the 2nd century Roman novelist, Apuleius, describes the appearance of an Isis cult initiate who is clothed in a costly vestment, holding in his right hand a lighted torch, and wearing "a comely … chaplet from which the palm-tree leaves jetted like rays of the sun" (1965, p. 250). This account helps us to understand the

4. For a more complete discussion of this motif see Corcoran 1988, pp. 129–36.

context of the irradiated crowns that are added to the portraits. It also helps to clarify the symbolism of the candle (Petrie 1911, p. 4) held in the modeled hand of a contemporary cartonnage bust-piece with a gilded face in the collection of the Fitzwilliam Museum, Cambridge (Inv. E. 103.1911).[5]

Embellishments to portraits such as gilded lips, broad collars of gold, hands that hold garlands or vessels of Nile water, have been explained as last-minute additions before the portraits were enclosed within the funerary wrappings (D. L. Thompson 1982, p. 9). I should like to propose that these additions might have been made while the portraits were yet in the home to commemorate the cult initiation of the individual portrayed or to assist in the use of such portraits as channels or mediums. This suggestion is based on the premise that the inherently Egyptian sense of time as a cyclical process need not have precluded the idea of the transformation of an individual into a god while still alive (Wente 1971, pp. 178–79) and the possibility that certain offering formulae such as those from the Book of Gates and the Amduat might have been used in ancient Egypt to identify "a living person with beings in various states ... as ... participants in the sun god's voyage of renewal" (Wente 1971, p. 175).

The solar attributes of the portrait mummies invite a comparison of the use of the portraits in a domestic context with that of the anthropoid busts of the New Kingdom excavated at Deir el-Medineh (and elsewhere). Jean Keith-Bennett suggested that, in addition to an ancestral or votive function, these anthropoid busts "may have had more than one meaning for their users" (Keith-Bennett 1981, p. 50). Florence Friedman (1985, pp. 83–92) suggested that these painted, limestone busts were manifestations of the "*ꜣḫ ỉḳr n Rꜥ*." Friedman describes an "*ꜣḫ ỉḳr n Rꜥ*" as "principally one who enjoys a place in the solar bark and is its crew member" (ibid., p. 85). Hereby, we are reminded of a formula from the Amduat describing the "sorceries of Isis ... performed upon earth ... [by] one who is in the bark of Reꜥ" (Wente 1971, pp. 165–66) and we recall the hieroglyphic text on the footcase (Egyptian Museum, Cairo, Inv. CG 6839, above) exhorting the deceased to stand up on her feet to join Reꜥ in his bark.

The anthropoid limestone busts from Deir el-Medineh were highly painted and one (Brooklyn Museum Inv. 54.1), at least, of the females represented wears a podium headdress, a base, perhaps, for a papyrus crown — a golden circlet with "papyrus stems and umbels surmounted by discs"[6] — a crown, I believe, that has solar implications. Bernard Bothmer (1987, p. 29) has suggested that the female limestone busts from Deir el-Medineh might represent a deceased ancestor commemorated as the goddess Hathor, consort of the sun-god, creator-god, Reꜥ. It is noteworthy that in Demotic inscriptions on Roman period shrouds, deceased females are sometimes referred to by the epithet "the Hathor,"[7] not, as one might have expected, as "the Isis" as the female counterpart of "the Osiris." This use of the name Hathor accords well, however, with the syncretism of Hathor and Isis in the Roman period when Isis embodied cosmic characteristics to complement those of her solarized consort, Serapis.

In the Egyptian Museum, Cairo, is an enigmatic object (Inv. CG 33269) that is exhibited in the same case as portrait mummies. Its inclusion in the case is most probably coincidental, but serendipitous[8]. Edgar published the piece as a "schoolgirl" (1907, pp. 49–52), but the nude torso might represent a cult initiate at the moment of emergence from immersion, a bath in the waters of

5. A photograph of this object appears in Parlasca 1966, pl. 5.1.

6. See Wilkinson 1971, p. 152. A line drawing of Brooklyn Museum Inv. 54.1 appears in figure 68 on page 153.

7. For a list of examples see Mark Smith 1987, pp. 129–31. Add to this list the inscription from the shroud of Museum of Fine Arts, Boston, Inv. 54.993.

8. Parlasca (1969, p. 31 and pl. 5,2) includes this aedicula painting among those paintings in his corpus of mummy portraits.

creation being a prerequisite to cultic rebirth.[9] The food offering painted on the front of the "schoolgirl's" niche is reminiscent of a New Kingdom stela depicting an individual offering to an *ꜣḫ i͗ḳr n Rꜥ* bust.[10]

There is certain physical evidence for the portrait mummies having been kept for some time before being buried (D. L. Thompson 1982, pp. 8 and 28, note 8). Petrie noted rain damage, scratches, missing inlaid eyes, broken cartonnage that was repaired, and even a grafitto on the feet of one mummy that he considered to have been drawn by a child (Petrie 1911, pp. 2–3; Petrie 1889, p. 15). In addition to remarks by Herodotos and Diodoros on the Egyptian custom of keeping mummies above ground (Petrie 1889, p. 15), literary evidence for keeping the mummy of a loved one comes from a 2nd century A.D. Greek novella that describes how a forlorn widower embalmed his dead wife in "the Egyptian style" and kept her body with him.[11] That wrapped mummies were kept, and presumably presented with offerings (the widower brought his wife's mummy out to join him in his meals), suggests a similarity in the posthumous use of portrait mummies and the *ꜣḫ i͗ḳr n Rꜥ* anthropoid busts.

A comparison with the function of "abbreviated" statuary, like the anthropoid limestone busts, and an attempt to coordinate visual documents with native Egyptian religious texts provides tantalizing links between ancient Egyptian traditions and the use of "mummy portraits" from the Roman era. Although early Christian writers expressed doubt and some Egyptologists remain skeptical of evidence of the belief of the ancient Egyptians in the ability of an individual to become a god while alive on earth or of an individual's ability to assume non-human forms, evidence suggests that this might well have been the cult function in a domestic context for the so-called Faiyum mummy portraits.

9. Sauneron (1980, p. 50) discusses the similarity between this phase of the initiation rites of a 21st Dynasty priest with the initiation of Lucius into the Isis cult. See also Wente (1971, pp. 177–78), who discusses the goal of ritual death and rebirth in the Book of Amduat and the Book of Gates in relation to the initiation of Lucius.

10. D'Abbadie 1946, p. 135, fig. 1. See also a discussion of the *akh* in relation to food offerings in Friedman 1985, pp. 86–91 and Wente 1971, pp. 167 and 177.

11. Reardon 1989, p. 159. I thank my colleague Dr. Richard Jasnow for this reference.

a

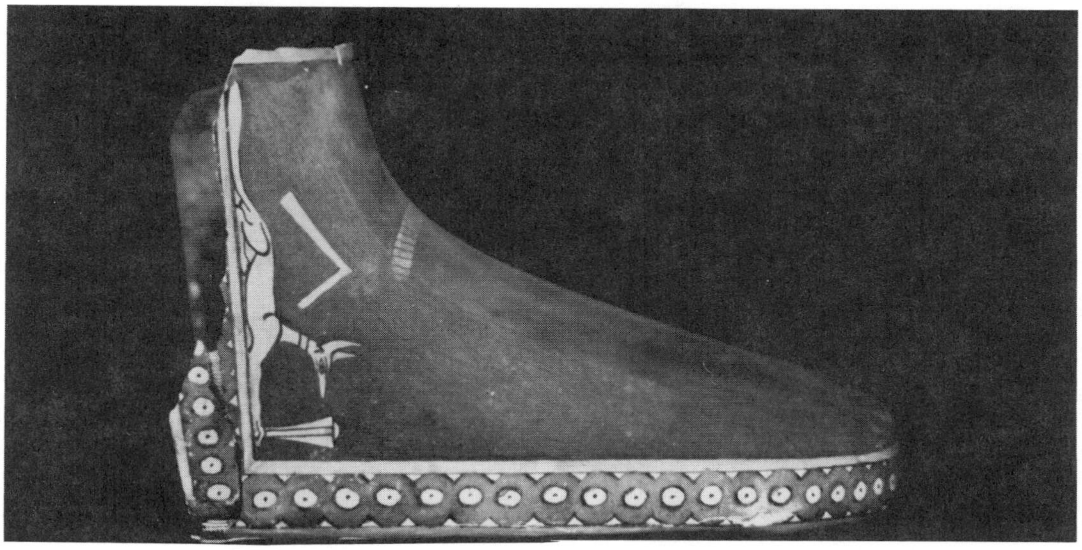

b

Photographs of a Cartonnage Footcase (Egyptian Museum, Cairo, Inv. CG 6839):
(*a*) Top View; (*b*) Side View.

CHAPTER 8

THE LAKE OF MOERIS: A REPRISE

EUGENE D. CRUZ-URIBE
Northern Arizona University

A. Gardiner, in an article published in *JEA* 29 (1943, pp. 37–50), argued on the basis of a review of the occurrences of the word *ḥn.t* found in hieroglyphic and Demotic texts, that the word was equivalent to the Greek word *LIMYN* and proffered the translation "lake, swampy land," as opposed to the earlier rendering "canal." Gardiner reiterated the same arguments in later publications (1947, p. 7* and 1948, p. 29). He thus takes the phrase *tꜣ ḥn.t n Mr-wr* to mean "the lake of (the town) Moeris." Gardiner argued that the Coptic *HONE* (*CD*, p. 690a) likewise would not mean "canal," but rather "lake, swampy land."

I began this investigation of the term *tꜣ ḥn.t Mi-wr* on the basis of a footnote by the late Charles Nims in his doctoral dissertation from 1937. Before his death Prof. Nims and I began a collaborative effort to revise his dissertation for publication to include additional texts from Philadelphia in the Faiyum currently housed in the collections of the British Museum and the University of Michigan (Ann Arbor). In going over his manuscript notes it was clear that Nims did not agree with Gardiner's conclusion and in his brief note in *JEA* 33 (1947, p. 92), Nims refers to additional Demotic examples of *tꜣ ḥn.t n Mi-wr*, but refers to *ḥn.t* by the Coptic form *HONE* only.

In *Appendix A*, is a list of the variety of translations given by Egyptologists and Demotists for the term *ḥn.t*. As clearly shown there is hardly agreement on the translation or meaning. One should note in particular the reference from the *Oracular Amuletic Decrees* (Edwards 1960); there *ḥn.t* is found between *itrw*, "river" and *ḫꜣs*, "runnel" in the series of terms refering to water.

In *Appendix B*, is a list of the towns found in the Demotic texts which have the phrase *tꜣ ḥn.t n Mi-wr* and the side of the *ḥn.t* on which these towns lie.

If we accept the translation of *ḥn.t* as "lake" there are some discrepancies. Dime, as the northernmost town in the Faiyum, would always lie north of the "lake," Moeris. Likewise, Tebtunis on the far south geographic point in the Faiyum would always be south of the "lake." But the town of Philadelphia would lie to the true east of any "lake" as it is situated at the far eastern edge of the Faiyum. If my understanding of *Pr-grg-Ḏḥwty* is correct, it straddles the *ḥn.t* and is both north and south of it. We should note that the town of Hawara, located at the point where the Bahr Yussef enters the Faiyum depression, is stated to lie north of the "lake." These items suggest that the term "lake" cannot be accepted as a reasonable translation of *ḥn.t* in the Demotic texts.

Gardiner's translation of "lake" derives from his understanding of the Greek *LIMYN* to mean "lake." The translation "swampy land, marshland" perhaps derives from the fact that Bell (1943, p. 46) noted that *ḥn.t* parallels the usage of *DRYMOS* which is a papryological term used to indicate a marshy area that over time became desiccated and supported a variety of agricultural products or activities such as grasses, pasturage, grain cultivation, left fallow, etc. (see Bonneau 1979a, pp. 181–90). The term *LIMYN* on the other hand refers to the technical condition where there is stagnant water which occasionally forms, but is not perennial. It can also refer to an irrigation basin and is the area or land recovered from the waters after each inundation (Bonneau 1971, p. 76). Bonneau (1971, p. 75, no. 354) suggests that *DRYMOS* is to be equated with the Egyptian *pḫw*, "marshlands" (*CDME*, p. 92), while *LIMYN* without a doubt corresponds to *ḥn.t* (*CDME*, p. 115).

In light of the evidence discussed thus far the translation of *ḥn.t* as "lake, marshland" cannot be accepted. I would equate, following Bonneau, "marshland" with *DRYMOS*. I would follow Gardiner and others in equating *ḥn.t* with *LIMYN* up to a point. While *ḥn.t* can have a variety of meanings ("watercourse, canal, recovered land," etc.), in the phrase *tꜣ ḥn.t n Mi-wr* we should return to the translation "canal" as it accords well with the hieroglyphic, Demotic, and Coptic usages. The deciding factor in this case is the added appellation *n Mi-wr*, "of Moeris," which must refer to the town site Gurob as suggested by Gardiner.

We should keep in mind that the classical authors note that the Faiyum was fed by a *canal* off of the river Nile (see Diodorus Siculus I.52; Strabo VIII.17, I.4; and Herodotus II.149). Strabo (VIII.17, I.37) also notes that the Lake of Moeris is large enough to bear the inundation and not overflow into the inhabited and planted parts of the Faiyum. To this author the text suggests that the translation of *ḥn.t* as "marshy/swampy lands" would be an inaccurate picture of the extensive cultivated areas in the Faiyum. The intent of the Ptolemies, as well as numerous pharaohs before, in developing the lands of the Faiyum for irrigation, precludes suggesting that they were attempting to produce marshlands. Rather the *canal* of Moeris acted as the supplier of water for controlled irrigation works. Flooded fields during the inundation would be similar to "marshlands," but it would seem illogical for the Egyptians to designate the locations of towns on the basis of a temporary natural phenomena.

It is well known that during the reign of Ptolemy III Euergetes that an extensive canal network was developed (Crawford 1971, p. 109). Crawford suggested that the Argaitis Canal, also known as the canal of Euergetes, was perhaps the Greek name for the canal of Moeris. Bresciani and Pestman (1965, pp. 173–74) argue that the canal of Moeris must be identified with the Bahr Yussef. Thus, recent studies with maps of the Faiyum have shown only the Bahr Yussef as the principal canal leading from the Nile to Birket Qarun (e.g., Thompson 1988, p. 2 and Bianchi, ed. 1988, p. 12).

It would appear that the wide distribution of towns in the Faiyum north and south of the *ḥn.t Mi-wr* favors our adoption of Preisigke's opinion that the name "canal of Moeris" was applied to the main canal network of the Faiyum (Spiegelberg 1908, p. 42, note 3). That all towns on the Moeris canal so far known are either on the north or south bank, except for *Pr-grg-Ḏḥwty* which may have straddled the canal, would indicate that the chief canals of the Faiyum were thought of as always running east-west, just as the Nile was always considered to run north-south, without taking into consideration its turns.

In conclusion, I would agree with Gardiner that the name Moeris refers to a town Moeris, which is to be identified with the site of Gurob (Lloyd 1976, p. 34, no. 1 and Crawford 1971, p. 43). The term *ḥn.t* can be understood as meaning "canal." Finally the phrase common in many Demotic texts, *tꜣ ḥn.t n Mi-wr*, is to be translated "canal of (the town) Moeris" and refers principally to the Bahr Yussef, but by extension, to all of the principal canals in the Faiyum which served as part of the extensive irrigation system.

One may challenge these conclusions if one takes note of the study by G. Garbrecht (1986, pp. 1–22). Garbrecht takes note that various studies have shown that the level and area occupied by the Moeris Sea/Lake Moeris varied a great deal throughout ancient times up through the present century. Given the right circumstances of high Nile levels causing major flooding into the Faiyum and the building of certain strategic dykes, or other man-made water controlling devices, the size of a "Lake" Moeris could conceivably allow it to extend such that it would match the "north" and "south" designations mentioned earlier. However, the necessary circumstances to make that "Lake" appear as needed by Gardiner's argument are not forthcoming from the evidence we have observed. A fuller discussion of this topic will appear shortly in the forthcoming volume *The Archive of Tikas, Demotic Texts from Philadelphia in the Fayum*.

APPENDIX A: BIBLIOGRAPHIC DISCUSSIONS OF THE TERM *ḥn.t*

1. Yoyotte (1958, pp. 428–29) followed Gardiner and noted that place names with reference to the "lake of Moeris" are to be found on the borders of the lake.
2. Edwards (1960, p. 25 and xxii) following Gardiner, translates *ḥn.t* as "swampy lakes" as the amuletic decrees distinguish between *mr*, "canals"; *itrw*, "rivers"; *šd.t*, "wells"; *bwꜣ.t*, "swamps"; *ḫꜣꜥ mḥ*, "pools left by the inundation"; *ḫꜣs*, "runnels"; and *ḥnw*, "swampy lakes." We should note however that the sole occurrence of *ḥn.t* in the amuletic decrees places *ḥn.t* between *itrw*, "river" and *ḫꜣs*, "runnel."
3. Yoyotte (1962a, p. 88, no. 4) notes that *ḥn.t* is not exactly "canal" nor "lake," but a natural branch of water in a flat area where water can stagnate, i.e., a marshy area.
4. Vergote (1962, pp. 69–71), after reviewing the evidence presented by Gardiner and the Greek evidence, argues that it is not certain that *ḥn.t* means "lake," and it may be "canal" or a "branch of water," a watercourse or the like.
5. Goedicke (1963, pp. 83–84) examines several hieroglyphic texts and argues for the translation of *ḥn.t* as "watercourse."
6. In his translation of the Late Egyptian story "Apophis and Seqenenre," Wente (1973, p. 79, no. 4) adopts the translation "canal."
7. Černý (*CED*), takes *ḥn.t*/*HONE* to mean "swampy lake" following Gardiner.
8. Westendorf (*KHwb*, p. 378) likewise follows Gardiner.
9. Cauville (1983, p. 127, no. 5) suggests that *ḥn.t* means "arms/branches of water."
10. Lesko (*DLE*, vol. 2, p. 120) cites the studies of Gardiner and Goedicke, but only gives question marks for the translations of "swampy lake," "canal," and "watercourse." He then blindly accepts Wente's translation "canal."
11. Vycichl (*DELC*, pp. 304–05) notes that *HONE* in Coptic has three meanings "canal," "water of heaven," and "basin." He argues that Goedicke is closest to the mark in explaining the meaning of *ḥn.t* and that it must mean "branch" of the Nile, or "canal" on the basis of an inscription from Edfu.

   Among Demotic scholars the same variance of meaning is also found.

12. H. S. Smith (1958, p. 93) translates "canal of Moeris."
13. Reymond (1966–67, p. 475, no. 28) translates "swampy land of Moeris" following Gardiner.
14. Lüddeckens (1968, p. 21, no. 34) translates "Moeris-Kanal," but notes in his commentary that, following Yoyotte, *ḥn.t* means neither "canal" nor "lake" but a "standing, low-lying, water course."
15. Zauzich (1974, p. 73) gives the translation "canal," but in a later article (1977, p. 154) gives "marshland."
16. This latter is followed by Harrauer and Vittmann (1985, p. 68).

APPENDIX B: LIST OF TOWNS FROM DEMOTIC TEXTS WHICH HAVE BEEN NOTED TO BE ON THE NORTH OR SOUTH SIDE OF THE *tꜣ ḥn.t n Mi-wr*

1. Tebtunis, on the south side, P. Cairo 30612/4, (Spiegelberg 1908a, pls. 21–22); P. Cairo 30617a/3 (Spiegelberg 1908a, pl. 27).
2. Dime, on the north side, (for discussion see Reymond 1965–66, pp. 433ff., and Reymond 1966–67, pp. 464ff.).
3. Heliopolis, on the south side, P. Michigan Dem. Inv. No. 4244.5c/5 (unpublished, see Nims 1947, p. 92).
4. *Pr-grg-Šw*, on the south side, P. Köln 2411/6 (Lüddeckens 1968, p. 11).
5. *Ps*, on the south side, P. Lille 29/2 (Sottas 1921, p. 58).
6. *Pr-grg*, on the south side, P. Mil. Vogliano 24/5 (Bresciani and Pestman 1965, pp. 169–80).
7. *Pr-grg-Ḏḥwty*, on the south and north side, P. Lille 49/10 and 71/9 (this appellation is uncertain; de Cenival 1973, p. 122, suggests that the town simply had a north and south half; however, it is also possible that the town straddled the *ḥn.t*).
8. Hawara, on the north side, P. Ash. dem. 13/2 (Reymond 1973, p. 96).
9. Philadelphia, on the north side, P. Tikas 7 (Cruz-Uribe, in press).
10. An unknown town in the division of Themistes (possibly Heliopolis), on the south side, P. Loeb 64–65/3 (Spiegelberg 1931, pl. 35).

Reymond (1965–66, p. 438) has already noted that all towns in the Faiyum are listed as being either north or south of the *ḥn.t n Mi-wr*.

CHAPTER 9

THE *KBN.WT* VESSELS OF THE LATE PERIOD

JOHN COLEMAN DARNELL
The Oriental Institute

A. B. Lloyd (1972a, 1972b, 1975a, 1977, and 1980) has taken up the problem of the early history of the trireme in a series of articles, and has suggested that there is Egyptian evidence for the existence of the trireme in the sixth century B.C. In *JEA* 58 (1972a, b), Lloyd proposed that beginning with the Saite period we have the Egyptian word for Greek-style warship — *kbn.t* — and attempted to use a portion of the Saite and Ptolemaic evidence for *kbn.t* in support of Herodotus' statement that Necho had triremes built. Although in this original article Lloyd does not suggest that *kbn.t* is always to be read specifically as "trireme," in a later article (1975a, p. 59, note 116) he refers back to his *JEA* 58 contribution as justification for rendering *kbn.(w)t* in the Elephantine Stele of Amasis as "triremes." Elsewhere, Lloyd summarizes his work on the proposed Egyptian lexicographical evidence for the trireme only slightly more cautiously: "In Egyptian texts from the Saite period we find references to ships called *kbn.wt* which are beyond all reasonable doubt war-galleys built for ramming of a totally un-Egyptian type."[1] Van't Dack and Hauben have followed this definition; of *kbn.wt* they conclude:

> Or à partir du temps des Saïtes, on l'a régulièrement employé pour désigner les galères de guerre baties d'après des modèles étrangers et munies d'un éperon, plus particulièrement les trières. Sous les Ptolémées le terme désigne également des types plus grands que les trières (Van't Dack and Hauben 1978, pp. 70–71).

D. Jones (1988, p. 148) also followed Lloyd's lead, and defines the term *kbn.t* as "later used to describe trireme"[2]

Herodotus in Book II.159.1 claims that Pharaoh Necho had τριήρεες constructed. According to de Meulenaere, whom Lloyd cites at the beginning of his original discussion of *kbn.t*,

> met de door Herodotos vermelde τριήρεες moeten ongetwijfeld *kbn.t*-schepen bedoeld zijn, waarvan men den naam reeds in de 6de dynastie aantreft; het waren grote zeeschepen die in den Saïtischen en Ptolemaeischen tijd ook wel als krijgsschepen gebruikt werden (de Meulenaere 1951, pp. 60–61).

De Meulenaere doubted a Greek dominance in the Saite navy, and suggested that Herodotus rather artificially and incorrectly rendered Egyptian *kbn.t* by Greek τριήρεες. Lloyd took up de Meulenaere's suggested equation of the τριήρεες of Herodotus and the Egyptian *kbn.wt* vessels, but turned de Meulenaere's argument around—for Lloyd, Late Period Egyptian *kbn.t* would translate correctly and specifically Greek τριήρεες.

1. Lloyd 1975b, p. 33; for *kbn.wt* in the index in 1988a, p. 329, Lloyd provides the rendition "ramming war-galleys."

2. *LÄ* V, col. 605, also follows Lloyd's view of the *kbn.wt* ships of the Late Period.

The term *kbn.t* is used in a number of texts to refer to Greek-style warships, triremes amongst them, in the Ptolemaic period. Lloyd is not correct, however, in making of this the exclusive and primary meaning of the word in the Ptolemaic period, and he is not correct in attempting to use the term in an argument for the presence of warships of Greek design, even triremes, in the Saite navy. The evidence shows that the term *kbn.t* throughout the Late Period retains its original meaning of "ocean-going vessel" (see Bietak 1988, p. 37). In the Saite and Persian period attestations of *kbn.t*, the term encompasses more than simply warships, and when specific operations are described, ramming and ship to ship combat is not even suggested. *Kbn.t* does not mean "warship"; even when describing elements of the Ptolemaic high seas fleet it does not always signify vessels of the size of a trireme. The word does not ever *denote* "warship" (although a vessel of war, among others, can be a *kbn.t*), and any attempt at utilizing the word in a discussion of the trireme, or of Greek involvement in the Saite navy, is misdirected.

The purpose of this essay is not to enter into the argument concerning the time and place of the trireme's invention, but to examine the purported Egyptian lexicographic evidence for the trireme.

I. THE PTOLEMAIC EVIDENCE

ONLY ONCE IS THE TERM *KBN.T* TRANSLATED INTO GREEK, AND IT IS NOT TRANSLATED AS "TRIREME" OR "WARSHIP" SPECIFICALLY

Lloyd does not discuss this occurrence of the term. In the Nabaireh version of the Decree of Memphis, Ptolemy V Epiphanes "took care to send out troops, horses, and *kbn.t* ships in opposition to those who came in order to fight against Egypt, on land as well as on sea."[3] The context suggests warships, and the detailed determinative of *kbn.wt* shows a Hellenistic warship. The term *kbn.t* here is rendered as *br* in Demotic and νῆες in Greek (Spiegelberg 1922a, p. 123 no. 106; Daumas 1952, p. 274, notes 1 and 2). The word is not translated as "trireme" in the Greek version of the decree, showing that a simple equation of *kbn.t* with trireme is incorrect. The Greek νῆες, avoiding an adjunct such as μακραί, is also noncommittal as to whether the vessels were warships or not.[4] Furthermore, the term is rendered in Demotic as *br*, the βᾶρις, a river craft (Casson 1971, p. 341). Neither the Greek nor the Demotic version uses a term which clearly designates a warship, and the Demotic intends small river craft to be understood. This would be only the second attestation of *kbn.t* as referring to a vessel in use on the Nile,[5] and the use here is explicable with reference to the divisions of the Ptolemaic navy, and the strategy of defense in the Delta (see the following section).

3. *Urk.* II.179.7-8; Spiegelberg 1922, p. 47; Ptolemy V elsewhere dispatches other *kbn.wt* vessels. See the discussion of his Year 23 stelae in the next section.

4. According to Lloyd 1975a, p. 59, citing Morrison and Williams 1968, p. 245, "the word ναῦς 'by itself commonly means a *trieres*.'" Certainly, as *GE-L*, p. 1422, indicates, πλοῖον "when distd. from ναῦς, without Adj., mostly *merchant-ship*, or *transport*, as opp. ship of war." However, we do not have a group of clear merchantmen mentioned for which νῆες might be the martial counterpart. As far as ναῦς referring to a warship, in contrast to πλοῖον, note that ναῦς is "rare in non-literary Hellenistic Greek,... πλοῖον being generally used" (ibid., p. 1162). If ναῦς here is simply an attempt at using a more "literary" term for πλοῖον, then even an implied yet undemonstrable use of ναῦς in contrast to unmentioned merchantmen is even more unlikely.

5. A vessel in the funereal crossing of the Nile in the Eighteenth Dynasty Theban tomb (#49) of Neferhotep is labeled a *kbn.t* (Davies 1933, pls. 22–23). *Wb.* V.118.6 states that the *kbn.t* here is a bark carrying a sarcophagus, but this is an error. When examined, the bark is referred to by the common term *nšm.t*. The word *kbn.t* is found in a text spoken by men on a small boat, who refer to the women on the larger craft behind them as being on a *kbn.t*. Is the vessel an actual ocean-going vessel (it is shown as larger than the other boats), or is there some allusion here to Hathor of Byblos (*nb.t kbn.t*), who assists the dead in his journey by making his steering oar (CT spell 61 = *CT* I, p. 262)?

THE TERM *KBN.T* REFERS TO OCEAN-GOING VESSELS

In two Ptolemaic examples, the term *kbn.t* is used in parallel with terms for riverine craft. According to the *Wb.*, the term *kbn.t* can have the meaning "warship." The *Wb Beleg.* volume gives only one reference for this meaning, the naos Louvre C 123. In a portion of the laudatory text, Ptolemy II Philadelphus is:

wsḫ m kbn.wt ꜥšꜣ q(ꜣ)q(ꜣ).w (*Urk.* II.77.15)

These *kbn.wt* and *q(ꜣ)q(ꜣ).w* vessels are warships, as the martial tenor of the text in which this excerpt is found suggests. *Wb Beleg.* V.14.8 should also have cited the parallel text on the stele fragment Berlin 14400. In a list of epitheta, the ruler (Ptolemy Soter ?) is said to be:

ꜥšꜣ
mšꜥ *ḫrp-qnw*
kbn *dp(.w) nw ỉtr* *ꜥḥꜥ[yw n ꜥḥꜣ (?)]*

These two texts indeed show *kbn.t* as a term for warships, but they also reveal that even here, this is not the primary meaning of the term. The Berlin epithet contains two pairs of terms describing divisions of the Ptolemaic host. The first pair lists the two basic divisions of the land based forces, the army (*mšꜥ*) and the cavalry (*ḫrp-qnw*); the second pair describes two major divisions of the naval forces. The *dp(.w) nw ỉtr* stand for the Nile squadrons, which suggests that *kbn.wt* must be the high seas fleet of the Mediterranean, Red Sea, and the Indian Ocean (Van't Dack and Hauben 1978, pp. 60–66). Similarly, in the Louvre C 123 text, the *q(ꜣ)q(ꜣ).w* are river craft,[6] parallel to the *kbn.wt* representing the ruler's ocean-going fleet. Neither *q(ꜣ)q(ꜣ).w* vessels nor *dp.w nw ỉtr* denote warships, but indicate rather riverine craft, warships from the contexts in which the terms are employed.[7] Similarly, *kbn.t* retains its original meaning of ocean-going vessel, known as a warship only through the context in which the word is employed.

What might at first appear to be an exception in our corpus to the use of *kbn.t* to refer to an ocean-going vessel occurs in the Nabaireh version of the Decree of Memphis. In the section of the decree mentioned above (R 12 = Spiegelberg 1922a, p. 47; *Urk.* II 179), describing the measures which Ptolemy V took to protect the borders of Egypt, the king is said to have sent out infantry, cavalry, and boats. The Greek νῆες is suitably vague and all inclusive (see above and note 9). The Demotic *br*, however, the βᾶρις, suggests a riverine craft. On the basis of the Demotic text, the corresponding hieroglyphic *kbn.t* could refer to βᾶρις craft as well as riverine vessels. These,

6. *Wb.* V.14.5–8; Boreux 1924, pp. 231–34; Jones 1988, pp. 95, 146–47; Van't Dack and Hauben 1978, p. 71. *Qꜣqꜣ.w* vessels do not appear ever to have been employed in the open sea. A fragment of a text of Necho from Elephantine (Junge 1987, pp. 66–67 and pl. 40c) preserves part of a list of the vessels forming apparently a flotilla accompanying the king on the occasion of a campaign against the Nubians, and lists among others a *qq.t*. Ch. Müller (1975, pp. 83–84) suggested that the vessels listed on the fragment were warships operating on the Red Sea (Spalinger [1979a, p. 603, note 29] assumes a victory procession is mentioned; he also suggests [1977a, p. 244] that the stele may provide "additional information regarding Necho's maritime policy" — this it does not provide). Given the presence of an apparent royal bark, numerous transport vessels, and no clear troop ships, for Junge "insgesamt macht die Flotte somit eher den Eindruck einer >>Hofflotte<< (1987, p. 67);" this is the more reasonable conclusion. The *qq.t* vessel(s?) mentioned here is but another example of the type as a river craft, not an example of an exceptional use of a *qq.t* vessel in the sea (according to Junge [ibid., p. 66 note *m*] a *qq.t* was "möglicherweise ein leichtes schnelles Schiff zur Befehlsübermittlung und postalischen Kommunikation—etwa ein >>Depeschenschiff<<"). Müller and Junge read *[pḥ (?)-] qq.t*; on the order of reading of the line fragments on the stele see Jansen-Winkeln 1989, p. 31.

7. According to Ch. Müller (1975, p. 84) the *q(ꜣ)q(ꜣ)* vessel as a "Kriegsschiff" is "gut belegt." This is incorrect; the *Wb.* cites only *Urk.* II.77.15 for the word used to describe vessels of war, and the *qq.t* vessel on the stele of Necho which Müller discussed may not even be a military vessel after all (see preceding note).

which Ptolemy V took to protect the borders of Egypt, the king is said to have sent out infantry, cavalry, and boats. The Greek νῆες is suitably vague and all inclusive (see above and note 9). The Demotic *br*, however, the βᾶρις, suggests a riverine craft. On the basis of the Demotic text, the corresponding hieroglyphic *kbn.t* could refer to βᾶρις craft as well as riverine vessels. These, smaller vessels for patrolling the mouths of the Nile, are to be expected in the context of defense of the Delta; larger ships, and most ocean-going vessels, would be unexpected.

When Antigonos Monophthalmos attempted to invade Egypt in 306 B.C., and Demetrios attempted landings on the Delta coast, Ptolemy Lagus used almost exclusively small vessels in his defensive river patrols (Seibert 1969, pp. 215–19; Hauben 1975–76, pp. 267–71).[8] Hauben notes that this parallels the strategy of Nectanebo II, and asks whether a lack of maneuverability on the part of triremes and polyremes, or a simple lack of triremes and polyremes, influenced Ptolemy's strategy (Hauben 1975–76, pp. 269-70, note 8 [citing Diodorus XVI.47.6]).

Hauben (1975–76, pp. 268–69, notes 5 and 6) points out that seagoing vessels could at times sail far up the Nile.[9] Many of the larger types of ancient warships, even triremes, were relatively light, and could be drawn on shore by their crews at night, a procedure necessary to maintain the speed and maneuverability of the vessel (Casson 1971, pp. 89–90).[10] The time for extensive operations on the Nile involving large and numerous vessels, regardless of their tonnage and draft was, however, limited. August and September appear to have been the months of the greatest traffic on the inundated Nile (see Bonneau 1964, pp. 96–101, 418–19); by January the level of the Nile was so low that the river was closed to larger vessels until July at the earliest.[11] The rushed

8. Diodorus XX.76.3 says that Ptolemy employed only riverine vessels; Pausanias I.6.6 does claim that some triremes were also used.

9. For the use of large vessels on the Nile only during the inundation, a logical but overlooked point, see Bonneau 1964, pp. 96–101 (note 2, p. 99 especially), 418–19.

10. Beaching was a precaution "taken to see that waterlogging did not add unwanted weight." As an indication of the maneuverability of a heavy laden cargo vessel (with a ram-like cutwater), see the mosaic from Sousse showing men wading ashore from an anchored vessel, carrying timbers (Dunbabin 1978, p. 270 ["Sousse 21"] and references); the men are not carrying lead ingots (see Meiggs 1982, pp. 529–30). According to Rostovtzeff (1926, p. 288, pl. 46, 2) "the mosaic furnishes a good illustration of the peculiar conditions of navigation in the shallow Syrtes."

11. According to Le Père 1822, 11 (*État moderne*) pp. 240–41: "La navigation du Nil dépend absolument des crues et du décroissement des eaux, qui en déterminent la durée; car elle cesse successivement pour les bateaux d'après leur tirant d'eau ... Pendant les derniers temps du décroissement du fleuve, c'est-à-dire pendant quatre à cinq mois de l'année, depuis janvier jusqu'à la fin de juin, le Nil est peu navigable: les bancs de sable y rendent fréquens les échouemens." See also the comments of Belon 1970, p. 101a. In this connection it is interesting to compare the evidence of the "Bodleian Archive on Corn Transport" from the 18th regnal year of Ptolemy Philometor (Reekmans and Van't Dack 1952, pp. 149–95). The earliest document in the archive (Papyrus Bodleian Ms. Gr. class. d. 107 = document no. 1) shows that a shipment of 750 artabae on Pharmouthi 24 (May 24) required more than one vessel for transportation (τὰ πλοῖ[α]). Perhaps two vessels were involved, for on Pharmouthi 29 (c. 69 = document no. 5), a single vessel carries just under half the Pharmouthi 24 load — 350 artabae ("the smallest cargo mentioned in our archive" [ibid., p. 178]). These loads suggest extreme caution and extremely low water levels; even vessels of 600 artabae capacity were small (Bonneau 1964, p. 98). The documents for late June show an increase in single vessel loads (c. 67 = document no. 3 [Pachon 18], 654 artabae; d. 108 + fr. c. 106 = document no. 4 [Pachon 22], 600 artabae; e. 105 = document no. 6 [Pachon], 250 artabae; c. 68 + fr. d. 109 + fr. e. 106], 1126 artabae). The largest, however (1126 artabae), may have been excessive for the time of year, and the vessel carrying that load is noted as shipwrecked. On July 28 (24 Payni) the water was at a sufficient height to allow a vessel loaded with 1300 artabae to proceed unhindered (d. 106 + fr. d. 109 = document no. 7). The best months for these shipments would have been August and September; navigation from January to late June would have been difficult, and these papyri demonstrate this. May and early June saw only small loads; shipments increase in size in June, although a prematurely large cargo is shipwrecked. By late July, when the river should have begun rising appreciably, the largest ship load of the archive is underway.

height of the Nile and to press on to Memphis with his fleet.[13] Because of the imminent fall of the Nile, Antigonos risked sending his navy to Egypt through the inclement Mediterranean weather, and departed Egypt in defeat at the end of November, when there remained for him no more than a month for moving his fleet to Memphis, where the fall of the inundation would have forced the invading vessels to remain until the coming July.[14] What Antigonos attempted was theoretically possible, and much later the fleet of an Arab Syria did raid Cairo.[15] Ptolemy's defenses were, however, sufficient to hold off the forces of Antigonos.

Ptolemy could not know how long Antigonos might harass Egypt, and long term coastal patrols sent against the would-be invaders would have to cope with the low Nile as well as with the inundation. If Antigonos succeeded in pushing up the Nile towards Memphis, Ptolemy's forces could hope to hold back the invasion long enough for the declining Nile to stop Antigonos' ships. Ptolemy's vessels would have to be small and light enough to remain operational after Antigonos' ships had all run aground. Vessels patrolling the Nile, and those attempting to enter the Nile from the Mediterranean, would also have to cope with the treacherous mouths of the Nile. According to J. M. Le Père, in the *Description de l'Égypte* :

> On appelle *boghâz*, en Égypte, les passes étroites et périlleuses des bouches du Nil à la mer. Ces bouches sont fermées par les sables que les flots de la mer, agités par les vents du large et combattus par le courant des eaux du fleuve, y déposent au point d'équilibre où ces forces viennent se briser. Ces bancs de sable varient suivant les saisons et l'action plus ou moins grande des vents, en sorte que ceux qui forment la barre qu'on trouve ordinairement aux bouches du Nil, changent souvent de position, et rendent sans cesse nécessaires aux navigateurs les soins d'un pilote ... mais cette surveillence continuelle d'un pilote n'est pas toujours suffisante pour prévenir les accidens (Le Père 1822, pp. 236–39).

Even during the height of the inundation these *boghâz* could be treacherous (Le Père 1822, p. 238).[16] Patrol vessels would need to be capable of operating within the *boghâz* while attacking ships were running aground, and should be able to venture easily out of the mouths of the Nile. The short period of the high Nile, the lack of maneuvering space within the channels of the Nile, and the *boghâz* at the mouths of the Nile, all suggest the use of small vessels for year round defense of the Nile. This was in fact the situation which obtained during the Roman period, when small craft

13. Bonneau (1964, pp. 77–78) misunderstood Antigonos' strategy, and assumed that the inundation prevented the naval operations of Demetrios. These were hampered by Ptolemy and his small vessels. The operations which the officers decline to carry out due to the inundation (Diodorus XX.76, cited by Bonneau, p. 78, note 1) are land operations, proposed as a last hope of invasion after the failure of the primary, naval plan.

14. Compare the text cited by Bonneau 1964, p. 99, note 2. The desire to take advantage of what remained of the high Nile in order to reach Memphis with an ocean-going fleet explains why Antigonos risked his fleet and then withdrew when he did. This supports Hauben's view of Antigonos' primary strategy.

15. al-Maqrizi, *Al-Mawâ'iẓ wal-I'tibâr bi-Dhikr al-Khitat wal-Âthâr* II 181, 6 et passim (1853); Le Père (1822, p. 241) points out that a caravelle of 24 cannon sailed from Damietta to Cairo in 1778 during the inundation. Ocean-going ships were often outfitted at Cairo during the Middle Ages (see Popper 1951, pp. 11–15).

16. The *boghâz* of Damietta was less dangerous than that of Rosetta; according to de la Laune (as quoted by Douin 1922, p. 15): "Le Bogaz de Damiette, plus resserré que celui de Rosette, offre une passe plus commode. Il y a toujours au moins 7 pieds d'eau. De gros bâtiments, et même des chébecs de 14 pièces de canon le passent en tout temps avec la précaution de s'alléger auparavant..." Invading warships carrying men, equipment, and supplies, operating under active opposition from land and river based forces, would have difficulty discharging their loads before entering the mouth of the river, and then taking on their cargo again before proceeding upriver. Seibert states: "Der Auftrag der Flotte [des Antigonos] lautete zunächst, Truppen an Land zu setzen" (1969, p. 218). As Hauben has remarked, however, the fleet was meant to proceed to Memphis. Considering the problems caused by the *boghâz*, the army would need to land in order to lighten the vessels and protect them from the Lagid forces, as the fleet navigated through the treacherous Nile mouths.

such as ἄφρακτα, δίκροτοι, and μονόκροτοι were routinely employed for patrol duties on the Nile (Hauben 1975–76, p. 269, note 6).[17] The Byzantines made use of *dromonaria* and *akatia* in patrolling the mouths of the Nile, and "two-banked craft were never assigned such duty" (Casson 1971, p. 154, note 63).[18]

Primarily the difficulty of operating large ships in the narrow confines of a river choked with small enemy vessels, rather than any consideration of the draft of larger vessels, is likely to be behind Ptolemy's apparently exclusive use of small vessels in defending Egypt against the planned naval invasion by Antigonos Monophthalmos.

Br is not a term which would apply to a trireme, and the context of riverine defense speaks against the use of triremes, and large warships in general. The *kbn.wt* vessels mentioned in the Nabaireh text correspond to small, traditional Egyptian vessels in the Demotic text (Casson 1971, p. 341).[19] To be consistent with their task on the Nile, and in keeping with the corresponding Demotic *br*, the *kbn.wt* should be small vessels. How does one explain this use of the term *kbn.t,* which should designate an ocean-going vessel?

Under certain conditions, vessels of the high seas fleet, almost always smaller ratings of the fleet, could be assigned duty on the Nile, augmenting the ποτομοφύλακες (Rostovtzeff 1940, pp. 367–76; Hauben 1975–76, p. 269, note 6; Van't Dack 1976, pp. 79, 97–98; Van't Dack and Hauben 1978, pp. 61, 80). These πλοῖα θαλάσσια could conceivably be referred to as *kbn.wt* vessels in hieroglyphic Egyptian, and were of Greek design, consistent with the determinative given to *kbn.wt* in the Nabaireh text.[20] From the general νῆες of the Greek text, the Demotic and hieroglyphic editions of the decree of Memphis detail the two sorts of craft which Ptolemy used in his defense of the Nile—riverine craft such as the κοντωτά καὶ ὅσα σμικρότερα ἄλλα which figure in Appien's description of the navy of Ptolemy II Philadelphus (Van't Dack 1976, p. 99, note 5; Van't Dack and Hauben 1978, p. 69), the Demotic *br*; and small ratings of the ocean-going fleet assigned duty on the Nile as πλοῖα θαλάσσια, the triremes mentioned by Pausanias as part of Ptolemy's defensive fleet, the hieroglyphic *kbn.wt*.[21] In the context of defense of the Delta, these small ocean going

17. Note the single banked galley filled with soldiers on patrol in the inundated Delta in the Palestrina mosaic (see conveniently Strong 1976, p. 72, fig. 29; the color illustration in Bowman 1986, p. 11, fig. 1; and the close-up in Casson 1971, fig. 116).

18. The naval engagements carried out by the Byzantine Emperor Leo against the Arab fleets in 717 and 718, operating out of the Golden Horn, illustrate well the advantages of a few vessels engaging great fleets of large vessels in a confined water where maneuvering space and not depth of water was the major issue. Jean Coppin gives a brief account of Nilotic pirates, who toiled with motives different from those with which we may hope the earlier Nile patrols operated, but with the same object — stopping large vessels on the Nile: "Comme nous fûmes proches de la pointe de l'îsle de Delta, où le Nil fait ses deux branches, l'on nous avertit de nous tenir davantage sur nos gardes, parce que les voleurs y sont le plus souvent avec des petits batteaux" (1971, p. 174 = [41]).

19. According to Van't Dack and Hauben (1978, p. 70) "il est probable que beaucoup de ces punts [the κοντωτά which Ptolemy Lagus used to defend the Delta] et des autres σμικρότερα étaient d'origine indigene."

20. Compare graffiti at Gebel Silsileh apparently showing these smaller warships patrolling the Nile (see Preisigke and Spiegelberg 1915, pls. 10 [#158], 15 [#233]).

21. This parallels Ramses III's description of his preparation of the Delta against the Sea Peoples, large *mnš* vessels and smaller *br* boats being sent to block the mouths of the Nile (*MH* I pl. 46, line 20 = *KRI* V 48, 8–9). If the determinative given to *br* in the Medinet Habu text actually does show a lion's head at the prow of the boat, then the Egyptian vessels depicted in the sea battle scene may be *br* coasters. This could then explain the "peculiar" elements which disturbed Casson (1971, pp. 37–38). The use of *br* vessels to carry soldiers is attested elsewhere from the Ptolemaic period (Merzagora 1929, p. 127, note 6). Compare also G. Möller's interpretation of the type of marine troop λαβαρεῖς mentioned by Aristagoras. Möller (1920, p. 78) suggests that Egyptian *br*, Greek βᾶρις may be an element in the word, and Lloyd (1988a, p. 187) on this basis suggests "'men of the baris, boatmen' (?)." On the parallelism between *kbn.t* and *br*, see also below, note 54.

warships would easily fill a gap in the capabilities of the lighter *br* craft. According to Brémond, concerning the port of Rosetta:

> les marchandises gros(s)es et de grand poids sont portées sur de longs batteaux, plats au fonds, dict *germes*, que peuvent sortir sur ces bans de sable, et qui pèchent peu d'eau, mais au moindre mauvais tamps, en mer, sont facilles à naufrager en ceste coste orageuse (1974, p. 14 = [37]).

Such flat bottomed riverine vessels would be ideal for patrolling the mouths of the Nile, but would require augmentation by the small vessels of the ocean going navy in order to engage an incoming fleet and to pursue a retiring enemy.[22] As a precedent for using small craft defending the mouths of the Nile, one can cite Ptolemy Lagus; for patrolling the mouths of the Nile with triremes at sea, one could perhaps cite Ptolemy Lagus again, and certainly the thirty triremes which Alexander left in Egypt under the command of Polemon, charged with guarding the Nile mouths (Hauben 1972, p. 63).

The vessels of Ptolemy's fleet were probably of Greek and Phoenician manufacture, so a translation of *kbn.wt* as "warships of non-Egyptian design and manufacture" is connoted, yet the primary meaning of *kbn.t* is "ocean-going vessel," and even in the Nabaireh text of the decree of Memphis *kbn.t* retains this meaning.

THE *KBN.WT* VESSELS ARE OFTEN ASSOCIATED SPECIFICALLY WITH THE LEVANT

The only Ptolemaic example of *kbn.t* for which Lloyd attempts to discuss the word in the context of the Egyptian text is on the Satrap Stele of Ptolemy Lagus (*Urk.* II.15.3).[23] The portion of text in question is *Urk.* II.15.2–10:

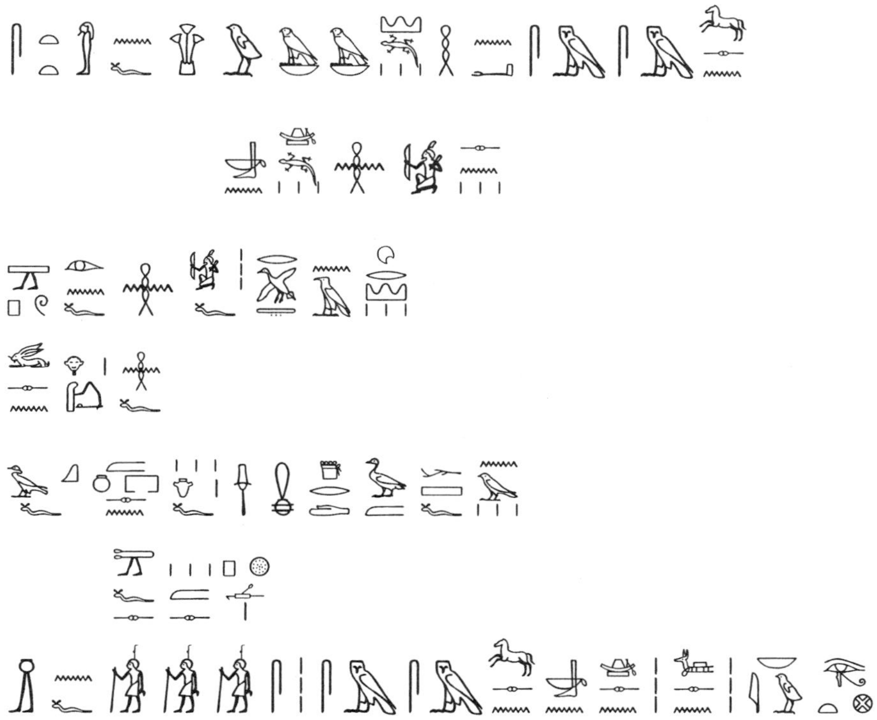

22. A connection with the sea is also provided by the use of *wꜣḏ-wr/ym*/θάλασσα in describing the origin of the foes against whom the *kbn.wt* were sent out.

23. The stele is dated year 7 of Alexander II.

Lloyd renders this section as:

> He mustered the Greeks in great numbers together with their horses and many *kbnt*-ships with their crews. He marched with his army against the land of Syria. They [sc. the Syrians] fought against him when he entered amongst them, his heart being stout like a falcon in pursuit of *šfnw* birds, so that he conquered them in one battle. He brought back to Egypt all their chiefs, their horses, their *kbnt*-ships and their treasures (1972a, p. 274).

For Lloyd, the first *kbn.wt* vessels mentioned in the section are those of Ptolemy, the others being the vessels of Antigonos. By rendering *Ḥꜣw-Nbwt* as "Greeks," he associates Ptolemy's *kbn.wt* vessels with Greek crews.[24] According to Lloyd, the *kbn.wt* vessels manned by crews of the *Ḥꜣw-Nbwt* refer to "the Ptolemaic battle fleet of Greek war galleys" (Lloyd 1972a, p. 275).

Vandersleyen has shown, however, that the term *Ḥꜣw-Nbwt* does not mean exclusively "Greeks," even during the Ptolemaic period; from his investigation, "il resort que Haou-nebout n'a jamais eu dans l'usage le sens spécifique de <<Grecs>>" (Vandersleyen 1971, pp. 139–74).[25] Not expecting that Ptolemy should assemble Phoenicians in preparation for an expedition into Asia, Vandersleyen suggests that the passage begins with a shortened version of a standard *Königsnovelle* conceit — an uprising occurs, is reported, and the king in righteous rage storms forth to crush the enemy. Vandersleyen proposes that this is the content of lines *Urk.* II.15.2–3, wherein he would read *Ḥꜣw-Nbwt* as the subject of *sṯwt*, and *n* as "contra." For him the *Ḥꜣw-Nbwt* are the foes of Ptolemy, and both mentions of the *kbn.wt* vessels refer to the conveyances of the Asiatic foe.

24. Brugsch already rendered *Ḥꜣw-Nbwt* here as "Ioniens" (1871, pp. 3, 10).

25. Vandersleyen concludes [pp. 152–53] that *Ḥꜣw-Nbwt* must be rendered as "Greeks" only in the Second Decree of Philae and in the Harris Stele. Perdu (1985, p. 107, note *o*), discussing line 10 of the "Stele of Naples," revives the suggestion of Vercoutter (1949, p. 201) that the late writings of *Nbw* in *Ḥꜣw-Nbw* as though it were to be read *Nb.wy*, "the Two Lords," are examples of a new meaning applied to the term during the Ptolemaic period: "ceux qui sont autour (dans l'entourage) du double maître," the Greeks supporting the king. This "new etymology" cannot be demonstrated, and from the time of Ptolemy II Philadelphus "ceux qui sont autour du double maître" would have suggested an Egyptian translation of the Greek οἱ περὶ τὴν αὐλὴν ἐπίλεκτοι μάχιμοι, the native Egyptian bodyguard established by Ptolemy II (*Urk.* II.42.5–11; Winnicki 1989a, pp. 228–29). The conclusion of Desroches-Noblecourt and Kuentz (1968, p. 149, note 70) is to be retained: the writings of *nbw* as *Nb.wy* are examples of "la confusion, phonétique et graphique, du duel masculin avec le pluriel masculin et féminin." The text which Perdu discusses refers to Sematawtefnakht's preservation by Heryshef-Re during the *ꜥḥꜣ n Ḥꜣw-Nbw*, with the determinative . Perdu reads "l'offensive des Grecs"; he assumes that the battle of Issos is meant (1985, p. 108, note *t*; Limme (1983, pp. 326, 328) also reads *Ḥꜣw-Nbw* in this passage as referring to people). *Ḥꜣw-Nbwt* can refer both to "un type de population" and is found "opposé à *tꜣ* et à *ḫꜣst*, ce qui en fait une région naturelle" (*LÄ* II, col. 1053). The determinative of *Ḥꜣw-Nbw* in the Stele of Naples allows for the term being purely geographic. Taking *ꜥḥꜣ* as referring not to a single battle, but encompassing a number of engagements, reading "war, campaign, state of war," *ꜥḥꜣ n Ḥꜣw-Nbw* should be understood as "the Levantine campaign," encompassing all of the battles from Issos through Gaza (for a late example of *ꜥḥꜣ* referring to a state of war over a potentially long period of time, compare Papyrus Krall IX 10–12, where *ꜣḫ* will be in the district and *mlḫ* in the city until the armor is brought out of the city of Djura). Issos was a shock to the Persian held Levant, but only with the fall of Gaza and the reduction of Persian sea power was the fall of the Egyptian satrapy inevitable. The reason for Alexander's drive to Egypt was the control of the eastern Mediterranean littoral, and *ꜥḥꜣ n Ḥꜣw-Nbw* well describes the campaign which began at Issos and ended at Pelusium (Ehrenberg 1926, pp. 8–13; Fuller 1954, pp. 93–94). Rather than referring back to *Ḥꜣw-Nbw*, the *sn* of *smꜣ⸗sn* in the following line (11) could refer to Asia, *Stt* in line 10 (in note *r* on p. 108, Perdu indeed recognizes that here "le pays vaut pour ses habitants suivant une métonymie d'un emploi courant dans les textes égyptiens" [compare *sn* referring back to lands also given purely geographic determinatives in Vercoutter 1949, p. 155: #48]). Also possible is a reading of *sn* in *smꜣ⸗sn* as a use of the third person plural suffix pronoun as a writing of the passive (*NÄG* § 269; *KDG* §326; *DG* §248), *⸗sn* here written as a classicizing archaism for *⸗w*/ΟΥ. The passage in question on the Stele of Naples should be read: "During the Levantine campaign, when you drove back the Asiatics, you protected me. Millions were slain round about me, but not one could lift his hand against me."

We might not expect Ptolemy to gather together "Phoenicians" before an expedition into Syria-Palestine, but grammatically this is the best understanding of the passage. A reflexive use of *stwt,* "to assemble," appears to be otherwise unattested, and taking *stwt* as a passive is little improvement, suggesting that the *Ḥꜣw-Nbwt* were roused by some nameless Syrian foe. If a reflexive use of the verb were allowed, for the sake of argument, the *Ḥꜣw-Nbwt* might well "assemble" against someone, but what of the *kbn.wt* vessels? The components of the military force listed in lines *Urk.* II.15.2–3 are arranged in a chiastic manner: people (*Ḥꜣw-Nbwt ꜥšꜣw*) and their conveyances (*smsm=sn*); conveyances (*kbn(.wt) ꜥšꜣw*) and their people (*mšꜥ=sn*). *Ḥꜣw-Nbwt* and *kbn(.wt)* are parallel, either coordinate objects, or coordinate subjects. It is thus not possible to read that the *Ḥꜣw-Nbwt* assembled against Ptolemy together with the paraphernalia of war; rather one would have to understand that the *Ḥꜣw-Nbwt* and *kbn.wt* vessels assembled against Ptolemy. The independent action imparted to the ships when *Ḥꜣw-Nbwt* is taken as a subject of *sṯwt* is both unexpected and undesirable. For the preposition *n* as "against" a person, Vandersleyen (1971, p. 148, note 5) cites Erman, *NÄG* §600 no. 5 and *Wb.* II.193.11. As these authors have recognized, there are occasions on which the object of the preposition *n* must be understood as being acted "against," yet this is not so much a meaning inherent in the preposition as a function of the translation into English, based on the nature of the action performed "*n*, someone."[26] The reflexive use of *stwt* being otherwise unattested, this point is moot. All things considered, the best understanding of *Urk.* II.15.2–3 is: "He (Ptolemy Lagus) assembled numerous Phoenicians and their horses, numerous *kbn* vessels and their crews."[27]

Accepting Vandersleyen's understanding of the *Ḥꜣw-Nbwt* as Phoenicians, but rejecting his rendering of the passage from the Satrap Stele, we find that Ptolemy I assembled certain Phoenicians, with cavalry, and *kbn.wt* vessels with crews, before he went out against Syrians,[28] who also disposed of Phoenician vessels (*kbn.wt* ships). This does not present the problem which compelled Vandersleyen to his suggestions regarding the passage; rather, the Satrap Stele actually alludes to specific events in 315 B.C., which reveal that Ptolemy Lagus did indeed assemble Phoenicians and their vessels, and which relate the origin of the *kbn.wt* vessels which Ptolemy later captured from the "Asiatic" foe.

26. On *n* "adversatif," see also Perdu 1985, p. 106–07, note *n*.

27. If *Ḥꜣw-Nbwt* were read as the subject of a verb *stwt* with a meaning other than "to assemble," one could suggest *stwt n* with Meeks 1979, p. 276, no. 79.2837, citing *KRI* II 242, 8, as "se joindre à, s'associer à." This would yield "The numerous *Ḥꜣw-Nbwt* … were allied with him/took his part."

28. Vandersleyen (1971, p. 149), recognizing that there is no clear referrent for the *sn* of line *Urk.* II.15.5 (*wn=sn ḥr ꜥḥꜣ ḥnꜥ=f*), suggests that "*sn* s'expliquerait par une allusion aux nombreux personnages cités au début, mieux qu'avec la terre de *Ḫꜣr* qui désigne une région et non un peuple." Vandersleyen can do this by assuming that the *Ḥꜣw-Nbwt* are the enemy, and array themselves against Ptolemy. As the text must be read to say that Ptolemy Lagus assembled the *Ḥꜣw-Nbwt*, the enemy and the referent for *sn* in line 5 must be sought elsewhere (the *sn* in *wn=sn ḥr ꜥḥꜣ ḥnꜥ=f* should have the same referent as the *sn* in the immediately following *ꜥq=f m-ẖnw=sn*; *ꜥḥꜣ ḥnꜥ* here is thus better understood as "to fight with" in its hostile use, and not "to fight with" as rendering assistance [in which use the *sn* of *wn=sn ḥr ꜥḥꜣ ḥnꜥ=f* could have referred to the *Ḥꜣw-Nbwt* whom Ptolemy had assembled]; on *ꜥḥꜣ ḥnꜥ*, see Morschauser 1985, p. 173, note 399). In spite of Vandersleyen's misgivings, a country name can represent its inhabitants and provide a referent for a pronoun referring to them (see below, note 38) — the *sn* of *wn=sn ḥr ꜥḥꜣ ḥnꜥ=f* could refer back to *Ḫꜣr*. In the present text there is yet another possibility. In note *a* on p. 15 of *Urk.* II, Sethe notes that the signs of the apparent *n(y) Ḫꜣrw* in *pꜣ tꜣ n(y) Ḫꜣrw* are arranged as 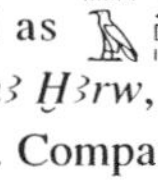, which suggests the possibility of reading the group as *nꜣ Ḫꜣrw*, the whole as *pꜣ tꜣ* (*n* — haplography) *nꜣ Ḫꜣrw*, "the land of the Syrians," *nꜣ Ḫꜣrw* being Ptolemy's enemies, and the referent for *sn* in lines *Urk.* II.15.5–6. Compare line 22 of Stele Cairo 50048 (Gauthier and Sottas 1925): Ptolemy takes care of the divine images of Egyptian deities which were carried off from Egypt *r pꜣ tš pꜣ ỉšr pꜣ tš nꜣ Ḫr.w* in the time of the Medes — *pꜣ tš nꜣ Ḫr.w* parallel to *pꜣ tꜣ nꜣ Ḫr.w* (see also line 9 of the same stele, and Spiegelberg 1922a, p. 219, no. 469; p. 220, no. 477).

According to Diodorus XIX.58, Antigonos entered Phoenicia in 315 B.C. intent on acquiring a fleet. He found it necessary to arrange for the construction of new vessels because, according to Diodorus, Ptolemy Lagus had shortly before taken all of the Phoenician vessels to Egypt. This is what the Satrap Stele records in *Urk*. II.15.2–3 — Ptolemy collected Phoenicians, their horses, and their ships.[29] Following this mention of preparatory defensive measures taken in the year 315 B.C.,[30] the line beginning *šm pw ỉr.n=f* commences the description of the events of 312 B.C., the year of Ptolemy's victory at Gaza.[31] After the battle, Tyre and Sidon abandoned Antigonos' side and joined Ptolemy. Sidon was one of the three Phoenicians cities (the others being Tripolis and Byblos) in which Antigonos had set up naval arsenals for his new fleet (Diodorus XIX.58). There Ptolemy would have found some of the new "Byblian" vessels of Antigonos.[32] The capture of *kbn.wt* vessels from the "Asiatic" enemy mentioned in *Urk*. II.15.9 thus alludes both to Antigonos' construction of a fleet in Phoenicia beginning in 315 B.C., and to Ptolemy Lagus' capture of Antigonos' Phoenician naval arsenals following the battle of Gaza in 312 B.C. The pithy text of this small portion of the Satrap Stele fits well with what Diodorus Siculus tells us of Phoenician naval allegiances and activities between 315 and 312 B.C.[33] The *Ḥ3w-Nbwt* of the stele are Phoenicians, and the *kbn.wt* are the ships which Ptolemy pulled out of the Phoenician ports in the face of Antigonos' advance. *Kbn.t* is here used in the old sense of "ocean-going vessel," and in reference to vessels constructed in Phoenicia, and initially operating from there — all nuances of the term *kbn.t* are understood and exploited in the text of the Satrap Stele.[34]

29. For horses and native cavalry in later Ptolemaic Coele-Syria (specifically in the Ammonitis), see Rostovtzeff 1922, pp. 25–26, 167–68; Préaux 1939a, pp. 214–15; for Levantine land forces in the early Ptolemaic period, compare the Jewish soldiers mentioned in the "Letter" of Aristeas, § 13; on foreigners in general in Ptolemaic forces, see Peremans 1972, pp. 67–76, and Van't Dack 1976, pp. 90–95; on the ships, see Van't Dack and Hauben 1978, pp. 84–85. For Phoenicians in the Saite military, see below, note 70.

30. As Seibert (1969, pp. 143–44) points out, Ptolemy's evacuation of Phoenicia shows that the new ruler of Egypt was "rein defensiv eingestellt."

31. The gathering of men, horses, and ships should not refer to the preparations for the battle of Gaza, for naval operations directly connected with this action are unattested. Bouché-Leclerq (1903, p. 47, note 2; p. 106, note 1) recognized this, and also connected the references to ships with the year 315 B.C., but assumed a reference to "la victoire remportée en 315 par Polyclitos à Aphrodisias, sur la côte de Cilicie." For him, however, the *kbn.wt* gathered by Ptolemy and those which he captured from his foe all refer to vessels in action in 315 B.C., the section being for him a jumble of events from 315 and 312 B.C. Bouché-Leclerq (ibid., p. 52, note 3) incorrectly assumes that the retreat by Ptolemy out of Syria-Palestine is mentioned in the Satrap Stele by the bringing back of spoils recorded in lines *Urk*. II.15.9–10.

32. Diodorus XIX.62 states that Antigonos' fleet in 315 consisted of 120 new, Phoenician-built vessels, and refers to him leaving some at Tyre. Ptolemy may have captured all of Antigonos' Tyrian squadron following Gaza.

33. Lloyd (1972a, pp. 273–74) simply states that "the text [the Satrap Stele] concentrates on the military campaigns in Syria between 320 and 312 B.C. but it also hints at the wide-ranging and highly successful naval operations conducted by Ptolemy in the Eastern Mediterranean."

34. Phoenician naval engineers are attested working at Alexandria (Fraser 1972, pp. 429–30), and the timber for Ptolemaic vessels — even the completed vessels themselves — were furnished by foreign cities (Rostovtzeff 1922, p. 123; Wilcken 1925, pp. 93–99; Préaux 1939a, p. 41); the use of native Egyptian wood in Ptolemaic warship construction is attested once (Fraser and Roberts 1949, pp. 289–94), but only for the ἐντορνεία, an upper defensive work, not the hull (see also Casson 1971, p. 89, note 59). For the sort of wooden ship's parts which Nepherites I sent to Agesilaos, see Kienitz 1953, pp. 79–80. Note that in India, Alexander had a fleet manned by Phoenicians, Cypriots, Carians, and Egyptians — Egyptians and *Ḥ3w-Nbwt* (Arrian VI.1.6).

The section of the Satrap Stele discussed here (the portion given in *Urk.* II.15.2–10) should be rendered:

He assembled numerous Phoenicians and their cavalry,
numerous *kbn.wt* -vessels and their crews.
He advanced with his host against the land of the Syrians;
they fought against him;
he entered among them, violent like a falcon[35] in pursuit of small fowl,[36]
with the result that he conquered them at once.
To Egypt he brought all their chiefs, their horses, their *kbn.wt* vessels, and
all their marvels.

Also of bearing on the discussion of the meaning of *kbn.t* in the Late Period is the observation that the naval affairs of the Ptolemies were to a large extent in the hands of Egyptians and Levantines.[37] Many non-combattant sailors were Egyptians, and the ἐπιβάται appear to have been predominantly Egyptian "pendant toute la période hellénistique, jusqu'aux derniers jours de l'empire lagide" (Van't Dack and Hauben 1978, pp. 84–89, 90–92).[38] Along with this strong Egyptian presence, Phoenicians must have filled many sailing and marine roles; Van't Dack and Hauben (ibid., p. 89) quote Plutarch's account of a centurion speaking to Antony, before the battle of Actium, of his desire to fight on land rather than in ships Αἰγύπτιοι καὶ Φοίνικες ἐν θαλάσσῃ μαχέσθωσαν (Antonius 64.2).[39] Whatever a vessel's design origin, it is unlikely that Greeks were ever predominant in the complement of a Ptolemaic fleet, but Phoenicians may have been present in sufficient numbers for one always to suspect the influence of the ethnicity of a ship's crew in the use of the term *kbn.t*. The *kbn.wt* vessels of the Ptolemies were probably not filled with Greeks.[40]

Two stelae dated to year 23 of Ptolemy V Epiphanes refer to *kbn.wt* vessels operating in the *wꜣḏ-wr*, under the command of Aristonikos (Daressy 1911, p. 6, line 28 of the stele; idem 1917, p. 178, line 15 of the stele [Cairo Museum No. d'entrée 44901]).[41] As Daressy understood the text, the stelae apparently refer to preparations which Ptolemy made for receiving from Rome the expected allotments of former Seleukid held lands, allotments expected but never received. Later there is mention of Aristonikos' capture of the Phoenician city Arados, apparently utilizing these same

35. Literally "*sḫm* of heart like (that of) a falcon." For *sḫm ib* as "violent," see Piankoff 1930, p. 37; Fecht 1972, pp. 139–40.

36. Reading *šfn.w* as a form of *šf* (as did *Wb.* IV.455.3 *Beleg.*; this equation was questioningly suggested in *Wb.* IV.460.3); the translation is that of Edgerton and Wilson 1936, p. 60, note 4a for *MH II*, pl. 68, 4.

37. Many of the vessels of the early Ptolemaic navy were constructed in Asia Minor and Cyprus (Wilcken 1925, pp. 93–99).

38. See Winnicki (1989a, p. 227, note 46) on the possibility that the Egyptians involved in the Chremonidan war were "die Mannschaft der Expeditionsschiffe."

39. On the Cypro-Phoenician fleet of Alexander, a portion of which was detached under Polemon to guard the mouths of the Nile, see Hauben 1972, pp. 58–65, and the references cited there.

40. Line 9 of the Naukratis stele of Nectanebo (text in Erman and Wilcken 1900, p. 130) appears to associate maritime imports into Egypt, as well as the *wꜣḏ-wr* itself, with the *Ḥꜣw-Nbwt* (see Vandersleyen 1971, p. 146).

41. On the date of the stelae, Walbank 1979, p. 189, note 128, and references given there. On Aristonikos, see Otto 1934, p. 2, note 6 and Chevereau 1985, p. 194. It has not yet been possible to examine these stelae in the Cairo Museum. The stele which Daressy published in *RdT* 38 appears to show the *kbn.wt* vessels followed by *by.w* vessels (see D. Jones 1988, p. 136 [#27], to which add the Year 23 Stelae references). In *RdT* 33 (p. 6, line 28), the *n* of *kbn(.t)* appears to be written after *kby* (note that the *k* over the *b* has become a gold sign) and before *by(.w)*, probably a copying or typesetting error (less likely is an orthography of *kbn.t* without the *n* [for *kbn.t* as *kby.t*, see James 1962, p. 101, note 16 (= XX B, 11)] as the *nw*-pot would then be superfluous).

forces.[42] Aristonikos recruited for the Ptolemaic host in Greece,[43] and some of these *kbn.wt* vessels which the Year 23 stelae record as operating in the *wꜣḏ-wr* may have come with their mercenary crews from Greece. Most of the ships' crews, however, are likely to have been composed of Egyptians and Phoenicians. Although Epiphanes may have needed troops from Greece, he was in the position to offer Egyptian vessels and their crews to the Achaean league (Bouché-Leclerq 1903, pp. 395–98). The theater of operations with which the stelae are concerned is Phoenicia. The *kbn.wt* vessels here are warships, and perhaps also transport vessels, plying the eastern Mediterranean, fighting and landing near Byblos itself. Although they were warships and probably of Greek design, their crews are not likely to have been Greek, and they are foremost ocean-going vessels in the eastern Mediterranean, as were the old *kbn.wt* ships.

All of the Late Period examples of the term *kbn.t* which Lloyd cites do appear to refer to warships; other examples which he does not cite refer to transport vessels.

THE TERM *KBN.T* REFERS TO CARGO VESSELS

None of these examples are discussed by Lloyd, and until now only one has been mentioned in connection with a study of *kbn.wt* vessels in the Late Period. In the Pithom Stele of Ptolemy II Philadelphus, the term *kbn.t* occurs three times, always with a rather detailed determinative. Two of these occurrences (*Urk.* II.86.10 and 87.11) are within a long section recording the martial prowess of the king. While detailed, neither determinative gives any indication of the presence of a ram. In the section of the stele dealing with the foundation of *Ptolemais theron*, πρός τῇ θήρᾳ τῶν ἐλεφάντων (Strabo, *Geography* 16.4.7) in Abyssinia,[44] Ptolemy II Philadelphus dispatches a group of ships down the eastern canal and into the Red Sea. The flotilla is described as "his great fleet, consisting of four *kbn.w(t)* ships" (*Urk.* II.100.15). The foundation of *Ptolemais theron*, as later described in the stele, indicates that the expedition brought farming equipment and cattle, presumably transported by the four *kbn* vessels, a task for which triremes, and warships in general, were not suited.[45] Furthermore, if one examines the determinative given to *kbn.t* in this passage, neither hint of a ram nor evidence of an elaborate aphlaston aft is given. The vessel is a round bottomed transport ship.[46] Just as the vessels which the pharaohs dispatched to Punt were *kbn.t* ships, so the flotilla which Ptolemy II sent to the Red Sea consisted of *kbn.t* ships. Again *kbn.t* retains its old meaning.

Two final Ptolemaic examples of the word give further evidence for *kbn.t* in the old sense of eastern, ocean-going vessel. Kurth (1980, pp. 153–67) has examined the use of the term *kbn.t* in a wine offering scene in *Edfu* III 241, 11–242, 2, and attempts to use the occurrence of the term *kbn.t* in the epitheta of Ptolemy VIII to date the assumed original version of the scene and its annotations to the Saite period. Kurth's understanding of the meaning of *kbn.t* in the scene must be questioned. Ptolemy VIII in the wine offering scene is referred to as "king of Egypt, ruler (*ḥqꜣ*) of Fenekhu, who controls (*sỉp*) the *kbn.t* vessels in the sea." Kurth, following the works of Lloyd, renders *kbn.t* here as "*kbn.t* -Kriegsschiffe (griechische Kampfschiffe)," and concludes that this is a reference to Egyptian control of the sea. The determinative could refer to a warship, but the context does not

42. For the fate of Phoenician Arados under Ptolemy VI, see Otto 1934, p. 66 (and note 4).

43. Perhaps mentioned in line 23 of the decree (Daressy 1911, p. 7).

44. On the location of *Ptolemais theron*, see I. Hofmann 1975, pp. 85–94; Darnell (forthcoming), and the references cited there.

45. On elephant transports, see Krebs 1965, pp. 96–101.

46. The sign in fact closely resembles the determinative provided for *kbn.t* in the earliest attestations of the word, in the Old Kingdom text *Urk.* I.134.15 and 17, which itself recounts a voyage to Punt. *Wb.* V.118.5 mistakenly lists the occurrence of *kbn.t* in *Urk.* II.100.15 as an example of the term *kbn.t* referring to a warship.

necessarily call for this. In the scene, the goddess Uto is referred to as the one "to whom the Fenekhu sail (south), bearing their wine...."[47] Wine offering scenes in the Ptolemaic period mention Phoenicia and Syria as the origins of the offered wine first in the reign of Ptolemy III,[48] and the wine in this scene, as Kurth recognized, is coming from the Levant.[49] The Levantines sail to Uto with their wine, and Ptolemy controls the *kbn.t* vessels in the sea. There should be a connection; perhaps the *kbn.t* vessels are those of the Levantines, in which they bring their wine to Uto. This is further suggested by an associated text, *Edfu* III 240, l. 14, in which Ptolemy VIII is referred to as "the one who brings in presents from the lands of Asia."

The following example has thus far been overlooked in the discussion of the nature of the *kbn.t* vessels in the Late Period, and has a bearing on the Edfu text: In a list of adorations of Mut on the Ptolemaic gate into the enclosure of Mut at Karnak (Sauneron 1983, pl. 13, line 12; Bouriant 1890, p. 168, lines 10–11; discussed in Vandersleyen 1971, pp. 149–50 and Vercoutter 1949, no. 43), a *kbn.t* vessel is mentioned in relation to Syria: "Hail to the mother of gods and men, to whom come the 'Byblians' in the sea, laden with the goods of Syria (*tꜣ-nṯr*)."[50] The following line appears to be related (plate 13, line 13): "Hail to the mother of gods and men, to whom come the *Ḥꜣw-Nbwt* in adorations, fear of her pervading their hearts." The Byblians here carry Syrian goods, and the mention of these Syrian traders called forth the following reference to the fearful adoration of the Levantines. These Byblians are not men of war, for they are "laden with the goods of Syria." In the Edfu text, the Levantines bring wine, and Ptolemy VIII controls the *kbn.wt* vessels; in the Karnak text, these thoughts are joined—the *kbn.wt* vessels bring the goods of the Levant. The *kbn.wt* vessels in both texts should be cargo ships.

As published in *MIFAO* 107, the determinative for *kbny* in the Karnak text is rather strange.[51] There appears to be an aphlaston aft, common in warships but infrequently found on merchantmen; at the prow there is a protrusion and a vertical element, which in general recall the ram and horn of a warship. The protruding "knife" is above the water line, at gunwale level, not suitable for a ram, and the hull is round, more suitable to a fat merchantman than to a warship. An inspection of the actual hieroglyph at Karnak reveals a somewhat more respectable vessel (see fig. 9.1), and one which appears to have a ram. The *kbn.t* vessel determinative in the Edfu text could pass for a warship. The contexts in which both ships are found suggest merchantmen, yet the determinatives show vessels with the rig of war (though one has the rounded hull of a freighter). These seeming contradictions suggest that the *kbn.wt* vessels in both texts were thought of as merchant galleys, such as the κυβαίδιον vessels carrying wine from Palestine to Egypt in Nikanor's letter to Zenon and Krition, PSI 594.

Figure 9.1. Vessel from the Ptolemaic Gate into the Enclosure of Mut at Karnak

47. Of Wadjyt, *Edfu* VII 165, 13, reads: *ỉỉ n≈s Fnḫw ḥr ỉnw≈sn*.

48. See Poo 1984, pp. 153–56, 227–29 (for example, on the Bab el-Amra, *Urk*. VIII.47.9–11).

49. On the importation of wine during the Ptolemaic period, see Préaux 1939a, pp. 186–87; on wine from Syria-Palestine, Tcherikover 1937, pp. 23–25.

50. On *tꜣ-nṯr* as Syria, see Spalinger 1979, p. 292, note 48, citing Sethe 1906, pp. 356–63 (p. 361, note 3), and Schäfer 1931, pp. 734–35; see also Kuentz 1920, pp. 178–83.

51. Although it is nearer the mark than the shape given by Bouriant 1890, p. 168.

These vessels (Greek *histiokopoi*; Latin *actuariae*) could have an aphlaston, and were at times naval auxiliaries. *Akatoi* galleys could have a pointed cutwater, and Caesar records (*Bell. Alex.* 44.3) their use as warships in an emergency (Casson suggests that the pointed cutwater could easily be converted into a ram).[52] *Sammelbuch* 9571, line 6 (2nd century A.D.) records an *akatos* running between Ashkalon and Alexandria. Papyri Cairo Zenon 59002 and 59672 record that merchant galleys of the κέλης sort ran with some regularity between Egypt and Syria in the mid-third century B.C. A vessel in a mosaic from Tebessa in Algeria, dating to the 2nd or 3rd century A.D., and perhaps named *Fortuna Redux*, is a merchant galley with an aphlaston, a protruding, ram-like cut water, and a full cargo of amphorae.[53] This vessel, with the silhouette of a man-of-war and the cargo of a merchantman, a merchant galley probably of the *akatos* type, is the sort of ship referred to in the Edfu and Karnak texts here under discussion.[54]

Ptolemy VIII Euergetes II, as the controller of the *kbn.wt* vessels, insures that the wine of the Levant reaches Uto. As is appropriate to the scene, Ptolemy emphasizes not his martial prowess, but his organization of trade allowing the income of the Levant to reach Egypt. This is in keeping with the character of the wine offering scenes of Ptolemy VIII at Edfu, as characterized by Götte (1985/86; 1986, pp. 63–80) — the texts of the scenes of Ptolemy VIII emphasize the organizational abilities of the king as they relate to the internal prosperity of Egypt. Here Ptolemy VIII refers to the merchant marine, not the fleet of war. The *kbny* vessel depicted in the adoration of Mut at Karnak has its combination of warlike and mercantile features explained when it is seen as a merchant galley.[55]

52. The passenger carrying φάσηλος could be fitted out as a warship with a ram (compare the φάσηλος τριηριτικοῖς mentioned by Appian, *Bell. Civ.* 5.95 — see Casson 1971, p. 168, note 58). Discussing the presence and absence of pointed cutwaters on merchant vessels, Casson (1971, p. 174) concludes that "so far as we can tell, no difference in function was involved; indeed, the ancient artists seem to go out of their way to show the two types together performing the same work" (so even in mythological scenes — see Dunbabin 1978, pl. 61: no. 154). Besides rams, merchant galleys could be fitted out with other elements of the warship's standard gear; the earliest contemporary attestation of the *dolon*, the emergency rig of warships (Casson 1971, pp. 237–38; Kreutz 1976, p. 84, note 21), is as part of the equipment of a *kubaia* merchant galley in Papyrus BM Zenon 2139, 6 (Skeat, ed. 1974, pp. 231–32).

53. Casson 1971, fig. 140 (also pl. 137, the mosaic from Althiburus, 3rd or 4th century A.D., showing the front of a vessel with a ram and a load of amphorae). A sculpted version of this sort of vessel, with a pointed cutwater and a full load of kegs, probably transporting wine on the Moselle, was found at Neumagen (see Göttlicher 1978, pp. 86–87 [#520], pl. 41). Köster (1923, p. 154) describes the vessel as a merchant ship with a "Sporn." This, along with other features, disturbed Moll (1929, p. 23), for whom "das Schiff, das sehr idealisiert ist, ist kaum das gewöhnliche Transportschiff der Mosel und der Rhine. Die Bauform ist zu sehr einer Trireme nachgeahmt." He concludes that the model did not depict an actual vessel. For Göttlicher (op. cit.) "der Widerspruch des Kriegschiffes zu seiner zivilen Ladung ist bisher ungeklärt." These objections to the veracity of the carving are, in the light of the depiction of *Fortuna Redux* alone, unfounded. Two vessels similar in appearance to the Neumagen wine ship are depicted in an early Christian fresco from the necropolis of Cagliari (Wulff 1918, p. 92, fig. 74). One of the two vessels has the old styled *artemon* ("a sail of fair size hung on a mast often nearly as high as the mainmast" [Casson op. cit., p. 240), suggesting that it was a large ship. These early Christian parallels suggest that the Neumagen vessel was a known type, which could run quite large. A further plastic representation of what may be a merchant galley with a round, fat hull and a ram-like cutwater is a bronze model from Syria (Göttlicher op. cit., p. 84 [#505], pl. 40).

54. The use of *kbn.t* to refer to ocean-going merchant galleys suggests another reason for the use of *kbn.t* as the hieroglyphic rendition of Demotic *br* in the Nabaireh version of the Decree of Memphis. *Br* vessels in use as coasters along the eastern Mediterranean littoral are attested in the Report of Wenamun (Gardiner 1932, p. 62, 14; p. 63, 2, et passim). Edgerton and Wilson 1936, p. 54, note 20b, rendered the *br.w* which Ramses III dispatched for the defense of the Delta as "coasters", and if the term could be so used during the Ptolemaic period (for which there does not appear to be any clear evidence), the *br* vessels and *kbn.t* ships which Ptolemy assigned to patrol the mouths of the Nile might all be rendered as "coasters."

55. For the indistinct line separating the battle fleets and merchant marine of Ptolemaic Egypt, see Lesquier 1911, p. 256; Rostovtzeff 1922, pp. 122–25.

If the epithet of the king had been "to control the sea with *kbn.wt* galleys," it might have been a good martial epithet; as it is, "to control *kbn.wt* vessels in the sea" is not quite so martial, for whatever the sort of vessel, it is the control of the shipping, not the sea, which is emphasized. This would be expected for Ptolemy VIII;[56] *sỉp kbn.wt* is not "ein direkter Bezug zur Seeherrschaft" (Kurth 1980, p. 165) and there is no reason to see a Twenty-sixth Dynasty original behind this epithet.[57]

According to Lloyd the "growing suspicions" that *kbn.t* means trireme "are transmuted into absolute certainty by writings of the word elsewhere in *Urkunden* II," citing the orthographies of *kbn.t* in *Urk*. II.23.9, 77.15, and 179.7. This absolute certainty is dashed by the round-bottomed expedition transports of *Urk*. II.86.10 and 87.11, and the merchant galleys from Edfu and the Mut Precinct.

None of the Ptolemaic examples of *kbn.t* speak for understanding the word as indicating a trireme or a warship of Greek or other non-Egyptian design. All of the Ptolemaic attestations of *kbn.t* are consistent with the use of the term in the Eighteenth Dynasty. The Ptolemaic evidence provides no support for interpreting the Saite examples (and the one Persian period example) of *kbn.t* as indicating "war-galleys built for ramming of a totally un-Egyptian type" (Lloyd 1975b, p. 33). The Saite and Persian period examples of *kbn.t*, like those of the Ptolemaic period, are consistent with the uses of the term in the New Kingdom.

II. THE SAITE AND PERSIAN EVIDENCE

THE TERM *KBN.T* REFERS TO OCEAN-GOING VESSELS

On the statue of Udjahorresnet,[58] the owner of the statue is said to have borne, under Amasis and Psammetichus III, the title:

ỉmy-r kbn.wt nswt

"Overseer of the royal *kbn.wt* ships"

Lloyd (1972a) makes much of this. According to him, this title does not occur before the Saite period, which thus makes it "novel." He goes on to suggest that the archaizing Saite rulers would have employed this "novel term" only if "something completely new had appeared which needed a

56. The reference to Syria-Palestine in a text of Ptolemy VIII Euergetes II could also be an allusion to the attempted recovery of Syria by Ptolemy VI Philometor (Bagnall 1976, p. 13), a usurped reference by Ptolemy VIII to the lost Syrian holdings which Ptolemy VI almost reclaimed, and an allusion to the disputed dowry of Ptolemy VIII's mother, Cleopatra the daughter of Antiochus IV.

57. Kurth (1980, p. 160) also assumes that the presence of the toponym *ỉm.t* in the epithet *nb.t ỉm.t* of Wadjyt indicates "daß wir den historischen Hintergrund der hier untersuchten Aussagen des Textes in der 26. Dyn. zu suchen haben." The disrepair in which the temple of Imet lay during the Ptolemaic period (Petrie 1888, pp. 7–8) does suggest that the use of the toponym Imet in a divine epithet during the Ptolemaic period is anachronistic. We can not conclude from this, however: "daher muß der historische Hintergrund des Textes in einer früheren Zeit gesucht werden" (Kurth 1980, p. 160). The toponym Imet survives the decline of the actual town and remains in use into the Roman period (Beinlich 1990, pp. 83–84; *LÄ* II, col. 401, note 258; Helck 1974, p. 196; Drioton 1942–3, pp. 2, 5). Wadjyt Mistress of Imet is attested several times at Edfu (see Cauville 1987, p. 42), and in *Edfu* V 99, 2–12 she is the recipient in another wine offering scene (see Gutbub 1962, p. 55, note 2). Imet was a wine growing area (*LÄ* IV, col. 925, note 10), and this along with its proximity to Pelusium (on wine import at Pelusium, see Fraser 1972, pp. 149–50) could explain the association of Wadjyt Mistress of Imet with Phoenicia and Phoenician wine (on Wadjyt, Mistress of Imet, and Phoenicia see Sethe 1917, p. 321; idem 1928, p. 179, note 70e; and Gutbub 1962, p. 71, note 4).

58. See the bibliography given by Chevereau 1985, pp. 101–02 (and the summary of his career on pp. 330–31).

novel expression to describe it." In his view, the old term *kbn.t* was resurrected in order to describe a new type of vessel which was in some way similar to the old *kbn.t* vessel.

The exact title *ỉmy-r kbn.wt nswt* is indeed known only from the statue of Udjahorresnet. If we examine the title in the light of the Saite titles for "fleet admiral," it is not so much a novelty as a false archaism produced by the Saite rulers whom Lloyd correctly characterizes as "a consciously archaizing body of men" (1972a, p. 272). The hieroglyphic examples of the title "admiral of the fleet" have been collected by Chevereau (1985, pp. 271–73);[59] the titles which he assembles, with the number of individuals for whom they are attested, are:

1)	*ỉmy-r ꜥḥꜥ.w n ꜥḥꜣ nswt m wꜣḏ-wr* "Overseer of the Royal Fleet of War in the Sea"[60]	1
2)	*ỉmy-r ꜥḥꜥ.w nswt* *ỉmy-r ꜥḥꜥ.w (n) nb Tꜣ.wy* *ỉmy-r ꜥḥꜥ.w* [61] "Overseer of the (Royal) Fleet	2 1 2
3)	*ỉmy-r kbn.wt nswt* "Overseer of the Royal *Kbn.wt* Vessels"	1
4)	*ỉmy-r ḥwꜥ.w nswt* "Overseer of the Royal *Ḥwꜥ.w* Vessels"[62]	3
5)	*ḥry n ꜥḥꜥ.w n nb-Tꜣwy* "Chief of the Fleet of the Lord of the Two Lands"	1

Of the nine examples, five specify the ships involved by the general term *ꜥḥꜥ.w* for "fleet" (on one occasion qualified by *n ꜥḥꜣ*). The three examples of the title employing *ḥwꜥ* as the term for the vessels are directly parallel to the five with *ꜥḥꜥ*, the terms *ꜥḥꜥ* and *ḥwꜥ* being treated as synonyms during the Saite period (Goyon 1969, p. 167, note 1). Lloyd states: "The title does not occur before the Saite Period. In the New Kingdom the expression for Admiral of the Fleet was  *ỉmy-r ꜥḥꜥ.w n nsw* [*sic*]" (1972a, p. 272). Chevereau's list suggests that this, and *ỉmy-r ḥwꜥ.w nswt*, remained the common form of the title throughout the Saite Period; *ỉmy-r kbn.wt nswt*, so far as the available evidence shows, was an eccentric title.

The title of Udjahorresnet can, however, be shown to be simply a restatement of the first, elaborate title listed above: *ỉmy-r ꜥḥꜥ.w n ꜥḥꜣ nswt m wꜣḏ-wr*. Leaving aside the adjunct *n ꜥḥꜣ*, "of war," we are left with the bare description of the fleet as *m wꜣḏ-wr*, "in the sea." Egyptian ships on the sea, specifically warships of Amasis and Psammetichus III operating against the Persians, would

59. He follows Lloyd in assuming that *kbn.t* means "trireme" (p. 272); see also Naguib 1982, 69–75.

60. Without entering into the presently fashionable discussion of *wꜣḏ-wr*, the reading "sea" for the Ptolemaic period is justified by the use of *wꜣḏ-wr* corresponding to Greek θάλασσα and Demotic *ym* in the bilingual decrees (Daumas 1952, p. 227; D. Müller 1961, pp. 61–67; see also Cannuyer 1990, p. 17, note 15, citing Beaux 1988, pp. 197–204). Note also that the Ptolemaic vessels in the *wꜣḏ-wr* under the command of Aristonikos referred to in the year 23 stelae of Ptolemy V appear to have operated off Arados, in the Mediterranean. As for the Saite period, the "Naukratis Stele" refers to the imports entering Egypt at Naukratis as (line 9) *ḫ.t nb(.t) pr(.t) m Wꜣḏ-wr Ḥꜣw-Nbwt* (text: Erman and Wilcken 1900, p. 130; see also Vandersleyen 1971, p. 146, and Lichtheim 1976, pp. 139–46); this would admit extending the *wꜣḏ-wr*/θαλασσα/*ym* equation of the Ptolemaic trilingual decrees back into the Saite period.

61. One of the holders of this title, Sematawtefnakht, was also an *ỉmy-r ꜥpr (n) nswt*, which suggests that his title *ỉmy-r ꜥḥꜥ.w*, although unqualified by a reference to the ruler, did refer to a high level of naval command, not the lower echelon *ỉmy-r ꜥḥꜥ.w* of the New Kingdom (Goyon 1969, p. 169, note 5).

62. The title *ḫrp qq.t* which Chevereau also lists, reading "commandant de la flotte de guerre" (1985, pp. 134–35) is actually a title of responsibility for riverine traffic, there being no evidence that *qq.t* ever refers to an ocean-going vessel (see above, notes 6–7).

fall under the old term *kbn.t*, a seagoing ship plying eastern routes. Rather than the use of a novel title to indicate a new sort of vessel, Udjahorresnet's title is an archaism, an attempt at translating *ỉmy-r ʿḥʿ.w m wȝḏ-wr* into something more archaic, in the end a false archaism, producing a title for which we have no attestation in quite that form.[63] The definition of *kbn.t* in this context is not, however, peculiar. *Kbn.t* here indicates a seagoing ship, not whether it was a trireme or even a warship.[64]

Lloyd assumes that Udjahorresnet's title referred to command of warships,[65] as Chevereau assumes that all of the Saite titles "Commander of the Fleet" listed above refer to martial offices. These assumptions are unlikely to be correct. Goyon concluded that the Late Period title *ỉmy-r ḥwʿ.w nswt*, along with the related forms employing *ʿḥʿ.w* and *kbn.wt,* referred primarily to the control of merchant vessels (Goyon 1969, p. 159–71).[66] As he recognized, in order to show that *ʿḥʿ.w* vessels were true warships it was necessary to append the word *ʿḥȝ*, in the Ramesside period as well as in the first Saite title listed above. For Goyon, *kbn.t* is "le terme qui désigne caractéristiquement a basse époque le navire de commerce maritime;" he concludes that the title of Udjahorresnet was that of an official active "dans le domaine du transport par mer" (1969, p. 168, note 5). *Kbn.t* meaning "ocean-going vessel" fits the merchant marine as well as the fleet of war, and the probable hybrid of the two which composed the Saite royal fleet. *Kbn.t* as "trireme" or "ramming war-galley" in a title referring at least in part to a merchant fleet, and encompassing all of its component vessels, is unlikely. Of all the Saite titles for fleet commander listed above, Goyon concluded that *ỉmy-r ʿḥʿ.w nswt n ʿḥȝ m wȝḏ-wr* might refer to "une flotte de trières" (1969, p. 169).[67]

63. The use of the term *ḥwʿ* in titles of the Saite period also appears to be archaizing (Goyon 1969, p. 167).

64. Note that Chevereau (1985) incorrectly states that Posener (1936) gives evidence for the use of *kbn.t* to refer to a warship already during the Ramesside period. Although *mnš* vessels do appear in martial passages of the time, the *kbn.t* is not attested as a warship until the Late Period.

65. Posener (1936, p. 9, note *e*) assumed that the *kbn.wt* vessels in Udjahorresnet's title refer to "bâtiments de guerre, sens que *kbn.t* prend fréquemment a l'époque ptolémaique." Posener appears to have recognized, however, that "navires de mer" remained the basic meaning of *kbn.wt.*

66. The *ỉmy-r ʿḥʿ.w* and *ỉmy-r ʿpr nswt* Sematawtefnakht was one of the *ʿȝ n mryt* of Heracleopolis, a controller of shipping in Upper Egypt (Mokhtar 1983, pp. 25–26, 131–34 and Jones 1988, p. 118). One of the *ỉmy-r ḥwʿ.w nswt*, Heqawemsaf, was also an *ỉmy-r pr.wy-ḥḏ n Ḫnw* (Chevereau 1985, p. 100).

67. If Udjahorresnet's title *ỉmy-r kbn.wt nswt* is a version of Hor's title *ỉmy-r ʿḥʿ.w nswt n ʿḥȝ m wȝḏ-wr* (without the specification *n ʿḥȝ*), there may be a further Levantine connection to Udjahorresnet's office. Hor was perhaps a military governor of Syria-Palestine (so Chevereau 1985, p. 92, note a), being a *ḫrp ḫȝs.wt Ḥȝw-Nbwt* and a *mḥ-ỉb n nswt m ḫȝs.wt Ḥȝw-Nbwt*, and Udjahorresnet may have been similarly concerned with the Levant. Note that Hor's title *mḥ-ỉb n nswt m ḫȝs.wt Ḥȝw-Nbwt* is a late and somewhat abbreviated parallel to Djehuty's title *mḥ-ỉb n nswt ḥr ḫȝs.t nb(.t) ỉw.w ḥry(.w)-ỉb nyw wȝḏ-wr* found on his gold bowl in the Louvre (N. 713: *Urk.* IV.999.9; Lillyquist 1988, pp. 26–27, figs. 40–43). Lillyquist (ibid., p. 25) states that the title *mḥ-ỉb n nswt ḥr ḫȝs.t nb(.t) ỉw.w ḥry(.w)-ỉb nyw wȝḏ-wr* is attested only once, that being on the Louvre bowl of Djehuty. This ignores the Saite parallel. Hor's title is found on a naophorus statue discovered by Petrie at Tell el-Yehudiyeh (Petrie 1906, pp. 18–19, pls. 15 and 20), which speaks against Lillyquist's belief that the Louvre bowl should be a forgery of the early 19th century, as do many other details.

Given the occurrence of the title *ỉmy-r kbn.wt nswt* only once, Lloyd would also have to assume that triremes could also be included under the general heading of *ʿḥʿ.w*, as indeed Van't Dack and Hauben have suggested.[68] The exclusive equation *kbn.t* = trireme, Greek-style warship is lost.

THE *KBN.WT* VESSELS ARE ASSOCIATED WITH THE LEVANT

The Elephantine Stele of Amasis refers to Apries coming against the newly royal Amasis with "*kbn.wt* vessels filled with innumerable *Ḥ3w-Nbwt*." Originally for Lloyd "large numbers of *kbnt* -ships are mentioned in the same breath as Greek mercenaries (*Ḥ3w-nbw*) as part of the forces of Apries" (1972a, p. 272). This association of Greeks and *kbn.wt* vessels in a martial passage is one of Lloyd's arguments for rendering *kbn.t* as "trireme, Greek style warship." Following Vandersleyen, *Ḥ3w-Nbwt* may not be rendered simply and exclusively as "Greeks," but is to be understood as "Phoenicians, Levantines," indicating a geographic origin on the Asiatic littoral. The primary meaning of the term *Ḥ3w-Nbwt* is "Phoenicians, Levantines." Lloyd later takes note of Vandersleyen's work on *Ḥ3w-Nbwt*, and does not translate the term in a rendition of the relevant passage from the Elephantine Stele (Lloyd 1975a, p. 59, note 117). Lloyd's conclusion "that the term *Ḥ3w-nbw(t)* in the Elephantine Stele includes, without exclusively designating, H.'s Carian and Ionian mercenaries" is correct—a term for soldiers of coastal Asiatic geographic origin could reasonably include coastal dwelling Asiatic Greeks.[69]

There are problems with Vandersleyen's treatment of the passage, and he overemphasized the possibility that some of the *Ḥ3w-Nbwt* who filled Apries' *kbn.wt* ships were actual Phoenicians (Leahy 1988, p. 190, note 29).[70] *Ḥ3w-Nbwt* in the Elephantine Stele probably refers almost exclusively to Greek soldiers, but through a reference to geographic origin and not ethnicity. We know the ethnic makeup attributed to Apries' forces by Amasis and later tradition—Greek mercenaries. This does not mean, however, that the word may be rendered as "Greeks." If one accepts Vandersleyen's understanding of the term as implying a Levantine geographic origin, then the use in the Elephantine Stele of *Ḥ3w-Nbwt* with its eastern Mediterranean association can be seen as having suggested the use of the term *kbn.wt* — "Byblians" — to refer to the ocean-going vessels of Apries' force. Even were Vandersleyen's basic understanding of the term rejected, and a more general and hoary translation adopted, such as Iversen's "Transinsularians" (1987, pp. 54–59), we would in the Elephantine Stele have ocean-going vessels in use by ocean-going troops. A direct and exclusive equation of *Ḥ3w-Nbwt* with Greeks is not easily made, nor is the exclusive equation of the Late Period *kbn.t* with the Greek trireme; neither equation can here derive support from the other. The *Ḥ3w-Nbwt* of Apries may have consisted of Asiatic Greeks for the most part, and their ocean-going vessels may have included ramming warships, yet the term *Ḥ3w-Nbwt* does not denote exclusively "Greeks," but rather "Asiatic coastal dwellers"; nor does *kbn.t* mean "trireme" or "ramming war-galley," but "ocean-going vessel," with the hint of eastern routes. That *kbn.t* could be used of Asiatic Greek ocean-going vessels in no way supports a translation of *kbn.t* as "ramming

68. Van't Dack and Hauben 1978, p. 71 (this is also expressed by Chevereau 1985, p. 272, note *j*). That *kbn.t* vessels could be thought of as *ʿḥʿ.w* is demonstrated by the designations of Hatshepsut's Punt expedition vessels, ships of the same design referred to as *kbn.wt* and *ʿḥʿ.w* vessels (Naville 1898, pl. 72 [*kbn.wt* = *Urk*. IV.323.2]; pl. 74 [*ʿḥʿ.w* = *Urk*. IV.328.17]); this was still the case in the Ptolemaic period, as the Pithom stele shows (in lines 21–22 [*Urk*. II.100.15] the expedition vessels sent by Ptolemy II Philadelphus to found *Ptolemais theron* are referred to as generally as *ʿḥʿ.w* vessels and specifically as *kbn.wt* vessels).

69. For Carian mercenaries as Asiatics and grouped together with Syrian mercenaries, compare Cleomenes' questions to Sosibius: τίνας αγωνίας; ἤ δῆλον τοὺς ἀπὸ Συρίας καὶ Καρίας στρατιώτας; (Pol V.36; see the comments of G. T. Griffith 1935, pp. 127-28).

70. Leahy has shown that Cyprus' role in Apries' war with Amasis was not at all great. However, Saite rulers, Apries included, did employ Phoenicians in their naval forces (on Apries and Phoenicia, see Kitchen 1986, p. 407 and note 967; for Phoenicians in the Saite host, see Kienitz 1953, p. 40, note 1 and Thompson 1988, p. 83).

war-galley" or "trireme." The fact that the Ptolemaic examples of *kbn.t* do not support a rendering of the term as "trireme," or even "warship" in general, as the basic meaning of Late Period *kbn.t* speaks strongly against forcing such a specific translation on the term in the Saite period.

In the Elephantine Stele there is an association of people considered by the Egyptians to be ultimately of "transinsularian" or Levantine geographic origin — *Ḥ3w-Nbwt* —with *kbn.wt* ships, ocean-going "Byblians," a use of the term *kbn.t* which is neither unexpected nor novel nor of any bearing on the use of Greek style warships in Saite Egypt. Some of the *kbn.wt* vessels of Apries may have been warships of Greek design, but we have no way of knowing.[71] Of whatever design the ships were, they were probably almost all used as troop transports, and no naval battles involving ramming are anywhere suggested.[72]

Spalinger points out that the vessels of Apries naval force are termed *kbn.wt*, whereas the ships of the later, anonymous enemy of Amasis are referred to as *ʿḥʿ.w*. Spalinger considers that these are different sorts of vessels. This is not certain, however, as *kbn.wt* ships can be referred to as *ʿḥʿ.w* (see above and note 68); this previously attested variation of terminology — *kbn.t* and *ʿḥʿ* referring to the same vessel — in the Elephantine Stele does not provide additional information on the nature of the *kbn.wt* vessels of Apries.

As a further example of the association of *kbn.wt* ships with the Levant, the portion of the Satrap Stele of Ptolemy Lagus (dated to year 7 of Alexander II) referring to the reign of Chababesh during the Persian domination mentions the Egyptian ruler instituting measures *r ḫsf kbn(.wt) nt Stt r Km.t*, "in order to repel the *kbn(.t)* vessel(s) of Asia from the Blackland" (*Urk*. II.16.7–14).[73] Based on this passage, Spalinger says "this evidence from the Satrap Stele indicates that *kbn.wt* ships were employed by the Persians (undoubtedly through their Phoenician allies) before the invasion of Alexander the Great" (Spalinger 1978a, p.149, note 42).[74] These are Asian craft, not Greek warships.

THE PERSIAN PERIOD ATTESTATIONS OF *KBN.T* REFER TO EXPEDITION VESSELS

In line 17 of the stele of Darius from Tell el-Maskhoutah, a *kbn.t* ship is sent to explore the eastern canal (Posener 1936, pp. 50–63).[75] In line 15 of the stele of Kabrit (Posener 1936, pp. 63–81, 99; pls. 5–13) a *kbn.t* ship is mentioned following reference to the excavation of the canal, perhaps the same *kbn.t* as that mentioned in line 17 of the stele from Tell el Maskhoutah. In lines 16–17 of the stele of Kabrit, *kbn.wt* vessels are said to travel to Persia. In line 19 of the same stele, *kbn.wt* vessels are said to be *ʿpr ẖr [...]* (the same description in the stele of Suez, line 19 [Posener 1936, pp. 81–87]). Again these are uses of the *kbn.wt* vessels in the area of the Red Sea, *kbn.wt*

71. Spalinger (1979a, p. 603, note 29; idem 1977, p. 231, note 33; idem 1978, p. 149, note 42) recognized that Lloyd's use of the Elephantine Stele of Amasis was incorrect; unfortunately Spalinger also accepted that the term *Ḥ3w-Nbw* could be rendered simply as "Greeks." Even a body of Greek soldiers might not use exclusively Greek vessels for their conveyance; consider the makeup of the fleet of Alexander the Great on his arrival in Egypt (noted by Vandersleyen 1971, p. 145, note 2; see also above in the section on Egyptians in the Ptolemaic navy).

72. Herodotus II.163 and.169 mentions only the land battle of "Momemphis" as the single and decisive encounter between the forces of Apries and those of Amasis. Diodorus I.68 gives Marea as the site of the battle (see Leahy 1988).

73. On this section of the stele, beginning *Urk*. II.16 and continuing through .18, see Spalinger 1978, pp. 147–52 and Ritner 1980, pp. 135–37.

74. According to Goedicke (1985, p. 38), the *kbn.wt* vessels which Chababesh sought to ward off from Egypt are "clearly triremes," although nothing in the text hints at this.

75. There appears to be a fragmentary mention of a *kbn.t* vessel again in line 20. On the canal see Spalinger 1978b, pp. 20–21 (and the references cited there in note 35), and Hinz 1975, pp. 115–21. Posener concluded that the canal itself is being explored; Golenischeff had earlier suggested (1890, pp. 99–109) that a trip into the Red Sea was described.

expedition ships like those dispatched to the area by Hatshepsut. The vessels of lines 16–17 of the stele of Kabrit travel both the Red Sea and the Indian Ocean, and the *kbn.wt* vessels of line 19 of this stele are loaded with some sort of cargo. Lloyd does not discuss these occurrences of *kbn.t,* in which *kbn.t* refers to expedition vessels and cargo ships.

The pre-Ptolemaic examples of *kbn.t* are not all warships, and no example of the term in a martial context specifies ramming as one of the vessel's functions. Although the evidence which we now possess suggests a certain lapse in the use of the term between the New Kingdom and the Saite period, the Late Period revival of *kbn.t* appears also to have resurrected the earlier meanings and uses of the term. There may remain areas of dispute regarding the term *kbn.t* in the Late Period, but these disputes must involve the use of the term at all times. The Late Period *kbn.t* was, on the evidence of the available texts, employed in the same situations as the *kbn.t* vessel of the Eighteenth Dynasty.

III. A SIMILARITY BETWEEN THE *KBN.T* AND THE TRIREME?

It remains to examine whether or not one can say with any certainty that there was a similarity between the old Egyptian *kbn.t* vessel and the trireme.

Lloyd (1972a, p. 272) quotes Säve-Söderbergh (1946, 88ff.) as stating that the old *kbn.t* was a "fast-running galley." Why would Säve-Söderbergh, discussing the *kbn.wt* ships in the Punt expedition reliefs of Queen Hatshepsut at Deir el-Bahri, make such a statement? Nothing in either the depictions nor in the accompanying texts provides any such information. If we read well the page on which Säve-Söderbergh makes this statement, and check all of his references, we find the answer. Earlier on the page on which he terms the *kbn.wt* vessels "fast-running galleys," Säve-Söderbergh mentions, by way of a footnote, an article by Crum suggesting an etymological connection between the hieroglyphic *kbn.t* and the Coptic ϭΙΝΟΥΗⲖ vessel. We thus know that Säve-Söderbergh was acquainted with the particulars of the Coptic ϭΙΝΟΥΗⲖ, and from this it is easy to see how he thought "fast-running galley" to be an appropriate designation of the *kbn.t* vessel.

Crum (1931, pp. 453–55) suggested that the Coptic ϭΙΝΟΥΗⲖ may have descended from the hieroglyphic *kbn.t*. In the Paris Glossary 44, 54b, the word ϭΙΝΟΥΗⲖ is given as ⲀⲣΟΜⲀΝΙΜ, the Greek δρομάδιον, which Crum rendered as "vaisseu rapide." From ⲀⲣΟΜⲀΝΙΜ = ϭΙΝΟΥΗⲖ < *kbn.t*, Säve-Söderbergh derived his description of the *kbn.t* as a "fast-running galley." The Coptic ϭΙΝΟΥΗⲖ is used of merchant ships, but a military use is easily supportable, given the correspondence to the Greek δρομάδιον, and the possibility that the word survived as a loan word in Old French *gainele*, *gamele*, *ganguemele*, adopted by the Crusaders to describe their own vessels.[76]

However, the connection between ϭΙΝΟΥΗⲖ and *kbn.t*, necessary for Säve-Söderbergh's description of the *kbn.t*, is impossible. *CED* (p. 333) and *KHwb* (p. 460) have cited Crum's suggestion questioningly. Osing, however, accepted Crum's etymology for ϭΙΝΟΥΗⲖ (1976, pp. 311, 475, 856 [note 1320]). According to *DELC* (pp. 342–43), concerning ϭΙΝΟΥΗⲖ, "*il ne peut pas* y avoir rapport avec *kbn.t*"; Vycichl suggests that *nw* or *nb* < *ww* is just possible, and that **g-w-l*, etc., may be the root of ϭΙΝΟΥΗⲖ (Jones [1988, p. 292] follows *DELC*). *DELC* compares Arabic, *gal*, "go, turn, run, etc." ϭΙΝΟΥΗⲖ might have been used of a trireme, as it surely was of the δρομάδιον; the ϭΙΝΟΥΗⲖ and *kbn.t*, however, appear to have nothing to do with one another, and the *kbn.t* cannot on the basis of any evidence be called a "fast-running galley."[77]

76. Roquet 1973, pp. 19–23. Note that *DELC* (p. 343) cites Roquet incorrectly, misunderstanding him as attempting to derive ϭΙΝΟΥΗⲖ from *gainele*, rather than the reverse, as is the case. See also Helderman 1988, pp. 57 and 58, notes 17–18.

77. The δρόμων was apparently a lateen-rigged vessel (Casson 1971, p. 153 and Kreutz 1976, p.83), as were the ships of the Crusaders, including most likely their *gaineles* (see inter alia Kreutz 1976; Bonino 1978, pp. 9–28; and Pryor 1984, pp. 363–72).

IV. CONCLUDING REMARKS

The Saite and Persian attestations of the term *kbn.t* are:

1) Elephantine Stele of Amasis
Ḥ3w-Nbwt/Phoenicians are the occupants of the *kbn.wt* vessels, employed by Apries at the time of his final conflict with Amasis. This was a land battle, with no recorded engagement of rival fleets involved. The *kbn.wt* here mentioned are likely to have been used solely as troop transports.

2) Title of Udjahorresnet
Kbn.t is attested in the title *ỉmy-r kbn.wt nswt*, a version of the title *ỉmy-r ˁḥˁ.w (n ˁḥ3 nswt) m w3ḏ-wr*. The title probably refers to control of the merchant marine.

3) Tell el-Maskhoutah Stele of Darius
A *kbn.t* vessel is dispatched by Darius to explore the eastern canal connecting the Nile and the Red Sea. This is the *kbn.t* ship as an expedition ship.

4) Kabrit Stele of Darius
In lines 16–17 of this stele, *kbn.wt* vessels are said to have sailed between Egypt and Persia, and in line 19, *kbn.wt* vessels loaded with some sort of cargo are mentioned. These are attestations of the *kbn.wt* as expedition and cargo vessels.

5) Suez Stele of Darius
In line 19 there is a reference to *kbn.wt* vessels as cargo ships, laden with some cargo.

6) Satrap Stele of Ptolemy Lagus
The earlier ruler Chababesh takes steps "to repel the *kbn.(w)t* vessels of Asia" from the Delta coast.

No naval engagements requiring ramming are mentioned or implied. All of the *kbn.wt* are ocean-going, and in two of the four examples, Asiatics are associated with the vessels. An expedition boat is called *kbn.t*, as were the Punt expedition ships of Hatshepsut. In the title of Udjahorresnet, the *kbn.wt* for which he exercised responsibility were probably merchant vessels, or a combination of military and transport ships. None of the determinatives of these Saite and Persian attestations of *kbn.t* are extraordinary, and none give any indications that the vessels were of a foreign design.

The Ptolemaic attestations of *kbn.t* are:

1) Satrap Stele of Ptolemy Lagus
Ḥ3w-Nbwt/Phoenicians are the occupants of the *kbn.wt* vessels.

2) Berlin Stele 14400
In a martial epithet of Ptolemy I Soter (?), *kbn.t* is parallel to *dp.w(t) nw ỉtr*, both summarized by *ˁḥˁ[.w n ˁḥ3 (?)]*.

3) Naos Louvre C. 123
In a martial epithet of Ptolemy II Philadelphus, *kbn.t* is parallel to *q(3)q(3).w*, "river craft."

4) Pithom Stele
In lines 4 and 6, *kbn.wt* vessels are mentioned in laudatory epitheta suggesting that they are warships, but the detailed determinatives show no evidence of rams; those in line 4 are said to be "in the sea."

5) Pithom Stele
In line 22, the *kbn.wt* vessels are cargo ships sent on the expedition into the Red Sea to found *Ptolemais theron* in the elephant hunting grounds.

6) Ptolemaic gate into the Mut Inclosure at Karnak
In a text from the reign of Ptolemy II Philadelphus, a *kbny* vessel is said to be "laden with the goods of Syria"; the *Ḥ3w-Nbwt* are mentioned in the next line.

7) Nabaireh version of the "Decree of Memphis"
In lines 18–19 of the hieroglyphic text, Ptolemy V Epiphanes is said to have sent out *kbn.wt* vessels to guard Egypt from foreign incursions, apparently in defense of the Nile mouths. The term is translated in Demotic as *br*, and in Greek as νῆες.

8) Year 23 Stelae of Ptolemy V Epiphanes
Kbn.wt vessels are mentioned along with other forces in a section mentioning Apameia and the *w3ḏ-wr*. Later there is a passage describing the capture of the Phoenician city Arados. These vessels appear to have been under the command of Aristonikos.

9) *Edfu* III 241, 17-242, 1
In a wine offering scene of Ptolemy VIII Euergetes II, *kbn.wt* vessels are mentioned in such a context as to suggest that they are merchant galleys carrying wine from the Levant to Egypt.

Even for the Ptolemaic period, a time for which no one would deny the presence of the trireme in the Egyptian navy, *kbn.t* never means exclusively "trireme." The word is used with full understanding of its original meaning — an ocean-going vessel. Rather than being a novel way of referring to a new ship design, *kbn.t* in the Ptolemaic inscriptions reveals the use of an old term with a perfect understanding of its original meaning. The only association of the term *kbn.t* with a ram in a martial context is in Ptolemaic examples 2 and 3, and this association is based solely on the appearance of the determinatives. In both examples, *kbn.t* is parallel to a term for riverine craft, showing that the primary meaning of *kbn.t* in both examples 2 and 3 is "ocean-going vessel." In examples 6, 7, and 8, the determinatives of *kbn.t* all show pointed cutwaters, but the passages in which the word occurs all refer to merchant ships; merchant galleys, which not infrequently sported ram-like cutwaters, are meant. In example 5, cargo/expedition ships are indicated, and the determinative shows a round cargo vessel without a ram.[78]

Kbn.t does not mean "trireme," but the term is related to the introduction of the trireme into Egypt. The voyage of Wenamun witnesses a decline in Egyptian influence, even trade, in Phoenicia at the end of the Ramesside period, and only in the Late Period do we again find indications of Egyptian interest in Levantine timber and ocean going vessels (i.e. the gift of timber made by Nepherites I to Agesilaos [see above, note 34]). There was an increased concern for naval armaments at the time of the Greco-Persian conflicts, and Egypt found it necessary to acquire timber for the construction of vessels of the new Mediterranean sort, first to arm her Greek allies and to protect her Persian overlords, and later to support her adopted Ptolemaic rulers.[79] Egypt's arming with Persian and Greek triremes — often of Phoenician wood and often of Phoenician construction — lead to the revival of *kbn.t*, through timber purchases and ship construction in the Levant.[80] The renewed Egyptian interest in Levantine wood and ocean-going vessels coincided with the

78. De Meulenaere (1951, p. 61, note 53) lists only examples 1, 2, and 3 (and number 4 of the Saite/Persian examples) as attestations of the Ptolemaic use of the term *kbn.t* to designate a warship.

79. As is often pointed out "Egypt's woodlands could not supply the long timbers that were needed to build warships" (Meiggs 1982, p. 133).

80. The vessels of the Persian navies were essentially Phoenician (Meiggs 1982, pp. 82–84).

introduction of the trireme, and with Egypt's involvement with the competing Mediterranean fleets of the Greeks and the Persians; the term *kbn.t* was revived by the introduction of the trireme and other Mediterranean style warships, but *kbn.t* does not mean "trireme."

After 200 B.C., none of Egypt's warships were Phoenician built, or built of Phoenician wood (Meiggs 1982, pp. 133–36, 145). This period, during the reign of Ptolemy V Epiphanes, coincides with the last references but one to *kbn.wt* vessels.[81] After 200 B. C. the Ptolemies still had warships, and probably some mercenary Phoenicians as crew members and even shipwrights, but Egypt's wood supplies thereafter came principally from Cyprus (Meiggs 1982, p. 84). The time range of the attestations of *kbn.t* in Egyptian texts of the Late Period corresponds to the period of Egypt's renewed interest in Phoenician and Greek warships at the end of the first millennium B.C., and corresponds to the periods during which she had access to Phoenician timber and technology.

Kbn.t describes seaworthy vessels, be they vessels of war, trade, or exploration. There was no Egyptian word denoting "trireme" specifically, or "warship of foreign design" in general, even during the Ptolemaic period. The Ptolemaic evidence shows that an attempted equation of the Late Period *kbn.t* and the Greek trireme/Greek warship is incorrect; such an equation can hardly be forced upon *kbn.t* in earlier texts.

81. For the use of *kbn.t* from the reign of Ptolemy VIII Euergetes II, and its significance, see above, pp. 78–81.

CHAPTER 10

ABOUT THE ORIGINS OF EARLY DEMOTIC IN LOWER EGYPT

OLA EL-AGUIZY
The University of Cairo

In examining some Serapeum stelae on which Mr. Mohamed Ibrahim, one of our Egyptian colleagues, studying in France, is working; I noticed the presence of writing resembling to a great extent the abnormal hieratic script of Upper Egypt. A close examination of the other Serapeum stelae already published by Malinine, Posener, and Vercoutter (1968) revealed similar characteristics, as well as some early Demotic signs appearing in hieratic texts of the Twenty-fifth Dynasty.

The first group of these stelae dates back to the Twenty-second Dynasty (Sheshonq V). These are as follows :

Stele 30, year eleven of Sheshonq V (pl. 10.1a). You can notice in the first line the word *wn* and the group *pꜣj⸗f* both resemble abnormal hieratic.

Stele 33, year thirty-seven of Sheshonq V (pl. 10.1b). Only the two lines in front of the head of the bull are interesting to our purpose, they show strong similarities with abnormal hieratic specially the writing of the god *Ḥr* and the group *sꜣ n* and the writing of the word *hꜣrw*.

Stele 42, same date as previous (pl. 10.2a). This stele is quite interesting as we notice four lines of hieratic, then at the end of the fourth line the writing becomes more cursive with signs resembling abnormal hieratic namely: *ḥrj* and *pr*. The two following lines which seem to have been inserted later have a style which in its general aspect and slanting writing, reminds us of abnormal hieratic. At a close examination of the signs, many similarities have been observed.

Stele 58, from the Twenty-second Dynasty also (pl. 10.2b). A hieroglyphic stele with two lines of graffiti in two different styles of writing: the first closer to hieroglyphs, while the second is much more cursive using forms resembling abnormal hieratic. It is clear from the context that the two lines were written by the same scribe who simultaneously used two different styles of writing.

The second group of stelae (nos. 159 and 160) date to the twenty-fourth year of Taharqa (Twenty-fifth Dynasty) . These are hieratic stelae in which I could notice some signs written in the early Demotic style (pl. 10.3a, b).

The Memphitic stele Louvre C. 101 from the eighth year of King Psammetichus is also interesting for the study of the origins of Demotic in Lower Egypt. It is a hieratic stele which was said to bave been copied from a Demotic original (pl. 10.4; Malinine 1975, pp. 168–73).

The similarities between the signs in these stelae and abnormal hieratic and early Demotic signs are demonstrated more clearly in table 10.1. The two columns on the left show examples from the Serapeum and C. 101 Stelae; those on the right show their parallel in abnormal hieratic and early Demotic.

The abnormal hieratic signs have been chosen from the documents published by Malinine (1983) Louvre E 3228e, d, b; E 2432, BM 10113 (Reich 1914); and a few examples from Papyrus Vienna D 12003 (Malinine 1973) and Papyrus Leiden K 128 F1942/5.15 (Vleeming, 1980). As for the early Demotic examples they are mainly chosen from Papyri in the Egyptian Museum, Cairo.

DESCRIPTION OF TABLE 10.1

The Standing Man with Raised Hand in Invocation. The first sign (Twenty-second Dynasty) resembles the early Demotic form which is the result of the natural evolution of the sign. The second and third signs from Stelae 159 and C. 101 respectively have no parallel in abnormal hieratic or early Demotic but are closer to the stereotyped form which appears in the Ptolemaic period for this and other human forms.

The Seated Child with Hand to Mouth. The resemblance of this sign to its abnormal hieratic and early Demotic parallels is quite clear.

The *nfr* Group. This group has no abnormal hieratic parallel in the chosen documents, but is quite similar to early Demotic examples.

The *nḥ* bird. The straight slanting line, representing an abbreviated body line above the angle which represents the legs, is noticed in early Demotic examples and also in early Ptolemaic examples from Upper Egypt (30601, 2); except for the length of horizontal line which is a feature characterizing all horizontal lines in Demotic. This slanting line does not show in the unique abnormal hieratic example.

The god *Ḥr* on both Serapeum stelae and stele C. 101 clearly resembles abnormal hieratic.

The *bꜣ* bird. The curve representing the head of the bird on Stele 58 (Twenty-second Dynasty) and in Stele C. 101 is clearly noticed in abnormal hieratic examples. The development of this form will give the common Demotic form in which the same curve has changed its direction reaching down to the horizontal line.

The form of the letter *ḫ* is similar to both abnormal hieratic and early Demotic.

The roundness of the letter *h* is similar to early Demotic.

The *pr* sign on Stele 42 is closer to the abnormal hieratic examples, the development of which will give the early Demotic form.

wn. The example on Stele 30 is identical to the abnormal hieratic one. We know that the Demotic form is probably the result of the ligature of both upper and lower signs.

st. The angular lines on Stelae 159 and 160 are closer to the early Demotic examples, while abnormal hieratic has always two parallel lines.

ḥrj. The example of Stele 42 has its equivalent in both abnormal hieratic and some of the early Demotic forms which represent a normal evolution of the sign.

ḏd. We notice that the abnormal hieratic document BM 10113, which has many early Demotic features, omitted the vertical stroke following the group *ḏd*; while, on the contrary, Papyrus 30657, which might be considered an early Demotic text with some abnormal hieratic influences, still keeps the stroke. Therefore the writing of *ḏd* on stele C. 101 without the vertical stroke is an early Demotic feature.

wꜣḥ. It is well known that this group has a characteristic writing in abnormal hieratic, magnifying the roundness above the swab. The origins of this writing could be traced back in hieratic. Its writing in C. 101 is closer to Demotic as its zigzaged lines represents the swab itself joining with the following phonetic complement. The simplification of this zigzaged line will lead directly to the early Demotic form of the sign.

The writing of *ntj* on Stele C. 101 clearly resembles early Demotic.

rḫ. On Stele C. 101 without the separate slanting line above is closer to abnormal hieratic than Demotic.

pꜣj=f. We have here writings of this group from different periods: the first, from the Twenty-second Dynasty; the second, a hieratic example from the Twenty-sixth Dynasty and on the other side an abnormal hieratic example from the Twenty-fifth Dynasty and lastly an early Demotic example. It is clear that the writing of the Twenty-second Dynasty is similar to that of the Twenty-fifth Dynasty and is an outcome of the ligature of the second element of the hieratic group, followed by the elimination of the first element of the group in the early Demotic example.

ir. The signs on the Serapeum Stelae from the Twenty-second Dynasty have equivalents in abnormal hieratic. The tendancy to ligature the two elements of the group already begins in Stele 33 and is the main feature in early Demotic.

ʿnḫ. The writing of this group, whether from the Twenty-second or Twenty-fifth Dynasty, is similar to both abnormal hieratic and early Demotic.

Finally, the resemblance of the group *sꜣ n* with its abnormal hieratic counterpart, and that of *rsj* with the early Demotic one is unquestionable.

The study of theses similarities yielded the following facts:

1) Most cursive signs added to, or written on stelae of the Twenty-second Dynasty have great affinities with the abnormal hieratic script of Upper Egypt. Some of them, in the natural course of evolution of the writing, show similar forms in early Demotic also, such as: *ḫ*, *pr*, *ḥrj*, seated child with hand to mouth, *pꜣj=f*, *ir*, and *ʿnḫ*.
2) The style of most of the signs appearing in hieratic texts of the Twenty-fifth Dynasty and on the stele C. 101 from the Twenty-sixth Dynasty are closer to that of the early Demotic signs, such as: *ntj*, *wꜣḥ*, *ḏd*, *rsj*, and the standing man with raised hand in invocation.
3) Some signs from the stelae of the Twenty-second Dynasty are closer to early Demotic than abnormal hieratic; while a few signs from the C. 101 stele are closer to abnormal hieratic, such as *rḫ*, *sꜣ n*, *Ḥr* and *bꜣ*.

CONCLUSION

These facts prove that, at least since the end of the Twenty-second Dynasty, a cursive writing quite similar to abnormal hieratic was also used in Lower Egypt.

In accordance with Malinine's definition of abnormal hieratic, i.e. the "final stage of development of the cursive Neo-Egyptian Hieratic," the palaeographical study previously undertaken in my Ph. D. thesis has also proved that abnormal hieratic signs have shown a normal gradual development from their hieratic originals, generally simplifying the lines of the hieratic sign by rendering it more compact or by omitting some of its original lines.

This development is a normal graphic process to which any script reaching such a degree of abbreviation is submitted. Therefore, it would only be normal that hieratic, either in Upper Egypt or Lower Egypt, underwent the same graphic transformations. It is well known that the various stages of the abnormal hieratic script of Upper Egypt can be traced back as far as the New Kingdom, while this continuity is not evident for Lower Egypt.

Now, since the evolution of the hieratic script of Upper Egypt has followed a gradual and logical pattern of simplification generally influenced by historical factors, it might also be assumed that the hieratic script of Lower Egypt must have passed through similar phases leading to a cursive writing similar to abnormal hieratic.

The study of a larger number of similar stelae might yield more evidence proving the use of this cursive writing in Lower Egypt.

It is also worth noting that the few signs resembling early Demotic on the Twenty-fifth Dynasty stelae have intermingled with a good hieratic style, i.e. with well-formed signs.

Such a style must have co-existed in Lower Egypt with a more cursive one, and might probably be considered as the origin of the early Demotic script which was born in this part of the country.

Thus, I would suggest that Demotic is not — as Malinine assumed — derived from a different cursive branch of hieratic used in Lower Egypt; but rather from one of two hieratic styles used in Lower Egypt itself. The first of these styles, being the natural development of late hieratic, had become too cursive to go on being used. The second, closer to the hieratic originals, devoloped into early Demotic, by a gradual and normal simplification of well-formed hieratic signs.

As for the Louvre Stele C. 101, in which hieroglyphic, hieratic, and Demotic signs appeared, I would suggest that it was copied from a hieroglyphic original and not from a cursive one. This copying must have been done by a scribe familiar with the Demotic script. Nevertheless, this stele — as Malinine suggested — proves that Demotic was already known in Lower Egypt from the beginning of the Twenty-sixth Dynasty.

Finally, as shown in table 10.1, the Demotic simplification of the sign is not different in Lower, Middle, or Upper Egypt. This proves that Demotic is the result of one single pattern of abbreviation, and that geographical distinctions are not really significant.

Table 10.1. Comparison of Hieroglyphic Signs to Abnormal Hieratic and Early Demotic Forms.

Hieroglyphs	*Serapeum Stelae*	*Stele C. 101*	*Similar to Abnormal Hieratic*	*Similar to Early Demotic*	*Abnormal Hieratic*	*Early Demotic*
	St. 42; St. 159	2		X		C. 50071, 1
	St. 160		X	X	E 3228e, 8; BM 10113, 6	C. 50064, 2; C. 50059, 7; C. 30657,4
	St. 58; St. 160			X	E 3228, 17	C. 50071, 3; C. 50058, 4; C. 31061, 3
	St. 42; St. 33			X	BM 10113, 6	Pap. Rylands 1, E, K; C. 30601, 2
	St. 33; St. 42	6; 8	X		E 3228d, 7	C. 50080, 2; C. 50058, 6; C. 50144, 2
	St. 58	8	X		E 3228d, 2; E 3228d, 11; E 3228d, 19	

Table 10.1. Comparison of Hieroglyphic Signs to Abnormal Hieratic and Early Demotic Forms (*cont.*).

Hieroglyphs	*Serapeum Stelae*	*Stele C. 101*	*Similar to Abnormal Hieratic*	*Similar to Early Demotic*	*Abnormal Hieratic*	*Early Demotic*
	St. 33		X	X	E 3228d, 11; BM 10113, 2	C. 50100, 5; C. 50065, 11; C. 30665, 4
	St. 42			X	E 3228e, 4; E 3228e, 2	C. 50079, 2; C. 50058, 3; C. 50144, 2
	St. 42	3	X	X	E 3228e, 3; BM 10113, 2	C. 50066, 6; C. 50058, 2; C. 50150b, 2
	St. 30		X		E 2432, 8	
	St. 159; St. 160			X	E 3228d, 3; BM 10113, 2	C. 31045, 1; C. 50058, 6; C. 31062, 9
	St. 42		X	X	E 3228e, 19	50066, 10; 50058, 7; 50059, 5; 50146, 4

Table 10.1. Comparison of Hieroglyphic Signs to Abnormal Hieratic and Early Demotic Forms (*cont.*).

Hieroglyphs	*Serapeum Stelae*	*Stele C. 101*	*Similar to Abnormal Hieratic*	*Similar to Early Demotic*	*Abnormal Hieratic*	*Early Demotic*
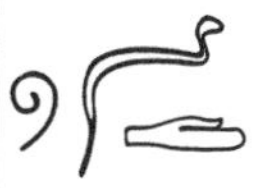		 2		X	 E 3228d, 2 E 3228e, 7 BM 10113, 1	 C. 50068, 1 C. 50059, 4 C. 30657, 1
		 5		X	 E 3228b, 8, 13 BM 10113, 2	 C. 31054, 9 C. 30657, 1
		 4		X	 E 3228d, 8 BM 10113, 5	 C. 50066, 8 C. 50059, 7 C. 50151, 5
		 2	X		 E 3228e, 8 Vienna D 12003, 12	 C. 31045, 4 Louvre E 9294 + 0
	 St. 30	 5	X	X	 Papyrus Leiden F1942/5.15, line 18	 C. 50058, 7
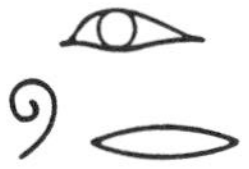	 St. 42 St. 42	 2	X	X	 E 3228e, 19 BM 10113, 5	 C. 50066, 2 C. 50059, 6 31062, 8

Table 10.1. Comparison of Hieroglyphic Signs to Abnormal Hieratic and Early Demotic Forms (*cont.*).

Hieroglyphs	*Serapeum Stelae*	*Stele C. 101*	*Similar to Abnormal Hieratic*	*Similar to Early Demotic*	*Abnormal Hieratic*	*Early Demotic*
	 St. 42 St. 33 St. 58	 3	X	X	 E 3228e, 12 BM 10113, 2 E 3228e, 6	 C. 50097b, 2 C. 50058, 4
	 St. 42 St. 160		X	X	 E 3228c, 7 Vienna D 12003, 1	 C. 50064, 3 C. 50058, 7
	 St. 33	 5	X		 E 3228e, 3	
		 5		X		 C. 50100, 7 C. 50059, 4 C. 50150b, 1

a

b

Two Stelae from the Reign of Pharaoh Sheshonq V (Twenty-second Dynasty):
(*a*) Stele 30 from Year 11; (*b*) Stele 33 from Year 27

PLATE 10.2

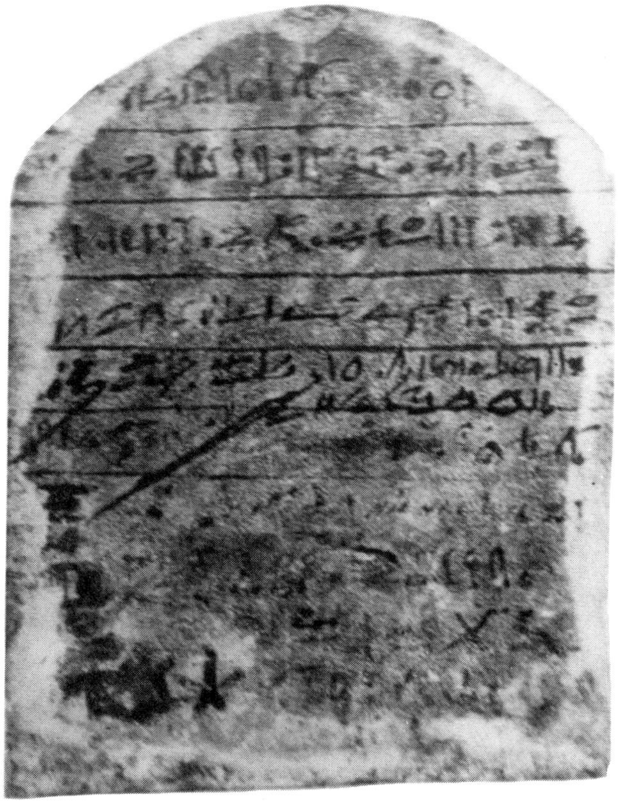

a

b

Two Stelae from the Twenty-second Dynasty: (*a*) Stele 42, Year 37 of Sheshonq V; (*b*) Stele 58

a

b

Two Stelae from Year 24 of Pharaoh Taharqa (Twenty-fifth Dynasty): (*a*) Stele 159; (*b*) Stele 160

PLATE 10.4

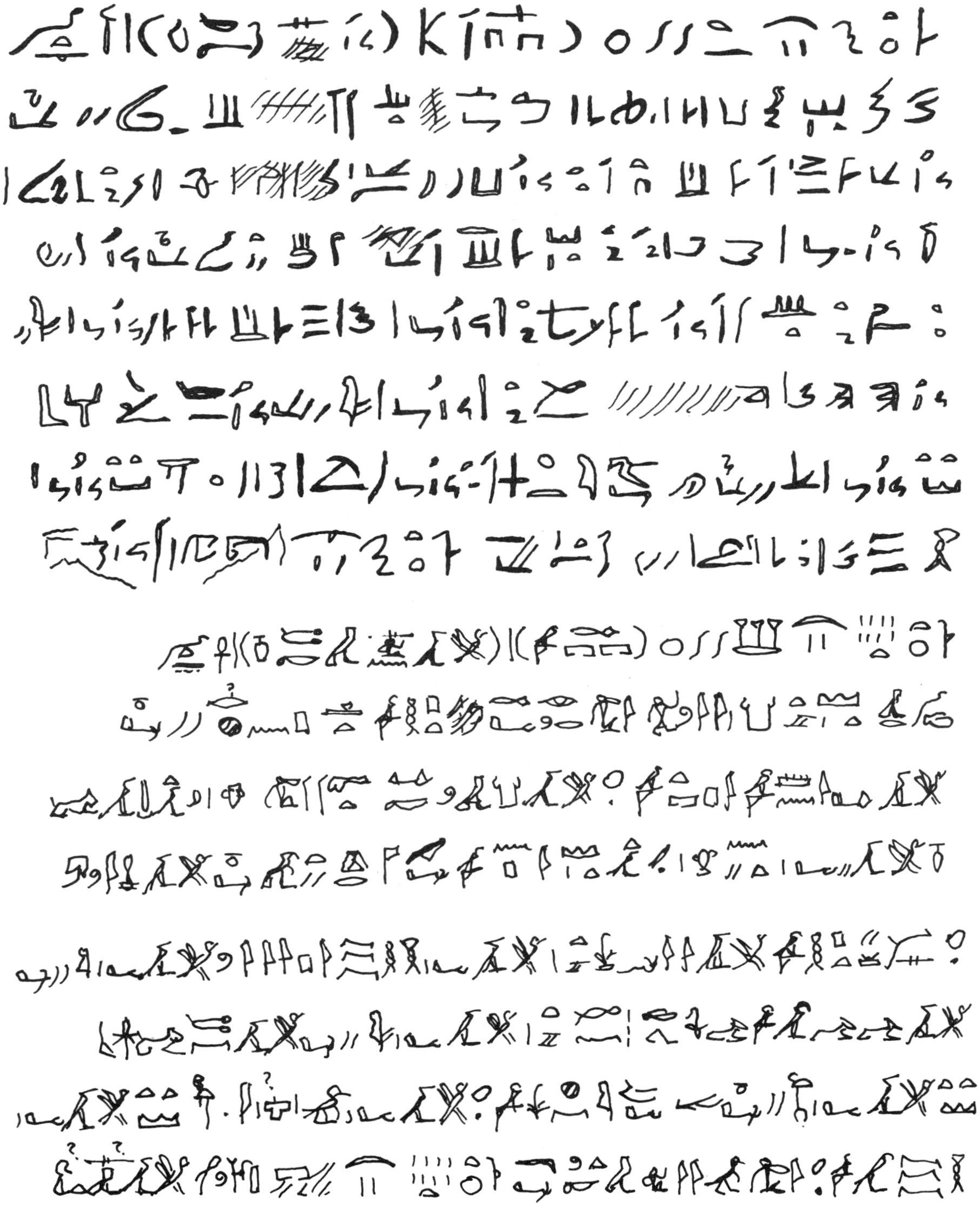

Louvre Stele C101

CHAPTER 11

THREE MIRRORS WITH DEMOTIC INSCRIPTIONS

ADEL FARID
Egyptian Museum

The three mirrors, which I am publishing here, belong to a group of metal objects with Demotic inscriptions.[1] These metal objects include vessels, boxes, coins, musical instruments, censors, mirrors, statues, sistrums, and tablets. In general, these objects bear votive inscriptions or other inscriptions on a variety of themes.

1. Mirror, Inv. Nr. E 1856, Musées Royaux d'Art et d'Histoire, Brussels (pl. 11.1)[2]

Provenance	Unknown
Measurements	17.3 × 11.9 × 0.4 cm
Material	Bronze
Inscription	Demotic inscription of two lines
Bibliography	Unpublished

The Demotic Inscription (see fig. 11.1 for a facsimile drawing)

Transliteration:

1) *Ḥwt-Ḥr tj ʿnḫ n Ta-Ḏḥwtj*
2) *Ta-Prt*

Translation:

1) Hathor may give life to Ta-Thoth,
2) daughter of Prt

Commentary:

For Hathor, see Daumas, *LÄ* II, cols. 1024–33.

For the personal name *Ta-Ḏḥwtj*, cf. *PN* I, p. 363, Nr. 14; and

 Ταθωτις, Ταθωυθις

For the personal name *Prt*, cf. Ranke 1935, p. 134, Nr. 14, 18, and 20:

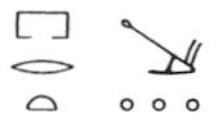

The personal name *Prt* is not mentioned in *Dem. Nb.*

1. For metal objects with Demotic inscriptions see the second part of my Ph.D. dissertation (1985). For mirrors, cf. Ch. Müller, *LÄ* V, cols. 1147–50. Not a single mirror with a Demotic inscription was mentioned in this article.
2. For the photograph of the mirror from Les Musées Royaux d'Art et d'Histoire, Brussels, I would like to thank Mr. Luc Limme.

2. Mirror, Nr. 292, Collection of King Farouk, the former King of Egypt (fig. 11.1 and pl. 11.2)

Provenance	Dendera
Measurements	22.2 × 15.2 cm
Material	Gilded Silver
Date	Roman period
Scene	The god Horus-*smꜣ-taui* or the god Ihj brings a sistrum to the goddess Hathor
Inscription	Demotic inscription of four lines
Themes of the inscription	Strategos inscription, Votive inscription
Bibliography	Unpublished

The Demotic Inscription (see fig. 11.3 for a facsimile drawing)

Transliteration:

1) *[m-bꜣḥ] Ḥ.t-Ḥr nb.t iwn.t Is.t tꜣ ntr.t ꜥꜣ.t n-tr.t Ptlwmjs*
2) *pꜣ srtjḳws pꜣ ḥm-ntr Ḥr pꜣ ḥm-ntr Ḥ.t-Ḥr pꜣ ḥm-ntr Ihj*
3) *[pꜣ ḥm-ntr Is.t] pꜣ ḥm-ntr n nꜣ ntr.w n ḥ.t-ntr*
4) *[iwn.t-]tꜣ-ntr.t*

Translation:

1) Before Hathor, mistress of Dendera, Isis, the great goddess,
   from the hand of Ptolemaios
2) the strategos, the prophet of Horus, the prophet of Hathor, the prophet of Ihj
3) [the prophet of Isis], the prophet of the gods of the temple of
4) Dendera

Commentary:

I have identified strategos Ptolemaios, the dedicator of this mirror, with strategos Ptolemaios, son of strategos Panas and grandson of strategos *Pꜣ-šr-Bꜣst* (Psenobastis). Strategos Ptolemaios has another Egyptian name:

Hieroglyphic: *Pꜣ-šr-pꜣ-ḫj* 

Demotic: *Pꜣ-šr-pꜣ-ḫj* 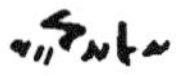

Strategos Ptolemaios has left thirteen Demotic and two hieroglyphic inscriptions.

The Demotic Inscriptions

1) Stele Cairo CG 31083 (Spiegleberg 1904, p. 10 and pl. I)
2) Stele Cairo CG 31092 (ibid., p. 23 and pl. IV)
3) Stele Cairo CG 31093 (ibid., pp. 24–25 and pl. IV)
4) Stele Cairo CG 31130 (ibid., p. 51 and pl. XIII)
5) Stele Cairo CG 50044 (Spiegleberg 1932, pp. 14–16 and pl. II)
6) Stele Cairo CG 50045 (ibid., pp. 17–18 and pl. II)
7) Stele Cairo JE 44305 (Spiegelberg 1912, pp. 36–39 and pl. 2, 1)
8) Stele Cairo 10/5/50/1 (Bresciani 1960, pp. 119–26)
9) Mirror Cairo JE 46375
10) Mirror King Farouk Collection, Nr. 292
11) Bronze tablet BM 57371 (Shore 1979, pp. 138–60)

12) Bronze tablet BM 57372 (ibid.)

13) Stele Stockholm MME 1970:2 (Wångstedt 1984, pp. 271–72 and pl. 37)

The Hieroglyphic Inscriptions

1) Statue Cairo CG 690 (Borchardt 1930, pp. 34–35 and pl. 127)

2) Statue Cairo JE 45390 (Daressy 1916, pp. 268–70)

3. Mirror Cairo JE 46375 (figs. 11.2 and 11.3; pls. 11.3 and 11.4)

Provenance	Dendera
Measurements	30.8 × 25.8 cm
Material	Gilded Silver
Date	Roman period
Scene	The goddess Hathor seated, holding in her right hand the *ʿnḫ* sign and in her left hand a scepter.
Hieroglyphic inscription	*Ḥwt-Ḥr nb.t iwnt ir Rʿ nb.t pt ḥnwt ntrw nbw* Hathor, mistress of Dendera, Eye of Reʿ, mistress of heaven, mistress of all gods.
Demotic inscription	Three lines
Themes of the inscriptions	Strategos inscription, Votive inscription
Bibliography	Unpublished

The Demotic Inscription (see fig. 11.6 for facsimile drawings)

Transliteration:

1) *n-tr.t Ptlwmjs sꜣ Ptwlmjs pꜣ mr-mšʿ pꜣ snjns pꜣ sn n Pr-ʿꜣ pꜣ ḥm-ntr Ḥr pꜣ ḥm-ntr Is.t pꜣ ḥm-ntr*

2) *Ḥ.t-Ḥr nb.t iwn.t ir.t Rʿ nb.t pt ḥnwt ntrw nbw ḥnc sn=f Swḏꜣ=f-pꜣ-ʿꜣ pꜣ snjns pꜣ sn n Pr-ʿꜣ*

3) *pꜣ ḥm-ntr Ḥr pꜣ ḥm-ntr Ḥ.t-Ḥr pꜣ ḥm-ntr Is.t ḥnʿ Swḏꜣ=f-pꜣ-ẖm pꜣ mr-mšʿ ḥnʿ sn=f [Swḏꜣ=f-pꜣ-ljlw]*

Translation:

1) From the hand of Ptolemaios, son of Ptolemaios, the strategos, the Syngenes, the brother of the king, the prophet of Horus, the prophet of Isis, the prophet of

2) Hathor, mistress of Dendera, Eye of Reʿ, mistress of heaven, mistress of all gods, together with his brother *Swḏꜣ=f-pꜣ-ʿꜣ*, the Syngenes, the brother of the king,

3) the prophet of Horus, the prophet of Hathor, the prophet of Isis, together with *Swḏꜣ=f-pꜣ-ẖm*, the Strategos, together with his brother [*Swḏꜣ=f-pꜣ-ljlw*]

Commentary:

The beginning of the Demotic text is somewhat broken but the word is clear and the reading is certain.

It is pointed out in line 1 of the Demotic text of the Egyptian Museum mirror that strategos Ptolemaios is the son of Ptolemaios 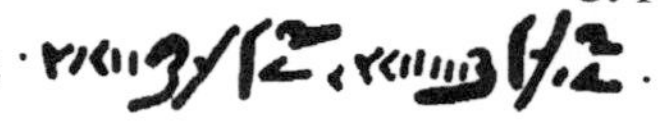. Now the question remains: who is this Ptolemaios, the father of our strategos Ptolemaios? The Egyptian sources (hieroglyphic and Demotic) offer us the names of two strategoi called Ptolemaios who lived in Dendera:

1) Strategos Ptolemaios, son of strategos Panas and grandson of strategos *P3-šr-B3st*;

2) Strategos Ptolemaios-*p3-šr-p3-ḫj*, father of strategos *Ḳwrks* (statue Cairo JE 45390).

Daressy copied the inscription of the other name of Ptolemaios as follows and he deciphered it *Pa-Khrod-ka*. The letter *Ḳ* is written in the hieroglyphic inscriptions of the statue Cairo JE 45390 in the personal name of strategos *Ḳwrks* three times; twice on the naos, which *Ḳwrks* bears or carries with his hands, and the third time in the inscription on the back pillar of the naophorous statue of *Ḳwrks*:

1)  2)  3) 

After a careful examination of the original hieroglyphic inscriptions on the statue Cairo JE 45390, I discovered that the letter *Ḳ* in the personal name in Daressy's copy is certainly not *Ḳ* at all, but *P*. So the personal name should be as follows: , that is the hieroglyphic equivalent of the Demotic name *P3-šr-p3-ḫj*. The *Wörterbuch* (III, p. 237) lists the word *ḫj* . The *Wörterbuch* also lists the sign as a determinative of this word. So this hieroglyphic sign should be read as *ḫj*, and not as *ḳ3*. So the old reading of *P3-ḫrd-ḳ3*, *P3-šr-ḳ3* in Daressy and the other scholars who followed him (Spiegelberg, Henne, Van't Dack, Bengston, de Meulenaere, A. Farid [1989, pp. 155–68, pls. 10–11], Ranke [*PN* I, p. 119, no. 8], and Peremans and Van't Dack [1950, p. 29, no. 237]) should be corrected as *P3-šr-p3-ḫj* , which is the correct reading of the personal name in the Demotic texts of the BM Tablets 57371 and 57372.

Daressy (1916, pp. 268–70) who has published the hieroglyphic inscription of the statue Cairo JE 45390, identified Ptolemaios *p3-šr-p3-ḫj* with strategos Ptolemaios, son of strategos Panas and grandson of strategos *P3-šr-B3st* (Psenobastis), and he dated the statue at the end of the Ptolemaic period and before the Roman conquest of Egypt. Four scholars followed the opinion of Daressy: namely Spiegelberg (1922b, pp. 88–92; 1926, pp. 27–34), Henne (1935, p. 38), Van't Dack (1949, pp. 3–44), and Bengston (1967, p. 224). De Meulenaere (1959a, pp. 19ff.) has argued that the two Ptolemaios are two different persons:

1) Strategos Ptolemaios called *P3-šr-p3-ḫj* who lived during the Ptolemaic period and

2) Strategos Ptolemaios, son of strategos Panas and grandson of strategos *P3-šr-B3st* who lived at the beginning of the Roman period.

But my opinion is that the two names belong to one person, Ptolemaios *p3-šr-p3-ḫj*. Shore (1979, pp. 138–60) has recently published two important Demotic texts, both engraved on bronze tablets found at Dendera, BM 57371 and BM 57372. Both Demotic texts include the name *P3-šr-p3-ḫj* called Ptolemaios. Tablet BM 57371 also refers to his three sons, namely:

1) Strategos *Swḏ3=f-p3-ʿ3* called … 

2) Strategos *Swḏ3=f-p3-ḫm* called … 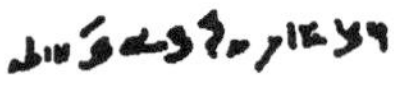

3) Strategos *Swḏ3=f-p3-ljlw* called *3sjgns* 

The mirror from the Egyptian Museum, Cairo JE 46375, lists four sons of Strategos Ptolemaios:

1) Strategos Ptolemaios 

2) Strategos *Swḏꜣ=f-pꜣ-ꜥꜣ* 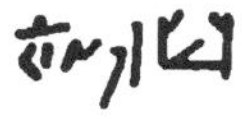

3) Strategos *Swḏꜣ=f-pꜣ-ḫm* 

4) Strategos *Swḏꜣ=f-pꜣ-ljlw* 

Zauzich (1980, pp. 189–90) has published a review of Shore's article and he certainly corrected some of Shore's readings, but his last suggestion to consider *Swḏꜣ=f* , , as a verb form and not as a personal name is certainly not correct. *Swḏꜣ=f* is most definitely a personal name. There is no doubt about that at all. This is clear from the context of both Demotic documents: the bronze tablet (BM 57371) and the gilded silver mirror (Cairo JE 46375). We notice here that these persons bear double names, one Egyptian and the other Greek. After a careful study of the Demotic texts of both Cairo JE 46375 and BM 57371, I have come to the conclusion that the persons in both documents are identical. The problem is that the Egyptian Museum mirror (JE 46375) lists four sons of Ptolemaios, while the tablet (BM 57371) lists three sons of Ptolemaios called *Pꜣ-šr-pꜣ-ḫj* . The other problem is that the Egyptian Museum mirror gives the eldest son as Ptolemaios, while the British Museum text (line 52) names *Swḏꜣ=f-pꜣ-ꜥꜣ* as the eldest son of strategos Ptolemaios called *Pꜣ-šr-pꜣ-ḫj* . I would like to suggest that strategos Ptolemaios, the eldest son of strategos Ptolemaios called *Pꜣ-šr-pꜣ-ḫj* died, then the second son *Swḏꜣ=f-pꜣ-ꜥꜣ* became the eldest son, otherwise how can we explain his nonexistence in the bronze tablet BM 57371. I would also suggest that the mirror from the Egyptian Museum is older than the British Museum tablet. We notice also that *Swḏꜣ=f-pꜣ-ꜥꜣ* did not have the title *mr-mšꜥ* on the Egyptian Museum mirror but he has the title *mr-mšꜥ* on the British Museum bronze tablet. This fact suggests that *Swḏꜣ=f-pꜣ-ꜥꜣ* received the title *mr-mšꜥ* (strategos) only after the death of his elder brother Ptolemaios.

The Demotic texts of the two bronze tabltes (BM 57371 and BM 57372) refer to strategos Ptolemaios with double names: one Egyptian, the other Greek. Both texts denote the two names as follows: *Pꜣ-šr-pꜣ-ḫj* called Ptolemaios.

Bronze tablet BM 57371, line 24 *Pꜣ-šr-pꜣ-ḫj ḏdjt n=f [Ptlwmjs]* 

Bronze tablet BM 57372, line x + 9 *Pꜣ-šr-pꜣ-ḫj ḏdjt n=f [Ptlwmjs]* 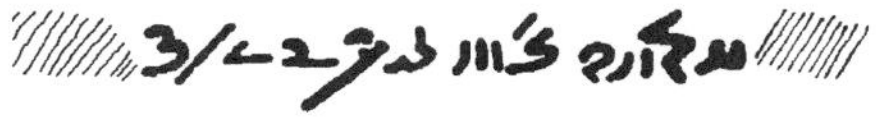

The statue Cairo CG 690 lists three generations of the family of strategos Ptolemaios, son of strategos Panas and grandson of strategos *Pꜣ-šr-Bꜣst* (Psenobastis) namely:

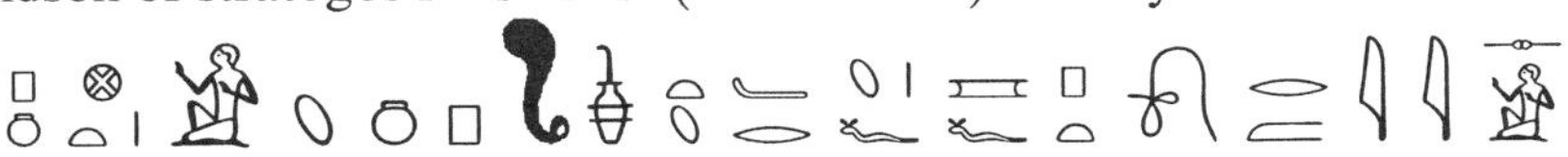

Grandfather  *Pꜣ-šr-Bꜣst* (Psenobastis)

Father  *Pꜣ-n-niwt* (Panas)

Son  Ptolemaios

On the statue of strategos *Ḳwrks*, son of strategos Ptolemaios called *Pꜣ-šr-pꜣ-ḫj* (Cairo JE 45390), it seems that the hieroglyphic writing of *Pꜣ-šr-pꜣ-ḫj*  is equivalent to the Demotic writing *Pꜣ-šr-pꜣ-ḫj* of the same name. Owing to the similarity of the titles between strategos

Ptolemaios, son of Panas and strategos Ptolemaios, son of Ptolemaios and because both come from Dendera and because the palaeography of the Demotic text of the Cairo Museum mirror JE 46375 refers to the Roman period, I have come to conclude that strategos Ptolemaios is the son of strategos Ptolemaios called *P3-šr-p3-ḫj*, and the grandson of strategos Panas, and the great-grandson of of strategos *P3-šr-B3st* (Psenobastis). According to the hieroglyphic and Demotic documents we can reconstruct the genealogy of this family as follows:

P3-šr-B3st + ?

|

P3-n-niwt (Panas) + ?

|

Ptolemaios (*P3-šr-p3-ḫj*, *P3-šr-p3-ḫj*) + ?

|

Ptolemaios — *Swḏ3=f-p3-ʿ3* — *Swḏ3=f-p3-ḫm* — *Swḏ3=f-p3-ljlw*

The first personal name *Ptlwmjs* is so engraved  while the second personal name *Ptwlms* is so written . The scribe probably has written it in this manner to distinguish between the father's name and the son's name. Ptolemaios has three titles:

1) *p3 mr-mšʿ*  Strategos

2) *p3 snjns*  Syngenes

3) *p3 sn n Pr-ʿ3* 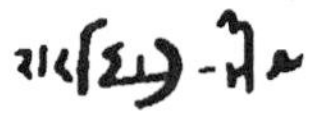 Brother of the King

De Meulenaere has proved that the titles *mr-mšʿ wr* and *wr ʿ3 n mšʿ* designate a strategos. He argued also that the title *mr-mšʿ* could be an abbreviation of *mr-mšʿ wr*. He concluded futher on that the combination of the two titles *mr-mšʿ* and *sn-nsw* designate a strategos of a nome. Ptolemaios has other priestly titles:

1) *p3 ḥm-ntr Ḥr*  The prophet of Horus

2) *p3 ḥm-ntr Is.t*  The prophet of Isis

3) *p3 ḥm-ntr Ḥ.t-Ḥr nb.t iwnt ir.t Rʿ nb.t pt ḥnwt ntrw nbw* 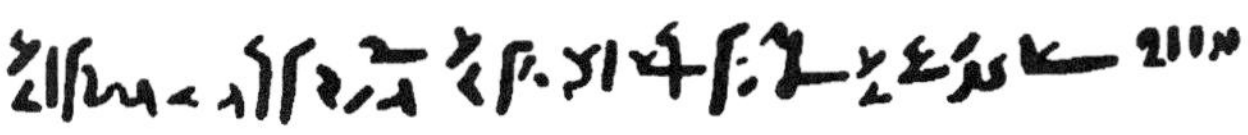 The prophet of Hathor, mistress of Dendera, Eye of Reʿ, mistress of heaven, mistress of all gods.

According to the Demotic text of the mirror Cairo JE 46375, Ptolemaios has three other brothers, all of whom were strategoi. These four brothers are mentioned as follows:

1) *Ptolemaios* 

2) *Swḏ3=f-p3-ʿ3* 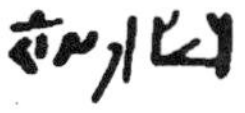 who has two titles:

a) *p3 snjns* 

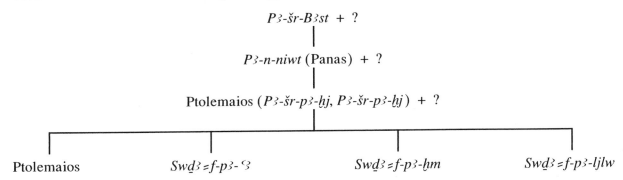

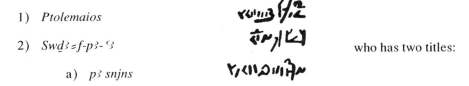

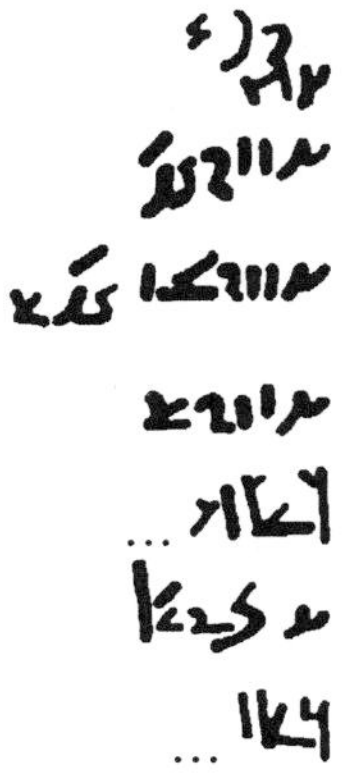

b) *pꜣ sn n Pr-ꜥꜣ* — and another three priestly titles:

c) *pꜣ ḥm-ntr Ḥr* — The prophet of Horus

d) *pꜣ ḥm-ntr Ḥ.t-Ḥr* — The Prophet of Hathor

e) *pꜣ ḥm-ntr Is.t* — The prophet of Isis

3) *Swḏꜣ=f-pꜣ-ḫm* — who has one title:

pꜣ mr-mšꜥ — Strategos

4) *Swḏꜣ=f-pꜣ-ljlw*

The titles of *Swḏꜣ=f-pꜣ-ljlw* cannot be seen on the mirror because the corrosion has not been cleaned from the handle of the mirror where the Demotic inscription should be continued.

We know that strategos Ptolemaios and his four sons each have two names: one Egyptian, the other Greek:

1) Ptolemaios = *Pꜣ-šr-pꜣ-ḫj* (Demotic)  *Pꜣ-šr-pꜣ-ḫj* (hieroglyphic) , the father

2) Ptolemaios = ...

3) *Swḏꜣ=f-pꜣ-ꜥꜣ* = ...

4) *Swḏꜣ=f-pꜣ-ḫm* = ...

5) *Swḏꜣ=f-pꜣ-ljlw* = *ꜣsjgns*

The name of the dedicator of the naophorous standing statue Cairo JE 45390 is *Ḳwrks*. Since *Ḳwrks* is a Greek name, it probably is to be equated either to *Swḏꜣ=f-pꜣ-ꜥꜣ* or to *Swḏꜣ=f-pꜣ-ḫm*. We have to exclude their brother Ptolemaios, because Ptolemaios is a Greek name. We will have to wait for new documents to find out the Egyptian name of Ptolemaios and the other Greek name of one of his brothers. An important question which must be asked here: Since we know from the titles of the four sons of strategos Ptolemaios that all four were strategoi at the same time, did all four act as strategoi in Dendera or in different nomes?

De Meulenaere (1959, pp. 18–23) argued that there is a difference in the titles between the hieroglyphic inscription of the statues Cairo JE 45390 of strategos Ptolemaios-*Pꜣ-šr-pꜣ-ḫj* and the Demotic inscription of strategos Ptolemaios, son of strategos Panas, and grandson of strategos *Pꜣ-šr-Bꜣst* (Psenobastis). The hieroglyphic inscription of the statue (Daressy 1916, pp. 268–70) reads:

mr-mšꜥ sn-nsw Ḳwrks sꜣ Ptwlmjs ...... ḥm-ntr itjw (njswt-bjtjw) ḥnꜥ twt=sn wꜥb n gꜣ=sn sn-nsw Ḳwrks sꜣ n mr-mšꜥ Pꜣ-šr-pꜣ-ḫj

Strategos and syngenes *Ḳwrks*, son of Ptolemaios ...... prophet of the kings of Upper and Lower Egypt, together with their statues, priest of their chapels, the syngenes *Ḳwrks*, son of strategos *Pꜣ-šr-pꜣ-ḫj*.

The Rosetta Stone (Demotic lines 22–23) mentions also (Spiegelberg 1922b, S. 56):

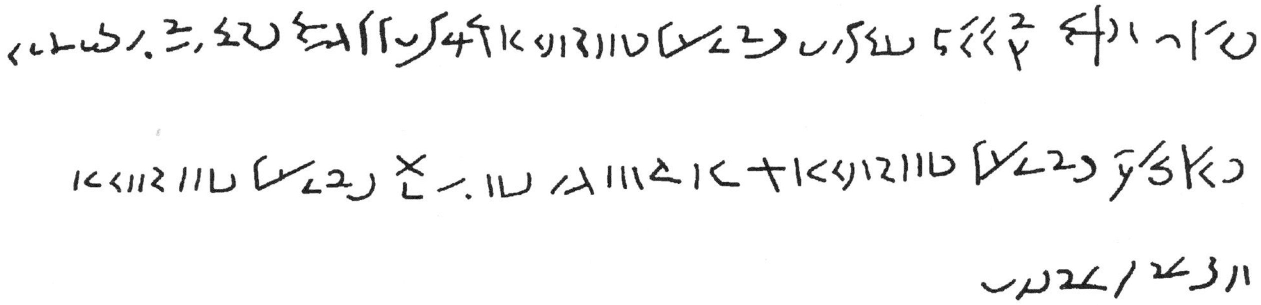

mtw=w dit ꜥḥꜥ wꜥ twtw n Pr-ꜥꜣ c.w.s. Ptwlmjꜣs ꜥnḫ ḏt pꜣ ntr pr ntj nꜣ-ꜥn tꜣj=f mt-nfrt mtw=w ḏd n=f Ptwlmjꜣs nḏ Bḳj ntj iw pꜣj=f whm Ptwlmjꜣs iir nḫt Kmj

and they will erect a statue of the king L.H.P. Ptolemaios living forever, the god Epiphanes Eucharistos and they will call it Ptolemaios savior of Egypt, whose translation is Ptolemaios, who protects Egypt

De Meulenaere argued that the title *Pr-ꜥꜣ* in the Ptolemaic period was replaced by the title Caesar in the Roman period:

> Il y a meme certains indices qui font supposer que l'appellation 'Pharaon' ete remplace a l'epoque romaine par celle de 'Cesar.' Ainsi, Psenamounis, grande pretre de Ptah sous Auguste, figure-t-il comme prophete de Cesar dans l'inscription de Petoubastis. Que l'on songe aussi a Panas et Ptolemee, qui sont appeles 'agent de Cesar,' tandis que Menkare, pere de Montesouphis, etait, lui, 'agent du Pharaon' (de Meulenaere 1959, pp. 23–24).

But we know that the title *sn-n-Pr-ꜥꜣ* "Brother of the Pharaoh" was still in use in the Roman period, as the following examples attest:

1) Sandstone socle of the granite statue Cairo JE 46320 = CG 50047 of strategos *Pa-mnḫ*, son of strategos *Hjꜣrgs-Pꜣ-ꜥšm*: *pꜣ sn n Pr-ꜥꜣ* (Spiegelberg 1932, pp. 19f., pl. XI)

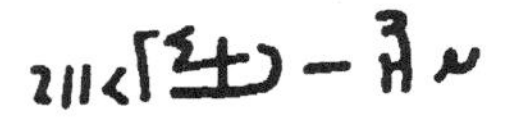

2) Stele Berlin 22468 of strategos *Pꜣ-ꜥẖm-Pa-šw*, son of *Pꜣ-ꜥẖm-rmt-bḥdt*: *pꜣ snjns pꜣ sn n Pr-ꜥꜣ* (Spiegelberg 1927, pp. 27–34; Farid 1989, pp. 155–68, pls. 10–11)

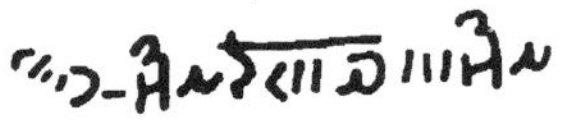

3) Stele Cairo CG 31083 of strategos Ptolemaios, son of strategos Panas: *pꜣ snjns pꜣ sn n Pr-ꜥꜣ* (Spiegelberg 1904, p. 10, pl. I)

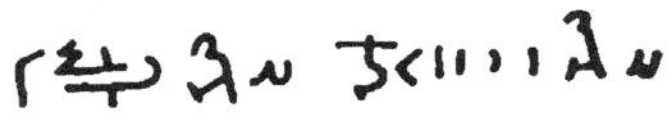

4) Stele Cairo CG 31092 of strategos Ptolemaios, son of strategos Panas: *pꜣ sngns pꜣ sn n [Pr-ꜥꜣ]* (Spiegelberg 1904, p. 23, pl. IV)

5) Stele Cairo CG 31093 of strategos Ptolemaios, son of strategos Panas: *pꜣ sngns pꜣ sn n Pr-ꜥꜣ* (Spiegelber 1904, p. 24f., pl. IV) 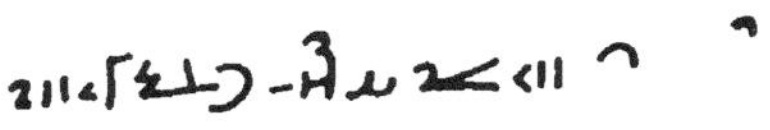

6) Trilingual Stele Cairo CG 50044 of strategos Ptolemaios, son of strategos Panas: *pꜣ snjns pꜣ sn n Pr-ꜥꜣ* (Spiegelberg 1932, pp. 14–16, pl. XI) 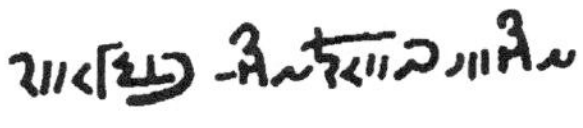

7) Stele Cairo CG 50045 of strategos Ptolemaios, son of strategos Panas: *pꜣ snjns pꜣ sn n Pr-ꜥꜣ* (Spiegelberg 1932, pp. 17f., pl. XI) 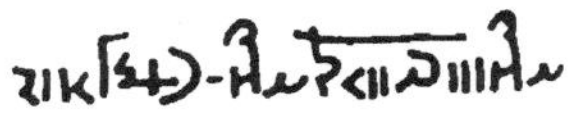

8) Stele Cairo CG 31137 of strategos Lysimachos: *pꜣ sn n Pr-ꜥꜣ* (Spiegelberg 1904, pp. 53f., pl. XV) 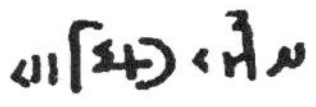

9) Mirror Cairo JE 46375, strategos Ptolemaios, son of strategos Ptolemaios: *pꜣ snjns pꜣ sn n Pr-ꜥꜣ* 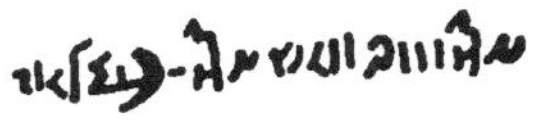

10) Mirror Cairo JE 46375, line 2, strategos *Swḏꜣ=f-pꜣ-ꜥꜣ*: *pꜣ snjns pꜣ sn n Pr-ꜥꜣ* 

11) Bronze Tablet BM 57371, line 53, strategos *Swḏꜣ=f-pꜣ-ꜥꜣ*: *pꜣ sn n Pr-ꜥꜣ* (Shore 1979, pp. 143–51) 

If de Meulenaere is right, the title *sn n Pr-ꜥꜣ* should have been replaced by *sn n Kjsrs*, which did not happen. Also the title *sẖ Pr-ꜥꜣ iw=f ip*  was still in use in the Roman period, and if de Meulanaere were right, the title should have been replaced by *sẖ K̠jsrs iw=f ip*, which did not happen. See the following examples:

1) Stele Cairo CG 31099 of *ꜥn-m-ḥr* called *Pꜣ-sẖn*: *sẖ Pr-ꜥꜣ iw=f ip* (Spiegelberg 1904) 

2) Stele Louvre E 13074 = Bibliotheque Nationale no. 126 (C48) = Louvre Museum E 13074: *sẖ n Pr-ꜥꜣ iw=f ip* (Spiegelberg 1908b, pp. 144–47, pls. I–II, Nr. XLI) 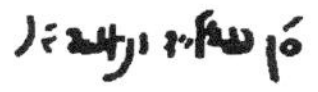

3) Bronze Tablet BM 57371,

line 16: *sẖ n Pr-ꜥꜣ iw=f ip* 

line 22:*sẖ n Pr-ꜥꜣ iw=f ip* 

(Shore 1979, pp. 143–51)

Figure 11.1. Facsimile Drawing of Gilded Silver Mirror with Demotic Inscription from the King Farouk Collection (Nr. 292; Now in the Egyptian Museum, Cairo).

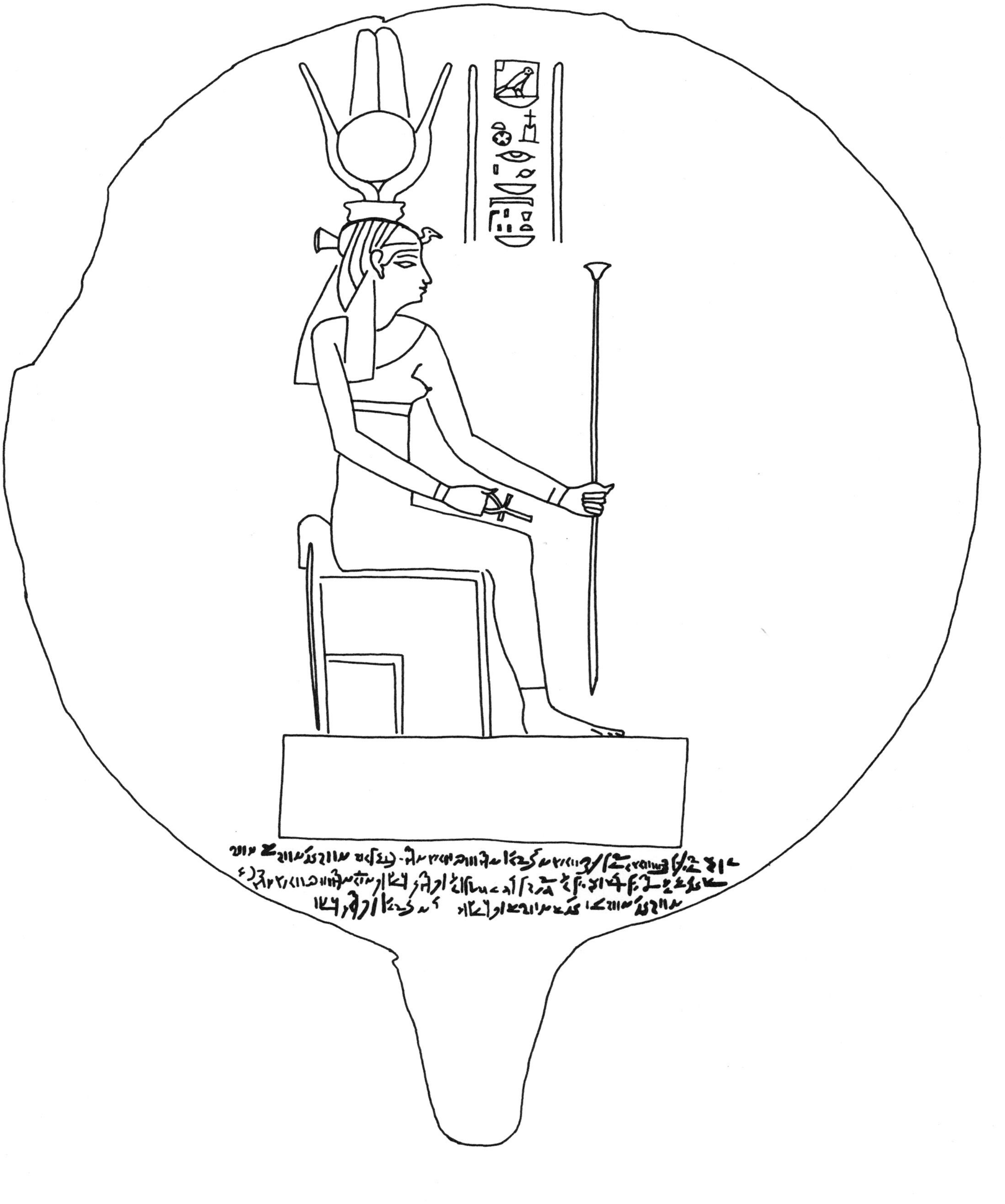

Figure 11.2. Facsimile Drawing of Gilded Silver Mirror with Demotic Inscription from the Collection of the Egyptian Museum, Cairo (JE 46375).

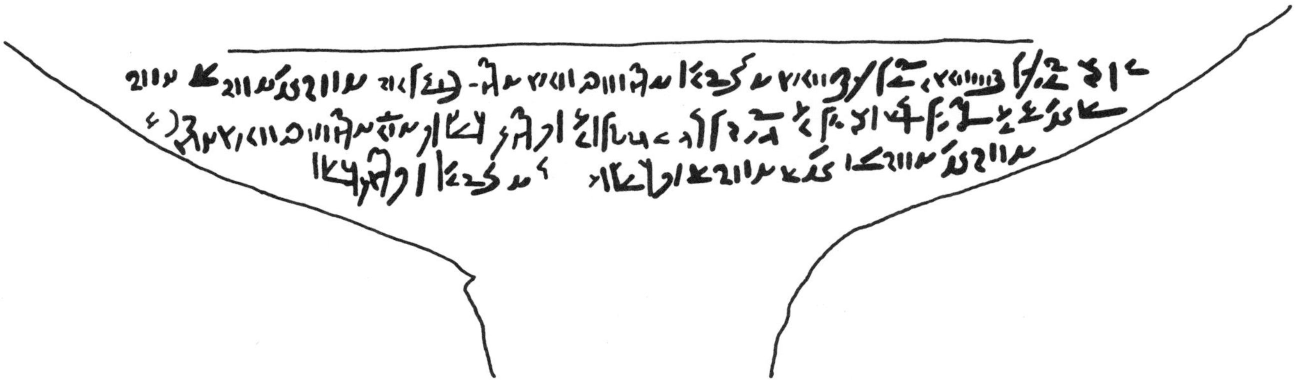

Figure 11.3. Detail of Demotic Inscription on Gilded Silver Mirror from the Collection of the Egyptian Museum, Cairo (JE 46375).

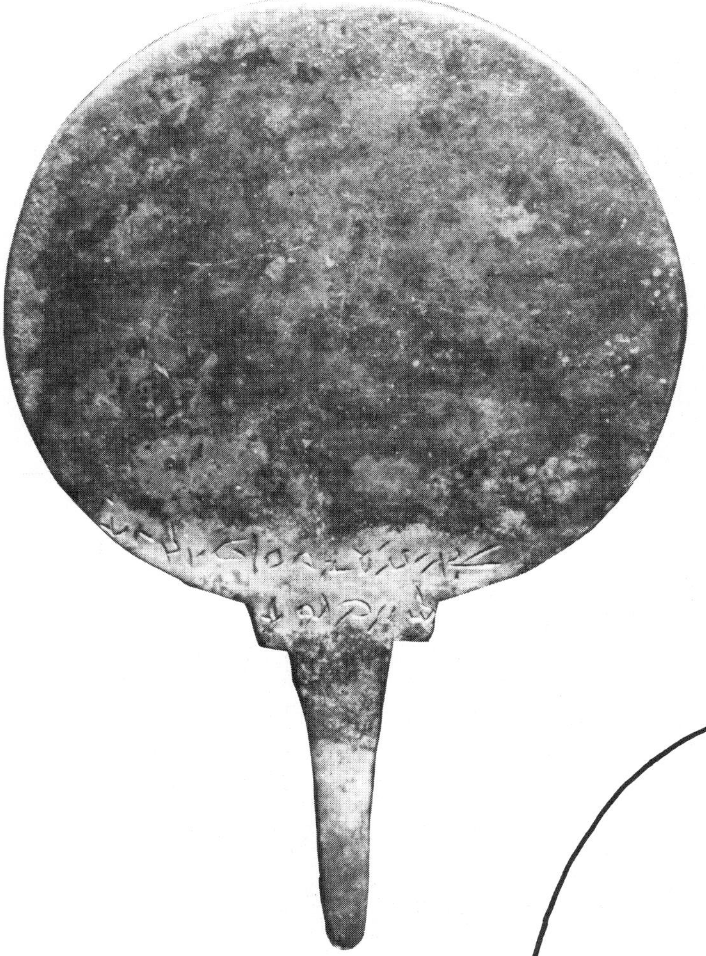

a

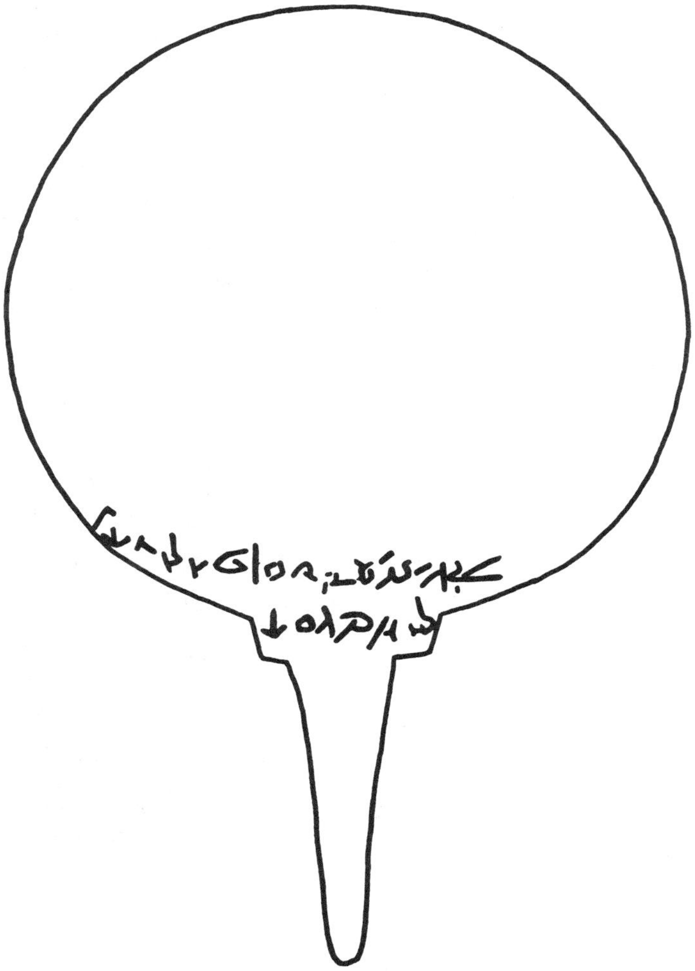

b

Bronze Mirror with Demotic Inscription from the Collection of Musées Royaux d'Art et d'Histoire, Brussels (Inv. Nr. E 1856): (*a*) Photograph; (*b*) Facsimile Drawing

Photograph of Gilded Silver Mirror with Demotic Inscription from the King Farouk Collection (Nr. 292; Now in the Egyptian Museum, Cairo).

Photograph of Gilded Silver Mirror with Demotic Inscription from the Collection of the Egyptian Museum, Cairo (JE 46375).

PLATE 11.4

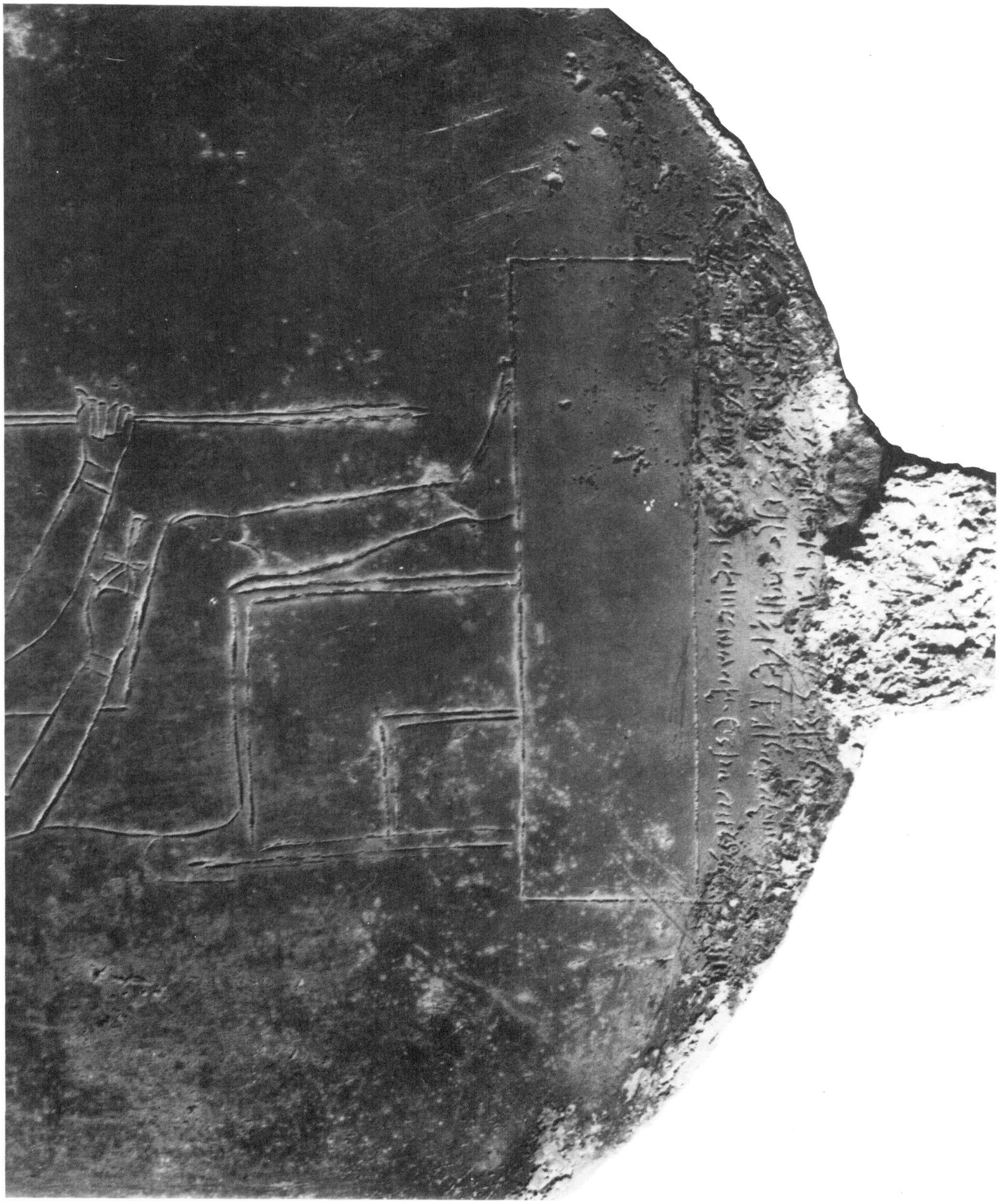

Detail Photograph of the Demotic Inscription on the Gilded Silver Mirror from the Collection of the Egyptian Museum, Cairo (JE 46375).

CHAPTER 12

THE WANDERING PERSONNEL OF THE TEMPLE OF NARMUTHIS IN THE FAIYUM AND SOME TOPONYMS OF THE MERIS OF POLEMON*

PAOLO GALLO
University of Pisa

In 1938 an archive of 1555 ostraca was found at Medinet Madi, the ancient town of Narmuthis, in the south of the Faiyum.

Several remarks about the discovery and the general content of this archive have been made already (see *ODN* and Gallo 1989, pp. 99–123); therefore I think that it will suffice to recall briefly that the ostraca were found in a building within the enclosure of the temple dedicated to the local goddess Renenutet, and that all of them date to the Roman period, about the second century A.D. Unfortunately, as the originals have disappeared (*ODN*, p. 1), we now possess only photos of these texts. The photographic archive is kept at the University of Pisa and studied by the team directed by Professor Edda Bresciani.

The main peculiarity of these ostraca is that they are written sometimes in Demotic, sometimes in Greek, and very often Greek and Demotic mixed in the same text (Bresciani and Pintaudi 1987, pp. 123–26). The contents are various: we have school texts, medical prescriptions, astrological texts, lists of various objects and materials, tax receipts, accounts, and juridical matters.

The subject of this paper is an unusual group of texts whose content reveals in detail some little-known aspects of the administration of an Egyptian temple in the Roman period.

We sometimes find quite cryptic "telegraphic style" texts, such as the following:

TEXT A (see fig. 12.1a)

OMM VOGLIANO NO. 431 = *ODN*, TEXT NO. 3

Transcription	*Translation*
1. *šm r*	1. Go to
2. *Tš Niw.t-*	2. Tosh, Nar-
3. *Rnmwtj.t Tꜣ-rs*	3. muthis, Ta-resi

* Last year my stay in Paris coincided with the lectures on the Faiyum held by Professor Jean Yoyotte at the Ecole Pratique des Hautes Etudes, V^e section. He offered me precious suggestions while I was working on this paper, and encouraged me to publish it; I wish to express here my gratitude to him. I am also indebted to Professor Françoise de Cenival and my friend Michel Pezin, who kindly showed me the writing of some toponyms occurring in unpublished papyri in Paris and Lille.

Transcription	Translation
4. *j Rꜥ-*	4. Ro-
5. *snt qṭj ẖr*	5. senti. Go around according
6. *pꜣ rḫ ssw nb*	6. to the instruction, every day.

NOTES

Lines 5–6 *qṭj ẖr pꜣ rḫ*. Another example of the same expression can be seen in *ODN*, text no. 27.6–7; as shown by the determinative, the word *pꜣ rḫ* "what is known" or "what is to be known" concerns a written document, hence the translation of "instruction"; an instruction that in this context could be a very practical one.

This obscure and short text contains two orders clearly sent to someone by his superior; the first task of the addressee is to go to some locality near Narmuthis, whose identification will be discussed in detail in the second part of the paper; the second order is to travel according to a written instruction, "every day." This statement leads us to suppose that the tour in the mentioned villages lasted more than one day; this interpretation seems confirmed by other clearer texts such as the following two:

TEXT B (see fig. 12.1b)

OMM VOGLIANO NO. 661 = OMM ARCH. PISA NO. 821

Transcription	*Translation*
1. *sw wꜥ šꜥ sw 5*	1. (From) the first until the fifth,
2. *Tš sw 6 šꜥ*	2. (at) Tosh; (from) the sixth until
3. *sw 15 ẖn*	3. the fifteenth, in
4. *Pꜣ jꜥl*	4. The river;
5. *hrw 10 — kj-ḏd — sw 16*	5. (from) the tenth — error — (from) the sixteenth
6. *šꜥ sw 25 r Rꜥ-*	6. until the twenty-fifth, to Ro-
7. *snt sw 5*	7. senti; the fifth,
8. *... e Pꜣ-Jgn*	8. ... to *P3-Ignt* (?);
9. *t (?) sw 10 ḥtj*	9. The tenth, a period
10. *r Niw.t-Rnmwt.t*	10. to Narmuthis

NOTES

line 5 *kj-ḏd*. Here used to introduce a correction. The scribe wrote *hrw* instead of *sw*, and 10 instead of 16.

line 7 *sw 5*. Of course the fifth day of the following month.

line 9 *ḥtj*. Cf. *EDG* 338.3; the meaning of "period, moment" is well shown by the texts published by Parker (1959, columns VII, line 11; VIII, line 13; IX, line 14).

TEXT C (see fig. 12.2a)

OMM VOGLIANO NO. 990

Transcription	*Translation*
1. *e.ir s.t.w (r) tj*	1. ....towards the places (to) deliver
2. *ꜥꜣ*	2. (the) precious goods:
3. *Pꜣ-glg-Sbk*	3. Kerkesoucha,
4. *Pꜣ ꜥt rs*	4. The southern edge of the cultivations,
5. *Qs Pꜣ-sj*	5. Qos, Pa-si,
6. *<Pꜣ-sj> Te*	6. < Pa-si >, Tem,
7. *m Pꜣ-glg-*	7. Kerke-
8. *Tꜣ-wr.t sm*	8. thoueris, (the) herb (and)
9. *... nb e-nt šꜥt*	9. every ... that is cut

NOTES

Line 1 *e-ir*. Apparently this document begins with a preposition; therefore we have to suppose that the first part of the text was written on the other side of the sherd or upon another ostracon.

s.t.w. This word has the hieratic determinative for a building, different from the verb *ij* "to come" (cf. the writings in *ODN*, texts nos. 15.3 and 28.16).

(r) tj. The preposition *r* introducing final clauses is often omitted in the texts of this archive, e.g. *tw-s nꜣ nkt n-nt.e šw tj* Ἥρων, "here there are the things that are useful, (to) give (to) Eron" (cf. Gallo 1989, p. 103, text A, line 1).

Line 2 *ꜥꜣ*. Hieratic word to be transcribed 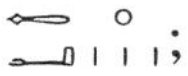; I do not know of any Demotic occurrence of this term. It is very probably a variant of the hieroglyphic term , var. , 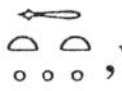,which indicates not only the precious stones but also, in a wider sense, the whole of the exotic precious things needed for religious and funerary rituals (aromas, frankincense, pigments, oils, etc.; cf. Meeks 1979, 77.0568 and 78.0621). This meaning matches the contexts of these ostraca, where pigments and substances pertaining to cult are often handled as goods to be distributed by the clergy of Narmuthis to the minor sanctuaries of the neighbouring villages (see below).

Line 6 < *Pꜣ-sj* >. The second *Pꜣ-sj*, being a repetition, is to be eliminated. In our ostraca the last word at the end of a line is often repeated entirely at the beginning of the following line; probably the scribe was worried that the first writing was not clear enough (cf. for instance *ODN*, text no. 27, lines 2–3: [32/32]; Gallo 1989, text E, lines 7–8: [*mšꜥ/mšꜥ*]; an example in Greek: Vogliano, Cinotti, and Columbo 1953, p. 511, text 1, lines 22–23: καταπλε/ῦσαι καταπλεῦσαι.

Line 9 *šꜥt*. Paleographically, a reading *bk* is possible also; *šꜥt* is preferable because the word seems to refer to the substantive *sm* "herb" of the line above. I think that the action of *šꜥt n sm*, the "cutting of the herb," the "harvesting," may correspond to the parallel Greek expression χορτηγία λέγειν attested by an unpublished ostracon of the archive.

Such texts form a category still little known at this time. They must be considered as true "agendas" for persons who have to follow the orders of a superior. In this case, they have to travel to villages situated near Narmuthis. It is noteworthy that the motion verb *qtj* "to turn, move in circle" (*EDG*, p. 552.4) is often used (cf. e.g. text A), to suggest the idea of the circular itineraries followed by these persons.

Who were these "wandering" people? And why did they have to travel so frequently to other localities? Several ostraca may shed some light on the matter. One of the tasks of these itinerant travellers was to provide the smaller adjacent villages with materials that probably were difficult to find and could not be producted locally. These goods were exported to the neighbouring villages by the bigger and better supplied temple of Narmuthis. The ritual nature of most of the materials leads us to suppose that they were sent mostly to the little sanctuaries of the villages. Ostracon D may furnish an idea of this kind of text containing lists of goods.

TEXT D (see fig. 12.2b)

OMM ARCH. PISA NO. 4 = GALLO 1989, PP. 109–16, TEXT C

Transcription

[Lines 1–8 omitted]

9. *k.t-md.t wʿ šm nḥḥ r Tš*
10. *wʿ šm] ḥmꜣ r Tš ʿjq šw 10 gʿl*
11. *5 r Tš wʿ šm qmꜣj r Tš k.t-md.t*
12. *ibd III šmw sw wʿ šʿ sw 15 tḥb*
13. *ẖn ḥ.t-ntr r wn hrw r-bnr lwš*
14. *e ʿnḫ gꜣ r (?) bw-ir tj-k tḥb*
15. *wʿ.t ẖr-qlm wʿ.t*
16. *rpj ḏjt ʿn wʿ*
17. *lḥm n ḏt*
18. *ḥtj ḏt (?)*

Translation

[Lines 1–8 omitted]

9. another thing: a little oil for Tosh,
10. [a little] salt for Tosh, ten dry breads and
11. five cakes for Tosh, a little gum for Tosh. Another thing:
12. (from) the first day of Epiphi until the fifteenth, do aspersion rites
13. in the temple to be a day (?) out ; take care
14. of the flower bunch, also, (if ?) you did not perform aspersion rites;
15. an under-garland, some
16. leaves of olive tree. A
17. branch of olive tree,
18. *ḥtj*-plant (?).

Among the transported materials more often mentioned there are gum, castor oil for lamps, salt, votive garlands, eggs, different kinds of bread, cakes, pigeons, tree branches, olive oil, and cloths. Mainly they are objects pertaining to worship, which we know already mostly from Greek papyri (see Lewis 1983a, p. 105 [P. Oxy. 1211 and P. Oxy. 2797]) and from some Demotic documents concerning religious associations (de Cenival 1972a, pp. 16–20).

Some texts refer to the trade of less common goods, such as pigments: arsenic powder, cinnabar, indikon, Synopes-earth, copper powder, and others. One of these texts (publication forthcoming) says that the pigments are to be brought to the village of Ro-senti. We may suppose that these colours were used to paint frescoes, linen, or mummy cartonnages.

The economic nature of these exchanges of goods is still unclear. We do not know yet if the minor sanctuaries bought or simply received these materials from Narmuthis's temple stores. We hope that further studies on this archive will help to solve this question.

Another problem concerns the identity of these travellers and their status. We have seen that they remained in some localities for five days, and in some cases even for ten or fifteen days. Text B shows that the person spent forty days in different villages before coming back to Narmuthis. Consequently, it is clear that the delivery of goods could not be the only purpose of these people. Some ostraca seem to suggest that another task of their visits was to collect taxes and to attend to some local business. But ostraca such as text D reveal that these men were priests, whose degree, unluckily, is unspecified. In lines 12–13, we read that the man has to perform the aspersion rites (*tḥb*) in the temple for a period of fifteen days. It is very likely that the sanctuary meant here is that of the village of Tosh mentioned in the previous lines (9–11). Have we to suppose that the clergy of Narmuthis was also charged to perform the rituals in the sanctuaries of the neighbouring villages? Although rare, this phenomenon is already attested in some zones of Egypt during the Roman period. In Papyrus Oxy. 2782, dated to the second-third centuries A.D., a hierophant orders a priestess of the village of Nesmeimis to go to another village, Sinkepha, to perform the rituals:

> Marcus Aurelios Apollonios, hierophant, to the ritual basket-carrier of [the village of] Nesmeimis, greeting. Please go to [the village of] Sinkepha to the temple of Demeter, to perform the customary sacrifices for our lords the emperors and their victory, for the rise of the Nile and increase of crops, and for favourable conditions of climate. I pray that you fare well (Lewis 1983a, p. 85).

These unusual Demotic texts from Medinet Madi allow us a glance at the everyday life of the priests of an Egyptian temple of Roman period. On the whole, we receive the impression that during the second century A.D. the economy of several sanctuaries in the western area of the Meris of Polemon depended upon the temple of Narmuthis. The content of the Greek ostraca, although not yet sufficiently studied, seems to confirm this point of view (Vogliano 1939, p. 88)[1]. Some of the texts lead us to suppose that the clergy of Narmuthis was not only charged to supply the adjacent minor sanctuaries, but sometimes also to celebrate sacred rituals there.

A LIST OF SOME OF THE TOPONYMS OCCURRING IN THE ARCHIVE OF NARMUTHIS

The villages and little towns mentioned in this archive were situated in the Meris of Polemon, with the exception of two or three villages, which were probably in the Meris of Themistes, close to the boundary with Polemon. Some toponyms occur here for the first time while others, already known from Greek sources, are mentioned for the first time in Demotic in these texts. For these reasons I have thought it useful to give a list of the toponyms which occur more frequently.

I. 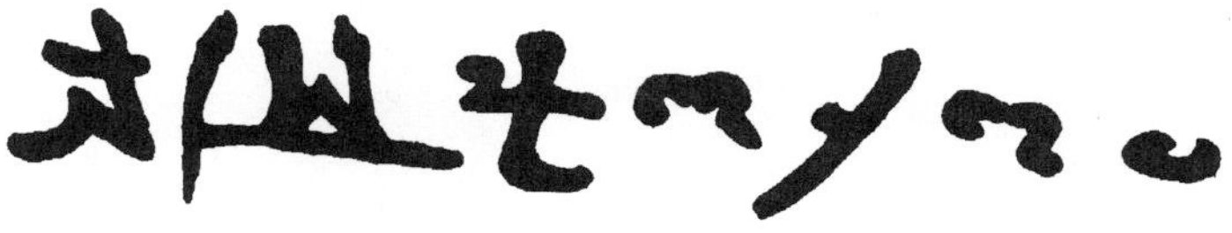 *Pꜣ-glg-Sbk* = Κερκεσοῦχα

A village in the Meris of Polemon (*DGT*, III, pp. 108–09), whose land bordered on that of Ἄρεως κώμη at the southwest (Daris 1984, p. 105).

1. Vogliano wrote, about the duties of the high priest of Narmuthis which are often mentioned by the Greek ostraca: "... d'un document de ces archives il résulterait que le personnage en question avait aussi la juridiction sur les temples de moindre importance de la région et devait en assurer le fonctionnement."

II. 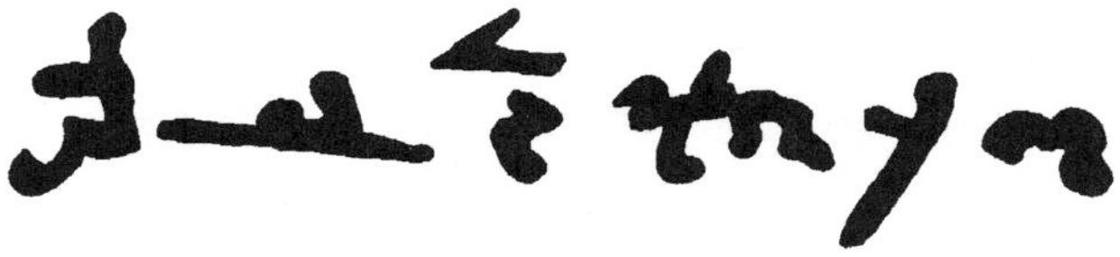 *(Pꜣ-)glg-Tꜣ-wr.t* = Κερκεθοῆρις

A village in the Meris of Polemon, generally identified with Kom Shamsin (*DGT*, III, p. 99). The presence of a προφητὴς Ἄρεως in the village suggests a proximity to Areos kome, where the cult of Ares is attested (*DGT*, I, p. 199)[2].

III.  *Mn-nfr* = Μέμφις

A village of the Meris of Polemon (*DGT*, III, p. 262; Daris 1984, pp. 107 and 119).

IV.  *Qs* = Κῶς ?

The village of *Qs* is mentioned also in other Faiyum papyri: Papyrus Dem. Inv. Sorbonne 539, line 1; Papyrus Dem. Inv. Sorbonne 1208b, line x + 5 (unpublished). On the basis of these occurrences, the toponym  in Papyrus Dem. Lille 29, line 2, also is to be read *Qs*;[3] Papyrus Lille 29 specifies the geographic position of the village: *dmj Sbk Qs ẖn tꜣ dnj.t Tmjsts ḥr ʿt-rsj [Mr]-wr n pꜣ tš ꜣrsjnꜣ*, "the town of Sobek, Qos, in the Meris of Themistes, on the southern edge of the canal of Moeris, in the Nome of Arsinoe." It is noteworthy that the southern edge of cultivations (*ʿt-rsj*) is mentioned in connection with *Qs* also in our text C. In a Greek papyrus of the sixth century A.D., a village named Κῶς is mentioned among other villages close to Narmuthis (Wessely 1904, pp. 97–98; *DGT*, III, p. 174). For this reason, in spite of the lack of more ancient Greek citations, its identification with the Demotic *Qs* might be possible.

V.  *Tꜣ-btn* = probably Τεβέτνυ

A village of the Meris of Polemon, identified with the Arabic village of Defednu (*DGT*, IV, pp. 375–76). For the hieratic writing of 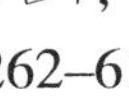, see *HP III*, no. 318. *Tꜣ-btn* is mentioned already in an early Ptolemaic papyrus (262–61 B.C.), where its name is written  (Papyrus Dem. Berlin 13637, lines 9 and 23; Cheshire 1986, p. 36). As the toponym seems to preserve its peculiar writing intact until the Roman period, there is no strict reason to consider it an early occurrence of the name of Tebtunis, as has been done (Cheshire 1986, pp. 36–39); the Demotic name of this town, *Tꜣ-nb-Tn* or *Tꜣ-nb-Tꜣ-Tn*, differs totally from

2. The cult of the "megistos theos Ares" in this village is attested by Papyrus Tebtunis III, 926.

3. Being read *Ps*, this toponym has been wrongly identified with the Greek village of Πισαί. See Sottas 1921, pp. 58 and 64 (note 2) which is equivalent to de Cenival 1972a, pp. 3 and 13–14 (notes 2 and 4).

our toponym, and had been written in its correct form since the third century B.C. Therefore, we could simply suppose that *Tꜣ-btn* indicates a different locality. Actually, a big village called Τεβέτνυ in the south of the Meris of Polemon is mentioned in Greek papyri from 255–54 B.C. (Daris 1984, p. 103, note 6 and following). Its Demotic name has never been found, but it must have had one, because the Greek form Τεβέτνυ clearly reveals an Egyptian origin, and *Tꜣ-btn* seems to correspond exactly to the spelling of the Greek name.

VI.  *Pꜣ-sj* = Πτολεμαὶς Μελισσουργῶν ?

With the scribal variant , this village is mentioned also in some other papyri from the Faiyum: Papyrus Dem. Inv. Sorbonne 1279a, recto, col. II, line 5 (unpublished) and Papyrus Dem. Inv. Sorbonne 575, recto, line 16 (unpublished). Probably the village was situated in the southwest of the Meris of Polemon, close to that of Themistes. We already know of two other Egyptian towns with this name: the first one is Πτολεμαὶς ἡ Ἑρμείου, in the nome of Thebes, whose Demotic name is just *Pꜣ-sj* (Gardiner 1947, pp. 39*–40*). A second *Pꜣ-sj* is quoted in an autobiographical hieroglyphic text, where the toponym refers to a fortified town in Syria (*pꜣ tꜣ n Ḫꜣr*) whose Greek name was Ptolemais (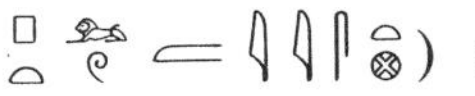) and which is probably to be identified with Ptolemais-Akko (Quaegebeur 1989, pp. 94–95 [column 2 of text] and pp. 105–07). The fact that in both cases the Egyptian toponym *Pꜣ-sj* refers to towns called Ptolemais in Greek is quite curious indeed, and leads us to wonder if we have to suppose a correspondence with a Ptolemais also as far as our *Pꜣ-sj* of the Faiyum is concerned. In this case, the Demotic toponym might refer to Ptolemais Melissourgon, "Ptolemais of the bee-keepers," which seems to be the only Ptolemais in the Meris of Polemon (Daris 1984, p. 101). The Greek papyri often quote its name close to those of Tebetnu and Kerkesoukha (Daris 1984, pp. 105–06), villages which are also recorded in our ostraca — cf. nos. I and V. For the toponym *Pꜣ-sj* an etymology from the word *sꜣw* "beam" has been suggested recently (Quaegebeur 1989, p. 105); the term could refer to the wooden docks built by the Ptolemaic kings on the shore near their foundations (Quaegebeur 1989).

VII.  *Rʿ-snt*

The first part of this toponym has a very unusual paleographic shape. What I suggest is to consider the group  a writing of the prefix *rʿ*- "act of,"[4] here followed by the ʿain  as phonetic complement, and by the abstract determinative .[5] The entire name, then,

4. Cf. *EDG*, p. 242, where some similar Roman writings of the first sign are recorded.

5. The word *rꜣ*, written  in our ostraca, could have influenced this writing of the prefix *rʿ*- because of its similar pronunciation. For *rꜣ*, cf. Gallo, 1989, text C, line 8 and the note on p.114.

might be transcribed in hieroglyphs as follows: . If my interpretation is right, the toponym should signify "Action of founding," and could be identified with the Faiyum locality of 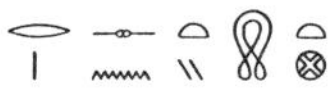 mentioned in several hieroglyphic texts (Yoyotte 1962b, pp. 119–21).[6] The geographical position of *Rꜣ/Rʿ-snt* in the Faiyum becomes quite clear now from the contents of our archive. Ro-senti occupies a very pre-eminent position with regard to Narmuthis: in our archive this toponym is the most frequently mentioned, more than Narmuthis itself; the priests went so often to Ro-senti to bring or to take away goods from there, that, no doubt, we have to place Ro-senti in the immediate neighborhood of Narmuthis, maybe at only a few hundred meters from the temple; the possibility that this name indicates an ancient district of the town cannot be excluded. Other evidence seems to confirm the proximity of *Rꜣ/Rʿ-snt* to Narmuthis. The so-called "Book of the Fayum," dated to the Roman period, presents *Rꜣ-snt* as a place sacred to the god Thot (Yoyotte 1962b, p. 120); and the cult of Thot-Ibis is actually attested in the neighbourhood of Narmuthis by the Greek papyri, which repeatedly quote the name of a large sanctuary of Ibis-Thot, Ἰβιῶν εἰκοσιπενταρούρων, beside the name of Narmuthis (Wessely 1904, pp. 75–77).[7] Also, frescoes and graffiti representing ἰβιοβοσκοί have been found in a chapel at Kom Madi, only a few thousand meters from Narmuthis (Bresciani 1980, pls. XVIII–XIX).

VIII. 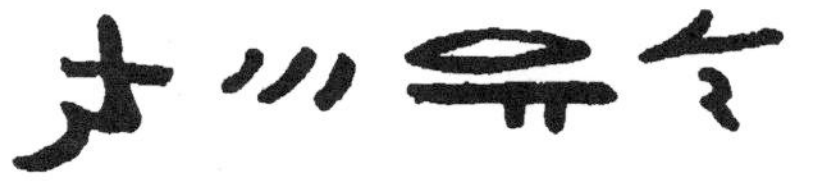 *Tꜣ-rsj*

Several places called *Tꜣ-rsj(t)* are known all over Egypt. The toponym, well studied in its hieroglyphic and Demotic occurrences, means literally "the watch-tower" (Yoyotte 1958, p. 417; Vleeming 1987, pp. 157–59).[8] Last year Professor Yoyotte reconsidered this toponym; in his opinion *Tꜣ-rsj(t)* might refer to the posts of police placed on the boundaries that separated one nome or administrative district from another. The ancient Egyptian *Tꜣ-rsj(t)* survived in Arabic toponymy as ترسا (Tirsa; seeYoyotte 1972a, pp. 7–8). A village called Tirsa still exists in the Faiyum on the road between Sennuris and Sanhur; of course, it is too distant to be identified with the *Tꜣ-rsj* mentioned in the ostraca. The geographical position of this Tirsa, situated exactly on the ancient boundary line between the Meris of Themistes and that of Herakleides, seems to confirm Yoyotte's hypothesis. Consequently, the *Tꜣ-rsj* quoted in our archive might refer to the guard post placed on the boundary between the Meris of Polemon and Meris of Themistes, to which Narmuthis was very near.

6. Our interpretation of the first group as *rʿ-* "act of," agrees with Yoyotte's intuition, cf. p.120, note (4): "A l'origine Rꜣ-snty comme d'autre toponymes en rꜣ a pu etre un terme d'acception générale formé à partir du prefixe rꜣ- (ZÄS 77, 3–7): 'le fait de fonder', 'la fondation par excellence.'"

7. The *status quaestionis* on this Ibion and its location has been summarized in Bernand 1981b, p. 69–70.

8. For a new Demotic occurrence in P. Champollion 9, line 3, see Devauchelle 1988, p. 13 (the author reads *tꜣ rb.t*).

IX.  *Tš*

In our texts the toponym Tosh occurs very often in the lists mentioning other villages near Narmuthis. The meaning of "nome" is therefore unlikely in these contexts, also because *Tš* is never preceded by the article *pꜣ* as it should be. It is known that the hieroglyphic toponym  could indicate not only the Faiyum basin itself, but also its capital, the town of Crocodilopolis (Yoyotte 1962b, pp. 104, 106–07). Such identification cannot be excluded completely, although it seems hardly likely. As all of the villages quoted together with Tosh are in the south of the Faiyum, Crocodilopolis seems to be quite out of the route; on the other hand, the quantity and quality of the goods taken to *Tš* (e.g. see text D) are a quite meagre tribute for the capital of the nome. For these reasons I presume that Tosh is the name of a village situated somewhere in the southwest of the Meris of Polemon (Gallo 1989, pp. 114–15), where the priests of Narmuthis also had to perform sacred rituals.

X. 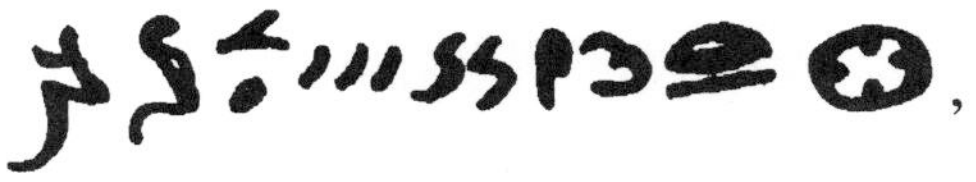, var. 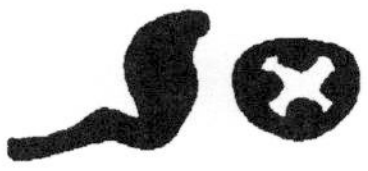 *Niw.t-Rnmwtj.t* = Ναρμοῦθις

Literally, this toponym translates as "the town of the goddess Renenutet." We do not know if this is the original form of the town's name. Undoubtedly, in this case the hieroglyphic ⊗ corresponds to the Greek spelling Να-. But Greek toponyms beginning with Να- derive in general from the plural of the Egyptian possessive article *nꜣ(j/w)*, e.g. Ναθώ = *Nꜣj-tꜣ-ḥwt* "Those of the temple"; Ναύκρατις = *Nꜣ(j)-Krṯ* "Those of Krt"; Τσενενή = *Tꜣ-st-nꜣj-Niwt* "The place of those of Thebes"; etc.[9] For this reason *Niw.t-Rnmwtj.t* might be a late reinterpretation of a more ancient form *Nꜣj-Rnn.t* "Those of the goddess Renenutet" (Spiegelberg 1903a, p. 87), where  could have been replaced by ⊗ because of its similar pronunciation.[10] The case of Naukratis, literally "Those of Krt," supports this hypothesis: since the Twenty-sixth dynasty its name always has been written correctly by means of the possessive article *nꜣj(w)*, in hieroglyphic as well as in Demotic;[11] but in the Naucratis Stele (Thirtieth dynasty) we find the form 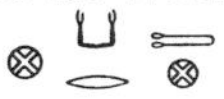, which reveals the learned interpretation of a hierogrammateus and is to be translated "The town of Krt" (Stele Cairo 34002, line 13; for bibliographic notes, cf. Lichtheim 1976, pp. 139–46).

9. For the particle *nꜣj (w)* in toponymic expressions, cf. Spiegelberg 1918a, p. 110, 1903a, pp. 86–88; for Natho, cf. *LÄ* IV, col. 354; for Naukratis, cf. *LÄ* IV, cols. 360–61; for Tsenenè, cf. Meeks 1972, p. 113, note 213.

10. The exact phonetic value of the hieroglyphic ⊗ is uncertain, cf. *Wb*, II, p. 210. In Coptic *njw.t* gave ne- as well as the possessive article *nꜣj(w)*, cf. *KHwb*, p. 118; it is noteworthy that in some late Demotic papyri *njw.t* is often written as *njꜣ/nꜣj*, a word that usually means "time," Coptic nei, cf. M. Smith 1987, p. 66.

11. A plate of the occurrences of Naucratis' name is in de Meulenaere 1951, p. 101. The transcription of P. Dem. Cairo 31169, line 26, is to be corrected: the toponym is written 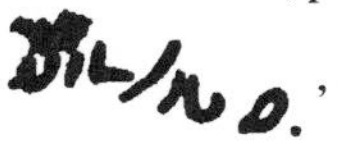, as well as in P. Dem. Louvre E. 3266.7 , cf. de Cenival 1972b, pl. VIII and pp. 23, 40 (the author reads *dmḏ Krḏ*). In both cases, the first sign of the word does not represent *njw.t*, but the plural possessive article *nꜣj(w)* in its early form, cf. *EDG*, p. 203.

The scribes of Narmuthis refer to some villages using "fictitious" toponyms instead of their real Demotic or Greek name; this renders their identification more difficult. Such "fictitious" toponyms are formed by the hieroglyph *Njw.t* plus the name of the foremost divinity of the meant locality (another example is that of *Niwt-Imn*, cf. Gauthier, DG III, p. 76). They clearly reflect the influence of Narmuthis' name. The use of *Njw.t* seems to suggest that these settlements were quite big. They are:

XI.  *Niw.t-Sbk*, "The town of the god Sobek"

As the cult of Sobek is attested everywhere in the Faiyum, it is difficult to decide with certainty which place is meant here. It could refer to the capital of the Faiyum, Greek Κροκοδείλων πόλις, but also to a locality closer to Narmuthis, as Kerkesouka or Tebtunis.

XII.  *Niw.t-Nj.t* "The town of the goddess Neith"

As mother of Sobek, Neith was worshipped everywhere in the Faiyum. As this goddess is often identified with Thoeris by the Egyptians and with Athena by the Greeks (Quaegebeur, Clarysse, and van Maele 1985, pp. 217–32), *Niw.t-Nj.t* could refer to the big village of Kerkethoueris, quoted elsewhere in this archive (cf. toponym no. II), or to that of 'Αθηνᾶς κώμη, situated in the Meris of Themistes, but near to the boundary with Polemon.[12]

XIII.  *Niw.t-Stẖ* (?)

This obscure locality is represented by means of a donkey's head. While the other toponyms are mentioned in several texts, this one occurs only once in a school text (*ODN*, text no. 17). It could have been invented by the student himself in doing the exercise, but in

12. *DGT* I, p. 30. We know very little about gods and cults in Athenas kome. At the moment only a private cult of Isis is attested there, cf. Rübsam 1974, p. 61. Therefore it is impossible to know exactly if the village derived its name from the Alexandrian Demotic of Athenieus or from the name of the goddess Athena. However, the two possibilities do not exclude each other necessarily. The foremost god of the village of Areos kome, whose name might also derive from Alexandrian Demotic (cf. Fraser 1972, p. 44), was actually Ares, see below, note 13. In our case, therefore, we cannot exclude completely that *Niw.t-Nj.t* is a learned Egyptian reinterpretation of the Greek toponym Athenas kome. For the real Demotic name of Athenas kome (*Nꜣj-ꜥ-Tmtjs* or *Pꜣ-ꜥ-Tmtjs*) see now Clarysse 1987b.

his mind the toponym could refer to a real village all the same. In the Roman period, often the ass represents the god Seth; yet we do not have any evidence for the cult of Seth in the Faiyum. Are we to suppose that the toponym refers, less strictly, to a village where a god having an aggressive character was worshipped? The war god, Ares, actually was venerated in the village of Areos kome, nearby Narmuthis.[13] We know, however, that in the *interpraetatio graeca* Ares corresponds to the Egyptian god Onuris-Shu (cf. Wilcken, UPZ no. 81), a deity who has never been found associated with the god Seth in Egyptian texts.

13. *DGT* I, p. 199. The cult of the *megistos theos Ares* in this village is attested by Papyrus Tebtunis III, 926.

a

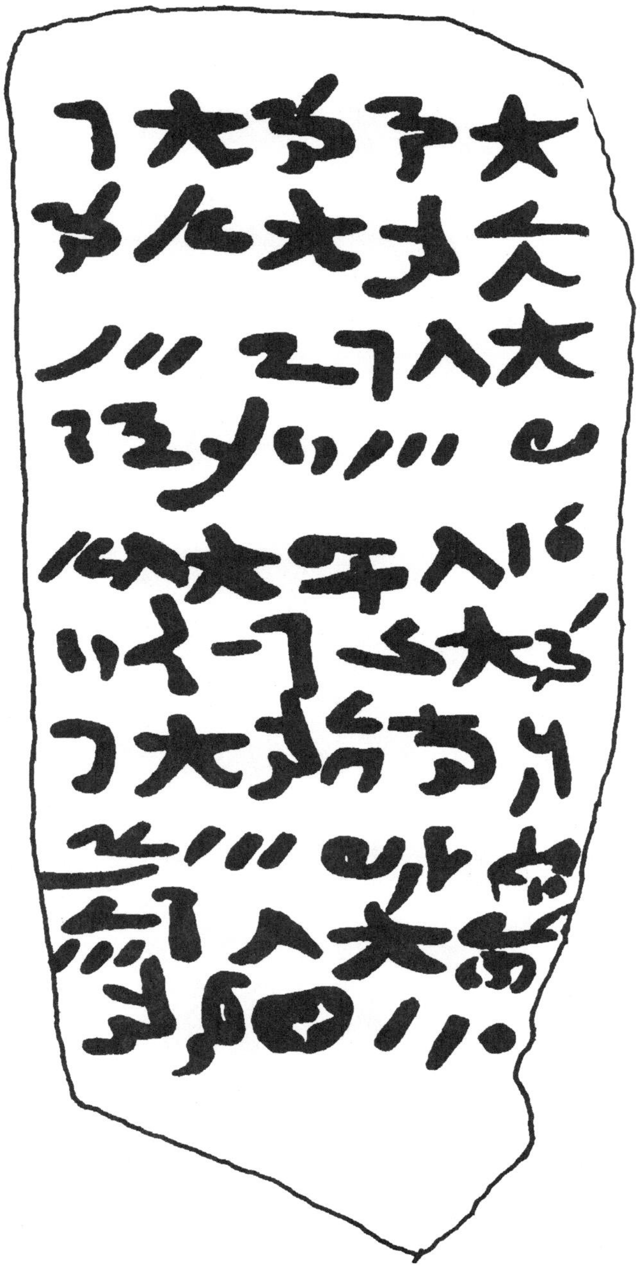

b

Figure 12.1. Facsimile Drawings of Demotic Ostraca: (*a*) Text A, OMM Vogliano no. 431 = *ODN*, Text no. 3; (*b*) Text B, OMM Vogliano no. 661 = OMM Arch. Pisa no. 821.

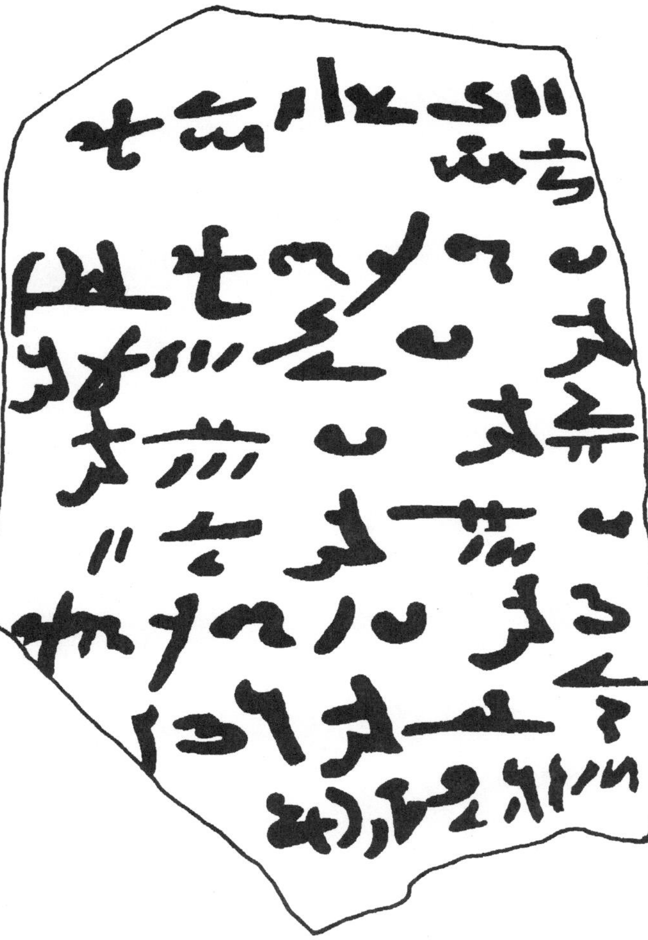

a

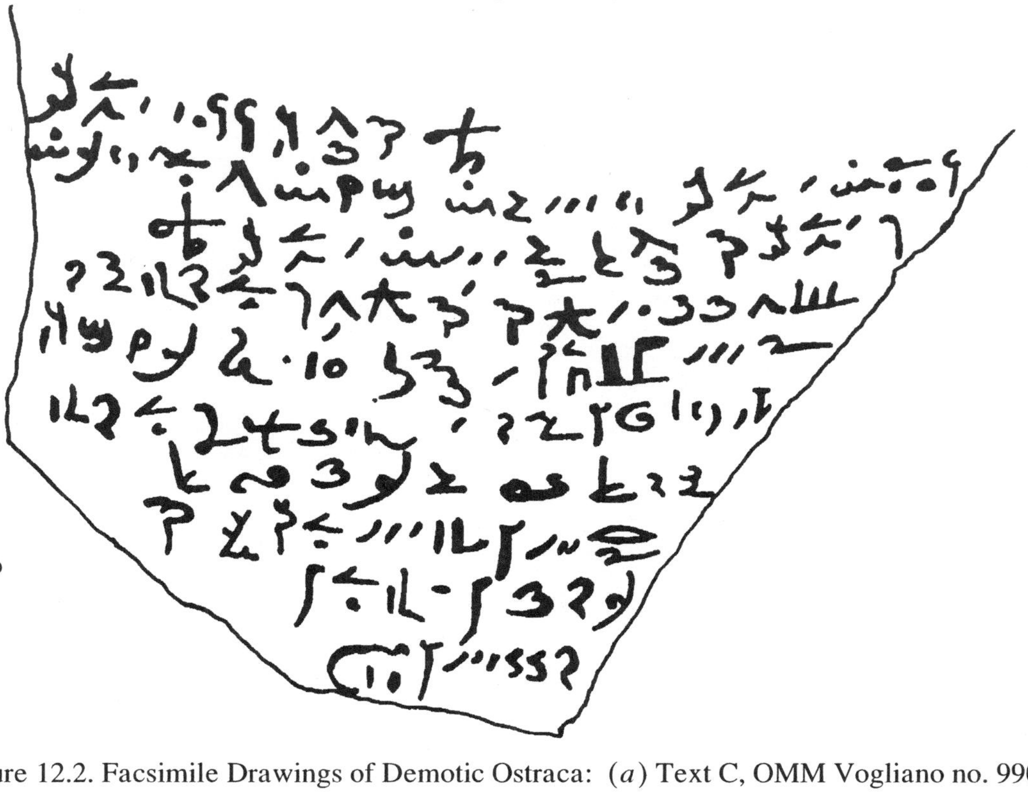

b

Figure 12.2. Facsimile Drawings of Demotic Ostraca: (*a*) Text C, OMM Vogliano no. 990; (*b*) Text D, OMM Arch. Pisa no. 4 = Gallo 1989, pp. 109–16, Text C

CHAPTER 13

EGYPTIANS, GREEKS, ROMANS, *ARABES*, AND *IOUDAIOI* IN THE FIRST CENTURY A.D. TAX ARCHIVE FROM PHILADELPHIA: P. MICH. INV. 880 RECTO AND *P. PRINC.* III 152 REVISED

ANN ELLIS HANSON
Department of Classical Studies, The University of Michigan

During the reigns of Augustus and his Julio-Claudian successors the city of Alexandria not only retained its economic position as the leading emporium of the eastern Mediterranean, but also its political dominance over Egypt, for it was administrative center of the newly constituted Roman province.[1] In a suburb of Alexandria, Juliopolis/Nikopolis, lay the principal Roman military encampment, home to three legions until 23 A.D. when the force was reduced to two legions and support troops (cf. Hanson 1980a and 1980b). The Roman conquerors overlaid a new stratum on the ethnically diverse populations that characterized Alexandria from its inception. Ethno-cultural considerations were important determiners for Augustus and his Julio-Claudian successors, when they went about conferring political and economic privileges in Alexandria and throughout the province. As the dominant elite, Roman citizens were everywhere exempt from the payment of the poll tax (λαογραφία) and other capitation taxes (χωματικόν and ὑική), levied on males between the ages of fourteen and sixty-two.[2] The next, most favored group within the Roman tax structure were the citizens of the so-called Greek cities—Alexandria, Naukratis in the Delta, and Ptolemais in Upper Egypt, for they too enjoyed the exemption from the poll tax, as well as the privilege of continuing to use Greek civic institutions. Alexandrian citizens not only bore Greek names and spoke the Greek language, but they also claimed that education in the Greek gymnasium and the holding of prestigious magistracies in the *polis* were traditional in their families. Less privileged in the Roman tax structure were those with metropolite citizenship.[3] Romans assessed these citizens of the district capitals, or *metropoleis*, at a half-rate for capitation taxes and yet, at the same time, they extended to them many of the same Greek civic institutions that had under the Ptolemies been reserved for the so-called Greek cities. By so doing, the Romans were not only expressing their own approval of life in cities, but they were also acknowledging the extent to which the Greek settlers who had flocked into the countryside in the third century B.C., to live alongside native Egyptians, had, in the course of time, successfully fused to produce a city-dwelling and bicultural

1. For a convenient summary, see Bowman 1986, pp. 21–43; for a more complete bibliography, see *passim* in Geraci 1983.
2. Still valid is the overview by Wallace 1938a, pp. 96–134, 140–45.
3. See the description of metropolitan citizens in Lewis 1983a, pp. 36–64.

population. Egyptians acquired Greekness to the extent that personal names and language were no longer dependable distinguishers between Egyptians and Greeks by the beginning of the second century B.C. (*WChres.*, no. 50, pp. 78–79), and immigrant Greeks were being transformed by their Egyptian experiences, as many took Egyptian wives and participated in the worship of Egyptian cults.[4]

Augustus and his Julio-Claudian successors did not, however, privilege all inhabitants of Alexandria and the Greek cities, for they denied exemptions from capitation taxes to the non-Greek *politeumata*, taxing these groups at the highest rate. That is, members of the "foreign" *politeumata* paid the poll tax at a rate that was paid by Egyptian peasants, whether those peasants lived in their villages, or had migrated to the *metropolis* or to Alexandria. As an institution, the Ptolemaic *politeuma* provided non-Greeks with a means to maintain a degree of separateness while living within a Greek city, for the *politeumata* fostered socioreligious continuity and guaranteed some degree of juridical and corporate independence (cf. Thompson Crawford 1984, pp. 1069–75). One of the oldest and largest *politeuma* in early Roman Alexandria was that of the Jews, and we learn much about the violence that Romans encountered when Alexandrian citizens attacked the Jews who also inhabited the capital.[5] We can view these outbreaks in the Julio-Claudian period from contemporary sources that present the Jewish, Greek and Greco-Egyptian, and Roman viewpoints—in, for example, Philo Judaeus and Flavius Josephus, the earlier chapters of the *Acta Alexandrinorum*, papyri from Abusir el Melek, as well as the Emperor Claudius' letter in response to an embassy of Alexandrian Greeks to his court in Rome. Ethnic tensions energized and also enervated daily life in the grand city, as groups clashed and then withdrew from open confrontations, only to clash again, when divisive issues offered an opportunity.

I. THE GRECO-EGYPTIAN PEASANTS OF PHILADELPHIA

In contrast to the citizens of Alexandria and other city-dwellers, the peasant populations of the *chorá* seem to present a more placid and homogeneous face in the Augustan and Julio-Claudian periods. The majority of those who inhabited the villages and countryside of the Faiyum were peasants, and they paid capitation taxes to their Roman overlords at the highest rate. Roman rulers no doubt preferred to assume that a stable and stodgy homogeneity characterized taxpaying peasants, for such a view simplified their exploitation of the province. The trained eyes of Faiyum villagers, however, were able to see with considerable clarity the gaps that separated the elite from the poorer residents in each and every village. Money and power characterized the village elite at Philadelphia and their acquisitive habits awakened in them a degree of sympathy for their new Roman masters, as providing an atmosphere in which their own agricultural efforts and their money-lending flourished.[6] To be sure, village differed from village, and the veneer of Hellenism in Julio-Claudian Philadelphia was more pronounced than, for example, at the more affirmedly Egyptian Soknopaiou Nesos with its priestly elite (D. Samuel 1981, pp. 389–403). At Philadelphia the choice of an Egyptian or a Greek name was in the Julio-Claudian period a matter of personal preference or family tradition, rather than a key to professional and financial advancement. Thus,

4. See, e.g., Pomeroy 1984, pp. 103–24 (Apollonia alias Senmonthis, wife of Dryton); D. Thompson 1988, pp. 212–65 (the Sarapieion archive); and von Staden 1989, pp. 26–31 (on the "frontier" environment of Alexandria that made it possible to set aside conventions of the city-states in "old Greece").

5. The bibliography on the Jewish community of Alexandria is deservedly immense; I have relied here for discussions of anti-Semitism in Kasher 1985 and *CPJ* I–III. Cf. also Saddington 1975, pp. 112–37 and Foraboschi 1988, pp. 807–40.

6. This was the conclusion I drew in my "Village Officials at Philadelphia: a Model of Romanization in the Julio-Claudian Period," 1989b, pp. 428–40.

under the Emperor Claudius, Horion, son of Petosiris, served as collector of capitation taxes, as one of the *praktores argyrikôn*, along with two men with quite Greek names—Maron, son of Pylades, and Nemesion, son of Zoïlos.[7] The *praktores argyrikôn* not only collected capitation taxes, but they were themselves also peasant taxpayers, assessed capitation taxes at the highest level; their names appear on the tax rolls. At other times, however, their names also appeared on lists of those who were exempt from one or more capitation taxes for a specific year, presumably a privilege facilitated by their public service as tax collectors and compilers of the taxing lists.[8]

Insofar as the village elite can be identified from private papers in the tax archive, that elite mirrored the multiculturalism of Alexandria. Two offices in the village were particularly important in raising the tax levies for Rome: that of the *komogrammateus*, or village scribe, who dealt with the census declarations at the local level and who compiled the lists of those liable to capitation taxes and other public duties; and that of the *praktores argyrikôn* who collected the moneys. A letter that the *komogrammateus* of Philadelphia, Herakleides, wrote to Nemesion the *praktor* reveals that the two men cooperated closely with one another, as Herakleides instructed Nemesion to take care of the interests of a certain group of men during his own absence from the village.[9] The implication of Herakleides' concern is that these were influential men in the life of the village. The list includes both Nikanor the citizen, a man with a Greek name and metropolitan privileges, and Nepheros the bull-burier, a man with an Egyptian name and occupation. The *praktor* Nemesion also shared business interests with men bearing the Romanized names Lucius and Longinus.[10] The *tria nomina* that marked Roman citizens occur in the archive only when Nemesion's superiors in the Roman bureaucracy were being addressed.[11] Lucius and Longinus, who bear only a praenomen or a cognomen, seem to be villagers that have acquired a veneer of Romanization through contact with the troops of occupation—such as had done the men who appear on lists of ἐϲτρατευμένοι.[12] These were not soldiers, or even sailors in the fleet, since the men's names remained on the tax rolls. They seem rather to have supplied support services to the Romans at Juliopolis/Nikopolis, and their adoption of Roman names perhaps replayed earlier times, when Egyptians adopted Greek names and habits in the century that followed the coming of Alexander and his Macedonians.

The language of both the public and private documents in the tax archive is Greek. Many of the documents were prepared by or were addressed to one of the *praktores*, Nemesion, son of Zoïlos. Nemesion used the Greek language not only for his public business, but also for his private correspondence. If he had a wife, her name was probably Thermouthis, and she wrote to him in crude and misspelled Greek about family and business matters, keeping him abreast of local

7. For these men in documents from the archive already published, see, e.g., *P. Gen* 2.91.7 and 14, *P. Mich.* 10.582.1 (+ *BL* 7, p. 114) and 4.

8. See e.g. an exemption from dike tax for Maron and Nemesion in P. Mich. inv. 619v.28–29.

9. *SB* 14.12143 and summarized in Hanson 1989b, pp. 429–32.

10. For Lucius, see *SB* 14.11585 and in the *Appendix* below, P. Mich. inv. 880r.1 and 32 and *P. Princ*. 3.152.1, revised; for Longinus, see P. Mich. inv. 615. Men with similar Romanized names (but not the Roman *tria nomina*) also appeared in contemporary papers of the record office in another Faiyum village, Tebtunis: Maximos, son of Diodoros alias Papontos (*P. Mich.* V 273.1), Pompeios, son of Patron alias Primos (*P. Mich.* V 272.12).

11. E.g. *SB* 4.7461, letter of introduction from Dionysodoros, strategos of the Herakleides division of the Arsinoite nome, to his counterpart in the Herakleiopolite nome, Gaius Julius Iollas; and *SB* 4.7462, a petition Nemesion and five other *praktores* of neighboring villages addressed to the prefect Tiberius Claudius Balbillus.

12. Among the published texts, see *P. Ryl.* 4.595.114 (as parallel texts from the archive show, ἐϲτρατευμένοι is to be read, not ἐϲτραγευμένοι).

developments, including the activities of Lucius.[13] What is hard to determine is whether or not Nemesion could read or write the native Egyptian language. Only one document in the archive contains Demotic—fourteen much effaced lines on the verso of P. Col. inv. 90 that are without apparent connection to the text on the recto. On the recto is a Greek text, a sworn deed of surety, whereby a villager agrees to go bail for Nemesion for debts incurred by his father and mother. Nothing suggests, however, that Nemesion, or his colleagues, either wrote the fourteen lines of Demotic, or would have been able to read them, and the poor state of preservation of these lines (when compared to the well-preserved text on the recto) makes it likely that someone had tried to erase the Demotic lines. Evidence that Nemesion at least spoke Egyptian comes instead from accounts in the archive that also involve Lucius (for the texts, see the *Appendix* below). In late spring A.D. 56 an account shows that sixty-four drachmae were paid "for the price of two arourae of hay" to "Theon the farmer" and twelve additional drachmae for cutting the hay (880r.24–25). Some five years later in another account, written by Nemesion himself,[14] moneys are again paid to a certain Theon for cutting hay (*P. Princ* 3.152.31 and cf. 4), but this time Theon is styled *tabourios*, instead of *geôrgos. Tabourios* is otherwise unknown, either as a Greek name or a Greek denominative. *Tabourios* may, however, represent a Greek formation on the Semitic root *tbn* meaning "hay" or "straw," intended by Nemesion in the meaning "hay man" and inserted by him in his document instead of "farmer." No certain example of *tbn* or *tbr* in the meaning "hay" has been found in an Egyptian context; at the same time, a plant *tbr* has occurred, and although it is not the usual word for "hay," its meaning is not determined by context—thus making the derivation of *tabourios* from an Egyptian root possible.[15] If Nemesion could play with the language, giving the Semitic root (*tbn*/*tbr*) Greek formation as *tabourios* ("hay man"), the implication may well be that he spoke it, even if he failed to write Demotic in his public and private papers.[16]

To belong to the village elite of Philadelphia in Julio-Claudian times was to speak Greek and to be conversant with things Roman and with Roman acquisitive habits.

II. *ARABES* AND *IOUDAIOI* IN THE PHILADELPHIA TAX ARCHIVE

The site of Philadelphia was previously unoccupied, and the village was laid out in accordance with Hellenistic grid-patterns for city-planning (Viereck 1928, p. 7; cf. also E. Bernand 1975, pp. 196–97). Its position at the northeast corner of the Faiyum made it an important point of entry into this rich agricultural district; in the Roman period there was a customhouse in the village for collecting internal customs duties.[17] Philadelphia's proximity to the Nile nurtured its connection with localities to the north and with Alexandria, as well as diversified the village's economic

13. The letter of Thermouthis to Nemesion (*SB* 14.11585) is dated 7 July A.D. 59. The relationship between the two is not specified in the letter, but the first editor, Professor Herbert C. Youtie, concluded that Thermouthis was probably either the sister or wife of Nemesion.

14. For other texts in the archive written by the hand of Nemesion, see below on *P. Lond.* 6.1912, Claudius' letter to the Alexandrians, and also on *P. Princ.* I 13, below, note 30.

15. I thank Professor Bernard Lewis and Dr. Robert K. Ritner for advice on the matter: for the Semitic root *tbn*, see *JD* pp. 1644–45; for *tbr* as a plant, see Reymond 1976, col. 1/19—although Dr. Ritner assures me that the suggested translation "clematis" is most unlikely.

16. For an example of similar activity by a scribe writing accounts, cf. Youtie 1970, pp. 545–51.

17. Fifty-one receipts are known from the customhouse at Philadelphia, out of a total of ca. 900—or 5.6% of the receipts in Sijpesteijn 1987, pp. 102–43. Receipts for items exported from the village greatly outnumber receipts for items imported, and the exports included cereal grains, legumes, fodder, wood, and dates.

prospects.[18] The Zenon archive gives us a vivid picture of the village soon after its foundation, and the population of Philadelphia, as it appeared in the letters, consisted largely of immigrant Greeks, marked by their Hellenic names and their ethnic designations, and native Egyptians, whose names, even if transliterated into Greek characters, reflected their Egyptian language and their Egyptian origins. Zenon and his correspondents mention a large number of geographical places and the ethnic designations they employ span the Mediterranean from "Tarantine" and "Sicelot" in the west to "Arabic" or "Arabian" and "Indian" in the east. The geographical distribution of the ethnics also reflects Zenon's personal ties to the area around his hometown of Kaunos in southwestern Asia Minor and his business activities in Syria and Palestine on behalf of his employer Apollonios (see Pestman et al. 1981, Index XIIIA–D, pp. 477–509). The wide variety of geographical names employed in the Zenon letters also testifies to a lively interest in origins of peoples and commodities. It is not surprising that this diversity is lacking in the Julio-Claudian tax archive. The ethnics that are employed in these public tax registers, however, are either ones that designate villages within Egypt from which taxpaying peasants, currently resident in Philadelphia, originated,[19] or they are the designation *Arabs* (Ἄραψ); in the private papers of the tax archive, the letters and private accounts, there is also *Ioudaios*.

The *Arabes* of the Zenon archive derived their name from the eastern desert on the left bank of the Nile. The entire desert area was known as "Arabia,"[20] while the nome "Arabia" lay in the north part of this eastern desert, south of Pelusium (Bowersock 1983, pp. 144–47). These *Arabes* were apparently Semites in origin, although the names of *Arabes* in the Zenon corpus are either Greek or Egyptian (Boswinkel 1983, p. 35). The *Arabes* of the Julio-Claudian tax archive paid capitation taxes at the highest level and they were registered for tax purposes together with the other peasants of Philadelphia, for the village was their *idia*.[21] Their names are, for the most part, Greco-Egyptian, although Ἰώϲηποϲ, the father of Apelles (line 2), points to a Semitic origin (cf. *Iudaeus Apella* at Horace, *Satires* 1.5.100). This list of *Arabes*, a γραφὴ Ἀράβων, seems to parallel other lists compiled by the tax office of weavers (γέρδιοι), greengrocers (καρπῶναι), and other professions whose socioeconomic functions were of interest to the Roman government.[22] Some of the *Arabes* mentioned in the Zenon archive performed guard duties, and ἀραβοτοξόται performed such functions on both sides of the Nile from the early Ptolemaic period into the Byzantine times (e.g. *P. Hamb.* 3.225.33 and 39; *P. Harris* 2.200.3). The *Arabes* associated with Philadelphia in the days of

18. For the early Ptolemaic period, see Clarysse 1980, pp. 91–122, and for the Augustan period, Hanson 1984b, pp. 77–87. The tax archive paints a similar picture of dealings with localities in the Memphite nome and northward to Alexandria in the Julio-Claudian period. The weavers of Philadelphia figure frequently in the archive, and see also *P. Phil.* 1.

19. E.g. *P. Corn.* I 23a, a text that now joins P. Gen. inv. 221.

20. Strabo 17.803 (ἡ δὲ μεταξὺ τοῦ Νείλου καὶ τοῦ Ἀραβίου κόλπου Ἀραβία μέν ἐϲτι ...); for references in the papyri to both the area and the nome, see Abd-El-Ghany 1989, pp. 233–42, especially p. 235 and notes 15–16. See also *P. Köln* 2.107.6 and the note *ad loc.*

21. Cf. *P. Mich.* 12.638 (+ *BL* 7, p. 116 and Shelton 1978, pp. 283–86). Contrary to what is said in the *ed. prin.*, the text is a list of *Arabes*, registered for tax purposes at Philadelphia; the text is to be dated to the reign of Claudius on prosopographical grounds. I offer corrections to that text in lines 4, 5, 12, and 18: γραφὴ Ἀράβω(ν) / Ἀπελλῆ(ϲ) Ἰωϲήπο(υ) / Ἄγρων Πουώρε̣ω̣(ϲ) / (4) Ἀπολλώ(νιοϲ) Μύϲθ(ου) (δρ.) η / Παϲίων Ἀπολλω(νίου) / Ἕλλη(ν) Σαμβ(ᾶτοϲ) / Ἕλλην Ἁρφαή(ϲιοϲ) / (8) Ἄλκιμο(ϲ) Ἁρφαή(ϲιοϲ) / Πανετβ(εὺϲ) ἄλλο(ϲ) / Νεκφερῶ(ϲ) Πετεϲούχ(ου) / Χαιρή(μων) Ἁρφαή(ϲιοϲ) / (12) Σαμβ(ᾶϲ) Φάϲ̣ι̣το(ϲ) / Ἕκτωρ ἀδελφό(ϲ) / Ἕκτωρ Πανετβ(εύιοϲ) / Σαμβ(ᾶϲ) Ἕκτωρο(ϲ) / (16) Ὧροϲ Ὡρίωνο(ϲ) / Μύϲθ(αϲ) ἄλλο(ϲ) / Ἡρακλ(ῆϲ) (ὁμοίωϲ) Ἶβιϲ / Ἁτρῆϲ ὃϲ κ(αὶ) Διδυμᾶ̣τ̣(οϲ) / (20) Νεμε̣ϲ̣ίων Πανετβ(εύιοϲ).

22. Cf. e.g. *Arabes* in the rubrics of an alphabetical year ledger for A.D. 39/40, P. Mich. inv. 876 recto.44–51: Ἁρφαῆϲιϲ Μύϲθου Ἄραβο(ϲ) Ἄραψ ἀπολ(ύϲιμοϲ) / (45) Ἀπολλῶνιϲ Μύϲθου Ἄραβο(ϲ) .... / (49) Ἀπέλληϲ Ἰωϲήπου Ἄραβο(ϲ) / (51) Ἁρφαῆϲιϲ Ἕλληνοϲ Ἄραβοϲ ἀπολ(ύϲιμοϲ).

Zenon, however, were more often concerned with flocks of sheep and goats (Boswinkel 1983, pp. 36–37), and the same business interests may have occupied the Julio-Claudian *Arabes* of Philadelphia, although the notations and lists made by the tax bureau guarantee no more than that *Arabes* constituted a group of interest to the state. The Roman government early displayed concern with the flocks and herds of Egypt, as the many declarations from owners make clear, and taxes on the various aspects of pastoralism were a prominent motive for Roman bureaucratic preoccupation.[23] In the Julio-Claudian period there was considerable experimentation with finding the form of registration for flocks that would prove the more efficient, and the accounts of Lucius from A.D. 56/57 (see the *Appendix*, below), may have been kept with a view toward complying with the government regulation that required a supplementary declaration in Mecheir, in effect in precisely these years.[24]

In the Julio-Claudian tax archive the ethnic *Ioudaios* appears only in the accounts of Lucius, the *praktor* Nemesion's associate in agricultural matters, and *Ioudaios* most often characterizes a man named Isak. The name of Isak's father is never mentioned. Such an omission may indicate that his father's name was not known in the village and that while Isak frequented Philadelphia on business, he was not registered there for poll tax. Isak trafficked in sheep and goats, their hides, and their fleece, and he may have been the owner of the flocks; he was not a shepherd, as was Pnepheros who served Lucius for a monthly wage as both shepherd and agent (cf. below, the *Appendix*: 880r.26; cf. also 3, 32, 41, 43–44, 48, 56, 81; 152.8, 14, 32, 33). The two ethnics still in use in the tax archive from Julio-Claudian Philadelphia, *Arabes* and *Ioudaioi*, designate men apparently Semitic in origin and possibly involved with pastoralism.[25]

Claudius' letter to the Alexandrians was copied on the back of a papyrus belonging to the tax archive—a year ledger from A.D. 37/38, Gaius' second regnal year in Egypt. The hand in which the letter was copied is that of the *praktor argyrikôn*, Nemesion, son of Zoïlos (Hanson 1984a, pp. 1107–18). Professor Jacques Schwartz has recently drawn attention to the fact that there was little in Claudius' letter that would have interested a village tax collector.[26] That is, was it likely that Nemesion was interested in the exchanges of courtesies and privileges between Julio-Claudian emperors and Alexandrian citizens, either in the past or in the present?[27] Schwartz argued that it was Claudius' remonstrances to both Alexandrian citizens and to Jews resident in Alexandria (lines

23. Balconi 1984, pp. 35–60, and for more recent bibliography, see Hanson 1989a, pp. 61–69.

24. From late in the reign of Claudius and until late in the reign of Nero the registration required in Mecheir (26 January–24 February) had to be supplemented in Epeiph (25 June–24 July) of the same year, so as to take notice of newborn lambs born after a first declaration. See Balconi 1984, pp. 44–48, and Hanson 1989a, pp. 61–69. The accounts of Lucius contain records for the last four months of the year, from Pachon (26 April–25 May) to Mesore (25 July–23 August) in year 2 (= A.D. 55/56), and for the first five months that precede Mecheir, from Sebastos (29 August–27 September) to Tybi (27 December–25 January) in year 3 (= A.D. 56/57). The accounts also give special notice to young lambs (ἄρνεϲ).

25. Many have seen 'Αλαβάρχηϲ as a dissimulation of 'Αραβάρχηϲ—e.g. *CPJ* I, p. 49 and note 4, citing "Wilcken, Dittenberger, and others"; *LSJ*[9] *Addendum*, s.v. 'Αραβάρχηϲ. In the Julio-Claudian period several wealthy Alexandrian Jews served as *Arabarch*/*Alabarch*, including Philo's brother Alexander, father of the future prefect, and it is possible that *Arabarch* provides the piece of evidence that the designation *Arabes* could and did at times refer to *Ioudaioi*. But Abd-El-Ghany 1989, pp. 236–41, argues vehemently that two terms were distinct: the *Alabarch*, an important person in the Jewish community in Alexandria; the *Arabarch*, an official responsible for trading activity in the Red Sea ports and caravan routes and sometimes also epistrategos of the Thebaid. Cf. also Kasher 1985, p. 347, who recognizes only *Alabarch* as the name for the Jewish leader.

26. Butin and Schwartz 1985, pp. 127–29, and summarized in the introduction and notes to *P. Strasb.* 9.823.

27. Compare also the reprinting of columns one and five of Claudius' letter (*P. Lond.* 6.1912) as #16 in Pestman 1990, pp. 105–09; again the editor was concerned with the motive for the copying—"it is not known why the tax-collector of Philadelphia copied a letter addressed to the Alexandrians."

73–104) that were of interest to the *praktor argyrikôn* of Philadelphia and to his fellow villagers. Schwartz imagined that the new Emperor's concern for the civil strife that had broken out anew in Alexandria, the anti-Semitism of the city's Greek citizens, and the attempts of Alexandrian Jews to usurp privileges belonging to Alexandrian citizens were what concerned Nemesion, because these topics responded to anti-Semitism in his own village. Schwartz' reconstruction is not unattractive. The bond it posits between city and village aligns the embattled Jews of the capital with their fellows in the *chorá*, as is not only suggested in Claudius' letter (lines 96–97), but was visible in the continued responses of Jews in the countryside to the pogroms of the capital—late in the reign of Nero, after Titus' victories in Judaea and the institution of the Jewish tax, and again under Trajan (see the summary in Kasher 1985, pp. 18–28). Anti-Semitism in Faiyum villages early in the Julio-Claudian period would help to explain this apparent Jewish solidarity evident in the later decades of the first century. Attractive as Schwartz' reconstruction is, it relies on faulty readings in *P. Princ.* I to forge the joins between papyri from the tax archive,[28] his own *P. Strasb.* 9.823, and two letters from the Berlin collections, BGU 4.1078 and 1079,[29] published many years ago. The Strasbourg letter is mutilated at the beginning, and the names of both sender and addressee are lost; it was dispatched on 16 April 42. The first Berlin letter was sent from Sarapion, who was in Alexandria, to Sarapias in the *chorá* on 20 October 38 and the second was sent from Sarapion, now in the *chorá*, to Herakleides in Alexandria on 4 August 41. Sarapion's letter to Herakleides included the warning that Herakleides, like everyone else, "should beware of the Jews." The anti-Semitic sentiments of this letter were tied to Philadelphia by the rare name Νήδυμος (1079.4), the man who had carried an earlier letter from Sarapion to Herakleides. But Νήδυμος does not appear in *P. Princ.* I 13.xix.5, or anywhere else in the archive. The index to *P. Princ.* I does read Νήδ(υμος), but this represents a misreading of Νέςτου, an *epoikion* in the vicinity of Philadelphia.[30]

The tax archive from Philadelphia offers no clear and unequivocal evidence for anti-Semitism in the village in the years between the riots under Gaius and the unrest under Nero that culminates in Titus' sack of Jerusalem and the Jewish tax. The tax archive is, however, from precisely those critical years, and another aspect of the archive may add a small measure of support to Schwartz' suggestion that Nemesion copied Claudius' letter because of his interest in the Jewish question, even if the Berlin papyri cannot be linked with the village. As noted above, the only "foreign" ethnics employed in the archive mark Semites—*Arabes* and *Ioudaioi.* This is not proof of anti-Semitism at the local level. Nonetheless, the continued use of these particular ethnics does suggest a degree of separateness and a possible lack of amalgamation of Semites into the life of the village. The designations *Arabes* and *Ioudaioi* implied an alterity for Semites, even though their associations with the village extended back for generations. Should divisive issues arise, this separateness may have had the potential of blossoming into open conflict with resident or itinerant Jews, even as it did in Alexandria.

It has been customary, then, to see Claudius' letter as an Alexandrian document: it was certainly that to Bell, to Tcherikover, and to a first generation of scholars. But the letter is likewise a village document and a text from the tax archive: as a village document, Claudius' letter testified to the interests of the elite class at Philadelphia—the men for whom the tax collector Nemesion no doubt copied the letter onto the back of a tax roll. The interests of this group extended to Alexandrian problems and to their Roman imperial solutions. When viewed at close range, Julio-

28. See the warning of Browne, *P. Mich.* 12, p. 43: "... but many of them [texts from the Philadelphia tax archive], unfortunately, cannot yet be safely used by historians and other scholars."

29. Reprinted as W*Chres.* 59 and 60, and the latter as also *CPJ* 2.152.

30. I offer the revised reading of *P. Princ.* I 13.xix.5 (= line 559; 1990, pp. 259–83). This account was also written by Nemesion.

Claudian Philadelphia was a mirror of the capital, and not so much the homogeneous group of tax-paying peasants it seemed when viewed at a distance. To local residents the village was a community with its own power structure, and the elite at its summit was keenly attuned to the Roman good will that permitted them to enrich themselves through the acquisition of influence and worldly goods, provided they also collect the taxes owed to Rome from fellow villagers and preserve the *Pax Romana* in the surrounding countryside. The Semites for whom the village served as political and/or economic center had apparently not blended with its Greco-Egyptian population, for theirs were the only ethnic designations still in current use in the public and private documents of the tax archive. The Emperor Claudius had tried to reestablish peace between Jewish and Greek communities in Alexandria through the provisions and admonitions of his letter, although subsurface tensions continued, waiting to flare up when opportunity offered. Schwartz was probably correct that similar tensions existed at Philadelphia under Julio-Claudian emperors.

APPENDIX: ACCOUNTS OF LUCIUS

I. P. MICH. INV. 880 RECTO[31]

The recto contains four columns of accounts. Top and bottom margins are preserved, although an extensive lacuna at the beginning of the line mars the text in the first column after line 13. The fourth column on recto and the last to be preserved at right has also lost between six and ten letters along its right margin. The document, which begins with a heading at the top of column I, line 1, may be lacking only the fifth and final column, presumably a record of expenditures for year 3 to parallel the record of expenditures for year 2 (lines 23–31). The accounts were written in a large and fluid hand, one of the most readable of the archive. The scribe wrote in a manner similar to, or identical with, the second scribe (m. 2) of *P. Mich.* 12.640, a list of tax collections for A.D. 55/56. The text on verso consists of ten columns: eight columns list tax payments, arranged by villages and names of *cheiristai*, or at other points, by names of individual taxpayers; two columns also contain lists of arrears of poll tax, as does an additional column placed on the recto by the scribe of the verso. Although that column was written on the recto of the papyrus, it is connected by subject matter to the text on the verso and is not reproduced here. This aspect of the papyrus illustrates the ease with which public accounts of the tax bureau were mixed with private accounts involving Nemesion and his associates.

The accounts on the recto begin with records for the last four months of regnal year 2 of Nero (lines 1–31) and continue with records for the first four months of regnal year 3 (lines 32–82). In each year the composition of the flock in the care of Pnepheros the shepherd is first tabulated (lines 1–9 and 32–53); lambs are given special notice and ewes are counted separately from rams. These tabulations may have been kept with a view toward complying with governmental regulations in this period that required not only a declaration of sheep and goats in Mecheir (26 January–24 February), but also a supplementary registration in Epeiph (25 June–24 July) to include newborns. Receipts follow (lines 10–22 and 54–82) and then expenditures (lines 23–31, but apparently lost for year 3). The last date mentioned in the account is Epeiph of regnal year 3, providing a *terminus post quem* of 24 July 57 for the composition of the accounts.

PHILADELPHIA | 70.2 × 29 CM | AFTER 24 JULY 57

Column I

λόγος προβάτων Λουκίου β (ἔτους) Νέρωνος Κλαυδίου Καίσαρος
Σεβαστοῦ Γερμανικοῦ Αὐτοκράτορος, Παχών·
Πνεφερῶτι ποιμένι πρόβ(ατα) θηλυκὰ νγ, ἀρσενικ(ὰ) κζ, ἄρνε(ς) κβ,

31. Professor G. Michael Browne graciously yielded to me his right of publication, and I have had the benefit of his preliminary transcript.

(γίν.) ϲύμμικ(τα) πρόβ(ατα) π, ἄρνε(ϲ) κβ,
τούτων διεφθάρη{ι} Παχὼν διὰ τοῦ αὐτοῦ ποιμένο(ϲ) θηλυκ(ὰ) πρόβ(ατα) β,
Παῦνι θηλυκ(ὸν) πρόβ(ατον) α,
Μεϲορὴ{ι} ἀρϲενικ(ὸν) πρόβ(ατον) α, καὶ ἄρνε(ϲ) β, (γίν.) πρόβ(ατα) θηλυκ(ὰ)
γ, ἀρϲενικ(ὸν) α, ἄρνε(ϲ) β,
(γίν.) ϛ, καταλείπ(εται) πρόβατα θηλυκ(ὰ) ν, ἄρϲενικ(ὰ) κϛ,
ἄρνε(ϲ) κ, (γίν.) ἀριθμοῦ ϙϛ.
λήμματοϲ τῶν ἀπὸ Παχὼν ἕωϲ Μεϲορὴ{ι} β (ἔτουϲ)
Νέρωνοϲ Κλαυδίου Καίϲαροϲ Σεβαϲτοῦ Γερμανικοῦ Αὐτοκράτοροϲ
Παχὼν τ̣ι̣μῆϲ δερμάτων γ διὰ Σακολάο̣υ̣ Ἰουδ(αίου) (δρ.) ιβ
̣ ̣ ̣ ̣ [ ] ὁ̣μ̣ο̣ί̣ωϲ Ἰ̣ϲ̣ά̣κ[ι] Ἰ̣ο̣υ̣δ̣α̣ί̣ωι διὰ Πουωρέω̣(ϲ) Παβό(τοϲ)
[ ] ̣ (δρ.) η
[ ] ̣
[ ] ̣ ̣ ̣
[ ] ̣ ̣
[τιμῆϲ] θηλυκ(οῦ) α, ἀρϲ[ε]ν̣ι̣κ(ῶν) γ (δρ.) ν
[τιμῆϲ] θηλυκ(οῦ) α, ἀρϲ[ε]νικ(ῶν) β (δρ.) μ
[τιμῆϲ] θηλυκ(οῦ) α, ἀρϲ[ε]νικ(ῶν) α (δρ.) μ
[Πνε]φ̣ερῶτ(οϲ) [ ]
[(γίν.)] (δρ.) ρν

Column II

τούτων ἀνηλώμ(ατοϲ), Παχών·
Θέωνι γεωργῶι τιμῆϲ χόρτου ἀρο(υρῶν) β (δρ.) ξδ
κόπτρα τῶν προκειμ(ένων) [[̣]] ἀρο(υρῶν) β (δρ.) ιβ
Πνεφερῶτι ποιμένι μιϲθοῦ μηνῶν δ, ἀνὰ (δρ.) ιϛ (δρ.) ξδ
τιμῆϲ οἴνου κεραμίων β (δρ.) ϛ
βαλανευτικοῦ, ἡμιαρταβίου (δρ.) γ
κατ' ἄνδρα ζυτηρᾶϲ τοῦ αὐτοῦ ποιμένο(ϲ) (δρ.) ι
(γίν.) (δρ.) ρνθ καί ὑπὲρ δαπα-
νήματοϲ (δρ.) θ ἐν Λουκίου
γ (ἔτουϲ)· ὁμοίωϲ λόγοϲ προβ(άτων) Λουκίου δι(ὰ) Πνεφερῶ(τοϲ) τοῦ αὐτο(ῦ)
ποιμένοϲ
μηνὶ Σεβαϲτῶι π̣ρ̣ό̣β(ατα) θηλυκ(ὰ) ν, ἀρϲενικ(ὰ) κϛ, ἄρνε(ϲ) κ
(γίν.) πρόβατα οϛ, ἄρνε(ϲ) κ.
τούτων διεφθάρη{ι} διὰ τοῦ αὐτοῦ ποιμένοϲ
τῶι αὐτῶι μηνὶ Σεβαϲτ[ῶι] π̣ρ̣ό̣β(ατα) θηλυκ(ὰ) β, κ̣α̣ὶ̣ ἀ[ρὴ(ν)] α,
(γίν.) διεφθαρμ(ένα) πρόβ(ατα) β̣, ἀρὴ(ν) α·
Φαῶφι Ἀ̣θ̣ὺ̣ρ ἄρνε(ϲ) γ, (γίν.) ἄρνε(ϲ) γ [ ] ̣ ̣ ̣ ̣ ̣ ( ) δ̣ ̣ ̣
Ἀθὺρ ἐ̣ν̣ τ̣ῶ̣ι̣ τεϲϲαρακ[ον]τ̣α̣ρ̣ο̣(υρικῷ) διὰ Θ̣έ̣[ωνοϲ ?] ̣ ̣ ̣ ̣ ̣ κ̣α̣ὶ̣
διὰ τοῦ αὐτοῦ Πνεφερῶτο̣ϲ̣ ποιμ(ένοϲ) Ἰϲ̣ά̣κ̣ι
Ἰουδαίωι εἰϲ πρᾶϲιν [πρ]όβ(ατα) ἀρϲεν̣ι̣κ(ὰ) γ.

Column III

Τῦβι διὰ Ἀπολλῶτοϲ τοῦ Σωϲίππου καὶ Πνεφερῶτοϲ
τοῦ αὐτοῦ ποιμένοϲ τῶι αὐτῶι Ἰϲάκι Ἰουδαίωι

ὁμοίωϲ εἰϲ πρᾶϲιν, ἀπολογία προβάτ(ων) θηλυκ(ῶν) ε
καὶ δέρματοϲ ἀρνίου ἑνόϲ,
(γίν.) πρόβ(ατα) πεπραμένα η, καὶ δέρμ(α) α
καὶ ἐν τῶι Ἑκατονταρουρικῶι (m. 2) \`Μεϲιῶτ̣ο̣ϲ´ (m. 1) διὰ Πνεφερῶ(τοϲ) ποιμ(ένοϲ)
καὶ Ϲαμβᾶτοϲ Ἀράβου ὁμοίωϲ εἰϲ πρᾶϲιν Ἰϲάκι
Ἰουδαίωι ἀρϲενικὰ πρόβ(ατα) δ,
(γίν.) θηλυκ(ὰ) πρόβ(ατα) ζ, ἀρϲενικὰ ζ, ἄρνε(ϲ) ε,
καταλείπεται πρόβατα θηλυκ(ὰ) μγ, ἀρϲενικ(ὰ) ιθ, ἄρνε(ϲ) ιε
(γίν.) π̣[ρό]β̣(ατα) ϲύμμικτα ο̣ζ
λήμματοϲ τοῦ αὐτοῦ γ (ἔτουϲ)
μηνὶ Ϲεβαϲτῶι διὰ Ἰϲάκεωϲ Ἰουδαίου καὶ
διὰ Πνεφερῶτοϲ ποιμένοϲ τιμ̣ῆ̣ϲ̣ ἐ̣ρί̣ω̣(ν) (δρ.) ιβ
κ̣α̣ὶ Ἰ̣ϲ̣ά̣[κι Ἰουδαίωι διὰ τοῦ αὐτο̣ῦ̣ π̣ο̣ι̣μ̣έ̣ν̣ο̣(ϲ)
αρ....... δ̣ (δρ.) γ
Φα̣ῶ̣φι Ἰ̣ϲά̣[κι Ἰο]υδα̣ί̣ω̣ι δέρματ(οϲ) ἀρνίου α (δρ.) β
Ἁθὺ̣ρ̣ ὁ̣μ̣ο̣[ίωϲ τῶι αὐτῶ]ι̣ Ἰϲάκι Ἰουδα[ίωι τ]ι̣μ̣ῆ̣ϲ ἀρϲενικ(ῶν) γ (δρ.) ζ
Τ̣ῦβ̣ι δ̣ι̣ὰ̣ [.....] ου καὶ τοῦ αὐτοῦ ποιμ(ένοϲ) [ ]
(Note at top, between columns iii and iv: [[ὡϲ εἰπὼν ποιμ( ) υ̣......]])

Column IV

Ἰϲ̣ά̣κ̣ι̣ ε̣ἰ̣ϲ πρᾶϲ̣ι̣[ν], ἡ αὐτὴ ἀπολογία π[ροβ(άτων) θηλυκ(ῶν) ε καὶ]
ἀρνίου δέρματοϲ [ ]
Μεχεὶρ ὁμοίωϲ ἐν τῶι Ἑκατονταρουρικ(ῷ̣) δι[ὰ Ϲαμβᾶτοϲ (?) or Πουώρεωϲ (?)]
Ἀράβου ἀρϲενικὰ πρόβ(ατα) δ [ ]
(γίν.) λήμματοϲ ἀργ(υρίου) (δρ.) ρπϛ̣ [ ]
καὶ ἀπὸ τιμῆϲ ἐρίων μηνὶ Ϲεβαϲτῶι [ ]
Πουῶρι ἐμπόρωι προβ(άτων) θηλυκ(ῶν) σ, ἀ[ρϲενικ(ῶν)
Χοιὰχ ὁμοίωϲ Πουῶρι ἐμπόρωι θηλυκ(ῶν) π, ἀ̣[ρϲενικ(ῶν)]
Τῦβι ὁμοίωϲ τ̣ῶ̣ι̣ α̣ὐ̣τῶι ἐμπόρωι θηλυκ(ῶν) . [ ]
Μεχεὶρ ὁμοίωϲ τ̣ῶ̣ι̣ α̣ὐ̣τ̣ῶ̣ι̣ ἐμπόρωι θηλυκ(ῶν) . [ ]
Φαμενὼθ ὁμοίωϲ τ[ῶι αὐτῶι ἐ]μ̣π̣ό̣ρ̣ωι θ̣η̣λ̣υκ(ῶν) . [ ]
Φαρμοῦθι ὁμοίωϲ τῶι αὐτ[ῶι ἐμπόρωι ? θη]λυκ(ῶν) ϲ, ἀρϲ̣[ενικ(ῶν)]
Παχὼν ὁμοίωϲ τῶι αὐτῶι [ἐμπόρωι ? θηλ]υ̣κ(ῶν) ., ἀρϲενικ(ῶν) [ ]
Παῦνι τῶι αὐτῶι ἐμπόρωι θη[λυκ(ῶν)., ἀρϲενικ(ῶν).]
Ἐπεὶφ τῶι αὐτῶι ἐ̣μ̣π̣ό̣ρωι θ̣η̣λ̣υ̣κ(ῶν) ν̣δ, [ ]
εἰϲ χιτῶνα Θεανίου [̣.̣]̣.... [ ]
(γίν.) ὑπὲρ ἐρίων ἀργ(υρίου) (δρ.) .. [ ]
γίνεται ἐπὶ τὸ α[ὐτό]
καὶ τὰϲ διὰ Πνε[φε]ρ[ῶ]το(ϲ).... ( ) [ ].. [ ]
γίνεται ἐπὶ τ̣ὸ̣ α̣ὐ̣τ̣ὸ̣..... [ ]

NOTES TO THE TEXT:

I 3. For Pnepheros the shepherd, agent for Lucius, see below, lines 26, 32, 41, 43–44, 48, 56, 61 (?), 81, and also *P. Princ.* 3.152.8, 14, 32, 33.

I 13. Read Παβῶ(τοϲ) and cf. *P. Princ.* 3.152.17. For Pouöris, son of Pabôs, merchant and agent for Isak, see also below, lines 69–77.

I 22. The total is correct for the items in lines 12–20.

I–II. The column of accounts, continued on recto by the scribe of the verso, was placed in the space between columns I and II.

II 24. For Theon the farmer ("hay man"?), see *P. Princ.* 3.152.4 and 31 and above, p. 132.

II 27–29. In addition to his wages, Pnepheros apparently also received an allowance of wine (line 27) and payment for minor capitation taxes (lines 28–29).

II 43. For Apollos, son of Sosippos, see also *P. Princ.* 3.152.26–27.

IV 63. Apparently a reference to the transaction in lines 45–46.

IV 65–66. Either [Cαμβᾶτοϲ] or [Πουώρεωϲ] / 'Αράβου, cf. above, line 49, or P. Mich. inv. 880v.196–97.

TRANSLATION:

Column I

Account of the sheep of Lucius for year 2 of Nero Claudius Caesar Augustus Germanicus Imperator, in Pachon (26 April–25 May 56):

Pnepheros the shepherd has 53 female sheep, 27 males, 22 lambs.

Total: 80 sheep in all, 22 lambs.

Of these, there perished in Pachon (26 April–25 May 56) through the same shepherd 2 females,

In Pauni (26 May–24 June 56) 1 female,

In Mesore (25 July–23 August 56) 1 male, 2 lambs. Total, 3 females, 1 male, 2 lambs.

Total, 6. Remainder, 50 females, 26 males, 20 lambs. Total, 96.

Account of receipts from Pachon to Mesore (26 April–23 August 56) of year 2 of Nero Claudius Caesar Augustus Germanicus Imperator:

In Pachon, for the price of 3 skins, through Sakolaos the Jew	12 dr.
... likewise to Isak the Jew, through Pouöris, son of Pabôs	8 dr.
(three lines badly damaged)	
... for the price of 1 female and 3 males	50 dr.
... for the price of 1 female and 2 males	40 dr.
... for the price of 1 female and 1 male	40 dr.
... through (?) Pnepheros	
Total, 150 dr.	

Column II

Expenditures of these items, in Pachon (26 April–25 May 56):

To Theon the farmer, for the price of 2 arourae of hay	64 dr.
For cutting the aforesaid 2 arourae	12 dr.
To Pnepheros the shepherd, wages for 4 months, at 16 dr. per month	64 dr.
For the price of 2 keramia of wine	6 dr.
For bath tax, hemiartabion	3 dr.
For beer tax for the same shepherd	10 dr.
Total, 159 dr., and for expenses, 9 dr.—on the estate of Lucius	

Year 3, likewise, account of the sheep of Lucius, through the same shepherd Pnepheros:

In the month of Sebastos (29 August–27 September 56), he had 50 females, 26 males, 20 lambs.

Total, 76 sheep, 20 lambs.

Of these there perished through the same shepherd in the same month of Sebastos 2 females, 1 lamb. Total lost, 2 females, 1 lamb.

In Phaophi and Hathyr (28 September–26 November 56), 3 lambs. Total, 3 lambs ...

In Hathyr (28 October–26 November 56), in the Forty-Arourae plot through Theon (?) and through the same Pnepheros the shepherd, to Isak the Jew, for sale, 3 males.

Column III

In Tybi (27 December 56–25 January 57), through Apollos, son of Sosippos, and Pnepheros the same shepherd to the same Isak the Jew, likewise for sale, the amount (?) of 5 females and 1 lambskin.

Total sold, 8 sheep and 1 skin.

And in the 100-arourae plot, through Pnepheros the shepherd and Sambas, Arab, likewise for sale to Isak the Jew, 4 males.

Total, 7 females, 7 males, 5 lambs

Remainder, 43 females, 19 males, 15 lambs, 77 in all.

Account of receipts of the same third year:

In the month of Sebastos, through Isak the Jew and through Pnepheros the shepherd, for the price of wool (?) 12 dr.

And to Isak the Jew through the same shepherd ...	3 dr.
In Phaophi to Isak the Jew for one lambskin	2 dr.
In Hathyr likewise to the same Isak the Jew for the price of 3 skins	7 dr.

In Tybi through ... and the same shepherd ....

Column IV

To Isak for sale, the same amount (?) of 5 female sheep and 1 lambskin.

In Mecheir likewise, in the 100-arourae plot, through [Sambas or Pouöris (?)], Arab, 4 males.

Total, for receipts, 186 dr. of silver

And from the price of wool in the month of Sebastos ....

To Pouöris the merchant for 200 females, ..., ... males....

[The text becomes fragmentary.]

II. *P. PRINC.* 3.152 VERSO (REVISED)

Like the preceding text, this papyrus also records capitation taxes collected by the tax office on one side and agricultural accounts that involve Lucius on the other. The latest date mentioned in the tax records was 27 October A.D. 57, while the accounts on verso list expenses for regnal years 2, 3, and 7 of Nero—A.D. 55/56, 56/57, and 60/61. Top and left margins are intact, as the blank space of 5 cm after the left margin and of 2.3 cm below top margin demonstrates. At the same time, damage to the surface of the papyrus brought the loss of about nine letters in the first column at left. The right margin is nearly intact, and only a letter or two is missing at right in the second column. Both columns break off at the bottom, and, in the absence of totals, it is impossible either to calculate how much text has been lost, or to know if the record is a complete one—or simply notes for some later, more elaborate document. The same scribe wrote both recto and verso, and the hand is that of Nemesion himself. In this instance he is writing very quickly, so that often individual letters are not fully articulated. Although they were unaware that the hand was Nemesion's, the first editors observed: "The scribe wrote an illegible cursive and many of the entries are difficult to decipher" (*P. Princ.* 3, p. 72). Because some of the same people appear in this account as in P. Mich. inv. 880r above, improvements can be made in the transcript of the *ed. prin*.[32]

32. The correction for line 4, suggested by Sir H. I. Bell and recorded in *BL* 3, p. 153, has been accepted into the text in modified form. The correction for line 15, suggested by E. W. Wipsyzcka and recorded in *BL* 5, p. 86, points the way to a correct reading of the text. I have also made corrections in lines 1, 4–7, 9–18, 21–22, 26, 28, 31–32.

P. PRINC. INV. AM 8915 31 × 23 CM A.D. 60/61

Column I

λόγος δαπάν]ης Ὑπερμένου μετὰ Λουκ(ίου)
τῆς αὐτ]ῆ̣(ς) μητρὸς τοῦ β (ἔτους)
Νέρωνο(ς) τοῦ] κυρίου
4 Θέωνι ταβ]ο̣υ̣ρίωι εἰς κοπὴν
ἐ]ρ̣γάζ(οντι) (δρ.) μη
] . . . ι̣ νο( )
] . . ος ἡμισείας (δρ.) θ
8 Πνεφερ]ῶ̣τ̣ει ποιμένει μισθοῦ
ἀν(ὰ) (δρ.) ις, μη(νῶν)] δ (δρ.) ξδ
] . . ἐ̣ρ̣γ̣ά̣του α (δρ.) γ
] τ̣ικ̣ο̣υ̣ (δρ.) γ
12] ἀρταβίας [[τοῦ γ (ἔτους)]] τοῦ β (ἔτους) (δρ.) λζ (τριώβ.)
] . . . α . . τῆς αὐτῆ(ς) μη(τρὸς) δ . . β( ) (δρ.) ι
Π]νεφερῶτο(ς) καὶ τ̣ῶν αὐτῶ(ν) (δρ.) ε
] . . ( ) ὑπὲρ ὑφάντρω(ν) (δρ.) ε
(After 2 cm left blank, several traces of writing)

Column II

17 Μεσορὴ{ι} Πουώρει ἐνπόρω(ι) Παβῶτος (δρ.) μ̣η̣[
(γίν.) τῶι Μεσορὴ (δρ.) ρμ
καταλείπετε ὑπὲρ δαπάνη(ς) (δρ.) λα (τριώβ. ?)
20 (ἔτους) γ Νέρωνος τοῦ κυρίου
ἀνήλωσις
Νεμεσίωνει Τιτᾶνος τῆ(ς) μη(τρὸς) Τα . . . τω̣( ) (δρ.) ξ[
τειμῆ(ς) ἄρακος παρὰ Θέωνο(ς) (ἀρτάβης) α (δρ.) γ (τριώβ. ?) [
24 παρὰ Φιλήμωνος . . ( ) (δρ.) ις[
σπόρω(ν) γ (ἔτους)
τειμῆς χόρτου χλωροῦ δι᾽ Ἀπολλῶτο(ς)
Σωσίπου [[ἀργυ(ρίου) (δρ.) λδ (δρ.)]] \`(δρ.) . [΄
28 τειμῆς χλωρῶν καὶ σπόρ(ων) (δρ.) [
. ανες . ω( ) τειμῆς σπερμάτω(ν) τ̣ῶ̣ν̣ ἀ̣π̣᾽ ἀ̣ν̣η̣(λώσεως) [[(δρ. ?)]] [
ζ (ἔτους) ζ (ἔτους)
Θύωνι ταβουρίωι τειμῆ(ς) χόρτο(υ) ἰς κοπ(ὴν) [
32 Πνεφερῶτι ποιμένει μηνὸ̣ς̣ . [
]ει ποιμένει διὰ Πνεφε̣[ρῶτο(ς)

NOTES TO THE TEXT:

II.19. Read καταλείπεται.

II 31. Read Θέωνι.

CHAPTER 14

THE PERSIAN CLAIM TO KUSH IN LIGHT OF EVIDENCE FROM LOWER NUBIA*

LISA A. HEIDORN
The University of Chicago

The Oriental Institute of the University of Chicago conducted a salvage excavation in 1964 at the fortress of Dorginarti, a site located at the northern end of the Second Cataract in Sudanese Nubia. The excavators believed that the fortress dated to an earlier pharaonic period; subsequent publications have dated Dorginarti either to the Middle or New Kingdom.[1] However, a reexamination of the archaeological materials from the site proves that they date rather to the Saite and Persian periods. Similarly dated ceramics and small objects have also been found elsewhere in the Sudan, as well as in Egypt and the Levant.

Lower Nubia during the period in question has been characterized as an unpopulated buffer zone situated between two hostile kingdoms. Low Nile floods and adverse political circumstances have both been blamed for this supposed lack of occupation.[2] But the textual and archaeological records show that Nile floods were at least adequate in the first half of the first millennium B.C. and that they were occasionally quite high;[3] also, the evident prosperity of the Kushite and Saite periods argues against consistently low Niles. The existence of Twenty-fifth Dynasty and Napatan remains at various sites in Lower Nubia in fact shows that there was settlement in the area for at least part of the period in question.[4]

A Saite fort at Dorginarti also proves that Lower Nubia was important during the seventh and sixth centuries B.C. Achaemenid inscriptions and representations indicate that Kush was part of the Persian empire; and a guardpost—constructed atop earlier remains at Dorginarti and surrounded by late sixth and fifth century pottery—may have served as a Persian-period frontier post until the end of the fifth century B.C.[5]

* This is an abstract of my article, "The Saite and Persian Period Forts at Dorginarti" (Heidorn 1991).

1. Dorginarti is dated to the late New Kingdom by the excavators, see Knudstad 1966, pp. 178–86.

2. The theory that Nile levels were low during the first millennium B.C. was first proposed by Firth 1915, pp. 21–22. See also the discussion and references in Adams 1977, p. 242. Bruce G. Trigger believes that political circumstances led to a hiatus; see 1965, pp. 112–14.

3. For discussions of the relevant nilometer marks at Karnak, see von Beckerath 1966, pp. 43–55; Legrain 1896a, pp. 111–18; Legrain 1896b; and Ventre Pacha 1896, pp. 95–107.

4. Note the redating of materials at sites in Lower Nubia (Vila 1980, pp. 175–78 and B. B. Williams 1990, pp. 31–49).

5. The account of the Napatan king Harsiotef (404–369 B.C.) suggests that neither Egypt nor Kush was in firm control of the region. However, Harsiotef campaigned against rebels in Lower Nubia (*ʿkin*) and pursued their leaders all the way to Aswan; see Grimal 1981, p. 54.

Traditional luxury goods continued to flow north out of Africa during the Saite and Persian periods in Egypt. Phoenician merchants on the Red Sea and their overland partners in the Levant participated in a lucrative trade network that connected Africa with the Near East.[6] Both the Egyptians and Persians may have sought to win control of the Lower Nubian routes in order to secure the safe conduct of trade and diplomatic expeditions travelling along these paths, and perhaps also to tap the profits of this trade in African luxuries.

6. Necho and Darius were both interested in constructing a Red Sea canal; part of their interest may have been a desire to obtain the products of Africa from the seaport connected to the African trade network. See also Lemaire 1987, pp. 49–60; and Bunnens 1985, pp. 121–33.

CHAPTER 15

ARCHIVES BILINGUES DE NOMARQUES DANS LES PAPYRUS DE GHÔRAN

SUZANNE HÉRAL
Katholieke Universiteit, Leuven / Paris - Sorbonne

La collection des Papyrus de Ghôran, actuellement conservée à l'Institut de Papyrologie de la Sorbonne à Paris, est le résultat des fouilles menées par Pierre Jouguet (1901, pp. 380–411)[1] en 1901 et 1902 dans le cimetière de Ghôran, au nord-ouest du petit Bassin de Gharaq, lui-même situé dans le sud-ouest du Fayoum.[2] Ces papyrus ont été extraits de cartonnages appartenant à une centaine de momies.

En 1989, dans le cadre d'un mémoire de maîtrise, j'ai eu l'occasion de procéder à leur recensement systématique, ce qui m'a permis de mesurer le caractère bilingue très marqué de la collection. En effet, sur un total de quelque 250 papyrus publiés, grecs et démotiques s'équilibrent presque, à concurrence de 135 contre 115, la légère prédominance apparente des grecs étant compensée par un nombre supérieur d'inédits démotiques: 300 environ contre 250 grecs.

Après ce travail d'inventaire, j'ai cherché à dégager de la collection des ensembles cohérents et significatifs comme, par exemple, des archives centrées sur un personnage principal. Deux figures de nomarques ont alors émergé de la masse, au travers de deux groupes de documents datant du milieu du IIIe siècle avant notre ère.[3]

Tout d'abord, une remarque sur le terme d'"archives" qui leur a été appliqué. Il ne s'agit pas d'archives au sens des archives de Zénon (cf. Orrieux 1985, pp. 41–54), qui ont été sélectionnées et rassemblées par la volonté d'un homme dans un but précis de conservation. Ici, au contraire, il a fallu tenter de reconstituer des séries, même incomplètes, de documents qui, après avoir été jugés périmés à une date proche de la fin du IIIe siècle avant notre ère, avaient été mis au rebut, livrés à la récupération et dispersés au hasard lors de la fabrication des cartonnages funéraires. L'objectif a été de recréer, même partiellement, les dossiers démantelés de l'archiviste antique, et d'essayer de retrouver la valeur instrumentale de chacun de ces documents qui, à un moment donné, ont servi à régler les affaires de la vie quotidienne dans diverses localités du Fayoum.

En second lieu, le titre de nomarque mérite lui-même quelques précisions, en raison de son ambiguïté fondamentale. Le découpage administratif de l'Égypte en nomes, héritage de l'époque pharaonique, a été maintenu par les Ptolémées. Mais, après la conquête, les gouverneurs de nomes, ou nomarques, ont vu leurs prérogatives diminuées au profit des stratèges, investis de l'autorité

1. *Notice sur les fouilles de Médinet-Ghôran et de Médinet-en-Nahas*, Bulletin de l'Université de Lille et de l'Académie de Lille, juillet 1902.

2. Voir la carte en *Annexe I*, où le site est orthographié Gurrān.

3. Publications: Boyaval 1973, p. 187 sq.; Cadell 1966; de Cenival 1967, pp. 99–107; 1968, pp. 37–51, 1978; pp. 1–3, 1984; Jouguet 1907–28; Sottas 1921.

militaire. Or, au IIIe siècle, on constate l'existence simultanée de plusieurs nomarques dans un nome de grande dimension comme le Fayoum. Des auteurs modernes[4] se sont attachés à résoudre cette apparente contradiction et sont parvenus à dégager la notion de nomarque de district, par opposition à celle de nomarque au sens classique et plein du terme, c'est-à-dire nomarque de nome. Certes, ce dernier subsiste, mais ses attributions ne concernent plus que la gestion du domaine foncier et l'organisation des travaux agricoles. De leur côté, les nomarques de district, soumis à l'autorité du nomarque de nome, sont chargés de la mise en oeuvre au plan local de la politique agricole décidée à l'échelon du nome. Les districts, ou nomarchies, portent le nom de leur titulaire du moment, suivant la formule ἡ τοῦ δεῖνος νομαρχία, ce qui permet de jalonner la carrière de ces fonctionnaires.

Essayons maintenant de situer nos deux nomarques dans leur cadre spatio-temporel. Ces deux personnages, au nom incontestablement grec, sont dûment répertoriés dans la *Prosopographia Ptolemaica*. Le premier par ordre chronologique est Diogénès, qui a exercé ses fonctions entre 258 et 250 dans un district comprenant le sud de la méris de Thémistos et une partie de la méris de Polémôn.

Les contours de sa nomarchie, indiqués par des traits horizontaux sur la carte en *Annexe I* (p. 155), ne sont proposés qu'à titre de simple hypothèse, à partir des points de repère que constituent les toponymes cités dans une série de *prostagmata* (voir Lenger 1967, pp. 145–55). Il s'agit d'ordres de versement en nature, émis par le nomarque en faveur de diverses catégories d'agriculteurs à titre d'avance pour les semailles. Hermoupolis apparaît comme le village le plus septentrional du district, puisqu'il appartient à la méris de Thémistos. D'autre part, à l'extrémité sud-ouest, on relève le nom de trois villages du Bassin de Gharaq: Théogonis, Talit et Kerkéosiris. Enfin, la localité d'Oxyrhyncha mérite une mention spéciale, car elle semble avoir été un centre administratif important, peut-être même le siège des bureaux du nomarque. Malheureusement, il n'est pas possible de la situer sur une carte. On sait seulement, d'après certains papyrus, qu'elle n'aurait pas été éloignée de Tebetnu.

Notre second nomarque, Aristarchos, est non seulement bien attesté, mais de plus, il a connu une carrière d'une longévité tout à fait remarquable, puisqu'elle s'étend de 250 à au moins 231 avant notre ère. Nous devons cette dernière date à Clarysse (1974, p. 84), qui a su reconnaître Aristarchos sous le "ghost-name" d'Abat[—] dans le P. Petrie I 16,2 daté de 231. Ainsi, grâce à cette date, Aristarchos devient le plus notable des nomarques de district connus à ce jour, puisqu'il a exercé ses fonctions au moins pendant vingt ans, sur une période comprenant les cinq dernières années du règne de Philadelphe et les dix-sept premières de son successeur, Evergète. Or, dans l'état actuel des connaissances, la durée de la nomarchie, en tant qu'institution, n'a guère excédé une trentaine d'années, entre 260 et 230 environ.

Ici, une petite mise au point me paraît utile. On a longtemps considéré Aristarchos comme le successeur immédiat de Maimachos, lequel aurait exercé ses fonctions dans le même district de 260 à 250. Cependant, le P. Petrie III, 49, dont Clarysse m'a signalé des fragments inédits, mentionne côte à côte sept nomarques différents, parmi lesquels figurent Maimachos et Aristarchos. Tous ces personnages sont cités en relation avec un décompte d'outils. Il faut donc supposer que Maimachos et Aristarchos ont dirigé au même moment deux nomarchies différentes. Cette observation corrobore d'ailleurs une constatation que j'avais faite avant d'avoir eu connaissance de ces nouveaux textes. En effet, j'avais noté que les attestations respectives de ces deux nomarques, dont on pensait qu'ils s'étaient succédé à la tête du même district, concernaient en réalité des zones nettement distinctes. Ainsi, le district de Maimachos comprenait notamment une partie de rive du Lac

4. Sur l'émergence progressive du concept de nomarque de district, voir: Preisigke et Spiegelberg 1914, p. 41; Seider 1938, pp. 11–42; Van't Dack 1948, pp. 147–161; 1951, pp. 5–38; et Peremans et Van't Dack 1953, pp. 75–81.

Moëris de même que les localités de Tanis et de Psennyris, repérables sur la carte, ce qui permet de le situer dans le nord-ouest de la méris d'Hérakleidès. En revanche, les toponymes cités dans les archives d'Aristarchos renvoient tous à des implantations situées dans le sud de cette méris. Hormis Exo Pseur, dont on sait qu'il se trouvait à la périphérie de Krokodeilôn Polis, capitale du nome, on relève les noms de Pharbaitha et de Sebennytos, deux localités proches de Perséa, village connu du sud de la méris d'Hérakleidès. A la pointe sud du territoire, Ptolémaïs Hormou (cf. Bonneau 1979b, pp. 310–26) a sans doute représenté le pôle d'activité économique le plus important de la nomarchie, en tant que port principal du Fayoum, par où devait transiter tout le trafic fluvial avec la vallée du Nil, c'est-à-dire tout le commerce avec Alexandrie. Mais là encore, la superficie du district d'Aristarchos, qui apparaît marquée de hachures verticales sur la carte en annexe, n'a qu'un caractère purement indicatif.

Voilà donc grossièrement esquissés les contours des deux nomarchies. Après avoir tenté de définir géographiquement le ressort respectif de nos deux nomarques, on est naturellement conduit à mettre en parallèle le contenu de leurs archives. A cet égard, trois types d'opposition se manifestent. Le premier concerne le plan matériel le plus concret, à savoir les cartonnages qui ont livré ces deux lots de documents. On peut dire que les archives de Diogénès (Diogénès = *Pros. Ptol.* I et VIII nº 882. Voir la liste de ses archives en *Annexe II*) ont bénéficié d'un concours de circonstances vraiment exceptionnel, si l'on considère que la presque totalité des papyrus publiés, soit 35 sur 38, sont issus de quatre pièces de cartonnage appartenant à la même momie, respectivement un masque, un plastron, une bande de jambe et une chaussure, en somme l'appareillage complet de la momie. A l'opposé, les archives d'Aristarchos (Aristarchos = *Pros. Ptol.* I et VIII nº 879. Voir la liste de ses archives en *Annexe III*) ont subi une forte dispersion au moment de la fabrication des cartonnages. Sur un total de 17 papyrus publiés seuls 9 d'entre eux portent un numéro d'origine correspondant au cahier de fouilles de Pierre Jouguet. Les pièces concernées sont trois plastrons isolés, autrement dit, chacun d'eux appartient à une momie différente.

Deuxièmement, sur le plan de la chronologie, on constate chez Diogénès une concentration massive des documents sur une période d'un an. Tous les papyrus, sauf un, sont datés de 251/250, ce qui correspond, en l'état actuel des connaissances, à la dernière année d'activité du nomarque. En revanche, dans les archives d'Aristarchos, la chronologie ne se laisse pas cerner de façon aussi claire. D'abord, près de la moitié des papyrus sont dépourvus de date. D'autre part la date, lorsqu'elle subsiste, pose parfois des problèmes de lecture. Enfin, on constate que sur un total de 26 papyrus, 13 seulement sont datés et s'échelonnent de 250 à 238. Mais sur la période de douze ans ainsi couverte, les cinq premières années prédominent par le nombre de documents représentés, ce qui correspond au début de la carrière de notre nomarque.

Enfin, les deux archives s'opposent l'une à l'autre par la nature de leur contenu documentaire. Les archives de Diogénès se partagent dans leur grande majorité entre deux types documentaires, qui recoupent exactement le clivage linguistique entre textes grecs et démotiques:

— du côté grec, une vingtaine de *prostagmata,* déjà mentionnés, qui sont des ordres administratifs adressés par le nomarque à un subalterne grec du nom de Thrasymédès;

— du côté démotique, une douzaine de déclarations de petit bétail, toutes établies suivant le même formulaire stéréotypé, pour le compte de contribuables égyptiens.

Par contraste, les archives d'Aristarchos ne renferment qu'un type documentaire unique: la lettre. A l'exception d'une lettre privée, il s'agit de lettres administratives provenant d'interlocuteurs variés, chacune illustrant à sa façon les différentes compétences du nomarque. En outre, le caractère bilingue de ces archives est nettement moins prononcé, puisque sur 17 papyrus publiés, 2 seulement sont démotiques.

Mais, sans s'arrêter à ces disparités somme toute superficielles, il est possible de discerner un point de convergence entre ces deux archives, un lieu où elles se rencontrent pour refléter les mêmes réalités, en l'occurrence le rôle tenu par certains subalternes des nomarques. On s'aperçoit qu'au niveau local, les nomarques sont amenés à faire appel à des auxiliaires de rang modeste, qui peuvent être aussi bien des Égyptiens que des Grecs. Au bas de l'échelle administrative, des éléments indigènes fournissent, en quelque sorte, la charnière nécessaire pour établir le contact avec la population. C'est dans cette perspective que nous examinerons les rapports des nomarques avec une première catégorie d'auxiliaire, le myriaroure.

La question des myriaroures a déjà fait couler beaucoup d'encre. Il importe avant tout de démystifier leurs fonctions, en les dissociant totalement de l'image prestigieuse d'Apollonios le dioecète, détenteur de la fameuse dôréa de Philadelphie, mais avant tout Ministre des Finances de Philadelphe. La conception la plus réaliste en la matière me paraît être celle exprimée par Criscuolo (1977, pp. 109–22; 1981, pp. 116–18). Selon elle, les myriaroures seraient de petits fonctionnaires locaux, experts en agriculture et responsables de la gestion de superficies théoriques de 10.000 aroures, soit environ 25 km^2. Leur position hiérarchique les placerait à un échelon intermédiaire entre les phylacites et les cômarques, c'est-à-dire dans les rangs des fonctionnaires locaux les plus modestes. Tel est du moins l'ordre de préséance qui ressort du P. Petrie II 42 (a) = III 43 (1), annonçant la promotion de Théodôros au grade d'ingénieur en chef des travaux publics du nome.

Maintenant, que nous apprennent nos deux archives sur les rapports entre nomarques et myriaroures? Précisément, dans une lettre du même Théodôros, adressée au nomarque Aristarchos[5] et datée de 247 (P. Sorb. inv. 113 = *SB* XII 10844), il est demandé au nomarque de procéder à certains travaux d'irrigation contrôlée après la saison des crues avec, notamment, le concours du myriaroure local.[6] Le nom de ce dernier n'est malheureusement pas précisé, la fonction étant jugée un moyen d'identification suffisant, et par conséquent, l'origine ethnique de cet homme nous reste inconnue. Or, si l'on en juge par le P.L.Bat. XX 38 daté de 253, la fonction de myriaroure était loin d'être réservée aux Grecs. En effet, ce texte fait mention de deux myriaroures placés sur un pied d'égalité, dont l'un, Andromachos, est manifestement grec, tandis que l'autre, Panouphis (*Pꜣ-nfr* ou *Pa-Inpw*) ne saurait être qu'égyptien. Le document en question dresse le relevé des terres placées sous l'administration de chacun des deux myriaroures, dont une partie est constituée de lots attribués à des clérouques. Cet élément se retrouve dans la lettre de Théodôros à Aristarchos, où il est prévu que le myriaroure anonyme agisse de concert avec les *neaniskoi,* probablement de jeunes cadets militaires, détenteurs de parcelles dans la zone concernée. Ceci ne fait que confirmer le rôle d'auxiliaire technique que devait jouer le myriaroure auprès du nomarque, notamment dans les opérations de mise en culture de terres agricoles.

Le seul myriaroure dont le nom apparaisse clairement dans nos deux archives est Sentheus, en égyptien très probablement *Smꜣ-tꜣ.wy,* qui est cité quatre fois dans les *prostagmata* de Diogénès (P. Lille 47 et 48, P. Sorbonne 23 et 30). Dans ces textes, Diogénès, pas plus qu'ailleurs Théodôros, ne s'adresse directement au myriaroure: il laisse ce soin à son subalterne grec Thrasymédès, qui devra avoir recours à l'entremise de Sentheus pour faire distribuer des avances en nature aux agriculteurs de quatre villages. Dans ces quatre cas, on retrouve la même formule διὰ Σενθέως μυριαρούρου καὶ κωμογραμματέως Παώφιος. Cette expression ayant donné lieu à controverse, je passerai en revue trois hypothèses différentes:

5. La lecture Ἱ̣π̣π̣άρχωι à la ligne 1 de l'editio princeps a été corrigée par Clarysse en Ἀριστάρχωι.

6. A la ligne 5 de l'editio princeps B. Boyaval n'avait pas reconnu le sigle habituel du myriaroure, qui a été identifié par Clarysse. Au lieu de καὶ τῶι ̣χ̣[.]κ̣. il faut lire καὶ τῶι μ(υρι)αρού(ρωι) καὶ.

— Cadell, éditeur des P. Sorbonne, s'est prononcée en faveur de l'existence de deux personnes distinctes: d'une part le myriaroure Sentheus, et de l'autre un cômogrammate du nom de Paôphis (1966, p. 89, note 3).
— Jouguet, gêné par la construction en chiasme où les deux fonctions se trouvent accolées, a préféré opter en faveur d'un cumul de charges et voir en Paôphis un toponyme (1907–1928, p. 213, notes 2–3). Cette hypothèse d'un cumul de charges est d'ailleurs reprise par Criscuolo dans son étude sur le cômogrammate (1978, pp. 45–48).
— Enfin, Clarysse m'a suggéré que, Paôphis n'étant pas un toponyme attesté, il serait préférable de l'interpréter comme le patronyme de Sentheus. *Sentheus Paôphios* pourrait correspondre en démotique à *Smꜣ-tꜣ.wy sꜣ Pa-Ḥp*. Or, ceci est précisément le nom du cômogrammate (*sẖ-dmj*) de Dionysias (*Tjwnss*), qui est l'auteur d'un compte de céréales portant sur plusieurs villages du Fayoum en l'an 18 d'Evergète, soit 229/228. Il s'agit du P. dém. Lille 110. Malgré l'écart de vingt-deux ans et le changement de lieu, Dionysias étant situé à l'extrême nord-ouest de la méris de Thémistos, on ne peut totalement exclure qu'il soit question du même personnage que celui mentionné dans les *prostagmata* de Diogénès.

Mais quelle que soit l'hypothèse retenue, le myriaroure n'apparaît que comme une tierce personne, dont un intermédiaire est chargé d'obtenir l'assistance technique pour la préparation de travaux agricoles relevant de l'autorité du nomarque de district. Or, historiquement, la fonction de myriaroure semble avoir été liée dans sa durée à l'existence de la nomarchie. En effet, il semble qu'on ne rencontre de myriaroures qu'au milieu du IIIe siècle avant notre ère, et notamment entre 253 et 247. C'est pourquoi, on est tenté de voir en eux des auxiliaires spécialisés des nomarques, leur vocation agricole s'inscrivant dans la vaste entreprise de mise en valeur du Fayoum lancée par Philadelphe.

Une seconde catégorie de subalternes retiendra maintenant notre attention, ce que j'appellerai les agents du contrôle des récoltes. A cet égard, deux documents peuvent être mis en parallèle, l'un grec et l'autre démotique, tous deux étant adressés au nomarque Aristarchos la même année 248, à propos du contrôle de deux sortes de récolte. Le premier est le P. Sorbonne 32, où un certain Agathinos, fils de Simôn, s'engage vis-à-vis du nomarque à faire rentrer dans le grenier royal l'intégralité de la récolte de sésame du village de Sebennytos. Comme tous les oléagineux, le sésame était soumis à un monopole d'État,[7] selon les modalités définies dans le *P. Revenue Laws* (cf. Bingen 1978a, pp. 19–27; 1946, pp. 127–48). Après avoir été estimée sur pied, la récolte devait être vendue dans sa totalité au fermier du monopole, à un prix fixé par règlement, mais c'étaient les agents de l'économe qui venaient en prendre livraison. Comme il est de règle pour toute obligation contractée envers le Trésor, l'engagement d'Agathinos est assorti d'un serment royal (cf. Seidl 1929, pp. 14–17), qui sert à le solenniser et à le rendre par là même plus contraignant. Le nomarque, destinaire du document, fait alors figure de représentant de l'autorité royale.

Le deuxième texte, le P. dém. Sorb. inv. 1186, se présente sous la forme d'un contrat en double expédition. Comme tout contrat démotique, il s'agit d'une déclaration unilatérale émanant du contractant envers l'autre partie, qui est ici le nomarque Aristarchos. Au terme de cet engagement, un garde ou phylacite (*rs*) du nom de *Ḥr-ḫb* (Harkhèbis en grec) s'oblige vis-à-vis du nomarque à faire rentrer dans le grenier royal, à une date déterminée, 200 artabes de blé produits sur le territoire du village de *Pꜣ-ꜥ-Išwr*. Le nom de ce village correspond probablement en grec à *Syrôn Kômê* (cf. Peremans et Van't Dack 1953, pp. 67–69), et dénote la présence d'une colonie de Syriens (cf. Vaggi 1937, pp. 29–32). Il est intéressant de relever qu'à la ligne 4 du second texte, qui représente

7. Sur le monopole de l' huile, voir Préaux 1939a, pp. 65–72.

le contrat effectif, par rapport au premier qui ne serait qu'une proposition de contrat, le titre du nomarque *p3 sḥn p3 ʿt mḫṯ* est suivi d'une expression mutilée *p3 rwd 3pwrns p3* .... Il ne subsiste de ce mot qu'un fragment du signe initial et l'éditeur suggère qu'il "pourrait appartenir au groupe ... qui sert à rendre en démotique le titre de dioecète," et dont nous devons depuis peu la résolution à J. Yoyotte.[8] Ainsi, Aristarchos serait le représentant légal d'Apollonios le dioecète, Ministre des Finances et autorité suprême en matière fiscale. Cette hypothèse ne paraît pas trop risquée, car le document en question concerne un engagement envers le Trésor royal, et la référence au dioecète remplacerait en quelque sorte le serment royal. Le produit à livrer, du blé, est soumis à un régime différent de celui des oléagineux. S'il n'y a pas monopole, il y a cependant contrôle et séquestre des moissons.[9] Ces opérations, qui peuvent être confiées à des phylacites (cf. Kool 1954, pp. 34–39), sont destinées à garantir le versement des fermages et des impôts dus en blé. La présence ici d'un phylacite égyptien n'a rien d'étonnant en soi, car dès le IIIe siècle les indigènes occupaient de nombreux postes dans les cadres inférieurs de la police (cf. Peremans 1972, p. 76). Enfin, dernière remarque sur ce contrat démotique, la présence d'une clause dite d'*hêmiolia,* pénalité de 50% prévue en cas de non-respect du délai de livraison. Cette disposition, encore inconnue à l'époque préptolémaïque (cf. Hughes 1952, p. 5), apparaît comme l'assimilation imposée d'une pratique juridique grecque, étrangère à la tradition égyptienne.

Ces deux exemples du contrôle des récoltes mettent en évidence la tutelle exercée par le nomarque sur des agents, même extérieurs à ses services. Le nomarque lui-même était tenu personnellement responsable des agissements de ses subordonnés, et en cas de fraude ou de manquement venant de ces derniers, il pouvait être condamné à verser une amende, par exemple au fermier du monopole de l'huile, si celui-ci estimait qu'il avait été lésé sur la quantité de la récolte livrée. Ce système répond au principe des "responsabilités en cascade"[10] mis en place par le pouvoir Lagide, dans le but d'éviter tout détournement de ses revenus.

Pour conclure, je retiendrai deux points qui ressortent de nos deux archives bilingues de nomarques:

1) l'importance du nomarque de district comme rouage du contrôle étatique de l'agriculture, d'un bout à l'autre du processus de production, et cela pour le plus grand bénéfice du fisc royal
2) le rôle particulier des auxiliaires égyptiens aux échelons les plus humbles de l'administration, qui étaient le lieu obligé des contacts, sinon des échanges, entre la classe dominante étrangère et la population locale.

Cependant, à la même période, certains Égyptiens avaient déjà réussi un début d'ascension sociale à l'intérieur du système. Témoin: Achoapis,[11] c'est-à-dire *ʿnḫ-Ḥp,* nomarque de district indigène qui fut, à partir de 244 et durant une quinzaine d'années, le collègue et le voisin d'Aristarchos dans une nomarchie du nord de la méris d'Hérakleidès.

8. Sur *sntj*, équivalent possible de dioecète, voir Yoyotte 1989, pp. 73–90.

9. Sur le séquestre des moissons, voir Préaux 1939a, pp. 126–29.

10. Sur la responsabilité des fonctionnaires, voir Préaux 1939a, p. 449.

11. Sur Achoapis, voir Übel 1968, p. 266, note 1 et *PUG* III 114.

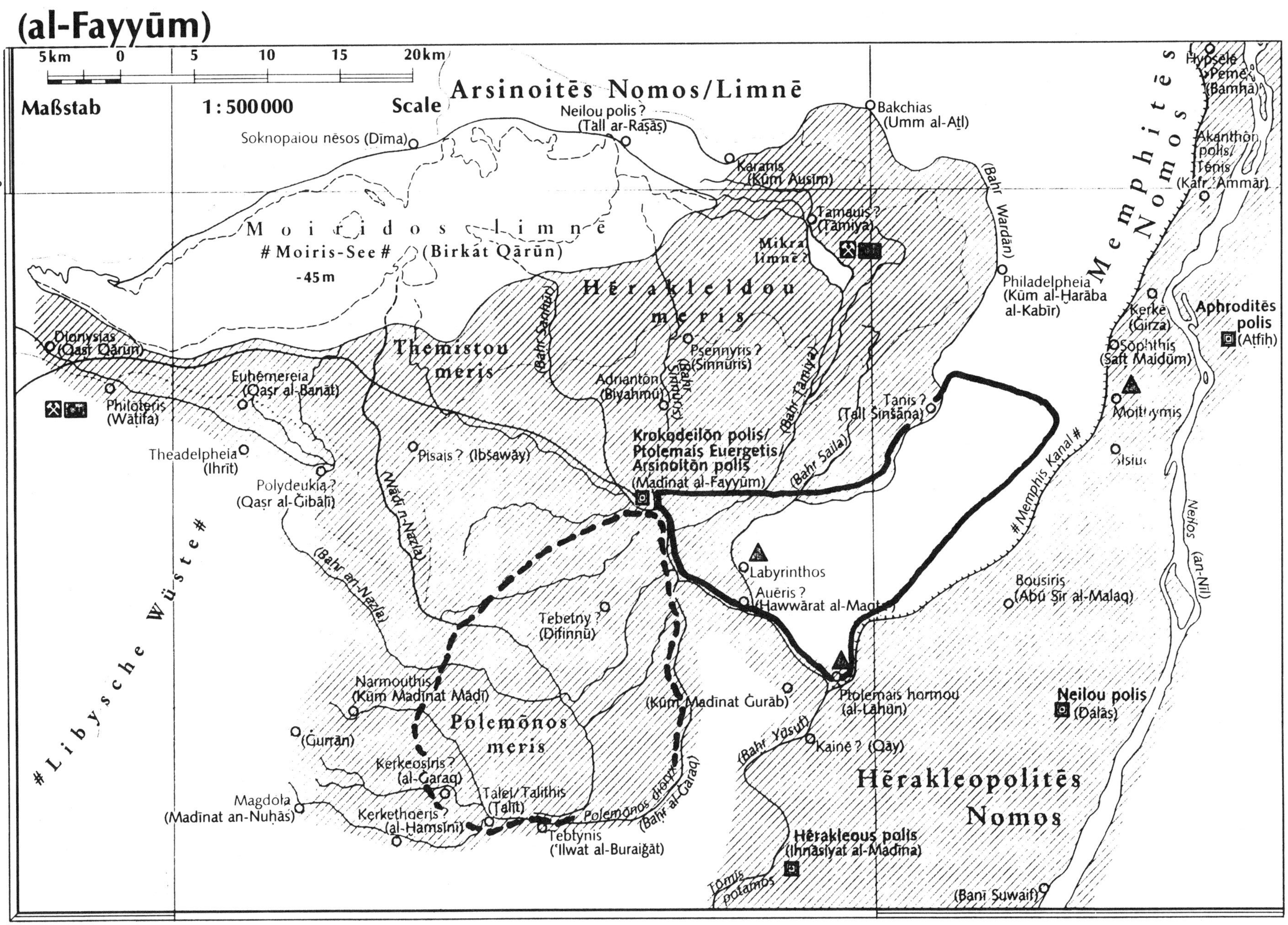

Figure 15.1. Le Fayoum; Key: – – – Nomarchie de Diogénès (localisation approximative); ——— Nomarchie d'Aristarchos (localisation approximative).

ANNEXE II

ARCHIVES DE DIOGÉNÈS

1) *Cartonnages d'origine*:

a) Papyrus publiés:
- Gh. 157 (masque):
  P. Lille 41, 42, 44, 45, 46, 47, 48, 49, 50, et 52.
  P. Sorbonne 22, 23, 24, 25, 26, 27, 28, 30, et 31.
- Gh. 158 (plastron):
  P. dém. Lille 12, 13, 14, 15, 16, 17, 18, 19, et 20.
- Gh. 159 (bande de jambe):
  P. Lille 39, 40, 43, et 51.
- Gh. 160 (chaussure):
  P. Sorbonne 19, 21, et 29.

b) inédits:
- Gh. 210 (chaussure): P. Sorb. inv. 571.
- Gh. 270 (débris d'un masque): P. dém. Sorb. inv. 1397 et 1398.
- sans numéro d'origine fiable:
  P. Sorb. inv. 298
  P. dém. Sorb. inv. 1294.

2) *Classement chronologique*:

P. Sorbonne 19	256 av. n.è.
P. Lille 39 à 51	251 av. n.è.
P. dém. Lille 12 à 20	251 av. n.è.
P. dém. Sorb. inv. 2301	251 av. n.è.
P. dém. Sorb. inv. 1196	251 av. n.è.
P. dém. Sorb. inv. 1248	251 av. n.è.
P. dém. Sorb. inv. 1294	251 av. n.è.
P. Sorbonne 21 à 30	251/250 av. n.è.
P. Sorbonne 31	250 av. n.è.

Papyrus publié non daté: P. Lille 52.

ANNEXE III

ARCHIVES D'ARISTARCHOS

1) *Cartonnages d'origine*:

- — Gh. 201 (plastron): P. Lille 12 à 17.
- — Gh. 183 (plastron): *SB* XII 10844 et 10850.
- — Gh. 17 (petit plastron): *SB* XII 10851.

2) *Classement chronologique*:

P. Lille 12	250 av. n.è.
P. dém. Sorb. inv. 1186	248 av. n.è.
P. Sorbonne 32	248 av. n.è.
SB XII 10850	248 av. n.è.
P. dém. Sorb. inv. 750b (inédit)	248 av. n.è.
SB XII 10844	247 av. n.è.
P. Sorb. inv. 2340 (inédit)	247 av. n.è.
P. Sorb. inv. 2698 (inédit)	247 av. n.è.
P. dém. Lille 108	247/246 av.
SB XII 10853	246 av. n.è.
P. Lille 13	244 av. n.è.
P. Lille 15	241 av. n.è.
P. Lille 14	238 av. n.è.

3) *Papyrus non datés*:

a) publiés: P. Lille 16 et 17.
SB XII 10851, 10852, 10854, 10855, et 10856.

b) inédits: P. Sorb. inv. 573, 2699, 2700, 2701, 2702, et 2703.

CHAPTER 16

SOME THOUGHTS ON THE SUBJECT "'STATE' AND 'CHURCH' IN PTOLEMAIC EGYPT"*

WERNER HUSS
Universität Bamberg

When Alexander tried to give Egypt a sort of temporary inner structure, he had to take into consideration that there were three politically relevant groups in the country: the military, the bureaucracy, and the clergy. Certainly, the military caused the least trouble. It was more difficult, on the one hand, not to push the enchorian bureaucratic ruling classes to the side and yet, on the other hand, not to give them too much authority. But the most delicate problem was the Egyptian "church"; with the "church" it was not possible — as it was with the general government, the treasury, and the military — to try to satisfy the Macedonian and the enchorian wishes by splitting their influence. Here the choice remained only between destruction and integration. Alexander rationally chose the second possibility.

I

In regard to this question, the Ptolemies agreed. It was in the interest of the "state" to win the "church" for the crown. If the "church" were won for the crown, then this would bring about a positive effect on the political attitudes of most of the native inhabitants vis-à-vis the regime. This was not to be doubted due to the great influence that the clergy possessed.

The means by which the Ptolemies tried to attain this goal were varied. Among these means were: tax reductions, suspensions of taxes, tax donations, granting of loans, gifts of several different kinds (especially for the building, extension, and maintenance of temples), granting of exemptions from legal-monopolistic regulations, granting of asylums, granting of privileges to priests, return of statues of the gods, the establishment of regular conferences of priests, freedom in drafting the decrees of the synods, the taking over of cult functions, acts of legitimation of the clergy who were dependent upon the pharaoh, and the enforcement of effective controls of the clergy (ἱερεῖς), the heads of the clergy (ἐπιστάται), and the notaries (*sẖw ḳnbt* = μονογράφοι) acting "in the name" of the clergy.

II

How did the "church" react to the attempts of the "state" both to accommodate and to discipline the former?

1. Without doubt, the "church" was ready to meet the advances of and to work with the "state." This can be seen in various ways.

* The text of this paper, besides some additions, is translated from German by J. Skinner, Universität Bamberg.

a) A first indication that the Egyptian clergy, at least, would not refuse to comply with the demands of the pharaoh can be seen in the fact that they — *nolentes volentes* — paid dues and taxes and bore the costs of board and lodging of the traveling pharaoh and his retinue.

b) One should also be reminded of the texts of the temple inscriptions and the relief depictions on the temple walls; the priests were most probably responsible for their form. The texts and depictions emphasized the continuity and legitimation of the Ptolemaic kingdom by the Egyptian gods, and in this respect laid the basis for the state (*tꜣ*) itself; these were important gifts in return from the "church" to the "state."

c) Furthermore, the priests approved the foreign, domestic, and religious policies of the government and thereby contributed to an important stabilizing factor in Egypt's political life.

d) Propagandistic protection of the flank coincided with the clergy's political support of the government. Propaganda by the "church" in support of the government was especially evidenced by the clergy's intended assimilation or identification of the rulers with the gods. In the same way, the clergy of Memphis set the birth dates of Ptolemy VI and Ptolemy IX and the enthronement of Ptolemy VIII on the same date as the birth date and enthronement of Apis bulls (*alii aliter*). Often enough the priests attested to the pharaoh that he corresponded to the traditional ideal of the pharaoh. The priests of Philae for example called Ptolemy VI the one "who protects Egypt, furnishes (?) the shrines, and upholds the laws." Egypt, the shrines, and the laws — an almost classical triad!

e) On special occasions the priests especially expressed their devotion to the pharaoh. The priests of Mendes held a funeral for Arsinoe II according to the ritual for the burial ceremony of dead rams, and the priests who congregated in Kanopos decided to conduct a funeral for the Princess Berenike based on the ritual for the burial of the holy bulls Apis and Mnevis. And not a few (above all Memphite) priests gave their daughters the dynastic names Arsinoe and Berenike.

2. The above mentioned pieces of evidence — especially the decrees of the synods — give the appearance of a clergy who faithfully served the government. This appearance is deceptive. There was opposition; opposition of different kinds and of different intensity. Above all the accidental discovery of the so-called "Demotic Chronicle" and the "Potter's Prophecy" reveals that the decrees of the synods, which appear to mirror the largely problem-free relationship between the "state" and the "church," only convey one side of the coin. The other side is unfortunately in bad condition.

   a) It may be somewhat of a surprise when I classify the Nektanebos legend found in the apocryphal *Vita Alexandri* as one of the documents that express a dissenting position to Alexander and his successors who ruled Egypt. Does not the Egyptian narrator of this legend support a pro-Macedonian line when he makes the Macedonian the son of the last native pharaoh? Scarcely. The Egyptian had Egyptian goals. Otherwise he would have hardly characterized Alexander as Αἰγύπτιον ἄνθρωπον κοσμοκράτορα βασιλέα. When he saw that Alexander had asserted himself in Egypt — and also against the Persian "arch-enemy" — and was legally crowned pharaoh, he asked himself the question: how could he interpret this event? He chose a solution that allowed a certain balancing out. On the one hand, he admitted that Alexander was the legitimate ruler; on the other hand, he admitted that Alexander was a ruler in such a way that he interpreted his rule as that of an Egyptian over Egyptians. In this way Alexander's rule was, for the Egyptians, more bearable. By considering this point we are justified in characterizing this document as a document lightly critical of a claim to power that was emphasized too strongly as Macedonian.

It would be very interesting to know to which clergy the author of this legend belonged. But here only conjectures are possible. Since Nektanebos II — other than in the "Demotic Chronicle" — is characterized as a positive figure and since the oldest son of Nektanebos II lived during the Ptolemaic reign in Iseion, the city of his ancestors, and had a respected position there, the assumption, as it appears, is not totally unfounded that the author of the legend also had his home in Iseion.

b) The "Dream of Nektanebos" is closely related to the "Legend of Nektanebos." Since the "Dream" — as far as we can know this — shows a tendency similar to the "Legend," it might also be interpreted in a similar way: a native priest tries to save what is possible for Egypt by connecting the figure of Alexander with that of Nektanebos.

c) One kind of opposition that was probably not at all uncommon can be seen in the history of the calendar reform found in the "Kanopos-Decree," a calendar reform that — as the later decrees show — came to nothing, and, in addition, perhaps in the fact, that most priests — in spite of the regulation of the same decree — did not present themselves as priests of the *theoi Euergetai.* This was an opposition without words, an opposition of silent protest!

d) But what did the priests of Philae think when, for example, during the reign of Ptolemy XII, they wrote the following text on the large pylon of the Isis Temple next to the depiction of the suppression of the enemy?

> It is Ptolemy on his throne as hero at the head of Philae, while he crushes the rebels (*bṯnw*) and cuts off the hand of the Trogodytes and binds the Nubians by their hair, who stabs the enemy before him with his knife and destroys the *Ḥ3wnbwt* with his club.

The priests were not at all forced because of a given traditional pattern to name the *Ḥ3w-nbwt*, the Greeks, in this connection! Consequently, they considered the Greeks to be enemies of the pharaoh (and thus of Egypt) in the same way as the rebels, the Trogodytes, and the Nubians. Although it should be warned against seeing a concrete political program in such texts, it is nevertheless quite clear that the priests of Philae had great reservations about the Greeks — probably more than this.

But had not the Pharaoh himself, who "destroys the *Ḥ3w-nbwt* with his club," belonged to the *Ḥ3w-nbwt*? Surely! Here is a certain tension that has not been, in my view, fully explained. In any case, according to the intentions of the priests of Philae, the pharaoh should (and "could") not come into the line of fire in the same way as the Greeks. After all, it was the pharaoh who had invested considerable sums in the building of the temple. But since the priests of Philae apparently longed for at least the removal of the Greeks from positions of power, they also opposed a government that was not ready to adapt itself to their liking.

e) One must also mention in this connection the fact that there are cases in Demotic, for example from the documents of Tebtunis, where the pharaoh's name was written — against the norm — without a cartouche and with the determinative of a foreign people. It is difficult to believe that the scribes who wrote these names — and the scribes worked "in the name" of the priests — acted on the one hand out of carelessness and on the other out of exactness in the way they did. Their conduct at least reveals rather a distancing if not outright opposition.

f) The "Demotic Chronicle" is for our purposes an important document but one that is also difficult to interpret: the language is sometimes consciously ambiguous, the meaning of several phrases cannot be adequately explained, and above all authors from different time periods wrote the text. If one wants to gain knowledge about the era from this document, one of the necessary prerequisites is to separate the various literary layers from one another. At least one must distinguish the oracle (*tp rꜣ*), which appears to some (Ed. Meyer) to be "as incomprehensible as a witch's magic spell," from the interpretation or interpretations. The last interpreter gave the "Chronicle" its final form during the Macedonian era. One of his most important statements is: "A man from Hnês (i.e. Herakleopolis) is the one who will rule after the foreigners (and) the Ionians." Another passage relates: "The prophet of Harsaphes looks forward to the time after the Ionians. (For) it became a conqueror in Hnês." The long-awaited native ruler, who will ascend the throne of the pharaohs after the Persians and Macedonians, will come from Herakleopolis (Megale). From the house of the "ship masters" of the city who were so mighty during the time of the Saites? We do not know. In any case he will "not abandon the law" according to the last exegete. He "has sacrifices brought (again) to the gods" and he "starts a rebellion ... ." Of course, the latter mentioned aspect is especially important from a political point of view. And although it is not absolutely certain that the Macedonians are meant by the "dogs" (*ꜣwꜣww*) and Alexander the Great by the "big dog" (*ꜣwꜣw ꜥꜣ*), the general direction in which the last revisor of the oracle thought is in any case unambiguous. Surprising is the fact — if it is a fact — that the last exegete brought the version of the "Chronicle" known to him up-to-date in the first half of the third century, i.e. in a time in which there were no political or military battles between those who supported the government and those who represented the interests of the native Egyptians. But if protest slogans against the government of the kind found in the "Chronicle" were echoed in less turbulent or completely quiet times, then this reveals that certain clerical groups were keeping alive under the surface the fire of hatred for the foreign rulers.

g) The "Lamb-Prophecy" is similar to both the "Chronicle" and to the "Potter's Prophecy." It originates most probably from the time of the Persians. The last interpreter, however, who revised the prophecy, was a priest who lived during the time of the Ptolemies, for in Column II, line 1 the expression "the Greeks" appears. Due to this topical reference to political events or conditions during the time of the Ptolemies, the prophecy received a new anti-Macedonian face.
The place of origin for the prophecy, which is contained in the text found in Dimeh (Soknopaiou Nesos), cannot be exactly determined. With certain reservations, the place where the document was found reveals that the clergy of Sobek of Soknopaiu Nesos belonged to the clergy which — at least at times and partly — exhibited anti-Ptolemaic feelings.

h) A gripping document of the fight of the Egyptian priests against the ruling Macedonian-Greek class and especially against the pharaoh, the spokesman for this class, is the "Potter's Prophecy." Both the anti-Greek and anti-governmental character of this document is beyond doubt. I would just like to mention a few expressions that can be connected with the Greeks: Τυφώνιοι, ζωνοφόροι, ξένοι (ἄνδρες) and ἀσεβεῖς as well as ἀσέβεια, ἀνομίαι, and παράνομον. To which degree the παραταλάσσ{ε}ιος π̣ό̣λ[{ε}ις] Alexandria is regarded as the perfect example for the un-Egyptian and the foreign, you can infer from the fact that in this document the ἀγάλματα were not brought back from Persia but from Alexandria "to Egypt."
It is beyond doubt that the "Potter's Prophecy" and also the interpretations contained in it originated from clerical groups. But in which? In my opinion, in those of the Thot-clergy

of Hermopolis. This conclusion derived from textual observation has been supported to a certain degree by the director of the papyrus collection of the Austrian National Library. Mr. Harrauer writes (3 November 1989): "... to G 19813 [= P_2] ... there exists a handwritten inventory slip from Wessely's days with the note 'papyrus from the year 1886.' That would mean: from ... Hermupolis Magna."

Accordingly, at least some of the clergy of Thot of Hermupolis were anti-Ptolemaic during certain time periods of the second century. They clothed their convictions in a royal novella and with the help of this literary work tried to become politically active. We do not know the extent of their efforts nor if their efforts to a certain degree were crowned with success. We can perhaps gather that their activities were not completely unimportant from the fact that three papyri were found with the text of the "Potter's Prophecy," a fact that is astonishing in view of comparable literary works.

III

Let us summarize briefly what has been discussed.

The official announcements — especially the decrees of the synods — mirror a picture of problem-free relationships between the "state" and the "church." This picture corresponds only partly to historical reality. When looked at as a whole, the relationships between the "state" and the "church" were far and away more differentiated and more complicated than these announcements suggest. The priests responded to the pharaoh's offer of cooperation partly with consent, partly with reluctance, and partly with rejection, even irreconcilable enmity. They expressed their convictions both by word and by image; they made "political propaganda."

It can be assumed that the clerical groups who were opposed to the government were more numerous and stronger than the few documents of this opposition indicate — this above all because more official announcements were preserved than the opposition's statements, which in many cases were not written down and which above all usually were not engraved in stone.

CHAPTER 17

DIE MEDINET HABU OSTRACA: EXCAVATION OF THE ORIENTAL INSTITUTE OF THE UNIVERSITY OF CHICAGO 1928/29

URSULA KAPLONY-HECKEL
The University of Marburg

Von allen mir bekannten Sammlungen ägyptischer Ostraka, die man in situ gefunden hat,[1] ist der Fund von Medinet Habu am umfangreichsten; er umfaßt mehr als vier einhalb tausend Texte und erstreckt sich vom Neuen Reich[2] bis hin in die Arabische Zeit:[3] Eine Masse, die für den Forscher ebenso bei Einzelfragen z.B. nach zeitgenössischen örtlichen Verwaltungspraktiken, wie bei der Zusammenschau wirtschaftlicher Entwicklungen unerschöpflich sein wird!

Die Medinet Habu Texte auf Tonscherben und Kalksteinplatten in Hieroglyphen, in Hieratisch, Demotisch, Griechisch, Koptisch und Arabisch sind durchnumeriert von Nr. 1 bis Nr. 4560. Man hat die einzelnen Schriftträger schon auf der Grabung Stück um Stück mit der Field Number und mit

1. Damit meine ich vor allem die unpublizierten demotischen und demotisch-griechischen (sic) Ostraka im Kelsey Museum in Ann Arbor; sie stammen aus dem Fajum, vermutlich aus Karanis, nach Clarysses brieflicher Auskunft vermutlich aus dem II. Jahrhundert v. Chr.
   Die bei den zweiten Deir-el-Bahri-Ausgrabungen des Metropolitan Museum of Art, New York am Hathor-Tempel und aus dem Grabungsschutt von Naville ans Licht gekommenen und unveröffentlichten Ostraka erstrecken sich zwar auch über eine Spanne vom Neuen Reich bis zur koptischen Zeit; ich habe die Grabungsfotos im Metropolitan Museum in New York durchblättern können; die Originale der demotischen Ostraka und wohl auch die z. T. recht hübschen hieratischen Texte sind in Kairo geblieben; die einschlägigen koptischen Ostraka befinden sich heute im Besitz der Columbia University, New York, wo ich — auf der Suche nach demotischen Acker-Amt-Texten aus Deir-el-Bahri — alle die vielen Tausende dankenswerterweise habe durchsehen können.
   Ich vergleiche das Medinet Habu Material vor allem mit der Sammlung von gut vierhundert unveröffentlichten demotischen Ostraka in Turin, die aus den italienischen Grabungen in Gebelein stammen. Im Gegensatz zu dem über viele Jahrhunderte strömenden Reichtum an Medinet Habu Ostraka beschränken sich die demotischen Gebelein-Belege auf die knapp einhundert Jahre dieser Ägyptisch und Griechisch gleichermaßen gut belegten Militärkolonie, die vom Beginn des II. Jahrhunderts v. Chr. bis zum Sacco di Tebe im Jahr 88 v. Chr. Bestand gehabt hat; die Turiner Ostraka bilden einen Schwerpunkt inmitten der sonst aus Ankäufen u.ä. stammenden zahlreichen Gebelein-Texte.
   Sodann gehören hierher die paar Dutzend unveröffentlichter Ostraka aus der Oase Chargeh, die sich im Metropolitan Museum befinden; sie reichen (nach brieflicher Aussage von G. Vittmann zu den Hieratischen Texten) von der 21./22. Dynastie über gut zwei Dutzend Demotische Belege mit wenigen Griechischen und Koptischen Texten bis in die christliche Zeit.
   In der Oase Dachleh hat man in den letzten Jahren mehrere hundert Ostraka gefunden, deren Fotos ich in Toronto einmal habe durchsehen können. Um Gegensatz zu den Chargeh-Belegen, wo sämtliche römischen Steuer-Quittungen fehlen, gibt es in Dachleh davon übergenug.
2. Es befinden sich unter dem unerfaßten hieratischen Material ein paar Tonscherben aus dem Mittleren Reich.
3. Es handelt sich bei dem arabischen Ostrakon Medinet Habu um ein Schreiben wegen "Schuhen."

der fortlaufenden Ostraka-Grabungsnummer versehen und jeweils zwanzig Fragmente oder mehr zusammen fotografiert. Publiziert hat Miriam Lichteim (OIP Vol. LXXX) 1957 davon 160 demotische Ostraka.[4]

Die sämtlichen Grabungsunterlagen, also auch die Grabungstagebücher und die Grabungsfotos, sollen mit Hölscher längst vor dem Krieg nach Berlin ans Ägyptische Museum gegangen sein.[5]

Von den Grabungsfotos befindet sich ein unvollständiger Satz von 214 guten Abzügen im Maßstab 4:5 in der Fotothek des Oriental Institute in Chicago, aber keine Negative. Aus den vorhandenen Grabungsfotos hat John Larson 27 Find Spot Nummern rekonstruieren können; für die demotischen Ostraka haben sich von den im Basement liegenden Originalen noch drei Field Nummern hinzufinden lassen, u.a. (mit Lichtheim) 30.130a für das Familienarchiv des *Ms-wr*; von dessen 39 Ostraka tritt kein einziges in den vorhandenen Fotos auf; Miriam Lichtheim hat aber schon 27 Belege davon publiziert. Vermutlich befinden sich alle Belege dieses Familienarchivs in Chicago.

Ende der fünfziger Jahre mußte von Dr. Hughes ein großer Teil der Ostraka ans Ägyptische Museum nach Kairo zurückgebracht werden. Eine Liste der zurückgebrachten Ostraka hat sich im Oriental Institute in Chicago bisher nicht gefunden. Ebensowenig sind uns bei unserer Durchsicht der demotischen Ostraka-Bestände des Ägyptischen Museums Kairo im Frühjahr und im Herbst 1983 irgendwelche mit MH gezeichneten demotischen Ostraka begegnet.[6]

Was steht uns also an Demotischen Ostraka aus Medinet Habu im Oriental Institute in Chicago zur Verfügung?

Erstens gibt es im Oriental Institute in Chicago an Medinet Habu Originalen 2086 Texte; davon sind 435 Stück Demotische Ostraka[7], inklusive 32 Griechisch-Demotische Ostraka und 12 Demotisch-Griechische Ostraka.

Zweitens sind aus den Fotos 364 Demotische Ostraka erreichbar, wovon 107 auch im Original vorhanden sind; also erbringen die Fotos einen Zuwachs von 257 Ostraka-Fotographien. Das ergibt 692, also knapp siebenhundert Demotische Ostraka Medinet Habu.

Davon hat, wie oben gesagt, Miriam Lichtheim (1957) 160 Nummern publiziert; in den Tempeleiden (1963) sind ca. 20 mit Faksimile oder im Katalog erfaßt.[8] Es bleibt also gut ein halbes Tausend Demotische Ostraka Medinet Habu übrig, die unerfaßt sind.[9]

4. Über die Koptischen Ostraka und die Publikation von Koptischen Medinet Habu Ostraka durch Stefanski und Lichtheim u.a. hat Terry Wilfong schon referiert.

5. Im Sommer 1989 gab es Leute, die hofften, die sämtlichen Unterlagen seien nach dem Mai 1945 zur Sicherheit nach Washington gekommen. Dr. Joachim Karig vom Ägyptischen Museum in Berlin-Charlottenburg, der u.a. deswegen am 24. Mai 1989 in Chicago vorsprach, hatte bis zum Symposium nichts Positives dazu melden können. Wie ich im Frühjahr 1991 brieflich von Brian Muhs erfahre, sind jetzt Nachrichten über den Verbleib der Unterlagen bei Terry Wilfong eingetroffen.

6. Nach der Tradition des Kairener Museums befinden sich die zurückgegebenen Medinet Habu Ostraka wohlbehalten (in den Holzkistchen der Rücksendung) in dem für nicht-ägyptische Wissenschaftler unzugänglichen Sous-sol oder im "deuxième" des Museums. Sie waren im März 1992 unauffindbar.

7. Das eben erwähnte Familienarchiv des *Ms-wr* befindet sich ganz in Chicago.

8. In beiden Fällen ist der Versuch unterblieben, Texte einer Verwaltungsinstanz oder aus einem Familienarchiv nebeneinanderzustellen und zusammen zu interpretieren.

9. Es liegt uns hier sehr daran, auf die Ostraka Bestände des Oriental Institute Museum Chicago und des Field Museum of Natural History, ebenfalls in Chicago, hinzuweisen. Man hat seinerzeit die Ayer Ostraka-Collection z.T. im FMNH und z.T. im OIMC erworben: Unter den 312 Ostraka des FMNH gibt es knapp 200 demotische Ostraka. Unter den etwa mehr als tausend Ostraka des OIMC gibt es mindestens 297 demotische Ostraka; das macht nochmals ein halbes Tausend aus.

Einen Überblick über die Demotischen Ostraka Medinet Habu und ihre zeitliche oder inhaltliche Zuordnung können wir hier nur in begrenztem Maß vorlegen; folgende Notizen sind bemerkenswert:

Die in Chicago erreichbaren Demotischen Ostraka Medinet Habu beginnen im zweiten Jahrhundert v. Chr. und gehen bis in die späte Römerzeit. U.W. fehlen alle demotischen Texte aus dem dritten Jahrhundert v. Chr. [Nach Notizen bei den griechischen Ostraka aus der Hand des verstorbenen Gräzisten Wilmot gibt es aber griechische Belege aus dem III. Jahrh. v. Chr.] Der Beleg des *P3-whr*, von Lichtheim (a.a.O.) als Nr. 12 publiziert, könnte der knappen Sprache nach ins III. Jahrhundert v. Chr. einzuordnen sein.[10]

Es ist für den Wert einer Medinet Habu Ostraka-Publikation ganz entscheidend, daß die Demotischen Ostraka mit ihrem Umfeld, d.h. zusammen mit den gleichzeitigen Griechischen Ostraka veröffentlicht werden. Daß dies für die späteren koptischen und die byzantinischen griechischen und koptischen Texte auch gilt, versteht sich von selbst.

Werfen wir noch einen Blick auf den Inhalt der demotischen Medinet Habu Ostraka: Zum großen Teil handelt es sich um Rechtsurkunden aus Familienarchiven; sie enthalten objektiv und subjektiv stilisierte Quittungen; sodann gibt es vierzig Tempeleide, knapp dreißig Acker-Amt-Quittungen, wozu vom Acker-Amt dreizehn Acker-Akten-Kladden[11] kommen, ein paar Briefverträge; ein paar Fragmente von Mumien-Listen mit einem Vertrag.

Des weiteren gibt es wie in jeder Ostraka-Sammlung aus Oberägypten Listen von Leuten, von Sachen, von Ausständen, vielerlei Notizen; diese Texte nennen wir Kladden oder rough drafts; wir sehen darin die Unterlagen zu den verschiedenen Amtsarchiven und Buchführungsarchiven.[12] Es gibt Ostraka-Briefe und u.a. auch schriftliche Anweisungen.[13]

Nur ein paar wenige Belege liegen außerhalb der Amtsakten, der Familienarchive und der Buchführungsarchive: Etwa das fragmentarische Onomastikon der Berufe, wo genannt sind:

> "Fisch-Mann," also "Fisch-Händler,"
> "Drogen-Mann," etwa "Apotheker" usw., wohl die einzige Schulübung.

Ein einziges Horoskop stammt aus dem 43. Jahr des Augustus.

Übrigens gibt es auch ein paar frühdemotische oder vorptolemäische nicht-literarische Ostraka.

Was gibt es nicht?

Ein Ostrakon mit einer historischen Erzählung oder mit einem anderen literarischen Text habe ich bisher nicht entdeckt, auch kein Gebet[14] und kein Orakel.

Es erheben sich mehrere Fragen:

Eine *erste Frage* mag sein:

Soll man das nach Kairo zurückgebrachte Medinet Habu Ostraka-Material in die Publikation einbeziehen oder soll man zunächst das Chicago Material erarbeiten?

10. Abgesehen von einem einzigen Paralleltext desselben Mannes in Straßburg (Nachlaß Spiegelberg im Oriental Institute in Chicago) kennt Brian Muhs, inzwischen sehr am Material aus dem III. Jahrh. v. Chr. interessiert, nichts Vergleichbares. Das ist ganz anders bei der Ayer-Collection und dem übrigen OIMC Bestand, wo er schon reichlich Belege aus dem III. Jahrhundert v. Chr. hat identifizieren können.

11. Dazu kommt ein weiterer griechischer Acker-Kladden-Beleg aus dem Oriental Institute Museum; solche griechischen Texte sind ganz rar!

12. So mit E. Seidl 1964, S. 16f.

13. Was es nicht gibt, sind schriftliche Auszahlungs- oder Liefer-Anordnungen, wie wir sie aus den unveröffentlichten demotischen Ostraka von Chargeh kennen. Erst recht nicht solche "Bring Wasser!" Anweisungen, wie sie Bresciani und Thissen in den Enchoria aus Oxyrhynchos veröffentlicht haben.

14. Ein Gebet auf Ostrakon gibt es im Ägyptisches Museen in Leipzig.

Mein Vorschlag ist, man erarbeite zuerst nur das in Chicago erreichbare, oben kurz vorgestellte Medinet Habu-Material, um in möglichst exakten kleinen Schritten und bald "Erfolge" zu erringen und sie melden zu können. Mehr Material aus Chicago, etwa aus der ehemaligen Ayer-Sammlung (jetzt im FMNH und im OIMC)[15] oder etwa auch aus Kairo läßt sich in absehbarer Zeit einarbeiten.

Natürlich erhebt sich die *zweite Frage* sofort:

Will Frau Kaplony das alles allein machen?

Nein, sicher nicht![16] Vielmehr liegt es mir sehr daran, nur einer in einem Team zu sein. Gedankenaustausch, Kritik und gegenseitiges Mutmachen sind wichtige Faktoren für unser Unternehmen. Die vorläufigen Pläne eines Teams haben sich vom September 1990 bis zum April 1991 folgendermaßen entwickelt: Zu Brian Muhs/Philadelphia und Linda Ricketts/North Dakota[17] hat sich inzwischen im Frühjahr 1991 Dominic Montserrat/London gemeldet.

Die *dritte Frage* geht um den ersten Termin.

Das nächste Mal möchte ich im Frühjahr 1993[18] für ein paar Wochen im Team am Oriental Institute in Chicago mit den jungen Team-Kollegen zusammenkommen. Linda Ricketts ist an griechischen und demotischen Ostraka der jüngeren Ptolemäerzeit interessiert, Brian Muhs ist am III. Jahrh. v. Chr., Dominic Montserrat an den Griechischen Ostraka[19] interessiert.

Vierte Frage:

Wie ist die Veröffentlichung gedacht?

Wie Sie am thebanischen Acker-Schreiber Sesostris[20] gesehen haben, ist es fruchtbar, thebanische Ostraka nach Verwaltungsinstanzen und/oder nach Familienarchiven zusammenzustellen. So geht mein Vorschlag dahin, zunächst um einen gut belegten Schreiber[21] oder um eine gut belegte Familie herum ein paar Texte zu gruppieren, die Zeitgenossen dazuzusuchen und zügig in Rapports und kurzen Aufsätzen das Material zu erschließen.

15. Natürlich wäre wünschenswert, weitgehend das thebanische OIM Material und den FMNH Bestand heranziehen. Übrigens steht im Oriental Institute in Chicago auch Spiegelbergs Nachlaß zu den Straßburger Ostraka zur Verfügung, an denen zur Zeit niemand arbeitet.

16. Auf den Rat von H.-J. Thissen werde ich zuerst das MS der Gebelein-Acker-Akten (vgl. unser Referat in Third International Congress of Demotists, Cambridge 1987) abschließen und noch an anderen Gebelein-Texten arbeiten. Übrigens war es K.-Th. Zauzich, durch den ich von schwierigen, ja unlösbaren Gebelein-Garten-Arbeitsquittungen an die thebanischen Acker-Arbeitsquittungen und damit an das Medinet Habu Material in Chicago gekommen bin! Vielen Dank!

17. Dr. Linda Ricketts ist im August 1991 verstorben.

18. Nicht im Mai 1992, wie im September 1990 unverbindlich besprochen.

19. Die Griechischen Ostraka sind für Herrn Prof. Wikgren reserviert. Dies Problem wird sich im Jahr 1993 durch einen persönlichen Besuch bei ihm klären lassen.

20. Das Referat am Vortag hatte den Titel: "Der thebanische Acker-Schreiber Sesostris, Sohn des Anchoapis."

21. Damit wird dem Diskussionsvorschlag von S. Allam entsprochen, mit dem Untersuchen von Ämtern zu beginnen; das sei für die Rechts- und Wirtschaftsgeschichte am wichtigsten.

CHAPTER 18

DER THEBANISCHE ACKER-SCHREIBER SESOSTRIS, SOHN DES ANCHOAPIS

URSULA KAPLONY-HECKEL
The University of Marburg

Die Nachrichten über die Ackerland-Vermessung im vorptolemäischen Theben sind rasch aufgezählt: Jeder kennt die Gräber der 18. Dynastie von Menna und seinen Kollegen, wo man mit dem Meß-Strick das Getreidefeld auf dem Halm vermißt. Geschriebene Dokumente zur Ackerland-Vermessung aus dem Neuen Reich und der Spätzeit speziell für Theben fehlen.

Das ändert sich im II. Jahrhundert v. C.: Es gibt da zweierlei Ostraka-Texte, die thebanische Ackerland-Vermessung betreffen. Zum einen kennen wir jetzt neunundfünfzig demotische Ostraka mit Ackerflächen-Berechnungen, mit Listen von Leuten und Acker-Aruren, mit Listen von Nachbarn. Wir nennen sie Acker-Amt-Kladden. In den Kladden sehen wir die Unterlagen zu Amtsarchiven aus der Landwirtschaftsverwaltung, also Unterlagen zu Papyrus-Akten der Verwaltung.[1] Wir lassen die Acker-Amt-Kladden beiseite.

Zum anderen existieren da die *r-rḫ=w* Texte. Wir definieren sie heute als Acker-Arbeitsquittungen. Den Terminus Arbeitsquittung kann man zuerst 1899 bei Ulrich Wilcken[2] in den griechischen Ostraka finden, und zwar für Damm-Arbeiten. In unserem Fall der *r-rḫ=w* Texte handelt es sich um Quittungen für geleistete Feldbestellung, die wir in Zusammenhang mit Zwangspacht-Maßnahmen von Ptolemaios VI. Philometor sehen möchten.

Eine solche Acker-Arbeitsquittung sagt aus:

"Dem NN, S. des NN, werden × Aruren anerkannt."

1. Einschlägige griechische "Acker-Vermessungspapyri" sind für Mittel- und Unterägypten belegt (vgl. Anm. 11ff. unseres Referats "Thebanische Acker-Amt-Quittungen" für das Internationale Rechtshistoriker-Symposion "Grund und Boden in Altägypten" in Tübingen, Juni 1990); sie existieren in Demotisch in vielen unveröffentlichten Papyrus-Fragmenten für Gebelein (in Arbeit, vgl. unser Referat in Third International Congress of Demotists, Cambridge 1987), fehlen aber u.W. bisher für Theben. Wir können diese thebanischen Ostraka-Kladden nur nach der Paläographie datieren und versuchen, sie in die späte Ptolemäer- und die Römerzeit einordnen: viele Belege sind fragmentarisch und sehr schwer verständlich.

2. Wilcken 1899, vol. I, p. 129.

Das bedeutet: NN hat × Aruren gepflügt, gewässert und eingesät; er bekommt dies bei der Inspektion der aufgegangenen Saat im Frühjahr quittiert.

Eine Acker-Arbeitsquittung enthält auf jeden Fall:

1. Das Regierungsjahr ohne Angabe des Herrschers;
2. den Schreiber mit Namen und Vaternamen, aber ohne Titel, sowie die Namen eines oder mehrerer Zeugen mit Vaternamen (vor dem Sacco di Tebe in 88 v.C. unterschreiben meist mehrere Zeugen);
3. vom Farmer den Namen und den Vaternamen;
4. die Ackerlage und/oder den Gesamt-Acker;
5. die Größe des Teil-Ackers in Aruren oder Bruchteilen davon.

Die Acker-Arbeitsquittung kann wahlweise die Größe des Gesamt-Ackers angeben, dessen (Acker-)Herrn mit Namen, eventuell mit Vaternamen, den Ertrag in Weizen-Artaben pro Arure und den Gesamt-Ertrag des Teil-Ackers in Weizen-Artaben, gelegentlich in Ölsaat-Artaben.

Bisher haben wir 163 Acker-Arbeitsquittungen für Theben gesammelt und können folgende Fragen klären:

1. Wie hat man die *r-rḫ=w* Texte zu datieren?

   Sie beginnen in der Regierung von Ptolemaios VI. Philometor[3] und reichen bis in die frühe Römerzeit. Es fehlen *r-rḫ=w* Texte aus dem III. Jahrhunderts v.C.[4] und aus der Zeit nach Augustus.

2. Wo werden die *r-rḫ=w* Texte ediert?

   Die *r-rḫ=w* Schreiber schreiben nichts als *r-rḫ=w* Quittungen; jegliche anderen Dokumente aus ihrer Hand fehlen. Also werden die thebanischen Acker-Arbeitsquittungen von einer selbständigen Institution ediert; wir nennen sie "das thebanische Acker-Amt." Für den hauptamtlichen Schreiber verwenden wir den Arbeitstitel "Acker-Schreiber"; wir nennen die *r-rḫ=w* Quittungen daher auch *Acker-Amt-Quittungen (AAQ).*

3. Wie verteilt sich das Material im thebanischen Raum?

   Das thebanische Acker-Amt spaltet sich in Theben-Ost und Theben-West. Der Acker-Schreiber von Theben-Ost gebraucht ein anderes Formular als der von Theben-West: Der von Theben-Ost startet nämlich die Acker-Amt-Quittung mit Regierungsjahr,-monat und -tag,

3. Vgl. de Meulenaere 1967, S. 297–99.

4. Das lässt sich u.a. an den Personennamen erkennen.

während sein Kollege im Westen und in Erment mit der Formel *r-rḫ=w* beginnt und mit dem Datum schließt.

4. Wieviel Acker-Schreiber sind nebeneinander tätig?

   Nach unseren Unterlagen ist in Theben-Ost wie in Theben-West jeweils nur ein einziger Acker- Schreiber im Amt.

5. Wird bei der Ackerland-Beschreibung zwischen dem rechten und dem linken Nilufer unterschieden?

   Wir teilen hier nur soviel mit: In Theben-West ist in der Regel der Terminus "Hoch-Acker" gebraucht. In Theben-Ost fehlt der "Hoch-Acker" ganz; hingegen wird hier meist für Teil-Äcker aus den Feldern anderer Männer und mehrfach für sehr kleine Stücke "Uferstreifen" quittiert.[5]

6. Was erfährt man über den Verbleib der Acker-Amt-Quittungen?

   Die einzelnen Farmer bewahren ihre Acker-Amt-Quittungen zusammen mit den Getreide-, Geld-, Nekropolensteuer-Quittungen und Tempel-Eiden sorgfältig im Familien-Archiv auf. Das wissen wir aus dem am West Gate[6] gefundenen umfangreichen Familien-Archiv der *Ms-wr* Familie in Medinet Habu; zu den publizierten Belegen gehören nämlich noch vier unpublizierte Dokumente: Drei schwierige Acker-Amt-Quittungen und ein Tempel-Eid.

7. Gibt es griechische Parallelen aus Oberägypten?

   Nein, nicht unmittelbar zu den *r-rḫ=w* Texten.[7] Sehr wohl aber zur Zwangspacht; das sind die griechischen επιγραφη-Getreide-Quittungen. Es fehlt uns hier die Zeit, das Problem der Zwangspacht aufzurollen.[8]

Um Ihnen die Acker-Amt-Quittungen an praktischen Beispielen zu illustrieren, lege ich zwanzig *r-rḫ=w* Texte[9] vor, die der Acker-Schreiber Sesostris,[10] S. des Anchoapis, unterschrieben oder geschrieben hat. Von den 20 Belegen stammen sechs aus der Medinet Habu Grabung des Oriental Institute der University of Chicago; d.h., dies sind in situ Funde aus Theben-West; die übrigen 14

5. Vgl. Kaplony-Heckel 1990, Tabelle V und VI.
6. Field No. 30.130 a, Find Spot R 8; vgl. Lichtheim 1957, S. XIII.
7. Wir haben bei unserer gewiß noch unvollständigen Suche nach Parallelen bisher erst eine einzige griechische Acker-Akten-Kladde gefunden, und zwar im Royal Ontario Museum in Toronto, 1976, Nr. 240 = ROM 906.8.629.
8. Vgl. die einschlägigen Referate auf dem Internationalen Rechtshistoriker-Symposion im Juni 1990 in Tübingen.
9. Die unbekannten Texte sollen in absehbarer Zeit mit Photographien in den Enchoria erscheinen.
10. Wir wählen für das spätptolemäische *S-n-Wsrt* die übliche Namensform des Mittleren Reichs, also Sesostris.

Texte verteilen sich heute über die Museen in Cairo,[11] Chicago[12] (das Field Museum und das Oriental Institute Museum), Leipzig,[13] London,[14] Oxford,[15] Straßburg, und Toronto.

Sechzehn davon sind exakt zu datieren: Wie schon de Meulenaere (a.a.O.) an den publizierten Belegen beobachtet hat, gehört dieser Acker-Schreiber Sesostris in die Zeit des VI. und des VIII. Ptolemäers.

Wir stellen außerdem fest: Gemäß der von uns beobachteten Tradition der Acker-Schreiber[16] beginnt Sesostris als Zeuge: Er signiert als dritter Zeuge Nr.1 (D 23) im Jahr 30; das ist der 28. April[17] 151 v.C.[18] Damit sind alle Regierungsjahre 26, 27, 28, 29 und 30 der übrigen Belege automatisch für Ptolemaios VIII. an zu setzen. In die Regierung des Ptolemaios VI. gehört sicher

11. Unser Dank gilt Herrn Direktor Dr. M. Muhsen für alles Entgegenkommen.

12. In Chicago liegen aus der ehemaligen Ayer-Sammlung ein Text im Field Museum of Natural History, zwei Texte im Oriental Institute Museum der University of Chicago; dort befinden sich auch, wie eben erwähnt, aus der Grabung des Oriental Institute Chicago in Medinet Habu 1928/29 vier Original-Ostraka, ebenda im Photo-Archiv die Ausgrabungsphotos von zwei weiteren, die man nach Cairo zurückgeschickt hat.

Ebenfalls im Oriental Institute in Chicago haben sich aus dem Nachlaß Spiegelberg vier Belege in Spiegelbergs "Normalschrift" als Acker-Arbeitsquittungen von der Hand des Sesostris identifizieren lassen; die Jahreszahlen sind z.T. ungewiss.— Spiegelberg kannte die Acker-Amt-Quittungen noch nicht und bezeichnet sie meistens als "Rechnungen." — Ich bin dem Oriental Institute zu großem Dank verpflichtet, daß ich dies hochinteressante und so ergiebige Material in Ruhe habe studieren können.

13. Zuletzt hat sich von der Hand unseres Sesostris eben im Mai 1990 ein Beleg in der Universitätsbibliothek Leipzig gefunden. Dort liegen im ganzen vier west-thebanische (DO Leipzig UB 2021, 2022 + 2025, 2026) und drei ost-thebanische (DO Leipzig UB 2024, 2027, 2028) Acker-Amt-Quittungen.

14. Der Beleg aus London DO BM 43.553 ist eben als Nr. 2 in der Kaplony-Heckel 1990,veröffentlicht worden; dort sind Übersetzung und Interpretation noch ungenügend.

15. Von den einschlägigen "Theban Ostraca" hat schon Herbert Thompson 1913 drei Belege veröffentlicht, die heute z.T. in Oxford, z.T. in Toronto liegen.

16. Vgl. Paus, den S. des Harthotes, der bei Sesostris sieben Mal als Zeuge gegenzeichnet, um dann im Jahr 36 (d.i. Frühjahr 134 v. C.) als Acker-Schreiber mit DO Cairo JdE 51457 die ausführlichste aller Acker-Amt-Quittungen auszustellen: Er gibt wie in Lichtheim 1957, Nr. 121 *pꜣ ḥtr* und *pꜣ wꜣj* an und verzeichnet im ganzen sechs Teil-Äcker; auch ein "Ibis-Futterplatz" ist darunter genannt.

17. Es ist der "vierte Frühjahrsmonat," also stets ein Monat, aber kein Tag angegeben; wir setzen trotzdem das Tagesdatum an und vermuten, daß zu diesem Tag die Acker-Kontrolle begonnen hat; ob sie sich über den ganzen Monat ausdehnt, ist uns ungewiß.

18. Ebenso signiert er als erster Zeuge Nr.2 (MH 4210), wo das Editionsjahr verloren ist.

auch das Jahr 36 von Nr. 8 (D 7), d.i. der 26. Februar 146 v.C.; denn im Jahr 36 des Ptolemaios VIII. ist schon ein anderer Schreiber belegt.[19] Nur vier Belege[20] bleiben offen.

Gehen wir weiter zu den Zeugen-Unterschriften![21]

Da sind von den sechs Söhnen des Harthotes, die in *r-rḫ=w* Texten vorkommen, fünf in der Amtszeit des Sesostris belegt; einige lassen sich auch im Papyrus-Archiv von Deir-el-Medine als Zeugen wiederfinden, z.B. Petamenophis, der S. des Harthotes; er fällt in der Zeugenliste von 171 v. C.[22] durch seine kräftige junge Unterschrift auf. Von den zwanzig Texten des Sesostris hat eben dieser Petamenophis, S. des Harthotes, elf Belege gegengezeichnet; er unterschreibt jedesmal an letzter Stelle, gerade als wäre seine Unterschrift für die ganze Arbeitsquittung der Stempel, das "Tüpfelchen auf dem i."[23]

Die Verbindung der Acker-Amt-Zeugen zum Tempel-Notariat bestätigt wohl auch die Acker-Amt-Quittung Nr. 7 (D 1) mit der Zeugen-Unterschrift des Notars Harsiese, S. des Chestefnachte:[24] Das Jahr 35 von Nr. 7 (D 1) liegt innerhalb seiner Schreiber-Amtszeit von den Deir-el-Medine Papyri.[25]

19. Z.B. Paus, S. des Harthotes (Cairo JdE 51457), Totoes ohne Vaternamen (Kaplony-Heckel 1990, Tabelle V.)

20. Für vier Belege stehen beide Regierungen zur Wahl:

Ptolemaios VI. Philometor (181–145 v. C.):

*	Jahr 32	=	149 v. C.	Nr. 4 (Str 1088)
**	Jahr 34 *ibd 3 prt*	=	28. März 147 v. C.	Nr. 5 (Lpz 2022 + 2025)
***	Jahr 35 *ibd 2 prt*	=	26. Febr. 146 v. C.	Nr. 6 (MH 4085)
****	Jahr 35 *ibd 2 prt*	=	26. Febr. 146 v. C.	Nr. 7 (D 1)

und Ptolemaios VIII. Euergetes II. (170–116 v. C.):

*	Jahr 32	=	138 v. C.	Nr. 4 (Str 1088)
**	Jahr 34 *ibd 3 prt*	=	25.März 136 v. C.	Nr. 5 (Lpz 2022 + 2025)
***	Jahr 35 *ibd 2 prt*	=	23.Febr. 135 v. C.	Nr. 6 (MH 4085)
****	Jahr 35 *ibd 2 prt*	=	23.Febr. 135 v. C.	Nr. 7 (D 1)

21. Fünf Männer mit ägyptischem Namen signieren, ohne den Vaternamen hinzuschreiben; sie sind angesehene ältere Leute, wie Herieus und Harthotes; ob sie mit den Männern identisch sind, deren Söhne in der gleichen Urkundengruppe der *r-rḫ=w* Texte als Zeugen auftreten, lässt sich vermuten; z.B. erscheint zweimal Nechutes, der S. eines Herieus.

22. P. Deir el Medine 3 v 11.

23. Auch der Zeuge Amenothes, S. des Psenthotes, aus Nr. 11 (DO MH 1621 = Lichtheim 1957, Nr. 121) mag mit dem gleichnamigen Zeugen derselben Zeugenliste identisch sein. Damit wären diese beiden Männer von 171 bis 143 v.C., also 28 Jahre lang, sowohl beim Tempel wie am Acker-Amt als Zeugen tätig.

24. Vgl. de Meulenaere, a.a.O.; Zauzich, Schreibertradition, s.v.

25. Er hat dort im Jahr 22 des Ptolemaios VI. (159 v.C.) den DP Deir el Medine 4 (Zl.26) und im Jahr 36 des Ptolemaios VIII. (134 v.C.) DP Deir el Medine 9 (Zl.9) geschrieben.

Ein eigenes Problem bilden die drei Zeugen mit griechischem Namen, Herakleides, Ptolemaios und Philippos, die das Setzen des Vaternamens ebenfalls für entbehrlich halten.[26]

Damit verlassen wir "die Schreibstuben" und gehen auf die Felder! Was notiert damals Sesostris über die Lage der Äcker?

In zwölf Belegen gibt er das "Hochland von Djeme" an, zweimal den "Lagerplatz der Handwerker;" einmal ist beides kombiniert.[27] Es ist auffällig und kaum ein Zufall, dass bei Sesostris die Größe des Gesamt-Ackers fehlt,[28] wie wir sie später in Theben-West wie in Theben-Ost oft genug vermerkt finden.

Der nächste und letzte Schritt führt uns zu den Leuten,[29] denen man für die Bestellung der Felder die Acker-Amt-Quittungen ausgestellt hat. Es gibt da zwei Fragen:

1. Was für eine gesellschaftliche Position können wir für diese west-thebanischen Farmer erkennen?
2. Gibt es eine Regel für die Größe der Teil-Äcker innerhalb eines Familien-Archivs?

Von den 20 Belegen des Sesostris wählen wir drei Familien-Archive,[30] nämlich das des Theon, das des Phagonis-des-Jüngeren und das des Psenatymis.

a. Das Familien-Archiv des Theon[31] besteht aus zwei griechisch-demotischen Getreide-Quittungen und einem (demotischen) *r-rḫ⸗w* Text, alle drei für seinen Sohn Apollonios ausgestellt. Sesostris quittiert ihm mit der Acker-Amt-Quittung Nr. 8 (D 1) für das Jahr 35 "drei Aruren" auf dem Hoch-Acker von Djeme und vermerkt "ihm allein." Wir wissen nichts über Apollonios, als daß er einen griechischen Namen und Vaternamen hat, und daß die beiden Getreide-Quittungen einen demotischen Nachtrag mit "Datum-Getreidemenge" enthalten. Darf man aus dieser Kombination schließen, daß Apollonios zwar lesen kann, aber nur Demotisch? Gehört er also zu den Priester-Familien von Theben-West? Hatte er früher

26. Es wäre gut, man könnte sie als griechische Beamte identifizieren, die ab und zu in Theben-West inspizieren; aber unsere erste Sucherei in den griechischen Belegen der Theban Ostraca und in der Prosopographia Ptolemaica hat noch nichts Rechtes erbracht.

27. Den "Lagerplatz der Handwerker" kennt man auch aus Berliner und Londoner Papyri.- Ein- oder zweimal ist die Ackerlage vergessen.- Die restlichen Texte sind an der betreffenden Stelle kaputt.

28. Vgl. unsere Übersicht Kaplony-Heckel 1990, Tabelle V und VI. Ob man das Fehlen der Gesamt-Acker-Aruren als Hilfsmittel zur Datierung von *r-rḫ⸗w* Texten nutzen kann, wissen wir noch nicht.

29. In Tübingen (vgl. oben) war noch von Kleinbauern die Rede; das muß man jetzt ablehnen.

30. Überaus interessant sind auch die Probleme um das Archiv der Familie des Phibis, hier mit Nr.1 (D 23), dem ältesten unserer 20 Texte, mit einer Acker-Amt-Quittung des Psemmonthes, S. des Phibis, belegt; es gehören mit einiger Sicherheit in dasselbe Archiv noch die unveröffentlichten demotischen Ostraka D 43 und D 6, beides *r-rḫ⸗w* Texte für einen Phibis, S. des Psemmonthes, vom Jahr 2 und vom Jahr 7, sowie die GDO G 18, G 19, G 20, und G 21.

31. Das Familien-Archiv des Apollonios, des S. des Theon, besteht aus Nr.7 (D 1), sowie aus GDO G 23 und 24 der Theban Ostraca: Apollonios zahlt im Jahr 26 im Herbst einmal $9\frac{5}{12}$ Artaben Weizen ein, fünf Tage später $17\ \frac{7}{12}$ Artaben, zusammen also 27 Artaben Weizen. Er bekommt mit der Acker-Arbeitsquittung Nr. 7 (D 1) für das Jahr 35 drei Aruren auf dem Hoch-Acker von Djeme quittiert, mit dem Vermerk "ihm allein."

einen ägyptischen Namen? Er könnte der Sohn eines Priesters sein, der Soldat (mit einem neuen griechischen Namen) geworden ist, und der jetzt auf seine Alten Tage daheim in Theben-West seßhaft wird.[32]

b. Für das Familien-Archiv[33] des Phagonis-des-Jüngeren haben wir bisher fünf *r-rḫ=w* Texte und eine Getreide-Quittung zusammengetragen, ausgestellt auf seine beiden Söhne Psemminis und Psennesis. Wie uns Brian Muhs/Philadelphia aufmerksam gemacht, gehört Phagonis-der-Jüngere in die große Pastophoren-Familie der Deir-el-Medine Papyri. Sein Sohn Psemminis ist der Großvater des erfolgreichen Totoes, des S. des Zmanres, aus dem Deir-el-Medine-Archiv: Psemminis verkauft im Jahr 137 v. C. Liturgien-Tage innerhalb der Familie und wird dabei als *wn*-Priester, also als "Schreinöffner," bezeichnet.[34]

Wie gross sind hier die Teil-Äcker?

Ist ein Sohn des Phagonis-des-Jüngeren der einzige Farmer, werden ihm an "Hochacker" quittiert:

3	$\frac{5}{8}$	Aruren,[35]
11	$\frac{1}{4}$	Aruren[36] und
4	$\frac{7}{8}$	Aruren,[37] hier zusätzlich
	$\frac{1}{4}$	Arure auf dem "Lagerplatz der Handwerker."

Bilden die Brüder eine Genossenschaft, quittiert man ihnen

17	$\frac{1}{16}$	Aruren Hochacker.[38]

32. Man sieht, wir haben hier dieselben Probleme wie bei den Militärs in Gebelein. Soll man Apollonios in die Militärs einreihen? Etwa von Theben-West?

33. Es sind dies die Acker-Arbeitsquittungen vom Jahr 36: Nr. 8 (D 7), vom Jahr [20? oder 30?+]6: Nr.10 (Str 1992), vom Jahr 27: Nr.14 (OIM 6979) und vom Jahr 28: Nr.16 und 17 (OIM 7003 und FMNH 31.632-161), sowie eine Getreide-Quittung vom Jahr 33 (MH 137, unveröffentlicht).

34. DP Deir el Medine 8, vgl. DP Deir el Medine 9!

35. Nr. 14 (OIM 6979)

36. Nr. 10 (Str 1992)

37. Nr. 17 (FMNH 31.632-161)

38. Nr. 16 (OIM 7003)

c. Das Familien-Archiv des Psenatymis[39] besteht aus drei *r-rḫ=w* Texten.[40] Hat ein Sohn kultiviert, quittiert ihm Sesostris

1 $\frac{1}{2}$ Aruren[41] und

1 $\frac{3}{4}$ Aruren[42]

Arbeiten Sohn und Enkel zusammen, quittiert ihnen Sesostris

14 Aruren.[43]

Vielleicht sind hier die $1\frac{1}{2}$ Aruren ein halber "Drei-Aruren"-Teilacker.[44]

Wie die Aruren-Angaben aus den drei Familienarchiven erkennen lassen, kommt zwar ein "drei Aruren"-Acker oder die Hälfte davon mehrfach vor; es fehlt uns aber bisher ein Schlüssel, das Rätsel um die Größe der Teil-Äcker mit all den verschiedenen Aruren-Bruchteilen zu lösen.

Kommen wir zum Schluß!

Für unsere Kenntnis der spätptolemäischen Verwaltung und der einheimischen Gesellschaft in Oberägypten sind die *r-rḫ=w* Texte oder Acker-Arbeitsquittungen/Acker-Amt-Quittungen eine wahre Fundgrube: Die Acker-Vermes sung von Theben befindet sich in ägyptischer Hand. Die großen west-thebanischen Priesterfamilien sind in die Zwangspachtmaßnahmen des Pharao miteingeschlossen.

Die jetzt zusammengetragene Menge an thebanischem Material macht es möglich, für Theben-West wie für Theben-Ost das Acker-Amt und die Familien-Archive im einzelnen zu studieren. Hoffentlich können die in situ gefundenen Medinet Habu Ostraka dafür genützt werden.

39. Einen Mann dieses Namens kennt man auch aus den Zeugen-Unterschriften des DP Deir el Medine 8 v 9, vom Jahr 137 v. C.; aber wir brauchen mehr Anhaltspunkte, um den dort genannten Psenatymis, S. des Peteharpres, mit Psenatymis, dem Vater des Amenothes in Nr. 2 (MH 4210), des [Amen]othes in Nr. 6 (MH 4085), und der Brüder Belles und [...]esis in Nr. 19 (Str 674) zu identifizieren.

40. Nr. 2 (MH 4210), ein Fragment ohne Jahr, ist sicher vor das Jahr 150 v.C. einzuordnen, weil Sesostris noch als erster Zeuge und nicht schon als Acker-Schreiber signiert; Nr. 6 (MH 4085) vom Jahr 35 (26. Febr. 146 v.C.) und Nr. 19 (Str 674) vom Jahr 29 (141 v.C.).

41. Nr. 2 (MH 4210)

42. Nr. 6 (MH 4085)

43. Nr. 19 (Str 674)

44. Vgl. die "drei-Aruren" von Apollonios und von anderen *r-rḫ=w* Texten der Theban Ostraca!

ANHANG I: DIE ZWANZIG BELEGE, ZEITLICH GEORDNET

A. AUS DER REGIERUNG DES PTOLEMAIOS VI. PHILOMETOR

Sesostris als Zeuge:

Nr. 1: D 23	Jahr 30 *ibd 4 prt.*	28. April 151 v.C.
Nr. 2: Medinet Habu 4210	[Jahr ...:]	(vor 150 v.C.)

Sesostris als Ackerschreiber:

Nr. 3: BM 43553 (FS Lichtheim Nr. 2)	Jahr 31:	150 v.C.
Nr. 4: Straßburg 1088	Jahr 32:	149 v.C.
Nr. 5: Leipzig UB 2022 + 2025	Jahr 34 *ibd 3 prt.*	28. März 147 v.C.
Nr. 6: Medinet Habu 4085	Jahr 35 *ibd 2 prt.*	26. Februar 146 v.C.
Nr. 7: D 1	Jahr 35 *ibd 2 prt.*	26. Februar 146 v.C.
Nr. 8: D 7	Jahr 36 *ibd 3 prt.*	27. März 145 v.C.

ANHANG I: DIE ZWANZIG BELEGE, ZEITLICH GEORDNET (*Fortgesetzt*)

B. Aus der Regierung des Ptolemaios VIII. Euergetes II.

Nr. 9: Cairo JdE 51253	Jahr 26:	144 v.C.
Nr. 10: Straßburg 1992	[Jahr 2]6:	[144 v.C.]
Nr. 11: Medinet Habu 1621 (Lichtheim 1957, Nr. 121)	Jahr 27:	143 v.C.
Nr. 12: Medinet Habu 2806	Jahr 27:	143 v.C.
Nr. 13: Straßburg 687	[Jahr 27?:]	[143 v.C.]
Nr. 14: OIM 6979	Jahr 27 *ibd 4 prt.*	26. April 143 v.C.
Nr. 15: Medinet Habu 1480 (Lichtheim 1957, Nr. 122)	Jahr 27 *ibd 4 prt.*	26. April 142 v.C.
Nr. 16: OIM 7003	Jahr 28:	142 v.C.
Nr. 17: Field Mus. 31.632-161	Jahr 28 *ibd 4 prt.*	26. April 142 v.C.
Nr. 18: Medinet Habu 2686	Jahr 29:	141 v.C.
Nr. 19: Straßburg 674	Jahr 29:	141 v.C.
Nr. 20: D 25	Jahr 29 *ibd 2 prt.*	25. Februar 141 v.C.

ANHANG II: DIE ZWANZIG BELEGE, NACH MUSEEN GEORDNET

DO BM 43555 [publ.: Kaplony-Heckel 1990, Nr. 2]	Nr. 3
DO Cairo JdE 51253 [unveröffentlicht]	Nr. 9
DO D 1 (Oxford) [publ.: H. Thompson 1913, 46 pl.IV]	Nr. 7
DO D 7 (Toronto) [unveröffentlicht]	Nr. 8
DO D 23 (Toronto) [publ.: H. Thompson 1913, 44 pl. IV]	Nr. 1
DO D 25 (Toronto) [publ.: H. Thompson 1913, 46 pl. IV]	Nr. 20
DO Field Museum of Natural History (Chicago) 31.632-161 [unveröffentlicht]	Nr. 17
DO Leipzig UB 2022 + 2025 [unveröffentlicht]	Nr. 5
DO Medinet Habu 1621 [publ.: M. Lichtheim 1957, Nr. 121]	Nr. 11
DO Medinet Habu 1480 [publ.: M. Lichtheim 1957, Nr. 122]	Nr. 15
DO Medinet Habu 2686 [unveröffentlicht]	Nr. 18
DO Medinet Habu 2806 [unveröffentlicht]	Nr. 12
DO Medinet Habu 4085 [unveröffentlicht]	Nr. 6
DO Medinet Habu 4210 [unveröffentlicht]	Nr. 2
DO Medinet Habu 6979 [unveröffentlicht]	Nr. 14
DO Medinet Habu 7003 [unveröffentlicht]	Nr. 16
DO Straßburg 674 [unveröffentlicht]	Nr. 19
DO Straßburg 687 [unveröffentlicht]	Nr. 13
DO Straßburg 1088 [unveröffentlicht]	Nr. 4
DO Straßburg 1992 [unveröffentlicht]	Nr. 10

CHAPTER 19

A FIRST CENTURY ARCHIVE FROM OXYRHYNCHOS OR OXYRHYNCHITE LOAN CONTRACTS AND EGYPTIAN MARRIAGE

TRAIANOS GAGOS, LUDWIG KOENEN, AND BRAD E. MCNELLEN
Department of Classical Studies, The University of Michigan

At the 1989 International Congress of Papyrology in Cairo L. Koenen presented a preliminary report on the Family Archive of Pausiris, son of Pausiris—hereafter referred to as Pausiris Jr.—a weaver who lived in Oxyrhynchos in the seventies of the first century. His surviving papers include those of his brother Dioskous and his father Pausiris Sr. A family tree may facilitate orientation:

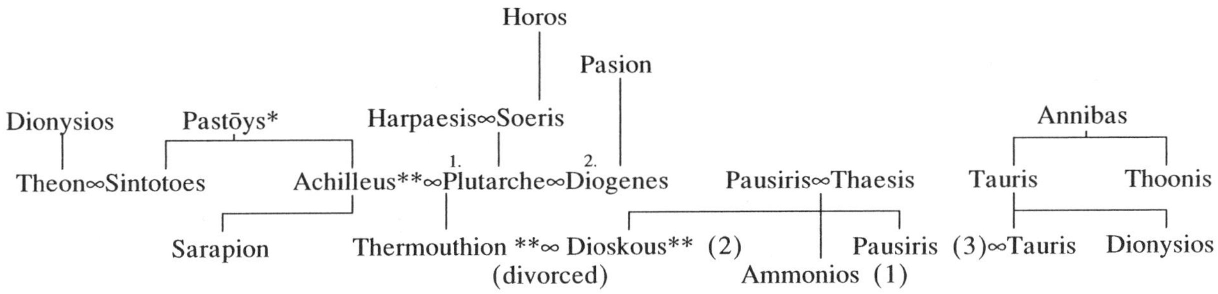

* Pastōys' name is also spelled Pestōys (#7.1).

** Dioskous, Thermouthion, and Achilleus appear also as Dioskourides, Thermouthis, and Achilliōn, respectively.[1] It is not certain that Achilleus, the father of Sarapion, is the same person as Achilleus, the father of Thermouthion.[2]

Most of the archive, which contains also papers of the two generations preceding Pausiris junior, was assembled by H. C. Youtie. The joint authors of this paper are presently preparing the

1. Dioskourides: #7.5; Thermouthis: *P. Mich.* 191 (note on line 21; here #9); Achilliōn: #10.1. For such minor variations in the forms of names see Youtie 1976, pp. 193–96 (1981, pp. 307–10); Sijpesteijn 1979, p. 253, note on P. Mich. inv. no. 3318, verso 12; Omar, *P. Sot.* 3.3, note; Koenen and Omar in introduction to *P. Turner* 21, notes 3 and 4; Koenen and Henrichs 1978, pp. 125f., note 150; Omar 1991, p. 221, note on #3.14 (P. Cairo SR 3732/28).

2. For Achilleus, alias Achilliōn, the husband of Plutarche and father of Thermouthion, see Jones and Whitehorne 1983, #25. A later Achilleus, son of Achilleus, married to Thaisous, had two children, Sarapion and Thermouthion (attested for A.D. 66 and 91/92; *PSI* 8.871.29 and *P. Oxy.* 38.2856.11; *Register* #27).

edition.[3] *Appendix II* includes an overview of the entire archive, an earlier version of which was distributed at Cairo.[4] Within the topics studied at the present convention, we wish to focus the discussion on one particular feature: our suspicion that the marriage loans from wives to husbands reflect an influence of Egyptian marriage practice. If we can make our case, this should urge us to be more cautious when we generalize and claim that, on the legal level, Greeks and Egyptians lived side by side without much interaction.

Among the total of twenty-three papyri,[5] which range from A.D. 49 to 78, there are sixteen loan documents concerning nine different transactions (##6–20). Three documents were issued by the agoranomoi (##8, 9, 11); the remaining documents, loan contracts as well as repayments, were written and executed through a bank at the Sarapeum in a form that was peculiar for Oxyrhynchos in the first century and was called: χειρόγραφον καὶ διαγραφή, "personal contract with bank-transfer" (##7.32f., 16.4f., 17.11, 20.17f.).[6] In these, a subjective homology (ὁμολογῶ) with *hypographai* is followed by a bank *diagraphe* that acknowledges the transaction.[7] The form of the document claims that the χειρόγραφον is a private contract between the parties without any institutional involvement and that the role of the bank is restricted to the execution of the financial transaction and to the attestation of this fact in the brief διαγραφή at the bottom of the document.[8] However, the formulaic character of the χειρόγραφον and, in particular, the unambiguous mention of the payment through the bank,[9] suggest that the documents were prepared and written by an employee of the bank. Alternatively, this could have been done by professional scribes who knew, and were specializing in, the specific documents used at the bank.

Twice, however, the texts employ a different terminology: in #10 (lines 9–10) κατὰ διεγβολὴν γεγονυῖαν κατὰ διαγρ̣[α]φήν διὰ τῆϲ αὐτῆϲ τραπέζηϲ, "in accordance with the document of payment which was issued according to a *diagraphe* through the same bank";[10] and in #18 (lines 11–12) the text reads χ̣ειρόγ̣ρ̣α̣φον διεγβολῆϲ διὰ τῆϲ αὐτῆϲ τραπ̣έ̣[ζ]ηϲ, "document of payment,

3. Our editorial work is greatly facilitated by the Duke Data Bank of Documentary Papyri, now available on CD ROM, No. 6 of the Packard Humanities Institute.

4. In the present paper all references marked with the # sign relate to the first column of *Appendix II*.

5. In *Appendix II*, twenty-two documents are listed, but #9 exists in two copies.

6. For the term see Wolff 1978, p. 97; add *P. Turner* 84.13 (and note) and *P. Oxy*. 49.3487.13 (and introduction), but it occurs occasionally elsewhere and in earlier times (see Wolff, note 75). See already Preisigke 1910, pp. 231–34.

7. See ##6, 10, 12, 13, 14, 15, 18, and 19 in addition to the documents just listed.

8. E.g. #12.30–33: date, followed by διὰ τῆϲ Ἀμμω(νίου) καὶ Ϲαρα(πίωνοϲ) καὶ (τῶν) μετό(χων) τρα(πέζηϲ) γέγο(νεν) ἡ διαγρ(αφή), "the bank-transfer has been made through the bank of Ammonios, Sarapion, and Co."; cf. ##14.35–39, 15.34–37, 17.34–39, 18.29–33, 19.25–26, 20.36–40.

9. E.g. ##6.3–5 ὁμολογῶ ἔχειν παρὰ ϲοῦ ἐπὶ τοῦ πρ̣ὸ̣ϲ Ὀξυρύνχων πόλε̣[ι] Σαραπιείου διὰ τῆϲ Ἀμμωνίου [τ]οῦ Ἀμμωνίου τραπέζηϲ, "I acknowledge that I have received from you through the bank of Ammonios son of Ammonios at the Sarapeum in the city of Oxyrhynchos"; cf. 7.6–9 and similarly 10.3–6.

10. Lines 8–13 δραχμὰϲ εἴ[κ]οϲι – – –, | ἃϲ εὐχρήϲτηϲά ϲο̣ι κατὰ διεγβολὴν γεγονυῖ|αν κατὰ διαγρ̣[α]φὴν διὰ τῆϲ αὐτῆϲ τρα|πέζηϲ τῷ Μ̣εχεὶρ μηνὶ τοῦ ἐνεϲτῶτο(ϲ) | ἕ̈κτου ἔτουϲ Νέρωνοϲ Κλαυδίου Καίϲαροϲ | Ϲεβαϲτοῦ Γερμανικοῦ αὐτοκράτοροϲ (January 27 – February 25, A.D. 60), ἣν καὶ | ἀναδέδωκά ϲ̣οι κεχιαϲμένην. The bank is the Sarapeum's bank of Ammonios son of Ammonios, and the χειρόγραφον in which this reference to the earlier document occurs is written a few months later (June 9, A.D. 60). The διεγβολή seems to indicate a document of payment issued "in accordance with the διαγ̣ραφή through the bank"; and the wording κατὰ διεγβολήν apparently refers to a document rather than to the actual payment. The phrase remains, however, ambiguous as to whether διὰ τῆϲ αὐτῆϲ τραπέζηϲ modifies this document (διεγβολή) or belongs to διαγραφή. But this makes little difference. The διεγβολή would thus be similar to what in the Oxyrhynchite documents is called χειρόγραφον, and the only difference that we can perceive is its connection with payment in cash. In the case of #10 the amount is small (20 drachmai). For other uses of the term διαγραφή, in particular for an official's order to the bank to accept a payment from a third party, see Drewes 1974, pp. 95–155, especially pp. 98–105 (we did not see his dissertation, 1970).

written personally, (issued) through the same bank."[11] These instances are among the earliest occurrences of the rare term διεγβολή.[12] Outside the Oxyrhynchites, the ἀντίγραφον διαγραφῆϲ, an excerpt from the bank's accounts, developed in the course of the second century into a form of a bank-document that incorporated all relevant information; in scholarly literature, it is called "selbständige Bankdiagraphe." The banks distinguished between their διαγραφαί and διεκβολαί, but we are no longer in the position to see a clear difference and, therefore, treat the two words as, at least, materially identical.[13] In the context of first-century Oxyrhynchos, however, the phrase χ̣ειρόγρ̣α̣φον διεγβολῆϲ (#18) for a document issued by the bank is significant, because χ̣ειρόγρ̣α̣φον clearly indicates a document which preserves the form of a transaction between private parties, just as it is the case with the phrase χειρόγραφον καὶ διαγραφή. But the term διεγβολή suggests a differentiation: at least in concept, the amount was paid by the bank to the payee in cash.[14] But in reality the χ̣ειρόγρ̣α̣φον διεγβολῆϲ of #18 has nothing to do with cash: the amount of a loan of 300 drachmai is the monetary equivalent for valuables which a certain Tauris lent to her husband (#13).[15] We suspect that *P. Tebt.* 2.395 of A.D. 150, which is phrased in the form of an objective bank-document and is not distinguishable from a "selbständige Bankdiagraphe," is called ἀ̣ν̣τ̣ί̣[γρα(φον)] δ̣ι̣ε̣κ̣β̣ο̣λ(ῆϲ), although, admittedly, the reading remains uncertain.[16] The document attests the repayment of a loan which seems to have been paid out in money; but it was paid back through the final delivery of one metretes of oil. The entire transaction was a prepaid sale of oil, and the bank was hardly involved in the delivery of the oil; it acted in this

11. #18 of August 15, A.D. 74, lines 9–14 δραΙχ[μὰϲ τρ]ιακοϲίαϲ κεφαλαίου, ἃϲ εὐχρήϲτηϲά Ι ϲοι κ[ατὰ χει]ρόγρ̣α̣φον διεγβολῆϲ διὰ τῆϲ αὐτῆϲ Ι τραπέ[ζ]ηϲ τῶι Τῦβι μηνὶ τοῦ ἐνεϲτῶτοϲ Ι ἔκτο[υ] ἔτουϲ αὐτοκράτοροϲ Κ̣αίϲαροϲ Οὐεϲπαϲιανοῦ Ι Cεβαϲ(τοῦ) (December 27, 73–January 25, 74), ἣν καὶ ἀναδέδωκά ϲοι κεχιαϲμένην. The bank is again the Sarapeum's bank, now of Ammonios, Sarapion, and Co. In analogy to the standard terminology of χειρόγραφον καὶ διαγραφή, the χειρόγραφον διεγβολῆϲ should not only have specified the details of the transaction from its typically subjective point of view, but also have initiated the bank's payment. The expression could be the full form for what is usually called χειρόγραφον (without διεγβολῆϲ), but it is more likely that the terminology refers to a payment in cash (cf. footnote 10, above).

12. Only *SB* 4.7465 is older (A.D. 44). For further documentation see footnote 13, below.

13. For recent discussions on the διαγραφή and the διεκβολή, see Drewes (1974, note 10), and Wolff 1978, pp. 95–105, especially p. 96, note 70 on the legal synonymity of the two expressions; for a list of διεκβολή documents see Bingen 1949, pp. 310–11, supplemented in 1983, p. 44 note to line 1, where L. Casarico epigrammatically notes: "con questo termine [διεκβολή] si indica sia l' operazione bancaria, sia il documento corrispondente" (for the papyrus published there see also *SB* 16.12728). To those lists add now *P. Münch.* 3.94 with note 7, BGU 15.2486 (note to line 1; cf. Hengstl 1991, pp. 237f., #4) and *SB* 12.10887, published by J. D. Thomas 1970, pp. 172ff.; on p. 176 note 15, Thomas correctly observes that the word διεκβολή "has not previously appeared in connection with payment of a dowry."

14. In *SB* 12.10887 (see footnote 13, above), a document from Tebtunis (119–138), Ptolema the daughter of Isidoros declares that she has no claims against Pasipsemis son of Asepsio to whom she had been engaged. Isidoros had paid the amount of eighty silver drachmai to Pasipsemis on account of a dowry κατὰ διεγβολήν by a bank, but the latter had paid the amount back to Isidoros διὰ χειρόϲ when Isidoros was still alive, and the marriage had never been consummated. Pasipsemis seems to have received cash from the bank, probably because he had no account there; and for the same reason he paid the amount back in cash directly to Isidoros.

15. This document will be discussed below in greater detail (*Section I* and *Appendix II*). The lower part of this document, which may have contained the docket of the bank, is unfortunately lost and, therefore, we do not know whether the bank called its transaction a διεγβολή or διαγραφή (cf. footnote 10, above and footnote 27, below).

16. We inspected the document in the Rare Books Collections of the Bancroft Library at the University of California at Berkeley. Back, lines 20f. can be read: ἀ̣ν̣τ̣ί̣[γρα(φον)] δ̣ι̣ε̣κ̣β̣ο̣λ(ῆϲ), Παπ̣π̣ί̣ω̣ν̣ο̣[ϲ] Ι – – – ἀπέχ̣(οντοϲ); the ed. princ. prints ἀ̣ν̣τ̣ί̣[γρα(φον)] διαϲτολ(ῆϲ ?) τ̣[ο]ῦ̣ Παπ⟨πί⟩ωνοϲ. In lines 12f. of the front side, we expect [κα]ὶ ἀκ[ύρο]υϲ ε[ἶ]ν[αι τ]ὰϲ Ι δι[αγρ]αφὰϲ [π]αντὶ τῷ ἐ̣π̣ι̣[φέρο]ν̣τι, although ἐ̣ν̣κ̣α̣[λέϲο]ν̣τι may be palaeographically easier according to a drawing we made in Berkeley; [κα]ὶ - - - τῷ [ ] [ ]ν̣τι edd. princ. The reading needs to be checked again on the original.

transaction merely as notary.[17] Hence, the term διαγραφή with its necessity of accounting and bookkeeping would have been difficult to use. In the case of a fictitious involvement of the bank, the διεκβολή with its connotation of cash was a more appropriate form.[18] The same considerations may have caused the Sarapeum's bank of Ammonios, Sarapion, and Co. to issue the loan document attesting Tauris' loan of valuables to her husband in the form of a χειρόγραφον διεγβολῆϲ (#10). Only the form of the document had changed between the Oxyrhynchos papyrus and *P. Tebt.* 2.395: the subjective homology (χειρόγραφον) issued by the bank had become an objectively phrased bank-document.[19]

All this, in particular the later terminology, needs further exploration. Here, however, we will focus on a different feature, as we have already indicated: in eight loan documents of our archive, out of the total of sixteen such documents, the information points to three loans from wives to husbands. We shall start with the latest marriage in the archive and proceed from there to the two earlier cases.

SECTION I

Our first case, text #13 (*Appendix I*) is a loan conceded by Tauris Jr. to her husband Pausiris Jr., who at the time was twenty-two years old. No date is extant. The loan consists of several objects valued at 300 billon drachmai. The repayment is due within thirty days upon request (lines 13–15). Such stipulations of periods, normally thirty or sixty days, are characteristic of marriage agreements and will reappear in the course of this paper.[20] Further, the penalty of an additional 50% of the capital, the *hemiolia*, will apply, as usual, should Pausiris not honor Tauris' request on time (18–19).[21] Moreover, Tauris has the right of exaction upon Pausiris and everything he owns (19–20). Following the usual form of chirographic loan receipts, he assumes the status of a Persian of the Epigone. Thus, as debtor, he was subject to personal exaction (also see *Sections II* and *IV*; cf. *Section V*).[22]

17. See Drewes 1974, p. 112, "διὰ τῆϲ Μέλανοϲ τραπέζηϲ in Zeile 3 und 4 bezeichnet die Bank als die Ausstellerin der uns vorliegenden Bescheinigung, nicht auch als Ausführende der Öllieferung; diese dürfte vielmehr unmittelbar von Soterichos an Pappion erfolgt sein." If this is right, *P. Fayûm* 96 (Wilcken 1912b, no. 313 of A.D. 143; Drewes, pp. 113f.), concerning a rent of five metretai, should be a διεκβολή, too, not a διαγραφή (none of these terms is mentioned in the document). Also cf. BGU 15.2486 of June 4, A.D. 93, the "copy of a bank draft," [ἀντίγρ](αφον) διεγβολ(ῆϲ) ἀπὸ τ(ῆϲ) Ἑρμογένουϲ καὶ | [τῶν με]τόχων τραπέζ(ηϲ) Διονυϲιάδοϲ, in which a certain Panephromis pays for a piece of equipment for his oil press which was delivered by two carpenters. The rest of the document is broken off, but it is possible that the payment was in kind.

18. In other διεγβολαί banks were clearly involved in the payment; a number of documents mention διεγβολαί in connection with other primary documents (*SB* 4.7465; *P. Münch.* 3.94; *P. Hawara* 303 [1913, p. 303]; *P. Ryl.* 2.174; *P. Tebt.* 2.389; BGU 2.445; *SB* 6.9216).

19. In the preceding paragraph the διεκβολή is, in principal, seen as a payment in which the payer has his bank pay cash to the payee. While our remarks aim at Oxyrhynchos in the first century, the comparison with later documents indicates that we assume that this remains the characteristic feature of διεκβολή elsewhere and in later times. With this explanation we return to Preisigke (1910, pp. 234–36), who has argued that the employment of the term διεκβολή implied that the bank paid in cash, while διαγραφή, as a more general term, could be used for both a transfer from account to account or payment in cash. The objections which have been raised against this view are not decisive (Mitteis, 1912a, p. 70; Drewes 1974, pp. 120f., 127–33, and 155).

20. See the introduction to *P. Yale* 1.64.

21. On the meaning of the *hemiolia*-clause, see Lewis 1945, pp. 126–39; Rupprecht 1967, pp. 76–79 and 90–104.

22. The same form is used by all other receipts with bank *diagraphe* in this archive; see ##6, 12, 13, 14, 15, and 20. It is only in #9 (*P. Mich.* 3.191–92), an objective, agoranomic receipt (ὁμολογοῦϲι), that the debtor is not qualified as Persian of the Epigone. In all loan receipts of the Tryphon Archive, also from first century Oxyrhynchos (reedited by Biscottini (1966, pp. 60–90 and 186–292) [= *Tryphon*]; see below *Section IV* and footnotes 37f., below), whether they are issued by a bank or by agoranomoi, the debtor appears as Persian of the Epigone or, in the case of women, as *Persine* (Bank: *P. Oxy.* 2.305 [*Tryphon* 6; *SB* 10.10222]; 2.267 [*Tryphon* 12; see *Section IV*], 2.319 [*Tryphon* 16; *SB* 10.10238]; *P. Oxy.* 2.304 [*Tryphon* 31; *SB* 10.10246]; 2.269 [*Tryphon* 34]; agoranomoi: 2.320 [*Tryphon* 35; J. D. Thomas 1975a, pp. 309–14; *SB* 14.11491], and 2.318 [*Tryphon* 36; *SB* 10.10249]).

Of special interest for us is a stipulation requesting payment of an additional 100 drachmai, "should a separation occur while you are pregnant" (15–17).[23] The phrase does not tell us whether Tauris was actually pregnant at the time or not, but the terminology clearly indicates that there is a connection between the loan and the marriage of the couple.

The loan consists of four objects altogether (9–13). They include a pair of gold earrings valued at 40 drachmai and a chain of 30 drachmai of uncoined silver; two rather expensive objects estimated at 160 and 80 drachmai, respectively, are obscured by damage to the papyrus. The total of these objects amounts to 310 drachmai, provided that we count the weight of the chain as its value. Thus, the objects exceed the stated capital by 10 drachmai. This is a first indication that the objects are real and the loan is not fictitious.[24]

The document is crossed out, so it must be the original. The loan was paid back by Pausiris, if not in reality, so at least in legal terms. There are two likely scenarios for such an action: either the marriage was dissolved or the present loan was replaced by a new loan arrangement. A repayment of a loan of 300 billon drachmas, issued through the same bank and dated August 15, A.D. 74, is indeed extant (#18). We have already assumed that this document concerns the return of the original loan which we just discussed (#13; see above, p. 184); and the assumption that texts ##13 and 18 are receipt and repayment documents of the same loan is attractive and economical. This pairing is also favored by the fact that, in the cases of five other loans which Pausiris Jr. and his brother Dioskous received, both documents, the original receipt and the repayment, are extant.[25] If, indeed, document #18 is the repayment of loan document #13, then the loan was made between December 27, 73 and January 25, 74. Moreover, the cancellation of Tauris' loan is unlikely to indicate a separation, since on December 28, A.D. 74 (#20), after the death of his wife's mother, Tauris Sr., Pausiris still looked after the financial interests of the latter's son Dionysios, the brother of Tauris Jr., who, at the time, was a minor.

Under this scenario we may therefore suspect that the loan of 300 drachmai, which Tauris Jr. had given to her husband Pausiris in December-January 73/74, eight months later (around August 15, 74) was replaced by a new, equally open-ended loan-contract or a marriage contract, possibly after the birth of a child—or, of course, that Pausiris pressured his wife into foregoing her claims.

23. For this clause, cf. also *Section IV* below.

24. As it will be argued below, Pausiris seems to have sold the objects and have used the money for paying some of his debts. If the objects were already sold before the present document was written, it is quite possible that Pausiris got 10 drachmai less than he had expected on the basis of the original estimate of the objects. But other explanations (like a deduction for depreciation) are also possible.

25. The following are the other pairs: ##6 and 10, 9 and 11, 12 and 17 (the repayment is 7 drachmai more than the amount of the loan, because the loan had become overdue and was extended; see table 19.1, p. 187); 14 and 16; 15 and 19. Only in two cases, one of the documents is missing, and there is a good possibility that the missing documents never made it into Dioskous' and Pausiris' archive. (1) Document #8 attests that Thermouthion paid back a loan which her grandmother Soeris had given to Achilleus, her son-in-law, the husband of Thermouthion's mother, and Thermouthion's father; after Achilleus's death Thermouthion had inherited part of her father's house and, with it, the father's obligation to the heir of his former mother-in-law (see *Section III*). There is a reference to the loan contract: lines 14–17: κατὰ ϲυνγ[ρα]φὴν τὴν τελειωθεῖϲαν | διὰ τοῦ ἐν Ὀξυρύγχων πόλει μνημονείου τῷ Φαρ|μοῦθι μηνὶ τοῦ ἐνάτου ἔτ[ου]ϲ Τιβερίου Κλαυδίου | Καίϲαροϲ κτέ., but the original parties were no longer alive when the repayment was made. (2) #20 is a receipt of December 28, 74 for a loan in which Pausiris Jr. invested money belonging to his wife's brother, a minor. This is the last contract in the archive, and soon afterwards, in any case before 78/79 A.D., Pausiris left Oxyrhynchos for an extended stay in Alexandria (see #22 and cf. #21). On the other hand, the archive is clearly not complete. #7.30–33 mentions a loan which Dioskous received from his wife's aunt, and none of the documents related to that loan is extant. Moreover, no documents have been found in which a loan of 105 drachmai was rescheduled and changed into a loan of 112 drachmai on or around Phaophi 23 (October 20, 73; cf. footnote 26, below). This also could be explained, but it is remarkable that the archive, as it has been assembled, has relatively few documents from Ammonios Sr. and Dioskous, and nothing from Ammonios Jr.

The return of the loan of 300 drachmai—fictitious under such circumstances—does not refer to the actual objects listed in the original loan document. While this may be explained as an omission of irrelevant facts, it could nonetheless mean that the original objects had either lost value or were no longer owned by the couple. At the time, Pausiris was in financial difficulties as the reconstruction of his transactions in A.D. 73/74 shows (see table 19.1). It cannot be assumed that we know of all of Pausiris' larger transactions in A.D. 73/74 (cf. p. 185, footnote 25); and, yet, a consistent picture seems to emerge. In May of 74, he paid back two loans which amounted to 160 drachmai (##16 and 17), of which the larger loan of 112 drachmai had been rescheduled once before, (##17 and 12) and the smaller loan of only 48 drachmai was three weeks overdue (#16).[26] Moreover, two weeks after the new arrangement with Tauris, he finally repaid another loan of 120 drachmai which was already 4½ months late (#19). Thus, his payments in May and August of A.D. 74 amounted to 280 drachmai, plus some interests. In other words, the loan from his wife was just enough to cover his other obligations. Tauris might have agreed to the sale (if indeed she had a say in it) in order to prevent an exaction of the debts from her husband in which she would have lost her jewelry anyway. And, on the positive side, the renewal could have further improved her standing in the family and the marriage.

Here we need to recall what we have already said at the beginning of this paper. The reference to the original document is phrased as κ[ατὰ χει]ρ̣όγραφον διεγβολῆϲ διὰ τῆϲ αὐτῆϲ τρα̣π̣έ[ζ]ηϲ, "according to a personal contract of payment, issued through the same bank." We understood that the presentation of the various objects which Tauris gave to her husband was done privately. The bank could have estimated the values; but if it did, this was a service which was not mentioned in the documents. The essential service provided by the bank was the legal paperwork: the draft of the personal contract (χειρόγραφον) and a docket.[27] The form of the document was that of a διεκβολή, which, if we understand it correctly, was regularly used when the bank paid out the amount in cash, and the payee needed not to have an account at that or any other bank. The use of this form for transactions which did not involve any payment through the bank and, in this sense, were fictitious, was a natural extension of an available form and process to provide legal validity to such transactions which originally fell outside the competence of the bank. It is part of the development in which by the end of the first century private banks had finally obtained the full power of public notary, that hitherto had been reserved to the state and was mainly exercised by the agoranomoi.[28]

26. The loan of 112 drachmai was originally for 105 drachmai which Pausiris received on Pharmouthi 23 (April 18, 73). After the loan had become overdue, it was changed into a loan of 112 drachmai on or around Phaophi 23 (October 20, 73). Apparently on the day the loan became due, the document for the repayment was prepared (Germanikeios [Pachon] 22 [May 17, 74]). It was repaid on the next day (Germanikeios [Pachon] 23 [May 18, 74]) with interests in addition to the principal. The increase of the principal from 105 to 112 drachmai apparently reflects the interest for the original loan period plus the overtime, altogether six months. At the usual rate of 1% per month, the monthly interest for 105 drachmai was probably rounded up to 1 drachma 1 obol, which for six months adds up to 7 drachmai.

The two loans which Pausiris paid back on Germanikeios [Pachon] 23 (May 18, 74) were in the total amount of 160 drachmai, plus interest. The most valuable item conceded to Pausiris in the loan from his wife Tauris Jr., was estimated at precisely 160 drachmai, and Pausiris apparently obtained the 160 drachmai in a lump sum from the sale of that item. Moreover, when he took out the loan of 48 drachmai on Mecheir 17 (February 11, 74) shortly after he had received the loan from his wife (Tybi [December 27, 73–January 25, 24]), he might have done so with a view toward selling that item.

27. See footnote 15, above, on the fact that we do not know how the bank worded the docket. If #18 is indeed the repayment of the loan of document #13, the bank docket on document #13 must have contained the word διεκβολή (instead of διαγραφή) so that the repayment document (#18) could refer to it as διεκβολή.

28. This is the same development which finally empowered the banks to issue "selbständige" bank diagraphai; cf. Wolff 1978, p. 100 and Preisigke 1910, p. 278.

Table 19.1. Pausiris' Transactions in A.D. 73/74.

Doc. No.	*Inv. No.*	*Date*	*Business Details*	*Creditor*	*Amt. in Billon Drachmai*	*Balance of Outstanding Loans Billon*	
						Excluding Tauris' Loan	*Including Tauris' Loan*
12	84	April 18, 73	Loan due June 24, 73	Papontōs	105	105	105
		June 24, 73	Loan #12 overdue	Papontōs		105	105
cf. 17	88	<October 20, 73	Rescheduling of #12	Papontōs>	{(105)		
					112	112	112
13	92	Between December 27, 73 and January 25, 74	Open-ended loan in jewelry and other goods	wife Tauris	300	112	412
14	86	February 11, 74	Loan due April 25, 74 (see #15)	Dieuches	48	160	460
15	85	March 8, 74	Loan due April 25, 74 (see #14)	Eudaimōn	120	280	580
		April 25, 74	Loans ##14 and 15 overdue	Dieuches and Eudaimōn		280	280
16	90	May 17, 74	Late repayment	Dieuches	(48)**	232	532
17	88	May 18, 74*	Repayment	Papontōs	(112)**	120	420
18	89	August 15, 74	"Repayment"	wife Tauris	(300)	(180)	120
			<New contract, open-ended>	wife Tauris	300+	120	420
19	91	August 28, 74	Repayment, $4\frac{1}{2}$ months late	Eudaimōn	(120)**	0	300

* #17 was originally prepared for May 17, 74.

** The payments of loan documents ##16, 17, and 19 (48 + 112 + 120 drachmai) amount to 280 drachmai to which some interest may have been added. These payments were just covered by his wife's loan of 300 drachmai; see footnote 26, p. 190.

Finally, we mention a slight variation of our first scenario. Contrary to our assumption, the loan contract by which Tauris lent her husband jewelry in the value of 300 drachmai and which contains a stipulation with regard to pregnancy (#13), may not be the contract drawn up when Tauris moved in with Pausiris, but a partial rewording of another earlier contract which has not arrived to us. Perhaps, eight months after the first contract, Tauris was pregnant. Hence the first contract (now lost) was canceled by the extant repayment document (#18). Instead, a new loan was worded, repeating the itemization of Tauris' valuables, but adding a new protection clause in the case of separation during pregnancy. This contract was later canceled, in this scenario probably by divorce. Before the end of August of A.D. 75, Pausiris moved to Alexandria where he stayed for at least three years, and it is indeed uncertain whether he ever returned home (#22). His wife remained in his mother's house (#21), but how long she waited for him, we do not know.

SECTION II

We turn now to the second couple, Thermouthion and Dioskous, Pausiris' older brother. Thermouthis gave her husband first a loan of only 20 silver and billon drachmai through a bank at the Sarapeum on January 27, A.D. 60 (#6), payable two months later. The customary *hemiolia* penalty was stipulated for late payment. Just three months after the first loan, on April 18th of the same year, when the first loan was overdue, she granted him a second loan of 200 drachmai, payable without interest in sixty days upon Thermouthion's request (#9 = *P.Mich.* 3.191–92).[29] We

29. For δάνεια without interest see Rupprecht 1967, pp. 81f. Loans between family members were not necessarily interest-free; see Pestman 1971, pp. 7–29, esp. 16–17 and note 38 referring to a loan between husband and wife, in which 30% interest was charged (P. dem. Louvre 2443 of 250/249 B.C.). In the Ptolemaic period, the common and permissible interest rate was 2% per month, i.e. 24% or 25% *per annum*, depending on whether the loan period was calculated in the Egyptian or the Macedonian calendar. Thus the Ptolemaic interest rate was double the 1% monthly interest which was commonly charged in Roman times; see Rupprecht 1967, p. 74.

have already mentioned that such periods are characteristic of marriage agreements (see p. 184, footnote 20). The money for the second loan originated from Thermouthion's sale of her father's share in a house that she had inherited from him.[30] Because the transaction was related to the house sale, it was also handled by the agoranomoi.[31]

Both loan contracts contain stipulations for the exaction upon Dioskous and all his possessions; the first loan, executed through the bank, gives Dioskous the status of a Persian of the Epigone, thus placing him into a very vulnerable position (see *Section I*, footnote 22 and *Section IV*; cf. *Section V*). This is particularly remarkable, as only 20 drachmai were involved. Both loan documents are canceled, and we have the receipts for the repayment of both loans. The first receipt was issued by a bank at the Sarapeum on June 9, A.D. 60 (#10), more than two months late and over seven weeks after Thermouthion had given her husband the second loan. But the document does not mention a payment of the *hemiolia* (see p. 184, footnote 21). Nevertheless, Dioskous is protected against future claims from this loan by the usual phrases.[32] Most likely Thermouthion forgave him the payment of the penalty.[33] The repayment of the second loan was notarized by the agoranomoi on March 11, A.D. 61 (#11 = *P. Mich.* 3.194). We understand that Thermouthion had requested repayment of the loan, in this case clearly because of divorce, since document #11 calls him her ex-husband.

To sum up: Thermouthion gave her husband first a loan of 20 drachmai, and shortly afterwards, when she had inherited and sold a house, another 200 drachmai; the latter loan was open-ended and repayable within sixty days upon her request. The first loan, scheduled for the short period of two months, was paid back some time after Thermouthion had made her larger loan and, although the payment was late, the *hemiolia* seems to have been forgiven. It is likely that the first loan indicates a trial period of the marriage. Both loans were secured by the right to exaction.

SECTION III

The third case emerges from the background transactions of documents ##7–9. It concerns the parents of Thermouthion (see *Section II* above) and a loan of 140 silver and billon drachmai which her father Achilleus had received from Soeris, the mother of his wife Plutarche, between March 27

30. That Achilleus owned only part of the house is said in #7 where, after his death, his sister Sintotoes is reimbursed by his daughter Thermouthion for 14 drachmai which she has paid for her brother's tax dues and, probably in addition, for an undisclosed amount which she has advanced for repair costs of the house; these expenses were divided between herself and Thermouthion: lines 15–19 ὡϲαύτωϲ δὲ καὶ | τὸ ἐπιβάλλον ϲοι μ[έροϲ ἧ]ϲ ἐποι[ηϲά]μην δα|πάνηϲ ἐπιϲκευ[ῆϲ τοῦ ἐ]πιβά[λλον]τόϲ ϲοι (Thermouthion) | πατρικοῦ μέρου[ϲ οἰκί]αϲ καὶ αὐλῆϲ κοινῶν | καὶ ἀδιαιρέτων, πρ[όϲ] με τὴν Ϲιντοτοέα | καθ' ἕτερον μέροϲ, τῶν ὄντων ἐπὶ τοῦ πρὸϲ Ὀξυρύγχων πόλει ἐν λαύρᾳ Ἱππο|δρόμου κτἕ. "(I) also (paid) your share of the costs for the repair, which I had made, for the portion of the house and the courtyard that you inherited from your father, an undivided and common property—while the costs for (the) other portion fall to me—that is located at the Sarapieion in the city of Oxyrhynchos, in the Hippodrome quarter," etc. For κοινῶν | καὶ ἀδιαιρέτων, normally modifying τὸ μέροϲ, see *P. Soterichos* 26.8 n. (S. Omar); *P. Vindob. Worp* 5.11–12 and 10.11–12; Weiss 1908, pp. 359–65. Since the house was "undivided," the repair costs had to be shared by both parties. Three other references to this house are more ambiguous: #8.21 and #9.11f. (= *P. Mich.* 3.191 and 192.11f.) πατρικοῦ αὐτῆϲ μέρουϲ οἰκίαϲ. The other part of the house belonged to Sintotoes, Achilleus' sister and Thermouthion's aunt. In all likelihood, the house was once owned by one of the parents of Sintotoes and Achilleus.

31. The agoranomos in Ptolemaic and Roman Egypt functions as a public notary before whom a wide variety of documents is drawn up; see Raschke 1974, pp. 349–56 and 1976, pp. 17–29.

32. Document #10.13–20 ἣν (sc. the διεγβολὴν γεγονυῖαν κατὰ διαγρ[α]φήν, see footnote 10, above) καὶ | ἀναδέδωκά ϲοι κεχιαϲμένην. διὸ | οὐθὲν ἐνκαλῶι οὐδ' ἐνκαλέϲωι οὐδ' ἐ|πελεύϲομα[ί] ϲοι οὐδὲ ἄλλ[οϲ] ὑπέρ μου | περὶ μόνων τούτων μὴ ἐλαττου|μένηϲ μου [ἐν] τῷ δικαίῳ ὧν ὀφείλει<ϲ> | μοι κατὰ δαν[εί]ου ϲυγγραφῆϲ (instead of ϲυγγραφὴν) ἐφ' οἷϲ περιέχει.

33. We cannot be even sure that, in reality, Dioskous paid anything. The repayment could be fictitious. But then we would expect that the bank would have handled this as a διεκβολή.

and April 25, A.D. 49, when their daughter Thermouthion was already at least one year old. As was just mentioned (*Section II*), Thermouthion inherited her father's share in a house, while her mother Plutarche was remarried to a certain Diogenes.[34] Subsequently, Thermouthion sold her part of the house. On April 18, A.D. 60, she not only did pay 200 drachmai to her husband, as we have seen (*Section II*), but also repaid the 140 drachmai to her mother Plutarche who had inherited this claim from her mother Soeris (#8).[35] Thermouthion paid the appropriate interests. This does not imply that the original loan was with interests, but interests may have accumulated after her father's death or, possibly, after a subsequent grace period (see *Section V*). We can only guess what Plutarche did with her money. Within the framework that appears in these documents, it is fair to assume that she may have lent it to her new husband Diogenes.

SECTION IV

Now, we leave our archive and come to Tryphon, another weaver in Oxyrhynchos, and his second wife Saraeus[36] with whom he was living without 'marriage contract' (ἀγράφωϲ). The case of *P. Oxy*. 2.267 (*Tryphon* 12) of A.D. 37 is well known and much discussed.[37] It is the same type of χειρόγραφον with *diagraphe* through a bank at the Sarapeum as that found in the archive of Pausiris. The situation and the main provisions of the χειρόγραφον are briefly summarized as

34. Since the phrase ὁ γενόμενοϲ καὶ μετηλλαχὼϲ ἀνήρ (occurring in #9 [see footnote 35, below]) has been misunderstood in the past (see the introduction to *P. Yale* 1.64 [pp. 200f.]), it may be appropriate to remark that this is a ἓν διὰ δυοῖν, which, hence, does not imply a divorce before the death. There are many examples which preclude a divorce; here it is sufficient to refer to *P. Merton* 1.13.7f. But it is also fair to say that the same introduction to the Yale papyrus already anticipated some of the conclusions which we now reach on the basis of new evidence. See *Section V*.

35. Document #9 (*P. Mich*. 3.191/192) refers to this repayment and the receipt which Plutarche gave to Thermouthion (#8); the wording seems to imply that the repayment of Thermouthion's debt to her mother Plutarche took priority over Thermouthion's loan to her own husband: Lines 8–20 (ὁμολογεῖ) ἡ – – – Θερμούθιον μὴ πλείω δεδωκέ|ναι τῷ – – – αὐτῆϲ ἀνδρὶ Δ[ι]οϲκοῦτι | ἀπὸ τιμῆϲ οὗ πέπρακεν – – ȝ – πατρικοῦ αὐτῆϲ μέ|ρουϲ οἰκίαϲ – – ȝ – δραχμῶν διακοϲίων κεφαλαίου ἕνεκα τοῦ τὸ λοιπὸν τῆϲ τιμῆϲ | ἐξωτίαϲθαι (read ἐξοδίαϲθαι) ὑπ' αὐτῆϲ τῇ μητρὶ αὐτῆϲ Πλουτάρ|χῃ – – – εἰϲ ἃ ὄφειλεν (read ὤφειλεν) αὐτῇ ὁ – – ȝ – τῆϲ μὲν Θερμουθίου πατὴρ τῆϲ δὲ Πλουτάρχηϲ | γενόμενοϲ καὶ μετηλλαχὼϲ ἀνὴρ Ἀχιλλεὺϲ Παϲτωῦτοϲ, ἀκολούθωϲ ᾗ προεῖται αὐτῇ ἀπο|χῇ – – –. Document #9 does not even mention the fact that Achilleus had actually received his loan from Soeris, Plutarche's mother.

36. In a reconstruction of *P. Oxy*. 2.321 (= *Tryphon* 13 [see footnote 22, above]; CPG I 16; *SB* 10.10235), a badly damaged papyrus, Vandoni has suggested that Saraeus was the wet nurse of the daughter of Tryphon and Demetrous, his previous wife, who then took his wife's place after the latter had left Tryphon (1975, pp. 331–36). When—according to this theory—Saraeus moved in, the nursing contract, then seven months into a second year, was replaced by a loan contract by which Saraeus lent 40 drachmai to Tryphon over a period of five months (*P. Oxy*. 2.267 [= *Tryphon* 12]); the loan was fictitious and corresponded to the wages of five months of nursing. Since no date is extant in *P. Oxy*. 2.321, there is little to prove or disprove this theory, which essentially proceeds from the assumption that the loan of *P. Oxy*. 2.321 is so unusual that it needs to be explained by peculiar circumstances. This very assumption is doubtful since similar contracts have appeared. Moreover this theory does not take the valuables into account which were estimated as another 32 drachmai and which were an additional portion of Saraeus' loan. For further objections against Vandoni's theory see Whitehorne 1984, pp. 1267–74, in particular pp. 1268f. and footnote 7. None of these is decisive, but they render Vandoni's ingenious explanation as not very likely.

37. The archive as a whole has been published and discussed by Biscottini 1966, pp. 60–90 and 186–292; the papyri which in the Oxyrhynchos volume were only described were reprinted in *SB* 10.10220–10223; 10234–10249); see also Duttenhöfer 1991, pp. 264–66. For *P. Oxy*. 2.267 see already footnote 36, above, and the brief discussion of the text in Kutzner 1989, pp. 36–38 and 61. The most interesting discussion before Biscottini is in Wolff 1939, pp. 69–72. Biscottini (1966, p. 201, note 3) misrepresents Wolff's argument by suggesting that Wolff considers *Tryphon* 12 to be a *donatio ante nuptias* on the part of Tryphon, a thesis which Biscottini herself supports. But this very position has been rejected by Wolff: "This excludes the opinion of some writers that the loan was fictitious and really a *donatio ante nuptias* made by Tryphon to Saraeus" (quoted by Biscottini as: "I think ... that the loan was fictious (sic!) and really a *donatio ante nuptias* made by Tryphon to Saraeus"). For earlier (and partly outdated) discussions, see e.g. Brewster 1927, pp. 132–54; 1931, pp. 194–95; and 1935, pp. 25–29; Arangio-Ruiz 1930, p. 73.

follows. Tryphon acknowledges (ὁμολογῶι ἔχειν) that Saraeus has given him a loan of 40 drachmai in cash and 32 drachmai in valuables, in particular a pair of earrings and a white robe. Tryphon states the total amount of 72 drachmai, "to which nothing has been added at all, concerning which I am satisfied" (αἷϲ οὐδὲν τῶι καθόλου προϲῆκται, ὑπὲρ ὧν καὶ ϲυμπέπειϲμαι),[38] two clauses which have caused debate. The first clause on its own is common in Oxyrhynchite loans—found also in #14 of our archive[39]— and it is not specifically connected with marriage. The second clause is more problematic, in particular since, at this point of the contract, there is not much reason for the debtor to state that he is satisfied or in agreement with the loan which he receives from the woman with whom he lives, when his own obligations are yet to be specified. ϲυμπέπειϲμαι does occasionally occur in contracts, but we are not aware of any use of the phrase in loan contracts.[40] We should therefore stress that the two clauses in combination occur in Demotic contracts after mentioning the receipt of money or objects, especially also in "maintenance" or marriage contracts as in the phrase: "I have received it (sc. *ḥd n ỉr ḥm.t*, "the money to become a wife"; or the *nkt.w n s.ḥmt* "the goods of a woman") from your hand, my heart is content with it, (for) it is complete, without any remainder."[41] In the Greek translation of a sale of revenues from the performance of rites at a number of graves, the satisfaction clause is rendered as follows: [καὶ ἐ]δεξάμ[ην] παρὰ ϲοῦ τὴν τούτω[ν τιμὴν ἐκ πλήρουϲ] ἄνευ παντὸϲ [ὑπ]ολόγου. ἀπηυδόκηϲάϲ με.[42] "I have received from you the price for these (revenues) in full and without any deduction; you have pleased me." In the translation of another sale the corresponding phrase is πέπε[ι]κάϲ με ἀργυρίω (read -ρίου) τῇ τι[μῆι] τῆϲ ὑπαρχού[ϲ]ηϲ μοι οἰκία[ϲ – – –, "you have convinced me (= you have satisfied me) with the price in silver for the house which belongs to me."[43] In sum, ὑπὲρ ὧν καὶ ϲυμπέπειϲμαι in Tryphon's χειρόγραφον, where it follows the list of the money and the objects he has received from Saraeus, is a translation of the Egyptian formula and equivalent to "my heart is satisfied." We shall return to this later.

38. Lines 9f. For the traditional interpretation of the second clause see the original commentary by Grenfell and Hunt in the Oxyrhynchos volume (1899, p. 247); Wolff agrees with them and notes: "In naive frankness Tryphon admits that it was the goods brought to him by Saraeus that had persuaded him to enter into another union" (1939, p. 70); cf. also Biscottini 1966, p. 201 and note 2.

39. "L'espresioni αἷϲ οὐδὲν τῶι καθόλου προϲῆκται ... serve a precisare che la somma indicata rappresenta «l'ammontare totale del debito»," Zingale in note on *PUG* 2.62.7; see e.g. *P. Oxy.* 2.305.9 (*Tryphon* 6; *SB* 10.10222), 2.267.9 (*Tryphon* 12), 2.319.7f. (*Tryphon* 16; *SB* 10.10238), 2.304 (*Tryphon* 31; *SB* 10.10246), 2.269.5 (*Tryphon* 34), 2.320 (*Tryphon* 35; J. D. Thomas 1975a, pp. 309–14; *SB* 14.11491), 2.318 (*Tryphon* 36; *SB* 10.10249), 47.3351.6, 49.3485.9, 36.2774.8, 34.27744r.11; *P. Oxy. Hels.* 86r.1.8; 36.1; *P. Yale* 1.64.10 (see *Section V*); *P. Princ.* 2.32.9f.; *P. IFAO* 1.14.7. In the present archive, the phrase occurs in ##12.8; 14.10f.; 15.9f. For the precise meaning see the following argument.

40. Cf. *P. Mich.* 5.318/319/320.1f., 4, and 6 (of A.D. 40) οἷϲ καὶ ἐξ ἀναγνώϲεωϲ ϲυνπέπιϲμαι; *P. Ryl.* 4.600.21 ϲυνπέπιϲμε (read ϲυνπέπιϲμαι; agreement to co-lease). Closer come phrases like *P. Grenf.* 2.74.11 (4th century) τάλαντα ×, ἅπερ ἀπέϲχον, ἐφ' οὗ καὶ ϲυν[επείϲ]θην. Precisely the absence of real parallels has prompted *ad hoc* explanations (see footnote 38, above).

41. This phrase occurs in marriage contracts of type "A" and "B" in Pestman's typology (1961, p. 24, §§ 18–20 and p. 34, § 15, and especially pp. 92ff.; see also "diagram A" and "diagram B". In type "C" the same clause follows a list of the man's entire property. He is said to have "sold" it to his wife: "You have contended my heart with the money for all and everything that I possess and that I shall acquire ... I have received it completely, without remainder; my heart is content with it" (§ 22; Pestman 1961, pp. 39f. and "diagram C"). By this phrase the recipient of a loan certifies that (s)he has received the full amount and that possible silent charges (like interests) are already deducted from the nominal amount; this is quite similar to the modern practice of paying out a loan with the deduction of points. Cf. footnote 39, above.

42. *UPZ* 2.177.32–33 from Thebes (136 B.C.); cf. lines 3f. ἀπηυδ[όκη]ϲάϲ με [τῆϲ τι]μῆϲ – – –. The Demotic text of this bilingual contract is P. Berl. 5507 (*EDL* II 1.71ff.); see Pestman 1961, p. 96.

43. *SB* 1.5231 from the Arsinoites (A.D. 11), first copy 3; cf. second copy 3.

Tryphon promises to return the total of 72 drachmas after five months. As usual, non-payment will result in the penalty of *hemiolia*, and exaction would be upon Tryphon and all his property. And in order to give Saraeus even greater security, Tryphon took upon himself the status of a Persian of the Epigone, as did Pausiris and Dioskous when, in similar circumstances, they gave loan documents to the women with whom they lived (see *Section I* with footnote 22 and *Section II*; cf. *Section V*). In the case of a separation during the five month period of the contract, Tryphon should immediately return to Saraeus the earrings or their cash value; the rest of the "loan" would be repayable at the end of the contracted period of five months.[44] The value of the earrings was to be ἐν τῇ ἴσῃ διατιμ[ή]cει, "in the same estimated value (as the original earrings)." The phrase occurs occasionally in (later) Greek marriage documents.[45] Egyptian maintenance contracts stipulate similarly although with more words: "Then I shall give you similar goods ... or the value of them in money to what is written above."[46]

The stipulations of Tryphon's χειρόγραφον continue: should the couple separate during a pregnancy of Saraeus, Tryphon would have to pay an additional amount. We recall that this stipulation occurs also in the loan from Tauris to Pausiris (above, *Section I*). By June/July of A.D. 37 (June 25–July 24) Saraeus was pregnant (*P. Oxy.* 2.315 [*Tryphon* 17; *SB* 10.10239]), and this pregnancy could very well have been Tryphon's reason for giving her the feeling of at least some security through the contract we have been discussing.[47] But the contract was silently extended for six years, long beyond the original term of the loan, and it was not before June 9, A.D. 42 that Tryphon finally returned the loan. Thus the social function of Saraeus' loan to her husband was not exhausted by providing minimal security during the pregnancy. While the couple did not make a marriage contract, the loan contract fulfilled a comparable, albeit limited, function.[48]

When Tryphon returned the loan, the marriage continued, and we may assume that the extant contract was replaced by a new one. The situation bears many similarities with that of Thermouthion and Dioskous where an originally small loan of 20 drachmai for two months was shortly afterwards replaced by a bigger loan that could be revoked only by the woman. It seems

44. The essentially correct interpretation was given by Whitehorne 1984, p. 1272: "Saraeus is not penalized by this clause, but the exact opposite. She is instead being given a double option—the possibility of taking early repayment of part of the loan in the event of separation and the opportunity to take it in cash." We are not entirely sure whether cash was Saraeus' or Tryphon's "option" (cf. footnote 46, below). Moreover, there might not have been a choice if the earrings had been sold (cf. above, *Section II*). For the older view see e.g. Wolff 1939, p. 70; thus also Kutzner 1989, p. 37 ("Diese Regelung sicherte dem Mann—wenn auch nur für fünf Monate—den Bestand der Ehe."). Normally the repayment and return of goods was due either immediately or after a period of days, usually sixty, reckoned from the day the woman requested separation (see *Section II*); but this is a short-term contract, where the same stipulations were not appropriate as in an open-ended contract.

45. *P. Mich.* 15.700, a marriage contract in the form of a 'selbständige' bank *diagraphe* of A.D. 143 (provenance unknown), stipulates the receipt of a dowry of 40 drachmai, marital cohabitation, the man's obligation to provide for his wife, and the return of the dowry in the event of separation; this includes τὸ[ν] – – – κιτῶ̣ν̣α̣ (read χιτῶνα) ἐν τῇ ἴcῃ διατιμήcει. An Arsinoite marriage contract of A.D. 190 uses the same phrase for the ἱμάτια which were to be returned in the event of a separation (*CPR* 1.27 [*Stud. Pal.* 20]).

46. Thus in Pestman's type "A" § 28 (see footnote 41, above): "Then I shall give you similar goods as your *nkt.w n s.ḥmt* (above)mentioned or the value of them in money to what is written above" (1961, pp. 24 and 98f.). Pestman stresses that it is the husband's option to return goods of similar value or to pay her the value the objects had at the time when the deed was drawn up.

47. Thus Whitehorne 1984, p. 1270. But see also Vandoni's theory (1975).

48. Tryphon clearly states that he wishes to include the stipulation about pregnancy in the loan contract *because* of the fact that he and Saraeus were living in an unwritten marriage: lines 18–20 ἐπεὶ δὲ cύνεcμεν | ἀλλήλοιc ἀγράφω[c] προcομολογῶι, ἐὰν ὡcαύτωc ἐκ διαφορᾶc | ἀπ[αλλαγ]ῶμεν ἀπὸ ἀλλή[λων] ἐνκύου c[ο]ῦ οὔcη[c], ἕωc ἄν coι | [– – – . The sentence contains no clue as to whether Saraeus was pregnant at the time when this document was drawn up (after Whitehorne 1984, p. 1271); this can only be suspected on the basis of *P. Oxy.* 2.315 (see above).

that the shorter and smaller loan covered an initial trial period of the marriage when the financial stakes were kept low.[49]

SECTION V

Our next case is *P. Yale* I 64, the draft of an agoranomic loan document (called δάνειον as is #9 [*P. Mich.* 3.191–92] of our archive) of December 75–January 76 from Oxyrhynchos. Here, a certain Thaesis daughter of Besas gives her husband Aperōs an open-ended loan of 212 drachmas, αἷϲ οὐδὲν τῷ καθόλου προϲῆκται, i.e.'complete.'[50] The money was part of 300 drachmai which she had received from the sale of priestly income.[51] The loan was returnable within sixty days after the woman's request.[52] As is usual, *hemiolia* threatened Aperōs in case he should not return the loan on time, and he was to pay interest for any time after the grace period of sixty days.[53] Similarly, after the death of her father, Thermouthion had to pay interest for the loan which her mother had previously given her father (see *Section III*). Aperōs and his entire property were subject to exaction (see below, footnote 53), as was usual. And he stylized himself as a Persian of the

49. Here we return to Wolff's notion that *P. Oxy.* 2.282 indicates a trial union and in that much a trial marriage; but Wolff refutes the notion that "the trial marriage was an institution of the Greco-Egyptian legal system" (1939, p. 72). In any case, the system was flexible enough to provide the minimum security for the women in such unions and, thus, to make "trial marriages" socially viable.

50. For this formula, see above, *Section IV* and footnote 39; cf. footnote 41. Τῦβι in line 2 is followed by an empty space reserved for the numeral of the day. The lower part of the papyrus, beneath a paragraphos after the last line (29), is blank, enough to indicate that the document was never signed. The first editors were baffled by the absence of the signature (see their note on line 29). B. E. McNellen has inspected the papyrus in the Beinecke Library and checked the suggestions appearing in the following footnotes; smaller corrections will be made silently. In addition, we note that line 3 is exdented and line 17 ἀφ' ἧϲ is corrected from ἐφ' ἧϲ. We thank R. Babcock for his generous permission to check the papyrus and for providing us with a photograph. The papyrus needs to be flattened and reedited.

51. Lines 10–15 (cf. footnote 50, above): αἵ (sc. the 212 drachmai) εἰϲι ἀφ' ὧν ἔϲχεν | ἡ Θαῆϲι⟨ϲ⟩ τῇ ἐνε̣ϲ̣τώϲῃ ἡμέρα̣ μετὰ κυρίου τοῦ ἀνδρὸ̣[ϲ] | Ἀπερῶτοϲ πα̣ρ̣' (καὶ ed. princ.) Ἀμόιτοϲ ὑοῦ (read υἱοῦ) Λευκίου νεωτέρου ἱερέωϲ | Διὸ̣ϲ̣ κ̣αὶ Ἥραϲ καὶ Ἀπόλλωνοϲ καὶ Κόρηϲ καὶ Διονύϲου | κα̣ὶ τ̣ῶν ϲυνεϲτίων θεῶν ὑπὲρ ἐκϲτάϲεωϲ λειτουργιῶν ἡμερῶν δραχμῶν τριακοϲίων. "This amount of drachmai is part of the 300 drachmai which Thaesis has received today in the presence of her κύριοϲ, her husband Aperōs, from Amois, the son of Leukios Jr., the priest of Zeus, Hera, Apollo, Kore, Dionysios, and the associated gods, for the sale of her liturgical days … ."

52. See above, *Section II* and footnote 20; cf. *Section I* (thirty days). For more, see below.

53. Lines 19–23 in amended reconstruction (cf. footnote 50, above):

ἐὰν δὲ μὴ̣ [ἀποδ]ῷ καθὰ γέ-
20 γραπται, ἀποτειϲάτω ὁ δεδανειϲμέ̣[νοϲ Θαῆ]ϲ̣ι̣ τὸ{ν}
μὲν δάνειον μεθ' ἡμιολίαϲ καὶ τ̣[οῦ ὑπὲρ τὰϲ ἀπὸ] τ̣ῆϲ
παρανγελείαϲ ἡμέραϲ ἐ̣ξήκοντ̣[α ὑπερπεϲόντοϲ]
χρ̣όνου τοὺϲ καθήκονταϲ τ[όκουϲ τῆϲ πράξεωϲ οὔ-]
24 ϲ̣[ηϲ] Θαῆϲι ἔκ τε τοῦ δεδα[νειϲμένου καὶ ἐκ τῶν]
ὑ[π]α̣ρχόντ[ω]ν αὐτῷ πάν̣[των καθάπερ ἐκ δίκηϲ]

Lines 19f.: supplements are from the ed. princ. Lines 21f.: καὶ [τόκουϲ μετὰ τ]ῆϲ | παρανγελείαϲ edd. princ. Lines 22f.: τοῦ ὑπερπεϲόντοϲ] | χ[ρ]όνου edd. princ. (with correction of a typographical error). Line 23: τ̣[ῆϲ πράξεωϲ edd. princ. Line 25: [ὑπα]ρχόντ[ω]ν αὐτῷ πάν̣[των edd. princ. The end of the line has been restored by the present authors.

For the reconstruction cf. phrases like τοῦ ὑπερπεϲόντοϲ χρόνου τοὺϲ καθήκονταϲ τόκουϲ (BGU 11.2116.6f.; *P. Oxy.* 2.269 [*Tryphon* 34 (footnote 37, above)], 2.318 [*Tryphon* 36; *SB* 10.10249], 2.320 [*Tryphon* 35; J. D. Thomas 1975a, pp. 309–14; *SB* 14.11491], and 47.3351.11f.; cf. *SB* 3.7169.16; *P. Oxy.* 2.319 [*Tryphon* 6; *SB* 10.10238]; also in the present archive: ##12.14f. and 14.17f.) or τόκουϲ τοῦ ὑπερπεϲόντοϲ χρόνου τοὺϲ καθήκονταϲ (*P. Oxy.* 2.305 [*Tryphon* 7; *SB* 10.10222]; cf. *P. Oxy.* 2.304 [*Tryphon* 31; *SB* 10.10246]); also cf. τοῦ ὑπερπεϲόντοϲ ὑπὲρ τὸν ἐνιαυτὸν χρόνου (BGU 14.2395.25 and 70f.) and the reconstruction of *CPR* 7.39.3–5 τὸν τόκον – – 3 – τοῦ ὑπ[ερπεϲόντοϲ χρόνου τοῦ λογιζομένου] ἀ̣πὸ τοῦ ἐϲομένου Ἁθὺρ μηνὸϲ – – – and *P. Coll. Youtie* 1.10 [καὶ τοῦ ὑπερπεϲόντοϲ μετὰ τὴν δ]η̣λουμένην προθεϲμίαν [χρόνου (cf. *P. Strasb.* 1.52. 11f.).

Epigone, thus accepting the weak position of a debtor against whom quick action and even personal exaction was possible (cf. *Section I*, footnote 22, *Section II*, and *Section IV*). Unfortunately the end of the papyrus, in particular lines 26–29, is heavily damaged, but we suspect that the loan proper concluded with a μὴ ἐλαττουμένου clause, sufficient enough to tell us that Aperōs was already in debt to his wife.[54]

SECTION VI

Next we refer to *P. Oxy.* 49.3487 of October 1, A.D. 65, a χειρόγραφον with bank diagraphe, again issued by a bank at the Sarapeum of Oxyrhynchos. It is a receipt for 32 drachmai, constituting a partial repayment of a loan of 72 drachmai; almost two years earlier in the month of Hathyr, between November 28 and December 27, A.D. 63, a woman called Taÿsoreus had lent this amount to Sarapion with whom, at the time of the partial repayment, she lived together κατὰ [ν]όμους, i.e. according to "common law."[55] The original loan transaction was again in the form of a χειρόγραφον with bank *diagraphe.* The partial repayment is said to diminish neither (1) the woman's right to an exaction of the remaining 40 drachmai plus interest nor (2) her rights under a promised "contract of cohabitation," which, it is added, will remain enforceable.[56]

54. Lines 26–29 can be reconstructed as follows:

26 κ[ατὰ μη]δὲν ἐλ[α]ττουμένης τ[ῆς Θαήσιος ἐν τῇ πρά-]
ξει ὧν ὀφείλει αὐτῇ ὁ δεδα[νεισμένος κατὰ ....]
...ειαν καὶ διαγραφὴν τραπ[έζης
κυ[ρ]ία ἡ συγγραφή. [

Line 26: κ[ed. princ. Line 27: ξει [...]οφε [...]φα ed pr. Line 28: the first two letters are most likely λε (with a splash of ink over the stroke connecting them; alternatively με, as suggested by ed. princ.); most likely 27f. κατὰ ἀσφά]|λειαν καὶ διαγραφὴν rather than συγγραφήν (..γραφη[ed. princ.). Line 28: τραπ[έζης ἐφ' οἷς περιέχει? Cf. e.g. *P. Fam. Tebt.* 9.21.

ἀσφάλεια is a special term which, since the beginning of the imperial period, is used for χειρόγραφον (Wolff 1978, p. 159 and footnote 78). We have not found a precise parallel for the phrase κατὰ ἀσφά]λειαν καὶ δι-αγραφήν, but the term should be more or less synonymous with κατὰ χειρόγραφον καὶ διαγραφήν. Cf. *P.Oxy.* 1.104. 29, a will of A.D. 96, drawn up before the agoranomos, which mentions διὰ τῆς τοῦ ἐνοικισμοῦ [διὰ τρ]απέζης ἀσφαλείας. For the immediate context, see, e.g., *P. Turner* 17, the repayment of a loan of A.D. 69 in the form of a χειρόγραφον καὶ διαγραφή, Lines 19–22: κατὰ μηδ(ὲν) | μὴ ἐλαττουμένου μου ἐν [τῆι πράξει ὑπὲρ ὧν ἄλλων | ὀφείλει ὁ προ[γε]γραμμένος 'Α[ρθοῶνις κα]θ' ἑτέρας ἀσφάλειας.

55. Lines 4f.: τῶι συνόντι μοι κατὰ [ν]όμους ἀνδρί; cf. *P. Mich.* 5.254/255 dupl. r. 8 ἡ συνοῦσά μοι κατὰ νόμους γυνή; similarly *P. Vindob. Tandem* 27.2 and *SB* 10.10572.5; for more examples see Sullivan's note on *P. Oxy.* 49.3487.4. Mainly because the phrase refers to the νόμοι in general, not to a specific contract, Wolff explained the expression as an indication of ἀγράφως συνεῖναι (1939, pp. 54 and 67 and footnote 238). People living together were respected as "married," and, if the phrase has any meaning, it should refer to people living together according to custom (in contrast to people who could claim a specific contract). Sullivan has no concrete explanation, but notes that "the question remains whether this is a pious gesture or a reference to some definite law or laws." Both possibilities are hard to imagine. In the latter case we would expect the definite article, and the former has no place in a first-century χειρόγραφον with bank diagraphe.

56. Lines 19–25: μὴ ἐλαττουμέ|νης μου ἐν τῇ πράξι τῶν λοιπῶν δραχμῶν | τεσσεράκοντα κεφαλαίου καὶ τῶν ἀπὸ τοῦ | νῦν τούτων τόκων, ἔτι δὲ καὶ ἐν τῶι δικαί|ωι ἧς ὀφείλις μοι τῆς συμβιώσεως συγγραφῆς κυρίας οὔσης ἐπὶ πᾶσι τοῖς δι' αὐτῆς δε|δηλωμένοις. Cf. Lines 31–33: μὴ ἐλατ[τ]ουμένης μου ἐν τῇ πράξει τῶν | λοιπῶν δραχμῶν τεσσαράκοντα καὶ ἐν τῷ | δικαίῳ ἧς ὀφείλεις μοι συγγραφῆς ὡς πρόκειτ(αι). We see no real way to understand the second part of the stipulation in the sense of ἐν τῶι δικαίωι ὧν ὀφείλις μοι κατὰ τὴν συμβιώσεως συγγραφήν (cf. #10.18f. quoted in footnote 32, above). The phrase ἐν τῶι δικαίωι is rare. Closest is the occurrence in *P. Oxy. Hels.* 29.41–43 μὴ ἐλλαττουμένου | τοῦ Ἡρᾶτος καὶ Διογένης ἐν τῶι δικαίῳ | οὗ ἔχουσι πρὸς ἑατοὺς ὁμολογήματος | ἐφ' οἷς περιέχ[ε]ι πᾶσι. Here the genitive refers to the rights under an existing agreement. Hence we are not inclined to take ἐν τῶι δικαί|ωι ἧς ὀφείλις – – – συγγραφῆς as a claim on the part of the wife to be offered a marriage contract (with an objective genitive). For the meaning of συγγραφῆς κυρίας οὔσης as expressing the enforceability see Hässler 1960 and Wolff 1978, pp. 145f.

This stipulation constitutes the core of our difficulty to understand this transaction. The μὴ ἐλαττουμένηϲ clause usually expresses either that, in the case of a partial repayment of a debt, the remaining claims from the same contract are not diminished, or that, in the case of a full repayment of a debt, claims from other loans should not be affected by the present repayment.[57] Here both intentions appear to be combined. But, in light of the practice just described, protection of rights under another contract is inappropriate in the case of a partial repayment. Moreover, the idea of a reference to rights under a promised, not yet existing contract, is equally unusual, in particular, since then the future contract is even qualified as being enforceable.[58]

The promised contract itself is called a ϲυμβιώϲεωϲ ϲυγγραφή. This term is implied in *P. Fam. Tebt.* 21.10f. of A.D. 122, where two references to the same document occur, first with the phrase κατὰ ϲụνγραφὴν γ[ά]μου, "in accordance with a marriage contract," then with κατὰ τὴν αὐτὴν ϲυμβίωϲιν, "in accordance with the same marriage (contract)." This is the closest parallel we have found. The term clearly recalls ϲυγγραφὴ ϲυνοικιϲίου, a document of mainly Ptolemaic times that, if we follow Wolff (1939, pp. 11–34), was connected with the *ekdosis* of the woman by her father or another close relative.[59] Such a marriage contract could be supplemented by a ὁμολογία (or ϲυγγραφὴ ὁμολογίαϲ), dealing mainly with the dowry, or by other related contracts. Moreover we know of a number of legal pledges that promised women a ϲυγγραφὴ ϲυνοικιϲίου.[60] For example, *P. Tebt.* 3.815 fr. 4 r. I 1–10 (228–221 B.C.) is the abstract of a receipt of a dowry given under condition that the husband will make ϲυγγραφὰϲ ϲυνοικεϲίου; should he not do so, he would have to return the dowry.

Closer in time and milieu are *P. Mich.* 2.121.IV 7.1–8 (pp. 72–74) of A.D. 42 from Tebtunis, *SB* 12.10924 of A.D. 114 from Theadelphia,[61] and *P. Oxy.* 49.3491 of A.D. 157–158. The first of these documents is the abstract of an objective homology, contained in the grapheion's roll (τόμοϲ ϲυγκολλήϲιμοϲ). A husband, described as Persian of the Epigone, acknowledges to his wife, τῇ προούϲῃ καὶ ϲυνούϲῃ αὐτῶι γυναικί, that he has received from her (and her nephew acting as her κύριοϲ) the amount of 700 drachmai in addition to what he had already received twenty years earlier "according to another, an alimentary, contract," καθ' ἑτέραν ϲυνγρ(αφὴν) τροφῖτιν, finalized in the same grapheion. The original items given to her husband consisted of 560 drachmai, paraphernalia, some 14 arourai of catoecic land, and a female slave. The new loan (if this is the right term) increases the already substantial amount of what the wife had already handed over to her husband. The *SB* papyrus is very fragmentary and comes from Theadelphia; it is an objective homology, and the husband, again taking the status of a Persian of the Epigone, acknowledges to his wife, τ[ῇ προούϲῃ κ]ạὶ ϲυνούϲῃ αὐτῶι [γυ]ν[αικί], that he has received from her 200 drachmai in addition to the dowry of 40 drachmai which he already owes her according to a marriage

57. The latter is the case in #7.30–33. See Rupprecht 1971, pp. 100f.; Häge 1970, p. 195–205, especially p. 204.

58. "None the less, the phrase is odd, especially since οὔϲηϲ might imply that the contract already exists" (Sullivan in his note on line 23). This is not a problem of grammar as the participle participates in the futurity expressed by ὀφείλειϲ. The problem rather lies in the legal concept of stipulating, in a partial repayment of a loan, that the same repayment will not infringe on rights under a not yet existing contract that will be enforceable, if it ever comes into existence.

59. Wolff 1939, pp. 11–34; while the *ekdosis* was definitely a Greek custom as Wolff stresses, it was one practiced by many people including the Egyptians; see Pestman 1961, pp. 8–11 "giving in marriage." This could be done by the father or another close relative. But at the same time we must admit that the Egyptian law lacked a concept of the woman being transmitted from the *patria potestas* into that of her husband. Therefore, Egyptian women were able to conduct their own business, without a κύριοϲ (except in contracts written in Greek). Cf. Allam 1990, pp. 1–34.

60. Wolff 1939, pp. 10f.; Häge 1968, p. 163; and Sullivan in his note on *P. Oxy.* 49.3487.23.

61. Originally published by Kießling 1970, pp. 243–45.

contract completed through the same grapheion that notarizes the present transaction. And finally, the Oxyrhynchos papyrus, an *ekdosis*, lists not only a rich dowry (including valuables) and paraphernalia (more valuables) but also additional possessions which the woman, or the children of the couple, will inherit from the wife's parents; the wife also receives under the new contract land and a house, while her husband holds the right to the use of both. More gifts follow, but our interest focuses on another aspect. The extant contract is actually a renewal of a previous contract, and the dowry and the paraphernalia as well as the land and the house were given by the parents some nine years earlier when the couple started to live together. The earlier contract is called a "privately written contract" (χειρόγραφος ϲυνγραφή),[62] the renewal a "contract concluded publicly in the street," i.e. before the agoranomoi. The old contract is canceled.[63] In short, one marriage contract is succeeded by a second one which adds the transfer of more possessions in addition to what was given in the earlier transaction; and coincidentally, the legal form of the second contract reflects socially higher standards (see also *Section VII*).

In the last-mentioned three cases marriage contracts of different forms precede later loans and new marriage contracts, and we may assume that the later stipulations aimed at strengthening the position of the woman in the marriage.[64] In the case, however, of *P. Oxy.* 49.3487 of A.D. 65, on which our present discussion focuses, a loan precedes the pledge of a marriage contract which would probably change the status of the marriage from "unwritten" to "written" and thus certainly enhance the social and legal status of the woman. The abnormal feature that still remains in this case is the fact that the marriage contract does not yet exist but has only been pledged by the husband. The pledge could have been an oral one; but it could also have been stipulated in the original receipt of the loan, just as the above-mentioned receipt of dowry in *P. Tebt.* 3.815 pledges a ϲυγγραφὴ ϲυνοικιϲέου. Under this assumption, the combination in Taÿsoreus' receipt of a μὴ ἐλαττουμένηϲ clause, which safeguards her rights under another contract to be executed in the future, with a preceding portion of the same clause, which protects her rights under the original loan contract, becomes not only understandable, but also essential from her point of view. Taken together, both parts of the clause deny that the present partial repayment could have any effect on

62. This phrase has no parallel, but is probably synonymous with ἰδιόγραφοϲ ϲυνγραφή, a term which several times occurs in the context of marriages; see Wolff 1978, pp. 124f., note 92 and pp. 136f., note 2, also *Section VII* and footnote 67, below. The editor of *P. Oxy.* 49.3491, Bülow-Jacobsen, refers to Wolff 1975 (pp. 349–56), where the discussion deals with documents which were composed as objective homologies (in the third person), but have the date at the end—contrary to the practice of the agoranomoi and the grapheion. Thus these "private protocols," which were relatively popular in Oxyrhynchos, mix features of an objective homology with those of a subjective one. In the passage discussed here (*P. Oxy.* 49.3491.3) the scribe seems to have been uncertain about the correct terminology (see the passage as quoted in footnote 63, below).

63. *P. Oxy.* 49.3491.3–5 ᾧ προϲύνεϲτιν κατὰ ⟦χρηματιϲ⟧ χειρόγραφον ϲυνγραφὴν γεγονυῖαν τῷ ιβ (ἔτει) | Ἀντωνίνο̣υ̣ [Καίϲαροϲ τοῦ κυρίου ἣν] ἀνέδοϲαν ἀλλήλ(οιϲ) εἰϲ ἀκύρωϲιν ἀρκούμενοι τῇδε τῇ διὰ δημοϲίου ϲυνγραφῇ ἐν ἀγυιᾷ [ ] | γ(υναῖκα) γαμετήν, ἐφ' ᾗ ἔϲχ[εν (ἔϲχ[η(κεν) ed.)] ὁ γαμῶν ἅμα τῇ ϲυνελε(ύϲει) παρὰ μὲν τοῦ πατ(ρὸϲ) ἐν φερνῇ – – –," with whom she (a certain Chairemonis) has been living previously in accordance with a privately written contract concluded in the twelfth year of Antoninus Caesar the Lord, which contract they have given to each other for cancellation, while they content themselves with the present public contract, executed in the street, under which contract, at the time when they moved together, the bridegroom received from the father Herakleides as dowry … (translation adapted from the editor's rendering *mutatis mutandis*). The language is dense and even unclear. ἐφ' ᾗ should refer to the last mentioned contract, i.e. to the one which we read; only in this contract it makes sense to list the dowry and the paraphernalia, because the previous contract has been rendered for cancellation. On the other hand, the phrase ἅμα τῇ ϲυνελε(ύϲει) refers to the time of the first contract, and dowry and paraphernalia were actually given under the earlier contract. Hence, the present contract is a renewal and confirmation of the earlier one, but adds new stipulations. Moreover, it is notarized, a quality which the earlier contract seems to have lacked. Cf. line 12, where the rights of the husband to the possessions are confirmed by ὡϲ καὶ προέϲχ(εν); the editor reads προέϲχ(ε), but there follows punctuation and, then, εἰ̣[ϲ].

64. This fact, is for example, stressed by clauses like ἕξει ὁ γαμ(ῶν) ἐφ' ὅϲον ϲύνεϲτ(ιν) τῇ γαμο(υμένῃ) (*P. Oxy.* 49.3491.12).

the original receipt of the loan. One problem remains: the stipulation regarding the enforceability of the future contract. If the marriage contract were in existence, the phrase would have been appropriate. The scribe clearly had difficulty in adjusting standard legal phraseology to the concrete situation of the present case.

To sum up the discussion on *P. Oxy.* 49.3487, we can now reconstruct the situation as follows. At some point towards the beginning of their marriage, Taÿsoreus had made a loan to her husband in the usual form of a homology with bank *diagraphe*, in which her husband acknowledged not only the receipt of the full amount of the money, but also pledged that after some time he would offer his wife a formal marriage contract. Two years later, the wife might have needed some of the money for reasons of her own. Recalling the loan would have been tantamount to a request of separation. The couple did not have that on their minds, at least not yet. The partial repayment, therefore, was connected with an affirmation of their intention to enter a written marriage at a later date.

There is one final point that now can be taken up. The 32 drachmai of the repayment are part of the principal of 72 drachmai. Hence, it seems that at the time of the repayment no interest was paid.[65] But the remaining 40 drachmai will carry interest which amounts to less than 5 drachmai per annum, hardly an amount of much economic importance. Thus we may spin the story a little farther. By requesting a partial repayment and interest for the remainder of the loan Taÿsoreus might have served notice to her husband that her patience was running out and that he should better offer the pledged marriage contract soon.

SECTION VII

Finally we turn to *P. Lund* 6.3 (*SB* 6.9353) of unknown provenience,[66] a "privately written contract" (see p. 195, footnote 62), dated to a day between March 27 and April 25 of A.D. 139. The upper part of the document is lost, but it is clear that a man, probably styled as a Persian of the Epigone, acknowledges receipt of valuables in the estimated value of 528 drachmai which are to be returned at the end of the year, on August 28.[67] The acknowledgment that is typical for loan χειρόγραφα is followed by this declaration on part of the recipient of the loan: "I give to your daughter the proper marriage contract through the public notary."[68] Then follows a stipulation that the man who has received the 528 drachmai will return them within sixty days, if the relationship breaks up and the woman wishes to request repayment of "the dowry": 16–18 (ἐὰν) κ[α]ὶ ἡ (name

65. This conclusion is not completely certain. Theoretically it is possible that the original 72 drachmai included the interest for the first two years.

66. The nature and the form of the document points to Oxyrhynchite origin.

67. Lines 1–10: [(ὁ δεῖνα – – – Πέρϲηϲ τῆϲ ἐπιγονῆϲ τῷ δεῖνι – – – χαίρειν. ὁμολογῶ ἔχειν παρὰ ϲοῦ – – – (list of valuables, only ἀργυρ is still extant referring either to silver or money) – – – ἐν διατιμήϲει] |7 [δραχμῶ]ν π[εντακοϲ]ίων ε[ἴ]κ[οϲι | ὀκτώ, (γίνονται) (δραχμαὶ) φκη, [ἃϲ καὶ ἀποδώϲω ϲοι] | ἐπαγο[μ]ένων πέμπτηι τ[οῦ] | ἐνεϲτῶτοϲ ἔτου[ϲ]. Our reconstruction of this part of the document proceeds from the following facts: (1) the text is called a ἰδιόγραφοϲ ϲυγγ[ρ]αφ[ή] (line 31); (2) the date in lines 9f. should refer to the due date of a loan, according to the formulaic character of such texts; the editor saw merely traces of thirteen letters after the number; (3) the date which the editor reconstructed from insignificant remains of line 6 has no function in the context and cannot be reconciled with the date at the end of the document; (4) instead, line 6 needs to explain the following amount of drachmai in the genitive; and (5) the 528 drachmai are an estimated value. This is supported by lines 18–25, where it is said that within sixty days from the request for the repayment of the 528 drachmai the creditor is allowed to receive the goods "[in the] same evaluation that corresponds to the evaluation to which you (the creditor) are entitled": ἀποδώϲω τὰϲ | ἀργ(υρίου) (δραχμὰϲ) φκη ἐν ἡμέραϲ ἑ[ξ]ή|κοντα ἀφ' ἧϲ ἐὰν ἀπα[ιτ]ηθῆ[ι], χωρὶϲ πάϲη[ϲ] ὑπερθέϲε[ωϲ ἐξόν]|τοϲ ϲοι ἔχειν [τ]ὴ⟨ν⟩ διάλυϲιν [ἐν τῆι] αὐτῆι διατειμήϲει κατὰ | τὴν διατίμηϲιν τῆϲ ὑπα[ρχ]|ούϲηϲ περὶ ϲέ. We tentatively understand the last words as τὴν ὑπά[ρχ]|ουϲαν περὶ ϲέ, but remain skeptical because of the additional problem of the word division. Be this as it may, it is clear that the items given by the creditor are subject to an estimate of their value.

68. Lines 11–13 καὶ γράφομαι τῆι αὐτῆι θυγα[τρ]ί ϲου διὰ δημοϲίου τὴν καθήκουϲαν τοῦ γάμου ϲυγγραφήν.

of eight letters) βούληται τῆϲ φερνῆϲ ἀπαίτ[ηϲιν] ποιεῖϲθαι (see also p. 196, footnote 67). He also accepts the stipulation of *hemiolia* penalty for the case of delayed repayment of the principal, while the father has the right of exaction on the debtor and his property.

Thus the following situation emerges. A father lends to the husband of his daughter valuables equivalent to 528 drachmai for roughly four months; the husband promises to give his wife a public marriage contract within this period; with regard to this marriage contract the amount of the loan is regarded as a dowry. Should the marriage break up during the four months trial period, the loan must be repaid in sixty days, as is usual. In short, this document provides another example of a short trial marriage under a loan contract. In this case the husband acknowledged his contractual obligation to change the private loan contract, in which not even a private bank was involved, into a marriage under a public contract within the period of the loan. The situation is thus very similar to the one we discussed in *Section VI*.

To summarize the main features: from the first to the second century loans from wives to husbands were relatively common in Oxyrhynchos. The specifics of these loan contracts, issued through banks, agoranomoi, and in the form of unnotarized private contracts, were flexible. In a few cases their economic and social function is clearly visible in stipulations concerning separation during pregnancy or in a pledge on part of the debtor that he will give his wife a more formal marriage contract. In other cases the nature of the contract is revealed by their character as open-ended loans: only the wife could ask for the return of the money, thus presumably either initiating a divorce or reacting to the husband divorcing her. The need to return the money should have made divorce more difficult for the husband and, thus, should have created some security for the woman. This practice gives an advantage to the woman. Divorce, even then, was costly for the husband.

The repayment of such open-ended loans was normally due thirty or sixty days after the wife's request. In some cases, such loans were preceded by shorter and smaller loans marking a trial period; at least in one case, the loan arrangement preceded a marriage contract. The marriage could be based on a series of subsequent loan contracts and thus easily be adjusted to the changing economic situation of the family. Because of this feature, not every "repayment" and cancellation of a loan document indicates a divorce, and the payment of an outstanding loan could be fictitious, that is the prerequisite for a new contract with adjusted terms and enhanced status. The wife could also try to use the loan as an instrument to coax her husband into an improvement of the status of their marriage.

The loans, consisting either of money or goods, were not accompanied by written marriage contracts. If they were, these contracts would have been mentioned in the loan documents, which always refer to background transactions. Thus, the marriages in which loans from wife to husband were practiced were ἄγραφοι, as is specifically said in Tryphon's contract (*Section IV*); but they could lead to a written marriage, as we suspected in the cases of Taÿsoreus and Sarapion and the couple of *P. Lund* 6.3. On the other hand, a loan arrangement did not preclude either a simultaneous or subsequent marriage contract as we saw in the case *P. Oxy.* 49.3487 (*Section VI*). In the absence of marriage contracts, the loan agreements became an indirect legal base for such marriages.

The husbands were free to use the loans for their operations, and this fact confirms that these were real loans, not fictive ones. Hence, they are neither *donationes ante* nor *propter nuptias*. The ultimate ownership rested with the woman, and her heirs could claim the money. The usual penalties for delayed payments applied, but none of our documents indicates that the *hemiolia* was actually paid. To the contrary, in a mutual agreement marriage loans could be silently extended. But the wife retained the right of exaction upon the husband and all his property, which, however, would only have happened in unfriendly separations. Normally, these loans seem to have been interest-free; but under particular circumstances the wife could ask for interest (see *Section VI*).

In many respects these loans can be regarded as the equivalent to a dowry, and once the loan is called by this name (*Section VII*). Dowries conform to Greek as well as Egyptian practice. In a divorce the dowry had to be repaid in reasonable time. On the other hand, a woman could forfeit her entire dowry (φερνή) or half of it, at least according to Ptolemaic Greek and Roman marriage contracts respectively. The specific character of loans precluded forfeiture. Moreover, marriage loans were in accordance with Egyptian customs. Earlier, we saw that two phrases occurring in one of the loan documents originate from Egyptian formulas (*Section IV*). Here we return to the more significant of these clauses: "I have received from you the price for these (revenues) in full and without any deduction; you have pleased me." This sentence was used in Egyptian marriage contracts, but not exclusively so. Moreover, Egyptian maintenance contracts of Ptolemaic times regulated not only the maintenance of the wife and contained stipulations regarding children, but also contained the husband's receipt of a loan from his wife. Depending on the type of contract, this loan is called "the money to become a wife" (*ḥd n ỉr ḥmt*) or "the goods of a woman" (*nkt.w n s.ḥmt*). "The money to become a wife" had become a small, symbolic amount of 10–14 drachmai of silver, a deflation from earlier payments. It is in the context of the acknowledgment of the receipt of these loans that the husband uses phrases like: "I have received it (the money or the goods) from your hand, my heart is content with it, (for) it is complete, without any remainder." For the case of divorce, the Egyptian marriage contracts stipulate that "on your day you demand from my hand the above 500 (*deben*) of money, I shall give it to you thereupon, on a day within thirty days after it being claimed from my hand which you will do."[69] In Greek subscriptions such "loans" are called δάνειον and, closer to the Greek approach, φερνή ("dowry"). Moreover, in the Egyptian marriage contracts the husband pledges his entire property as security for his wife's claims (type "B," §23 Pestman [n. 41] pp. 34 and 115). Contractually the woman is put in a stronger position: "All and everything that I possess and that I shall acquire is a security ... for the (?) money (?) above described; I shall not be able to say to you: 'I have acted for you [in accordance with] all stipulations above(mentioned)' (while) this deed (is) in your hand" (thus in §§23f. of type "B," Pestman p. 34).

None of the documents which deal with loans related to an "unwritten marriage" shows any sign of *patria potestas*. The nature of the documents as homologies, concluded either at private banks or with the agoranomoi, would allow a father only a very limited role. He could only enter the procedure as κύριος, since conflict of interest precluded a husband to act in this role when he himself would be the recipient of the loan or would repay the loan. This is a particularly striking fact in cases where a husband acted as κύριος in related contracts, but not in loans where he could be regarded as beneficiary. In such cases we find a brother (#6), the husband of the mother (##9 and 11), or a maternal uncle (##13 and 18). We have not identified enough loans from wife to husband to render the absence of fathers significant. But it is nevertheless important to realize that the procedure itself minimized the role of a woman's family. "Unwritten marriages" provided no need for *ekdosis*, neither by the father nor by any member of her family. Women could very much act on their own (also see p. 194, footnote 59).

The legal interpretation of what the woman gives her husband as "loan" is a substantial contribution on the part of the Egyptian tradition to the marriage practice of early Roman Egypt. This is not to say that our loan documents are hidden Egyptian maintenance contracts. There is no element

69. Thus in marriage contracts of Pestman's type "B," § 18 (1961, pp. 34, 66–69, and "diagram B"). The connection of this request for repayment with divorce is clear in the following phrase: "If I repudiate you as a wife or that you repudiate (me) I shall give it (back) to you on the day on which you will demand it in return from me (or) a day within 30 days (after) the day (of) (re)claiming the above-(mentioned) money, 110 (*deben*)" (quoted by Pestman, p. 67). See Pestman for the entire matter of the Demotic maintenance contracts; and cf. above, *Section IV*. In Greek marriage contracts it is usually a period of sixty days within which the dowry has to be returned (Kutzner 1989, pp. 31f.) In this point, the Greek and Egyptian marriages are not very different.

of maintenance in them; nor has maintenance or even provisions for children any space in ordinary loan documents. On the other hand, maintenance is implied and can be seen as the husband's *obvious* obligation for receiving a loan free of interest; it needs not to be regulated. Making use of the Greek institution of banking and consequently restricting the provisions to the loan is in a sense a reversal of the primary intention of maintenance contracts, which, according to their name, served primarily this function. And yet, turning the loan into the main provision of a kind of substitute marriage contract also allowed the survival of an important element of the Egyptian legal tradition when it was no longer customary to write maintenance contracts. In a way, the marriage loans of Oxyrhynchos are the result of a combination of this Egyptian element with Greek fiscality and specifically private banking.[70] At the same time the use of private banks became also a milestone in the development of banks as notary public, as we have seen earlier, and thus, in the century after the Ptolemaic rule, marks a shift from the state to the private sector.

Addendum: The marriage contract *P. Babatha* 18 of April 5, 128, acknowledges a (fictive?) payment of 300 drachmai by the groom towards his bride's "dowry"; the dowry is paid in accordance with the husband's obligation to maintain his wife and their prospective children. In addition, the dowry contained jewelry and clothing in the value of 200 drachmai, which the bride brought with her. The total amount of 500 drachmai is regarded as a debt which the wife may call back whenever she chooses. She (and her agents) have the right to εἴϲπραξιϲ, and the husband is liable with all his property. Also see *P. Babatha* 17 of February 21, 128, a loan of 300 drachmai by Babatha to her husband. The partial similarities of these transactions with the Egyptian and Oxyrhynchite institutions studied in the present paper seem to be obvious, but need further study.

70. For the general question of the relationship between the Greek and the Egyptian cultures in Egypt and the vast literature on this topic, it may suffice to refer to L. Koenen's paper on "The Ptolemaic King as a Religious Figure" which, in 1988, was delivered at a conference on Hellenism at the University of California, Berkeley, and which is forthcoming in the Proceedings of that conference, to be published by the University of California Press.

APPENDIX I

LOAN OF VALUABLES FROM WIFE TO HUSBAND (TEXT #13: P. MICH. INV. NO. 92)

Inv. 92 (see pl. 19.1) 21.2 × 16.4 cm Dec. 27, A.D. 73 – Jan. 25, A.D. 74

Παυϲῖριϲ Π[α]υ[ϲ]ί̣ρ̣ι̣ο̣ϲ̣ τοῦ Ἀμμων[ίου] μητρὸϲ Θαήϲιοϲ
τῆϲ Διοϲκ[οῦτοϲ] τ̣ῶν ἀπ' Ὀξυρύγχω[ν πό]λεωϲ, Πέρϲηϲ
τῆϲ ἐπιγο̣νῆ[ϲ, Τα]ύρει μητρὸϲ Ταύρι[οϲ] τῆϲ Ἀννίβατο(ϲ)
[τῶν] ἀπὸ τῆ[ϲ αὐτ]ῆϲ πόλεωϲ μετὰ [κ]υρίου τοῦ πρὸϲ μητρὸ(ϲ)
αὐ[τῆϲ] θείου [Θοώνι]οϲ τοῦ Ἀννίβατοϲ χαίρειν. ὁμολογῶι
ἀ̣π̣[έχε]ι̣ν̣ παρὰ ϲ̣οῦ [ἐπὶ] τ̣οῦ πρὸϲ Ὀξυρύγχων πόλει Cαραπιείου
διὰ τῆϲ Ἀμμ[ωνίου κα]ὶ Cαραπίωνοϲ καὶ τῶν μετόχων τραπέζηϲ ἀργυρ[ίου Cεβαϲ]τοῦ νομίϲματο[ϲ δραχμὰϲ] τριακο-
ϲίαϲ̣, (γίνονται) [ἀρ]γ̣[υ(ρίου)] (δραχμαὶ) [τ̄, κεφαλα]ί̣ου, ἐ̣ν αἷϲ ἐϲτιν
ἐν[ω]τίων χρ[υ]ϲῶν ζεῦ-
γοϲ ἓν ἐν ϲυντειμήϲει δραχμῶν τε[ϲϲαρ]άκον̣τ̣α [κ]αὶ ἅλυ-
ϲιν ἀργυρίου ὁ̣λ̣κ̣ῆϲ ἀϲήμου δραχμῶν τ̣ρ̣ιάκο̣[ν]τ̣α̣ κ̣[α]ὶ̣ ...
ἐν ϲυντειμήϲ̣ει̣ δραχμῶν ἑκατὸν [ἑξ]ήκοντα καὶ κα̣ ̣ -
[̣ ̣ ̣]ενα δραχμῶν ὀγδοήκοντα. τὸ δὲ προκείμενον
κ[ε]φ[άλ]α̣ιον ἀποδώϲω ϲοι ἐν ἡμέραιϲ τριάκοντα ἀφ' ἧϲ ἐὰν
ἀπαιτηθῆ̣. π̣ροϲομολογῶ δὲ καὶ ἐα̣[ν] ἀ̣παλλ̣αγ̣ὴ γένη-
ταί ϲου ἐνκ̣ύ̣ο̣υ̣ οὔϲηϲ ἀποδώϲειν ϲοι χωρὶϲ τοῦ προκειμένου
κεφαλαίου εἰϲ τὴν τῆϲ λοχείαϲ δαπάνην ἄλλαϲ ⟨ἀ⟩ργ(υρίου) δ̣ρ[αχ]μ̣[ὰ]ϲ̣ ρ̣.
ἐὰν δὲ μὴ ἀποδῶι [καθάπερ γέγ]ρα̣[πτ]α̣ι, ἐ̣κ̣τ̣[ίϲω] ϲοι τὸ προκίμενο(ν)
κεφάλαιον μεθ' ἡμ[ιολίαϲ, τῆϲ πράξεώϲ ϲοι οὔϲηϲ ἔκ τε ἐμοῦ]
κ[αὶ] ἐκ τ[ῶ]ν̣ ὑπ[α]ρ̣χ[όντων μοι πάντων. κυρία ἡ χεὶρ πανταχῆ ἐπι-]
φ̣ε[ρ]ο̣μ̣ένη [καὶ παντὶ τῷ ἐπιφέροντι
— —

3: Αννιβατ^ο

4: μητρ^ο

5: read ὁμολογῶ

9: [τ̄ part of the overscore is visible, but there is no appreciable trace of the letter.

9–13: We expect 9 εἰϲιν and, subsequently, 10f. ἅλυϲιϲ (and more nouns in the nominative). The scribe is falling back in the accusative with which he began his description of the loan (8 [δραχμὰϲ] τριακοϲίαϲ).

13: ἕνα? Read προκείμενον

"Pausiris son of Pausiris, grandson of Ammonios, his mother being Thaesis, daughter of Dioskous, of the city of Oxyrhynchos, a Persian of the Epigone, to Tauris, her mother being Tauris daughter of Annibas, of the same city, who is acting with her guardian, her maternal uncle Thoonis son of Annibas. I acknowledge that I have received from you at the Sarapeum in the city of Oxyrhynchos through the bank of Ammonios, Sarapion, and Co, [the capital sum of] three hundred [drachmai] of Augustan silver coinage, [that is 300 drachmai of silver], which includes one pair of gold earrings, forty drachmai in value, a chain of a weight of thirty drachmai of uncoined silver, [(something)], one hundred and sixty drachmai in value, and [(something)], worth eighty drachmai. I shall repay the aforesaid capital to you within thirty days of request. I further acknowledge that if there is a separation while you are pregnant, I shall pay you, aside from the aforesaid capital, another 100 drachmai of silver for the expense of childbirth. If I do not make repayment [as written, I shall pay] you the aforesaid capital with a penalty of one-half, [and you have the right of exaction upon me and everything] I own. [This document is enforceable wherever it is pro]duced [and for everybody producing it."

APPENDIX II

TABLE 19.2. THE ARCHIVE OF PAUSIRIS, SURVEY OF DATA.

No.	Inv./Publ. No.	Document from (a) to (b)	Status	Kyrioi (a) and (b)	Hypographeis (a) and (b)	Transaction	Amount	Period	Date	Documents Referred To: Background	Offices, Signing Officials	Same Main Hands (##)*
Pausiris son of Ammonios												
1	*P. Mich.* 3.170 (# 72)	(a) *Pausiris* son of Ammonios of *Hippeon Parembole* quarter (b) Apollonios and Didymos, topo- and komogrammateis				Registration of apprenticeship with village officials		Beginning 8/29/49 (from beginning of tenth year of Claudius)	9/9 or 9/16/49 (Sebastos [Thoth] 12 or 19, tenth year of Claudius)	Pausiris Sr. gives his son *Ammonios*, a minor, into an apprenticeship with Apollonios son of Apollonios of the same quarter to learn the weaving trade (cf. #3)	Didymos and Apollonios	
2	*P. Mich.* 10.598 (# 74)	(a) Melas and Theon, tax-farmers (b) *Pausiris* son of Ammonios				Receipt of four installments of the weavers' tax	Total 32 drachmai	6/20/–10/27/49 (Epeiph 26, year nine of Claudius to Phaophi 30, year ten)	10/27/49 (Phaophi 30 year nine)			
3	*P. Wisc.* I 4 (bottom damaged)	(a) *Pausiris* s. of Ammonios and (b) Apollonios son of Apollonios, weaver				Apprenticeship contract; obj. mutual homology; 100 drachmai penalty for breach of contract by Pausiris plus 100 drachmai payment to treasury; also penalty for missed work	14 drachmai for clothing, and 5 drachmai monthly for food, paid by the father	One year	8/29-9/27/52 (Thoth ?, thirteenth year of Claudius)	Pausiris Sr. gives his son Dioskous, a minor, into an apprenticeship with Apollonios (cf. #1) to learn the weaving trade		
4	*P. Mich.* 3.171 (# 73)	(a) Helene daughter of Horion (b) Panechotes and Ischyrion, farmers of the weavers' tax		Epinikos son of Theon (husband); cf. #5		Registration of apprenticeship with tax farmers		Beginning 8/29/58 (from beginning of fifth year of Nero)	9/26/58 (Sebastos [Thoth] 19, fifth year of Nero)	Helene gives Amoitas, a minor, her nephew (father deceased), of Hermaion quarter, into apprenticeship with *Pausiris* son of Ammonios, of *Hippeon Campus* quarter (subunit of *Hippeon Parembole* quarter) to learn the weaving trade	Panechotes, tax farmer	
5	*P. Mich.* 3.172 (# 81)	(a) *Pausiris* son of Ammonios, of *Hippeon Parembole* quarter (b) Theon, farmer of weavers' tax				Registration of apprenticeship with tax farmers		Beginning 8/29/62 (from beginning of ninth year of Nero)	10/19/62 (Phaophi 22, ninth year of Nero); accepted on 10/20 (Phaophi 23)	Pausiris Sr. gives his son Pausiris Jr., a minor, into apprenticeship with Epinikos son of Theon of Hermaion quarter (cf. #4) to learn the weaving trade	Theon, tax farmer	
Dioskous son of Pausiris												
6	# 79	(a) Dioskous, son of *Pausiris* (b) Thermouthion daughter of Achilliōn (= Achilleus)	Persian of the Epigone	Sarapion, son of Achilleus (brother?)	Stratonikos son of Apion	Receipt of loan; cheirographon with bank *diagraphe*; hemiolia penalty; *praxis* clause	20 drachmai (Ptolemaic and Augustan coins)	Two months, Mech. 1–Pham. 30 (1/27–3/26)	1/27/60 (Mecheir 1, sixth year of Nero)	Loan from wife to husband. Invalidated, repaid by #10.	Sarapeum's Bank of *Ammonios son of Ammonios*	
7	# 80	(a) Sintotoes daughter of Pastōys (or Pestōys) (b) Thermouthion daughter of[†] Achilleus (Achilleus is Sintotoēs' brother)		(a) Theon, son of Dionysios (*husband*) (b) Dioskourides (= Dioskous) son of Pausiris	Ischyrion, son of Ischyrion	Payment for expenses; cheirographon with bank *diagraphe*; the payment does not affect the interests and the right of exaction for another loan which Sintotoēs had given to Dioskous (= Dioskourides)	14 drachmai and unspecified expenses for work, (in Ptolemaic and Augustan coins)		3/5/60 (Phamenoth 9, sixth year of Nero)	Expenses: (a) for poll and trade taxes owed by deceased father; (b) Thermouthion's share of repair expenses for part of house in *Laura Hippodromou*, inherited from father; reference is made to the cheirographon with *diagraphe* of the loan given by Sintotoēs to Dioskous	Sarapeum's Bank of *Ammonios son of Ammonios*	

* Only the identifications about which the authors have presently reached consensus are listed here.

TABLE 19.2. THE ARCHIVE OF PAUSIRIS, SURVEY OF DATA *(cont.)*.

No.	*Inv./Publ. No.*	*Document from (a) to (b)*	*Status*	*Kyrioi (a) and (b)*	*Hypographeis (a) and (b)*	*Transaction*	*Amount*	*Period*	*Date*	*Documents Referred To; Background*	*Offices, Signing Officials*	*Same Main Hands (##)*
8	# 78	(a) Ploutarche, daughter of Harpaesis and †Soeris daughter of Horos (b) Thermouthion daughter of †Achilleus son of Pastōys		(a) Diogenes son of Pasiōn (husband) (b) Dioskous, son of Pausiris		Repayment of loan and interests; obj. homology notarized by agoranomoi (ἐν ἀγυιᾷ); penalty clause for future accusations (100 drachmai to be paid to Thermouthion, 100 drachmai to the treasury)	140 drachmai plus interest (Ptolemaic and Augustan coins)		4/18/60 (Pharmouthi 23, sixth year of Nero)	Loan by Soeris, Ploutarche's mother, to Achilleus her son in law, in acc. with contract notarized by the public registry of Oxyrhynchos in Pharm. (3/27–4/25/49); the money originates from Thermouthion selling her deceased father's share of a house in the *Laura Hippodromou* to Didymos son of Didymos (the sale was made with her husband Dioskous as kyrios). The loan is probably equivalent to loans from wives to husbands.	Andromachos, associate of Chairemon and Sotades, agoranomoi	9 inv. #75
9	*P. Mich.* 3.191–92 (# 75/76); two copies	(a) Dioskous son of *Pausiris* and (b) Thermouthion daughter of †Achilleus son of Pastōys and Plutarche daughter of Harpaesis		Diogenes, son of Pasion (husband of Thermouthion's mother Plutarche)		Receipt of loan, obj. mutual homology notarized by agoranomoi (ἐν ἀγυιᾷ); without interest; *praxis* clause. This document is called *daneiou syggraphe* in #11	200 drachmai (Ptolemaic and Augustan coins)	Within sixty days after recall	4/18/60 (Pharmouthi 23, sixth year of Nero)	Loan from wife to husband. The money originates from Thermouthion's sale of her deceased father's share of a house in the *Laura Hippodromou* to Didymos son of Didymos (the sale was made with her husband Dioskous as kyrios); the rest of the proceeds were paid by Thermouthion to her mother Plutarche as repayment for the loan which Achilleus (Plutarche's deceased husband and Thermouthion's father) owed to Plutarche; see #8, here called "receipt" (ἀποχή); #191 is invalidated, repaid by #11	Andromachos, associate of Chairemon and Sotades agoranomoi	inv. 75 = #8
10	# 77	(a) Thermouthis (= Thermouthion) daughter of Achilliōn (= Achilleus) (b) Dioskous, son of *Pausiris*		Stratonikos, son of Apion	Stratonikos, son of Apion (note: the kyrios acts as hypographeus)	Repayment of loan #6 cheirographon with bank *diagraphe*	20 drachmai (Ptolemaic and Augustan coins)	About 4½ months	6/9/60 (Pauni 15, sixth year of Nero)	The original loan made by *diekbole* (cf. #18) in accordance with a bank *diagraphe* in Mech. 1/27–2/25; sc. on 1/27/60) was invalidated and returned; Thermouthion retains all rights with regard to another loan (*daneiou syggraphe*), sc. #8	Sarapeum's Bank of *Ammonios* son of *Ammonios*	18
11	*P. Mich.* 3.194 (# 83)	(a) Thermouthion, daughter of Achilleus and Plutarche (b) Dioskous son of *Pausiris* (ex-husband)		Diogenes, son of Pasion (husband of Thermouthion's mother Plutarche)		Repayment of loan [#9]; obj. homology notarized by agoranomos; penalty clause for future accusations (100 drachmai to Dioskous and 100 drachmai to the treasury).	200 drachmai (Ptolemaic and Augustan coins)		3/11/61 (Phamenoth 15, seventh year of Nero)	Loan from wife to husband, see #6. The money of the original loan came from Thermouthion's sale of her father's share in a house in *Laura Hippopodromou* (the sale was made with her husband Dioskous as kyrios) and in acc. with an homology between Thermouthion and Dioskous (through the public registry) in Phar. (3/27–4/25/60, sc. on 4/18) conc. 200 dr., i. e. #9	Epimachos, agoranomos	
						Pausiris son of Pausiris						
12	# 84	(a) Pausiris son of *Pausiris* and Thaesis (b) Papontos son of Chrysos son of Heraklas	Persian of the Epigone		Zōilos son of Horos son of Zōilos	Receipt of loan; *cheirographon* with bank *diagraphe*; hemiolia penalty; overtime interest; *praxis* clause	105 drachmai (Augustan coins)	More than two months (about ten weeks), 4/18–6/24/73 (Pharmouthi 23–Pauni 30)	4/18/73 (Pharmouthi 23, fifth year of Vespasian)	Repaid with overtime interest by #17 (112 drachmai); invalidated	Sarapeum's Bank of *Ammonios, Sarapion and Co.*	14, 16, 17

TABLE 19.2. THE ARCHIVE OF PAUSIRIS, SURVEY OF DATA *(cont.)*.

No.	*Inv./Publ. No.*	*Document from (a) to (b)*	*Status*	*Kyrioi (a) and (b)*	*Hypographeis (a) and (b)*	*Transaction*	*Amount*	*Period*	*Date*	*Documents Referred To; Background*	*Offices, Signing Officials*	*Same Main Hands (##)*
13	# 92 (lower part broken off)	(a) Pausiris son of *Pausiris* and Thaesis (b) Tauris daughter of Tauris daughter of Annibas	Persian of the Epigone	Thoonis son of Annibas (maternal uncle)	(End of document lost)	Receipt of loan; *cheirographon*; the bank's action is broken off; hemiolia penalty. Additional stipulation: payment of 100 drachmai by Pausirus for childbirth in case of separation. #18 calls this document a *cheirographon diekboles* (cf. #6).	300 drachmai (Augustan coins) actually in valuables including gold earrings and a silver chain; the itemized objects total 310 drachmai	Within thirty days after Tauris' request (paid back on 8/15/74 [Kaisareios 22, year six of Vespasian]), see #18	2/27/73–1/25/74 (Tybi, sixth year Vespasian)	Loan from wife to husband providing security to Tauris in case of separation, particularly during her pregnancy. All objects were apparently sold and the proceeds used for paying the loans ##12 (= 17), 14, and 15. The document is invalidated, but the marriage continued. Repaid through #18	Sarapeum's Bank of *Ammonios, Sarapion and Co.*	
14	# 86	(a) Pausiris son of *Pausiris* and Thaesis (b) Dieuches son of Kephalon son of Dieuches	Persian of the Epigone		Zōilos son of Horos son of Zōilos	Receipt of loan; *cheirographon* with bank *diagraphe*; no charges to be added to the principal; hemiolia penalty; overtime interest; *praxis* clause	48 drachmai (Augustan coins)	Two months (2/1—4/25; Mecheir 17-Pharmouthi 30)	2/11/74 (Mecheir 17, sixth year of Vespasian)	Repaid through #16 where the original loan contract is said to have been invalidated. The extant copy is not invalidated.	Sarapeum's Bank of *Ammonios, Sarapion and Co.*	12, 16, 17
15	# 85	(a) Pausiris son of *Pausiris* and Thaesis (b) Eudaimon son of Horos son of Phatres	Persian of the Epigone		Sarapion son of Ammonios	Receipt of loan; *cheirographon* with bank *diagraphe*; no charges to be added to the principal; interest to be paid monthly; *hemiolia* penalty; *praxis* clause	120 drachmai (Augustan coins)	About six weeks; 3/8–4/25/74 (Phamenoth 12–Pharmouthi 30)	3/8/74 (Phamenoth 12, sixth year of Vespasian)	Invalidated, repaid by #19.	Sarapeum's Bank of *Ammonios, Sarapion and Co.*	
16	# 90 (top broken off)	(a) Dieuches son of Kephalon (b) [Pausiris son of *Pausiris*]			Sarapion, son of Achilleus (note: Dieuches signs himself, too, but βραδέως)	Repayment of loan #14; *cheirographon*, no bank *diagraphe* on this copy; original document (#14) invalidated and returned.	48 drachmai (Augustan coins)	Almost three weeks late (due on 4/25 [see #14])	5/17/74 (Germanikeios = Pachon 22, sixth year of Vespasian)	The original loan for which the delayed payment is made (#14) is called *cheirographon kai diagraphe*	Sarapeum's Bank of *Ammonios, Sarapion and Co.* (but this copy is not signed)	12, 14, 17
17	# 88	(a) Papontos son of Chrysos son of Heraklas (b) Pausiris son of *Pausiris* and Thaesis			Sarapion, son of Achilleus	Repayment of loan #12 with interest; *cheirographon* with bank *diagraphe*	112 drachmai (Augustan coins)	Seven months 9/28–10/27/73 (Phaophi) to 5/18/74 (Pachon 23)	5/17/74 corrected to 5/18 (Germanikeios [= Pachon] 22nd corrected to 23rd, sixth year of Vespasian)	The original loan (#12), a *cheirographon* with bank *diagraphe*, has been invalidated and returned. The repayment is for #12, a loan of 105 drachmai. After it had become overdue, it was renewed in Phaophi, probably on Phaophi 23 (October 20), and 7 drachmai added for the first six months of the loan (Parmouthi 23–Phaophi 23, 4/18–10/20/73)	Sarapeum's Bank of *Ammonios, Sarapion and Co.*	12, 14, 16
18	# 89	(a) Tauris daughter of Tauris daughter of Annibas (b) Pausiris son of *Pausiris* son of Ammonios and Thaesis daughter of Dioskous		Thoonis son of Annibas (maternal uncle)	(a) Stratonikos son of Apion son of Stratonikos (for Tauris) (b) Apion son of Apion by adoption son of Stratonikos	Repayment of loan #13; *cheirographon* with bank *diagraphe*	300 drachmai (Augustan coins)	Eight months, 12/27/73–1/25/74 to 8/15; (Tybi–Kaisareios 22 [i.e. Mesore 22])	8/15/74 (Kaisareios 22; sixth year of Vespasian)	The original loan document issued by the bank (#13) is called *cheirographon diekboles* (cf. #10); invalidation and return of original document. Whether the "repayment" of this loan from wife to husband was followed by another loan (or other contract) is not known	Sarapeum's Bank of *Ammonios, Sarapion and Co.*	10

TABLE 19.2. THE ARCHIVE OF PAUSIRIS, SURVEY OF DATA *(cont.)*.

No.	*Inv./Publ. No.*	*Document from (a) to (b)*	*Status*	*Kyrioi (a) and (b)*	*Hypographeis (a) and (b)*	*Transaction*	*Amount*	*Period*	*Date*	*Documents Referred To; Background*	*Offices, Signing Officials*	*Same Main Hands (##)*
19	# 91	(a) Eudaimon son of Horos son of Phatres (b) Pausiris son of *Pausiris*				Repayment of loan #15 with interest, *cheirographon* with bank *diagraphe*	120 drachmai (Augustan coins)	About six months, i.e. $4\frac{1}{2}$ months late	8/28/74 (Epag. 5, sixth year of Vespasian)	Repayment of loan #15 on last day of the year; the original "*cheirographon* issued through the same bank" is invalidated and returned	Sarapeum's Bank of *Ammonios, Sarapion and Co.*	
20	# 87	(a) Teres son of Sarapion son of Teres (b) Pausiris son of *Pausiris* son of Ammonios	Persian of the Epigone		Stratonikos son of Apion son of Stratonikos	Receipt of loan; *cheirographon* with bank *diagraphe*; the repayment will be made for the account of Dionysios (a minor; brother of Tauris Jr., Pausiris' wife); penalty clause for damage ("double"); interest may be due (cf. the phrasing of the indemnification clause protecting Pausiris [?])	60 drachmai (Augustan coins)	Determined by the coming to age of Dionysios	12/28/74 (Tybi 2, seventh year of Vespasian)	The money for the loan became available at the death of †Tauris daughter of Annibas, the mother of Tauris Jr. (Pausiris' wife) and Dionysios, a minor. †Tauris Sr. had lent 120 drachmai to Nike daughter of Harsiesis for the right of habitatition in Nike's house (antichretic loan; *cheirographon* with bank *diagraphe*; date damaged). At the termination of the habitation Nike repaid the principal of the loan now to Pausiris who acted for the estate of Tauris Jr. and Dionysios; Pausiris returned to Nike the receipt of the original loan (a bank *diagraphe*; between 2/25 and 3/26/74, Pham., sixth year of Vespasian). On behalf of Dionysios, Pausiris then invested Dionysios' share of 60 drachmai in the present loan to Teres. Another contract concerning another 60 drachmai was probably issued for Tauris Jr. The money of the original loan to Nike belonged to an estate managed by †Tauris Sr. on behalf of her children.	Sarapeum's Bank of *Ammonios, Sarapion and Co.*	
21	# 93	(a) Pausiris (b) Thaesis				Private letter on business matters including an antichretic loan (probably letting space in the family house where the mother lived).			4/10, year ?, most likely after #18	Persons living with Thaesis: Dioskous, Tauris, Senammonia. Other persons: Harpalos, Heraklas		
22	# 94	(a) Dioskous and *Ammonios* sons of *Pausiris* and Thaesis of *Hippeon Parembole* (b) Symmachos and associate amphodarchs of *Hippeon Parembole*				Sworn declaration that brother Pausiris is staying in Alexandria			4/26–5/25 (?), 79 (Germanikeios [?] = Pachon, tenth year of Vespasian)	reference to edict of C. Aeterninus Fronto (see *P. Oxy.* 36.2756) "about those staying in Alexandria" in connection with the continued obligation to pay the poll tax.		

PLATE 19.1

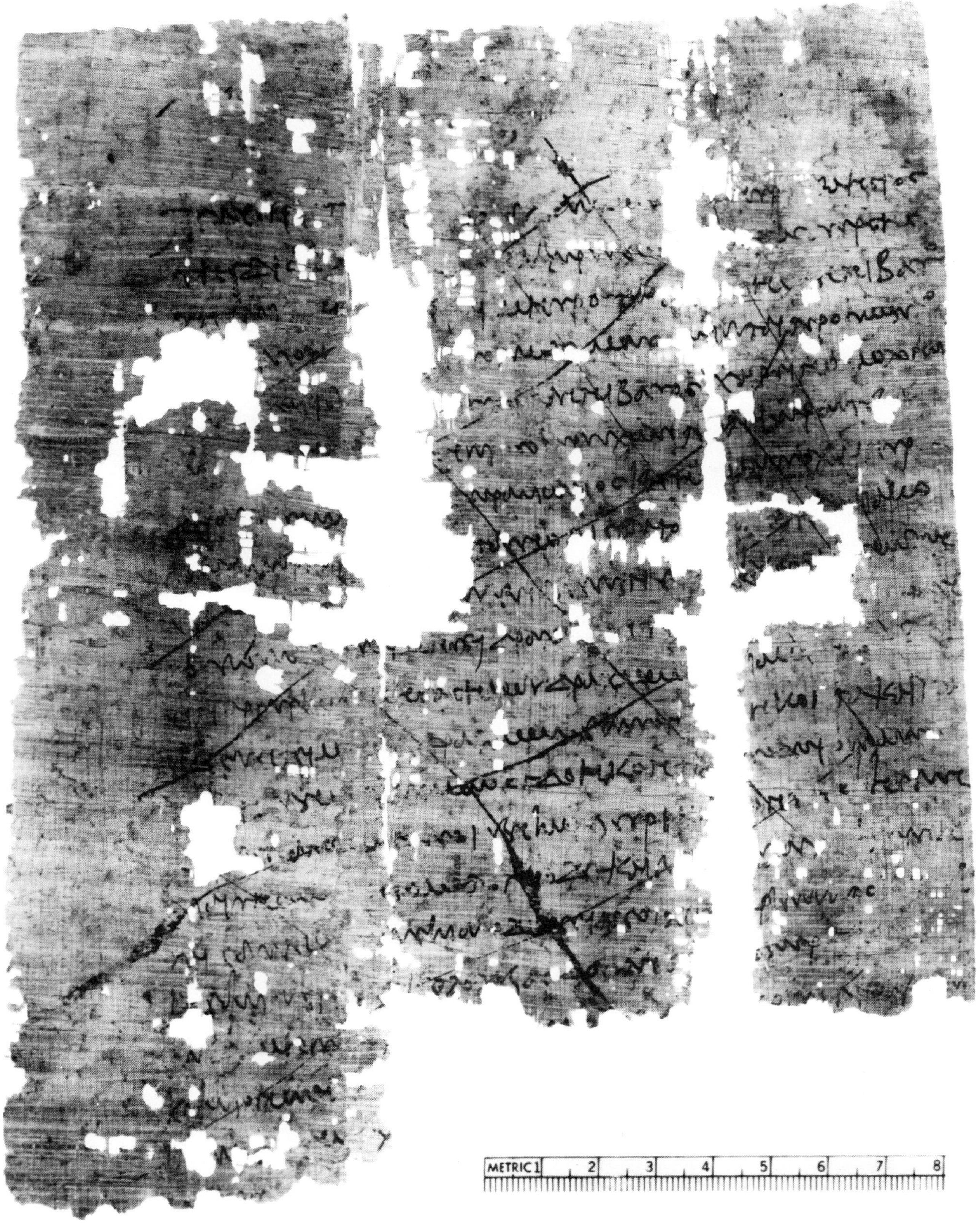

First Century Archive from Oxyrhynchos, Document #13 (P. Mich. inv. No. 92); Courtesy of the Special Collections Library, The University of Michigan, Ann Arbor. Note: the width of the vertical break on the right side is misleading, especially in the lower area of the document.

CHAPTER 20

DIE ÄGYPTISCHEN PRIESTER DES PTOLEMÄISCHEN KÖNIGSKULTES (ZUSAMMENFASSUNG)

EDDY LANCIERS
Katholieke Universiteit, Leuven

In der Entwicklung des ägyptischen Königskultes der Ptolemäerzeit sind mehrere Phasen zu unterscheiden. Obwohl die Theoi Soteres bereits am Anfang der Regierung des Ptolemaios II. vergöttlicht waren, wurden sie erst ab 215 in den griechischen eponymen Königskult aufgenommen. Im ägyptischen Milieu findet man ebenfalls nur spärliche Zeugnisse für eine Verehrung des Ptolemaios I. und der Berenike I. Ptolemaios II. schloß im 14. Regierungsjahr — d.h. wohl 272/1 — den Kult der Theoi Adelphoi an den eponymen Kult Alexanders in Alexandrien an. Unter seiner Regierung hat der Kult der ptolemäischen Herrscher auch einen Platz in den ägyptischen Heiligtümern erworben. Da der ägyptische Königskult unter Ptolemaios II. eingeführt wurde, und die Theoi Soteres nicht retroaktiv in diesen Kult integriert worden sind, fängt die Reihe der vergöttlichten Königspaare in den Titeln der örtlichen ägyptischen Priester mit den Theoi Adelphoi an. Wie aus abgekürzten Formeln deutlich hervorgeht, gelten die vergöttlichten Ptolemäer in diesen Fällen als synnaoi Theoi der lokalen Hauptgottheit.

Im Hinblick auf die Verehrung der Theoi Adelphoi als Theoi synnaoi in den ägyptischen Heiligtümern wäre zu erwarten, daß dieses Königspaar auch in den Titeln der ägyptischen Priester, die ein Amt im Rahmen des Königskultes innehatten, an erster Stelle genannt sein würde. In den meisten Fällen aber fängt die Reihe der vergöttlichten Ptolemäer in den Titeln dieser Priester mit den Theoi Euergetai an. Dies scheint auf die Bestimmung im Kanoposdekret zurückzugehen, daß jeder einzelne Priester sich öffentlich als Kultdiener der Theoi Euergetai zu präsentieren hatte. Spätere Ptolemäer haben diese Bestimmung in ihren Dekreten wiederholt. Zeugnisse für solche Titel eines Priesters des Königskultes findet man in allen Teilen Ägyptens bis zum Ende der Ptolemäerzeit, aber im Hinblick auf die allgemeine Tragweite der Verordnung sind sie alles in allem doch eher karg. Da die Priester den Titel eines Königspriesters aber vor allem in ihren demotischen und hieroglyphischen Titulaturen, und dann nicht nur in ihren offiziellen Urkunden, sondern auch in Graffiti, auf Bildern, Sarkophagen u.ä. erwähnt haben, rechtfertigt nichts die Annahme, daß sie ihre Stelle im Rahmen des Königskultes nur bei ihren Beziehungen mit den Behörden der Dynastie hervorheben wollten.

Die ägyptischen Priester hatten den täglichen Kult vor den großen Statuen und den kleineren, in Schreinen aufbewahrte Kultbildern der Ptolemäer zu versorgen. Außerdem brachten sie den vergöttlichten Königspaaren Opfer dar, besonders aus Anlaß der auch in den ägyptischen Heiligtümern zu feiernden dynastischen Festen. Beim Vollziehen von Ritualen und Handlungen, die seit alters her zum Kult der traditionellen ägyptischen Götter gehörten, kam der ägyptische Klerus somit fortwährend mit der Idee der Göttlichkeit der ptolemäischen Herrscher in Berührung, die zweifellos von Alexandrien aus zur Legitimation der griechisch-makedonischen Oberherrschaft propagiert wurde. Obwohl auch für einige frühere Pharaonen an bestimmten Stellen des Landes Kultbilder aufgestellt worden waren, ließ man jetzt fremden Herrschern in allen ägyptischen Heiligtümern einen Kult zukommen. Über die tiefer liegenden Gefühle der ägyptischen Priesterschaft dem Königskult gegenüber bleiben unsere Quellen stumm, so daß man nur Mutmaßungen äußern kann. Daß ein Teil der Priesterschaft anfänglich nur widerwillig am Kult der Ptolemäer teilgenommen hat, wie E. Winter auf Grund einer Untersuchung der Tempelreliefs bezüglich des Königskultes angenommen hat, ist wohl nicht ganz auszuschließen. Die ständige Wiederholung der Kulthandlungen sowie deren Anlehnung an herkömmliche Kultformen müssen letzten Endes aber dazu beigetragen haben, die Göttlichkeit der ptolemäischen Dynastie im Bewußtsein des ägyptischen Klerus zu verankern.

Eine Zurückhaltung der Priester gegenüber dem Königskult hätte man mit der Gewährung wirtschaftlicher Vorteile zu beseitigen versuchen können. Daß die Ptolemäer für den dynastischen Kult neue Opfergüter gestiftet haben, hat sich jedoch nicht bestätigen lassen. Auch die nominell für den Vollzug des Königskultes bestimmten Abgaben scheinen nicht immer, und jedenfalls nicht ohne den Umweg über die Staatskasse, den ägyptischen Heiligtümern zugeflossen zu sein.

CHAPTER 21

VISITORS TO ELEPHANTINE: WHO WERE THEY?

HERWIG MAEHLER
University College, London

In Ptolemaic and Roman times, the temple of Khnûm on the island of Elephantine was a major religious center, though not nearly as prominent as, e.g., the temple of Ptaḥ at Memphis or the Isis Temple on Philae. What makes it such a fascinating site nonetheless is the fact that a large number of inscriptions and graffiti both in Greek and in Demotic have survived on blocks which have come to light over the past twenty years in the excavations conducted by the German and Swiss Institutes. These inscriptions and graffiti are valuable because they tell us something about the people who carved them, i.e. about the visitors to the temple of Khnûm (see Jaritz 1980).[1] Some of them are still unpublished, and several of these present problems of interpretation for which I cannot offer convincing solutions.

On Elephantine, Khnûm was worshipped together with Satet and Anuket, two Nubian goddesses with whom he formed a triad. To the Greeks, Satet was Hera, while Anuket was Hestia. Several Ptolemaic inscriptions on blocks of altars were found reused in a brick wall underneath the temple terrace, where they had been used as filling material when the terrace was built in the first century B.C. One inscription (see Maehler 1970, pp. 170f. and pl. 58b) reads:

Βασιλεῖ Πτολεμαίωι καὶ βασιλίσσηι Κλεοπάτραι
τῆι ἀδελφῆι καὶ βασιλίσσηι Κλεοπάτραι τῆι γυναικὶ
Θεοῖς Εὐεργέταις καὶ τοῖς τέκνοις καὶ Χνούβει
καὶ Ἥραι καὶ Ἀνούκει καὶ Ἴσει καὶ Διονύσωι καὶ τοῖς ἄλλοις
θεοῖς πᾶσι ὑπὲρ Πτολεμαίου τοῦ Πτολεμαίου
τοῦ Εὐμενοῦς τῶν πρώτων φίλων καὶ στρατηγοῦ
καὶ Πτολεμαίου καὶ Τιμάρχου καὶ Καλλικράτου τῶν ἰσοτίμων
τοῖς πρώτοις φίλοις τῶν υἱῶν αὐτοῦ Ἀσκληπιάδης
Ἀμμωνίου Μακεδὼν τῶ⟨ν⟩ διαδόχων καὶ φρούραρχος
Ἐλεφαντίνης

To King Ptolemy and Queen Cleopatra his sister and Queen Cleopatra his wife, the Benefactor Gods, and their children and Khnûbis and Hera and Anukis and Isis and Dionysos and all the other gods, in the name of Ptolemy, son of Ptolemy, grandson of Eumenes, *strategos* and of the "First Friends," and of Ptolemy, Timarchos, and Kallikrates, of those equal in rank to the "First Friends," his sons; Asklepiades, son of Ammonios, the Macedonian, of the "Deputies," garrison commander of Elephantine — *scil.* has set up the altar.

1. Reconstruction of the terrace and its balustrade is now well under way, see Jaritz 1990, pp. 248f. and pl. 53b.

The dedicant, Asklepiades son of Ammonios, has the lowest rank in the court hierarchy, that of *diadochos*, but as garrison commander, *phrourarchos*, of Elephantine he was a local dignitary of some prominence. The person on whose behalf he made the dedication is a *strategos*: is this Ptolemy, son of Ptolemy and grandson of Eumenes, a military *strategos* (J. D. Thomas 1975a, p. 38) or, as Mooren believes (1977, p. 116), a *strategos* of more than one nome? He might have been a son of Ptolemy son of Eumenes who lived at the royal court at Alexandria in the time of Epiphanes (Polybius XVIII 53.8, see F. Walbank *ad. loc.*). Chronologically, this would be possible, since the inscription, addressed to Ptolemy VIII and both his sister, Cleopatra II, and his niece, Cleopatra III, can be dated to c. 140 B.C., at any rate after his marriage to Cleopatra III in 143 or 142 B.C. The court title *isotimos tois prôtois philois* ("equal in rank to the First Friends") appears between c. 145 and 120 B.C. (Mooren 1977, pp. 22–23).

Even more interesting is another inscription, also on a Ptolemaic altar (Maehler 1970, pp. 169f. and pl. 58a):

> Βα]σιλεῖ Πτολεμαίωι καὶ βασιλίσσηι Κλεοπάτραι τῆι ἀδελφῆι Θεοῖς Φιλομήτορσ[ι
> καὶ τοῖς τούτων τέκνοις καὶ Χνούβιδι καὶ Ἥραι καὶ Ἀνούκει καὶ Διονύσωι
> ὑπερ Βοήθου τοῦ Νικοστράτου Χρυσαορέως τοῦ ἀρχισωματοφύλακος καὶ
> στρατηγοῦ τὸν βωμὸν Χαιρέας Μέλανος Βοιώτιος φρούραρχος
> Ἐλεφαντίνης

> To King Ptolemy and Queen Cleopatra his sister, the Mother-loving Gods, and their children and Khnûbis and Hera and Anukis and Dionysos, in the name of Boethos son of Nikostratos, of Chrysaoris, chief bodyguard and *strategos*; Chaireas son of Melas, the Boiotian, garrison commander of Elephantine, (has set up) the altar.

This dedication must be somewhat earlier, at any rate before 145 B.C. Here another garrison commander, Chaireas, set up an altar on behalf of Boethos, and this man is relatively well known from other inscriptions and from papyri (*Prosopographia Ptolemaica* I no. 188 = II 1869). It seems that he held the post of *strategos* for more than fifteen years, first under Philometor and Cleopatra II, then under Euergetes II, and eventually also as *epistrategos* or governor of all Upper Egypt. The same Boethos is also mentioned in an inscription of the gymnasium at Kôm Ombo, where he is called *strategos*, as here; it is a dedication to Ptolemy VIII, Cleopatra II, and Cleopatra III (Wilcken 1913, pp. 415f.). However, at some stage the names of Ptolemy VIII and Cleopatra III were erased, no doubt during the civil war of 131–127 B.C., and it seems possible that Boethos sided with Cleopatra II against her brother. He was a prominent official and a member of the Greek upper class which backed Cleopatra II, whereas her brother, Ptolemy VIII, relied more on the Egyptians. This may explain why Boethos' successor as *epistrategos* of the Thebaid was not a Greek or a Macedonian but an Egyptian, Paôs, in office by late 131 B.C. — the only Egyptian to become *epistrategos* under the Ptolemies (*Prosopographia Ptolemaica* I no. 197).

Apart from these complete blocks, fragments of at least three more Ptolemaic inscriptions have been found. One of them is a dedication, similar to the first one, to Ptolemy VIII and his two Cleopatras by a "First Friend" (*prôtos philos*), whose name is lost (Maehler 1970, p. 171).[2] Another very fragmentary inscription, which was found very recently and is still unpublished, was addressed to "Queen Cleopatra" (Βασ[ιλισ]σηι Κ[, i.e. Cleopatra III), or to Cleopatra III and her son, Ptolemy IX, who both visited Elephantine in 115 B.C., by the priests of Aswan (οἱ ἀπ[ὸ Σ]υή[νης). A large block with a bilingual inscription (Greek and Demotic), discovered in 1989 and also still unpublished, is dedicated by Pelaias son of Bienkhi, chief priest and πρῶτος στολιστής of the temples of Elephantine, Bigge, and Philae (τῶν ἐν Ἐλεφαντίνηι καὶ τῶι Ἀβάτωι καὶ Φίλαις

2. Another fragment of this inscription has since been found, see Junge 1987, p. 81 and pl. 49b.

ἱερῶν).[3] A fragmentary stele shows the king and queen (Ptolemy IX and Cleopatra III) worshipping Khnûm, who is accompanied on the left-hand side by Satet, on the right by Anuket. Unfortunately, the name of the dedicant is lost with the rest of the inscription (C. Müller 1975, pp. 82f. and pl. 28c).

Looking at these Ptolemaic inscriptions, together with those published earlier and collected in Dittenberger's *OGIS*, one gets the impression that in the second century B.C. Elephantine was visited by a number of fairly high ranking officials, as the sanctuary attracted dedications by the local garrison commanders or the chief priest, on behalf of στρατηγοί and ἐπιστρατηγοί, and in 115 it was visited by Queen Cleopatra III herself and her son and co-regent, Ptolemy IX Soter II. On the other hand, there is not a single visitor's graffito by an ordinary person. We shall meet some ordinary and humble people only when we turn to the graffiti on the temple terrace of the early Roman period: there we shall find a very different set of customers. But first let me say a brief word about the function of the terrace and the adjoining nilometer.

Khnûm was the Lord of the First Cataract, where the source of the Nile was supposed to be. The Egyptians believed that deep down in the river bed, at the foot of the Cataract, there was a hole which produced the extra water which made the Nile rise (see Herodotus II 28 and Lloyd's [1976] commentary; Kees 1980, pp. 408f.), and so the god of Elephantine was believed to be responsible for creating and controlling the Nile flood. It is therefore not surprising to find his temple connected to a nilometer. It is right next to the temple terrace, to the south of the temple. In fact, there are *two* nilometers on Elephantine: one on the east side, east of the temple of Satet, and this is the one which was rediscovered in 1870 and used in the later 19th century, up to the time when the old Aswan dam was built (i.e. 1912). It is not, however, the nilometer described by Strabo (XVII 817.48) who calls it a φρέαρ ("tank" or "well"). Strabo's description fits only the other nilometer, the one below the terrace of the temple of Khnûm which was discovered in the 1970s in the recent German and Swiss excavations (Jaritz 1982, pp. 324–28 and pl. 71a; Jaritz and Bietak 1977, pp. 47–62 and pls. 11–13). This one is indeed a "tank," or rectangular well, dug into the rock and lined with sandstone blocks; it measures 11.25 × 8 meters. It may have served as a "Holy Lake" of the temple. On its long northern and southern sides, narrow steps lead down to the bottom. Its lower part is contemporary with the Khnûm temple (Dynasty Thirty and Ptolemaic), while the later phase is contemporary with the temple terrace which seems to have been built under the last Ptolemies and was certainly completed by the fourteenth year of Augustus (see below). This nilometer had been filled with a large number of blocks from the balustrade of the temple terrace above, which had been destroyed (for the sake of the metal grips which linked the blocks) and thrown down into the well. Among them were several shrines or chapels (ναΐσκοι) and obelisks, as well as blocks with inscriptions and graffiti, both in Greek and in Demotic (Jaritz 1980, pp. 66ff. and pls. 33–36). From these blocks it has been possible to reconstruct the whole balustrade which surrounded the terrace on three sides.

Among the Greek and Demotic inscriptions and graffiti, there are two *topos*-inscriptions which marked the places of market stalls on the temple terrace. One is in Greek: Δημητρίου καὶ Ἑρμίου καὶ τῶν ἀδελφῶν ὁ τόπος αὐτῶν, "This is the place of Demetrios and Hermias and their brothers (Jaritz, Maehler, and Zauzich 1979, p. 138 [G24]); the other is in Demotic: *ʿṯḫ.w tws bꜣḥ Ḫnm pꜣ mꜣʿ tꜣ wm ʿṯḫ.w tws*, "The brewers, in front of Khnûm, at the place of the feast of Khnûm, the brewers" (Jaritz, Maehler, and Zauzich 1979, pp. 150f. [D2]). The Demotic inscription ends just one meter to the left of the Greek one. On this spot the brewers sold their beer to the visitors who came to the temple terrace, which they call "the place of the feast of Khnûm." This recalls a

3. It now almost completes the inscription, of which part of the Demotic text was already known from a fragment found in the courtyard of the local museum, see Junge 1987, pp. 79f. and pl. 51a.

graffito at Philae: "We spent eight days feasting on the *dromos* of Isis, on wine, beer, and meat, the people of the whole city making merry" (F. Ll. Griffith 1935, p. 116: Philae no. 416.13).

The top block of one of the shrines (C) on the balustrade was left unfinished; the central piece should have been carved to form the winged sun-disc; instead, a name, Περικλῆς, was scratched onto it. Was this a visitor, or the name of the sculptor who was supposed to have carved the sun-disc? (The name, Perikles, was not common in Egypt.) More important is another inscription, along the top edge of the same block (Jaritz, Maehler, and Zauzich 1979, p. 146 [G44] and pl. 21b):]μίων ἦλθε L ιδ¯ Καίσαρος Φαμενώθ [, "...mion came, year 14 of Caesar, Phamenoth x." This is clearly a visitor's inscription, and it provides a precious *terminus ante quem* — the only precise date so far —: by February/March of year 14 of Augustus (16 B.C.), the terrace and the shrines must have been completed.

Most of the other graffiti are *proskynemata*, recording the worshipper's name if he was literate, or the outline of one or both of his feet, to record the place where he stood while worshipping the god, and to remain in the god's presence.[4] One visitor has drawn the outline of his left hand with the Greek word λῃστοῦ inside it (i.e. "the robber's" hand), perhaps as a joke.[5] One of the Demotic *proskynema*-graffiti is also interesting (Jaritz, Maehler, and Zauzich 1979, p. 149 [D1] and pl. 21c): *p3 rn nfr n Pa-ẖnm s3 Stm-n=j-ẖnm*, "The beautiful name of Pakhnûm, son of Setemnaikhnûm," *scil.* remains here forever. The same two names occur, in reverse order (Setemnaikhnûm, son of Pakhnûm), in two Demotic graffiti at Philae dated A.D. 21 and 30 (Griffith 1937, pp. 53f.: Philae nos. 54.5–6 and 57.3–4, dated A.D. 30 and 21 respectively); there Setemnaikhnûm's title is "superintendent of the singers of Isis of the Abaton (= Bigge) and Philae." His father, possibly the visitor who carved the graffito at Elephantine, would have lived in the second half of the first century B.C., which would agree with the *terminus ante quem* of 16 B.C. for the completion of the terrace.

Among the unpublished graffiti on the floor of the temple courtyard there are several drawings of gazelles or antelopes (the animals sacred to Anuket and Satet), a *tabula ansata* with τοπω / απολι / βοιηϲ written into it,[6] a "monotheistic" message which reads εἷς θεός, "one god," a formula frequently found also on magical gems from Egypt, and a very fine drawing, covering several blocks, of a dancing man with receding, curly hair.

The graffiti in Greek outnumber those in Demotic about eleven to one (so far, over eighty Greek, seven or eight Demotic). A majority of the personal names are Greek, such as Apollonios son of Archias, and the Perikles already mentioned. Many names are common Egyptian names, like: Psansnôs, Psenpouêris, Pakhnûbis, Pekysis son of Peteêsis, or Horion. A fair proportion, however (and this has been a surprise), appear to be Roman: Aelius, Ursus, Valerius, Quadratus, Nemesianus, Iulius and Iulia, Serenus, Antonius, and one *ALEAS*, even appears in Latin script. They are puzzling: Did Roman names become fashionable in Upper Egypt? There is not a single instance of the normal Roman *tria nomina*: were they really Romans? Were they soldiers? What are we to make of Psais son of Ursos? I do not know the answers, but I did note that among the inscriptions in the quarry of the Gebel Tingar, some 35 km north of Aswan, very similar

4. The Greek and Demotic graffiti from the temple terrace were first published by Jaritz, Maehler, and Zauzich (1979, pp. 125–54 and pls. 20–30), where a reconstruction of the balustrade may be found on p. 126; the graffiti on the floor of the forecourt will be published soon. On the meaning and the various types of *proskynemata*, see Geraci 1971, pp. 1–211.

5. Hands are very rare, but there is another example on a block from the entrance gate to a sanctuary of Mandulis in Ayuala (Lower Nubia) now being reconstructed on Elephantine; see Jaritz and Laskoeska-Kusztal 1990, p. 179, fig. 8 (G11), and p. 182.

6. Is Τοπω a proper name, "Topô from Libya" (Λιβοίης = Λιβύης)? Or should one assume two spelling mistakes and read τόπον ἀπολαβοίης, "may you receive a (burial-)place?"

combinations of names occur (Sayce 1891, pp. 48f.):[7] there is a Iulios, a Marios son of Psenkhnomis, a Klôdios son of Ammonios, a Kalasiris son of Tyrannos, and a Triadelphos son of Horos. And since Roman soldiers worked in the quarries of Mons Porphyrites and Mons Claudianus, they may also have worked in the quarry of Gebel Tingar, and left their names there. That might suggest that the Roman names among the graffiti at Elephantine also refer to soldiers.

Some of the late graffiti on the terrace floor produce common Coptic names, like Abraham, Iakôb, Andreas, and possibly Makarios. Many other graffiti makers seem to have been illiterate, since they simply scratched the outlines of their feet, or of one foot, into the pavement, to show posterity where they had been standing while praying to Khnûm. On the whole, they seem to have been very ordinary and humble people, much more modest than the garrison commanders or chief priests who dedicated the Ptolemaic inscriptions. The reason for this very obvious difference in the social class of the temple's customers is not clear, but — if I may end this paper on a speculative note — I shall offer two hypothetical suggestions.

First, I suspect that the temple of Elephantine lost some of its importance in the transition from the Ptolemaic to the Roman period, when high-ranking visitors continued to visit neighboring Philae but apparently not Elephantine. The temple which Augustus had built on Philae, and the "Kiosk" which Trajan added later, might suggest that under the Roman administration Philae was upgraded at the expense of Elephantine.

On the other hand, there might be a more technical reason for the absence of the common visitors' graffiti from the Ptolemaic evidence: before the terrace was completed in the early years of Roman rule, there may not have been a paved *dromos* of stone blocks, let alone a terrace floor and balustrade, into which visitors could have scratched their names, or the outline of their feet: there may have been just a mud path.

7. Sayce mistook the quarry for a necropolis and interpreted the rock inscriptions as tomb inscriptions; it seems much more likely that they record the names of quarry workers. See Jaritz 1981, pp. 241–46 and pls. 39–42.

PLATE 21.1

a

b

Graffiti on the Floor of the Temple Terrace of Khnûm at Elephantine: (*a*) εἶς θεός, (One God); (*b*) τοπω / απολι / βοιηϲ Written into a *Tabula Ansata*.

a

b

Graffito on the Floor of the Temple Terrace of Khnûm at Elephantine Depicting a Dancing Man: (*a*) Full View, (*b*) Close Up of Man's Head and Torso.

CHAPTER 22

DEMOTIC CONTRACTS AS EVIDENCE IN A COURT CASE?

CARY J. MARTIN
University College, London

The Demotic papyri from Saqqara, found during the Egypt Exploration Society's excavations between 1964 and 1976 in the Sacred Animal Necropolis, represent one of the richest and most varied finds this century. Their discovery in rubbish dumps by the entrance to the catacombs of the Mothers of the Apis and near the main temple area has been documented in the pages of the *Journal of Egyptian Archaeology*[1] and does not need elaboration here. It is, however, worth recalling the diversity of their subject matter, which has contributed to the great interest which has been shown in the papyri.

The literary texts are now perhaps the best known, thanks to their masterly publication by Professor Harry Smith and Dr. John Tait in the first volume of *Saqqara Demotic Papyri* (1983). Letters and pleas to deities are well advanced in their preparation, thanks to the same two editors, while dream-texts and papyri of a magical or mystical nature are progressing under the penetrative eye of John Ray, who has also given us the fascinating *Archive of Ḥor* (1976).

Temple day-books, itemizing income and expenditure, accounts and lists, not surprisingly have been paid little attention to date, but the legal and administrative texts have been worked at more attentively, although very little has been said about them in print up until now. Originally they were to have been published by George Biggs, a student of Professor Smith, and by Professor Pierce. The latter, in fact, had worked through all of these texts and his preliminary transliterations are the starting point for anyone studying the papyri today. Professor Pierce, however, became preoccupied with other matters and brought his work on them to an end. To facilitate their preparation, the texts were then divided into two categories. The first comprised the legal protocols and related material, which were studied by my wife, Ruth Martin, under the guidance of Professor Smith, before they were passed over to the present writer. The second category is made up primarily of the contracts, which have subsequently been worked on by Dr. Sven Vleeming.[2]

Undoubtedly, one of the principal reasons why these papyri have passed through so many scholars' hands is their lamentable state of preservation. It is often difficult to decipher with any confidence more than a few lines and frequently it seems impossible to state with certainty the precise nature of a particular text. This latter point also applies to the papyrus which is the subject of

1. See in particular Emery 1965, pp. 3–8; 1966, pp. 3–8; 1967, pp. 141–45; 1969, pp. 31–35; 1970, pp. 5–11; and 1971, pp. 3–13; and Martin 1973, pp. 5–15; and 1974, pp. 15–29; see also H. S. Smith 1974a, pp. 21–63 and Martin 1981.

2. Vleeming, however, does not intend to publish the papyri (personal communication, 14 November 1990).

this paper, Saqqara 71/72-DP 132. With this text, however, the task is not one of trying to make sense of a few partially preserved lines. Rather, it is quite the reverse. The text, while far from complete, is well preserved. What it contains, however, is open to interpretation.

Saqqara 71/72-DP 132 measures 20.1 cm wide by 26.2 cm high and is light brown in color. There are two joins on the sheet; the first is at the right-hand edge and the second approximately 6 cm in from the left-hand side. The text on the front is written parallel to the fibers and consists of two columns. Of the first column, only the last 3 cm or so of the ends of twenty-four lines are preserved. The second column is missing the ends of the lines and it is difficult to assess exactly how much is lost, although it would not appear to be more than a few centimeters. The first column is not the beginning of the text and an unquantifiable number of columns is missing. The same is true of the end of the papyrus, where the text at the bottom of the second column will have continued at the top of the following column.

The two columns of text on the front are divided into five sections. Column 1 contains the end of a section, followed by a second, quite small, section and then section 3 which continues at the top of column 2. Section 4 consists of nineteen lines, while of section 5 we have the first three lines, which would have continued at the top of the next, missing, column. Between each section there is a gap of 2 cm.

A full translation of the papyrus is not yet ready. Work is far from complete and there are many still unresolved readings. What first attracts one to the papyrus, however, is the manner in which the sections begin, or, to be precise, the manner in which the two sections to which the opening words are extant begin. Section 4 commences as follows:

> Another (writing) from the hand of [that is Demotic *ky n-dr.t*][3] Ankhḥep son of Ḥor, the prophet of Arsaphes, (and of) Tjaienimou son of X [the father's name is unclear], makes 2 people. Its copy.

The following line continues:

> Ankhḥep son of Ḥor, the prophet of Arsaphes, (and) Tjaienimou son of X, makes two people, are they who say to ... [The end of the line is missing].

Section 5 has an identical format. It begins as follows:

> Another (writing) from the hand of Imḥotep son of Ḥorkhonsu. Its copy. Imḥotep son of Ḥorkhonsu [The rest of the line is lost, but doubtless continued "is he who said to ..."].

The detail of section 4 is concerned with the delivery of some money, emmer, and other products to the ships of a certain Paptaḥ, which are moored by the quay in the district of Herakleopolis. The language of the text is full of clauses which are familiar to us from countless legal texts, for example:

> The money, the emmer [...] which we will not give to the representatives of Paptaḥ in the time aforementioned in accordance with everything aforementioned, [we will give it in the month] which is after the month in question, compulsorily without delay.

And further on:

> The representative of Paptaḥ is the one who is to be believed concerning everything which he will say with us in the name of [everything aforementioned].

Of particular interest is line 22 of the column, where the two individuals state that they "are far from the temple-domain of Imḥotep son of Ptaḥ together with the [temple-domain of Osorapis]." The last deity is restored on the basis of an earlier section. In other words, Ankhḥep and

3. The reading *n-dr.t* is a suggestion of Zauzich and Vleeming, for a sign which I was inclined to see as *sẖ*; cf. de Cenival 1984, p. 23, note 4,2.

Tjaienimou are saying that by delivering the money and the foodstuffs to Paptaḥ, they are fulfilling an obligation to the two temple-domains.

Section 4 is the best preserved of the five sections, but what can be gleaned from the others? Section 5 is concerned with some land or produce belonging to the "House of Bastet, mistress of Ankhtaoui" and to some fruit-gardens "in the temple-domain of Sothis ... in the house of Sothis." Section 3, which continues from column 1 into column 2, seems to deal with the leasing of some land from a year 16 to a year 17, the rent for which is to be paid to the "temple-domain of Imḥotep son of Ptaḥ (and) the temple-domain of Osorapis." That this section is related to the following section 4 is confirmed by the fact that it is the representative of Paptaḥ "who is to be believed [concerning everything] which he will say with us in the name of everything aforementioned." Few traces remain of sections 1 and 2, but the name Paptaḥ does occur twice more.

The back of the papyrus contains only one column, divided into two sections. The first section will have begun on the preceding column so its opening words can only be surmised. The beginning of the first line of section 2 is missing, but the name of the father of an individual can be made out, followed by what looks to be, "they said, may they write to me," and then something which is unclear.

The first section of the back deals with the delivery of some foodstuffs, including emmer, fowl, and wine, to the ships of Paptaḥ. Penalties are specified for late delivery and "the representative of Paptaḥ is the one who is to be believed [concerning everything which] he will say with us in the name of everything aforementioned." The contracting parties, whose names are lost, state that they are far ... from the temple-domain of Imḥotep son of Ptaḥ and from the temple-domain of Osiris, lord of Rosetau.

The second section appears to deal with the leasing of land. The phrase, well known from instruments to describe the length of a lease of land, that is "from the water of year 16 to that of year 17," occurs, followed by a statement on payment to the house of Paptaḥ. What the rental might relate to, however, is unclear. It is certainly more than an average parcel of land, as the quantities are huge—over 6000 artabae of emmer.

All seven sections of this papyrus, therefore, concern the same individual, a certain Paptaḥ whose father's name may be Ankhrenef. Because other columns of text existed on either side of the sheet, it seems more than likely that this is only a small part of a document which detailed a large number of transactions relating to Paptaḥ; the presence of Paptaḥ's name, in similar circumstances, on both the front and the back makes this assumption probable. The detail of the sections is concerned principally with the delivery of foodstuffs and in contexts which are strongly reminiscent, at least in some cases, of instruments of lease. Delivery is often to the ships of Paptaḥ, moored by the quay at Herakleopolis, and is to be effected by his agents. By ensuring delivery the contractors appear to be fulfilling their obligations towards certain temples in the necropolis area.

So what should one make of this text? The title to this paper makes reference to one possibility, that is that the text is a register of Demotic contracts brought forward in a court case. The reason for this supposition is the manner in which sections 4 and 5 on the recto begin, that is with the words, "another (writing) from the hand of X son of X," followed by the words "its copy." This is reminiscent of the famous Siut law suit, where, when documents were brought as evidence to court, the text read: "he produced a document of X before us. Its copy." There then followed the detail of the instrument (H. Thompson 1934, p. 25, P. BM 10591, B [= recto], col. vi, line 21).

Now, the wording within the sections of the Saqqara papyrus do bear all the markings of legal contracts. Familiar phrases abound, but it would not be true to say that they are contracts verbatim. They could be synopses, but they are not literal contracts. In the Siut archive, on the other hand, the documents produced as evidence are as good as verbatim, only the protocols effectively being omitted.

An alternative interpretation would be to see the text as an official register of documents relating to transactions involving Paptaḥ. In this case it would have been Paptaḥ who would have given to the authorities the documents, presumably as a way of registering his transactions. Wilcken has surmised that there were two documents involved in a deposition, one to be kept in the office of registration and one to have been retained by the contracting parties (1927, p. 606). Pierce, on the other hand, has suggested (1972, p. 182) that there may have been only one document, which was either kept in the registration office for safekeeping or simply retained long enough for the desired data to have been noted. If the latter were the case, could the Saqqara papyrus be a part of such a register?

There are two texts, one Greek, one Demotic, which are worth making reference to at this point. P. Paris 65 contains information on how Demotic contracts were to be entered in the records of the Greek administration in 145 B.C. (reedited by Pestman 1985, pp. 17–25). It shows that the Demotic contract was brought to the registration office where a Demotic abstract was made, to which the names of the contracting parties and a description of the agreement were added in Greek. These data (i.e. the Greek) were also entered in the public register. Under the Demotic contract itself, a Greek subscription was made to record that the agreement had been registered and a Greek subscription was also entered under the Demotic abstract, mentioning the date of the contract and its Greek subscription.

The second text is a recently published Demotic register, P. dem. Lille 120 (de Cenival 1987, pp. 1–9),[4] which probably belongs to the first part of the Ptolemaic period. This text bears the date of registration, the specification of the type of contract, sometimes what it was concerned with, and the name of one of the contracting parties. In other words, it carries exactly the same information in Demotic as P. Paris 65 tells us the public register in 145 B.C. should contain in Greek. Changes took place in the registration requirements at the end of 146 B.C., so the use of Greek in one register and Demotic in another should cause no surprise. We should also note the differences in time and place. Neither text, however, describes a public register, whether in Greek or in Demotic, which bears much resemblance to the format of our Saqqara papyrus. The various sections of the Saqqara text, on the other hand, are not dissimilar, bar the absence of the Greek data, to the descriptions of the Demotic abstracts of each contract to which P. Paris 65 refers. Given that we are looking at texts which relate to procedures at different times and in different places throughout Egypt, it is worth considering whether the Saqqara papyrus contains a list of such abstracts.

A third possibility is to see the papyrus as an administrative text, drawn up by temple officials to document the activities to be carried out on the temple estate over the year. In this case Paptaḥ would have been the temple official delegated to attend to the matters in question and the text would have been a record of the tasks to be performed and the names of those responsible to him for their fulfillment.

Saqqara 71/72-DP 132 is without doubt an intriguing text. Further study into it and the other papyri will be needed before it can be properly understood, but it aptly illustrates some of the riches to be found in the hundreds of fragments of legal and administrative texts from the Sacred Animal Necropolis at North Saqqara.

4. I would like to thank Joe Manning for bringing this text to my attention.

CHAPTER 23

ANCESTOR CULTS AT TERENOUTHIS IN LOWER EGYPT: A CASE FOR GRECO-EGYPTIAN OECUMENISM

ROGER V. MCCLEARY
The Kelsey Museum of Archaeology, The University of Michigan

BACKGROUND

With the generous support of the J. Paul Getty Trust (Los Angeles), the Kelsey Museum of Archaeology at the University of Michigan (Ann Arbor) is bringing to completion a major research project on the archaeological finds from a "reconnaissance" of the necropolis of ancient Terenouthis at Kom Abou Billou, in Lower Egypt (see figs. 23.1–2).

Some 2000 artifacts were recovered there by Dr. Enoch E. Peterson in the spring of 1935. At that time the University of Michigan's extensive excavations at Karanis and Dimay in the northern Faiyum were coming to a close and Terenouthis was reconnoitered as a potential successor.

In a period of about thirty-five days Peterson uncovered four major sections on the western periphery of this extensive *kôm* and it is this varied funerary material of several periods that is to be published under the auspices of the Getty Trust.

THE SITE

Kom Abou Billou is located on the fringes of the Libyan Desert about 2 km west of the Rosetta branch of the Nile. This necropolis dates as early as the late Old Kingdom, ca. 2300 B.C. (Farid 1973, pp. 21–22). Indeed, Kom Abou Billou and its nearby riverine metropolis (see fig. 23.2) are among the oldest occupied sites in Lower Egypt; and the present-day name of the riverside urban area, El-Tarrana (under which ancient Terenouthis today lies) contains the consonantal skeleton of its pharaonic period predecessor: **Ta-Renenût*, "the domain of Renenut" (Hermann 1963, p. 171).

The necropolis eventually covered an area of several hectares and is today bisected by a 40-meter-wide irrigation canal (Hawwass 1979, pp. 75–76). A succession of surface investigations and excavations has visited the site from 1887 (F. Ll. Griffith 1890, pp. 60–65) to the present (cf. *Orientalia* vols. 40–48, "Fouilles et travaux ...," *s.v.* Kom Abou Billou).

Dr. Peterson discovered hundreds of tombs and excavated a series of forty barrel- and pyramid-roofed mudbrick tomb structures in the course of his trenching operations, along with some 180 intact inhumations, often intrusively interred in later times when the tomb field was covered by the wind-blown sand of the Libyan Desert. These adventitious burials, as well as those made at the time of the tombs' building, were scattered in random patterns below, beside and above these tomb-chapels in the desert fill. No burial, contemporary or subsequent, was made within the actual mudbrick superstructures of these podium-tombs. A reconstruction of the *incunabula* of Peterson's unwritten site report in the Archive of the Kelsey Museum will be included in the first volume of the Terenouthis site report.[1]

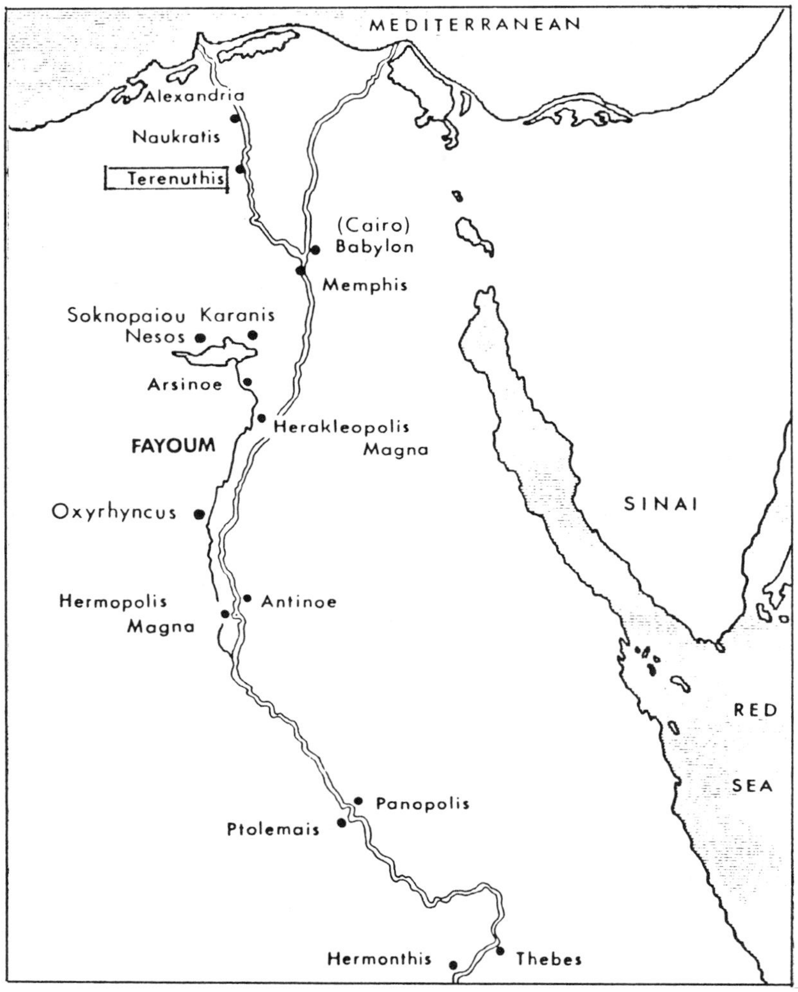

Figure 23.1. The Nile Valley South to the Thebaid.

Among Peterson's site data are many photographs taken by him of the tombs and especially their frescoed facades. This documentation is crucial, for within hours of the uncovering of the soil-moistened plaster and mudbrick structures they dried out to the point of disintegrating; only the photographs and some fragments of the plaster facades of several tombs remain. For the purposes of illustrating this presentation only two of the decorated facades are considered (see pls. 23.1–2).[2]

1. To be published in 1992, along with studies on all categories of burial-associated objects and miscellaneous surface- and in-fill finds, including: some 200 funerary stelae; 480 mostly legible coins and in many cases in the hand of the deceased; many pottery pieces, including two with pigment residue left by tomb-decorators; amulets in various media; several ostraca, one with hieroglyphs and one in Greek; a few glass *balsamaria*; several terracotta figurines; over 200 faience *ushabti* figurines and other miscellaneous faience pieces; fifty moulded clay lamps and some with figured *discoi*, and miscellanies of metal objects: magical orifice coverings, jewelry, and utility pieces. Most of this trove of grave goods is associated with discrete burials and all data related to these finds are to be presented according to database assorting and concording.
2. Full art-historical and technical analyses of all extant fragments of painted plaster from the tombs will be presented in Volume I of the Terenouthis Reports by Dr. Thelma K. Thomas, Curator at the Kelsey Museum of Archaeology, in the aforementioned forthcoming report.

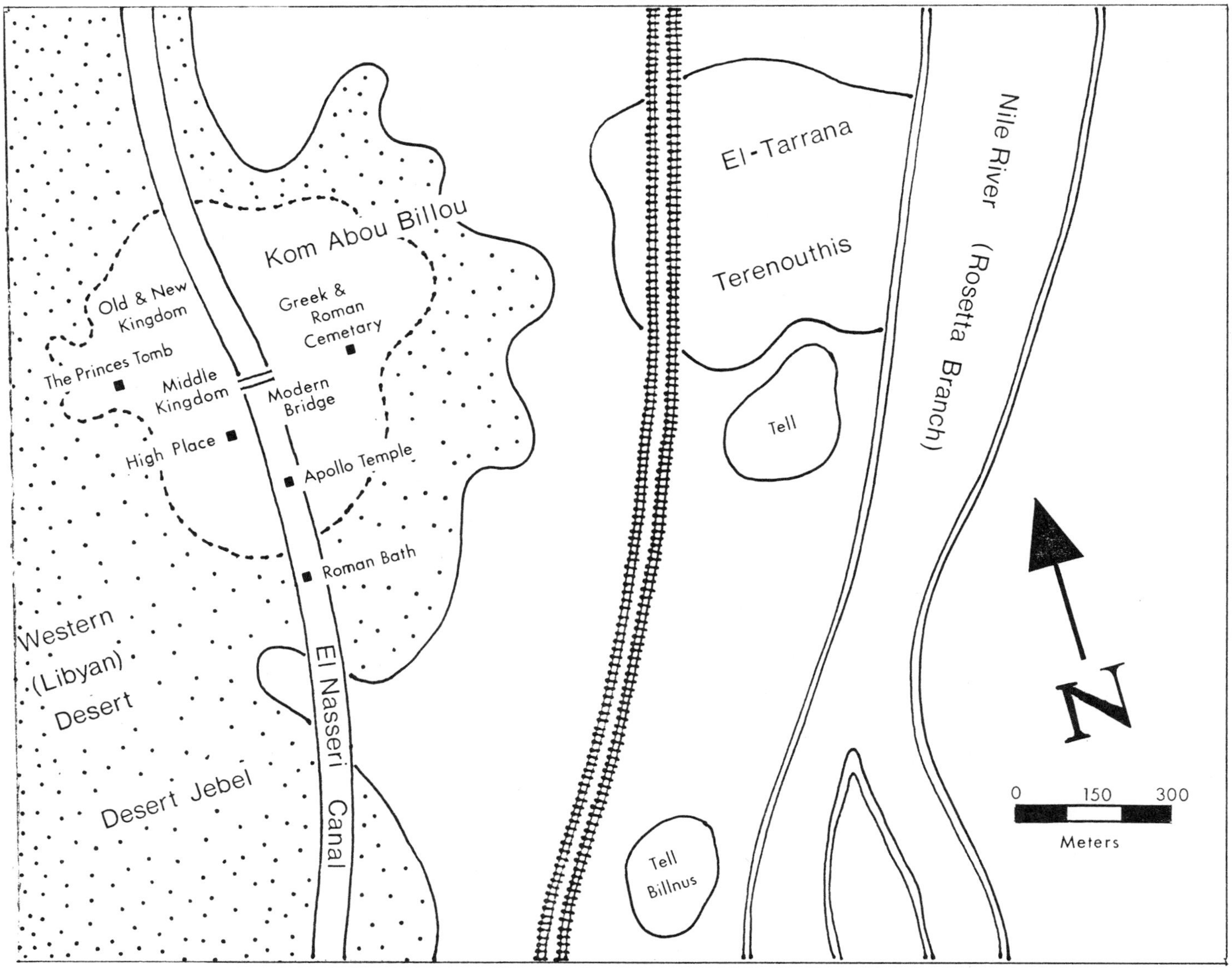

Figure 23.2. Ancient Terenouthis, Kom Abou Billou, and Vicinity.

GRECO-EGYPTIAN FUNERARY BELIEFS

That fundamental changes in the realm of funerary beliefs were afoot in Ptolemaic period Egypt is clear. At Kom Abou Billou (the best preserved necropolis of Lower Egypt), for instance, the appearance of "Charon's obols" in the hands of the dead demonstrates the sudden (mass?) adoption of a "foreign" custom, by at least the early decades of the first century A.D.[3]

But some aspects of the native Egyptian funerary religion were retained as fundamental. Most notable is the importance of the god Anubis. His images dominate not only the hundreds of Terenouthis funerary stelae but as well the decorative ensembles represented on the frescoed tomb-facades. This is a good indication that this necropolis was long controlled by the priests and

3. The presence of "Charon's silver" on most of the interments at this necropolis is not otherwise documented in the few Ptolemaic period cemeteries that are known; e.g., cf. Grenfell, Hunt, and Hogarth 1900, with surveys of several cemeteries adjoining Faiyum towns, such as Kasr el-Banât (Euhemeria) and Harît (Theadelphia); Petrie 1889, including a survey of Hawara, the necropolis of Ptolemaic and Greco-Roman period Arsinoe-Crocodilopolis, the administrative capital of the Faiyum.

leading families of Greco-Egyptian origin.[4] Additionally, the ancient Egyptian cult of mummification was practiced at this site; and thus Anubis' priestly corporation and its *taricheutai* (literally "fish-dryers"), who prepared the dead, were likely at the center of the collective religious authority during the early imperial period.

It should be mentioned that from the early Ptolemaic period there were intimate cross-identifications among Anubis, Thoth (Djehuty), and Hermes, the psychopompos of the Greeks. Eventually, through the processes of syncretism, Anubis and Hermes were identified as essentially one: Hermanubis (Grenier 1977, pp. 9ff., and especially pp. 23 and 27).

The dominance of Anubis at this Greco-Egyptian site is found in the ubiquity of two basic manifestations: as a smallish, domestic canine sitting or recumbent in close proximity to his charges or as the anthropomorphic Hermes of the Greeks. In the former manifestation Anubis' animal presides over the scenes of banqueting, incense offering etc., fictively taking place both "within" the scene and in actuality being performed "before" the tomb structure, where the rites of the cult of the immortal ancestor were celebrated.

This canine guardian is none other than Anubis, "the Opener of the Ways" (= the literally named Wepwawet of pharaonic period belief), who accompanies and guides the deceased on the danger-fraught journey into the underworld and eventually into the presence of Osiris. Before Osiris, the dead were judged and, even at this critical juncture in the process of becoming an immortal, Anubis stayed by the side of his initiate (see fig. 23.3; Grenier 1977, p. 186).

On plate 23.1 this traditional image of Anubis is seen both on the stele (in situ) and painted on the left edge of the barrel-roof's half-tympanum. In the latter scene, this once feared "Lord of necropolis" follows the image of the deceased, who holds the Anubis creature by a tether. This apparent trivialization of Anubis is found in all popular funerary arts of the early imperial period; e.g., on painted mummy shrouds, coffins, cartonnage masks, et cetera. This does not necessarily indicate that Anubis' role was diminished; rather it is an indication that Anubis was made accessible to his adherents in what appears to have been a popular revival of the pharaonic period funerary beliefs, that coincided with the remarkable growth of this necropolis in the first three centuries A.D.

Keeping in mind the pre-eminence accorded Anubis, albeit in his pseudo-pharaonic, theriomorphic guise at this necropolis, the presence of a Hellenistic visualization of Hermes (on pl. 23.2, left side) is remarkable. Depicted in the Helleno-Roman style of the mid-second century, a nimbed Hermes stands in an exaggeratedly relaxed *contrapposto* stance facing the viewer in a foreshortened presentation.

He holds forth (towards the niche = portal of the tomb) his *cadeucas*, conducting the himation-clad deceased (to the far left with the head missing). The latter — presumably Isidora — walks in step behind Hermes and moves with him "towards" her anticipated bliss, represented by the prospectively portrayed image of a banqueting Isidora at the rear of the niche. This simultaneous portrayal of the dead at various stages of their afterlife experience is commonplace in pharaonic period funerary art, e.g., in illustrated "Books of the Dead" and on tomb reliefs, et cetera.

The tomb owner's biographical data are recorded in a painted inscription on the rear wall of the niche: a 32-year-old woman called Isidora (derived from Demotic **T3-3st* and translated into a Greek compound-name, literally "the gift of Isis," cf. Vergote 1954, p. 4). She is depicted as a well-to-do (and somewhat corpulent) banqueter, who libates with a *kantharos* in her right hand (*pars familiaris*) in the direction of Hermes Psychopompos.

4. For the Ptolemaic period, compare J. H. Johnson (1986, pp. 79–82), who presents an analysis of the surviving marriage and land conveying contracts, including inventories of revenue-generating priestly holdings of tombs, their chapels, and even towns containing necropolis workshops, primarily at Memphis/Saqqara (pp. 80–81). It is very likely that a seigneurial upper middle class survived the socio-economic ruins of Egypt after the fall of the Ptolemies to become the Greco-Egyptian middle and upper classes of the Roman period.

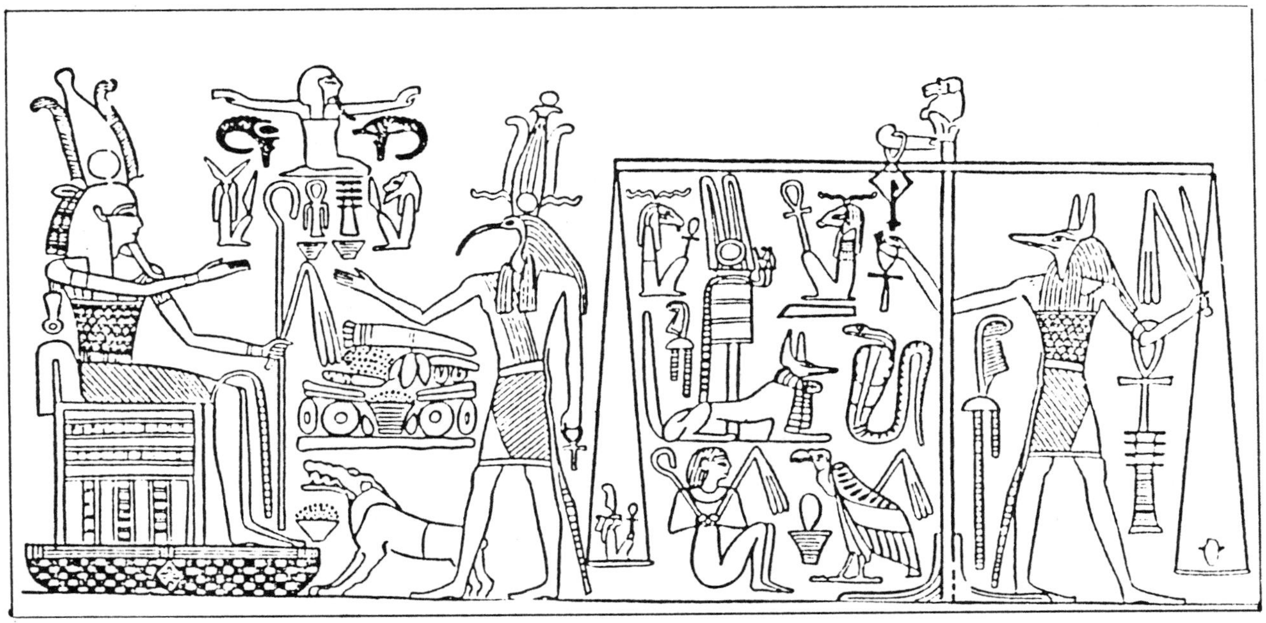

Figure 23.3. Line Drawing of an Illustrated Vignette of Chapter 125 of the *Book of the Dead* Showing the Climax of the "Weighing of the Soul" (Psychostasis) Before the Osirian Tribunal.[5]

At the same time, her invocation is more immediately directed towards the depictions of two Anubis canines that sit alertly atop kiosk shrines, painted on the plastered inner jambs of this deeply recessed niche (not visible in the photograph). Anubis is shown here in his role as protector of the necropolis ("*Inpu tpy ḏw.f* = Anubis, who is upon his mountain"; Grenier 1977, pp. 4, 5–7 and plates).

The mid-second-century date of the tomb (based on stylistic and palaeographic considerations) is significant, for it was at this time that the prosperity of Egypt under the "good emperors" crested (Préaux 1956, pp. 311ff.). The vital Greco-Egyptian town culture, that is reflected in the elaborate tomb monuments of this site and in the contemporary papyrological sources, was well adjusted to the Roman provincial system, and the upper strata of Greco-Egyptians increasingly emulated the dominant eastern, Helleno-Roman provincial culture. It is this period of relative affluence and class confidence in which a non-Egyptian image of Hermes could be juxtaposed with that of Anubis on a tomb (MacMullen 1964, pp. 187–89).

Conclusions drawn from the available site data indicate that this type of classical Hermes figure (or that of any Greek god or goddess) is absent from earlier (i.e first century) burial contexts at this necropolis. The presence of a sophisticated painting style, as well as its "foreign" iconography on

5. The heart of the deceased, Nitsi-ta-nebti-taui, is shown (balance's right pan) in exact equilibrium with a counterweight figure in the form of Maat, the goddess of Truth (left pan). Djehuty (Thoth), the ibis-headed god of learning and reckoning faces the enthroned figure of Osiris and delivers the verdict of the scales. It is to be noted that even at this critical point, when the verdict of the deceased's ordeal is being registered with the judge of the dead, Anubis simultaneously remains at his post steadying the *gnomon* of the scale (suspended from a horizontal "feather of Truth," upon the end of which Thoth's cynocephalos ape familiar crouches) so that the true reading is verified, should the balance's beam waver from its "true" alignment. Anubis thus stays with his initiates from the time he magically embalms them, while conducting them into the underworld and to Osiris' judgement seat, and then, in the final critical moments of the taking and delivering of the deceased's "justification" by ordeal. The ubiquity of Anubis in his popular guise as a domestic canine (derived from the animal oracle cults?) on the stelae and tombs of Terenouthis (as on all manner of popular funerary paraphernalia in this period) is thus in proportion to his critical roles at each stage in the process of becoming an immortal. Papyrus of Nitsi-ta-nebti-taui, dated to the late Nineteenth Dynasty, from Thebes (Piankoff and Rambova 1957, p. 15, fig. 35).

this tomb facade, belonging to a member of the prosperous Greco-Egyptian society of Terenouthis, suggests either a tolerance on the part of the authorities or a diminution (or end?) of their control over the builders and decorators of the tombs at this necropolis. It can also be postulated that either Isidora or her family was content to pay a superior artist to decorate a tomb with non-Egyptian scenes of the conducting of the deceased into and through the underworld — a crucial transition.

At the same time, however, a local artist was employed to embellish the tomb with traditional images showing the familiar Anubis canines guarding Isidora's blissful banqueting (on the inner jambs of the tomb's niche and not visible on pl. 23.2). This coincidence of purely classical- and pseudo-canonic (Egyptianizing) elements on tomb monuments of the mid-second century A.D. can be linked to the "stylistic dualism" that has been detected in Egypt's provincial arts, at this time.[6]

By contrast, in the previous century, overtly classicizing art was absent from the artistic repertoire of styles found on the stelae and tombs. This is not to say that classically derived elements and motifs were not present in the religious scenes; e.g., Greek dress, banqueting accoutrements, and furniture, incense-offering paraphernalia etc. "Foreign" elements, however, were fully integrated into the tomb's symbolic and structural contexts, that derived from a conscious revival of pharaonic period ideology and ritual usages. For example, the stelae were set into the upper-zone niches of the tombs with barrel and pyramid roofs and were intended to function magically as the "false door" emplacements of the Old Kingdom's mastaba tombs, that is, as portals to and from the Underworld.

This subordination of "foreign" elements of composition is further demonstrated by the artisans' and builders' application of a local version of the ancient Egyptian technical aesthetic of proportional modular gridding to both the stelae and the tomb facades.[7] The "foreign" motifs were thus embedded in a matrix of very ancient Egyptian artistic, religious and functional intentions.

Another instance of this Egyptianizing at Kom Abou Billou would be the presence of the tables of offering at the eastern ends of the tombs (often with central troughs), which are analogues to the stone offering tray (ancient Egyptian *ḥtp* {𓊵} and cf. the extended meaning of this commonly encountered hieroglyphic term: *ḥtp* {𓊵𓏌𓏌} i.e. "offerings" presented to the dead), placed before the "false door" and its statuary or relief images of the deceased in the cult chapels of mastaba tombs. At Kom Abou Billou, Dr. Peterson and later excavators have found numerous domestic pottery vessels. Many of the 200 pieces recovered by Peterson, especially the closed forms such as *choes*, were purposefully pierced at the base, apparently for direct-to-earth libations. That an elaborate cult of the ancestors, involving food offerings to the dead and communal cult meals for the living, operated at this necropolis in the Greco-Roman period is proven from this and many other strands of circumstantial evidence, that will be adduced in the forthcoming Terenouthis site reports.

RELIGIOUS TOLERANCE IN PROVINCIAL EGYPT

With the coming of Rome and its cosmopolitan empire, Egyptians of all races and cultures must needs have begun adjusting to the new order. As elsewhere in the empire this accommodation was accompanied by a revival of local religious fervor. This has suggested that in response to the challenges posed by Hellenism, and in turn the influences of Rome's provincial system, the people of these eastern cultures apparently retrenched themselves (reaction formation?) within their ancestral religions (Avi-Yonah 1961, pp. 79ff.).

6. Griffiths 1982, p. 249 *et passim*, a discussion of the stylistic dualism issue.

7. My research of the 200 funerary stelae in the Kelsey Museum's collections has revealed the presence of a modular grid used by the artisans of the lapidary workshops operating in Terenouthis' vicinity. By this archaizing means they sought to recreate the technical aesthetic of Egypt's most ancient "sacred engravings." Full explication of the "Terenouthis Canon" will appear in the first of the Terenouthis reports.

At this Lower Egyptian site, apparently, this manifests as a resuscitation of the ancient Egyptian cult of the immortal ancestor. Though the Egyptians (Greco-Egyptians) adopted Greek dress (men and women), hairstyles (women's "melon-coiffure") as well as Roman hair fashion (e.g. males' short-cropped military cut), these aspects of personal appearance in everyday life were but minor adjustments to the overall pharaonic-derived symbolic matrix of the tomb structures, with their Egyptianizing iconography and archaizing, canonic, technical aesthetic (modular gridding).

The admission of non-Egyptian elements of decor, beginning about the first quarter of the first century and manifesting in the hybrid Osirian religious observance by the mid-second century A.D., was limited to the aforementioned minor outward aspects of contemporary provincial life. It was the revived ancient Egyptian religious culture that induced the sudden expansion and popularity of the local necropolis of Terenouthis and allowed, as discussed above, non-Egyptian aspects of everyday life to enter surreptitiously (and in terms of the pseudo-canonic artistic revival, anachronistically) into the popular arts (Alexandrian-influenced) incorporated into the tombs.

Undoubtedly this pharaonic-derived funerary religion of the clerics aided the emergent Greco-Egyptian stratum of provincial Egyptian towns, like Terenouthis, to define their place in the rigid social hierarchy of provincial Romano-Greek society. And given the reverence and indeed awe in which Greeks and Romans in their turn held Egypt's solar funerary mysteries, the rather sudden revival of a pseudo-pharaonic cult of the ancestor at this necropolis would, at the very least, have gained the grudging respect of their overseers.[8] Respect of whatever degree would also have validated the communal/class struggle for recognition of the Greco-Egyptian middle and upper classes, emerging during the early centuries of *Pax Romana.*

One might also mention here the near total substitution of Greek inscriptions in the Attic epitaphic style (= an eastern provincial phenomenon) for the Demotic vernacular, by the first century A.D. This adoption of Greek by most of the prospering townsfolk of Terenouthis is a telling index of a collective will to adjust and to survive — if not to achieve a parity — among the exclusivistic official classes, the outward elegance of whose Hellenistic period luxury clothing, household furnishings, and accoutrements (items of class status) they adopted.

There are subtle indications that as the mid-second century arrived the collective confidence of the Greco-Egyptians developed to the point of opening their necropolis to foreigners. This is instanced in two isolated cases, the first, a North Syrian funerary stele with the "mains supines" motif.[9] The second is another very late second-century gravestone, the presence of which suggests that near or at this necropolis a Roman infantryman, named T(itus) Helvius Tacitus, apparently succumbed en route of march and was buried among foreigners (he was of the Celtic *gens* Helvii), with a purely Roman style headstone. Uniquely, at this necropolis, the epitaph is written in proper Latin in *scriptura capitalis* with serifs, suggesting the work of his legion's *lapidarius.*[10]

8. Concerning the revival of sun-worship in the eastern empire, see: *OCD*, 495 *s.v.* Helios; Ferguson 1970, p. 44; Hajjar 1971 vols. I–II *passim*, an in-depth survey of the recrudescence of sun cults in the Roman East and beyond. Of great significance is Philo's contemporary autopsy of the mystico-philosophical sect called the Therapeutae, who lived in communes in the northwest Delta around and beyond Lake Mareotis (just west of Alexandria), reported in *De vita contemplativa* xi.89ff. Notable is their worshipping of the rising sun with upraised arms, reminiscent of the *orans-thuraîos* ("the orant who is at the threshold") pose found on many of the Terenouthis stelae and elsewhere in provincial Greco-Egyptian funerary art.

9. Illustrated in el-Nassery and Wagner 1978, cat. no. 5 and pl. lxx.5, and the motif's meaning is discussed by Cumont 1933, pp. 385ff.

10. KM inv. no. 21194 (= Cat. No. 203) in the forthcoming Terenouthis Report Volume I.

TOLERANCE AND OECUMENISM

Openness to non-Egyptian influences was well established at the beginning of the Roman period necropolis at Kom Abou Billou, as seen for example, in the popular adoption of the "Charon obol" and the affecting in public of Greek and Roman clothing, hairstyles, banqueting parapherna-lia, et cetera. The cohesion of this otherwise submissive Greco-Egyptian society was substantially reinforced by the revival of a pseudo-pharaonic ancestor cult, with all its components, e.g., the shamanistic cult of mummification. In this expression of their national heritage the Greco-Egyptians came as close as they ever would to a revival of their past culture, under Rome's watchful administrative eyes.

But, that very cult of the ancestor, with its graveside rituals of communion and propitiating ancestors, was also a commonplace phenomenon throughout the eastern Empire and in Rome itself (Alföldi-Rosenbaum 1971, pp. 92–93 and notes). What set the Greco-Egyptian observance apart from its counterparts elsewhere was the aura of ancient Egyptian mystery infused into the revived rites and archaizing surroundings of same.

Moreover, the magico-religious cult of mummification and its elaborate and anciently cele-brated rites would have provided cachet to this local funerary *cultus*, and at the same time, a com-mon ground of identification for prospective initiates. For apart from these Egyptianizing trappings, the essential elements of the cult of the ancestor as practiced throughout the eastern Mediterranean empire of Rome were manifest: burial obsequies, lunar festivals of the dead, oracular interviews with propitiated ancestors, and communal sacral banquets at tombside.

A hypothetical visitor from an eastern provincial town, such as Anemurium on the south coast of Asia Minor, would have recognized the intent of the rituals and their attendant communal meals celebrated in front of the tombs, on which in many cases the deceased was shown as a libating banqueter in Greek dress upon a Greek-style banqueting couch (*kline*), or an incense-offering cel-ebrant, or a pious *orans*-figure greeting the rising sun and/or communing visitors. It would have been an instantaneously recognized paradigm of ancestor worship, the *mysterium* of the ancient Egyptian *cultus* notwithstanding.[11] Reciprocally, the Greco-Egyptians would have recognized these common beliefs and practices that they witnessed at the no less public obsequies for the dead among their neighboring resident aliens.

The phenomenon of syncretism that, as mentioned earlier was widespread in Ptolemaic Egypt, was no less present in the Roman period. At the end of the Ptolemaic period, for instance, there is the celebrated case of the learned, mystical, Faiyum priest, Isidoros, whose Isiac aretalogies sought through mythopoeic synthesis to amalgamate into the province of this goddess all the powers of Fate, effectively elevating Isis to the rank of a henotheistic "God" (Vanderlip 1972, pp. 93–95 and pls. 11–13). Though this theopoeic permutation was a localized phenomenon and restricted in its influence, this contrived melding of religious doctrines and identities is the leading edge, so to speak, of a continuous trend in certain priestly circles in the *chora* to align their multivalent theol-ogy with responsive aspects in the religious inventories of the less complicated "barbarians." It seems to be a bivalent process of religious acculturation that at once is manipulative of the foreign beliefs and superstitions of Egypt's occupiers, and over time, preconditioning the priestly circles of Egypt to be accepting of "the foreign" in their midst.

The common ground of fascination and interest (which in the event provided astute Egyptians and Roman syndics alike with a potential for a perpetually lucrative service industry) was found in the two areas of greatest personal religious concern: death and the afterlife. Here, Egypt's millennia-old Osirian mysteries were attractive, from pre-Homeric times, to foreigners. The task of

11. Alföldi-Rosenbaum 1971, pp. 92ff. and cf. Dentzer 1982, pp. 2ff., with detailed discussions of the origins and distribution of the sacred banqueting motif.

attracting these foreign residents was made the easier by the innate superstitiousness of the displaced miscellanies of immigrants and their Egyptian-born descendants. The Romans were no less attracted to the *arcana* of Egypt's oracle and funerary cults, and many resident Romans opted for Egyptianizing burial paraphernalia — just to be on the safe side. It is in this context of pervasive religious acculturation that Egypt's "death industry" revived and with it the fortunes of the Egyptian and Greco-Egyptian middle and upper classes.

Concomitantly, the admission to the Egyptian funerary mysteries of "foreigners" entailed long term consequences. For the Greeks, Romans, or whoever would eventually broaden the participation in the ethnic-Egyptian/Greco-Egyptian control of the local funerary cults, and eventually insinuate doctrines and notions of "foreign" afterlife beliefs.

A case in point would be the widespread notion in second-century Egypt that the Osirian judgement took place in the astral regions — an idea diametrically opposed to the Egyptian funerary belief in the underworld judgement.[12] This heterodox view is clearly expressed in the ceiling paintings in the tomb of a Petosiris, a grandee of ancient Trimunthon in the Dakhla Oasis, in the mid-second century A.D (Osing et al. 1982, p. 96 *et passim* and pls. 38–39). Underlying this transference of the apotheosis of the soul to the astral plane (shown on these elaborately painted ceilings as a crested ibis [*ibis comata*] or series of same ascending into the cosmos, ruled by Greco-Babylonian and Greco-Egyptian constellations) was the zodiacal lore of the Roman East (introduced into Egypt in the late Ptolemaic period), and which at some point in the early imperial period was wedded to the Osirian mysteries — contradictions notwithstanding.

There is strong indication from this and other artistic and social indices that a profound convergence of Egyptian and non-Egyptian funerary theologies took place by the second century. This is also the time that the "Stil-Dualismus" i.e. the harmonious coexistence of Egyptianizing and pseudo-Egyptian styles in art is detected.[13] In the historical context of a growing Greco-Egyptian town culture during the prosperous second century, the tailoring of Egyptian mysteries for the understanding and adherence of foreign initiates was a logical outcome.

At Terenouthis this convergence, as it might be termed, was registered in the workshops of its necropolis. The presence of a Helleno-Roman decorative program with Greco-Egyptian embellishments (as instanced on the tomb of Isidora) responds to the mixed theological trends of the middle decades of the second century A.D. To the extent that the priestly and lay stewards of the revived solar Osirian mysteries celebrated at this necropolis were amenable to admitting non-Egyptian elements into their previously strictly regulated preserve, it can be stated that tolerance of religious diversity existed at this necropolis.

In the larger context of the apparent harmonizing of Egyptian, Greco-Egyptian, and fatalistic eastern theologies, this openness (whether for altruistic or venal purposes) might be characterized as oecumenical. It was not the oecumenism of a proselytizing religion but a local tradition both responsive and at the same time attractive to the aspirations of people surviving in a period of spiritual insecurity, social malaise, and moral *anomie*. Over a period of several generations, the Greco-Egyptian town culture, that flourished up to about the third quarter of the second century of Roman rule, accommodated its cherished Osirian mysteries both to monied adherents and, unsuspectingly, to their contending religious ideologies.

12. Kákosy 1979, pp. 350–51, a discussion of the popular conception in the Greco-Roman period of the function of the temple as the earthly palace of a god, where he or she celebrated their bliss in banqueting — a notion surely born of the pharaonic period's ritualized attending upon the gods' daily physical needs by their phyles of priests and devotees. It was simply a case of the transference of this archaic concept to the popular conception of the actual tombs, where the people as "justified" survivors of the Osirian judgement also hoped to celebrate as gods, eternally.

13. Griffiths 1982, p. 249, with a balanced discussion of the stylistic dualism theories regarding the popular funerary arts in Greco-Roman period Egypt. The Terenouthis evidence broadens this theoretical reconstruction.

PLATE 23.1

Facade with Fresco Decoration. Unnumbered Tomb with Limestone Funerary Stele (KM 4-4206) in situ, Area 10, Kom Abou Billou. Close-up view of the tomb showing the method by which a funerary stele was placed/slotted in the recessed niche within the solid mudbrick construction of the barrel roof. The frescoed facade is organized by framed (painted) zones according to a standard program. In the lower zones, beside and just above the table of offerings are symbolic elements in bilaterally symmetrical arrangement: at either edge of the field are two sheaf-like containers of floral arrangements that are reminiscent of the very ancient Egyptian tradition of presenting floral clusters and garlands for the dead; against the white background to either side of the table of offerings an undulating vine-scroll is deployed, that is comparable to the use of vine-scrolls in the early imperial period, e.g. the *Ara Pacis*. In the center, perched uneasily on extended off-shoots of the vine are affronting doves. On the surface of the cornice-like area that mediates between the tomb's base and roof areas there is a formal "peopled-scroll" motif that is found in the Fourth Style's decorative ensembles, e.g. in the Neronian *Domus Aurea* in Rome. Helmet-clad heads alternate with "ascending" imperial eagles — the latter associated with the neoplatonic idea of the ascent of the soul during apotheosis, just as Ganymede was translated to Olympus by Zeus in the form of an eagle. In its siting between the upper and lower zones of the tomb itself, this motif is entirely appropriate, as the survival of the dead in both the Underworld and the astral regions was part of the dualistic afterlife ideology of both pharaonic and post-pharaonic Egypt. In the half tympana to either side of the stele's niche were two enframed fields of composition: to the right are the remains of a boating scene; to the viewer's left, the headless figure of a chiton- and himation-clad officiant placed in a standing-pivoting position relative to the viewer and to the tomb-niche. Directly behind this offering-bearer is a profile figure of an Anubis animal that holds up its left paw (*pars sinistra*) likely in approbation to the offices of the ancestor cult that are shown in progress. The presence of the stele with its *orans*-figure within the niche completes the symbolism of this funereal iconographic program.

PLATE 23.2

Close-up of the Upper Section of an Unnumbered Tomb with Frescoed Half Tympana and, Unusually, a Frescoed Back Wall of the Niche Substituting for a Limestone Stele (KM 4-4205). An on-axis view of the niche and upper facade of an unnumbered tomb with remains of the fresco decorations. Of significance is the fresco on the niche's rear wall which imitates a carved funerary stele of stone. In this instance the deceased is shown as a banqueting immortal who reclines upon a richly upholstered *kline* and raises a loop-handled, footed *kantharos* (likely representing a metalware piece) in libation gesture, directed at the viewer and the gods of the underworld. The hastily brushed on inscription identifies the owner as "Isidora, ... aged 37 years of age" who died on the "10th day of Choiak." To either side of this skillfully painted simulation of a relief stele are formal compositions: to the viewer's right are the remains of a now headless recliner within a Nile boat, moving "towards" the niche; to the left, a masterful rendition of a classico-Hellenistic set piece of a relaxed standing Hermes (Hermanubis?) carrying a *cadeucas* in his left arm and leading a partially visible chiton- and himation-clad figure towards the "portal" to the Underworld, the niche. In this facade fresco decoration is seen in literal pictorialization the funerary ideology of the Greco-Egyptian population of Roman period Egypt, an ideology that fused the ancient Egyptian and Greek concepts related to the transition to the afterlife as a voyage across the Nile to the "western regions" and as a journey led by a *psychopompos*, respectively. On stylistic grounds, the painting style, as also the palaeography of the inscription, e.g. the elongated oblique *hastae* of the alphas forming characteristic apices, suggest a mid 2nd century date, i.e. about or soon after the period of the Hadrianic neo-classical *renovatio*, that is especially noticed in provincial "minor arts." Cf. G. Grimm 1974, pl. 27, no. 18, a classicizing stele dated to the period of Hadrian, from Terenouthis.

CHAPTER 24

BIBLIOGRAPHY AND DESCRIPTION OF DEMOTIC LITERARY TEXTS: A PROGRESS REPORT

JAN MERTENS
Katholieke Universiteit, Leuven

The organizers of the Symposium asked us to present, for a wider audience of Egyptologists, Hellenists, and papyrologists, a project on which my colleague, Mr. Tassier, and I are currently working.

The aim of the project is to put together a kind of corpus of Demotic literary texts and — in doing so — to present a general view on Demotic literature as we know it. In fact, Demotic literature (the term is used in its broadest sense) seems to be neglected. In his *Grundzüge einer Geschichte der altägyptischen Literatur*, for example, the Egyptologist, Hellmut Brunner (1966) devotes only five percent of his text to Demotic literature. Although we must admit that many Demotic texts are very fragmentary we think that such treatment does not do justice to the great amount of literary texts that have survived and to the richness of the material. Some statistics included in this paper illustrate this statement.

The features of the project were presented during the Third International Conference of Demotic Studies in 1987 and were later published in *Göttinger Miszellen* (Mertens and Tassier 1988, pp. 49–55). At present we have collected 535 items. This is a tentative figure since many Demotic literary texts remain undiscovered in papyrus collections all over the world.[1] Still we think that this provisional figure gives already an impression of the great amount of texts in the native literary tradition during the Late and Greco-Roman periods. And Demotic texts form only a part of that tradition.

One should also look at the number of hieroglyphic and Hieratic literary texts of these periods. At this moment there is no corpus of such texts. The catalogue made by Madeleine Bellion (1987) can be used for such a purpose, at least for the papyri. The book catalogues, written on the walls of some temples of the Greco-Roman period, are another source of information. There are recent studies by Grimm (1989, pp. 159–69) on this subject and a new book which is published from the "Nachlass" of the late Siegfried Schott (1990). Of course, one should not overlook the literary texts themselves, written on the temple walls. All of these elements should be brought together to judge the importance of the native literary tradition.

1. For instance, in Vienna and Copenhagen. Compare contributions by Karl-Theodor Zauzich and Michel Chauveau during the conference.

As of August 1990, we have collected 535 Demotic literary and para-literary texts,[2] distributed as follows:

Table 24.1. Distribution of Demotic Literary and Para-Literary Texts.

GENRE	*NUMBER*
Narrative	136
Poetical	2
Wisdom	39
Historical/Prophetical	12
Religious	24
Mythological	12
Funerary/Mortuary	36
Magical	18
Omen Literature	27
Juridical	8
Medical	11
Mathematical	7
Astronomical/Astrological	44
School Exercises	38
Onomastica and Word-lists	28
Scientific (others or not specified)	80
Possible Literary Texts	13
TOTAL NUMBER	535

The numbers given in table 24.1 reveal the following tendencies:

1) There is a great continuity in all text categories. Nearly every genre of the classical pharaonic literature is represented in Demotic except for the traditional "Lamentations" genre and the love poems.

2) Within the Greco-Roman the same tendency is observed. Most text categories continued to exist well into the Roman period (second century A.D.). About sixty percent of the known Demotic literary texts are dated to the Roman period.

3) A quarter of the texts are narrative. This genre is certainly more diverse than the two Setne texts and the three or four texts from the so-called "Petubastis/Inaros-cycle" that are most often quoted.

At the Cambridge meeting in 1987 Mr. Tassier and I rather boldly stated that we could finish the English manuscript by 1990. Unfortunately the progress of the project has been delayed by several factors. Since we both have jobs outside Egyptology now, we also have to finish the work in our spare time.

2. Published and unpublished texts, written on all sorts of material. The figure was already obsolete by the time the conference ended, since many colleagues signalized new texts. It also became clear that literally thousands of fragments, in different papyrus collections, are still not catalogued.

Originally we felt that we had to take into account as many unpublished texts as possible. Otherwise the overall picture would not be complete. During the conference, however, it became clear that the majority of Demotists were — for different reasons — not in favor of incorporating systematically unpublished texts; most of those present were in favor of the publication being made available as soon as possible. We finally accepted this view. Therefore, the catalogue will only contain published texts. Finally, we are reluctant to put forward a date for the actual publication. We hope that we shall be able to finish the project by 1995.

CHAPTER 25

A BILINGUAL ACCOUNT OF MONIES RECEIVED

JAMES H. MIDGLEY
Macquarie University

24 March 235 B.C.

Inv. 499 — Provenance unknown

The front of P. Macquarie inv. 499* contains a continuous Greek text and several lines of Demotic writing to the right and below, which are only partly preserved. Both the Greek and Demotic hands exhibit a similar style, so that the entire text may have been written by the same scribe. The hand may be compared, for general appearance, with that of PLB XX 13, recto (Plate XIII), 252 B.C. Because of the wavy, brushlike strokes, the Greek hand is extremely difficult to read.

Gesso and a necklace-pattern of brown marks on the front of the papyrus suggest that the fragment is from the lower corner of a chest piece. The back contains vestiges of at least one line of extremely abraded, scarcely legible writing (written ↓).

The Greek text records payments of money from the villages of Λητοῦϲ κώμη, Βερενικὶϲ Αἰγιαλοῦ, and perhaps another village (cf. lines 2–4 and notes), into the bank at Crocodilopolis, and that of a village, Arsinoe (cf. line 8 and note). The Demotic writing contains the phrase, "the monies which have been received" (cf. Demotic line c and note), which may indicate that the Demotic portion of the text is related to the Greek, but the only figures given in the Demotic do not appear to have any connection with the amounts recorded in the Greek column. However, the Demotic figures begin at a "day 19" (Demotic line e), where the Greek calculations end (line 10), and the Demotic also contains the geographical name, "The Place of Berenice," opposite the Greek village name Βερενικὶϲ Αἰγιαλοῦ (line 3), which would appear to show a relationship between the Greek and Demotic texts. Dr. Robert K. Ritner of the Oriental Institute, the University of Chicago, who kindly read the Demotic for me, reports that the reading of this village in our text appears to confirm that P. dém. Lille 6, which contains the only other Demotic attestation of *P3-ʿ-Brng3*, does refer to Βερενικὶϲ Αἰγιαλοῦ, as had been suggested by the editor of the Lille papyrus, and not to Βερενικὶϲ Θεϲμοφόρου, since the Lille text derives from the *meris* of Themistes, not that of Polemon. Βερενικὶϲ Αἰγιαλοῦ is attested in papyri in the third century B.C. and from the first to the eighth centuries A.D. As the name implies, it must have lain on the shore of Lake Moeris. According to the editors of P. Fay., it must have been situated to the northeast of Ḳaṣr el Banât (cf. line 3 and note).

* For permission to publish P.Macquarie inv. 499 here I thank Professor E. A. Judge of Macquarie University, Sydney, Australia.

The money amounts given in the account may tentatively be assumed to be silver, for no notation is present to the contrary. The "year 12" in line 1 may thus be taken to refer to the reign of Ptolemy III Euergetes (= 235 B.C.). What the payments represent remains unclear. They are not assessed by land area, as were, for example, rents on crown land, but by the day, at the rate of 18¾ drachmas. It seems reasonable to infer rent payments for groups of persons from the villages named, though no word occurs in the text which throws light on the purpose of the monies. The amounts are calculated beginning from the first day of the month of Mecheir, up to the nineteenth. The survey itself is dated in line 1 on the fifth day of Mecheir. Three specific periods are given, and the length of each can easily be determined from the arithmetic, since the totals are clearly read: 1) from the first "up to the 5th" (line 5); 2) from the first "up to the 13th" (line 7); 3) from the first "up to the 6th" (line 9). The total of nineteen days given in line 10 shows that the scribe did not take into account the five days listed for the unread word (village?) in line 5, but calculated only the number of days for which money was actually collected, the thirteen days' worth of payments going to the bank at Crocodilopolis, and the six days' worth of payments for the bank in Arsinoe.

FRONT

→ ("Ετους) ιβ Μεχεὶρ ε̄	[...] ... [...] *Pr-ʿꜣ*[a]
παρὰ Λητοῦς κώ(μης),	
Βε(ρενικίδος) Αἰγιαλọῦ{ν}	[...] ... *nPꜣ-ʿ-Brngꜣ*[b]
Πτ ... ιος	[...] ... *nꜣ ḥḏ.w ỉ-ỉr ỉw*[c]
ἕως ε̄	
ἐπὶ τὴν ἐν Κ(ροκοδίλων) (πόλει) τρ(άπεζαν)	
ἕως ιγ ἀν(ὰ) ιη (τετρώβολον) (ἡμιωβέλιον)	
(δραχμαὶ) Σμγ (τετρώβολον) (ἡμιωβέλιον)	
[ἐπὶ τ]ὴν ἐν Ἀρσινόηι	[...] ... ⌜NN⌝[d]
ἕως ς ἀν(ὰ) ιη (τετρώβολον) (ἡμιωβέλιον)	
(δραχμαὶ) ριβ (τριώβολον).	
(γίνονται) ιθ (δραχμαὶ) Τνς	
ḥsb. t 12 nPr-ʿꜣ[h]	[...] *sw 19 4*[e]
Ptrwmys ...[i]	[...] *sw 19 4*[f]
	[...] ⌜*sw 19 4*⌝[g]

— — — — — — — — —

2 Λητοῦς: not Λητους; κώ(μης): ꝁ

6 Κ(ροκοδίλων) (πόλει): κ̄ ∩; 7 ἀν(ὰ): ⁄; 7, 9 (δραχμαὶ): ⊢;
(τετρώβολον): ∫; 7, 9, 10 (ἡμιωβέλιον): c; 9 (τριώβολον): ∫; 10 (γίνονθαι): /

BACK

↓

] [ ] κι [

TRANSLATION

Year 12, Mecheir 5.
From Letous *kome*,
Berenikis-on-shore,
Pt ... ios.
Up to the 5th (of the month): (no entry)
To the bank in Crocodilopolis:
Up to the 13th (of the month), at $18\frac{3}{4}$ drachmas,
$243\frac{3}{4}$ drachmas.
To the bank in Arsinoe:
Up to the 6th (of the month), at $18\frac{3}{4}$ drachmas,
$112\frac{1}{2}$ drachmas.
Total 19 (days), making $356\frac{1}{12}$ drachmas.

DEMOTIC

a: [...] ... [...] Pharaoh
b: [...] ... of/to/for "The Place of Berenice"
c: ... the monies which have been received
d: [...] ... (end of a theophoric personal name)
e: [...] day 19 (of the month) - 4 (units of payment)
f: [...] day 19 (of the month) - 4 (units of payment)
g: [...] day 19 (of the month) - 4 (units of payment)
h: Regnal year 12 of Pharaoh
i: Ptolemy ...

NOTES TO LINES

1. (Ἔτουϲ) ιβ Μεχεὶρ $\overline{\ \ }$ε. 24 March 235 B.C. The alternative dates of 10 March 210 B.C. or 20 March 193 B.C. are rendered unlikely by the calculation of payments in silver with no reference to a conversion rate for copper (cf. line 7 and note). This spelling of Mecheir, however, is more common in documents of the second century B.C., whereas the spelling Μεχίρ prevails in the third century (Mayser 1970, p. 68, note 2).

a. [...] ... [...] *Pr-ꜥꜣ*. "Pharaoh." Dr. Ritner comments that the right hand traces are broken and unclear/dark in the photo. At the end of the line *Pr-ꜥꜣ* "Pharaoh" would suggest a column heading with preceding date.

2. παρὰ Λητοῦϲ κώ(μηϲ). I thank Professor Willy Clarysse for his corrections of this line, and also of lines 4, 6, and 8. Though a precise parallel for the name is wanting, it is nonetheless assumed that the village name is simply a variation of Λητοῦϲ πόλιϲ, on which cf. *DGT*, pp. 197–98. It should be pointed out, however, that Mayser gives no instance of παρά used in this way with the name of a village (cf. 1970, vols. 2.1, 2.2, 2.3, indices, s.v. παρά). However, if Λητοῦϲ is taken as a personal name, an impossible situation presents itself, for there is no attested personal name with the genitive Λητοῦϲ, except Λητώ (the goddess Leto). It is perhaps possible, if this is a personal name, to posit a nominative, Λητήϲ (following the declension of ἀληθήϲ, –οῦϲ), since there is attestation for a similar name, Λ̣ηπ̣ῆϲ, in *SB* V 7597 (second/first century B.C.). If it is a personal name, the

symbol following must be read as κω(μάρχου), rather than κώ(μηϲ). In Bilabel's list of symbols only the former usage is given, but it seems plausible that the abbreviation κω( ) could have been used in other ways as well (Bilabel 1923, col. 2302). The solution which construes Ληποῦϲ as a village name seems less problematic than the alternative.

3. Βε(ρενικίδοϲ) Αἰγιαλοῦ{ν}. The village was located in the meris of Themistes, on the southwest shore of Lake Moeris (cf. *DGT* 2.1, pp. 42–44; Supp. I, p. 79; Grenfell, Hunt, and Goodspeed 1907, p. 373; Papyrus Fay., p. 14 and 82.3 and note). The *nu* at the end of Αἰγιαλοῦ is apparently a scribal error. The Demotic opposite reads, "The Place of Berenice," which would appear to confirm the reading of the Greek abbreviation as the same village name, which is found abbreviated Β( ) Αἰγιαλ(οῦ) or Βερ( ) (cf. *PSI* VIII 966.3, 4).

4. Πτ ... ιοϲ. Professor Clarysse has suggested that this word is a village name certainly beginning with Πτ, but it has not yet been identified. *DGT* gives eighteen geographical names (vol. 4.2, pp. 198–200) which begin with Πτ–, but none ends in ιοϲ, as does the name here.

c. [...] ... *nꜣ ḥḏ.w i͗-i͗r i͗w*. "the monies which have been received (an idiom = lit., 'which have come')."

5. ἕωϲ ε̅. "Up to/Until the fifth" (of the month), presumably the fifth of Mecheir, the day on which the document was written (cf. line 1 and note). Apparently this notation applies to the village whose name remains unread, in the previous line (cf. note), but for some reason no figures were entered for it.

6. ἐπὶ τὴν ἐν Κ(ροκοδίλων) (πόλει) τρ(άπεζαν). The symbol κ̅ (the line above is arched) occurs in P. Petrie III 53 (1), line 15 for Κροκοδίλων πόλιϲ. The symbol following is the common sign for πόλιϲ, a dome over an omicron or dot (cf. Bilabel, line c (above, note 2), col. 2303). I thank Professor Clarysse for reading the sign for τρ(άπεζαν). Besides the central bank in Alexandria, there were central banks in the nomes, under which operated banks at more local levels, from the meris to the village (Préaux 1939a, pp. 280–97; cf. A. Calderini 1938, pp. 244–78).

7. ἕωϲ ιγ ἀν(ὰ) ιη (τετρώβολον) (ἡμιωβέλιον) (δραχμαὶ) Σμγ (τετρώβολον) (ἡμιωβέλιον) The letters α and ν in ἀν(ὰ) have been simplified into a symbol (cf. plate). 18¾ drachmas × thirteen days = 243¾ drachmas. Since the drachmas are not qualified as copper, it is reasonable to assume that they are silver. The silver standard was still in effect up to the first half of 210 B.C. (Reekmans 1948, pp. 15–43 and 1949, pp. 324–25; BGU VII, pp. 274–75). The 'year 12' of the text then, corresponds to 235 B.C., in the reign of Euergetes, instead of in that of Philopator or Epiphanes (cf. line 1 and note). Moreover, Professor Clarysse informs me that the Demotic hand (because of the spelling of Ptolemy in line i) cannot be dated before the reign of Ptolemy III.

8. [ἐπὶ τ]ὴν ἐν 'Αρϲινόηι. That τ]ὴν refers to an implied noun, τράπεζαν, is clear from the context (cf. line 6). Arsinoe is one of several Arsinoite villages which bore that name (cf. F. Preisigke Abschn. 16a, s.v. Αρϲινόη). It cannot be a reference to the nome capital, which occurs in line 6 (cf. note). The village may be identified with that mentioned in P. Ent. 25.10-11: κώμηϲ 'Αρϲινόηϲ, τῆϲ Θε-|[11] μίϲτου μερίδοϲ, τῆϲ ἐπὶ τοῦ χώματοϲ.

d. [...] ... ⸢NN⸣. Dr. Ritner informs me that this is the end of a theophoric personal name. Perhaps then, it is the Demotic for Αρϲινόη, which stands opposite in the Greek.

9. ἕωϲ ϛ ἀν(ὰ) ιη (τετρώβολον) (ἡμιωβέλιον) (δραχμαὶ) ριβ (τριώβολον). The money amount, 112 drachmas, 3 obols, is the correct product of 18 drachmas 4½ obols for six days. On the basis of this arithmetic, the very faint traces after ἕωϲ, which is itself obscure, are read as ϛ.

10. (γίνονται) ιθ (δραχμαὶ) Τνϛ. This is the last line of Greek writing. The traces are faint, but the totals can be calculated from the figures in lines 7 and 9.

e-g. [...] sw 19 4 "Day 19 (of the month) 4 (units of payment)." In line g only the top traces are preserved. The Demotic appears to be a continuation of the account from day nineteen, where the Greek account ends.

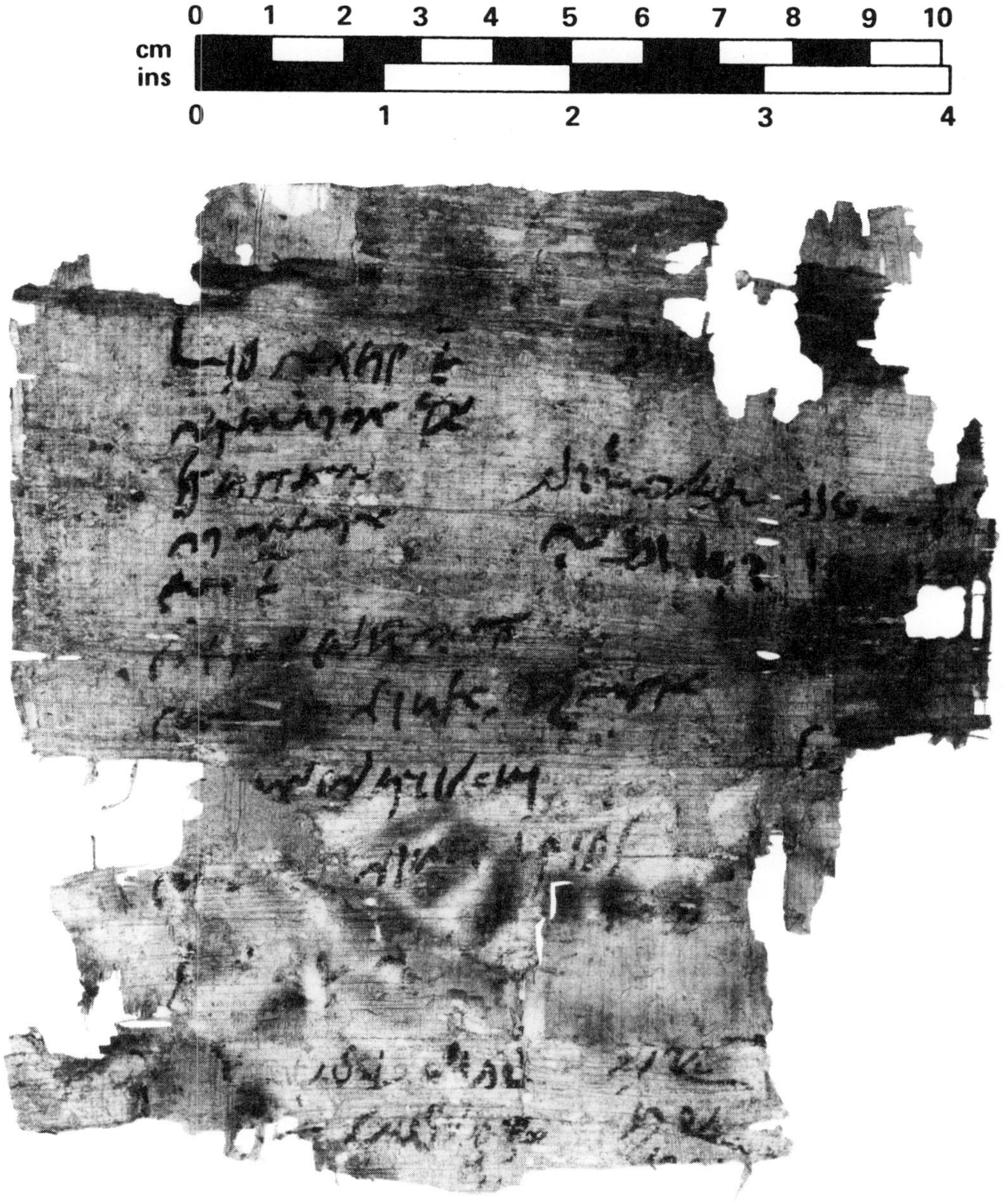

Photograph of Papyrus Macquarie inv. 499

CHAPTER 26

DEMOTISCHE TERMINI ZUR LANDESGLIEDERUNG ÄGYPTENS

RENATE MÜLLER-WOLLERMANN
University of Tübingen

Ausgangspunkt der folgenden Überlegungen war die Frage Van't Dacks, was denn das demotische Wort *tš* nun eigentlich bedeute (Van't Dack 1988, S. 382).[1] Impliziert war dabei die Frage, inwieweit demotische und griechische Verwaltungstermini, und das heißt, sowohl administrativ-geographische Termini als auch mit diesen gebildete Beamtentitel, kompatibel seien. Auf den ersten Blick muß nämlich einem Papyrologen — und nicht nur diesem — das demotische Begriffsinstrumentarium einigermaßen chaotisch erscheinen. Die Frage Van't Dacks ist denn auch eher von einem Demotisten, besser: einem Ägyptologen, zu beantworten als von einem Papyrologen, denn für derlei Fragestellungen sollte nicht nur das demotische Material, sondern auch das zeitgleiche hieroglyphische herangezogen werden. Im ersten Anlauf außer acht gelassen werden können hingegen die demotischen und kursivhieratischen Texte der Vorptolemäerzeit. Die Zeitgleichheit der herangezogenen Texte zu beachten ist nämlich wesentlicher als übereinstimmende Sprache oder Schrift. Auf dieses Problem wird noch zurückzukommen sein. Die Überlegungen sollen sich auch nicht auf das Wort *tš* alleine beschränken, sondern alle wichtigeren geographisch-administrativen Begriffe sollen miteinbezogen werden.

Doch beginnen wir mit dem Wort *tš*. Es dürfte Konsens darüber herrschen, daß *tš* dem griechischen νομός, allgemein mit "Gau" übersetzt, entspricht oder, vorsichtiger formuliert, entsprechen kann. Aber nicht jeder νομός heißt im Demotischen *tš*, er kann auch *qḥ* heißen. Da in Texten pharaonischer Zeit das Wort *qʿḥ.t* früher die Bedeutung "Gebiet" aufweist als das Wort *t(ꜣ)š*, könnte dieses Textmaterial den Schluß nahelegen, daß das eine Wort das andere ablöst. Die demotischen Texte widerlegen dies allerdings, denn dort können beide Begriffe nebeneinander stehen (s. z.B. Spiegelberg 1914a, S. 68 und Tafel III, Z. 4). Aber: Für ein und dasselbe Gebiet wird immer dieselbe Bezeichnung verwendet, sie werden also nicht promiscue benutzt, sondern variieren nach Lokalität. So heißt das Fayyūm immer *pꜣ tš ꜣrsynꜣ* bzw. *pꜣ tš n ỉm*, der Pathyrites immer *pꜣ tš n Pr-Ḥwt-Ḥr*, um nur die häufigst belegten zu nennen. Dagegen heißt der Gau von Koptos stets *tꜣ qḥ Qb.t* und der von Asyūṭ stets *tꜣ qḥ Syw.t*, auch hier wiederum nur die häufig belegten. Alle übrigen Gaue sind nur vereinzelt belegt.[2] Diese lokalen Varietäten haben gute ägyptische Tradition: Im Papyrus Wilbour, dem man seinen offiziellen, amtlichen Charakter wohl kaum absprechen kann, heißt der Verwaltungsbezirk von Hardai, in oder bei al-Qais gelegen, immer *qʿḥ.t*, der von Herakleopolis *w* (Gardiner 1948, S.

1. Professor Van't Dack sowie Professor Clarysse sei an dieser Stelle für wertvolle Hinweise gedankt.
2. Die Liste der Belege, die nur nachpharaonische Bezeugungen umfaßt und keinen Anspruch auf Vollständigkeit erhebt, findet sich im Anhang.

39f.). Es scheint, daß in der Spätzeit *w* jeweils durch *tš* ersetzt wurde und *q ʿḥ.t* jeweils als *qḥ* erhalten blieb. Die einzige mir bekannte Ausnahme stellt P. Rylands IX dar, der bezeichnenderweise kein offizielles Dokument ist; er verwendet vereinheitlichend *tš* (s. F. Griffith 1909, S. 406 [Index]). Eine eingehende Erklärung für den Wechsel in der Terminologie kann ich jedoch nicht anbieten. Zurück zu *tš* und *qḥ* in den demotischen Texten. Wenn beide einen νομός bezeichnen können, stellt sich anschließend die Frage, ob sie dies ausschließlich tun ober ob *tš* und *qḥ* auch andere geographische oder administrative Einheiten bezeichnen können. Um die Antwort gleich vorweg zu nehmen, dies können sie in der Tat, aber die Abweichungen sind relativ leicht zu erkennen und zu deuten. So kann *tš* in literarischen Texten unspezifisch verwendet werden, beispielsweise in der Lehre für Anchscheschonqi oder im Mythos vom Sonnenauge, wo mit dem *tš* einer Person seine Umgebung gemeint ist.[3] Die andere Ausnahme ist der Begriff *tš n Nw.t*. Er bezeichnet nicht den thebanischen Gau — hierfür gibt es kein einziges Indiz — sondern die Thebais. Er findet sich zumeist in Datierungsangaben, wo Ptolemais, der Sitz der eponymen Priester, als *m pꜣ tš n Nw.t* charakterisiert ist. Daß Ptolemais nicht im thebanischen νομός zu lokalisieren ist, vielmehr im größeren Gebiet der Thebais, liegt auf der Hand. Ein anderer unzweifelhafter Fall sind die Belege für den Strategen des *tš n Nw.t* im Familienarchiv von Asyūṭ, denn der dort genannte Noumenes ist in griechischen Texten als Stratege der Thebais bezeugt (Peremans und Van't Dack 1950, S. 25, No. 196; s. auch Mooren und Swinnen 1975, S. 29, No. 196). Ein drittes Indiz bildet der singuläre Beleg eines Schreibers des *tš n Nw.t Tꜣ-šd-rs* (P. Rylands XVII, 2), den ich als Schreiber der Thebais in *Tꜣ-šd-rs*, d.h. im Südbezirk, interpretieren möchte. Auf den Terminus *Tꜣ-šd-rs* wird später noch zurückzukommen sein. Bei *qḥ* beschränkt sich die Abweichung auf einen Fall. In einem Papyrus aus al-Ḥība ist ein *pꜣ sḥn tꜣ qḥ* belegt (CGC 50148, 6–7). Auf Grund des Fundortes sollte man annehmen, daß mit *qḥ* der Herakleopolitische Gau gemeint ist. Da dieselbe Person in einem fast zeitgleichen griechischen Papyrus derselben Provenienz aber als τοπάρχης bezeichnet ist (P. Hibeh I 75, 2–3), dürfte hier mit *qḥ* wohl eine Toparchie gemeint sein. Die in Frage kommende ist die Koitische, der innerhalb des Herakleopolites schon immer eine herausragende Bedeutung zukam und die gegen Ende der Ptolemäerzeit sogar in einen eigenständigen Gau umgewandelt wurde (Van't Dack 1988, S. 379 mit Anm. 8). Unter Berücksichtigung dieser überschaubaren und erklärbaren Ausnahmen kann also festgehalten werden, daß *tš* bzw. *qḥ* griechischem νομός entspricht.[4]

Einheitlicher gestaltet sich die Terminologie bei den administrativen Untereinheiten des Gaues, den Toparchien. Mit Ausnahme des Herakleopolites, wo τοπαρχία auch mit ἄγημα wiedergegeben werden kann (s. *DGT*, Supplement I, S. 5: Ἄγημα ἄνω und Ἄγημα κάτω), und dem Fayyūm, wo Sonderverhältnisse vorliegen, die später noch erörtert werden, zeigt sich folgendes Bild. Toparchien werden als *ʿ(.wy).w*, eigtl. "Häuser" oder "Plätze," bezeichnet. Diese Identifikation wurde bereits, allerdings ohne Beweisführung, von Sethe (Sethe und Partsch 1920, S. 264f.) und nach ihm und ohne Rückgriff auf ihn von Mattha (1945, S. 72) vorgeschlagen. Den Beweis hierfür liefert eine ptolemäische Bilingue aus Idfū, in der griechisches κάτω τόποι demotisch mit *nꜣ ʿ(.wy).w mḥ.ṱ(w)* wiedergegeben wird (Devauchelle und Wagner 1982, S. 90).[5] Alle übrigen mir bekannten Belege lassen nur vermuten, daß *ʿ(.wy).w* für τοπαρχία stehen könnte und keinen unspezifischen Ausdruck darstellt. Hierzu gehört z.B. ein ptolemäischer Papyrus, der wahrscheinlich aus Gabalain stammt und einen Dorfschreiber der südlichen Häuser des Gaues von Pathyris nennt (P. Berlin 13608, s. Spiegelberg 1930, S. 54).[6] Die gleiche Person ist zwar aus griechischen Texten nicht bekannt, aber eine südliche

3. P. BM 10508, 4, 20–21; 14, 21; P. Leiden I 384, 12, 4. Vgl. auch P. BM 10508, 5, 1–13. Vgl. des weiteren *pꜣ tš n pꜣ ꜣIḥwr* in Hughes 1951, S. 258–60; Clarysse und Winnicki 1989, S. 55f.; und *pꜣ tš n ꜣIst* in Griffith 1937, S. 53, und 1935, Tafel XVI (Ph. 55).

4. Daß *tš* auch die μερίδες des Fayyūm bezeichnen kann, wie Smith und Tait 1984, S. 48, vorschlagen, kann ich mangels Belegen nicht nachvollziehen.

5. Den Hinweis auf diese Textstelle verdanke ich Professor W. Clarysse. Vgl. auch seine Bemerkung in 1984, S. 1347.

6. Zur Person dieses Schreibers s. Vleeming 1984, S. 1053–56.

Toparchie des Pathyrites ist hinreichend abgesichert (*DGT* I, II, S. 128, und *DGT*, Supplement I, S. 42). In römischer Zeit wird in den thebanischen Steuerquittungen des öfteren eine Bank in den nördlichen *ʿ(.wy).w* genannt, an die Steuern gezahlt werden (Mattha 1945, passim; Lichtheim 1957, passim, v.a. S. 22). Da die Ostraka aus Madīnat Hābū stammen und Djeme in römischer Zeit zum Hermonthitischen Gau gehört (Bataille 1952, S. 64), kommt eine nördliche Toparchie als *nꜣ ʿ(.wy).w mḥ.ṯw* in Betracht. Allerdings ist für den Hermonthites keine κάτω τοπαρχία bezeugt, so daß eine definitive Absicherung nicht möglich ist. Außerdem ist in dieser Zeit eine Einteilung der Gaue in pagi vorherrschend. Auch ist eine Bank in dieser Gegend in den griechischen Texten nicht belegt, da das entsprechende griechische Formular in den Steuerquittungen anders gehalten ist. Bei anderen Belegen von *nꜣ ʿ(.wy).w* ist noch unsicherer, ob tatsächlich die administrative Einheit einer Toparchie gemeint ist oder nur eine unspezifische Gegend. *Nꜣ ʿ(.wy).w* stellt jedenfalls ein eindeutiges Pendant zu οἵ τόποι dar und bietet sich damit auch als Wiedergabe für τοπαρχία an. Verkompliziert wird der Sachverhalt dadurch, daß οἵ τόποι gelegentlich auch mit *mꜣʿ.w* wiedergegeben werden kann (Clarysse 1978, S. 7, und früher Sethe und Partsch 1920, S. 130f.). Üblicherweise entspricht jedoch der Singular τόπος dem demotischen *mꜣʿ*; dies wird jedoch nur bei hiermit gebildeten Beamtentiteln virulent. Für die pagi römischer Zeit ist kein demotisches Pendant bezeugt.

Völlig anders gestaltet sich die Unterteilung des Fayyūm. In ptolemäischer Zeit findet sich in den griechischen Texten eine Gaueinteilung in Nomarchien und drei μερίδες. Die Nomarchien sind durchweg mit Personennamen verbunden, was darauf hinweist, daß sie, zumindest ursprünglich, keine geographischen Begriffe darstellten, sondern Herrschaftsbereiche (A. Samuel 1966, S. 220–22). Darüber hinaus sind zwar Toparchen belegt, aber keine Toparchien. Möglicherweise umfaßten die Einflußbereiche der Toparchen nur einige Dörfer. In demotischen Texten wird μερίς einheitlich mit *tny.t* wiedergegeben; die Belege hierfür sind Legion. Daneben existieren zwei Untereinheiten des Fayyūm *ʿt*, nämlich *ʿt mḥ* und *ʿt rs tꜣ ḥny Mr-wr*.[7] Diese sind allerdings identisch mit den zahlreicheren griechischen Nomarchien (Peremans und Van't Dack 1953, S. 79). Da die Aufteilung des Fayyūm keine pharaonischen Vorläufer kennt, sind die Termini *tny.t* und *ʿt* neu geschaffen. So verwundert der Begriff *tny.t*, der in ähnlich großräumigem Sinn im administrativ-geographischen Bereich bis dahin unbekannt ist. Er dürfte eine direkte Übersetzung des Wortes μερίς darstellen. Andere Verwendungsweisen außerhalb des Fayyūm sind auch in griechisch-römischer Zeit nicht geläufig.[8] Eine Eins-zu-Eins-Zuordnung der beiden Wörter ist also gegeben. Die in griechischen Texten nicht bezeugten Toparchien lauteten demotisch wie im übrigen Ägypten *ʿ(.wy).w*, belegt sind allerdings nur die *ʿ(.wy).w bnr* (s. Reymond 1973, S. 13f. und 103f.). In römischer Zeit bleiben die drei μερίδες bzw. *tny.t* bestehen. Auf niederer Ebene finden sich in griechischen Texten zahlreiche Toparchien, die durchnumeriert sind, also den pagi im übrigen Ägypten entsprechen dürften. Hierfür ist kein demotisches Äquivalent bezeugt.

Für gauübergreifende Verwaltungseinheiten findet sich nur für die Thebais der Terminus *tš n Nw.t*, der bereits genannt wurde und der keinem Zweifel unterliegt. Als weitere Bezeichnung desselben Gebiets wurde *Tꜣ-šd-rs* in die Diskussion eingebracht. Dem sind allerdings gewisse Vorbehalte entgegenzusetzen. Zum einen findet sich dieser Begriff vorwiegend in Texten, auch demotischen Texten, pharaonischer Zeit (s. z.B. P. Louvre E. 7845A, P. Berlin P. 13582 und öfter). Zum anderen ist er in ptolemäischer Zeit nur in dem schon besprochenen Beleg eines Schreibers des *tš n Nw.t Tꜣ-šd-rs* und in Papyri aus Elephantine anzutreffen. In letzteren scheint ein *pꜣ Tꜣ-šd-rs* einem *ḥr.y Nw.t*, einem leitenden Beamten (hierzu s.u.) der Thebais, untergeordnet zu sein (P. Berlin P. 13543; s.

7. Die Vorschläge de Cenivals, *ʿt mḥ* als τοπαρχία ἄνω und *ʿt rs* als τοπαρχία κάτω zu interpretieren (1968, S. 48, und 1980, S. 201) leuchten nicht ein. Es werden nämlich jeweils die nördliche Toparchie als κάτω und die südliche als ἄνω bezeichnet; vgl. hierzu die Einteilung des Oxyrhynchitischen Gaues in Gomaà, Müller-Wollermann und Schenkel 1991, S. 20–22.

8. Vgl. aber Θερμουθέωνος μερίς im Oxyrhynchites: *DGT* II, S. 269.

Zauzich 1978). Dies bedeutet zum einen, daß *Tꜣ-šd-rs* und *tš n Nw.t* nicht identisch sein können — der oberste Beamte von *Tꜣ-šd-rs*, denn nur dies kann *pꜣ Tꜣ-šd-rs* meinen, kann nicht Untergebener eines leitenden Beamten desselben Gebiets sein. Zum anderen aber besteht oberhalb der Gauebene und unterhalb der Thebais keine weitere feste Verwaltungseinheit.[9] Also kann *pꜣ Tꜣ-šd-rs* nur entweder ein unspezifischer Ausdruck sein, was unwahrscheinlich ist, da ein spezifischer Verwaltungsbeamter genannt ist, oder *Tꜣ-šd-rs* sollte eine traditionelle Gau- oder Gebietsbezeichnung darstellen. In diesem Fall läge es nahe, den Gau von Syene oder die ihn umfassende Gegend so zu umschreiben. Für andere gauübergreifende Verwaltungseinheiten wie die Heptanomia oder das Delta sind keinerlei spezifische Termini bezeugt. Dies mag zum einen damit zusammenhängen, daß demotische Texte aus Mittelägypten und dem Delta relativ selten sind, hauptsächlich aber wohl damit, daß die Texte der höchsten Verwaltungsebene vorwiegend in Griechisch abgefaßt sind.

Der zweite Teil der Überlegungen — neben den Termini für Verwaltungseinheiten — betrifft die damit konstruierten Beamtentitel. Da ein und dieselben Personen sowohl in griechischen als auch in demotischen Texten auftreten können, scheint sich hier eine einzigartige Möglichkeit zu bieten, Eins-zu-Eins-Zuordnungen vorzunehmen. Jedoch zeigt sich recht bald, daß die hierin gesetzten Hoffnungen trügen. Die tatsächlichen Doppelnennungen sind weit geringer an Zahl, als man erwarten könnte. Nicht in Betracht gezogen werden sollen im folgenden griechische Beamtentitel, die transliteriert im Demotischen wiedergegeben werden wie z.B. στρατηγός (hierzu s. Clarysse 1987, S. 9ff.); sie werfen kaum Probleme auf. Gemeint sind vielmehr demotische Wörter ägyptischer Provenienz, die zumeist sehr unspezifisch erscheinen wie z.B. *sḥn* oder *ḥr.y*. In bezug auf *sḥn* haben Peremans und Van't Dack für die Ptolemäerzeit sehr klar aufgezeigt, daß einfaches *sḥn* einem οἰκονόμος entspricht, während *sḥn mꜣꜥ* "Orts-*sḥn*" einen ἄρχων bezeichnet, sei es ein Nomarch, Meridarch, Toparch oder Komarch, je nach dem, wie *sḥn mꜣꜥ* im folgenden näher spezifiziert ist (1953, S. 95ff.). Für die römische Zeit fehlen meines Wissens die Belege, um irgendwelche Aussagen zuzulassen. Problematischer ist die Bestimmung des *pꜣ ḥr.y*, zu dem verschiedenenorts bereits Überlegungen angestellt wurden (Smith und Tait 1984, S. 48; Van't Dack 1988, S. 285–87). Am häufigsten belegt ist der *pꜣ ḥr.y Nw.t*.[10] Die Schlüsselfigur hierzu ist ein *Ḥrmyꜣs pꜣ ḥr.y Nw.t*, der auf einem Holztäfelchen aus dem Jahre 110 v.Chr. aus Gabalain als Empfänger von Strafzahlungen genannt ist (DH Straßburg 13, s. Kaplony-Heckel 1966, S. 143f. und Tafeln 38f.). Dieser Mann ist mit Sicherheit identisch mit einer gleichnamigen Person, die in gleicher Angelegenheit in einem griechischen Papyrus aufgeführt wird und dort den Titel ὁ ἐπὶ τῶν προσόδων trägt (P. gr Amherst II 31, s. Betrò 1984, S. 41ff.). Die Titel *pꜣ ḥr.y Nw.t* und ὁ ἐπὶ τῶν προσόδων sind also als äquivalent zu betrachten. Letzterer bezeichnet einen leitenden Finanzbeamten und tritt seit dem 2. Jh. v.Chr. gerne zu dem des Strategen hinzu. Sein Funktionsbereich ähnelt dem des Thebarchen, der gleichfalls fiskalische Aufgaben hat. Der Titel Θηβάρχης würde sicherlich ein geeigneteres Pendant zu *pꜣ ḥr.y Nw.t* darstellen, aber solange die Identität von ὁ ἐπὶ τῶν προσόδων und Θηβάρχης nicht restlos geklärt ist, sollte die textlich nachweisbare Gleichsetzung von *pꜣ ḥr.y Nw.t* und ὁ ἐπὶ τῶν προσόδων beibehalten werden.

Als weiteres Problem stellt sich hier zudem wieder die Frage, ob mit *Nw.t* Theben oder die Thebais gemeint ist, ob es sich also bei *Ḥrmyꜣs* um einen Beamten von Theben oder der Thebais handelt. In beiden Texten sind aber die jeweiligen Titel die einzigen, die genannt sind, und lassen somit keine Deutung zu. *Ḥrmyꜣs* könnte jedoch noch weitere Titel besessen haben, die nur in diesem Kontext nicht genannt sind. Es sind denn auch in anderen griechischen Texten noch eine Reihe weiterer *Ḥrmyꜣs* belegt mit weiteren Titeln, u.a. Stratege und Nomarch des Thebanischen, Pathyritischen, und Latopolitischen Gaues (s. Mooren 1975, S. 249 [Index], in erster Linie kommt Nr. 0122 in Frage.). Die Gleichsetzung dieser untereinander und mit unserem *Ḥrmyꜣs* ist jedoch problematisch und bleibe dahingestellt. Angenommen aber, der Gaufürst der drei eben genannten Gaue sei identisch mit unse-

9. Daß einzelne Beamte mehrere Gaue gleichzeitig verwalten, ist davon unbenommen.

10. Zu den Belegen s. Van't Dack 1988.

rem *Ḥrmyꜣs*, d.h. *pꜣ ḥr.y Nw.t* bezeichne einen Finanzbeamten des Thebanischen Gaues und nicht einen der Thebais, so sollte doch verwundern, daß ausgerechnet dieser Titel als einziger genannt ist, wo es sich im Text jeweils um eine Angelegenheit in Gabalain handelt und *Ḥrmyꜣs* auch Gaufürst des Pathyrites war. Ein Beamter der Thebais aber, der finanzielle Angelegenheiten im Pathyrites regelt, ist hingegen durchaus denkbar. Die Indizien sprechen also dafür, in *pꜣ ḥr.y Nw.t* einen Beamten der Thebais zu sehen — J. Thomas bezeichnet ihn als niederen Strategen (1975b, S. 40f.). Diese Annahme wird gestützt durch die Belege des *pꜣ ḥr.y Nw.t* in den bereits erwähnten von Zauzich herausgegebenen Elephantine-Papyri (P. Berlin P. 15522, P. Berlin P. 13543). Dort ist er offenbar einem *pꜣ Tꜣ-šd-rs* vorgesetzt. Was immer letzterer im einzelnen auch sein mag, einen Finanzbeamten der Thebais anzunehmen liegt hier näher als einen Nomarchen des Thebanischen Gaues. Wenn nun *pꜣ ḥr.y Nw.t* ein Finanzbeamter der Thebais ist, stellt sich anschließend die Frage, was ein *pꜣ ḥr.y tš* ist. Der einzige Beleg, der zu dieser Fragestellung inhaltlich etwas abwirft, zeigt wiederum, daß er mit finanziellen Angelegenheiten befaßt ist (P. U.C. 31906, s. Smith und Tait 1984, S. 43–49). Welcher griechische Titel ihm entspricht, muß dahingestellt bleiben. Die übrigen Belege dieses Typs lassen vom Kontext her überhaupt keine Deutung zu. Festgehalten werden kann also nur, daß ein *pꜣ ḥr.y* wohl die Finanzoberhoheit über das Gebiet, das er verwaltet, ausübt.

Als Fazit ergibt sich, daß griechische Termini für geographische Verwaltungseinheiten im Demotischen in der Regel mit nur einem Wort wiedergegeben werden, griechische Beamtentitel hingegen oft mit mehreren. Dies mag u.a. damit zusammenhängen, daß die territorialen Einheiten in griechisch-römischer Zeit seltener einem Wechsel unterworfen waren als der zugehörige Beamtenapparat. Wechsel in letzterem wurde aber im Griechischen durch gleich bleibende Termini häufig kaschiert, man denke nur an die Funktionserweiterung beim στρατηγός. Das Ägyptische dagegen kann sich diesem Wechsel durchaus in anderer Weise anpassen. Verwiesen sei auf die verschiedenen Wiedergabemöglichkeiten von στρατηγός. Und es steht nicht an, in der demotischen Terminologie mehr Konsistenz zu erwarten, als von der Sachlage her gegeben war (s. hierzu A. Samuel 1966, S. 213–29, bes. S. 229).

ANHANG: BELEGE ZUR DISTRIBUTION VON *tš* UND *qḥ* IN VERBINDUNG MIT GAUNAMEN

tš n Nb:	P. Heidelberg 723
tš Dbꜣ:	P. Elephantine I, P. Elephantine V
tš n Pr-Ḥwt-Ḥr:	*passim*
tš n Hb:	Devauchelle und Wagner 1984, II, S. 18; Spiegelberg 1914a, S. 68f. und Tafel III
tš n Wḥe:	Spiegelberg 1914a, S. 68f. und Tafel III
tš Ḫmnw:	DP Michaelides A
tš n Ḥwt-nn-nsw:	P. Mallawi 483
tš ꜣrsynꜣ / tš n ỉm:	*passim*
tš Mn-nfr:	P. Berlin P. 13575
tš n Wn-ḫm:	P. Innsbruck
tš Šʿr:	P. Louvre E. 3334
qḥ Qb.t:	*passim*
qḥ Ḫn-Mnw:	Spiegelberg 1914a, S. 68f. und Tafel III; 1904, S. 160–62
qḥ Syw.t:	*passim*

CHAPTER 27

DEMOTIC AND GREEK OSTRACA IN THE THIRD CENTURY B.C.

BRIAN MUHS
The University of Pennsylvania

The Demotic script came into use in the seventh century B.C., but Demotic ostraca were rare until the third century B.C. Then between 275 B.C. and 225 B.C. Demotic ostraca became relatively common, particularly at Elephantine and Thebes, but also at other Upper Egyptian sites. After 225 B.C. Demotic ostraca became rare again until the second century B.C.[1]

Most of these third century B.C. Demotic ostraca are receipts for the payment of taxes. The use of receipts in Egypt was probably not a Ptolemaic innovation, since some Demotic receipts on papyri appear already in the sixth century B.C (listed in Thissen 1980, pp. 105–25). However, the relatively widespread use of receipts on ostraca in the third century B.C. may be related to the introduction of tax farming to Egypt by the Ptolemies.[2] Although Ptolemaic tax farmers merely underwrote the collection of taxes, in contrast to their predecessors in fourth century B.C. Athens who actually collected them, they still had an interest in maximizing the amount of tax collected and hence their profits (see Rostovtzeff 1941, pp. 327–30 and Bingen 1978a). The use of receipts on ostraca may then have developed to protect the taxpayers from overzealousness or even fraud on the part of the tax farmers.

The relative lack of Demotic ostraca after 225 B.C. may be due in large part to the revolt in the Thebaid between 205 B.C. and 186 B.C. However, it may be significant that the number of ostraca seems to diminish well before the beginning of the revolt.

Among the third century B.C. Demotic ostraca from Elephantine and Thebes, the most common receipts are for the *ḥḏ nḥb* or 'yoke tax,' the *swn nḥḥ* or 'price of oil,' and the *ḥḏ ḥmꜣ* or 'salt tax.' Receipts for these taxes are equally common at Elephantine and Thebes. Receipts for the *ḥḏ ʿrṱ* or 'forced labor tax'[3] and the *ḥḏ nḥy* or 'ivory tax' are common, but are found only at Elephantine. Receipts for the *ḥḏ mr ḫꜣs.t* or 'burial tax' are common, but are found primarily at Thebes. Other rarer receipts include those for the *tn in-šn* or 'veil tax,' the *ḥḏ ʿwy* or 'house tax,' the *ḥḏ ḥnk.t* or

1. Pestman (1967, pp. 2–8) cites two ostraca between 325 B.C. and 275 B.C., 110 ostraca between 275 B.C. and 225 B.C., six ostraca from between 225 B.C. and 175 B.C., 224 ostraca 175 B.C. and 75 B.C., and seven ostraca between 75 B.C. and 25 B.C. I have seen about 175 published third century B.C. Demotic ostraca from Elephantine and about 160 published third century B.C. Demotic ostraca from Thebes. In addition, I have examined about fifty unpublished third century B.C. Demotic ostraca from Thebes in the Oriental Institute collection and about twenty unpublished third century B.C. Demotic ostraca are described in Dr. George Hughes' *Catalog of Demotic Texts in the Brooklyn Museum* (unpublished manuscript).
2. Suggested to me by Dr. Robert Ritner.
3. Not 'scroll tax': see Devauchelle 1983, p. 32 and Shelton 1988a, p. 137.

'beer tax,' and the *ḥḏ tgy* or 'fruit tax.'[4] This variety of taxes differs from that found in contemporary tax registers from the Faiyum, which are dominated by the 'salt tax.' The absence of receipts for payments in kind, particularly grain receipts, also contrasts with later periods, when they become quite common.

The form of these receipts is very terse, usually only naming the taxpayer, the amount brought by the taxpayer, the tax for which it is brought, the scribe or scribes, and the date. They virtually never name the person or institution receiving the payment, for example, or any other additional information.

There are, of course, exceptions to this rule. The receipts for the *ḥḏ mr ḫ3s.t* or 'burial tax' name the person or persons being interred in the necropolis, as well as the person or institution which presumably receives the payment, which is the *mr ḫ3s.t* or 'overseer of the necropolis.' The most frequently named *mr ḫ3s.t* or 'overseer of the necropolis' is *Imn-rwš s3 Twtw*. In addition to *mr ḫ3s.t* or 'overseer of the necropolis,' he is also called the *rt* or 'representative' of *P3-di-Imn-nsw-t3.wy*, who is in turn called the *mr šn* or 'lesonis-priest,' the *ʿ3 n pr* or 'majordomo,' and possibly the *rt n pr Mnṯ* or 'representative of the estate of Mont.' The last suggests that the *ḥḏ mr ḫ3s.t* or 'burial tax' was ultimately paid to a temple rather than to the state, a conclusion which is supported by receipts for 'burial taxes' in which the phrase *r ḥw.t-nṯr* or 'for the temple' occurs where one would normally find the name of the tax (see Malinine 1961, pp. 137ff. and Wångstedt 1974–75, pp. 7–43).

Greek ostraca became relatively common in Egypt at about the same time as Demotic ostraca. Those from Upper Egypt include a large number of receipts for the payment of taxes, frequently with Demotic subscriptions. About half of these Greek and Greek-Demotic receipts are for the ἁλικῆς or 'salt tax'; the remainder represent a wide variety of less well attested taxes.[5] This variety of taxes differs from that found on purely Demotic receipts, but resembles that found on contemporary tax registers from the Faiyum insofar as they are also dominated by the 'salt tax.'

Unlike the Demotic receipts, the Greek and Greek-Demotic receipts provide the name of the tax collector, who usually but not always has a Greek name. Studies of Greek and Greek-Demotic receipts for the ἁλικῆς or 'salt tax' have shown that individual tax collectors are usually well attested for a few years, and then disappear. They have also shown that individual tax collectors regularly employed the same scribes to sign the Demotic subscriptions on their receipts (Remondon 1952, pp. 1–15 and Shelton 1988b, pp. 15–18). However, it should also be noted that the same scribes regularly sign purely Demotic receipts for the *ḥḏ ḥm3* or 'salt tax' in the same years. Clearly the same offices produced both the Demotic and the Greek receipts, at least in the case of the 'salt tax.'

4. From Elephantine there are twelve receipts for the *ḥḏ ʿrṯ* or 'forced labor tax,' one receipt for the *ḥḏ mr ḫ3s.t* or 'burial tax,' twenty-eight receipts for the *ḥḏ nḥb* or 'yoke tax,' forty-nine receipts for the *swn nḥḥ* or 'price of oil,' twenty receipts for the *ḥḏ nḥy* or 'ivory tax,' and forty-four receipts for the *ḥḏ ḥm3* or 'salt tax.' From Thebes there are fifty-eight receipts for the *ḥḏ mr ḫ3s.t* or 'burial tax,' thirty-nine receipts for the *ḥḏ nḥb* or 'yoke tax,' thirty-four receipts for the *swn nḥḥ* or 'price of oil,' and forty-one receipts for the *ḥḏ ḥm3* or 'salt tax.' From Elephantine and Thebes together there are three receipts for the *tn in-šn* or 'veil tax,' four receipts for the *ḥḏ ʿwy* or 'house tax,' ten receipts for the *ḥḏ ḥnk.t* or 'beer tax,' and four receipts for the *ḥḏ tgy* or 'fruit tax.' Taxes for which there are only one or two receipts have been omitted.

5. I have seen 127 published third century B.C. Greek and Greek-Demotic receipts on ostraca from Upper Egypt, and six unpublished examples in the Oriental Institute collection, of which fifty-eight have Demotic subscriptions, many of them unpublished. Sixty-four of these receipts are for the ἁλικῆς or 'salt tax,' eleven are for 'the tax of month ×,' five are for the ερεῶν or 'wool tax,' five are for ναύβια, a volume used to measure earth moved, presumably during compulsory labor, four are for the νιτρικῆς or 'soda tax,' four are for ἐλαίου or 'oil,' three are for the ἀπομοίρας, paid in wine, and three are for πυροῦ, paid in wheat. There are receipts for even rarer taxes, of which some may be alternate names for more common taxes.

So far these Demotic and Greek receipts on ostraca have been discussed as sources of information about the administration that issued them. However, they can also be used as sources of information about the taxpayers to whom they were issued. Admittedly, individual receipts do not provide much information about a taxpayer, but it is not uncommon to find several receipts belonging to the same taxpayer, particularly among the Demotic ostraca.[6]

These ostraca 'archives' are quite informative. The appearance of receipts for the *ḥḏ mr ḫ3s.t* or 'burial tax' in several Theban ostraca archives, for example, suggests a funerary occupation for the owners of these receipts, and indeed in a few cases they are explicitly titled *w3ḥ-mw* or 'choachyte.' The appearance of several owners of Theban ostraca archives together on lists of people on ostraca similarly suggests that they were members of the same small community, rather than a random sample of the presumably large population of Thebes.

Surprisingly, at least four of these Theban ostraca archives belong to people also named on Theban papyri from the third century B.C., not merely as witnesses, but as contracting parties. The papyri deal for the most part with the purchase or inheritance of houses and tombs. The numbers of tombs involved suggests that they were not for personal or familial use, but were instead a source of income, presumably in return for carrying out funerary rituals, an interpretation consistent with the title *w3ḥ-mw* or 'choachyte' occasionally given on the ostraca. The title usually given on the papyri, however, is *wn n Imn-ipy n pr-imnṯ Niw.t* or 'pastophore of Amenope in the west of Thebes,' a title often associated with but not the same as the title 'choachyte' (see Schönborn 1976). The locations of the houses is usually given as the 'Northern Quarter of Thebes,' either 'in the House of the Cow' or 'to the west of the temenos of the Temple of Mont Lord of Thebes,' although one group of papyri, the archive of Psemminis son of Bel, also deals with houses in Djeme, modern Medinet Habu. In fact, the lists of neighbors given to identify the houses makes it clear that most of the people mentioned in these papyri were neighbors, a conclusion consistent with the appearance of several of these people together on lists of people on ostraca.

I would like to suggest that the concentration of 'choachytes' and 'pastophores' in this community may be due to its location near the temple of Mont at Karnak. As I noted earlier, there is some evidence suggesting that the administration of the necropolis was run by a temple, specifically the temple of Mont. If this suggestion is correct, it would perhaps not be surprising to find a large concentration of 'choachytes' and 'pastophores' in the neighborhood.

6. Among the 220 Demotic ostraca from third century B.C. Thebes that I have seen, 140 belong to twenty-five individuals named on more than one Demotic ostracon. Among the 133 third century B.C. Greek ostraca from Upper Egypt, particularly Thebes, that I have seen, sixteen belong to four individuals named on more than one Greek ostracon. Five more belong to three individuals also named on Demotic ostraca.

CHAPTER 28

REPORT ON NEW DEMOTIC TEXTS FROM TUNA-EL-GEBEL

ABDEL-HALIM NUR-EL-DIN
Cairo University

During the cleaning operations and excavations undertaken by the archaeological mission of Munich University in Tuna-el-Gebel from 1979 to 1988, and by both Cairo University and Munich University since 1989, various materials were found, the most interesting of which were the coffins of the ibises, whether of stone or wood or in the form of jars.

Professor Sami Gabra, when excavating in Tuna-el-Gebel in the name of Cairo University in the 1930s, found thousands of ibis coffins, among which a few were inscribed in Demotic. Among the Demotic texts found at that time was the relatively long list of proper names registered on what seems to be a wooden coffin lid, which is now kept in the museum of the Faculty of Archaeology at Cairo University. This is the text which I shed light upon at the Third International Congress of Demotists at Cambridge in 1987. It consists of twenty-six lines on the recto and fifteen lines on the verso and is characterized by the almost consistent presence of the word *pꜣ nṯr* preceding proper names. In the same Cambridge congress, Professor Thissen, who was one of the participants in the Munich Archaeological Mission at Tuna-el-Gebel, informed me of the presence of somewhat similar texts written on ibis coffins discovered at Tuna by the Munich Mission and was kind enough to send me xeroxed copies of the facsimiles he made of these texts. Our joint mission working at Tuna since 1989 also came up with a great number of various kinds of ibis sarcophagi which also bear Demotic inscriptions.

Apart from the long text of the Cairo University Museum which might represent an official register of persons concerned, in one way or another, with the mummified ibises, our texts, as well as those of Thissen, are of simple form which could be summed up as follows:

1) *Wsir pꜣ-hb pꜣ nṯr* + a proper name
2) *ḥꜣ.t-sp* + *pꜣ nṯr* + proper names + *r in.w r Ḫmnw*
3) *pꜣ nṯr* + proper name(s) + *n-tr.t* (by the hand of) + proper name
4) *pꜣ nṯr* + proper name + *sẖ*
5) *pꜣ nṯr* + proper name
6) just a proper name

Apart from these inscribed coffins in which *pꜣ nṯr* followed by a proper name is a common feature, thousands of uninscribed ibis coffins also were found.

The breeding of the ibises and the different aspects of their cult, such as their feeding, death, mummification, and burial, have already been discussed by many scholars (Preisigke and Spiegelberg 1914, p. 33; Ray 1976, pp. 136ff.; de Cenival 1977, pp. 24ff.; and Smelik 1979, pp. 225–41), while the type of inscriptions we are dealing with have never been interpreted.

These inscriptions raise the following questions:

1) Who is *pꜣ ntr* in these texts?

2) Who are the persons mentioned after *pꜣ ntr*?

3) Why are some coffins inscribed while others are not?

As to who is the *pꜣ ntr*, I had suggested, at the Cambridge meeting in 1987 — but with some hesitation, that it indicates the ibis god itself. Since then, I have studied two other texts, from Tuna also, which might support this point of view. The first of these texts, in the Cairo University Museum reads: *Wsir pꜣ hb pꜣ ntr Pꜣ-tj-Ḫnm (sꜣ) Srtn*, "the deceased ibis, i.e. the god (of) *Pꜣ-tj-Ḫnm* son of *Srtn*." The second text, of which I have only a photograph, was found in the 1989 excavation season. It reads: *[...] pꜣ hb pꜣ ntr Ṯḥwtj-i-ir-tj=s sꜣ Ṯꜣj-n-im=w*, "The ibis, the god (of) *Ṯḥwtj-i-ir-tj=s* son of *Ṯꜣj-n-im=w*." The word *pꜣ ntr* in the first example seems to be in apposition to *Wsir* and *pꜣ hb*, while in the second example it is in apposition to *pꜣ hb*. Hence, we might conclude that *pꜣ ntr* is the *pꜣ hb* and that both represent the deceased or mummified ibis.

As for the second question concerning the identity of the persons named after *pꜣ ntr*, we notice in these inscriptions three categories of proper names: a name following *pꜣ ntr*, another sometimes following *r-in=w*, and a third following either *r-tr.t* or *sẖ*.

Three recommendation letters, found at Tuna-el-Gebel (see Zaghloul 1985) addressed by the priests of the temple of *Ṯḥwtj* at Tuna, to three persons living in the Faiyum, mention that the *wꜥb n Ṯḥwtj* and the *stmw n nꜣ hb.w* are asked to go to Hierakonpolis and other places in the Faiyum to collect and bring the mummies of the holy ibises to their resting place in Tuna. The text reads: *r in pꜣ hb ḫpr pꜣj=f wḏꜣ r Ḫmnw pꜣj=f ꜥ.wj-ḥtp*: "to bring the ibis who has died (whose death has happened) to *Ḫmnw* his resting place."

We know from previous studies concerned with the ibis cult that the *wꜥb n Ṯḥwtj* and the *stm.w-ꜥš* were the people in charge of breeding and caring for the living and dead ibises. It is clear from the previous text, that they were also charged with collecting their dead bodies from different localities in order to bring them to their burying place at Tuna-el-Gebel.

According to this text we might conclude that — in the texts under study — the name usually following *r in=w* or *r tr.t* must be that of the *wꜥb.w* or the *stmw-ꜥš*. This conclusion leaves only one alternative as to the name after *pꜣ ntr*: it must have been the name of the person dedicating the sacred animal to the god in order to receive his blessings and to immortalize his name (Preisigke and Spiegelberg 1914, p. 33; de Cenival 1977, pp. 24–29; and Smelik 1979, pp. 233–34).

This conclusion might help to clarify our third question: why are some coffins inscribed, while others are not?

Since the burying of ibises happened only once a year and the number of buried ibises at each yearly event ranged from hundreds to thousands, it would be possible to suggest that the inscribed coffins were those which had been dedicated by individuals, while the uninscribed ones were those of dead ibises which were mummified and buried without being dedicated, since the number of dedicators must have been much smaller than the number of buried ibises.

CHAPTER 29

THE BASILIKOS GRAMMATEUS

JOHN F. OATES
Duke University

In this paper[1] I wish to examine some aspects of the office of βασιλικὸς γραμματεύς as this bureaucratic designation occurs during the Ptolemaic administration of Egypt from the middle of the third century B.C. to the reforms of Augustus in 31 B.C. My concentration will be on the Greek documents of the third century B.C. with some indication of the importance of the Demotic evidence of the period and of both the Greek and Demotic evidence of the later Ptolemaic period. My remarks are reflections of problems that have bothered me in editing a series of Duke texts and do not represent even what could be called a "work in progress."

I hope, nonetheless, to raise questions which the evidence presents and which, if valid, call for a reevaluation of the office, duties, and status of the basilikos grammateus and, by extension, of other officials, e.g. the strategos and the oikonomos, in the Ptolemaic bureaucratic system. It seems to me that the evidence for this period shows a much different conceptualization than we have been inclined to impose on it in the past. Specifically we have unthinkingly used the model of the situation during the period of Roman domination to schematize that of the Ptolemaic period. A rereading of the evidence informed by a different point of view and different questions will, I believe, lead to a different appreciation of the nature and functioning of officials in the Ptolemaic system. This system was much less rigid and much more flexible than we have believed in the past and its dynamics more individualistic.

Let us then turn to the texts, primarily the Greek texts of the third century B.C., and examine what we find there. First we can observe that all βασιλικοὶ γραμματεῖς have Egyptian names and are clearly ethnically and culturally Egyptian; they are bilingual as well. (This situation obtains for the entire Ptolemaic period.) Furthermore, no one has ever questioned that the βασιλικὸς γραμματεύς is a translation of the Demotic for "scribe of the Pharaoh." This last fact is significant and I will return to it below.

There are approximately twenty-five to thirty Greek texts (see the *Appendix*) of the third century B.C. which mention the βασιλικὸς γραμματεύς or the βασιλικοὶ γραμματεῖς. I have excluded those mentioned in circulars addressed to various officials in numerous places, such as the Revenue Laws and which mention the βασιλικοὶ γραμματεῖς among other functionaries. I have excluded as

1. This paper remains virtually the same as that delivered to the Symposium "Life in a Multi-Cultural Society" at the Oriental Institute on September 6, 1990. I have added a few references and the *Appendix*. These two features do not make this presentation a work of scholarship and the disclaimer in the text remains valid. I would like to thank William H. Willis and Zola Packman for their comments and help. I am grateful to Klaus Maresch for discussion of the question and for making available unpublished Cologne material.

well dubious and uncertain readings. I have not attempted to come to terms with all of those which occur in the Petrie papyri.

There are certain characteristics of these documents which I wish to stress and which I will try to convince the reader are significant in reordering the thinking about the βασιλικὸς γραμματεύς. First, in a number of cases more than one basilikos grammateus appears and these basilikoi grammateis seem to be acting together. Second, it is extremely rare to find a basilikos grammateus associated with a geographical area and specifically with a nome. In numbers, there are seven cases where βασιλικὸς γραμματεύς are mentioned and seem to be working together (*P. Cair. Zen.* III 59387, *PSI* V 502, *P. Zen. Pestm.* 18, *P. Hib.* I 98, *P. Eleph.* 24, and *P. Lille* 1 [= *P. Zen. Pestm.* A]; perhaps also *P. Cair. Zen.* III 59472) and thus about twenty cases where a singular βασιλικὸς γραμματεύς works alone. In only two cases are there specific indications that the function of the basilikos grammateus is tied to a geographical location. In one the expression τοῦ νομοῦ (BGU III 1006) is used and the other is definitely ambiguous (*P. Cair. Zen.* II 59236). In the Greek papyri of the second and first centuries B.C. there is only one instance where the basilikos grammateus is attached to a place among more than 100 citations.

As to the function of the basilikos grammateus I have not tried to define or place his role in specific terms and it appears dubious that such can be determined without reference to other members of the Ptolemaic bureaucracy. The importance of the office can be noted from two instances: one, where Pankestor cannot plant some land because the basilikoi grammateis have not yet measured it (*PSI* V 502) and the other, where Zenon is called upon to mediate a dispute between a newly landed cleruch and the basilikoi grammateis about the correct mode of measuring his grant (*P. Cair. Zen.* I 59132). Both cases attest to the importance of the office and its holders. Furthermore, the basilikoi grammateis seem to be the only members of the bureaucracy for whom knowledge of both Egyptian and Greek was a requisite. We must also remember the social and political importance of the "scribe" in pharaonic Egypt. Professor Zauzich (1968) has shown the continued importance in the Ptolemaic period for the Demotic evidence. Thus we can safely think of the basilikos grammateus as an important part of the Ptolemaic system even if we cannot now be precise about the role of the office and its holders.

The evidence in the Demotic texts does not change this picture. I have not conducted a systematic search for all such texts and as many scholars know such a search is not easy for the Greek papyrologist/historian who does not have a knowledge of Egyptian and who is not familiar with likely places of publication of such texts (see the *Appendix*). In the texts I have examined, a designation of place of competence is rarely used and clearly there is no systematic scheme for so identifying such scribes. One other question causes me difficulties; apparently officials are designated "scribe" when "scribe of Pharaoh" may be meant. I will undoubtedly need help in assessing the Demotic evidence on the point (Pestman 1989, pp. 137–58).

What do we make of this evidence to interpret the role of the basilikos grammateus in the Ptolemaic bureaucracy? For a fresh approach to such a question, we must first look at the traditional view. All who work in the texts and history of Greco-Roman period Egypt know that during the period of Roman domination of Egypt the basilikos grammateus was the second in command in each of the nomes of Egypt and could act *vice* the strategos, the nome governor. These basilikoi grammateis were Alexandrian citizens and frequently Roman citizens as well. They normally served a term of three years in office, often succeeding to the office of strategos. If they did not immediately fill the higher office, then they served as a strategos later on although not necessarily in the same nome. The term of the strategos was normally three years and some served terms in more than one nome. These strategoi were also Alexandrians and frequently Roman citizens as well. It is very likely that each of the strategoi had served a term as a basilikos grammateus prior to service as a governor. Thus, during the Roman period to at least the middle of the third century, the scheme was neat and regular, but we must ask if this scheme has any relevance to the situation of the Ptolemaic period.

The only study dedicated to the basilikos grammateus is a Berlin dissertation by Biedermann (1913). I have not seen this work, for it does not exist in any North American library. We all know that the author had at his disposal but a fraction of the evidence available today and we know that he wrote at a time when most papyrologists/historians were not sensitive to (nor had enough evidence of) the great differences between the Ptolemaic system and that inaugurated by Augustus and used (with modifications) for nearly 300 years. It is evident from the comments of later papyrologists and historians of the Ptolemaic period that Biedermann projected the Roman scheme, one basilikos grammateus to a nome and no more, back into the Ptolemaic period. He has been followed by every editor of Ptolemaic texts, particularly when they try to explain away multiple basilikoi grammateis and to rationalize the cases where a basilikos grammateus serves for some years, then another basilikos grammateus is cited, and then the first reappears. Biedermann was aware of plural basilikoi grammateis in individual documents but apparently did not attempt to essay an explanation. (He knew of only two such texts out of the great quantity, even then, from the period 300 B.C. to A.D. 300.) Subsequent editors have used a variety of explanations for multiple basilikoi grammateis. Either the term is used of multiple subordinates of the basilikos grammateus of the nome or the basilikoi grammateis of more than one nome are acting together.

I do not think such explanations are adequate. They are not supported by any explicit evidence and run contrary to the usual principles of interpreting documentary texts. I believe any explanation must account for the existence of multiple βασιλικοὶ γραμματεῖς acting together, for the lack of geographical designation in almost all Ptolemaic texts, and must attempt to see what connection obtains between the earlier Egyptian office of "scribe," particularly the "scribe of Pharaoh" and the basilikos grammateus. It is true that the evidence does not explicitly define the role and place of the basilikos grammateus in the bureaucracy, but it does certainly suggest that the previous interpretation and comments of papyrologists have been overly schematic and overly simplified.

Eventually the answers, if there are any clear ones, will be found in connection with study of other offices in the Ptolemaic system of management. I do believe we have applied overly rigid schemes seeking a tidy organizational structure. After all neither Ptolemy I nor his son Philadelphus (nor the wizard dioiketes Apollonios) used the services of a management consultant firm for organizational advice and would not have understood such practice.

If we abandon the oversimplified explanation of the role of the basilikos grammateus, we must accept the consequences for other officials. Here I would refer to the στρατηγός and the οἰκόνομος. Leon Mooren has argued that the strategos continued to have military functions along side any civil functions. Royce Morris and I (1985, pp. 243–47) published a Duke text of 138 B.C. in which a strategos is bringing troops to a garrison.[2] I would suggest in fact that there was no hard and fast division between civil and military functions of the strategos, that in an organizational sense the strategos and the nome were not a fixed relationship. Once again it may be that Roman restructuring has imposed itself upon us. This last situation needs more work asking different questions and, as of now, it is difficult to trace any functional relationship between the Ptolemaic and the Roman strategos.

As for the οἰκόνομος, we cannot blame the Romans for our view; the oikonomos disappears as an essential function long before the Romans arrive. In this case our interpretation is mostly colored by Rostovtzeff's understanding of *P. Tebt.* III 703, for Rostovtzeff argued that this text was

2. *P. Duke inv.* G1974.5. The text was presented by Morris at the Seventeenth International Congress of Papyrology in Naples in 1983 and was thus known and commented on by Mooren (1984, pp. 1217–25).

addressed to an oikonomos by the dioiketes and thus gives us a guide to the duties of this official. I can only say here that the purposes of *P. Tebt.* III 703 remain obscure to me and that along with Revenue Laws papyrus, it is more instructive of bureaucratic theory than of practice. In any case the oikonomos also needs much more work in light of different questions.

I do not claim that his paper has provided any definitive answers, but I do hope that the questions I have raised are seen as valid and that the Ptolemaic bureaucracy needs once again to be studied from a different angle and formulated without reference to the developments of the Roman era. I believe we will find the situation was much more fluid and not nearly so organized as we thought and I also believe that reexamination of the texts will bring us a much clearer understanding of the Hellenistic mind and its approach to governance.

APPENDIX: LIST OF DOCUMENTS FROM THE THIRD CENTURY B.C. MENTIONING THE βασιλικοὶ γραμματεῖς

BGU III 1006

P. Cair. Zen. II 59132, II 59236, III 59387, and IV 59890

P. Eleph. 24

P. Gurob 8

P. Hamb. I 24

P. Hib. I 72, 98, 108, 153, and 156

P. Köln inv. 20764

P. Lille 1, 2, 3, 4, 22, and 23

PSI V 502 and VI 621

P. Tebt. III 705

P. Zen. Pestm. 12, 13, and 18

SB I 4309

Perhaps also *P. Cair. Zen.* III 59472

For some of the Demotic texts, see Clarysse 1978, pp. 5–8, with reference to the work of de Cenival 1973 and Sottas 1921. Both of these latter works concern the Lille Demotic material. See also Peremans and Van't Dack 1950 and Mooren and Swinnen 1975.

CHAPTER 30

ARAMAIC-DEMOTIC EQUIVALENTS: WHO IS THE BORROWER AND WHO THE LENDER?*

BEZALEL PORTEN
The Hebrew University, Jerusalem

In 1968 (pp. 334–43), I compared the schemata of Demotic and Aramaic conveyances, loans, and marriage documents. The similarities between the two systems, particularly with regard to conveyances and loans, was most striking. Noticing the near synonymity of so many words and phrases, scholars have lined up on either side of the question of which language was the lender and which the borrower. Divisions have often been along partisan lines, with Egyptologists lining up on the side of Egyptian primacy and Semitists on the side of Aramaic.[1] Since 1968 I have continued to gather trans-linguistic equivalents and have come up with over sixty examples, in addition to a dozen or so Demotic loanwords in Aramaic[2] and a few Aramaic loanwords in Demotic.[3] The Tale of Bar Punesh, to be published jointly with Karl-Th. Zauzich,[4] shows that Aramean scribes knew Egyptian literature and the late Demotic fragments of Aḥiqar show that Egyptian scribes knew Aramaic literature (see Zauzich 1976, pp. 180–85). The bureaucratic letter of Pherendates (P. Berlin 13540), so cleverly reedited by George Hughes (1984, pp. 77–84), shows how an Egyptian scribe could write a translational Demotic. However, it is neither in the literary nor in the epistolary field that our data are the richest, bur rather in the legal. I thus wish to present some thirty-five terms and phrases which may be considered translational equivalents because they occur in the same context. We turn first to P. Rylands 1, one of the earliest Demotic contracts (644 B.C.E.), and note ten expressions which have Aramaic equivalents; then cull a half-dozen expressions from four

* I am grateful to Jan Johnson for her helpful suggestions.

1. For references see Porten (1968, p. 334), to which add Rabinowitz (1956).
2. We may cite the following: *qnḥnty* (*TAD* B3.10:9, 3.11:5) = *qnḥ ntr*, "the shrine of the god" (Couroyer 1954b, pp. 558f.); *šnṭꜣ* (*TAD* B3.8:11) = *šnt*, "skirt, robe" (*EDG*, 516); *tmy*/*tmꜣ* (*TAD* B3.4:8, 3.5:10) = *tmy*, "town" (*EDG*, 632f.) or = *tꜣ my.t*, "the (divine) way" (*EDG*, 152f.); *tḥyt* (*TAD* B3.7:10, 13, 3.10:4, 13, 15) = *tꜣ ẖyt,* "the courtyard" (Couroyer 1954a, p. 252); *tmwꜣnty* (*TAD* B3.10:9) = *tꜣ my.t ntr*, "the way of the god" (Couroyer 1954b, pp. 557f.); *tshrꜣ* (*TAD* C1.2:1) = *tꜣ shr.t*, "the ship" (*EDG*, 445); *tqm* (*TAD* A2.1:7, 2.2:13, 2.4:12, 2.5:5, 4.2:10; B2.6:16, 3.3:6, 3.8:20) = *tgm*, "castor oil" (*EDG*, 662); *try* (*TAD* B3.5:3, 6, 3.10:4, 11, 3.11:6, 3.12:13, 21) = *tꜣ ry.t*, "the room" (Couroyer 1954a, p. 252); *try rsy* (*TAD* B3.11:3) or *dryrsy* (*TAD* B3.10:3) = *tꜣ ry.t rs*, "the southern room" (Couroyer 1954a, p. 252); *tqbt*/*tqbh* (*TAD* A2.1:5, 2.2:11) = *tꜣ qbt*, "the vessel" (*EDG*, 535; Porten 1968, pp. 267f.); and the words *hyrꜣ* (*TAD* B3.2:3, 5, 9) and *pmṭn* (*TAD* B1.1:12, 15) which appear to be Egyptian but for which satisfactory etymologies have not yet been found. For Demotic loan words in the Carpentras funerary stele cf. Gibson 1975, pp. 120–22.
3. We may cite, e.g., *šbyṭ* (*TAD* B2.6:9, 3.8:9, 6.2:2) = *šbyṯ* "shawl(?)" (*EDG*, 498).
4. The unrestored text is to be found in Cowley (1923, No. 71); for the restored text see provisionally Porten (1986, pp. 14–16).

Egyptian loan documents and deeds of obligation;[5] and finally cite nineteen selected expressions from diverse documents. The first two sets of comparisons show the degree to which the parallels are integral to the document as a whole and not merely coincidental whereas the third set shows the wide dispersion these parallels have.

P. RYLANDS 1

The operative part of both the Demotic and Aramaic contracts may be divided into three sections: transaction, investiture, and guarantees. The ten parallel expressions are almost evenly distributed among these three sections. The transaction section affirms that "I gave you" the property and "you have caused my heart to be satisfied" with the price. The investure clause asserts that the property "is yours," including "every kind (of property) in the (whole) land" related to it, and no one else "shall be able to control it except you." The guarantee clauses provide a warranty ("cleansing") against any suit and reassert that the property "above (written) is still yours." He who sues "in the name of" the property shall not be able to require the subscribing witness to appear outside his own town. The ten Demotic expressions are listed below in the left column in the order in which they appear in P. Rylands 1 and the parallel Aramaic expressions (all from the fifth century B.C.E.[6]) are given in the right column:

1. *tỉ=(y) n=k*, "I gave to you" (line 1).	*yhbt lk*, "I gave to you" (*TAD* B2.3:3, 2.7:2, 3.5:2f., 3.7:3, 3.10:2f., 3.11:2, 5.1:2, 5.5:2f.). This is the standard Aramaic expression of conveyance.
2. *mtw=k s.t* (*mtw=k s*), "They are (it is) yours" (line 2).	*zylk hw*, "It is yours" (*TAD* B2.7:7, 3.5:4, 3.10:11); one of the two standard Aramaic expressions of investiture.
3. *nt nb* (*n nk.w*) *n pꜣ tꜣ* (*ḏr=f*), lit., "every which (of property) in the world (to its limit)" = "every kind of property in the whole world" (lines 3, 5f.).	*kl zy ʾyty lh ʿl ʾnpy ʾrʿʾ klh*, lit., "all that he has on the face of the earth, all of it" = "all that he has on the face of the whole earth" (*TAD* B2.6:19f.); a unique phrase summarizing the property of the husband.
4. *tỉ=k mtr ḥꜣt=y*, "You have satisfied my heart" (lines 3f.).	*hwtbt lbby*, "You have satisfied my heart" (*TAD* B2.2:11, 2.9:8, 5.6:2f.); a standard formula of quittance (cf. Muffs 1968, pp. 142–72).
5. *bn-ỉw rḫ*, "shall not be able" (line 4).	*lʾ ykhl* (*TAD* B2.1:6, 2.2:12), *lʾ ykl* (*TAD* B2.6:31, 2.7:11, etc.), "shall not be able." This is the standard term of non-entitlement, followed by a verb such as *grh*, "institute lawsuit" (*TAD* B3.2:4, etc.; see Rabinowitz 1956, pp. 104f).
6. *ỉr sḫ.t*, "control" (line 4). This and the expression above combine in the clause, *bn-ỉw rḫ ẖrṱ.w sn.w rmt nb n pꜣ tꜣ ỉnk ḥꜥ(=y) mỉt.t ỉr sḫ.t n-ỉm=w pꜣy=k bnr* "Children, brothers, any man in the land, I included, shall not be able to control them except you."	*šlyṭ*, "control" (*TAD* B2.1:11, 2.4:11, etc.); standard expression of entitlement. It occurs once in a clause reminiscent of the Demotic one: *lʾ ʾyty ly br wbrh ʾḥrnn ʾḥ wʾḥh wʾnth wʾyš ʾḥrn šlyṭ bʾrqʾ zk lhn ʾnty wbnyky ʿd ʿlm*, "I have no other son or daughter, brother or sister, or woman or other man who controls that land except you and your children forever" (*TAD* B2.3:10f.; see Rabinowitz 1956, pp. 136–38; Yaron 1961, p. 103).

5. Malinine 1953, Nos. 2 (abnormal Hieratic; to be dated to 570 B.C.E. and not 568), 3 (Demotic; 499 B.C.E.), 4–5 (Demotic; 487 B.C.E. and not 498).

6. Almost all are quoted from *TAD* A, *TAD* B, and *TAD* C.

7. *ỉnk ỉ-ỉr tỉ nʿ=f n=k*, "I will cause him to be cleansed (= cleared) for you" (line 5). There is either an error or scribal confusion here, because it is regularly the object, not the person, which is cleansed; of the person it is said *tỉ wy=f r-r.k*, "(I will) cause him to be far from you." In P. Michigan 3523:6f. the scribe commits a similar error: *ỉw(=y r) tỉ nʿ=f (r)-ḥr*[*=tn*], "I will cause him to be cleansed for [you]," followed correctly by *ỉw(=y)* ⸢*tm*⸣ *tỉ wy=f r-ḥr=tn*, "If I do not cause him to be far from you" (Cruz-Uribe 1985, pp. 8f., 64). Later documents regularly use the verb *wʿb*.	*ʾnqh* (*TAD* B1.1:10), *ʾpṣl* (*TAD* B3.2:9, 3.4:20), "I will cleanse" (For comparison between Demotic and Aramaic warranty clauses cf. Porten and Szubin 1982, pp. 126f.; see also Yaron 1961, p. 105)
8. *nt ḥry*, "which is (written) above" (lines 5, 6, 6); abbreviation of full formula *nt sẖ ḥry*.	*zy ktyb mnʿl*, "which is written above" (*TAD* B2.1:10, 13, 3.4:17f, 3.11:10, 15, etc.); expression used in final clauses to refer to object of contract mentioned earlier.
9. *ỉw mtw=k ʿn šʿ ḏt*, "(the object) still being yours forever" (line 6).	*zylk ʾpm* (*TAD* B2.1:11, 3.5:22), *zylk ʾm* (*TAD* B3.4:16, 19), "(the object) still being yours." The variant Aramaic terms are known to us almost exclusively from this clause and the translation is from context; "nonetheless, moreover" would also be possible. The *clausula salvatoria* is a standard clause to indicate that though the penalty is paid the property remains in the possession of the recipient (see Yaron 1961, pp. 122f.; Skaist 1983, pp. 31–41).
10. *n rn n*, "in the name of (the disputed object)" (line 6). Elsewhere we have the expression *n rn(=y)*, "in my name" (e.g. P. British Museum 10846A:4 = Cruz-Uribe 1985, No. 15; also p. 61).	*bšmy*, "in my name;" referring to a suit brought by a third party in the name of the alienor (*TAD* B2.10:12f.). In one document the scribe wrote *bšm ʾrqʾ zk*, "in the name of that land" and then emended the clause to read *bšmy ʿl ʾrqʾ zk*, "in my name about that land," the word *ʿl* having been added supralinearly (*TAD* B2.2:14; for comparison see Kutscher 1977, p. 242; Rabinowitz 1956, pp. 107f.).

LOAN CONTRACTS

We may paraphrase the six parallel expressions in the loan contracts as follows:

1. You gave to me such and such an amount.
2. I shall give/repay you such and such an amount (comparison noted by Malinine [1950, p. 2] and by Pierce [1972, p. 42]).
3. If I do not repay you on time, a monthly penalty will be exacted.
4. If I do not repay, you may take as pledge enumerated items
5. until you are paid in full (see also Pierce 1972, p. 126.).
6. I cannot claim to have paid you as long as you hold this document (see Rabinowitz 1956, pp. 104f. and Pierce 1972, pp. 144f).

The Demotic expressions are listed in the left column and the Aramaic in the right column:

11. *tỉ=k n=ỉ*, "you gave to me" (Malinine No. 3:2, 4:2).

yhbt ly (*TAD* B3.1:3, 3.13:3), *ntnt ly* (*TAD* B4.2:1), "you gave to me."

12. *ỉnk tỉ(=y) s n=k* (Malinine No. 2:3), *mtw=(y) tỉ.t n=k* (Malinine No. 3:3, [4:2]), "I shall give to you."

ʾšlm wʾntn lk, "I shall pay and give to you" (*TAD* B3.13:4).

13. *n ỉbd nb rnp.t nb.t nt-ỉw=w ỉr=w ỉr-n=y*, "in all months and all years that they will be with me" (Malinine No. 2:5, 3:5f, [4:4], 5:6).

kl šnn wyrḥn[, "all (the) months and years[...]" (*TAD* B7.1:8; Yaron 1961, p. 109).

14. *pr ḥm ḥm.t šry šr.t ḥt ḥmt ḥbs nḥ bt*, "house, slave, handmaiden, son, daughter, silver, bronze, clothing, oil, grain" (Malinine No. 2:6; cf. 3:8, [4:6], 5:8).

by zy lbnn ksp wdhb nḥš wprzl ʿbd wʾmh śʿrn kntn wkl zwn zy tškḥ ly, "brick house, silver or gold, bronze or iron, slave or handmaiden, barley, emmer, or any food which you will find (belonging) to me" (*TAD* B3.1:9f.); *by zy lbnn ʿbd wʾmh mʾn nḥš wprzl lbwš wʿbwr zy thškḥ ly*, "brick house, slave or handmaiden, bronze or iron vessel, clothing or grain which you will find (belonging) to me" (*TAD* B3.13:11).

15. *šʿ-tw=f mḥ=w n pꜣy=f ḥt nt ḥry ḥnʿ nꜣy=w ms.wt*, "until he has filled [them] (= paid in full) with his silver which is (written) above and its interest" (Malinine No. 5:8).

ʿd ttmlʾ bkspk wmrbyth, "until you are filled (=paid in full) with your silver and its interest" (*TAD* B3.1:11, 17f; see Kutscher 1977, p. 243).

16. *bn-ỉw(=y) rḫ dd tỉ(=y) n=k ỉt ms [n].ỉm=w ỉw pꜣy sḫ n-ḏr.ṱ=k*, "I shall not be able to say, 'I gave you grain (and) interest thereof' while this document is in your hand" (Malinine No. 3:8f; cf. 4:7f., 5:9).

wlʾ ʾkl ʾmr lk lm šlmtk bkspk wmrbyth wsprʾ znh bydk, "And I shall not be able to say to you, saying, 'I paid you your silver and its interest,' while this document is in your hand" (*TAD* B3.1:11f.).

SELECTED TERMS

There follow nineteen selected legal terms which are paralleled in both languages. One of the most plastic terms is "do, make" — *ỉr* in Demotic and *ʿbd* in Aramaic (Nos. 17-19 below):

17. *ỉw=f (ỉr) n=t pꜣ hp n pꜣy sḫ ḥm.t*, "he will do for her the law of this document of wife(hood)" (P. Berlin 13593:8 [Elephantine]); said of one who seeks to expel the woman from the house of her husband.

wyʿbd lh dyn sprʾ znh, "and he will do for her the law of this document" (*TAD* B2.6:31, 3.8:32); said of one who seeks to expel the woman from the house of her husband (see Kutscher 1977, p. 46).

18. *ỉr qnb.t ỉrm*, "do suit with PN (= go to court with him)" (P. Louvre E 3228c:12 [Malinine 1951, p. 159]).

dyn ʿbd ʿm, "do suit with PN (= go to court with him)" (*TAD* B2.3:27).

19. *ỉr sḫ*, "make (= prepare, write) a document" (*EDG*, 140).

ʿbd spr, "make (= prepare, write) a document" (*TAD* B3.10:22; see Kutscher 1977, p. 242).

20. *ỉwṱ ḏd qnb.t nbt (md.t nbt) n pꜣ tꜣ ỉrm=k*, "without citing any document (or any word) in the world with you" (P. Rylands 8:10); at the conclusion of a penalty clause (see Cruz-Uribe 1985, pp. 68f.).

wlʾ dyn wlʾ dbb, "without suit or process" (*TAD* B2.3:14, 21f., 2.4:15, etc.); at the conclusion of a penalty clause (see Kutscher 1977, pp. 239f.; Rabinowitz 1956, pp. 82, 107; and Yaron 1961, p. 109). The Aramaic clause is compact whereas the Demotic parallel is expansive.

21. *nt sḫ ḥr pꜣ sḫ n sʿnḫ*, "which is written on the document of maintenance" (P. Hermopolis Law Code 4:21).

zy ktyb ʿl spr ʾnttky, "which is written on your document of marriage" (*TAD* B3.11:7).

22. *bn-ỉw(=y) rḫ ỉn ḏmʿ ỉs ḏ[mʿ mȝwy]*, "I shall not be able to bring an old papyrus (or) a ne[w papyrus]" (P. Rylands 4:3; restoration supported by P. Vienna 10157:7 as corrected by Hughes [1984]).
lʾ yk(h)l yhnpq ʿlyk spr ḥdt wʿtyq, "He shall not be able to bring out against you a new or old document" (*TAD* B2.3:15f., 2.7:11f.).

23. *ỉw=f ʿrq n=f ỉw=w tỉ wy=f r=f*, "If (defendant) swears for him, they will make (the plaintiff) withdraw from him" (P. Hermopolis Law Code 8:22).
ymʾty ly ... wrḥqt mnky, "You swore to me ... and I withdrew from you" (*TAD* B2.8:5–8).

24. *pḥ*, "arrive, reach; come to PN as an heir's share" (*EDG*, 137).
whʾ znh ḥlqʾ zy mṭʾk bḥlq, "And behold, this is the portion which came to you as a portion" (*TAD* B2.11:3; cf. 5.1:34).

25. *ỉw=w šn pȝ rmt ỉ-ỉr ỉr pȝ sḫ*, "They will ask (= interrogate) the man who made the document" (P. Hermopolis Law Code 4:10).
ršynkm ʾḥr šʾyltm, "We brought suit against you. Then, you were asked (= interrogated)" (*TAD* B2.9:7; cf. 7.1:3, 7.2:6; 8.7:2, 9, 8.8:5, 8, 8.10:6).

26. *pȝ ỉ-ỉr tỉ s n=y (n) ỉwy.t n pr.w ỉw=y gm.ṯ=w r=f*, "(the one who) gave it (= the house) to me as a pledge for grain which I find against him" (P. Hermopolis Law Code 6:12; the concluding idiom was "otherwise unknown" to Hughes [1984, see his additional notes]).
šlyṭ bʿrbny ... wtlqḥ lk ... wʿbwr zy thškḥ ly, "(you) control my pledge ... and may take for yourself (various objects including) grain which you will find (belonging) to me" (*TAD* B3.13:10f; 3.1:17; cf. 4.6:11). Despite the juxtaposition of "pledge" and "find," the Demotic and Aramaic combine the terms differently: the Demotic claimant "finds" the object owed (= the grain) while the Aramaic creditor "finds" the pledge.

27. *dmḏ s 2 ỉw=w rȝ wʿ*, "total, 2 persons, they being one mouth" (Malinine No. 9:4 [abnormal Hieratic]); brother and sister sell inherited property jointly.
kl tryn kpm ḥd, "total, two, as one mouth" (*TAD* B3.12:11); husband and wife sell property jointly (see Couroyer 1954b, p. 559).

28. *mtw=k s n ṯȝy (n) pȝ hrw r-ḥry šʿ ḏt*, "It is yours from this day upward unto eternity (= forever)" (P. Loeb 44:3).
zylky hw mn ywmʾ znh ʿd ʿlm, "It is yours from this day unto eternity (= forever)" (*TAD* B3.5:4; see Yaron 1961, p. 116); a standard Aramaic investiture clause.

29. *ỉw(=y) r tỉ n=k ỉḥ(.t) sḫm.t r pȝy=s smt n ⸢ỉḥ(.t)⸣*, "I shall give to you a ... cow according to her likeness of a ⸢cow⸣' (P. Berlin 13571:8); stipulation in warranty clause upon failure to cleanse property.
nntn lk byt ldmt bytk, "we shall give you a house in the likeness of your house" (*TAD* B3.4:21); stipulation in defension clause upon failure to cleanse property (for discussion of these two parallel clauses see. Porten and Szubin 1982, pp. 126f.).

30. *wn mtw=k ʾrṭb sw 10 ... ỉ-ỉr-n=y*, "You have 10 ardab wheat ... against me (= I owe you 10 ardab wheat)" (P. Rylands 21:10f).
ʾyt lk ʿly ksp krš [ḥd], "You have against me silver, [one] karsh (= I owe you 1 karsh silver)" (*TAD* B4.5:3; cf. 4.6:3; Kutscher 1977, pp. 242f. [citing inexact parallel]; Rabinowitz 1956, p. 104 [inexact and confused]; Yaron 1961, pp. 93, 108).

31. [*mn*] *mtw=k sp ỉ-ỉr-n=y n-ỉm=w*, "You do not have a remainder of them against me (= I do not owe you any more)" (P. Hermopolis Law Code 4:18).
lʾ ʾštʾr ln ʿlyk mn dmyʾ, "there does not remain to us against you from the price (= you do not owe us any more)" (*TAD* B3.12:6; see J. J. Rabinowitz 1956, p. 109 who cited F. Ll. Griffith 1909, p. 120, clause 6 = p. 256, clause 6).

32. *ỉn-nȝ rmt sḫt rmt r qt*, "If a man prevents a man from building" (P. Hermopolis Legal Code 7:18).
lʾ ʾkhl ʾklʾnk lmbnh ... hn klytk ʾntn lk ksp, "I shall not be able to prevent you from building ... If I prevent you, I shall give you silver ..." (*TAD* B2.1:6f).

33. *nt ỉ-ỉwd=f ỉ-ỉwd Bs(-n)-Mw*, "which is between him and Besenmut" (Malinine No. 9:8 [abnormal Hieratic]); expression indicating joint property (the parallel cited by Kutscher 1977, pp. 241f. is not apposite). — *nksn zy yhwwn byn tmt wbyn ʿnny*, "goods which will be between Tamet and Anani" (*TAD* B3.3:12f.); expression indicating joint property.

34. *ỉw=y ḫ3ʿ=t (n) ḥm.t mtw=y mst.ṯ=t mtw=y ḫn n=t k.t s.ḥm.t ḥm.t r.ḥr=t ỉw=y tỉ.t n=t*, "If I dismiss you as a wife, be it that I hate you, be it that I want another woman as wife instead of you, I shall give you ..." (Pestman 1961, pp. 22, 59–64). — *wy ʾmr śnyt lʾntty yhwyšmʿ lʿ thwh ly ʾntt ksp śnʾh brʾšh*, "And should he say, 'I hated my wife Jehoishma; she shall not be my wife,' silver of hatred is on his head" (*TAD* B3.8:21f.; cf. Yaron 1958, pp. 32ff.).

35. *n3 ḥn.w ... ḫr mṯk*, "the jars ... under (= for) mixed wine" (P.ʿOnchsheshonqy 4:18, 5:15; see also Husson 1982, p. 228). — *qpp 1 zy ḥwžn tḥt lbšyh*, "1 palm-leaf chest under (= for) her garments"; *qp zy ʿq 1 tḥt ḥmryh*, "1 wooden chest under (= for) her jewels" (*TAD* B3.8:17, 19).

CONCLUSIONS

There are at least four explanations for any or all of these equivalents: (1) the Aramaic borrowed from the Demotic; (2) the Demotic borrowed from the Aramaic; (3) both borrowed from a third source; (4) both evolved independently if coincidentally. While preliminary investigation suggests that some Demotic terms may be of Eastern origin, as maintained by Kutscher, Muffs, Rabinowitz, and (in part) Yaron, the data are not adequate to assert that other Aramaic terms, by chance attested in the fifth century B.C.E., derive from the Demotic. To pursue the investigation requires the joint effort of the Assyriologist, the Aramaist, and the Egyptologist. Ideally, we should be able to probe the Semitic background of every Aramaic term as Muffs (1968, pp. 142–72) did for *tib libbi* = *ḥ3t=y mtr.w* and see if the Demotic equivalent has roots in earlier Egyptian. By way of example we may take the last two terms presented: the double usage of *ỉ-ỉwd* would be considered due to Aramaic influence ("between you and between me") because early Egyptian uses only one, as in English "between you and me" (G. R. Hughes, orally), whereas *tḥt* in the sense of "for, containing" would be considered a Demotic *calque* because the word does not have that meaning elsewhere either in Aramaic or Biblical Hebrew. If this double conclusion is correct, it shows linguistic interpenetration and cross-fertilization on the micro-level, that of prepositions. It is certainly a real desideratum to unravel the mutual influence on the macro-level, that of legal systems.

CHAPTER 31

GRECO-EGYPTIAN DOUBLE NAMES AS A FEATURE OF A BI-CULTURAL SOCIETY: THE CASE Ψοσνευς ὁ καὶ Τριάδελφος*

JAN QUAEGEBEUR
Katholieke Universiteit, Leuven

1. INTRODUCTION

1.1. GRECO-EGYPTIAN DOUBLE NAMES

The phenomenon that one person is referred to by two different names, not to mention the patronym, is attested in Egypt from the Old Kingdom until the Roman period.[1] The development of a second linguistic and cultural community, especially after the invasion of Alexander the Great (332 B.C.), gave rise to a new type of double name, consisting of an Egyptian and a Greek component. Here we will pay attention exclusively to such Greco-Egyptian double names, without discussing other types of double names from Greco-Roman period Egypt.[2] Persons with an Egyptian and a Greek name are best known from Greek papyri,[3] but they also occur in Demotic[4] and hieroglyphic documents.[5]

The sociological background of the use of a Greek and an Egyptian name from the 3rd century B.C. onwards has not received full treatment here, because this aspect was studied in detail in connection with new examples of mixed marriages and of Egyptians adapting their names to their position within the Greek government service.[6]

* References to papyrological text editions are given according to Oates et al. 1985. For a handy reference to *BL* see *BLKon*.

1. See in general *LÄ* IV, s.v. Name (B. Expression de l'identité), cols. 322–23. For the hieroglyphic material of two periods detailed studies are available: P. Vernus 1986 and de Meulenaere 1966b, which is complemented by 1981, pp. 127-134.
2. The study of R. Calderini 1941, pp. 221–60 and 1942, pp. 3–45 is out of date. A new inquiry was announced by Leclercq (1963, pp. 192–94); cf. Leclercq 1975/1976, pp. 361–72.
3. The double names are registered in *OA* but not in *Nb*.
4. See e.g. several examples in Andrews 1988, pp. 193–99. It is not always easy to recognize if a Demotic name is indeed a transliteration of a Greek name, e.g. *Mꜣꜥ-Rꜥ* (Marrês) called *Ḥl-wn* (Hêrôn ?) in a Roman text from Tebtunis, cf. Botti 1956, p. 77. See *infra 3.2*.
5. See the list of de Meulenaere 1966a, p. 43. For a hieratic example see Quaegebeur 1986, pp. 74–76.
6. See the paper by W. Clarysse, "Some Greeks in Egypt," *Chapter 6* in this volume.

1.2. TRANSLATION OF NAMES

A second fact that deserves mention is the substitution of the Egyptian name by a Greek one. Several cases of translation of names in papyri from the Roman period have received special attention,[7] but one has to consider the use of a nickname as a particular aspect.[8] Elsewhere, too, on mummy labels for instance, a translated instead of a transliterated name is found in the Greek version.[9]

1.3. TRANSLITERATED AND TRANSLATED NAMES

Among the Greco-Egyptian double names known from Greek sources, we are here interested in particular in those that combine a transliterated Egyptian name and a Greek translation. Already this group has received attention several times, e.g. from Spiegelberg in a brief contribution entitled "Zu den griechischen Übersetzungen ägyptischer Eigennamen" (1925, pp. 6–8). As is well known, these double names often shed light on syncretism or on the identification of Egyptian and Greek gods or beliefs.[10] A complete updated list would be very useful but exceeds the aim of this article. Incidentally, such double names are also attested for gods.[11]

2. THE GRECO-EGYPTIAN DOUBLE NAME Ψοσνευς ὁ καὶ Τριάδελφος

Let us focus here on the Greco-Egyptian double name Ψοσνευς ὁ καὶ Τριάδελφος[12] "Psosneus also called Triadelphos," of which Spiegelberg has said: "In dem Beinamen Τριάδελφος eines Ψοσνευς ... liegt eine ungenaue Übersetzung vor" (1918b, p. 140).

Indeed, at first glance, one is inclined to interpret Ψοσνευς as "The two brothers," whereas Τριάδελφος means "The three brothers." Several authors have recognized in Ψοσνευς a variant of the well known name Ψανσνως which, as bilingual texts have since long shown, is a Greek transliteration of *P3-sn-snwy* "The two brothers" (see further).

On the other hand, already in 1911, Lambertz, in a short article "Zur Doppelnamigkeit in Ägypten," analyzed Ψοσνευς as *Π.χοσνευς "The three brothers" (p. 17), an interpretation that reappears in 1960 (p. 12) with Vergote, who proposed as phonetical explanation the reconstruction ⲡϣⲟ(ⲙⲛ̄ⲧ)-ⲥⲛⲏⲩ, "The three brothers."

It has to be noted that the combinations "two-" and "three-brothers" present a different structure in Egyptian: in *P3-sn-2* the figure comes at the end; in *P3-3-sn.w* it precedes the noun.

Since some doubt exists as to the interpretation of Ψοσνευς "Two or three brothers," it would seem best to start this examination with the name Τριάδελφος, whose meaning "The three brothers" can hardly be questioned.

7. See the text discussed in Wilcken 1908, pp. 123–24, 128–29 and reproduced in Wilcken 1912b, p. 76, no. 52 : Εὐδαίμων asks to change the names of his father and mother: Εὐδαίμων Ἥρωνος ἀντὶ τοῦ Ψοιτος καὶ ἀντὶ Τιαθρηους μητρὸς Διδύμης (cf. Quaegebeur 1975, p. 265). See also van Minnen 1986, pp. 87–92.

8. See Youtie 1970, pp. 545–51 (= 1973, pp. 1035–41). Compare Horak 1989, pp. 101–07.

9. Compare Quaegebeur 1978, pp. 249–50: Ἱέραξ = *P3-bjk* (Möller 1913, no. 5); Δίδυμος = *Ḥtr* (Möller 1913, no. 45); Διοσκορᾶς = *Pa-ntr* (Pestman 1965a, p. 50).

10. On several occasions I used Greco-Egyptian double names as an argument, e.g. for the identification of Month and Apollo and of Mut and Hera at Thebes, cf. Quaegebeur 1975/1976, pp. 463–78 or for the association of Heracles with the local god(s) of Herakleopolis/Ehnasiya, cf. Quaegebeur 1987, pp. 160–62. For syncretism in connection with minor gods and popular beliefs, cf. Quaegebeur 1983a, p. 311.

11. E.g. Σάτις ἡ καὶ Ἥρα, Ἀνοῦκις ἡ καὶ Ἑστία, etc. (*OGIS* I 130, 7–8); Σοκνεβτῦνις ὁ καὶ Κρόνος, et al. (cf. Ronchi 1975, pp. 596–97, 666; 1977, pp. 999–1000).

12. P. Lond. II, p. 28 no. 257, line 271 (Arsinoïtes).

2.1. "THREE BROTHERS" IN EGYPTIAN ONOMASTICS

2.1.1. Τριάδελφος, separate and in double names

The proper name Τριάδελφος has recently been the subject of a brief discussion which I would like to take as my point of departure (Heinen 1990, pp. 270–73; cf. Bingen 1989b, p. 366). The name is not found outside Egypt and clearly belongs to the native onomastic repertoire.[13] It is typical of the Roman and Byzantine periods (see Heinen 1990, p. 270). Without going further into the question of chronological and geographical dispersion, it may be noted that it appears, among other places, in Achmim and in the Faiyum, and is therefore not confined to a single region.

Several double names are known with the element Τριάδελφος, but in the present context I mention, besides Ψοσνευς ὁ καὶ Τριάδελφος, only one: Τριάδελφος ὁ καὶ Ψενθνευς,[14] as its second component, Ψενθνευς, shows a certain resemblance to Ψοσνευς.

2.1.2. *(P3)-ḫmt-sn(.w)* and related names

Can a pendant for Τριάδελφος be pointed out in Egyptian texts? Consultation of Ranke's *Ägyptische Personennamen* (*PN* I: 1935, *PN* II: 1952, *PN* III: 1977) yields only the reconstructed form **Ḫmt-sn.w* derived from the Greek transcriptions Χεμτσνευς and variants (1952, p. 310 no. 10). The name, however, had already been recognized on bilingual mummy labels, where *Ḫmt-sn.w* (without article) is rendered in Greek as Χεμσνευς (e.g. Spiegelberg 1901, p. 57* no. 413). Spiegelberg even wrote, in connection with Τριαδέλφη: "Übersetzung von Χεμσνευς oder genauer *Τχεμσνευς" (Spiegelberg 1901, p. 54*).

The name perhaps also appears on a hieroglyphic mummy label, where the element "brothers" would be written with three divine ideograms (Spiegelberg 1901, p. 19; Möller 1913, p. 13 no. 75). But the signs are too simplified for an identification of the gods on the basis of their faces and crowns.

In Demotic texts on mummy labels one also finds, in addition to *Ḫmt-sn.w*, the compounds *Pa-ḫmt-sn.w*[15] and *T3-šr.t-ḫmt-sn.w*.[16] Besides the form without article, however, there also exists a Demotic orthography with article: *P3-ḫmt-sn.w*; both forms are included in the *Demotisches Namenbuch*.[17] *P3-ḫmt-sn.w* can be rendered by Χεμσνευς as a variant of *Πχεμσνευς.[18] The same alternation, with and without article, is also found in other instances, for example in the brother-names *(P3-)sn-snwy* (in Greek: Σανσνως, Ψανσνως, etc. "[the] two brothers") and *(P3-) ftw-sn.w* (Φθουσνευς) "the four brothers."[19] There are yet more names that contain the element "brothers" or the numbers "two" or "four." As far as the number "three" is concerned, mention may be made here of *P3-ḫmt-iry.w*[20] "The three fellows" (man's name) and *T3-ḫmt-ḫbr*,[21] "The three friends" (woman's name).

13. *Nb*. 445; *OA* 322; see another example in Wipszycka 1988, p. 163 (father of Polykrates also called Petetriphis).
14. P. Mich. V 264 (I) (Tebtunis).
15. *Dem. Nb*. I 8, p. 557 (no Greek form, see however Παχεντσνευς infra).
16. Möller 1913, no. 37 bil. (= Σεμχενσνευς); no. 58 dem.
17. Example with article in Demotic: Mattha 1945, p. 184 no. 251/2 (Bodl. 1135); cf. *Dem. Nb*. I 3, p. 209 (no Greek form given).
18. See the bilingual ostracon Heidelberg 386 (Roman; probably from Edfu); this unpublished text was mentioned to me by W. Clarysse.
19. For presence and omission of the article, see Quaegebeur 1975, pp. 183ff. (Σαις, Ψαις, etc.); on *(P3-)ftw-Mnṯ* see Quaegebeur 1991, pp. 253–54.
20. *Dem. Nb*. I 3, p. 208 (Πχεμτερηυς); Spiegelberg 1901, p. 56*; *PN* II, p. 282 no. 26: Πχεμτερηυς (Vorschlag auf lautlichen Gründen). See also Bingen and Clarysse 1989.
21. Spiegelberg 1901, p. 55* no. 403.

2.1.3. Greek transliterations: Χεμτσνευς, etc.

For the Greek transliterations of "The three brothers," we must start from the bilingual data.[22] We have just seen that Χεμσνευς corresponds to *Ḫmt-sn.w*. From the compound *T3-šr.t-ḫmt-sn.w* rendered by Σεμχενσνευς,[23] one can further derive the variant Χενσνευς, which does indeed exist.[24] Preisigke's *Namenbuch*, s.v. Χεμσνευς,[25] brings together a whole series of variants, on the basis of which I have compiled the following selective survey:

t preserved:	Χεμτσνευς, Χεμτσνεους, Χεμτσνηυς,[26] Χμτσνηυ, Χμντσνηυ, Χεμτεσνευς, Χεμτοσνυ(ε)ις, Χεντοσνευς, Χεμθσενευς
t not preserved:[27]	Χεμσνευς, Χεμσνηις, Χενσνευς, Χεμψενευς, Χεμσονευς
Subst. sing.:	Χεντσανις (*OA* 341; *SB* III 7118), Χενσανις (Quaegebeur 1983c, p. 70)
Compounds:	
t preserved:	Παχεντσνευς (*Nb.* 294)
t not preserved:	Σενχεμσνευς (*Nb.* 378;*OA* 289), Σενχενσνηυς (*CEML* 788), Σενχονσνευς (*Nb.* 378), Σεμχενσνευς (*Nb.* 369)
Subst. sing.:	Σενχεντσαν (*Nb.* 378).

As the *t* of *Ḫmt-sn.w* must have been audible when carefully articulated, Χεμτσνευς may be regarded as a better transliteration than Χεμσνευς. The /t/ appears in all Coptic forms of the number "three," the more important of which are listed here:[28]

S(ahidic)	ϢΟΜΝΤ(Ε), Ϣ(Ε)ΜΝΤ, ϢΟΜΤ;
A(chmimic)	ϨⲀΜΤ(Ε)
F(aiyumic)	ϢⲀΜΤΕ.

Here I must confine myself to sundry remarks in connection with the Greek transliterations. As to the number "three," we see that χ as the initial consonant in the Greek renderings, issuing essentially from Southern Egypt, leans toward the Achmimic pronunciation. In a number of cases there is a partial assimilation of *m* > *n* before a dental consonant. The Achmimic *a-* vocalization, as found in Πχαμτερευς (= *P3-ḫmt-iry.w*; Bingen and Clarysse 1989, p. 46), is normally reduced to *schwa*. In a few instances we see that /s$^{\partial}$nêw/ is pronounced instead of /snêw/ due to the accumulation of consonants (Χεμθσενευς, Χεμσονευς, and Χεμψενευς with epenthetic *p*). Finally, note that the noun "brother," in its Achmimic form (CⲀN), can be used in the singular (cf. -σαν[ις]) instead of in the plural (CNHY).[29]

On the basis of the data now available it is not clear whether Ψοσνευς can be a new variant of Χεμ(τ)σνευς; therefore we still have to take a closer look at "The two brothers."

22. Spiegelberg 1901, p. 57* no. 413; compounds ibid., p. 43* no. 303. For other bilingual examples in the Louvre, see in general Boyaval 1976, passim (referring to *CEML*), while awaiting the publication of the Demotic texts by M. Chauveau. See also footnote 18, above.
23. See footnote 16, above.
24. *OA* 341 (*SB* VI 9418: III–IIa !).
25. *Nb.* 474; see also *OA* 340.
26. Quaegebeur 1971a, p. 166 and *BL* VII, p. 351 corrected from Χεμπνευς, Χεμπνηυς (*OA* 340).
27. Compare the omission of τ between ν and σ in other names, e.g. in Παμονσνως, variant of Παμοντσνως "He of the two gods Month."
28. *CD*, pp. 566b–67a mentions the proper name ϢMNTCNHY and refers to Τριάδελφος . Cf. *DELC*, p. 264. In Spiegelberg 1901, p. 57* no. 413, we find the Coptic forms: ϢΕΜN̄TCNHY, XΕΜN̄TCNHY, XMTCNHY; cf. Brunsch 1984, p. 149: XMNTCNHY and p. 151: ϢMNTCNHY.
29. Sethe 1916, pp. 56–57.

2.2. "TWO BROTHERS" IN EGYPTIAN ONOMASTICS

It is not my intention here to present the complete dossier. We will discuss the name solely in function of Ψοσνευς.

2.2.1. *(Pꜣ-)sn-snwy* rendered in Greek as Ψ/Σανσνως, etc.

Several authors have drawn up, or borrowed from one another, a list of various Greek transliterations of *(Pꜣ-)sn-snwy.*[30] In addition to Ψανσνως and Σανσνως, which are well known from bilingual texts and which are therefore beyond doubt,[31] we find a number of other forms, such as Ψενσνως, Ψονσναυς, Ψονσνευς, Ψοσνευς, Σανσνευς, Σονσναυ, et cetera. On the basis of a comparison with Coptic (see further) and on other phonetic grounds, it has been accepted that these are simple variants.

Some of these have been confirmed by bilingual data.[32] Thus we know for sure from a bilingual inscription on a mummy cloth the equivalence *Pꜣ-sn-snwy* = Ψονσνεου.[33] No one will doubt that Ψονσνεου is a non-Grecized form of Ψονσνευς, that is to say, a form without addition of a Greek ending.

There remains the question of the relationship between Ψοσνευς and Ψονσνευς. The disappearance of the ν before σ is a well-known phonetic phenomenon in Greek and is attested elsewhere in Greek transcriptions of Egyptian names. A case in point, besides the divine name Ψοσναυς (meaning "The two brothers" and to which we will return anon), is Χεσ- as a variant of Χενσ- for Chonsu (*Nb.* 475; *OA* 341).

2.2.2. The Greek translation Διάδελφος

Since Ψο(ν)σνευς can indeed be a rendition of the Egyptian name "The two brothers," the question arises whether there exists a Greek pendant. Parallel with Τριάδελφος as the translation of Χεμ(τ)σνευς, one could postulate for Ψο(ν)σνευς, "The two brothers," the form Διάδελφος. This name is indeed attested in the Faiyum in the 2nd–3rd centuries A.D. (BGU I 15, I, 5, 9; P.Oxy. XXII 2338, 58 [cf. Heinen 1990, p. 272] + *BL* VII [P. Laur. I, no. 4, 13]; P. Oxy. XII 1515, 8). It is a contracted form of the divine name Δύο 'Αδελφοί (P. Oxy. II 254) which is regarded, and in my opinion rightly so, as the translation of Ψοσναυς, the designation of a crocodile god (*SB* III 6154; Bernand 1981a, p. 100 no. 135), whose worship provided the basis for the Egyptian anthroponym "The two brothers."

I have dealt elsewhere with the connection of "The two brothers" with, on the one hand, the cult of crocodile gods and, on the other hand, the worship of the Dioscuri, the two sons of Zeus.[34]

2.2.3. Variants parallel to Coptic forms

Although a comparative study of the Greek transliterations and the Coptic pronunciation would lead us too far afield, let us take a brief look at the Coptic dialectal forms for the noun "brother"

30. Spiegelberg 1901, p. 35; *Nb.* 362; *CD*, pp. 343a, 347a; Hopfner 1946, p. 44 no. 55; Vergote 1954, p. 14 no. 71. Compare Quaegebeur 1969, p. 164. See also footnote 33. I have to refer also to the unpublished study, prepared under my supervision, by van Maele (1982).

31. See Spiegelberg 1901, p. 35* no. 236 (Σανσνως) and O. Tait II 562 (Ψανσνως).

32. For Ψενσωνς see Wångstedt 1969, p. 79 and for Ψοσναυς see P. Lille dem. II 71 (Greek part unpublished; reference W. Clarysse).

33. Thieme and Pestman 1978, pp. 134–35. In his review, Mussies (1983, p. 227) wrote: "In the discussion of the name Ψονσνέου (doc. 29) meaning 'The two brothers' it would be helpful for Hellenists to know that in Demotic and Coptic the numeral 'two' is regularly used with the singular (*pꜣ*-/π-), ..." One has to notice that the masculine article precedes the noun "brother" and not the number "two."

34. Quaegebeur 1983, pp. 312–16: Διοσκουρίδης ὁ καὶ Ψανσνως as an "interpretatio aegyptiaca." Compare P. Princ. I 8, V, 9: Διόσκορος ὅς καὶ Τεσνευς (Τε uncertain) probably to be corrected in Διόσκορος ὅς καὶ Ψο/εσνευς (Τεσνευς is a woman's name!).

and for the number "two" (*CD*, pp. 346b–47a; *KDG*, p. 20) in a simplified list, just by way of illustration.

"Brother"	S/B	ⲤⲞⲚ (S also ⲤⲈⲚ-)
	A/A2/F	ⲤⲀⲚ
	Plural, all dialects:	ⲤⲚⲎⲞⲨ (F also ⲤⲚⲈ(Ⲟ)Ⲩ).
"Two":	S(ahidic)/B(ohairic)	ⲤⲚⲀⲨ
	A(chmimic)	ⲤⲚⲞ
	A2 (Subachmimic)	ⲤⲚⲈⲨ
	F(aiyumic)	ⲤⲚⲈⲞⲨ

Let us consider the situation in the Faiyum, where our double name Ψοσνευς ὁ καὶ Τριάδελφος occurs. Here we regularly encounter the name Σανσνευς, a good Faiyumic form (compare Coptic ⲤⲀⲚ-ⲤⲚⲈⲞⲨ): first the noun in the singular followed by the number "two." As for Ψονσνευς and Ψοσνευς, also encountered in the Faiyum,[35] the noun ⲤⲀⲚ- could theoretically have lost its timbre and the o should then be interpreted as *schwa*.

If the first element of Ψο(ν)-σνευς renders, however, *Pꜣ-ḫmt-* "three," then the second component must correspond to "brothers," which in all dialects is /snêw/. And indeed, in the Faiyum -σνευς can transliterate both the number "two" and the plural "brothers." For "brothers" reference may be made to the name Πανεσνευς = *Pa-nꜣ-sn.w*, "He of the brothers," which appears in an interesting double name, Φιλάδελφος ὁ καὶ Πανεσνευς (*SB* IV 7368; *OA* 330).

Probably a distinction is to be made and was made in the Faiyum between, on the one hand, the Faiyumic Σανσνευς, "(The) two brothers," a new dialectal variant of the Sahidic, Ψονσναυς, and, on the other hand, Ψο(ν)σνευς, the local pronunciation of "The three brothers."

2.3. Ψοσνευς AND Ψενθνευς AS TRANSLITERATIONS OF *Pꜣ-ḫmt-sn.w*

It has already been noted that, besides Ψοσνευς ὁ καὶ Τριάδελφος, a second double name is attested in the Faiyum: Τριάδελφος ὁ καὶ Ψενθνευς (see *supra 2.1.1*). There is the obvious inclination to equate Ψοσνευς and Ψενθνευς via a simple syllogism. In addition, Ψενθνευς, because of the θ, is difficult to elucidate from the name "The two brothers" (θ is not a mere variant of σ). If Ψενθνευς can be a transliteration of *Pꜣ-ḫmt-sn.w*, we come back to the question whether Ψοσνευς cannot render *Pꜣ-ḫmt-sn.w* as well as *Pꜣ-sn-snwy*.

2.3.1. Ψοσνευς and variants: Ψομτισνευς, et cetera.

Here we must turn to a tax archive from 1st century Philadelphia which is being prepared for publication by Ann Hanson.[36] Without entering into detail I would like to draw attention to the following data. A man known as Ψοσνευς, son of Πραξίας, is mentioned in other documents with a somewhat different name; instead of Ψοσνευς, we find Ψομσνηους[37] and Ψομτισνευς. So Ψοσνευς Πραξίου = Ψομσνηους Πραξίου = Ψομτισνευς Πραξίου. The latter form is new and appears in Hanson's archive several times. The τι makes it impossible to explain the name as *Pꜣ-sn-snwy*. We further encounter the name Ψοντισνευς in Πετερμουθ(ις) ὃς κ(αὶ) Ψοντισνευς.

35. Compare Clarysse 1987a, pp. 19–20: "... a study ... has also shown that the typical Fayumic form of the name Ψονσνευς is indeed the usual one in the Arsinoites in the Roman period, but that in the Ptolemaic period we always find the Sahidic form Ψονσναυς. Could this mean that the Fayumic dialect as a whole came into being at the beginning of our era?" In fact we encounter in the Faiyum, beside the Sahidic Ψονσναυς, the good Faiyumic form Σανσνευς and we will see that Ψονσνευς is not necessarily another transcription of "The two brothers." I thank W. Clarysse for discussing with me this and some other questions.

36. Compare Hansen 1979, pp. 60–62. I wish to thank Ann Hanson most sincerely for the opportunity to consult and use this still unpublished material.

37. To be compared with Ψουμσνευς: *Nb*. 495 = BGU II 591, 4 (Ψουμσναυς, corrected in *BL* I, p. 55).

2.3.2. Ψοσνευς as a dialectal vocalization of *Pꜣ-ḫmt-sn.w*

If we omit the masculine article in the new variants of Ψοσνευς from the Faiyum, then -σο-, -σομ-, -σομτι-, and -σοντι- remain for the first element. Can it correspond with *ḫmt*, "three"? For Southern Egypt I found χεμ- and χεν-, in addition to a writing with τ (χεμτ, χεντ), sometimes followed by a mute vowel. Both ε and ο are known as such vowels; the ι in -σομτι-, -σοντι- to me seems, parallel with ε/ο in χεμτε/ο-, χεντο-, to prop up the τ.

So there remains only the σ opposite the χ. The alternation χ/σ can hardly pose a problem. One thinks immediately here of the dialectal differentiation in the Coptic rendition of the consonant *ḫ*. This dialectal variation is also known in Greek forms like πχημις/ψημις for *pꜣ ḫm*, "the little one" (Quaegebeur 1974a, p. 418). Comparison with the Coptic forms of the number "three" shows that in Southern Egypt (Achmimic) χ corresponds with ⳉ and in the Faiyum σ with ϣ.

The Faiyumic forms Ψομτισνευς and Ψομσνηους stand opposite Χεμτοσνευς and Χεμσνευς for the South. Ψοσνευς in the Philadelphia tax archive can only be a transliteration of a careless and shortened pronunciation of *Pꜣ-ḫmt-sn.w*, "The three brothers." I see the evolution as follows: Ψομτισνευς > Ψομσνηους > Ψονσνευς (this name exists but was always considered a transliteration of *Pꜣ-sn-snwy*) > Ψοσνευς.

Consequently, there is no reason to rule out the interpretation of Ψοσνευς as "The three brothers" in the double name Ψοσνευς ὁ καὶ Τριάδελφος, on the contrary. In fact, we already observed that there was probably in the Faiyum an opposition between the pure Faiyumic form Σανσνευς, "(The) two brothers" and Ψο(ν)σνευς, "The three brothers." But we cannot prove that Ψο(ν)σνευς renders in the Faiyum always *Pꜣ-ḫmt-sn.w*.

2.3.3. The rendering of /ts/ by θ?

We still have to take a closer look at the other double name: Τριάδελφος ὁ καὶ Ψενθνευς. The question here is: can Ψενθνευς be a transliteration of *Pꜣ-ḫmt-sn.w* and a variant of Ψοσνευς? I think the answer should be affirmative. To demonstrate that Ψενθνευς can be regarded as a variant of Ψοσνευς, the index of the Petaus archive must be consulted, where we find, besides Ψονθνευς, Ψομθνευς, and Ψονσνευς as well (Papyrus Petaus, p. 429). Are we to attribute to the θ the pronunciation /s/[38] or should we rather think of /ts/?

I think a good case can be made for θ as a rendition of /ts/. In the Petaus archive we encounter Θεμειτις as a variant of Τσεμιτ.[39] It is further well known that Θ, in addition to Τσ-, Σ-, and Χ-,[40] corresponds, at the beginning of many feminine names, with *Tš-* (Coptic ⲦϢ). On the other hand, we find that θ and other dentals in Greek words are sometimes rendered by *ts* in Demotic: Παρθικός : *Prtsygw* (Clarysse 1987a, p. 27 no. 58), Καλακάνθη : *Gꜣlꜣgꜣntsy* (Griffith and Thompson 1909, p. 122; Quaegebeur 1973, p. 99. Cf. F. Ll. Griffith 1937, p. 104). This point requires further examination because the θ in our case appears between consonants.[41]

The conclusion is that Ψοσνευς and Ψενθνευς in the double names discussed are best interpreted as transcriptions of *Pꜣ-ḫmt-sn.w*, so that the seeming antithesis between the two elements of the double name Ψοσνευς ὁ καὶ Τριάδελφος is resolved.

38. As I supposed wrongly in 1973, p. 98.

39. Papyrus Petaus, pp. 400, 427 and 429 (Ψονθνευς). Compare Παθωντις for Πατσωντις (?) in Wessely 1904 (reprint Milan 1975), p. 118 (reference P. Gallo).

40. For X = ϫ, see e.g. ⲠⲈϢϪⲀⲖ = Πεσχαλ: CPR XII, p. 88; ⲈⲖⲀϪⲒⲤⲦⲞⲤ: Pernigotti 1985, p. 92; cf. *CD*, p. 516a; Vergote 1973, p. 14 § 18; Kasser 1988, pp. 118–20 and 1980, p. 21.

41. Clarysse 1987a, p. 18: "The remarkable rendering of θ and τ by *ts* in Παρθικός and Σαρματικός seems to be typical of late texts and is closely paralleled in the London-Leiden magical papyrus. J. H. Johnson explains it as an indication of palatalisation of *t* and *th* before following *i*." Cf. J. H. Johnson 1976, p. 124.

3. FINAL CONSIDERATIONS

3.1. ASPECTS OF A STUDY ON THE "BROTHER-NAMES"

We have dealt with only a few elements of the extensive file on the "Brother-names," devoting special attention to the methodological and linguistic aspects. It has been argued that in the Faiyum Ψοσνευς should mean "The three brothers" rather than "The two brothers" and that *(P3-)ḫmt-sn.w* can be rendered in the Faiyum as Ψοσνευς and in Achmim as Χεμσνευς. Despite the criticism which has been leveled against my view that the Greek transliterations are fairly faithful renditions of the dialectal pronunciation (Brunsch 1977, pp. 212–13), a detailed study of the brother-names will make it possible to reconfirm the correctness of that position.[42]

The question as to which gods are behind the two, three, and even four brothers cannot be dealt with here.[43]

3.2. GREEK TRANSLITERATIONS AND TRANSLATIONS IN THE *DEM. NB*.

Consulting the *Dem. Nb.* for this study, I have found once again that the incorporation of Greek transliterations, except where bilingual documents are involved, is rather arbitrary. It is to be regretted that data from translated names have not been processed, and that double names are not mentioned as such. Yet this cannot alter the fact that the *Dem. Nb.*, as an inventory of Demotic names, remains an excellent research instrument.

3.3. IMPORTANCE OF AN INQUIRY ON DOUBLE NAMES

The analysis of Ψοσνευς ὁ καὶ Τριάδελφος illustrates clearly the difficulty of an inquiry into Greco-Egyptian double names. A comprehensive study of the use of double names in Greco-Roman period Egypt remains a desideratum, but the complexity of the problems, involving linguistic, sociological, as well as religious aspects, makes preliminary detailed studies necessary. Requisites are: a good knowledge of the two languages and of the various Egyptian scripts, as well as a familiarity with both cultures.

The syncretistic data already available, which can again be supplemented with a few new cases, must of course be integrated in the projected lexicon of information on Egyptian religion in Greek documentary texts (see e.g. Quaegebeur 1984, pp. 107–11).

42. Besides the detailed study of the alternation α/ο found in Ψαις/Ψοις, Σαις/Σοις (cf. ϢⲀⲒ/ϢⲞⲒ) and in the many compounds with *š3y*, see Quaegebeur 1974, pp. 418–19, where a distinction is made between standardized (koinê) forms and vulgar forms.

43. Horak (1989, p. 107) writes: "'Die beiden Brüder, Die drei Brüder, Die vier Brüder', bezeichnen Krokodilgötter im Fayum"; see already Kees 1956 (1st ed. 1941), p. 160. Compare Spiegelberg 1901, p. 36 and Hopfner 1946. Another interpretation for Τριάδελφος was proposed by Heinen (1990, pp. 270–73). The question needs further examination and exceeds the scope of this study.

CHAPTER 32

JEWS AND OTHER IMMIGRANTS IN LATE PERIOD EGYPT

J. D. RAY
The University of Cambridge

Egypt acted as a magnet for immigrants during most periods, but this is particularly true of the centuries beginning with the Twenty-sixth Dynasty and continuing to the end of Ptolemaic rule. Such newcomers were attracted by the potential wealth of the country, which was in marked contrast to conditions in the Aegean or in much of the rest of the Near East. In general, a pattern emerges of slow but steady assimilation to the culture, and even the religion, of the immigrants' new home. The Ionians, for example, are attested early (witness the new inscription from Priene published by Masson and Yoyotte 1988, pp. 171–80). However, if we consider the well-known Curse of Artemisia (= *UPZ* I 1), which dates from 311 B.C., we find that although the language of this text is Ionic Greek, the text can be transposed phrase for phrase into Demotic; indeed, it can almost be described as an ancient Egyptian text written in Greek. Another interesting example is given in the early (fourth century ?) papyri published by Zaghloul, where the affairs of an ibis-cult in Middle Egypt are in the hands of a man named Ariston (*ꜣrsṯn*). It is hard to imagine a more Egyptian occupation. The Carians, closely associated with the Ionians, show a similar pattern of Egyptianization. Graffiti left by Phoenician pilgrims at Abydos show the same features, and from a large but amorphous community of Aramaic speakers in Egypt we have the Carpentras Stele (Grelot 1972, no. 86), which is not only an Egyptian funerary prayer to Osiris, but even contains Egyptian words (*nb mꜣʿty, ḥsyw*) transliterated into Aramaic. This too can be seen as an ancient Egyptian text, in spite of its language. The now-notorious Amherst papyrus may represent a highly-developed example of this tendency; in many ways this text foreshadows the thought-world of later Greco-Egyptian magic.

The principal exception to this pattern of assimilation is the case of the Jews. These are known mainly from the archives at Elephantine, but have also left traces of their attitudes in the books of Ezekiel and Jeremiah, and in the story of Joseph, the archetypal history of an immigrant made good. The reasons for Jewish separateness are complex: one may suggest tighter family structure, the maintenance of links with the homeland, and possibly the codification of Jewish scripture. Certainly in late period Egypt Zeus could become Amun, and Thoth Hermes, but the Jewish God remains himself. Ionians and Phoenicians turned into *Ionomemphites* and *Phoinikaigyptioi*, but the Jews never became anything other than *Ioudaioi*.

CHAPTER 33

THE ADMINISTRATION OF LATE PTOLEMAIC EGYPT*

LINDA RICKETTS†
The University of North Dakota

Two archives of papyri and ostraca dominate the evidence for the end of the Ptolemaic period. The first is well known: it is the mummy cartonnage papyri out of the Herakleopolite, now in Berlin. Two editions of the late pieces appear in the Berlin series of texts; they are BGU VIII (Schubart and Schäfer 1933) and the recent BGU XIV, which includes the late land registers edited by Brashear (1980). The second "archive" is actually a collection of texts housed in several places and consists of ostraca out of Thebes in both Greek and Demotic. Publications of Greek texts by Milne (1913), Tait (1930), and now Shelton (1988b) have included several late ostraca. Examples from collections of Demotic texts at Oxford, London, and Toronto may be found in editions such as Thompson's (1913) for Oxford and Toronto, Wångstedt's articles, which take in several collections,[1] and Kaplony-Heckel's *Demotische Tempeleide* (1963), again with ostraca from many collections. Demotic pieces continue to surface, as witnessed by Richard Jasnow's recent edition of ostraca from the Mut precinct (Fazzini and Jasnow 1988).[2] This manufactured archive of Theban ostraca accounts for the largest number of texts out of Upper Egypt from Cleopatra's reign. Demotic ostraca are as significant in numbers as Greek ostraca in the collections — I am convinced, looking at the number of unedited texts locked away in museum storerooms. These Demotic texts, tax receipts, land allotments, and accounts, give us, as Janet Johnson (1987) has shown, our Egyptian view of the late Ptolemaic administration. The Demotic documents also allow insights from another direction into specific problems relating to royal chronology and Thebaid administration.

The Herakleopolite archive places in our best light the prosperity, in terms of land productivity, of the late Ptolemaic age, at least in this nome. This is contrary to accounts of Cleopatra's reign in classical authors. I proposed this prosperity in 1980,[3] and others have elaborated the point (Maehler 1983b, especially pp. 6–8 and Bowman 1985, pp. 285–86). The difficulties in the nome, from banditry and other upheavals, follow the dynastic struggles, as Maehler (1983b, p. 7)

* Due to her untimely death, Dr. Ricketts was unable to check the proofs of this article.

1. See Schneider 1985, pp. 163–71, for an index of Wångstedt's articles in *Orientalia Suecana*.

2. Jasnow dates most of the ostraca to the early Roman era, but there are a few late Ptolemaic pieces.

3. See Ricketts 1980. I note the profitability of the late Ptolemaic administration in a consideration of the transition to Roman rule in Egypt (ibid., p. 99) and BGU VIII 1760 is discussed with the *sitologoi* on page 54. The publication of the land registers in BGU XIV, however, made possible a discussion of the productivity in terms of specific land usage, and I addressed this land usage in a paper (1984), which is now in preparation as a chapter in a forthcoming study of the documents from Cleopatra's reign. Maehler's article (1983b), his inaugural lecture, supersedes the earlier effort.

has recently shown.[4] With the end of the dynastic conflicts (55 B.C. and again in 47 B.C.), affairs settled into the productivity witnessed by the late land registers and tax documents. A clear example of this is the now often quoted tax document, BGU VIII 1760, in which the Herakleopolite katoicics are stated to owe a good share of the tax in wheat due in a single year from the nomes to the central bureau: 71,360 artabas of the total 600,000 artabas.[5] The Herakleopolite, though, produced wheat at an overwhelming ratio: 54.9% of the cultivated land in registers 2441–2448 is devoted to wheat;[6] these land registers are in a single hand and probably represent a single year.[7] Barley, for the horses (a consistent reference), was secondary, along with other cereal cultivation.[8] Overall, in the registers, the productivity is evident, with some inundation (2441) and a lesser yield in a single register (2439) which might be attributed to a low Nile and a seasonal drought, perhaps

4. His examples for the dynastic conflict ending in 55 B.C. especially illustrate the point. Tinteris in 50/49 B.C., BGU VIII 1843, reflects better the insufficient flood of that year (see below, footnote 9).

5. The editors of BGU VIII thought that the payment from the chora of 600,000 artabas of wheat for the *phorologia* in BGU VIII 1760 must mean payment from the Herakleopolite only, even though the papyrus gives the chora as owing this figure. Maehler (1983b, p. 6) goes along with this interpretation of the editors, with the katoicics responsible accordingly for 71,360 artabas of the 600,000 artabas in wheat due from the nome. The tax is to be collected in two payments of 35,680 artabas from the katoicics. A consideration of the nome's productivity, however, shows that this reading, with 600,000 artabas due from the Herakleopolite, cannot be. BGU XIV 2434, an account list by toparchies from the Herakleopolite, gives 101,943½ (though it should read 101,953½) arouras of wheat as its total; and we could expect this to be the total area under wheat cultivation in the Herakleopolite according to the percentage of productive land in the nome in the land registers BGU XIV 2441–2448 and the percentage of land under wheat cultivation in the same registers. Figuring fifteen artabas per aroura as a high average yield, an annual production would total approximately 1,500,000 artabas of wheat, of which approximately 960,000 artabas would be available to the nome (such an amount would, moreover, support a population of about 100,000 using Crawford's [1971] reserved figure of 8.8 artabas per person annual consumption). Accordingly, 600,000 artabas of wheat would be a total annual taxable amount from the Herakleopolite, and therefore the nome's payment of this amount in BGU VIII 1760, in two payments of 300,000 artabas, according to the revised reading of chora as Herakleopolite, would exhaust its taxes. But there would be other assessments beyond the *phorologia* in the nome, and so the papyrus must record a payment of 600,000 artabas due from all of the nomes. Further, we would expect the katoicics of the Herakleopolite to pay a greater share of the assessment than the reading of the chora as the Herakleopolite would allow (ca. 12%). It is tempting to suggest that we have with the *phorologia*, the artaba tax levied at three-quarters an artaba per aroura (71,360 artabas per approximately 100,000 arouras); however, such a payment by the katoicics would put almost all the wheat cultivation in the nome under their direction, but perhaps the half payment of 35,680 artabas gives us the actual figure.

6. The percentage of wheat to cereal cultivation in the nome is taken from the amounts in land registers BGU XIV 2441–2448 ($1453\frac{9}{16}$ arouras of wheat). The percentage of wheat in the same registers to all lands, productive and unproductive, is 24.6%. Wheat commands the highest percentage of any known crop (unknown is 22.8%); *arakos* shows the second highest cultivation at 3.4% of all lands (200 arouras). Compare Brashear's commentary in BGU XIV, 1980, pp. 228–55 (Appendix V). Using land registers BGU XIV 2441–2448 for total land distribution and percentages, Brashear has wheat at $1665\frac{15}{16}$ arouras, 17.1% of all lands.

7. Brashear makes the observation of the same hand and the inventory roll in his introduction to the land registers BGU XIV 2441–2448 (1980, pp. 165–68).

8. Barley is 2.7% ($72\frac{5}{8}$ arouras) of the cultivated land in registers BGU XIV 2441–2448. Of all lands in these registers, barley holds only 1.2% (compare Brashear's commentary in BGU XIV, 1980, pp. 228–55). It is noteworthy, however, that another register BGU XIV 2439, lines 55–79, recording the lands of seven holdings in the nome, has a more even distribution of cereal crops, with wheat at 23.6% (119 arouras) and barley at 15.8% (79½ arouras); also, *olyra* is recorded at 80½ arouras (16% of the total recorded cultivation).

the same one attested in BGU VIII for 50/49 B.C.[9] There is nothing of the disaster in Cleopatra's reign, however, of which Seneca writes and modern authors suggest.[10]

I would like to add that a recent reconsideration of the age in another area, the originality of the art of the period (Ptolemy XII and Cleopatra VII), led by Robert Bianchi,[11] revises for us our understanding of its artistic contributions. The two revisions, economic and artistic, can stand together, as has been noted by Maehler (1983b, p. 5).[12] If there was a crisis of the age, it was not an economic one and not in a lack of creativity. The crisis may be found in Octavian's troops and another conquest.

A discussion of productivity and land usage in the Herakleopolite must acknowledge the groundwork set by Brashear in his commentary on BGU XIV.[13] Herakleopolite administrators, too, have been set out for prosopographical studies by others using the Herakleopolite papyri (see Van't Dack 1988). The nome *strategoi* Seleukos and Soteles have left considerable paperwork to follow for years 1 and 2 of Cleopatra[14] — including a plea by one, probably Seleukos, to be left alone and to send the paperwork to someone else (BGU VIII 1830, August 51 B.C.).[15] The first two years have the most documents in Cleopatra's reign, though Herakleopolite examples reach well into the 40s B.C.[16] The land registers are largely without year dates, though Brashear must be correct in proposing the βασιλίσσης of several registers with considerable private holdings (over 1285 arouras in one register) as Cleopatra VII.[17] The combined evidence for her reign shows an administration following the customary course and administrators who are Greek, at least at the

9. An insufficient Nile flood explains the problems the village of Tinteris was experiencing in 50/49 B.C. in BGU VIII 1843. A mobile work force had left Tinteris and the workers had returned home to pay their taxes. The abandonment of Hiera Nesos in BGU VIII 1835 may relate to the beginning of the drought (1835 is 51/50 B.C.) or to some unrest accompanying the dynastic struggle. For the dynastic struggle and BGU VIII 1835, see Maehler 1983b, p. 7; for BGU VIII 1835 and 1843, see Rostovtzeff 1953, vol. 2, p. 908. Pliny, too, in *Naturalis Historiae* 5.58, cites a drought, though in 48 B.C. rather than 50/49 B.C., and his figure for a critically low Nile (5 cubits or 7½ feet) should have caused more difficulties in terms of productivity, not witnessed in the Herakleopolite papyri (for example, BGU VIII 1760, at least for 51/50 B.C.; see above, footnote 5).

10. Seneca in *Naturalium Quaestionum* 4.16, says the Nile did not flood for two years, the tenth and eleventh of Cleopatra, but Seneca also says that this was a sign that Antony and Cleopatra's alliance would fail. For the alliance in 41 B.C., see now H. S. Smith's (1972, p. 186, Table 7) publication of an inscription from year 11 of Cleopatra's reign. In the same manner as Seneca, Pliny, too, gives the lowest level of the Nile in 48 B.C. as a sign that the river would avert the murder of Pompey by portent (*Naturalis Historia* 5.58; see above, footnote 9). We have in the evidence a reference to a low Nile in the beginning of 50/49 B.C. Of modern authors, Rostovtzeff is especially harsh towards Cleopatra's reign (see 1953, vol. 3, p. 1551, note 190). Concerning the inflation and currency about which Rostovtzeff writes, see now Clarysse and Lanciers 1989, pp. 117–32. I thank Dr. Clarysse for bringing this article to my attention. The authors refer to the doubling of prices (again) in 130–128 B.C. under the copper standard, prices that continue to Cleopatra's reign (130–30 B.C.). I would add that there was some stabilization imposed under Cleopatra VII, perhaps allowable because of the productivity.

11. Bianchi's recent address on the subject of late Ptolemaic art is described in *ARCE Newsletter* (Fall 1989), p. 25; and see Bianchi 1988.

12. Maehler discusses both art and documents of the period in his inaugural lecture.

13. Brashear's commentary follows his text editions in BGU XIV, pp. 222–26.

14. Seleukos (*PP* I 330) is evidenced as *strategos* from February 51 to February 50 B.C., Soteles (*PP* I 334) from May 50 to 49 B.C. In addition to the *strategoi* year 2 texts datable to Cleopatra VII, there are in the collection year 2 papyri which may be either Berenike IV or Cleopatra VII (BGU VIII 1779, 1780, and 1841); see Ricketts 1990, note 21.

15. The papyrus ends: μὴ ἐνοχ̣(λεῖν) (BGU VIII 1830).

16. The documents are listed in Ricketts 1980; an updated list, with Greek, Demotic, and hieroglyphic sources, is in preparation as part of a forthcoming study on the documents of Cleopatra's reign.

17. In land register BGU XIV 2438, the queen holds 1287½ arouras as βασιλίσσης. For the queen as Cleopatra, see Brashear's comments in BGU XIV 2441, p. 182, note 119.

nome level. When we look at the Herakleopolite population in her reign, Brashear's commentary again leads the way.

In the Greek evidence, the population involved in the productivity in the Herakleopolite was, of course, also Greek, and the katoicics stand out.[18] There are ethnics, and Latin names even begin to crop up at the end of the era, though what this appearance means is another matter.[19] Localities show Egyptian names; the toparchy Phebichis is notable for this and also, it appears, has poorer wheat production. As a note, because of this, the two toparchies remaining to be identified in the toparchy account list, BGU XIV 2434, must be Peri Polin and the Middle Toparchy; both lines in the account list show high wheat production, over 16,000 arouras of wheat each. Phebichis would be on another line in the account with missing lesser yields.[20] Presumably, what we have here are older settlements being incorporated or losing out to the katoicic settlement of the nome. We could wish for Demotic evidence to balance our approach.

There is a second similar archive of papyri for this period which has a few Demotic pieces. The archive is better known for the late second and early first centuries B.C., but the Tebtunis papyri at the Bancroft Library, the University of California, Berkeley, include documents that reach into the reign of Ptolemy XII. And more documents from Ptolemy XII and Cleopatra VII in this collection remain unpublished. Of the unpublished catalogued pieces from the first century B.C. that I have been able to look at, I noted accounts from the first part of the century and official records from Ptolemy XII — including a Demotic papyrus from year 13.[21] For Cleopatra's reign, at this point four documents are of interest: two published papyri which I have revised to Cleopatra VII (*P. Teb.* I 102 and 202);[22] and two unpublished papyri, a letter UC 2443 from the series marked box 19 and

18. In registers BGU XIV 2441–2450, the *kleros* holders show largely Greek names, while the farmers have more Egyptian names (see Brashear's appendices to BGU XIV, pp. 223–27, and his chart beginning on p. 229). Greek names in the Herakleopolite papyri presumably mean Greeks, and the katoicics must have enjoyed a high share of the prosperity. The problem of determining ethnicity from nomenclature has been dealt with by Crawford (1971); and Quaegebeur has defined the difficulties of nomenclature (1971a, pp. 158–72).

19. Along with Greek ethnics, we have Trogodytes and names in the evidence indicate some Jewish settlement in the nome (Onias in BGU VIII 1730; Alexander, son of Isakis, in *SB* V 7610). Latin names should show a Roman presence or are they an indication of status? For a consideration of Herakleopolite nomenclature, see Brashear's commentary to BGU XIV, pp. 222–26.

20. The amounts the two toparchies hold in wheat production in BGU XIV 2434 remain, though the names of the toparchies are lost; the amounts are $16,705\frac{5}{32}$ arouras and $16,133\frac{25}{32}$ arouras. Brashear, in his introduction to BGU XIV 2434, proposes Peri Polin, the Middle Toparchy, or Phebichis for the missing names. Only one other toparchy has a larger wheat cultivation in the register, Peri Tilothin at $17,246\frac{3}{4}$ arouras, so Phebichis with less wheat production should have far less an area than 16,000 arouras of wheat (Peran has only $3959\frac{1}{4}$ arouras of wheat in BGU XIV 2434). Phebichis is notable for references to barley production in the papyri; perhaps it is the region under cultivation in BGU XIV 2439 which has a more even distribution of lands under wheat and barley cultivation (see above, footnote 8).

21. The year 13 Demotic papyrus is UC 2530, the recto of *P. Teb.* II 288, a Greek text also from year 13. In addition to the catalogued papyri, there are, in the collection, other uncatalogued pieces whose origin, whether in regard to crocodile, box, city, or place in the collection, is unknown. One such mysterious group which came to my attention consists of nine pieces in a file folder marked UC 2411–2420; the catalogued UC 2411–2420 are otherwise located and known. These uncatalogued pieces in the folder show late hands and are in Greek and Demotic. I thank the University of North Dakota for providing me with a grant for research at the Bancroft Library, the University of California, Berkeley.

22. *P. Teb.* I 102 can be either Ptolemy XII or Cleopatra VII, though from the hand I might favor the latter, but it is a private hand. *P. Teb.* I 202 is Cleopatra VII; see Ricketts 1990, notes 27 and 37 and text. Both *P. Teb.* I 102 and 202 are from crocodile 29 (see below, footnote 23, for crocodile 29, box 19, and box 20).

box 20 (the last in the series, UC 2446 is dated A.D. 6),[23] and UC 1407, accounts, the verso of *P. Teb.* II 382, division of lands. The editors of the collection dated the accounts to around 30 B.C. to A.D. 1 (perhaps meaning through the early first century A.D.).[24] Although the Tebtunis accounts from the first century B.C. might be compared to the Herakleopolite accounts, and Demotic evidence to Greek, the comparison would be limited, of course, by the fewer Tebtunis examples.

Far more numerous are the examples from the late period, Ptolemy XII and after, in the second archive, the Theban ostraca. In my research, I have been interested especially in the Milne-Currelly collection housed in the Royal Ontario Museum and the Ashmolean Museum, and I would like to thank Dr. Nicholas Millet, Director of the Egyptian Department, the Royal Ontario Museum, and Dr. Helen Whitehouse, Keeper of the Antiquities, the Ashmolean Museum, for allowing me access to the ostraca and for their help during my research and photography. The difficulty with the ostraca, of course, is that when a regnal year is given in a text, the ruler is often not stated. Nevertheless, the late ostraca can be used as sources for the period in a general overview; those ostraca that can be dated may yield critical information for specific studies. Conclusions from two such studies deserve comment.

The first study involves the evidence for an Egyptian administrative family in the Thebaid. The Monkores family has been dealt with by Thissen (1977, pp. 181–91), and I have added a few comments about how the family seemed to fare better under Ptolemy XII than under Cleopatra VII.[25] Monkores family *strategoi* held several Theban nomes.[26] Active from the reign of Ptolemy XII,[27] the family survived to the Roman period (early Augustus) according to the Rhind papyrus. And subsequent publications by Wångstedt include an ostracon, which gives reference to what must be a later generation of the same family: Pamonthes, son of Pamonthes, who is the scribe, along with

23. The series includes UC 2441 through UC 2446 and runs from the first century B.C. (UC 2441–2443) to A.D. 6 (UC 2444–2446). The papyri are marked "from box 19" or "from box 20" (UC 2443) with no further description of origin. Besides the late sources box 19 and box 20, crocodile 29 is notable for papyri dating to the last Ptolemies. Crocodile 29 is the source of papyri for Ptolemy XII (including UC 2416, 112 or 76 B.C.) and Cleopatra VII (*P. Teb.* I 102 and 202).

24. The papyrus is of interest for Cleopatra's reign, because while it appears to be Roman rather than Ptolemaic, it is just Roman and so is evidence for the transition. The earliest papyrus from Augustus will remain *P. Oxy.* XII 1453, dated 1 Thoth, year 1 (31 August 30 B.C.).

25. The *epistrategos* Kallimachos' family is in Thebes under Cleopatra VII. For my comments on Monkores and Kallimachos, see 1982/83, pp. 161–65, especially pp. 162–63, note 8. And see now Ricketts 1990, notes 17 and 30.

26. Monkores' family held the Pathyrite, probably the Latopolite, the Ombite, and Perithebes (Monkores is *PP* I and VIII 283 and 284; his son, Kalasiris, *PP* I and VIII 266). For Monkores' family and Thebes and Monkores and the family of Kallimachos, now see Ricketts 1990, note 31.

27. For the evidence for Monkores' family, see Thissen 1971, pp. 181–91. *O. Theb.* D 22, naming Monkores, should be Ptolemy XII, however, not Augustus, so that Monkores I and Monkores II are the same individual in the manner of *PP* I and VIII 283 and 284. This dates Monkores to Ptolemy XII, his son, Kalasiris, to 55 B.C., and his other son, Pamonthes-Plenis, to year 5 of Cleopatra VII, 47 B.C. See Ricketts 1990, notes 15 (for *Med. Habu Graff.* 44 as 47 B.C.) and 17.

Kalasiris.[28] The ostracon takes the family to year 32 of Augustus, still holding on to the bureaucracy, and here we see the other side, continuity, in transition through Augustus.[29]

The second study deals with supporting evidence for the regnal year dating "year 30 which is also year 1" of 51 B.C. The year 30 in the dating belongs to Ptolemy XII; year 1 to Cleopatra VII (though their names do not appear), and the double era runs from 24 May through 15 July 51 B.C.[30] Cleopatra's year 1 precedes the double era 30 and 1 on one hieroglyphic inscription (*Bucheum* 13), and a second inscription and a papyrus, both in Greek, interrupt the double era with a year 1 dating (*I. Fay.* III 205 [Bianchi 1988, pp. 188–89], 2 July 51; *PSI* VIII 969, 6 July 51). Also, a year 30 ostracon in the Theban collection, *O. Theb.* III 30, is dated after Cleopatra's year 1 (4 March 51), and another series of Demotic Theban ostraca, from April to 3 June 51 may be Ptolemy XII (*O. Theb.* D 103, April [?]; D 100, 23 May; and D 24, 3 June).[31] The three datings, year 30, year 30 and 1, and year 1, overlap. And the discovery of another year 30 text, unpublished, in the ROM Theban ostraca, may lengthen the use of the single era year 30. The Demotic ostracon dated 27 June (Pauni 26), year 30, looks to be this era — late second century B.C. — arguably, but it is very close in appearance to the year 30 series.[32] I wish to thank Dr. George Hughes and Dr. Janet Johnson for examining closely for me the year date in this text, especially the somewhat troublesome day 26.[33] The document would extend the year 30 dating significantly, to the end of June 51 B.C., so that the purpose of the dual era as an indication of coregency, not honorific, would have to

28. Wångstedt 1968, pp. 33–34, no. 9. The ostracon is DO BM 31874. Kalasiris, son of Peftumonth, is one of the taxpayers; Pamonthes, son of Pamonthes, signs, year 32, 21 Pauni (A.D. 4). Another ostracon published by Wångstedt, from year 9 of Tiberius, has Pamonthes, son of Harsiese, son of Pelils; there is no office for Pamonthes in this text; see Wångstedt 1971–72, pp. 42–43, no. 16.

29. Studies now emphasize a change in policy in the Roman administration away from the Ptolemaic system. See Geraci 1983; Bowman adds other areas of change to the consideration in his review (1985, pp. 285–86) of Geraci. But the retention of administrators from Ptolemaic administrative families under Roman rule — in Pamonthes' case a powerful, Thebaid family — in a period that goes well beyond an early transition rather shows a remarkable continuity through Augustus (another example of the *strategoi* family is Ptolemaios, Roman *strategos*, son of Panas, Ptolemaic *strategos* [*PP* I 293]). It appears that strictly Ptolemaic court conventions, of course, were dropped, such as Ptolemaic titulature and court titles as Geraci has discussed. However, the regional administration continues, as the Pamonthes example shows, or was restructured in the case of the tax system to meet Roman expectations.

30. For the evidence and double era year 30 and year 1, see Skeat 1960, pp. 91–94.

31. For the dating of the year 30 series to Ptolemy XII, see de Meulenaere 1967, pp. 297–305. De Meulenaere dates the set according to the related pieces: *O. Wångstedt* 60, with Pikos, son of Ammonios and *O. Mattha* 81, year 28 of Ptolemy XII, with the same person. *O. Mattha* 81 also contains the phrase "the old district," as does *O. Theb.* year 30 group. An earlier date (Ptolemy X) is not considered and the related *O. Mattha* 275 still looks curiously Roman.

32. The ostracon, ROM D 259, a receipt of *Ḫnsw-Ḏḥwty*, son of *Pa-Mnṭ*, looks in some respects second century B.C., yet it is close to the year 30 series, though without "the old district," and also to a year 23 ostracon in the same collection, *O. Theb.* D 82, from Ptolemy XII. The year 30 Demotic documents extending to early June, or late June with the addition of ROM D 259, evidence the meaning of a coregency for the year 30 and 1 Greek texts, just as the year 1 Greek and hieroglyphic inscriptions evidence Cleopatra's rule before the double era in our papyri. The preference of the Theban scribes for Ptolemy's year over a coregnant queen's year can be seen again in year 2 of Berenike IV, when, although he is out of the country, Ptolemy's year stands before Berenike's year 2 in the evidence. See Ricketts 1990, note 15. Additional evidence in the Theban ostraca for this dual era from year 2 of Berenike IV has been brought to my attention by Dr. Ursula Kaplony-Heckel, and a follow-up note is in preparation. I wish to thank Dr. Kaplony-Heckel for allowing me to look at the manuscript for her recent editions of Theban ostraca from the British Museum (1990).

33. The day is Pauni 26, not 6; I thank Drs. Hughes and Johnson for their readings and critical comments.

be considered again. [34] Both regnal dates in use, from February through the end of June, should indicate a coregency, and so, in the Greek documents, the double era appears, the "year 30 which is also the year 1." (The era ended probably in late June or July with the death of Ptolemy XII which Caelius puts to the question on 1 August 51 [30 June 51, Skeat] in *Epistolarum Ad Familiares* 8.4.) The first of Cleopatra's double eras, then goes along with the other double eras of Cleopatra's reign: following Ptolemaic practice, they always mean a coregency.[35]

The significance of Demotic ostraca to late studies is shown, I believe, by these last two studies and, of course, there are Demotic inscriptions and statue inscriptions to supplement the ostraca. In conclusion, Demotic papyri may give us a basis of comparison of productivity in our future consideration of the Tebtunis and Herakleopolite archives, while the Theban ostraca already have allowed us to put back correctly in place a coregency of 51 B.C.

34. Skeat (1960, pp. 91–94) concluded from the Greek evidence and an Egyptian inscription (*Bucheum* 13) that the double era continues the last year of the former ruler, Ptolemy XII, with Cleopatra VII. I cited his argument in my earlier work (criticized by Criscuolo 1989, p. 325, note 1; though my interpretation is rather a discussion of the scholarship approaching the problem and I conclude with the papyrologists, especially Skeat, from primarily Greek evidence). With the Demotic year 30 series from *O. Theb.* now Ptolemy XII — and it appears to be so — and not earlier (Ptolemy X?), adding the June 51 piece ROM D 259, a coregency must be meant by the year 30 and 1.

35. For the last double era of Cleopatra's reign as a coregency with Caesarion, see Ricketts 1989, p. 46. As a result of this Congress presentation, I have learned from Dr. Jan Quaegebeur that the inscriptional evidence from Dendera which he has been studying supports the coregency of Ptolemy XII and Cleopatra VII. I thank Dr. Quaegebeur for allowing me to read the manuscript of his article soon to be published, "Cléopâtre VII et le temple de Dendera."

CHAPTER 34

IMPLICIT MODELS OF CROSS-CULTURAL INTERACTION: A QUESTION OF NOSES, SOAP, AND PREJUDICE

ROBERT K. RITNER
*The Oriental Institute**

In 1975, a study of the "Limits of Hellenization" by Arnaldo Momigliano began by noting that

> The philosophic historian will never stop meditating on the nose of Cleopatra. If that nose had pleased the gods as it pleased Caesar and Antony, ... we would have more books on Tutankhamen and on Alexander the Great. But a Latin-speaking Etruscologist, not a Greek-speaking Egyptologist, brought to Britain the fruits of the victory of Roman imperialism over the Hellenistic System. We must face the facts.[1]

* Dr. Ritner now holds the position of Assistant Professor of Egyptology in the Department of Near Eastern Languages and Civilizations, Yale University.

1. Momigliano 1975, p. 1. Ironically, Momigliano's pronouncements just preceded major museum tours of objects associated with both Tutankhamen and Alexander, generating a plethora of volumes on both rulers. From the Egyptological perspective, it is hard to imagine a need for yet "more books on Tutankhamen"; several new volumes and reeditions are appearing as this note is composed. Antagonism toward popular interest in Tutankhamen (at the expense of "proper" interest in classical Greece) also underlies the defensive inclusion of a sarcastic chapter on "The Treasures of Egypt" within Peter Green's impassioned apologia for "classical (Greek and Latin) education," *Classical Bearings* 1989, pp. 77–90. His presumption to critique the "value" of literary (p. 82) and religious (p. 90) writings, which he can neither read nor interpret, serves as a model of its kind. Egyptologists, who have only begun to penetrate the social, symbolic, and mythological complexity of these texts, will be struck to note that Green declares Budge's obsolete translation of *The Book of the Dead* "exemplary," and the same author's unreferenced and inaccurate *Egyptian Hieroglyphic Dictionary* "invaluable, but highly technical" (p. 86). Classicists' discomfort with Egyptian culture stems in large measure from the fact that it was not simply the lower levels of Greek and Roman society who praised or espoused Egyptian thought, but the very "torch-bearers" of "classical" civilization: Plato (cf. *Laws* 656), Pythagorus, Plutarch, Apuleius, Iamblichus, Marinos, Proclus, etc. This is, to quote Oscar Wilde, "the rage of Caliban at seeing himself in the glass." The fact that Egyptian philosophical speculation is expressed through complex symbolic *imagery*, rather than complex *vocabulary*, has frustrated expectations (held since the Renaissance) of discovering within Egyptian texts a simple confirmation of the universal validity of Greek philosophical categories and concepts. Egyptian discourse is not readily amenable to modern, "classically" trained rhetoricians, and the interest or devotion of a Pythagorus or Iamblichus is confusing, and not a little embarrassing. "This is the rage of Caliban at not seeing himself in the glass." Modern discomfort notwithstanding, the third century author Heliodorus felt constrained to explain Homer's knowledge of the gods by claiming that the father of Greek literature was really an Egyptian (*The Ethiopian Story*, III, §§ 14–15), and the same claim was made by the fourth century poet Olympiodorus of Thebes. Philosophical "significance" is a matter of taste and cultural predisposition.

Just precisely what facts are intended? The reference to Cleopatra's nose is an old cliché, appearing twice in the philosophical reflections of Blaise Pascal,[2] and even serving as the name of a new volume on "verbal shortcuts": *Cleopatra's Nose, the Twinkie Defense, & 1500 Other Verbal Shortcuts in Popular Parlance*.[3] Pascal uses the image only to reflect upon vanity and love, that is to say Caesar's chance attraction to Cleopatra, which had repercussions throughout the Roman world.[4] Momigliano uses this "verbal shortcut" for very different purposes; the image of the defeated Cleopatra serves to introduce the reasons for his complete exclusion of Egypt from a study on Hellenization (Momigliano 1975, pp. 3–4).

Momigliano declares that there was "no dramatic change in the Greek evaluation of Egypt during the Hellenistic Period"; all concepts were taken from the fanciful Egypt of Homer and Herodotus.[5] This is an extraordinary remark; Greeks now lived throughout Egypt, and whether they mingled extensively with the population or not, their experience will have been factual — not fanciful — and their concepts *will* have changed. When a Faiyumic gymnasium, the cultural guardian of Greek ethnicity, is dedicated to an Egyptian crocodile god, something has clearly changed.[6] Momigliano's comments suggest the image of a Greek fourth generation resident in the countryside scanning his Herodotus as though a Baedecker's Guide, hoping to discover where he lives, and who are his neighbors — or, perhaps, who is his wife.

Another reason given for ignoring the question of Egyptian-Greek relations in this period is the supposed decline of Egyptian culture, "because it was under the direct control of the Greeks and came to represent an inferior stratum of the population" (Momigliano 1975, pp. 3–4). Such an assessment follows one of the most enduring patterns used to explain cultural history, which may be termed the "Biological Model," or, if you will, culture as a plant: it sprouts, grows, flowers, and decays.

Whether expressed openly or merely implied, this notion underlies most discussions of Egyptian history to this day. The Old Kingdom equals the "sprout," the Middle Kingdom represents "growth," the New Kingdom is the "flower," while the Late period constitutes "protracted decay," and the Ptolemaic and Roman eras are certain "death." Loss of political independence is interpreted as a loss of cultural independence and vitality. Any evidence of subsequent change is viewed in terms of degeneration or foreign influence.

The traditional, basic histories of Breasted and Gardiner stop with the Persian conquest. Breasted applied a biological model quite literally, describing post-Persian Egypt as the "convulsive contractions which sometimes lend momentary motion to limbs from which conscious

2. See Davidson and Dubé 1975, p. 190; and the editions by Lafuma 1951, p. 232; and Stewart 1965, pp. 50–51.

3. Agel and Glanze 1990. The discussion of "Cleopatra's nose" is on p. 211.

4. Lafuma 1951, § 413-90, p. 232 (= Stewart 1965, §93, pp. 50-51): "Qui voudra connaître à plein la vanité de l'homme n'a qu'à considérer les causes et les effets de l'amour. La cause en est un je ne sais quoi. Corneille. Et les effets en sont effroyables. Ce je ne sais quoi, (*qu'on ne peut*) si peu de chose qu'on ne peut le reconnaître remue toute la terre, les princes, les armées, le monde entier. Le nez de Cléopatre s'il eût été plus court toute la face de la terre aurait changé." See also Stewart § 93 bis: "*Vanité* . La cause et les effets de l'amour: Cléopatre."

5. See Momigliano 1975, p. 3; and cf. p. 4: "But the Hellenistic Greeks preferred the fanciful images of an eternal Egypt to the Egyptian thought of their time." The transmission of the Egyptian fable of the lion and the mouse to "Aesop" disproves this contention (West 1969, pp. 161–83), as does the presence of a translated Demotic romance on Nectonebo among the reading materials of Apollonios in *UPZ* I, no. 81. Momigliano also suggests that the Greeks never viewed Egypt as a political power, inexplicably ignoring the significant Saite-Greek political maneuvers against the Persians.

6. For the stele in Trinity College, Dublin (*OGIS* 176), see Bevan 1968, p. 333. The depiction is purely Egyptian, with no attempt to modify the animal god for "Hellenistic" sensibilities.

life has long departed."[7] Gardiner noted that it might seem "ludicrous" to stop Egyptian history without mentioning the major Ptolemaic temples, but offered the reader a *superior* trade in the form of a final chapter on Egyptian *prehistory* (Gardiner 1961, p. 382). The attitude extends not merely to histories but to historians. Note how few Demoticists there are in world, how few contemporary Egyptologists extend their interests past Tutankhamen and the New Kingdom "flowering." In the past, Demoticists have been considered almost "suspect" to "mainstream" Egyptologists. It is perhaps worthy of reflection that Petrie did not commission a Demoticist to write the Ptolemaic volume in his series *A History of Egypt*, but instead turned to the Greek historian Mahaffy (1899). The presumption is, of course, that Ptolemaic history is *Greek* history; native Egyptian history was dead. Within Demotic studies, the response to such declarations of "premature death" has taken the form of numerous studies detailing and stressing the *vitality* of late, native culture, whether in terms of religion, literature, or even economics. In so far as cultural "vitality" is confused with cultural "purity," however, we run the risk of devaluing important examples of cross-cultural interactions. For the Egyptian historian, it should be remembered that the "flowering" of the New Kingdom occurred within a truly "multi-cultural" context, with Semitic influence from the court to the countryside, with clear influence in the military, religion, and literature. Such cultural borrowings in the New Kingdom are seen not as decay, but as cosmopolitan adaptations indicative of vitality. Need Ptolemaic Egyptian adaptations be seen as anything less?

The biological model which has so dominated Egyptian historiography has also had its influence in the writing of Greek history. With the loss of political independence to Alexander, Greek culture was once thought to have lost its authenticity, a notion enshrined in the contrast posed by the names "Hellenic" (genuine Greek) and "Hellenistic" ("would be" Greek).[8] Old notions of a Hellenistic "mixed culture" devalued the period in the eyes of Classicists. Like Demoticists, Greek Papyrologists have been viewed as "outsiders." In 1920, the great Hellenistic scholar Rostovtzeff still had to appeal for interest in the period, and insist that Alexandria was a legitimate continuation of Athens.[9] The necessity of the appeal is clear from the same scholar's appointment at the University of Wisconsin in Madison in the *Ancient History* department — the Classics department would have nothing to do with him.[10] Rostovtzeff stressed a vision of the Hellenistic world which was designed to win over the Classical historian, however. In this vision, a Greek "world culture" applied its "genius and innovation" to revivify older, withering civilizations. The *Greeks* were not in

7. Breasted 1905, p. 595. By a certain perverse irony, the official, posthumous portrait of Breasted poses the author with a statue of *post-Persian* date (Dynasty XXX).

8. For a concise discussion of the creation of the term "Hellenistic" by Droysen, and the concept's basis in the presumed fusion of cultures, see Préaux 1978, pp. 5–9. For the continued use of the notion of "Mischkultur," see the review of Maehler and Strocka, *Das ptolemäische Ägypten*, by W. J. Tait 1982, cols. 78–87.

9. Rostovtzeff 1920, pp. 161–78. Compare p. 161: "Such an epoch cannot be designated a period of decline. I take the liberty of affirming that people who know Athens and who are not thoroughly acquainted with Alexandria, Pergamon, and Antioch do not know Greece. They cannot fully realize the exceptional work of Greek genius."

10. Rostovtzeff's altercations with the local Classics Department are chronicled in Bowersock 1986, pp. 391–400, esp. p. 395. This reference was first brought to my attention by J. G. Manning.

a decline; they were the driving spirits of a new, if totalitarian, order.[11] The concept of bringing Western innovation to the withered East had long been a feature of the notion of "Hellenization," and was clearly based on the model of Nineteenth century European imperialism. As Alan Samuel has remarked: "Perhaps American ideas of 'manifest destiny' made the idea of the spread of Greek culture as welcome in the U.S. as Kipling's 'white man's burden' made it understandable in Britain" (A. Samuel 1989, p. 1). This colonial "parallel" was explicitly recognized by Bevan, who felt it necessary to stress certain differences between Ptolemaic Egypt and British South Africa or India (Bevan 1968, pp. 86 and 89). Nonetheless, Greek culture was to be viewed as superior, with a distinctly patronizing attitude toward the locals. Thus, when Bevan briefly notes the existence of Demotic documents, he remarks that they furnish important data for *native* life; the possibility does not occur to him that they could be of importance for the country as a whole, and they play almost no role in his history of Ptolemaic Egypt.[12] If Greek culture was to be saved from the biological model, Egyptian culture was still seen as a withering plant.

The evolving theories of Rostovtzeff added a new element to the older colonial model, clearly derived from his own, personal experience. From the East, the Greeks supposedly adapted and perfected the notion of "Oriental Despotism": a strong central power which demanded blind obedience, controlled private property, and desired to socialize or nationalize production.[13] It is at times difficult to know whether he is speaking of Ptolemaic Egypt, or of Marxist Russia, from which he had recently fled. For Rostovtzeff, the Egyptian was no longer patronized by a benign superior, but ruthlessly exploited by a monolithic government — he was a cultureless, powerless, second-class citizen to be pitied.

Such an image easily led to the perception of racial animosity between Egyptian and Greek, and fostered studies of local resistance to Hellenism, such as that of Eddy in 1961 and Momigliano in 1975.[14] The Egyptian was now seen as hateful, rebellious, and threatening, though still, of course, second class.

Our theoretical approach to Ptolemaic Egyptian society has changed much in the past fifteen years. Notions of racial animosity have been discounted, and, slowly, the vitality of local Egyptian tradition has been recognized.[15] A recent symposium on Cleopatra's Egypt in Brooklyn was entitled

11. Rostovtzeff 1920, pp. 161–78, esp. p. 161: "Such an epoch cannot be designated a period of decline"; and p. 162: "The Greek city states were gradually incorporated in the big monarchies of the East, infusing new forces into decrepit bureaucratic organizations. First of all, Greek genius supplied much constructive power in the building up of the Eastern political and economic system." The same dogmatic belief in Greek "genius" at the expense of supposed Egyptian "decrepitude" yet dominates the interpretation by Bagnall 1981, pp. 5–21. Bagnall proclaims "a fundamentally exploitative attitude on the part of the Greeks" who "had little true respect for Egyptian civilization as a living entity" (p. 21). Compare also p. 15: "Egypt afforded the economic opportunities; but they were created by the application of Greek conceptions of management and entrepreneurship to the Egyptian situation, not by long-standing Egyptian economic traditions." This conviction derives more from received convention than fact; see A. Samuel 1989, pp. 51–65. Bagnall's zeal to deny Egyptian influence in any aspect of Ptolemaic life leads him to rather peculiar distortions. The pronouncement (p. 20) that the underlying cosmology of magical texts derives exclusively from contemporary Hellenistic philosophy is an untenable exaggeration; the fundamentally Egyptian character of the magical papyri was evident even to Nock (1929, pp. 219–35), who suggested that unknown philosophers may have compiled the material. The "philosophy hypothesis" is in any case false, see further Ritner (forthcoming).

12. Bevan 1968, p. 159: "Numbers of demotic deeds have been found, which furnish important data for native life under Greek rule."

13. Rostovtzeff 1920, p. 162: "The Eastern state seemed to be quite incompatible with that of the Greek. The foundations of the Eastern state were a strong central power, an army of appointed, responsible officials, the blind obedience of the population, a tendency to make private property serve the interests of the State, and a desire to socialize and nationalize production."

14. For the impact of such thought in Egyptological writings, see Griffiths 1979, pp. 174–79.

15. An overview of these developments is found in A. Samuel 1989 and 1983.

ruthlessly exploited by a monolithic government — he was a cultureless, powerless, second-class citizen to be pitied.

Such an image easily led to the perception of racial animosity between Egyptian and Greek, and fostered studies of local resistance to Hellenism, such as that of Eddy in 1961 and Momigliano in 1975.[15] The Egyptian was now seen as hateful, rebellious, and threatening, though still, of course, second class.

Our theoretical approach to Ptolemaic Egyptian society has changed much in the past fifteen years. Notions of racial animosity have been discounted, and, slowly, the vitality of local Egyptian tradition has been recognized.[16] A recent symposium on Cleopatra's Egypt in Brooklyn was entitled "Cultures in Conflict," yet the question of cultural animosity was ignored by all speakers.[17] Old concepts of cultural synthesis or subjugation are giving way to theories of cultural separation.[18] While this separation should perhaps please everyone, allowing Greek and Egyptian culture to be "vital" independently, I fear that it can be taken too far, and am suspicious of the underlying motives in *overstressing* the absence of interaction, and wonder whether cultural "vitality" is again confused with cultural "purity."

Consider the 1989 discussion by Heinrich von Staden on the question of the influence of Egyptian medicine on the Alexandrian physician Hierophilus.[19] Von Staden admits certain similarities in terms of pulse taking, drugs, and disease theory, but his arguments are often carried by adjectives, not evidence: Egyptian pulse theory is dismissed as "struggling but insistent,"[20] Egyptian disease theory is "not alien" to the Greek (von Staden 1989, p. 5), the Egyptian physician's touch is "aggressive," the Greek's is "restrained" (von Staden 1989, p. 15). Egyptian enema treatments are said to represent "a pathological preoccupation with the anus ... bound to elicit an ethno-psychological study of Pharaonic Egypt sooner or later" (!!!)[21] It should be added that one Egyptian enema specialist is known to have had enough Greek patients to require the services of a well-paid interpreter; here at least there is cross-cultural preoccupation![22] Having accused the Egyptians of neurotic cleanliness,[23] von Staden then faults them as dirty, for not knowing soap (von Staden 1989, p. 15). Soap, as we know it, was invented in 1787 by the French surgeon Nicolas Leblanc, prompted by an earlier offer of a state prize by Louis XVI.[24] Until then, "soap" had been imported

15. For the impact of such thought in Egyptological writings, see Griffiths 1979, pp. 174–79.

16. An overview of these developments is found in A. Samuel 1989 and 1983.

17. "Ptolemaic Egypt: Cultures in Conflict" held December 2–3, 1988 at the Brooklyn Museum. Lecturers instead emphasized cooperation and cross-influence between cultures. A direct question posed by this author regarding the validity of the notion of "cultures in conflict" generated complete disavowal.

18. See A. Samuel 1989, passim; idem 1983, especially pp. 105–17 ; and Bagnall 1988, pp. 21–27.

19. Reviewed by myself 1989, pp. 39–40.

20. Von Staden 1989, p. 10. Egyptian influence here is said to be "not inconceivable."

21. Von Staden 1989, p. 12. This hyperbolic bombast derives from the author's distortion of Egyptian disease theory, which prescribed enemas and emetics for internal complaints in preference to bleeding. A reasoned analysis is found in Steuer 1948 and Steuer and Saunders 1959.

22. Admitted grudgingly in von Staden 1989, p. 26. The author insists that this must be an isolated case in Alexandria since "evidence of this kind is very rare"; in fact, evidence *of any kind* from Alexandria is "very rare" and generalizations about medical interactions are mere speculation. Bagnall 1981, p. 18, attempts to find in this transaction "deeper and darker aspects" of the Greek "exploitative attitude" since it involves mercenary motives. Bagnall is unaware of the theoretical basis of the Egyptian treatment, which is dismissed as "primitive" and "a toy" (in contrast to "Hellenistic science"): "I forbear to offer modern parallels to exotic practices like this becoming fashionable." Smirking remarks aside, the supposed "toy" of suppository and enema treatment remains a basic adjunct to modern medical practice; it is in no sense "exotic." Where, however, is the "Hellenistic science" of bleeding?

23. Von Staden 1989, p. 12: "legendary obsession with personal cleanliness."

24. A good, popular account of the tragi-comic development of modern soap is found in Bodanis 1986, pp. 206–09.

Though Mahaffy (1899, p. 191) and the Loeb editor Paton (1975, vol. 6, p. 335) kept the positive translation, Kunze emended the Greek to read "litigious" (πολυδικον),[24] while Bevan "charitably" assumed that Polybius meant: "The Egyptians at Alexandria might be rogues and cheats, but they did not violate the order of the city; they were civil rogues" (Bevan 1968, p. 100, note 3). Letronne kept the text and translated "submissive to the law," Kramer changed πολιτικον to απολιτικον "uncivilized," and most editors simply insert ου "not" before πολιτικον, yielding "not civilized."[25]

For Fraser, in his *Ptolemaic Alexandria* of 1972, emendation is said to be necessary (vol. 2a, pp. 144–45, note 184), and the Egyptians are described as "sharp-*tempered* and *un*civilized" (ibid., vol. 1, p. 61 [italics mine]). Building upon this rewritten text, Fraser constructs his entire framework of Alexandrian history, attributing the city riots of later years to the violence "inherent in the character of the Egyptianized population of the city" (implied proof of this assertion being Polybius).[26] Superior Greek culture had been weakened and destroyed through "the adulteration of Greek by Egyptian blood" (Fraser 1972, p. 84). By an ironic and devious rewriting of the sources to meet expected prejudices, the one group *not* stigmatized by Polybius as a factor in civic unrest has become the scapegoat for the city's demise. Fraser's analysis of the Jews is also interesting; they are said to be on a higher cultural level than the Egyptians, not because of their own culture which is irrelevant, but because they better ape the fashions of their cultural superiors. They were able to "acquire Greek culture of a superior level" (Fraser 1972, p. 57).

For Bowersock in 1990, the theory of a separation of cultures is confirmation of the Egyptians' "airless immobility" (p. 55),[27] overcome at last by the saving grace of Greek literature:

> Since demotic was not about to fill the intellectual and religious needs of Egyptians, it was thus ultimately Greek, despite long centuries of resistance to assimilation, that became the language in which Egyptians expressed themselves (Bowersock 1990, p. 57).

Egyptians redeem themselves for Bowersock by their assimilation as wandering Greek poets. As an aside, one should contrast the attitude of Gilbert Murray to Demotic literature in 1911. Professing himself "fascinated" by the tale of Setna, and regretting that "my own education has been neglected in the matter of Demotic," he went on to set the translation of Griffith into English verse as the poem *Nefrekepta*.[28]

24. Bevan 1968, p. 100, note 3. As Bevan notes, this emendation was accepted by Lumbroso.

25. A useful summary of this editorial contrivance is found in Walbank 1979, pp. 182–83. Walbank accepts the fabrication "{not} civilized." The image of the "exploited Egyptian" has influenced Egyptologists' interpretations of this Polybius passage as well. Thus, while W. Max Müller does not emend the text, he assumes that it must reveal "the surprise of Polybius that the Alexandrines of Egyptian race were somewhat different from the dull and apathetic mass of the other Egyptian natives"; see idem 1920, p. 9, note 1.

26. Fraser 1972, vol. 1, p. 800. Bagnall inverts the facts in 1981, p. 16, when he states that this passage in Polybius "has persuaded some moderns, most notably Peter Fraser, whose great *Ptolemaic Alexandria* is dedicated to the thesis that the Egyptian element was responsible for the decline of the city in practically all respects." On the contrary, it is the thesis of Fraser et al. which has reshaped the quote of Polybius!

27. Bagnall 1988, p. 24, also invokes the false image of a static Egypt, which could not adapt foreign elements without ceasing to be Egyptian. Such adaptations characterize Egyptian culture from the Predynastic Period. The unchanging nature of Egyptian culture is greatly over-emphasized by those who do not know it, and for whom everything Egyptian looks alike. A similar oversimplification can be directed to Greek and Latin materials, as embodied in the notion of "Greco-Roman culture."

28. Quotations on p. iii. Murray believed in the influence of Egyptian upon Greek literature, and his assessment of the Demotic novel is correspondingly flattering. Clearly, literary evaluation fluctuates with the bias of the critic, contra the absolute "truths" espoused in P. Green 1989, p. 82 and passim.

Consider finally the much-debated question of the "ethnicity" of Dryton's wife Apollonia.[29] Though she explicitly styles herself a "Greek" in both Demotic and Greek legal documents, it has been stated by Bagnall in 1988 that she cannot be Greek, since the "milieu" in which she lives *seems* Egyptian (p. 23).[30] This "milieu" includes, of course, her Cretan husband Dryton. Because Apollonia makes use of Egyptian documents, occasionally uses an Egyptian version of her name, and acts in an independent manner which defies standard preconceptions, Bagnall assumes that her claims to be Greek must be lies (and lies accepted at face value in open court): "In the case of the women, we cannot detect any motive other than social for the claim of Greek status, which was for them higher and more prestigious" (Bagnall 1988, pp. 23–24). By implication, no Greek woman would lower herself to using Egyptian practices — even if it meant the freedom to engage in commerce without a "kyrios" as intermediary. Conversely, Egyptian women must have craved the status of a cloistered Greek woman.[31] What then should one make of the lady Artemisia in one of the earliest preserved Greek papyri, *PGM* XL (see Preisendanz 1973, vol. 2, pp. 177–78)? Her Demotic-influenced petition to Oserapis is certainly reflective of an "Egyptian milieu." Do we make Artemisia a "Hellenizing Egyptian" in the fourth century B.C.?[32] Certainly not. When an individual is recognized as "Greek" to the satisfaction of both contemporary Demotic and Greek legal conventions, they *are* Greek to their contemporaries, whatever that ethnicity may have meant in Ptolemaic Egypt. Who are *we* to suggest that the ethnicity must be a fiction, just to meet *our* expectations?

Clear evidence of any sort of racial or cultural chauvinism is exceedingly rare for the Ptolemaic period.[33] In this regard, particular interest has been devoted during this conference to the preferential rate of assessing the salt tax for "Greeks" as attested in the Demotic Lille papyri from the Faiyum. This imbalance has been suggested by Dorothy Thompson to be a "benefit" for Greek-speakers, serving as an inducement for Egyptians to learn the Greek language. In contrast, Willy Clarysse has viewed the distinct rates as a form of institutionalized cultural "discrimination"

29. Discussion and references in Bagnall 1988, pp. 21–27, specifically attacking my own analysis (1984, pp. 171–88), and that of Pomeroy 1984, pp. 103–24 (now reprinted, 1989). Bagnall (p. 21) faults unnamed authors for supposed "lack of clarity, lack of sophistication," making itemized exception (p. 26, note 5) for those whom he assumes partake of his own interpretive bias. An excellent, spirited rebuttal by Pomeroy served as the plenary lecture for the annual convention of the American Research Center in Egypt held in Philadelphia on April 21, 1989. Bagnall rather misrepresents current assessments of the problem by suggesting that only Pomeroy accepts the notion of Greeks assimilating to Egyptian culture; see Lewis 1986, pp. 103 and 168, note 16 (a verbatim citation of my conclusions included as "an apt ending to the present chapter.") See now the discussion of Goudriaan 1988, pp. 131–33; and the clear example of "Egyptianization" documented by Clarysse within this volume, *Chapter 6*.

30. There is no great sophistication here; whether Apollonia were an "Egyptianizing Greek" or a "Hellenizing Egyptian" her "milieu" in rural Egypt would still be "predominantly Egyptian."

31. Greek trial depositions of ethnicity are also reduced to mere farce.

32. The phraseology of this petition derives directly from contemporary (and prior) Demotic exemplars invoking "the god Oserapis and the gods who sit with Oserapis" (*Wsỉr-Ḥp ỉrm nꜣ nṯr.w nt ḥtp ỉrm=f*); see further the remarks of John Ray in this volume, *Chapter 32*.

33. See A. Samuel 1983, p. 106: "the tone of the documentation ... by and large seems to suggest a rather comfortable relationship on the day-to-day level, with surprisingly few allusions to ethnic difficulties"; and ibid., n. 121: "it is important to note that derogation of the Egyptians is almost lacking from the Greek documentation, even in such texts as those of *UPZ* 8 which do attest disputes between Greek and Egyptian on ethnic bases." Nine examples (for 300 years) are listed in Goudriaan 1988, pp. 107–08, hardly justifying the remark that "the opinion the Greeks had of their Egyptian compatriots was often low." Accusations of ethnic discrimination may hide other motives (and spur official intervention), as recognized by Dorothy Thompson 1988, pp. 229–30. This is not to deny the existence of cultural pride or preference on the part of Egyptian or Greek. Certain tendencies toward "clannishness" are inevitable, if only because of the barriers of language and custom. It is perhaps useful to recall contemporary stereotypes disparaging British cooking (from the French point of view), or French organization (from the British point of view). These hardly reflect pervasive cross-channel "racism."

against Egyptians.[34] While the monetary distinction is fairly trivial (one obol, roughly a day's pay), the interpretive distinction between the designations "inducement" and "discrimination" is quite significant. The "facts" are noncommittal, falling ready prey to our theoretical biases. In either interpretation, however, the one obol difference need not reflect a sense of "racial superiority." If Greek-speaking Egyptians are admitted as "Hellenes" this is obvious. But I think that this need not reflect a sense of "cultural superiority" either, perhaps simply a recognition of cultural separation and numerical imbalance. If anything, it suggests a culture — or perhaps primarily a language — on the *defensive*; superiority does not need inducement.[35] The success of Greek administration in the developing Faiyum was to a large extent dependent upon bureaucratic scribes and interpreters fluent in that language. In any case, the Ptolemaic salt tax does not represent a consistent cultural policy, for the preferential rates were soon abandoned. Greeks and Egyptians were then taxed equally.

In the past, our theories have dictated our facts as often as our facts have dictated our theories. Theoretical bias has been unrecognized and its pervasive influence ignored. So long as we are willing to allow our preconceptions to structure our questions and answers, to rewrite the historians, or disbelieve the papyrus evidence, how will we ever find examples of positive cultural interaction between Egyptian and Greek? It will not matter whether we use Greek or Demotic evidence, or any evidence at all; we shall see only our long-ingrained stereotypes, and meetings like this one will have little purpose.

POSTSCRIPT

In discussions subsequent to the presentation of this paper, two issues were raised which are worthy of note and a brief response.

Diana Delia objected to the above characterization of racial antagonism as "rare," adducing the example of Juvenal, whose "anti-Egyptian" remarks are well known. Juvenal, however, is not relevant to the present discussion, since 1) he is of Roman — not Ptolemaic — date and quite different attitudes prevailed, 2) he is a satirist for whom ridicule — directed indifferently toward Roman, Greek or Egyptian — was an occupation, 3) he was in forced exile in Egypt and thus not disposed to be particularly charitable, and 4) he had been expelled from Rome precisely for his propensity to compose offensive remarks. Reasons of date and occupation also invalidate the (unmentioned) satires of Lucian, whose occasional Egyptian quips are evidence of the "Egyptomania" then popular in Rome. Relations between Greeks and Egyptians certainly deteriorated in Roman Egypt as a direct result of racial and economic distinctions imposed by Rome. This is a reversal of Ptolemaic policy, not an outgrowth of it.

Willy Clarysse's stated belief in the existence of "apartheid" in Ptolemaic Egypt ill accords with his own documentation of a governmentally-recognized "mixed" marriage between an Egyptian woman and a Greek Alexandrian citizen. Despite its basic meaning of "separateness" in Dutch and Flemish, the term "apartheid" in contemporary *English* usage conveys exclusively the nuance of South African practice in which mixed marriages or common use of fountains would be punishable by law. Nothing even vaguely similar existed in Ptolemaic Egypt.

34. See de Cenival 1984 (P. Dem. Lille 99, col. IVa, details the favorable assessments regarding Greek schools, pp. 20–21), and the respective articles by Thompson (*Chapter 40*) and Clarysse (*Chapter 6*) in this volume.

35. Preferential legislation for English in the United States, or French in Quebec, is not motivated by a sense of smug complacency, but by fear of ultimate cultural absorption within a larger foreign group.

CHAPTER 35

WRITING EGYPTIAN: SCRIPTS AND SPEECHES AT THE END OF PHARAONIC CIVILIZATION

ALESSANDRO ROCCATI
The University of Rome

1. Pharaonic Egypt strove to avoid linguistic confusion. In spite of the presence of a number of unknown languages in the country (a situation we can trace back on the base of the evidence from the first millennium B.C., when different cultures in Egypt are well attested), all written expression was devoted to one script and language (which we call Egyptian), thereby covering underlying varieties, possibly for the purpose of giving the impression of uniformity in a unified community. In the first millennium B.C. we witness in Egypt many foreign tongues spoken and written, but until the Ptolemaic period their use remains confined to individual minority cultures and never replaces the indigenous tradition. This latter, on the contrary, though accepting some input from the outside, endeavors to hide the influence and coexistence of several literate cultures beside it (Pestman, ed. 1985 and Pestman 1989, pp. 137–58). As a result we do not find in the native documentation a representation of actual speech, but rather a high register of expression through the different writing traditions (hieroglyphs, hieratic, and Demotic). To these, Greek is added in the Hellenistic period, as an exception to the above outlined situation. In its competition with Demotic, Greek is also felt to be a proper literary language, better reflecting actual language use than the former. This state of affairs largely conceals the lower layers of the population, who will emerge alone on the scene after the fall of the ancient world and the triumph of Christianity (Roccati 1989, pp. 49–56).

Like all the accepted languages of Christianity (Latin, Greek, etc.) Coptic constitutes an adaptation of a low register of speech to literature, which makes it difficult to reconcile its bond with the preceding cultural landscape.

2. As a result of the wider use of alphabets during the first millennium B.C., which encouraged the recording of individual languages, techniques of comparison and translation were developed; but true bilingual inscriptions are not found in Egypt before the Ptolemaic period (Roccati 1988, pp. 145–50). At that time the main impetus becomes the need for mutual understanding between Greeks and Egyptians, whereas Greek culture becomes more and more the dominant world culture. In such a situation there is less need for translating from Greek into Egyptian, mainly Demotic,[1] than from Demotic into Greek. Actually we know some works of native literature preserved in

1. For administrative pieces translated from Greek into Demotic, see Kaplony-Heckel 1974, p. 239.

Greek,[2] or in Demotic and Greek,[3] but no piece of Greek literature is known in Demotic although fragments of other non-Egyptian literature are preserved in Demotic (Zauzich 1976, pp. 180–85; Porten and Zauzich, in press). Only later, during the first two centuries of the Roman Empire, was there some demand for translating occasional Latin or Greek inscriptions into hieroglyphs;[4] these translations involve rather elaborate wording, reflecting a non-Egyptian compositional context.

On the other hand it need not be stressed how translation from Greek into Egyptian formed the bulk of early Coptic literature,[5] although it may be viewed as a continuation and a consequence of previous intense translating between Egyptian and Greek. Undoubtedly the process of massively transferring a cultural legacy from a non-Egyptian civilization into a new Egyptian society leads to the dropping of the ethnocentric attitude reflected in the high speech used from pharaonic down to Ptolemaic times (Grenier 1988, pp. 71–76); this, in turn, provides a clue for why so many Greek (loan-)words are found in the Coptic language.

We can summarize this situation by stating that works may be translated from Demotic into Greek and from Greek into Coptic, where Demotic and Coptic represent but two different faces of Egyptian and of scribal tradition. Recently, however, a claim has been advanced for the preservation of an ancient literary genre in Coptic; a text has been understood as a direct translation from Demotic into Coptic, as if they were two different stages of one and the same language.[6]

3. There are some texts in early Coptic literature which recall earlier local literature rather than works, of whatever origin, whose archetype would have been drawn up in Greek.[7] But the possibility of translating from Egyptian into Coptic is not without question because:

I. It is not likely that the pharaonic works could survive in the Christian tradition;

II. On linguistic grounds, late Demotic and early Coptic are so similar that they should not be treated as two distinct languages. Thus one text should not be translated from Demotic into Coptic, but rather transcribed, and this is what happens in the so called old Coptic texts.

Basically what distinguishes Demotic and Coptic is not so much the difference of writing and language but rather their participation in two different speech registers, high and low, depending on different language requirements. Therefore, according to the pharaonic usage, Demotic represents essentially a unitary language, even if the scribal tradition which was to name it arose in the north of Egypt, while Coptic is by nature divided into dialects.

A classification based on writing may be misleading. Not only do we have in (an adapted) Greek script a work in the traditional pharaonic language (Osing 1976; cf. 1987, p. 83), but old

2. "U" Leiden Greek Papyrus (Maspero 1911, p. 306: "L'aventure du sculpteur Pétêsis et du roi Nectanebo"); Oxyrh. Pap. XI 1381 (second century A.D.: "A Story of Imuthes"); Ammianus Marcellinus 17, 4, 17/23 (translation of the text of the Flaminian Obelisk at Rome). To this section belongs the History of Manetho (third century B.C.); perhaps Plutarch, "Peri Isidos," may be considered an elaborate translation of the Osirian myth (second century A.D.), but see also footnote 3.

3. De Cenival 1988; West 1969, pp. 161–83 (third century A.D.). Papyrus Carlsberg VII and Horapollo, *Hieroglyphika*, may be viewed in the same way: Winter 1991, cols. 91–94.

4. Obelisks from Munich, Naples, Benevento, and Piazza Navona and Pincio in Rome; cf. Winter 1991, cols. 86–87 and Derchain 1987.

5. Orlandi 1984, pp. 181–203. Charles 1916 (only two Ethiopic versions survive of an original, which was perhaps written in Greek, with some parts in Coptic (?), to be later translated into Arabic).

6. Funk 1976, pp. 8–21 ("Teaching of Silvanus," Nag Hammadi Codex VII 4 and Ms BM Or. 6003 = Ant BM 979); cf. Lichtheim 1983, p. 191. A resumée of the question is given by Cannuyer (1988, pp. 200–01). To be noted also is Thissen 1989, p. 238 (modern Coptic rendering of a Demotic text).

7. Lexa 1933, p. 106–16. Jensen 1950 might rest on older oral tradition. See also footnote 13, below.

Coptic should be considered Demotic transcribed in a pre-Coptic alphabet.[8] What makes a difference between a) these old Coptic texts and b) the Egyptian anthroponyms rendered in Greek script during the Ptolemaic age is that a) works on a written level but b) on an oral level.

That means that the passage from one linguistic layer into another is not impossible in everyday life, but it occurs outside the established literate traditions and develops inside the oral culture.

4. A similar problem is created by a Demotic literary text not written in Demotic, such as Papyrus Vandier, whose language has been variously classified as "néo-égyptien évolué" (Posener) or "early Demotic?" (Shisha-Halevi 1989, pp. 421–35) by scholars failing to realize that, since the second millennium B.C., writing is a variable independent from language.

Actually we should think about Demotic written not only in Demotic, but also in hieratic[9] and hieroglyphs (Yoyotte 1972b, pp. 254–59; Handoussa 1988, pp. 111–15) and Coptic (see footnote 8). Later on, Coptic was written not only in Coptic, but also in Greek (Crum 1939) and Arabic;[10] we might even consider as "Coptic" some late Demotic popular texts leaning towards a low register of speech.[11] Likewise the Coptic script was sometimes used to write Arabic (Casanova 1901, pp. 1–20 [thirteenth century: Wadi el Natrun]) and Demotic (see footnote 8).

Nevertheless it would be nonsense to imagine a text established in a literary form corresponding to a specific written format[12] which would be retold in different colloquial ways: probably this is the reason why the commentators of the "Teaching of Silvanus," which is written in Coptic but reminds one of earlier wisdom texts, thought at once of ordinary Greek wording. Any

8. Satzinger 1984, pp. 137–46. Quaegebeur 1982, pp. 125–36. For a magical spell rendered in Demotic and Coptic versions, see now DuQuesne 1991, p. 22. See also Lüddeckens 1972, p. 27 (an identical "demotische und koptische Urkundenformel").

9. Such are the literary piece published by Posener (1986) and the religious text treated by Schott (1954). On the latter see also Vernus 1990, pp. 153–208.

10. Cairo Coptic Museum no. 4091: Hymns for the whole year ...; the text is bilingual, Coptic and Arabic, the Coptic words being written in Arabic characters (thirteenth century).

11. For instance, the documentary texts published by Gallo 1989, pp. 99–123.

12. The case of M. Smith (1977, pp. 115–49), involving the Demotic transcription of an older hieroglyphic text reproduced in the Kharga Amun temple, can be understood as a transfer from hieroglyphs into a book script, here represented by Demotic instead of hieratic. Translation would be, of course, another matter, for which see my remarks 1987, pp. 81–83.

For the sake of comparison, I have asked for the opinion of Professor Finn Thiesen, a specialist of Urdu and Hindi at the University of Oslo, from whose kind answer (August 26, 1990) I can quote: " Spoken Hindi and Urdu are virtually the same language, but the written standards diverge. In the same way as an illiterate person will normally not understand literary language, Urdu-Hindi speakers who are literate in either Hindi or Urdu alone, will also in most cases be unable to understand texts which have simply been transcribed from Urdu to Hindi or vice versa.

"A good translation from f. ex. Urdu to Hindi should interfere as little as possible with the original text. I.e. it should try to preserve the Urdu flavour and change only such words and expressions as the translator feels will not be understood by the ordinary Hindi reader, and a difficult Urdu word should for this reason be replaced by a simple Urdu word known to the Hindi readers rather than by a puristic Hindi equivalent. Such translations exist, but they are not common. In most cases they have been made by the authors themselves (e.g. by Prem Chand).

"Most of the translations that I have seen, however, have been executed following almost the opposite principle. The translators seem to think that since this is a translation as many words as possible should be changed into puristic Hindi. The results are to my mind very unsatisfactory. The style is lost and the meaning often unnecessarily changed.

"Works of folk literature and also simple religious literature are often found in both Urdu and Hindi versions either identical (i.e. mere transliterations) or with only minimal changes.

"'Translations' of poetry are always mere transcriptions. Hindi 'translations' of Urdu poetry are very popular and much Hindi poetry too is, indeed, Urdu poetry written in the Hindi (devanagari) script."

difficulty, however, would be overcome, should we refer to the oral level, where high and low speech can easily alternate. A spoken tale could be transformed into a Demotic text at a given moment and into a Coptic text in another moment. In other words we may well think that in passing from the pharaonic to the Christian civilization, some texts long known by heart in the local milieu could be admitted into Coptic written notation, which does not imply by itself the cognizance of earlier written sources. The same objection applies to those who believe that texts rather than concepts should be compared between the Egyptian temple tradition and the Gnosis.[13]

If we should ever discover several written quotations of such an oral tradition, we ought probably to expect some differences in wording and format (actually this happens in the two known copies of the "Teaching of Silvanus").[14] That seems to demonstrate that in this field no written tradition was established yet.

5. This depiction of the scenery of language and script during the Roman period displays a complicated system of interrelations, but it is by no means abnormal; on the contrary it emphasizes phenomena which must have existed, but are less apparent, in other times and cultural situations as well. In particular we are reminded of the controversial situation of the "Wisdom of Ptahhotep" during the Middle Kingdom. There too, apart from the problems of dating (Luft 1976, p. 49), a rather obscure transmission of the text exists, which cannot be explained simply by text traditions (Burkard 1977, pp. 91–93, 194–209, and 230–42). Analogy with this suggested registering of earlier texts into Coptic script would seem to point out that the provenance of Ptahhotep (and other Middle and New Kingdom) texts was an oral tradition. This would allow for the substantial interpolations which have raised questions about the actual dating, and at the same time it would confirm the limited utilization of writing in the Old Kingdom, excluding texts written for communication and pieces of literature. But this topic is already dealt with in another place.

13. Derchain 1988, p. 258: "il faudrait comparer des textes, non des idées." Lately, however, Derchain has provided some correspondences between a Ptolemaic text and Asclepius (1990, pp. 25–27). These remind one of a Coptic version of Asclepius preserved in Nag Hammadi Codex VI (Parrott 1979, pp. 418–22). That would imply an origin from a Greek format, from which the Latin translation was also drawn. One might likewise think that in a bilingual milieu, where the Hermetic doctrine found its ground, several versions, including unwritten ones, might be in co-occurrence, at least for some texts. See Fowden 1986, p. 5 (a reference I owe to the courtesy of G. Filoramo).

14. See references in footnote 6; cf. Till 1955; furthermore Zandee 1981, pp. 515–31.

CHAPTER 36

FOREIGNERS IN THE DOCUMENTS FROM THE SACRED ANIMAL NECROPOLIS, SAQQARA

H. S. SMITH
University College, London

The documents from the Sacred Animal Necropolis, Saqqara, came to light in excavations by the Egypt Exploration Society, directed by the late W. B. Emery from 1964–71, and by G. T. Martin and myself from 1971–76.[1] Over 750 Demotic papyri were found, most of which were fragmentary (Smith and Tait 1983, especially pp. ix–xi). The locations in which they were discovered suggested that they had been finally dumped in the fourth century A.D. during the clearance of the ruined temple site preliminary to building a Christian monastic settlement (see Segal 1983, pp. 1–3). The internal evidence of the Demotic documents, however, suggests that they range in date from the sixth to the early third century B.C., and had previously formed part of an accumulation of rubbish of the very early Ptolemaic period (Smith and Tait 1983, pp. 4–5).

As many of the documents may not be published for some time,[2] I have assembled here a preliminary list of foreign ethnics, titles, and personal names, which occur in them; it makes no claim to completeness.[3] The following comments are intended to annotate the context of the quotations in the list, rather than to identify ethnicities or nationalities.

The papyri are quoted by their EES numbers, not by their EAO registration numbers.[4]

ETHNICS

S.H5-490 is a report in an early hand bearing the date 'Year 33, month 4 Proyet, day 6'; in view of this high year date, it should belong either to the reign of Darius I or that of Artaxerxes I. From the fragmentary text it concerns an army-commander (*mr-mš*ʿ) and some 'business' (*ʿš-sḥn*), but the context in which *nꜣ Mdy.w* 'the Medes' occurs is completely broken.

1. See Emery 1967, pp. 141–45; Emery 1968, pp. 1–2; Emery 1969, pp. 31–35; Emery and Smith 1970, pp. 1–3; Emery 1970, pp. 5–11; Martin 1971, pp. 1–2; Martin 1973, pp. 5–15; Martin 1974, pp. 15–29; H. S. Smith 1976, pp. 14–17; and Smith and Jeffreys 1977, pp. 20–28; see also Martin 1981, especially pp. 57–68 and Martin 1979, pp. 17–99.
2. The publication plans announced in H. S. Smith 1974b, pp. 256–58 have had to be modified and delayed owing to other unavoidable commitments that are certainly no fault of my colleagues who have so generously given time to the study of these documents. Publication is now in the hands of C. J. Martin, J. D. Ray, H. S. Smith, and W. J. Tait. A second volume is in a relatively advanced state of preparation.
3. While I am deeply grateful to the above-mentioned colleagues for allowing me to quote from papyri under their editorship, they are in no way responsible for the readings and interpretations given here. I wish, however, to acknowledge most valuable readings, corrections, and contributions from the following scholars: C. A. R. Andrews, S. M. Burstein, M. Geller, R. H. Pierce, J. D. Ray, R. K. Ritner, J. B. Segal, W. J. Tait, and K.-T. Zauzich.
4. For a clear account of the numbering systems used at North Saqqara, see Martin 1981, pp. 2–3. As this paper deals almost exclusively with Demotic papyri the prefix DP is omitted from the numbers.

S.71/2-136 is a complete letter, probably of the 4th–3rd centuries B.C., in which 'the Quarter of the Greeks' (*tꜣ ỉwỉ[t] n nꜣ Wꜣny*) is mentioned, a place known to have been in the district of Wenkhem, north of Memphis (Smith and Tait 1981, pp. 75–79). In S.H5-199, a fragmentary account, a plausible restoration suggests the reading 'the tax (*škr*) which they imposed before on the houses of the Greeks' (*nꜣ Wy[nn.w]*). In another account, S.H5-207, likewise of uncertain date, 'the food of the Greeks' (*pꜣ trp n nꜣ Wynn.w*) is mentioned among common Egyptian items. Another entry reads *rmt .rm. Ḏd-ḥr (sꜣ) Gre*; the presence of *rmt* and the fact that the damaged word is spelt with a 'foreigner'-determinative suggests that it may be an ethnic, but whether it should be read *Srmꜣlḥ* or *Prmꜣlḥ* is uncertain.[5]

Brief reference should be made here to the fifth century B.C. Aramaic papyrus S.H5-AP43, an official document in which 'Greeks and Carians' (*Ywnīn*, *Krkīn*) are mentioned three times in connection with the equipment of ships and, perhaps, the restraint of fugitive crew (Segal 1983, pp. 41–43, No. 26).

TITLES

The Iranian title *χšaθra-pavān* 'Satrap' occurs on an ostracon, S.75/6-7, reading : 1) *[........] ꜣrgstrꜣs ḫt(?) tꜣlnꜣ*, 2) *[........] Pꜣ-dỉ-ꜣst pꜣ ỉḫštrpny* (S. M. Burstein, forthcoming). Professor Stanley Burstein has now identified this satrap with the Peteesis appointed by Alexander the Great immediately after his conquest to govern Egypt jointly, as recorded by Arrian III.5.1ff.: "He then made his arrangements for Egypt; he appointed two Egyptians, Doloaspis and Petisis, and divided the country between them; but when Petisis presently resigned, Doloaspis undertook the whole charge." Professor Burstein's identification (forthcoming), surely correct, thus dates this mention of Alexander, written without either cartouche or 'foreigner'-determinative, to his first Egyptian year. Another mention of the title 'satrap' appears in S.H5-450, a fragmentary report or protocol, probably of fifth century B.C. date, which records a plea to a man named *Wšṯn*, beginning "I am the maidservant" followed by a lacuna, then *ḫštrpn tꜣ št rs* "the Satrap of the southern region" (reading due to J. D. Ray). The length of the lacuna is uncertain, so that the maidservant was not necessarily attached to the Satrap's person.

PERSONAL NAMES[6]

S.H5-269+284 is a letter addressed to a foreign generalissimo (*pꜣ ḥrỉ pꜣ mšꜥ*) named *Mytrḫꜣ* or *Šytrḫꜣ* by an Egyptian named Pediamun, almost certainly in the fifth century B.C.; the name may be Iranian (Smith and Kuhrt 1982, pp. 199–209).

S.H5-434 is a badly torn fragment of papyrus from what was originally probably a long and important document. On the front, it comprises the ends of the last sixteen lines of one column, followed by a two-line docket containing a date at the top of a blank area to the left; on the back it comprises the extreme ends of ten lines of one column, followed by sixteen incomplete lines of the next column. What survives is thus too partial for any clear idea of the original contents of the document to be gained. From the facts that certain documents and depositions are quoted within the text and that the text is divided into sections, in one instance headed by a day-date, and from its official style and the mention of *nꜣ wpṯy.w*, 'the judges,' it seems likely to be a record of judicial or administrative proceedings. The hand is a relatively early one, and the date-docket reads *ḥꜣt-sp 30 ꜣbd-2 ꜣḫt sw 16(?)*. No full summary can be offered here, but the following points are relevant to our subject.

1) In the Front, Col. 2, 1.2 under the date, and again in the Back, Col. 2, 1.10 at the end of a section, there occurs the group *Tꜣ-ḥmwḏn*, evidently, from the 'house'-determinative, a

5. C. A. R. Andrews informs me that a name *Prm*, possibly an ethnic, occurs in P. dem. BM 10661, line 3.

6. Iranian Etymologies for personal names in this article have now been critically reviewed, corrected, and amplified by Dr. Philip Huyse in a forthcoming article.

place-name. In a fragmentary Aramaic papyrus (No. 27: S.H5-AP15), Segal read in line 1 'at TḤMWṢN' and in line 5 'year 5 of Darius the King at TḤMWṢN' (1983, pp. 43–44). The two documents must surely refer to the same place, especially given the fact that both documents have a legal/governmental context. Segal did not suggest an identification for the place, and its etymology was unclear to him, as it is to me, though it is worth noting that the Aramaic *T* is represented by the Demotic feminine singular definite article *tꜣ*.

2) The name *ꜣršm* appears in the Front, Col. 1, 1 without context; in the Front, Col. 1, 1.12 in *ḏd ꜣršm my ḏd=w n=f*, "Arsham said: 'Let them say to him'"; in the Back, Col. 2, 1.1 in *pꜣ ḥḏ(?) r-ḏd ꜣršm pꜣỉ my dỉ=w* ..., "It is the money(?) of which Arsham spoke; let it be given ..."; in the Back, Col. 2, 1.9 in *ꜣršm r ỉn=w*, "Arsham to bring them ..."; and in the Back, Col. 2, 1.13 in *m-bꜣḥ pꜣỉ=n ḥry ꜣršm*, "before Arsham our Lord." Evidently, this Arsham was a person of great consequence to be thus addressed in judiciary or government proceedings at Memphis; it is highly tempting to identify this Arsham with the famous Persian satrap Arsames, who is attested in Aramaic documents from Egypt from year 37 (428 B.C.) of Artaxerxes I to year 17 (408 B.C.) of Darius II (G. R. Driver 1954, pp. 44–56). If so, S.H5-434 must date to Artaxerxes I, year 30, i.e. 435 B.C., and will contain the earliest reference to Arsames in Egypt.

3) In the Back, Col. 2, 1.7, in a new section following a day-date, *hrw(?) r-ḏd=f Mspṯ*, 'the day (on?) which he spoke, Maspat ...' (or '[to] Maspat'); in the Back, Col. 2, 1.11, at the beginning of another section, after a large group in the left margin (probably reading *Ḥr*), *ḥrw-bꜣk Mspṯ* ..., 'the deposition/letter of Maspat.' Letter 12 of the Aramaic leather documents edited by Driver (1954, pp. 33–35) is a complaint addressed by an Iranian noble, Widdapš, to Neḥtiḥur, Arsham's agent at Memphis, based on letters sent to him by his own agent, Maspat, concerning the non-delivery of Widdapš's Cilician serfs, and concerning the peculation of wine from his estate by Neḥtiḥur and oppression and robbery of 'my lady's' staff. A letter from Arsham to Pšamšek, son of ʿAḥ-ḥapi, in Babylon is mentioned in the text. It thus seems virtually certain that the Arsham and Maspat in S.H5-434 must be the same men as those in this Aramaic letter.

4) In the Front, Col. 1, 1.3 the name *ꜣrṯy* appears without context and again in the Back, Col. 2, 1.3 *ḏd=w n=ỉ(?) ꜣrṯy rḫ*, "They said to me: 'Arty knows ...'." In Driver's Letter 7, 1.10 (?) and Letter 13, 1.1 an important official ʿArtaḥay is named, though he does not appear in Letter 12 (1954, pp. 23–25, 35–36), but, given the approximate contemporaneity of the Aramaic letters, it seems possible that the Demotic *ꜣrṯy* is a defective rendering of ʿArtaḥay (cf. Greek Ἀρτάχαιος).

5) In the Front, Col. 1, 1.13 appears the phrase *ṯꜣỉ.ṯ=s ỉ.ỉr nꜣ Prsṯw.w*, 'take him/her/it to the *Prsṯw.w*,' occurs in a context which, conjecturally, might read: "Give orders concerning(?) their not sending (letters) to the (............) of the *Prsṯw.w*." As the word *Prsṯw.w* is determined with a 'speaking-man'-determinative, it is not likely to represent an ethnic name, and one would expect 'Persian' to be rendered by *rmt Prs*, as K.-T. Zauzich has pointed out to me; yet the meaning of the expression remains problematic.

6) However uncertain the content of S.H5-434, it seems to emerge that at least two, if not three Iranian high officials who appear in the Aramaic leather documents are mentioned in a document of Memphite provenance, probably to be dated to 435 B.C. As the provenance of the Aramaic leather documents is unknown, it seems not unlikely that these, too, came from Memphis, known to be the seat of Achaemenid government in Egypt.[7]

7. I am especially grateful to W. J. Tait for reading this document through with me, and to him, R. K. Ritner, and K.-T. Zauzich for valuable corrections and suggestions.

S.H5-43 is an oracle-question in an early hand, which reads: "O my great Lord, may he celebrate millions of *ḥb-sd* festivals! Is *Gyg*, the Syrian (*ʾIšwr*), the wife of *Brḳ*, to go to the land of Khor (*Ḫr*) in the first month of Akhet (day ...?) of this year? Let the document (*bꜣk*) be brought out to me."

The interest of this document is that an oracle-question entirely concerned with the affairs of foreigners should be addressed to an Egyptian deity, whatever his identity (Osiris-Apis?). Given the context, we must surely interpret the husband's name as the Semitic Barak, rather than the Egyptian *Brꜣ*, Belle ('blind [man]'); whether the wife's name is Semitic is less certain.[8] Probably the document is of the 5th–4th centuries B.C.

Foreign names appear among Egyptian names in several accounts and lists of personnel. In S.H5-202 there appear in the Front 1.1, *Bgbyṯ*, and in the Front 1.4, *Bgy*; these seem quite likely to represent the Iranian names Bagapat, which appears in Driver (1954, pp. 20–22), Letter 6, 1.1 and in Segal (1983, 77–79), No. 54, 1.11 (=S.H5-AP10), and Bagoḥay(= Iranian Bigvai, Greek Βαγώας), which appears in Cowley (1923, pp. 108–24), Pap. 30–32. In the same document, Back 1.1, ...*py sꜣt(?) Tꜣ-Ḫry*, the mother's name doubtless means 'the woman of Khor.' In S.H5-49, Back Col. 2, 1.9, likewise an account, a male person called *W/Šmgrṯ* appears; in S.H5-403, Front 11.1, 6, ... *sꜣ Brbry mwt=f W/Grwbš* occurs twice; in S.H5-366, Front 1.1, the reading *Grgr.šy* is somewhat doubtful; while in S.H5-478, ...*yrnḏhy* is perhaps incomplete. S.71/2-56, a list of names, includes in the Back 1.1, *Pꜣ-(n-)ḥy sꜣ Ḫrsm/n sꜣ Ḫym/šk*, in 1.2, *Pꜣ-(n-)Nt(?) sꜣ Ḥr sꜣ Ḫrsm/n mwt=f Tꜣ-(nt-)ỉmn*, in the Back 1.8, *ꜣm/štykꜣ/ḥ*; the first two seem clear cases of related persons of foreign ancestry who adopted Egyptian names. S.H5-17 lists in the Front 5–6, *Hwny sꜣ(?) Štḥṯ*, in the Front 1.10, *Grwšy*, in the Front 11.14–15, *Ḳsyn sꜣ Brꜣ/ḳ pꜣ šr n Tꜣ-by tꜣ s(t) n ṯbt*, '*Ḳsyn*, son of Barak/Belle, the child of Taby, the fishwife,' this last being in all probability the son of the Semite and an Egyptian woman; another possible instance of Barak appears in the Front 1.3. In an account, S.H5-198, Front 1.8, *Ṯꜣỉ-n.ỉm=w sꜣ Ḫfmṯ* appears and in S.71/2-31, Front 1.8, the name *Hgr*, borne by the Twenty-ninth Dynasty Pharaoh Hakor. In all these documents, the foreign names occur casually among Egyptian names, which are normally in the majority.

In legal documents also people with foreign names regularly occur as parties. In S.H5-174, Front 1.1, another *Bgy mwt=f Tꜣ-(nt-)ḥs* appears together with a man named *ʾIỉ-m-ḥtp sꜣ Ḥynꜣ*, an interesting instance, for in the first case we appear to have a man with an Iranian name with an Egyptian mother and in the second case the son of a foreigner who has taken an Egyptian name. In a report or protocol, S.H5-450, already quoted for the probable appearance of the title 'Satrap' in the Front, Col. 1, 1.2, we find, in the Front, Col. 2, 1.1, *Wšṯn* and, in 1.4, *Wšṯn ỉrm ꜣrṯ*..., apparently as actors in the proceedings; both perhaps represent Iranian names. Another report or protocol, S.71/2-140, Front 1.2, *wʿb Ḏd-ḥr sꜣ Wspyr*, exhibits as one of the parties a *wʿb*-priest with an Egyptian name born of a foreign father. In a legal instrument, S.72/3-35, Front 1.7, we meet the *mr-ꜣḥ.w Pꜣ(-nʾ-ỉḥy/Pꜣ(-n)-sy(?) sꜣ ꜣrṯkš*, an 'overseer of fields' with an Egyptian name but, apparently, an Iranian father. In a lease, S.H5-100, Front 1.4, another instance of *Hgr* as a private name occurs, while in a land-deed, S.71/2-51, Front 1.6, some fields belong to a man named *Ḳbrw*. S.H5-465, Front, Col. 2, 1.2, a fragment, yields *ꜣšwry*, 'the Syrian.' In a perfectly routine Egyptian letter, S.71/2-162, Front 1.2, asking the recipient (name lost) 'not to delay to hurry down (sc. to Memphis) this very moment,' a person named *Ḥrg(r)y* is mentioned, unfortunately in a damaged context. All these examples seem likely to belong to the 5th–4th centuries B.C. An account, S.72/3-46, Front, Col. 2/4, *Twrts*, and Front, Col. 2/5, *ꜣṯḥtrs*, yields two names which might well be Greek, e.g. Tyrtaios (or, if there is metathesis, perhaps the more common Diodoros or Theodoros) and Athenodoros (assuming omission of *n* before *t*, contrast *Dem. Nb.* I, 1.49). Whether this document is

8. J. B. Segal suggests a comparison with Assyrian *Ḳuḳu*.

of the fourth century or third century is uncertain, but, not unnaturally if the posited date-range for the archive is correct, Greek names seem very rare.

These names, eclectically selected, only serve further to emphasize the well-known fact that the population of Memphis in the 5th–4th centuries was of very mixed racial origin, and that it was a truly cosmopolitan city. Aside from the onomastic interest of the names, what is impressive is how foreigners and people of foreign parentage appear in almost every class of Egyptian document, however ephemeral, mixed with pure Egyptians, taking part in Egyptian religious practices, Egyptian legal cases, Egyptian official, social, and domestic life. The value of finds like the Saqqara papyri, containing many very fragmentary documents, almost worthless in themselves, is that they tend to illustrate this sort of intercommunal penetration more fully than smaller collections of documents of much greater individual worth.

LIST OF WRITINGS

In the first column the EES Saqqara Demotic Papyrus Number is given in the form S.H5-434 with DP omitted (= Saqqara, Grid Square H5, Demotic Papyrus 434) or S.71/2-56 (= Saqqara, Season 1971/2, Demotic Papyrus 56). This is followed by the side of the papyrus (Front or Back), the column number (if required), and the line numbers in which the foreign name appears, e.g. Fr. I/3 = Front, Col. I, line 3; Bk. 1, 8 = Back, lines 1 and 8. In the column headed *Transliteration*, the oblique stroke '/' means that the letters or symbols written immediately before or after the stroke are ***alternative*** readings of the same Demotic sign. Occasionally for clarity, alternative readings of the whole name are separated by the same diagonal stroke. Such alternative readings have been restricted to those which seem to me reasonably probable; I have not indicated every possible theoretical alternative which the Demotic script might allow. Dots within square brackets [...] indicate lacunae in the text. The Demotic writings are ***not*** facsimile copies and have no paleographical value; they are simply freehand 'normalschrift' from photographs or good copies, like those in *EDG*. Only ***one*** writing of each name or group is quoted, though all the references are given in the first column of the list. Where all available writings are damaged, I have conflated them in the copy.

Table 36.1. List of Writings.

Demotic Pap. No. Side/Line	*Transliteration*	*Demotic*
S.H5-269+284 Fr. 1	*M/Šytrhꜣ*	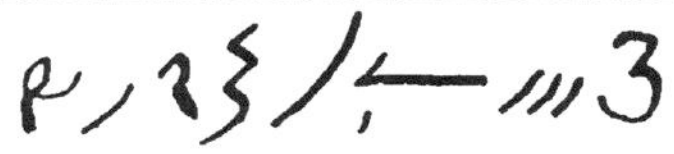
S.H5-434 Fr. I/1, 12, Bk. II/1, 9, 13	*ꜣršm*	
Fr. I/3, Bk. II/3	*ꜣrṯy*	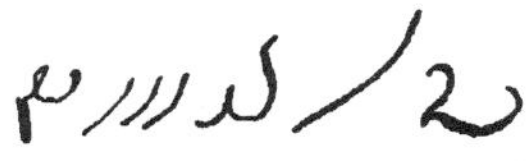
Fr. II/2, Bk. II/10	*Tꜣ ḥmwḏn*	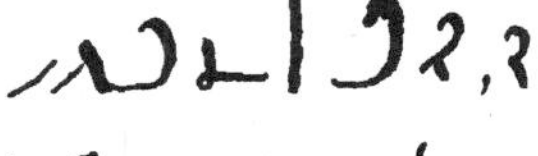
Fr. I/13, Bk. II/5	*nꜣ prsṯw.w*	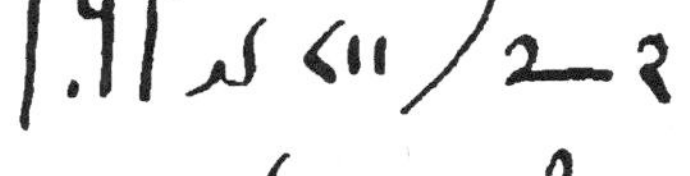
Bk. II/7, 11	*Mspṯ*	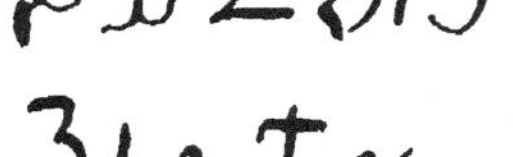
S.H5-43 Bk. 2	*Gyg tꜣ ʾIšwr*	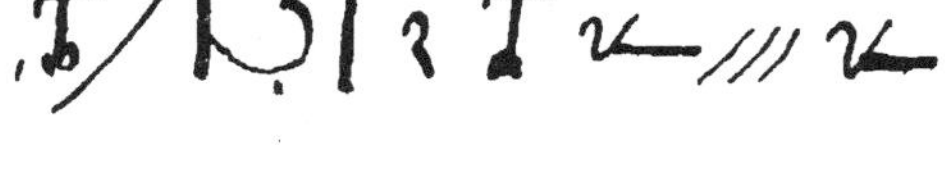

Demotic Pap. No. Side/Line	Transliteration	Demotic
S.H5-43 Bk. 3	*Brḳ*	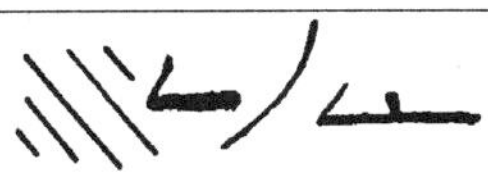
S.H5-202 Fr. 1	*Bgbyṯ*	
Fr. 4	*Bgy*	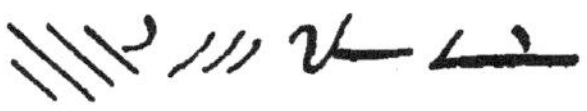
Bk. 1	*…]py sꜣ.t(?) Tꜣ-ḫry*	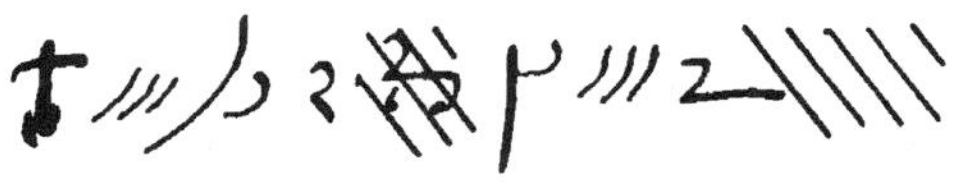
S.H5-49 Bk. II/9	*Wmgrṯ/Grmgrṯ*	
S.H5-403 Fr. 1, 6	*Brbry mwt=f W/Grwbš*	
S.H5-366 Fr. 1	*Grgr[.]m/šy*	
S.H5-478 Fr. 3	*…]yrnḏḥy*	
S.71/2-56 Bk. 1	*Pꜣ(-n)-ḥy sꜣ Ḫrsm/n sꜣ Hym/šk*	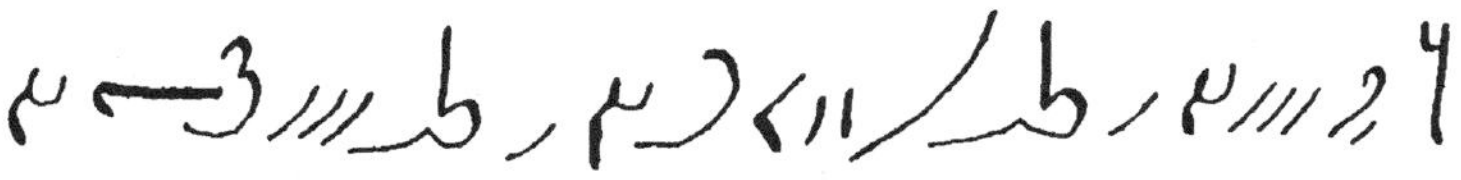
Bk. 2	*Pꜣ(-n)-Nt(?) sꜣ Ḥr sꜣ Ḫrsm/n*	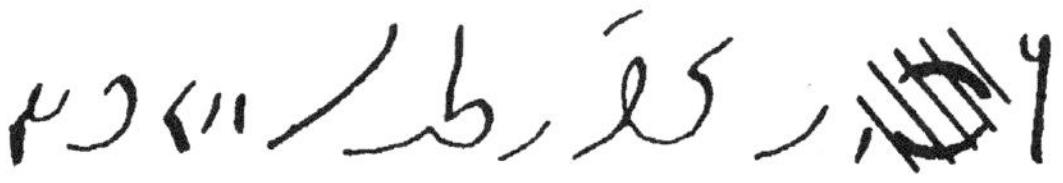
Bk. 8	*ꜣm/šṯykꜣ/ḥ*	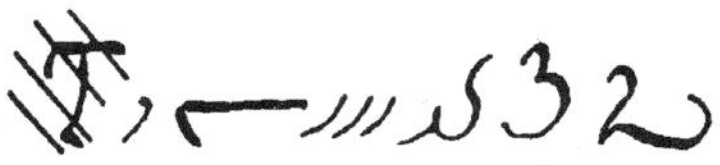
S.H5-198 Fr. 8	*Ḫfmṯ*	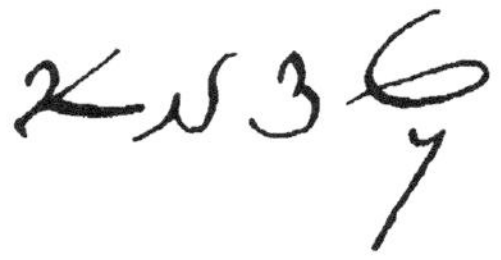
S.H5-17 Fr. 5–6	*Hwny sꜣ(?) Šṯẖṯ*	
Fr. 10	*Grwšy*	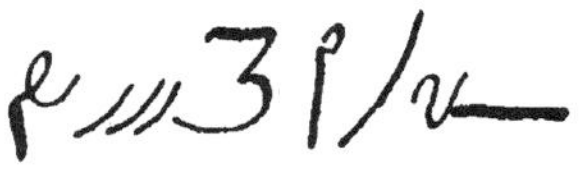
Fr. 14–15	*Ḳsyn sꜣ Brḳ*	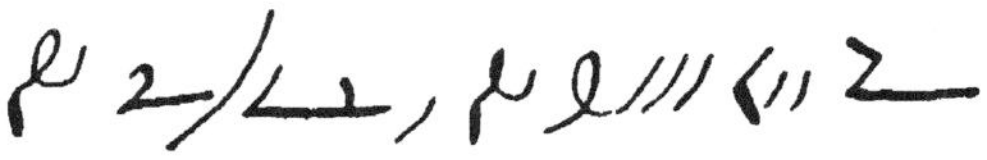
S.H5-100 Fr. 4	*Hgr*	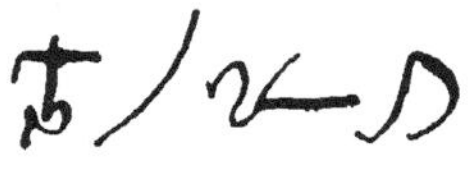
S.H5-174 Fr. 1	*…]Bgy mwt=f Tꜣ(-nt)-ḥs*	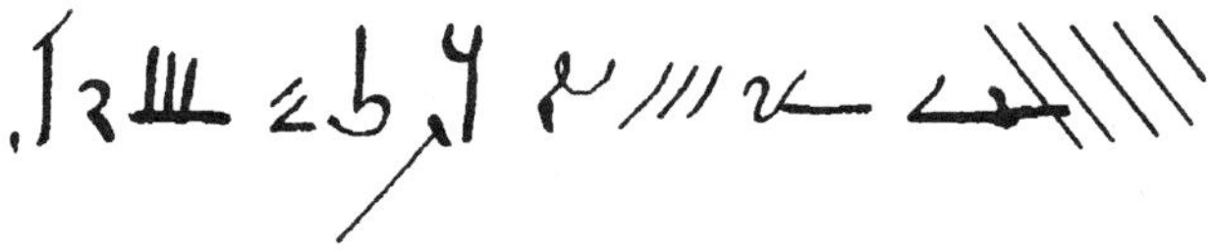

Demotic Pap. No. Side/Line	*Transliteration*	*Demotic*
S.H5-174 Fr. 1	*ʾIỉ-m-ḥtp sꜣ Ḥynꜣ/ḥ*	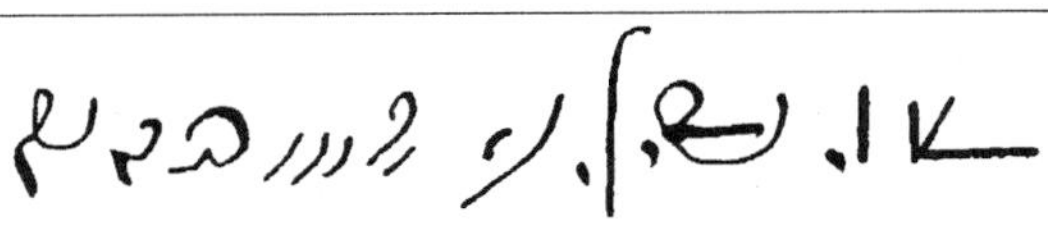
S.H5-450 Fr. II/4	*Wšṯn ỉrm (?) ꜣrṯ[…*	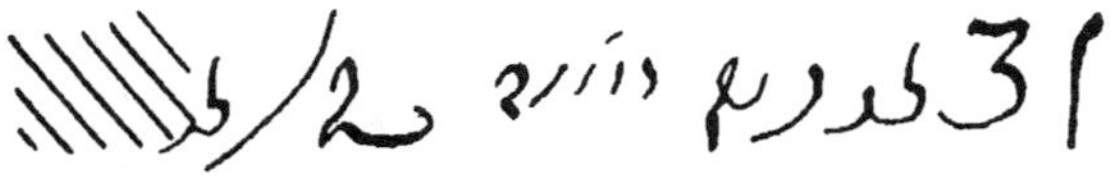
S.71/2-140 Fr. 2	*wꜥb Ḏd-ḥr sꜣ Wspyr*	
S.72/3-35 Fr. 7	*mr-ꜣḥ.w Pꜣ(-n)-ỉhy/ Pꜣ(-n)-sy sꜣ ꜣrṯkš*	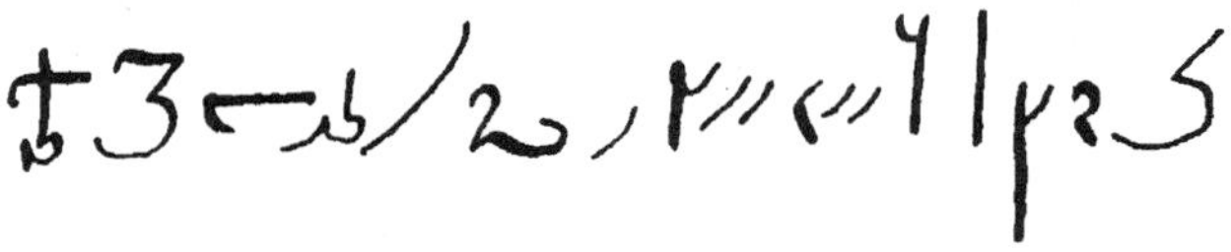
S.71/2-51 Fr. 6	*Ḳbrw*	
S.H5-465 Fr. II/2	*ꜣšwry*	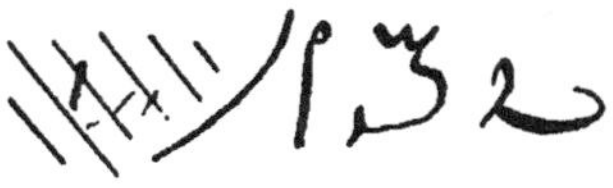
S.71/2-162 Fr. 2	*Ḥrg(r)y*	
S.72/3-46 Fr. II/4	*Twrts*	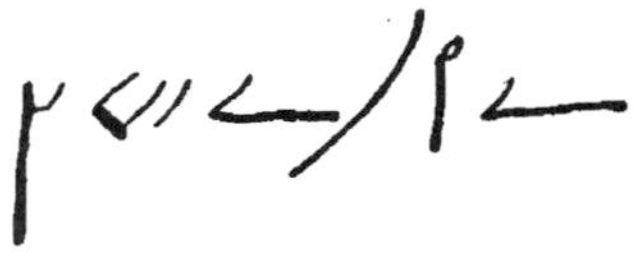
Fr. II/5	*ꜣṯḥḳ/trs/y*	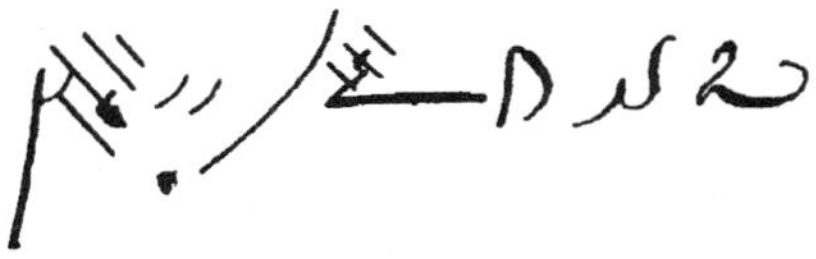

CHAPTER 37

DEMOTIC LITERATURE AND EGYPTIAN SOCIETY*

W. J. TAIT
University College London

This paper attempts to give a brief sketch of possible interconnections between work on Demotic literature and work on the social history of Late period and Greco-Roman Egypt. The aim is rather to raise some questions (and to identify a few problems) than to present a coherent survey. Some general and preliminary remarks are offered as to what Demotic literature might tell us about the multi-cultural life of late period Egypt, and consideration is also given to the extent to which, conversely, our knowledge of social history can help our study of the literature.

The term 'literature' as used here must be understood in a wide sense, embracing every kind of written text that is not, on common-sense grounds, to be classed as 'documentary.'[1] It may therefore be worth stressing the wide range of types of text this involves, that is to say, narratives (which themselves may be divided into several genres[2]); wisdom texts; mythological texts; religious rituals and instructional books; satire;[3] dream-interpretation, omen, and prophetic texts; astrological,

* I am most grateful to the organizers of *Life in a Multi-Cultural Society* and the Fourth International Congress of Demotists for the opportunity to give this paper, and my thanks are also due to the British Academy and to University College London for generous conference grants.

1. It is hard to arrive at a satisfactory definition of the terms 'literary' and 'documentary,' either for ancient Egypt or for any other culture (for a recent discussion, see Kaplony 1977). The present paper is not primarily intended as a contribution to literary criticism, and a pragmatic approach has been adopted. In practice, many (very reasonably) may prefer not to regard the Hermopolis Legal Manual (Mattha and Hughes 1975; essential bibliography: Allam 1986) strictly as 'literature,' although the approaches followed here ought not to mean that any such objections would be fatal to the whole discussion. Papyrus Rylands 9 (published, with full translation, by F. Ll. Griffith 1909) presents a genuine problem of classification — a practical rather than a theoretical one. The initial stimulus for its composition may have been a wish to document the circumstances of a particular dispute, perhaps for an immediate practical end, but it is hard not to feel that the writer was carried away by enthusiasm for his task, and that the finished product has as good a claim to literary status as many other texts (for a recent comment, see Wessetsky 1977).

2. It is difficult to judge whether or not the Egyptians themselves thought in terms of 'genres.' It can be observed that wisdom texts have more in common with one another than with other kinds of text. The same is true of certain groups of narrative texts — Setna texts for example — which are commonly referred to as 'cycles,' because they deal with one and the same named character. The known Setna stories show clear similarities to one another, above all in themes and structure. However, Demotic narratives of all types on the whole display a remarkable uniformity in style, vocabulary, and phraseology.

3. A paper on this topic, "Das demotische Gedicht vom Harfner als Produkt der Begegnung mit griechischer Literatur," was given at the symposium by Heinz-Josef Thissen.

magical, and medical works; legal manuals; word lists; and school texts. New finds[4] and the better exploration of existing collections[5] are steadily adding to this list, and filling out its details. The limitations inherent in any attempt to draw wide-ranging conclusions from the study of a single type of text are surely obvious: one cannot, for example, assess the significance of foreign influences on Demotic literature from a consideration of only one genre. In fact, this paper devotes a perhaps excessive proportion of attention to narratives and wisdom texts, at least in instancing texts to illustrate the problems addressed. The chief justification for such a bias is that there has been more relevant discussion of this material in the past. However, even to try to concentrate upon Demotic texts may lead to distortions or misunderstandings. It would be quite unwarranted to assume that the hieratic and hieroglyphic texts written during the same period may safely be left on one side, and the same may be said in respect of the Greek literary material from Egypt.[6] Yet there is no particular merit in disregarding documentary evidence, either. In fact, the only sensible course is to use the evidence of literary texts and of documents in conjunction. Thus the title of this paper is not an attempt to define a field of study: it is merely the title of a paper. Although the emphasis here is on broader issues, a certain amount of evidence for social history may be found embedded *within* Demotic literary texts. The famous First Setna narrative text[7] is unusually rich in this respect. It furnishes information, for example, on incest (unfortunately rather difficult to interpret), on literacy, and on marriage and the social role of women. Perhaps no rigid distinction can be drawn between studying the place in society of the texts, and using evidence about society incidentally included in them. Certainly the latter topic would deserve a paper of its own.

Before any worthwhile conclusions may be drawn, certain basic questions must be asked about the texts. Who wrote and who read them; when were they composed, copied, or read; and where? If satisfactory answers to these questions are not forthcoming, then at least some hypotheses must be entertained and tested.

As for *when*, the distribution of our evidence by date is wildly uneven. This is true both of published material, and of known unpublished material. We have massive finds from the second century A.D., and a little third century material. Before the Roman period, we are afforded only isolated glimpses, and nothing survives that may be assigned with complete confidence to a date earlier than the fourth century B.C. Until fairly recently, the history of Demotic literature up to the later Ptolemaic period was largely a matter of conjecture. Apart from certain religious books, there was no evidence for the continuance of literature in hieratic after about 1000 B.C. In the case of most types of text, there seemed to be a complete break between New Kingdom literature and Demotic literature. It was possible to argue that the latter was a fresh creation, and began only at some point in the Ptolemaic period. Many Demotists, including the present writer, preferred to speculate otherwise — that only the accidents of preservation concealed from us the earlier stages. However, the

4. The present writer has been concerned with the material from the EES excavations at North Saqqâra (see, so far, Smith and Tait 1983). Another example of the emergence of new types of material is furnished by the ostraca from Medinet Madi; the volume Bresciani, Pernigotti, and Betrò 1983 concerned material from excavations directed by Professor A. Vogliano, but work at the site has continued in recent years.

5. By chance, at the Congress, papers were given which concerned the Ashmolean Museum, Oxford, the British Museum, London (see *Chapter 2*), and the Carsten Niebuhr Institute, Copenhagen, but work is in progress upon literary material in many collections.

6. Nothing is said in this paper on the subject of Greek translations or adaptations of Demotic literary texts, which may certainly be reckoned to be part of the last stage of 'Demotic literature'; a sketch of this topic forms part of H.- J. Thissen, 'Graeco-ägyptische Literatur', *LÄ* II, cols. 873–78.

7. F. Ll. Griffith 1900; the most recent translation is that by Lichtheim 1980, pp. 125–38. A yet more recent translation of this text, and of others cited in this paper, no doubt is found in Bresciani 1990a, mentioned in her article (1990b), but this work is not yet accessible to the present writer.

lack of direct evidence was embarrassing.[8] New discoveries, both in Demotic and in hieratic, have done a little to close the gap between the two literatures. The Saqqâra papyri demonstrate that narrative, mythological, medical, and school texts were being written in Demotic at least a little before the Ptolemaic period.[9] It is a matter for debate whether or not they indicate an even longer history for the literature. The publication of Papyrus Vandier[10] has shown that a narrative text similar both in style and in language to Demotic examples could still be written in hieratic at a date when Demotic literature had, probably, already begun. This, of course, leaves many questions unanswered. There might have been a rapid and general switch from the use of hieratic to that of Demotic, for texts that were not perceived as religious, or the process might have been gradual and complex. It used to be plausible to suggest that the change might have been solely or primarily brought about by a wish to compose new texts in more up-to-date language than previously (or to 'translate' old texts into a more modern form), which would have been more feasible in Demotic script than in hieratic. However, P. Vandier provides only one of several indications that the position cannot have been as simple as this. It is conceivable that a change in educational practice might have been responsible; but then that change would itself require explanation. Further, it is obviously important to know something of the background of the literary tradition against which a work has been written: the significance for social history of any feature of literature will clearly be different if it is a new innovation than if it is entirely traditional.

Nearly all our Demotic literary papyri can be dated only on palaeographical grounds.[11] Although the study of the palaeography of these texts has its problems, the dating of most of our material is more or less generally agreed. The date of composition of the texts is another matter. That a text was composed earlier than our earliest surviving manuscript may be argued for several reasons, for example (i) that the grammar or vocabulary appears earlier than that of comparable manuscripts, (ii) that the text is transmitted in a corrupt state which suggests that many stages of copying have been involved, or includes direct evidence of variant readings or the collation of different manuscripts, (iii) that the contents indicate a particular date of composition.[12] What one

8. An early example of a different view may be found in the remarks of F. Ll. Griffith 1900, p. 1 (concerned solely with narrative texts): "But we must note the fact that while a considerable number of stories are extant in hieratic of the Middle and New Kingdoms, ten centuries follow between the end of the New Kingdom and the middle of the Ptolemaic rule (*circa* 1200[*sic*]–150 B.C.), during which this class of literature is entirely unrepresented by native documents." Griffith proceeded to suggest that "the art of the story-teller was by no means in abeyance"; although his remarks are brief, it seems fair to conclude from them that he supposed that there was a continuity in Egyptian narratives, but that this lay in oral literature. Perhaps much the same view can been seen in the (again, brief) comments of Reymond 1983 (see p. 42); cf. Brunner, 'Literatur,' *LÄ* III, cols. 1067–72.

9. Smith and Tait 1983. The few literary papyri from Saqqâra still awaiting publication include two mythological pieces (one concerned with the story of Horus and Seth), and one medical text; work on these is well advanced.

10. Posener 1986. Posener's cautious assessment of the date of the hand of the narrative text on the papyrus (p. 11) states that, at the most liberal estimate, the text cannot predate the Saite Dynasty. Plainly, however, he regarded a date lower than 664 B.C. to be probable.

11. Well-known exceptions are the First Setna text (see footnote 7, above), although the dating to year 15 (as the figure is generally read) of an unnamed king is of little help, and 'Bocchoris and the Lamb' (P. Vindob. D 10,000), for the colophon of which see Zauzich 1976b (for full publication of the text see Zauzich 1983). One Roman period hieratic text is dated by an elaborate colophon: text A in Botti 1959.

12. An example of a text to which the first two lines of argument have been applied is the Mythus vom Sonnenauge (Kufi) text (recent re-edition: de Cenival 1988). In the case of ʿOnchsheshonqy (Glanville 1955) Glanville (pp. xiii–xiv) maintained that the sound state of the text might indicate that "It is not altogether impossible that the composition and the manuscript are of the same date." Thissen has recently expressed approval of this approach (Thissen 1984, especially p. 11), whereas Lichtheim, in a brief comment in 1980, p. 159, is very cautious on the question (cf. Lichtheim 1983). The third line of argument (that based upon the contents) has been applied to many texts, but never with very clear-cut or universally accepted results, except in the obvious case of some astronomical material.

means by 'composition' is open to debate. Demotic more or less maintains the pharaonic tradition that 'authorship,' in its modern sense, is of no interest. That is to say that we do not find (and it would be very surprising to find) a literary text which bears an indication of the man who composed it. However, certain types of text may be ascribed to revered figures of the past, or to fictitious authors of other kinds. It is a little difficult to tell in what light the Egyptians viewed these ascriptions. The narrative introduction of P. BM 10508 credits its chief character, ʿOnchsheshonqy son of Tjainufe, with the composition of the wisdom text which occupies most of the papyrus (see footnote 12, above). There is good reason to discount the possibility that this name in any sense represents the author; and it would be unsafe to draw any conclusions from the fact that ʿOnchsheshonqy is a priest.[13] The possible relationship of Demotic texts with oral literature is problematic.[14] The suggestion may be offered that most of our texts did have an author: each was composed at a particular moment by a particular individual, and we do not have any 'transcriptions' of oral literature. The present writer is disinclined to see many of our texts as compilations or patchworks of already existing material. The unity of introduction and wisdom text in ʿOnchsheshonqy has been stoutly defended by Thissen (1984, pp. 10–13). Demotic narratives very frequently use the device of a story within a story. The First Setna narrative exploits this with great skill and subtlety, and indeed it is scarcely conceivable that the various 'episodes' of the story were not composed to belong together. The case of the Second Setna story[15] is less clear. Plainly, the author did not invent for himself the idea of a guided visit to the underworld, in which the contrasting and unexpected fates of a rich man and a poor man are revealed.[16] It is undeniable that the rest of the story would be perfectly coherent if the episode of the rich man and poor man were entirely omitted. However, it is probable that the general form and the details of the episode were contrived when the whole story was composed in its present form, rather than being mechanically incorporated as a pre-existing text. The Mythus vom Sonnenauge (Kufi; de Cenival 1988) text essentially consists of a series of animal fables embedded in a narrative, the mythological aspects of which make it virtually inconceivable that it could be anything but Egyptian in origin. The origin of the fables, however, is more debatable; they may well have had more than one source. The present writer has suggested that in at least one passage two versions of a fable have become muddled in our manuscripts (W. J. Tait 1976, pp. 41–44). It is natural to assume that narratives and some other kinds of text were designed for reading aloud, for oral performance, and certainly many texts share some features with oral literature, the most obvious being the use of certain kinds of repetition. Most narratives contain a very high proportion of direct speech, and this may have given scope for vivid performance.

As for *who*, part of the answer might at first sight seem straightforward. The two massive hauls of papyri that we have, one from Tebtunis,[17] and one from Dime,[18] came from temple-contexts, and the writers and readers of the papyri must, it might be said, have been priests. The present writer would hesitate to pass judgement on the Vienna material, but in the case of that from Tebtunis, it might be suggested that it is mistaken to describe it as coming from a temple 'library.' Such poor

13. For interpretations of the figure of ʿOnchsheshonqy, see especially the Einleitung to Thissen 1984.

14. For the same considerations in connection with earlier Egyptian literature, see for example Brunner, 'Literatur,' *LÄ* III, cols. 1067–72.

15. For the primary edition and a recent translation see footnote 7, above (Lichtheim's translation is on pp. 138–51).

16. See Lichtheim 1980, pp. 126–27, and Bresciani, 'Chaemwese-Erzählungen,' *LÄ* I, cols. 899–901; one might also note Doresse 1960.

17. For some of the problems concerning the provenance of papyri presumed to come from Tebtunis, see the Einleitung to the forthcoming first volume of *The Carlsberg Papyri* (in press).

18. The provenance of the Demotic texts in the Vienna collection also presents some problems. According to Reymond 1983, p. 43, certain Vienna Demotic literary papyri in some sense came from the town, or from the region, of Crocodilopolis (cf. Reymond 1976, pp. 21–30); however, her arguments are not always easy to follow.

information as we have on the various discoveries indicate that papyri were found in a wide variety of locations, which included priests' houses and caches by the great enclosure wall. There is no indication that any room could be identified as 'the' temple library. Generally, it is entirely impossible to tell where any one particular Demotic papyrus was found. At Edfu and elsewhere, some Greco-Roman temple inscriptions purport to tell us the titles of books held, although this information must be used with caution (see Burkard 1980, pp. 94–102). It is certainly not intended to deny here that *any* of the Tebtunis papyri could have come from a library, but in large part the material found seems more likely to have been the private property of the priests or in some cases to be from genizah-like dumps of outdated material. It may be suggested that the finds are rather short on the ritual papyri (liturgical material in the strict sense)[19] that might have been expected; however, it would no doubt be better to avoid making unwarranted assumptions about what would or would not be found in a temple library.

Would it, then, still be fair to say that the writers and readers must have been priests? Tebtunis was not inhabited solely by priests, and the priests were not the only literate inhabitants, if literacy is taken to include literacy in Greek. It does, however, make sense to ask if the priests might not have been the only people literate *in Demotic*. It is often suggested that under the Roman administration the use of Demotic as a documentary script was drastically curtailed, and professional Demotic documentary scribes ceased to exist; only the priests in the temples had any incentive to continue the use of the native scripts. This seems to be a reasonable view, but one would like to test it, and it may not be entirely correct. Roman period Demotic documents may help, but they have been somewhat neglected up to now. From Tebtunis, there may be a difference between those who wrote accounts in documentary Demotic hands, and those — explicitly priests — who wrote personal letters in an artificial literary Demotic hand.[20] Palaeography may be able to cast a little light, also. The Tebtunis material, although the bulk of it probably spans only 150 years, shows a bewildering array of different styles of hand. This in itself is a phenomenon requiring explanation.[21] However, it is possible to recognize small groups of very similar hands and also certain hands of individuals.[22] Because of this, it can be stated with confidence that the narratives, for example, were not written (that is, copied) by specialists, because other kinds of texts are written in the same hands. Thus the narratives cannot have been the preserve of professional story-tellers. On the other hand, there is no evidence yet of any overlap between the hands we find in the manuscripts of the stories and those of the medical texts.

19. The hieratic text A in Botti 1959, a copy of the 'Faiyum Papyrus,' is clearly 'instructional' rather than liturgical, and its colophon seems to indicate strongly that it was a private copy.

20. For example, P. Cairo 31220 and P. Tebt. Tait 22: see W. J. Tait 1977, pp. 71–78, and Brunsch's review 1978, with a re-edition of the Cairo text on p. 103.

21. The priests of Tebtunis in the earlier Roman period evidently did not lead secluded lives; but, even so, one might rather have expected that their Demotic hands would have conformed to a single, slowly developing style, especially if the temple school were the sole place where Demotic could be learnt. One possible, although only partial, explanation would be that the priests collected books written elsewhere; another would be that some of the writers themselves came from elsewhere. There is no evidence in the Demotic texts themselves to support either idea (and certainly, so far, all the Roman period Demotic texts studied seem to show the one unambiguous sign of the Faiyumic dialect, the systematic use of a special sign for *l* where other dialects would employ *r*). In fact, even if a highly pessimistic view were taken of the accuracy of our present understanding of the provenance and date of the Tebtunis and Dime material, the wide variety of hands from the Faiyum as a whole would still call for comment. The present writer must confess that he is not convinced by all the details nor by all the conclusions of the treatment of these questions, chiefly in connection with Vienna material, by Reymond in the two works (1976 and 1983) cited in footnote 18, above.

22. Volten (1951) first drew attention to these matters, in so far as they related to the task of distinguishing the fragments of individual manuscripts in the collection. It is likely that systematic work on the distribution of types of hand could in future provide useful results.

When we ask the same question — who wrote the texts — for the Ptolemaic period and earlier, we do not have even the beginning of a satisfactory answer. There is no reason to assume, as in the case of the Roman period, that literary texts will necessarily have been the work of priests. It is often pointed out that Demotic stories show a particular preoccupation with priestly life. This is the case in one of our earliest pieces of evidence, one of the two best preserved of the narratives from Saqqâra, *P. Dem. Saq. 1*. However, in the Egyptian late period, persons of status were very likely to exercise both priestly and other offices (a situation that had vanished in the Roman period), and several types of texts seem more to reflect this kind of milieu than any concern with what we should regard as 'spiritual' or even 'clerical' matters. In any event, Demotic narratives are even more preoccupied with the royal court, and yet it has not been usual to suggest that it was there that they primarily or initially circulated (although there is no reason to suppose that would have been out of the question — for the periods before the Ptolemies). Glanville first pointed out the characteristics of ʿOnchsheshonqy which seem to put "us into direct touch with peasant life in Egypt" (1955, p. xv), and explicitly suggested that the instructions "are written ... for the guidance of the peasant farmer" (Glanville 1955, p. xiv). Perhaps few now would seek to argue that this was the text's audience. In general, it seems that our limited knowledge of pre-Roman period Demotic literature suggests that there was a high degree of continuity between Roman texts and what went before. We may therefore guess either that the earlier literature was likely to have had the same priestly audience as the Roman, or that priests in the Roman period took over a previously more widely spread tradition. But it is still difficult to find grounds for choosing between these two possibilities.

As for *where*, again our surviving evidence is very unevenly distributed. The Roman period finds from the Faiyum predominate. There is some notable material from Hermopolis, from Achmim, and from Thebes, and there is fragmentary material from Saqqâra, which, for the most part, has tentatively been dated to the fourth century B.C. And of course there are texts of which the provenance is quite unknown. We are, therefore, scarcely in a position to judge if Demotic literature was being written all over the country in the same way. Just a few texts are known from more than one provenance (P. Spiegelberg [Pfründe], P. Insinger, Mythus vom Sonnenauge [Kufi], and the legal manual),[23] which shows that at least some texts could be widespread. One detailed point may be mentioned. Among the Inaros[24] texts, P. Spiegelberg is known from Upper Egypt and in three copies from Tebtunis. Although there are at least forty Inaros texts from Tebtunis, P. Krall (Bresciani 1964) does not seem to be attested among them, nor does the *Ägypter und Amazonen* text, of which two copies from Vienna have been published (Volten 1962).[25] One possible explanation is that these cycles of texts (apart from P. Spiegelberg, which was perhaps the earliest of the genre) were being composed locally for local consumption. It might be suggested that the actual date of composition of some, at least, might be placed in the Roman period, much later than is often suggested. However, the Demotic material from Tebtunis, as far as has yet emerged, has nothing local about its contents or subject matter. Some of the religious material in hieratic does show such

23. Papyrus Spiegelberg: Spiegelberg 1910; cf. Tait 1977, pp. 14–20. P. Insinger: bibliography and translation may conveniently be found in Lichtheim 1980, pp. 184–217 (add also her subsequent book (1983; cf. footnote 12, above). Mythus: see de Cenival 1988. The legal manual: see footnote 1, above.

24. To judge from his surviving notes, by the end of his life Volten had decided it would be better to refer to the texts often called the Petubastis cycle simply by the name of the character whose 'family' occurs in all of them. He had arrived at this position by stages: compare the title of his 1956 article: 'Der demotische Petubastisroman und seine Beziehung zur griechischen Literatur' with that of his 1962 book: *Ägypter und Amazonen: eine demotische Erzählung des Inaros-Petubastis-Kreises aus zwei Papyri der Österreichischen Nationalbibliothek*. Compare W. J. Tait 1977 p. ix, and Bresciani 1990b.

25. A partial translation is included in Lichtheim 1980, pp. 151–56.

a tendency, concerning itself with the local god Sobk (although it may be noted that the Faiyum papyrus,[26] much copied at Tebtunis, centers its attention upon Sobk of Crocodilopolis, and is not adapted to give any prominence to the town's own form of the god, Soknebtunis). The Roman period Demotic literary material, however, although proclaiming itself as having been written in the Faiyum by its dialect, does not show the slightest sign of being interested in local matters. By the very title of his volume *Stories of the High Priests of Memphis* (1900), F. Ll. Griffith implied a local origin for the Setna texts. This might be correct (and the first of the Saqqâra literary papyri also is chiefly set in the Memphite area). The text which most clearly seems to betray signs of a local origin and local interests is the Demotic Chronicle,[27] but this text had manifestly acquired a wider currency. Despite the fact that the text is, in a sense, of a unique type, it has many links with other Demotic material. In general, although there may well have been local compositions, the indications must be seen to be broadly against the idea that there were separate local literatures.

One or two other general statements may perhaps be hazarded. We know that just one or two Demotic texts had a substantial life, although the only dramatic example is the legal manual, which was in use, at least in some form, for almost a millennium, if we include estimates of its date of composition and the fragments of a Greek translation from Oxyrhynchus.[28] The general pattern, however, seems to be that new texts were constantly being written within the existing traditions, or, in the case of cycles such as the Setna stories, within the framework of an existing genre. We are beginning to have some indications that these traditions, and the modification which they underwent, may one day be traceable from the late New Kingdom through to the Roman period. It may be suspected, however, that many individual texts did not survive for long, and it is perhaps less plausible than some have argued that most of our texts must have been composed much earlier than our oldest surviving copy.

If a priestly context is accepted for the Roman period Tebtunis material, then some comments may be offered on the relations between Egyptians and Greeks. We know that the priests at Tebtunis in the earlier Roman period conducted a good deal of business in Greek.[29] It is therefore curious that the Demotic literary texts are virtually free of Greek words and expressions.[30] A similar position may be observed in Demotic material from elsewhere, although not in some texts published from the Vienna collections,[31] nor in P. London-Leiden (Mag.; Griffith and Thompson 1909), which is of later date than most of the Tebtunis Demotic papyri. If it is correct that a proportion of the texts were actually composed in the Roman period, then the lack of Greek influence on the vocabulary is remarkable. It contrasts with the situation in Demotic documents, although that does vary. That the priests were aware of Greek culture is evident. It is likely that the illustrated Greek herbal from Tebtunis was owned by the priests.[32] Yet there also comes from Tebtunis a Demotic herbal, quite unillustrated, showing no sign of Greek influence and virtually no Greek plant names.[33] It is perhaps to be dated to around the middle of the second century A.D.

26. Some of the hieratic versions are published in the volume edited by Botti (1959) cited in footnote 11, above. A study of the material by Beinlich is forthcoming at the time of writing.

27. Spiegelberg 1914b; cf. J. H. Johnson 1974, pp. 1–17; 1983, pp. 61–72; 1984, pp. 107–24.

28. See footnote 1, above and specifically Pestman 1983.

29. This can be seen from a mere glance at the section 'The priests of Soknebtunis' in P. Tebt. ii (Grenfell, Hunt, and Goodspeed 1907, pp. 54–116).

30. This matter was first brought into focus by Clarysse 1987a (especially p. 14).

31. See the texts published by Reymond 1976.

32. P. Tebt.ii.679 (Pack 1965, no. 2094); see J. de M. Johnson 1912. P. Tebt. Tait 39–41 (not 42) may possibly belong to the same papyrus.

33. P. Carlsberg 230, forthcoming in the first volume of *The Carlsberg Papyri* (in press).

The nature of the contents is very similar to that of P. London-Leiden, including the high proportion of magical material. One might have thought that a work of 'practical' use such as this would have been frequently augmented, updated, and adapted, and thus potentially receptive of Greek ideas and vocabulary. This is what we do see in the herbal material in P. London-Leiden. It is possible that there was a significant shift in this respect between the late second century and the middle of the third.

It seems likely that at least a few of the Inaros texts were written with an awareness of the Homeric poems. They take some very general idea from Homer (that there might be a feud over a suit of armour; that a hero might refuse to aid his king; that there is a land of women-warriors, so that a hero might find himself fighting its queen), and work this up into a narrative within Egyptian traditions. Beyond these broad ideas, the plots pay little regard to what actually happens in Homer, and the texts have virtually no interest in reproducing anything of the outlook or style of the Homeric poems. One small detail may be mentioned: battle scenes and single combats abound, and there are frequent general references to mass slaughter; and yet there seems to be not even a mention of the death of any one named hero.[34] That the stories are all more or less concerned with the deeds of heroes and with fighting may be a general feature either taken from Homer or in which it was intended to follow Homer; it is not yet clear whether or not this was a new departure in Demotic literature. There is no convincing precedent in New Kingdom narrative literature; for example, the story of the 'Taking of Joppa,'[35] in what little survives, shows no real interest in martial affairs. If there is any substance in the conjecture that P. Spiegelberg was the first of these texts, around which the others of the cycle grew, then it is remarkable that its central theme, a dispute over the rightful possession of a priesthood, is a traditional Egyptian one. It will not be surprising if other stories in the same cycle prove to take their ideas from other and not necessarily Greek sources. Thus the link with Homer seems casual, almost incidental. The general position is perhaps that Roman-period priests such as those at Tebtunis were not cut off from Greek culture, but their concern with it was curiously limited, and it is difficult to see anything of fear or resentment, let alone rebellion, in their literature.

To conclude: this paper, on the basis of some sadly uneven evidence, has tried to offer a few hypotheses, which may be shown to be more or less probable — or may be totally overthrown — as new material is studied, or old material re-examined. Fresh evidence, in the form of newly discovered texts, would be invaluable. But this will not automatically solve our problems. It is more important to ask the right questions.

34. Inaros' own death does not seem to be narrated in any of the texts, although it overshadows several of them, most obviously P. Krall (the dispute over his armour), and *Ägypter und Amazonen* (where there is some discussion of his burial), see p. 308, above.

35. In this context, it is, of course, curious that the text describes a stratagem that has been likened to that of the Trojan horse.

CHAPTER 38

GREEK AND DEMOTIC SCHOOL-EXERCISES

EMMANUEL TASSIER
Katholieke Universiteit, Leuven

Life in a multi-cultural society meant for the inhabitants of Egypt life in a multilingual society. For the Ptolemaic and Roman periods, this came down to, if we simplify somewhat the situation, the use of Egyptian (in the main written in Demotic) and of Greek. These two different languages require different teaching methods and an important source for our knowledge of the teaching methods in Egypt in this period are school-exercises, texts written by pupils or their teachers.[1]

Recently, Greek and Demotic school-exercises have in some aspects been studied and compared, for instance by Kaplony-Heckel (see footnote 1), Devauchelle (see footnote 1), and Maehler (1983a, pp. 191–203). The aim of this article is to call attention to some problems emerging from the study of this type of document and to suggest some tentative answers to questions recent studies have raised. I will concentrate on elementary education, although the line between the different stages of instruction is not always easy to draw.

First of all, it is worth stressing that we are in a better position to study and evaluate Greek school-texts than Demotic ones. The Greek material is much more abundant and we are able to place the bulk of the texts in their proper context, although many problems remain.[2]

For the Demotic exercises, we depend mainly on the texts themselves and we ourselves have to apply standards to classify texts as school-exercises. Possible criteria to be used are necessarily partially subjective: the contents of the text (they should be suitable for teaching purposes, as are, in our eyes, for example, word-lists and grammatical exercises), the material on which texts are written (potsherds and limestone tablets for instance are traditional surfaces for school-exercises in Egypt), and the poor quality of writing and grammar. I believe we sometimes take it too easily for

1. Recent studies on Demotic school-exercises, with ample bibliographies: Kaplony-Heckel 1974, pp. 227–46; Devauchelle 1984, pp. 47–59; J. H. Johnson 1990, pp. 86–96. The general treatment of Erichsen (1948) is still valuable. In Brunner, 1957, the then known Demotic material is placed in the overall context of Egyptian education, see especially pp. 78–80. Demotic grammatical exercises in the context of the study of ancient linguistics are discussed by Swiggers and Wouters 1990, pp. 10–46, especially pp. 20–24.

   Recently published school-texts are: O. Cairo inv. 12461, O. Cairo inv. 12462 (C), O. BM 86591, and O. BM 86596; cf. Nur el-Din 1987, pp. 199–204 and pls. I–II. P. Hamburg 33; cf. Brunsch 1987–88, pp. 5–9, with important corrections by Zauzich 1990, pp. 163–66. The Demotic ostraca excavated in El Kab seem to contain several school-texts, cf. Quaegebeur, (forthcoming B). The geographical list of O. Ashmolean 956 (cf. M. Smith 1988, pp. 78–84) is perhaps also a school-text.

2. Although the first edition appeared in 1948, the best general treatment of Greek education is still Marrou (6th ed., 1965; this edition was reprinted in two volumes in 1981 and the paging slightly differs from the original publication). The papyrological sources have been extensively used. Lists of Greek school-exercises: Zalateo 1961, pp. 160–235; Debut 1986, pp. 251–78. A recent publication of Greek school-texts is Harrauer and Sijpesteijn 1985.

granted that particular texts are school-exercises. For example, if we would find dreambooks — with their fixed pattern of introductory clauses — out of their context, there is a good chance that they would be considered as school-exercises. Maybe some texts which are now classified as school-texts ought to be reconsidered.[3]

We will now turn to three aspects of Greek and Demotic school-texts that have recently been discussed: word-lists, grammatical exercises, and the apparent absence of Demotic literary ostraca.

The use of word-lists as school-texts is well attested, both in Demotic and in Greek. In Greek there are lists of gods, personal names, occupations, and so on, which are sometimes classified alphabetically.[4] On the Demotic side, we possess lists arranged according to subjects: gods,[5] geographical lists,[6] occupations,[7] et cetera. For this practice we find many parallels in ancient Egyptian (cf. Gardiner 1947). In a way related to these texts are lists with compound nouns indicating persons and occupations:[8] compositions with *rmt* "man,"[9] *s-n* "man of,"[10] etc. On the other hand, we have some texts in which the words are arranged by the first sound: e.g. personal names beginning with *h*,[11] word-lists beginning with *ḏ*.[12] These texts stem both from the Ptolemaic period and from the Roman period. It has been suggested that this arrangement can be attributed to Greek influence (Kaplony-Heckel 1974). This cannot be excluded, but I do not exclude the possibility that the Egyptians have come to the principle of arrangement by the first sound on their own initiative.

An important piece of evidence in this respect is P. Saqqara 27, probably a school-text, where we apparently find a fixed order for the consonants (cf. now, Kahl 1991, pp. 33–47). In the text, birds are first said to be sitting on a plant; the first sound of the bird-name and of the name of the plant are each time the same, and each consonant is used only once. This can be compared with the manner English children learn their alphabet: a is for ape, b is for ball, c is for cat, et cetera.

Further in the text, birds are said to fly to a place, and again the same principle of matching sounds is used. The order of the consonants is partially different, but the text is very fragmentary. Anyway, it seems important that this text stems from the fourth century B.C., when Greek influence in these matters is even more difficult to assess than in the Ptolemaic or Roman periods. So, already in this period, the Egyptians knew the principle of arranging words with the same sound together.[13]

3. Compare e.g. Bresciani 1984, pp. 1–9 and pls. 1–2. Are all these lexical fragments to be considered school manuals?
4. E.g. in the well-known teaching manual "Livre d'écolier" (Pack 1965, no. 2642) we find in lines 38–47 a list of gods and in lines 58–66 a list of rivers. Pack 1965, no. 2716 is a list of personal names arranged alphabetically; Pack 1965, no. 2654 is an alphabetical list of occupations.
5. E.g. P. Cairo 31168 recto, cols. 1–6; P. Cairo 31169 recto, col. 4, line 10 – col. 10. Perhaps also P. Hamburg 33 verso, following the reconstruction of Zauzich 1990, pp. 163–66.
6. E.g. P. Cairo 31169 recto, col. 1, line 1 – col. 4, line 9; see also Zauzich 1987b, pp. 83–91. O. Ashmolean 956, cf. footnote 1, above.
7. E.g. P. BM 10856 fr. b.; cf. Bresciani 1963, p. 18 and pl. VII B. P. Berlin 23572 and P. Carlsberg 23; cf. W. J. Tait 1984, pp. 211–33 and pl. 31.
8. J. H. Johnson (1990, p. 88) catalogues these texts as grammatical exercises.
9. E.g. O. Cairo s.n.; cf. Hess 1897, pp. 147–49. O. Karnak LS 2; cf. Devauchelle 1984, pp. 47–49 and pl. 10.
10. E.g. P. Sorbonne 1318 a and b, to be published by M. Pezin; cf. Devauchelle 1984, p. 53.
11. P. BM 10852; cf. Bresciani 1963, pp. 15–16 and pl. VI.
12. P. Carlsberg 12 verso; cf. Volten 1952, pp. 496–508.
13. For the problem of an "alphabetical" arrangement of sounds, see the discussion of P. Saqqara 27 in the publication of the text: Smith and Tait 1983, pp. 209–13.

An important part of the corpus of Demotic school-exercises is formed by grammatical texts. There exists a great variety: verbs conjugated in different persons,[14] grammatical forms conjugated in one person in different sentences,[15] relative forms,[16] et cetera. In Greek, we find many examples of similar grammatical texts, for example complete conjugation schemes of verbs[17] and words and sentences declined in all cases.[18] That the Greek exercises served as an example for Demotic ones has been rejected because we have one or two examples of grammatical conjugational schemes from the Ramesside period.[19] Although these are isolated examples, the principle of these kind of texts would have been known (Brunner 1957, pp. 72–73; Kaplony-Heckel 1974, p. 232). There is, however, another and perhaps stronger argument against the assumption of Greek influence on Demotic school-exercises: Greek grammatical school-exercises are in fact a by-product of theoretical grammatical treatises. The most important, the "Techne Grammatike" of Dionysius Thrax, was written about the end of the second century B.C., and examples of conjugation schemes were added later (cf. Wouters 1979, pp. 33–37). The use of these schemes as school-exercises is only attested from the third century A.D. (Marrou 1965, pp. 255–57; Wouters 1979, pp. 17–18). At first, they were not even intended for beginners, but later they were indeed used by starting pupils. It has been suggested that this was due to the deterioration of the knowledge of Greek in the Roman period (Maehler 1983a, p. 201).

At any rate, as we possess grammatical school-exercises in Demotic from the Ptolemaic period, Greek influence is extremely doubtful. Influence the other way round, from Demotic grammatical texts on Greek texts is very improbable. But I think these facts show us that we have to reconsider perhaps part of the Demotic grammatical school-exercises. Maybe we have to ask ourselves if at least some of these texts are not in fact kinds of grammatical treatises,[20] in a way comparable to the systematic hieroglyphic sign-lists we know from the late period.[21] This does not exclude that material from these grammatical texts was also used in schools.

The last problem I want to touch upon briefly is the apparent absence of literary texts among school-texts. Already in a quite early stage, young pupils in Greek were confronted with classical Greek texts; fragments were used as reading and writing exercises, and in a later stage, the authors were intensively studied (Marrou 1965, pp. 231–32 and 243–54). When we turn to the pharaonic period, we learn for example from the mass of ostraca found at Deir el-Medineh and other places that in the Ramesside period literary texts formed the most important part of the curriculum, also for beginners (cf. van de Walle 1948; Brunner 1957, pp. 86–91). The pupils had to copy fragments of classical texts such as the "Kemit" (cf. Chappaz 1989, pp. 33–43) — the traditional school-book for beginners — the "Instructions of Amenemhat," the "Satire of the Trades," and so on.

The situation for Demotic is quite different. Apart from the ostraca from Medinet Madi, discussed below, there are some sixty literary ostraca — and texts on related materials, such as writing-boards — known. But of these, only a few are literary in a strict sense. There are the

14. E.g. O. Ashmolean 726; cf. Reich 1924, pp. 285–88 (number of the ostracon kindly provided by Dr. M. Smith). P. Vienna 6464; cf. Kaplony-Heckel 1974, pp. 244–45.

15. E.g. P. Berlin 13639; cf. Erichsen 1948. P. Carlsberg 12 verso, fr. a, lines 1–11; cf. Volten 1952.

16. E.g. O. Bodleian 683; cf. Kaplony-Heckel 1974, p. 246.

17. E.g. Pack 1965, nos. 2162–2165.

18. Pack 1965, nos. 2661, 2705, and 2706.

19. O. Petrie 28; cf. Černý and Gardiner 1957, p. 3 and pl. VII, no. 7. O. Cairo 25227; cf. Daressy 1901, p. 55.

20. The conjugation lists of P. Vienna 6464 (see footnote 14, above) could be taken into consideration.

21. P. Carlsberg 7; cf. Iversen 1958. The Sign Papyrus; cf. Griffith and Petrie 1889, pp. 1–19 and pls. I–VIII.

Krugtexte (Spiegelberg 1912c), there is a drawing board with a fragment from the Petubastis-cycle,[22] and a few wisdom-texts.[23] The religious and funerary texts on ostraca[24] are maybe partly school-texts, but may also have been written down for other purposes, which is certainly also true for magical[25] and astronomical[26] ostraca. On the other hand, texts as word-lists, grammatical texts, calculating exercises, and so on form the bulk of the known "literary" ostraca.

The Medinet Madi ostraca pose specific questions.[27] A great part of this material seems to originate from a school, but the interpretation of the texts is far from certain due to the difficulties in deciphering them.[28] Some appear to contain something like admonitions to the pupils,[29] but literary texts as tales or wisdom literature[30] are absent.

So, it seems that literature had not an important part in the "Demotic curriculum." Naturally, our picture of the situation may be blurred by the defective tradition of these kind of texts and excavations or finds in museums may compel us to alter our views. Yet, I would like to put forward an explanation based on the present evidence. In the Ramesside period, we found that literary texts were extensively used for instructional goals. It is important to note that the classical texts are written in Middle Egyptian, which means that they were grammatically obsolete in the Ramesside period. We have evidence that many pupils — and teachers — did not understand what they were writing down (cf. Brunner 1957, pp. 89–90). One of the important reasons why these texts were still taught is the fact that they were indeed "classical," venerated texts, already used for ages as school-texts (cf. Assmann 1985, pp. 35–52).

I believe that for Demotic the situation is quite different. First of all, we may assume that Demotic was in its early stage mainly a script for official and legal purposes. For narrative literature, religious texts, and so on, hieratic was still the script to use.[31] When Demotic was to be taught, there were simply no literary texts available. When a Demotic literature later emerged, from the fourth century B.C. onward, as we now know from the Saqqara papyri, this "new" literature perhaps did not have the same prestige as the classical tales in pharaonic Egypt — or as Homer and Euripides in the Greek schools. One could even suggest that texts such as word-lists or grammatical texts — if these are indeed texts meant to be used as teaching material — or texts

22. In the Fitzwilliam Museum in Cambridge; cf. Ray 1972, pp. 247–51 and pl. XLIII. Another limestone board with perhaps parts of a narrative text is published by Spiegelberg 1912a, pp. 32–34 and pl. I; and 1913, pp. 137–38.

23. O. BM 50627; cf. R. Williams 1977, pp. 270–71 and 1981, p. 3, note 3. O. El Kab 5 T 004; cf. Quaegebeur 1981, pp. 531, 536; and forthcoming B.

24. E.g. O. Corteggiani 1; cf. Menu 1981, pp. 215–16. O. Naville; cf. M. Smith 1977, pp. 115–49 and pl. XVIII. O. Uppsala 672; cf. Wångstedt, 1957, pp. 9–13 and pl. I.

25. E.g. O. Strasbourg 1; cf. Spiegelberg 1911, pp. 34–37. O. Karnak LS 7; cf. Devauchelle 1987b, pp. 139–40 and pl. I.

26. Compare Neugebauer 1943, pp. 115–26; Neugebauer and Parker 1968, pp. 231–35; Parker 1984, pp. 141–43 and pl. 23. O. Karnak NMB 2; cf. Devauchelle 1987b, pp. 137–38 and pl. I.

27. This bilingual archive from Medinet Madi in the Faiyum is only preserved in photographs. Some forty Demotic texts are published: Bresciani, Pernigotti, and Betrò 1983; Parker 1984, pp. 141–43 and pl. 23; Gallo 1989, pp. 99–120 and pls. I–III. An edition of a part of the Greek ostraca is in preparation by R. Pintaudi and P. J. Sijpesteijn.

28. Gallo (see *Chapter 12*), for example, has demonstrated that some texts seem to be instructions for itinerant priests.

29. So O. Medinet Madi I 10, 12, and 13; see Bresciani, Pernigotti, and Betrò 1983.

30. Although a few ostraca seem inspired by wisdom-texts, so O. Medinet Madi I 25 and 26; cf. Bresciani, Pernigotti, and Betrò 1983.

31. The Papyrus Vandier, edited by G. Posener (1986), seems to confirm this. The language of this hieratic papyrus, written towards the end of the sixth century B.C. or at the latest in the fifth century B.C., is similar to Demotic.

such as the bird-list of P. Saqqara 27, were by then fully established as school-texts, so that literature was no longer needed for elementary educational purposes.[32]

32. Professor W. J. Tait mentioned, in his paper given at this conference ("Aspects of the Orthography of the Saqqara Demotic Papyri"), the existence of some fragments in the Saqqara papyri (S.H5-DP 11 and S.H5-DP 285, excavation numbers kindly provided by Prof. Tait) that contain probably a list of personal names, written in a really large hand. Professor Zauzich also told him that in the Carlsberg collection in Copenhagen, there is a papyrus with personal names, also written in a large hand. These could indeed be some sort of calligraphic exercises.

CHAPTER 39

GREEKS OR COPTS?: DOCUMENTARY AND OTHER EVIDENCE FOR ARTISTIC PATRONAGE DURING THE LATE ROMAN AND EARLY BYZANTINE PERIODS AT HERAKLEOPOLIS MAGNA AND OXYRHYNCHOS, EGYPT

THELMA K. THOMAS
The University of Michigan

Art historians of Byzantine Egypt confront a state of desperate confusion over basic terminology. Whereas "Coptic" as used by philologists refers to the last phase of the Egyptian language, and "Coptic" as used by theologians refers to the Christological doctrine of Egyptian monophysite Christianity, art historical usage encompasses all that and more. Art historians employ the term to designate the arts of a rather open-ended historical epoch comprising late Roman, early Byzantine, and even later Arab rule of Egypt. Consequently, pagan arts are often identified by the "Coptic" label. The title of this presentation, however, reflects my concerns with a very specific art historical sense of "Coptic," which stands in contradistinction to "Alexandrian" stylistically, iconographically, ethnically, and culturally: whereas "Alexandrian" indicates Greek, or at the least Hellenistic, steeped in pagan learning, possessed of wealth and urban sophistication; "Coptic" indicates Egyptian, Christian, poor, and rustic.[1] The state of the art historical question is this: are our interpretations, chiefly of artistic style, accurate in elaborating upon the as yet untested notion of "Coptic" Egyptian versus "Alexandrian" Greek art? Are we correct in our assessment of, for example, all fourth-century A.D. Egyptian sculpture as responding negatively to Alexandrian artistic ideals, as being "anti-Hellenistic," therefore "Coptic" in style?

My investigations suggest that the artistic remains do not fit within the given art historical dialectic. Specifically, sculptures bearing pagan subjects which may be attributed to Greek urban centers are impossible to understand within the given Coptic, zealously Christian, poverty-stricken, rural setting. This paper focuses on such artistic remains from the cities of the interior of late Roman and early Byzantine Egypt: a group of limestone reliefs from monumental tombs from cemeteries associated with two of Byzantine period Egypt's most well-known *metropoleis* — Herakleopolis Magna and Oxyrhynchos (see pls. 39.1 and 39.2). I present here some old and

1. Badawy 1978; Beckwith 1963; DuBourguet 1964; Duthuit 1931; Farag 1976–77, pp. 22–42; Gayet 1902a; Strzygowski 1904; Torp 1969, pp. 101–12; and Wessel 1963.

readily available evidence for artistic patronage. What is new and noteworthy is that this evidence, chiefly documentary, has never been studied in association with the artistic remains.[2]

Before presenting the written evidence, two problems complicating the study of Byzantine period Egyptian art must be stated, and the funerary reliefs from Herakleopolis Magna and Oxyrhynchos in particular. In the first place, the hundreds of limestone sculptures from Herakleopolis Magna, Oxyrhynchos, and other similar sites were excavated quickly, and without adequate archaeological documentation. Often their place of discovery is unknown, and attributions must be made on the basis of technical affiliations. The excavators sought the remains of earlier periods or, at best, written records of all periods. As a consequence, although these late Roman and early Byzantine funeral complexes are now nearly impossible to reconstruct, the minutiae of the daily lives of their artisans and patrons were saved from rubbish heaps.[3]

Secondly, after their discovery and subsequent dispersal to museum collections throughout Egypt, Europe, and North America, these limestone sculptures began to deteriorate at a rapid pace. Detailed comparisons of chronologically arranged photographs point out the extent of damage suffered by each relief. A very few, exceptionally well-preserved sculptures indicate how completely the addition of polychromy transformed the visual effect of these sculptures. In other examples, the original appearance of these polychromed reliefs has been reduced to hard edges, harsh highlights and shadows, bereft of any of the softness originally imparted by the texture, coloring, and added detail of the polychromy. In more frustrating, poorly preserved examples, such photographic comparisons document how finely chiseled surfaces have deteriorated to the point of illegibility. I have dealt with polychromy and problematic surface damage on other occasions. It should be sufficient in this context to mention only that the stylistic evidence upon which we have based the Greek vs. Copt premise is misleading, and entirely inadequate (T. K. Thomas 1989, pp. 54–64 and 1990).[4]

My analyses of the physical evidence indicate that the manufacturing processes of the niched tombs could not have varied greatly between Oxyrhynchos and Herakleopolis Magna. Through several generations, between the late third and late fifth centuries, niche decorations of the same size were produced to fit into tombs constructed on the same basic scheme, consisting of a small, rectangular, niched chamber decorated with polychromed friezes and niche heads which were set into the walls at or above eye-level. Structural types, consistent dimensions, carving and painting techniques, and subject matter all indicate that we are dealing with a regularized genre of architectural decoration. It is clear, however, that no two tombs or decorative programs are exactly alike. And, it is significant that these frieze and niche decorations were, quite clearly, crafted by artisans willing to produce these large decorated tombs for individual patrons of any faith — so long as the patrons paid.

Although there is not enough archaeological evidence for the detailed reconstruction of individual niched tombs, there is enough documentary evidence to formulate a generic description of the historical circumstances behind their creation.

For the present purposes of this presentation, the papyri collected at these sites are more important than the contested stylistic evidence. The papyri offer a more complete picture of the multicultural setting. They preserve evidence of continuing traditional Greco-Roman arrangements in

2. This documentary information and the results of my physical analyses of the reliefs are presented in full in my dissertation (T. K. Thomas 1990).

3. Important excavation reports include Almagro and Presedo 1976, pp. 3–5; Breccia 1932, pp. 60–63, and 1933, pp. 36–44; Naville 1891 and 1894; Petrie 1905a, 1905b, and 1925; Petrie and Bruntun 1924; Presedo Velo 1976, pp. 94–96; Severin 1981; Wilcken 1903, pp. 294–336; and, of course, *The Oxyrhynchus Papyri* (1898–1990 [and continuing]; published in the series Graeco-Roman Memoirs by the Egypt Exploration Society).

4. The first discussion of this distressing phenomenon appears in Boyd and Vikan 1981.

the processes of artistic production and commissioning. Documentary texts record how craftsmen of diverse skills and training were contracted individually to work the limestone, baked brick, plaster, and paint from which the niched tombs were constructed.[5]

The documentary papyri further indicate that each tomb was constructed ad hoc according to specific orders placed by the patron who commissioned the tomb. The patron (or overseer, who might be one individual or a group of persons) undertook three separate activities: financing, supervising construction, and planning the decorative program.[6]

These and other documents specifying or suggesting costs entailed by the construction of the monumental tombs indicate that the "lower classes" who have been identified in previous art historical literature as the patrons of these monuments could not have afforded them.[7] Further damaging the "Coptic" claim to patronage is the fact that these documents are written in Greek, and the craftsmen — of the "middle classes" are often noted in these documents as being illiterate (possibly meaning illiterate in Greek). It is difficult to specify which of the main forms of Christianity the Christian patrons tended to follow. The imagery in the Christian funerary reliefs offers no clues as to Christological doctrine. The pagan imagery is clearly drawn from the traditional Greek repertory. The only possible commissioners of the niched tombs, then, were the wealthier, educated pagans and Christians who shared a common Greek or Hellenized outlook.

This, then, is the rub of the Greek or Copt question: whereas these reliefs have been termed "Coptic" because of art historical readings of their (incompletely preserved) style, on the basis of the written evidence their patrons must be identified as Greek, whether wholly Greek, of Greco-Egyptian descent, or Hellenized Egyptian.

Late Roman and early Byzantine monumental tombs at other metropolitan Egyptian sites are clearly related to the tombs at Herakleopolis Magna and Oxyrhynchos. The second century "Tomb of Isidora" in Hermopolis Magna consists of a small rectangular chamber with a niche inserted into the north wall just above eye-level. The crown of the niche is decorated with a shell. At the bottom of the niche is a shelf painted with the form of a lion-footed funerary couch or *kline*. To either side of the niche is an epigrammatic inscription composed in honor of the deceased, Isidora (E. Bernand 1969). The niched tombs at Herakleopolis Magna and Oxyrhynchos, and the other sites, bear similar inscriptions and/or decorations concentrated at their niches. Common to the Byzantine period Christian niched tombs at these, and other sites, are low shelves under the wall-niches: some seem to have served as funerary couches while others, defining the floor of the niche, are very small.[8]

Thus, archaeological and documentary evidence indicates that the Greco-Roman background for the construction and shaping of these tombs was pervasive in the metropolitan centers. Artisans and patrons carried on the traditions of their predecessors in the production and commissioning of these expensive niched tombs. Other written sources, chiefly literary, describe for us the funerary beliefs of these wealthy urbanites, explaining why — in the precursors and in the early Byzantine period Egyptian niched tombs — the niche received such attention which, coincidentally, has some

5. A select few are: P. Oxy. VII 1049 (second century A.D.) on specialized categories of stonemasons; P. Oxy. XLVI 3308 (A.D. 373) "Undertaking an Oath" taken by a stonemason as to where he might legally practice his trade; P. Fay. 36 (A.D. 111–112) "Tender for a Brick making concession"; P. Oxy. XX 2285 (A.D. 285) mentioning payment for bricks; P. Oxy. XII 1450 (A.D. 249–250), costs for plastering and painting; and P. Oxy. VI 896, (A.D. 316) "Painter's estimate" for a large project.

6. See, for example: P. Oxy. III 498 (second century A.D.) wherein overseers negotiate for redecorating parts of pre-existing overall programs; P. Oxy. XXII 2348 (A.D. 224) "Greek version of a Roman Will" wherein the deceased designates overseers for the tomb project and the expense to be borne by his estate; P. Grenf. ii.77 (third–fourth centuries A.D.) "Letter from Melas to Serapion and Silvanus" on expenses for a less grandiose burial.

7. Additional references are gathered together in T. K. Thomas 1990.

8. Similar examples from other Roman and Byzantine period Egyptian *necropoleis* may be found in, for example, von Bissing 1950, pp. 547–76; Donadoni 1938, pp. 493–501; Gayet 1902b; and Salmi 1945, pp. 161–69.

bearing on its requiring a considerably larger portion of the expense. The first of two inscriptions in the "Tomb of Isidora," for example, testifies that the architectural elements of the niche were more than strictly functional. They were symbolic as well. The niche and its architectural decoration formed a sanctuary for the deceased, much as temples formed sanctuaries for gods. The second inscription makes clear that, upon her death, Isidora was metamorphosed into a nymph.

Like their Greek and Roman period predecessors, the early Byzantine period Egyptian pagan funerary niches were frequently decorated with images of gods, heroes, and nature divinities and with motifs associated with those divinities. Half-shells, nymphs and Pan, Nile and Earth, Dionysius, Heracles, and Aphrodite are common images associated with the deceased in the pagan niche decorations. The pagan imagery has often been misinterpreted within a Coptic, entirely Christian setting, as lacking meaning, or as having willfully and subtly subverted the original pagan intentions, or as being syncretistic despite the lack of a single overtly syncretistic composition or motif. The explicit evidence from, for example, the inscriptions in the "Tomb of Isidora," suggest that these images retain their obvious import as attributes or portraits of the deified deceased. The formal devices employed to make the pagan scenes appear to emerge from within the crowns of the niches created an effective visual reference to the deification of the dead, as if the niche contained a cult statue looming out over the altar and sacrificers below.

The Christian niche decorations, treated to the same formal devices, would have appeared as windows presenting vivid visions of the paradise to which the deceased had ascended, and would have stressed the relationship between the shelf or altar below and the vault above as a path of communication between paradise and earth. The significance of the Christian funerary niches stems from the different tradition of church architecture in which the decorations commonly offer visions of the heavenly paradise, Christ, and the cross.

In conclusion, the written evidence and comparative monuments here introduced into discussions of "Coptic" art offer necessary information for discarding indiscriminate use of the term. The costs and unique qualities of the polychromed funerary niche decorations, in particular, argue that the patrons demanded specific products fitting their views of themselves: they commissioned and received niched tombs like those of their peers throughout Egypt, and, indeed, throughout the Empire, constructed according to the traditions of their ancestors and the laws of the realm. The evidence for artistic patronage, I believe, asks us to recast the Greek versus Coptic stylistic question, and asks us to confront such phenomena as why Western European art historians, usually so quick to appropriate anything Greek, have given this art to the Copts.

Niche Decoration from an Early Byzantine Period Tomb at Herakleopolis Magna Depicting a Nymph on a Sea Monster.
The Brooklyn Museum, 41.1226, Charles Edwin Wilbour Fund. Photograph courtesy of The Brooklyn Museum.

PLATE 39.2

Fragment of a Niche Decoration from an Early Byzantine Period Tomb at Herakleopolis Magna Depicting an Angel (or Angels) Presenting a Cross in a Wreath.
The Coptic Museum, Cairo. Photograph after G. Duthuit (1931).

CHAPTER 40

LITERACY AND THE ADMINISTRATION IN EARLY PTOLEMAIC EGYPT

DOROTHY J. THOMPSON
Girton College, Cambridge University

In the Oriental Institute in Chicago is a black basalt statue base from Upper Egypt in honor of Arsinoe, the wife of Ptolemy II Philadelphus. On the top is a detailed hieroglyphic dedication while on the front, in fine lettering, a briefer Greek dedication reads: *Arsinoes Philadelphou*, 'of Arsinoe Philadelphus.' Accepting the suggestion of Jan Quaegebeur that this dedication, from a priestly context, illustrates the receptivity of the native priesthood to the language of their new Macedonian rulers, I want here to explore further some of the implications of this suggestion (Fraser 1960, pp. 133–34; Quaegebeur 1988, p. 47). For the fact that an Egyptian dedicatory statue from the mid third century B.C. may, on the front face of its base, proclaim this dedication in Greek shows to what extent the language of the new rulers had become accepted during the first century of the Ptolemaic dynasty.

The general question with which I am concerned is that of literacy in Egypt in the period following Alexander. What happens when the long-established tradition of Egyptian literacy, a priestly and scribal literacy which was both highly valued and closely confined, is brought into contact with the more open, secular tradition of Greek literacy?[1] The context for such an exploration must be the reality of the Macedonian conquest of Egypt by Alexander the Great followed, on his death, by the satrapy of his general Ptolemy, son of Lagus, who, as Ptolemy I Soter, later became king of Egypt and all its people. Unlike the Persians earlier, the Ptolemaic rulers formed a resident dynasty with a closely controlled administration. How far that administration was based on Egyptian, Persian, or Greco-Macedonian models has already been the subject of much study, and there is more to do. Here my interest is more limited. What I want to look at is what happened in terms of language and literacy in the first hundred years of this new administration. How far can the language of the documents produced — ostraca, papyri, and inscriptions — and the identification of those who wrote them add to our understanding of the process by which Greek rule was established in this new Hellenistic kingdom? How important was literacy in this process? How was Greek literacy spread? What were the reactions of different groups within Egyptian society to this new state of affairs?

In a previous study (forthcoming) I concentrated on the first fifty years where surviving documentation is predominantly Demotic. In these early years, Greeks and Egyptians needed each other's cooperation and, as earlier under the Persians, collaboration came from the Egyptian

1. Egyptian literacy: Baines 1983, pp. 572–99, especially p. 581 and 1988, pp. 192–214; Goody 1986, pp. 32–35, 64–65 and 1987, pp. 30–44; and Finnegan 1988, p. 42. Greek literacy: O. Murray 1980, pp. 91–99.

literate classes, the priestly upper classes — men such as Manetho from Sebennytos, the historian of Egypt who wrote in Greek (Jacoby 1958, no. 609; Fowden 1986, pp. 52–54; and Mendels 1990, pp. 91–110), Nectanebo, a Ptolemaic military commander from the old royal family (de Meulenaere 1963, pp. 90–93), or the priest Wennofer whose sarcophagus lid (in Cairo) and statue (in Vienna) have both survived: "I spent my life on earth in the King's favor, I was beloved of his courtiers" and "at the time of the Greeks I was consulted by the ruler of Egypt, for he loved me and knew my intentions" are his boasts.[2] The Greeks would need to recognize this help — and so they did. Alexander's general Peukestas, in a terse order posted at Saqqâra, put sacred buildings out of bounds (Turner 1974, pp. 239–42), and the so-called Satrap Stele records endowments returned by Ptolemy to local temples in the neighborhood of Sais (*Urk.* II, pp. 11–22, note 9 and Bevan 1927, pp. 28–32, for translation). And there are other examples, both Greek and Egyptian, on stone and on papyrus, from the reign of Ptolemy I (Thompson, forthcoming, note 19).

This then, a picture of collaboration between the existing literate classes and the new rulers, is how I would characterize the first generation of Ptolemaic rule. There were, of course, administrative innovations (for instance, the Greek financial officers in early Theban Demotic texts [Quaegebeur 1979a, p. 47]) but it is only from the reign of Ptolemy II that evidence survives for the intensification of the bureaucracy which later characterizes Ptolemaic administration. And with this intensification came the growing use of Greek. The organization and collection of the salt-tax may serve as an illustration.[3] With very few exceptions, this tax was charged to all and levied by local tax collectors. In preparation came a series of household declarations with individuals listed (together with their animals) and, on the basis of these declarations and also their own research, lists of taxpayers recorded topographically were compiled by the tax collectors. In addition, analytical records were drawn up, grouping the local population by profession and status (*kat᾽ ethnos*) and forming the basis for summary compilations with the information simply in cash terms. When it came to tax payments, individual receipts were issued to the taxpayers and the collector kept day-by-day accounts of what he got in. Taxes were then paid over to the local bank at ten day intervals and separate accounts were kept of these drafts. Sometimes the same records could serve for other local taxes — especially the obol-tax paid by most adult males — and sometimes separate lists were made for different taxes. The form of these operations differs by area and over time, but overall the system is just as complex, involving as many written documents on either papyrus or ostracon, as that, say, of the regular land survey. The operation was recorded, at least in the third century, in either Demotic or Greek, and, as in the issue of receipts, sometimes both were used together. Indeed, the use of a rush, the standard Demotic writing implement, for the Greek records of *CPR* XIII shows how these local offices might function in both languages.

How far the nature of this Ptolemaic bureaucracy depends on a growth of literacy in the new Greek language with its more easily accessible script, or indeed the effect of this on the uses of Demotic, is something I am not yet ready to answer, though the question must surely be asked. What I do want to bring into the discussion here is the program of education which accompanied this gradual change of language. The problems of personnel and access to local information essential to successful control are among those faced by all imperial powers. And when Ptolemy son of Lagus, supported by a contingent of Macedonian troops from Babylon and by the corpse of the Conqueror, established himself in Egypt, these were among the problems he faced. Like the Persians before him, with their use of Aramaic, Ptolemy, it seems, determined to exercise rule in a new language. What he lacked at the start were sufficient administrators fluent in Greek to

2. For the sarcophagus lid, see Lichtheim 1980, p. 55. For the statue, see Quaegebeur 1980, p. 78.

3. Übel 1966, pp. 325–68 and 1969, pp. 62–66; Shelton 1976, pp. 35–39; and Bagnall 1978, pp. 143–46. *P. dem. Lille* III and *CPR* XIII add important new evidence in both Demotic and Greek.

exercise this rule. Education (as always?) was the answer to the problem, and from the reign of Ptolemy II Philadelphus on there is a growing body of evidence to suggest the scale of what I take to be a royal initiative.

Tax breaks played an important role in the process. Our earliest evidence to date is the Greek *Dikaiomata* papyrus which records a letter from Apollonios, *dioiketes* under Ptolemy II Philadelphus, to one Zoilos, passing on a royal decree to exempt from the salt-tax (the Ptolemaic form of the poll-tax) teachers of letters, physical education teachers, and the victors of certain, designated, national games (*P. Hal.* 1.260–64). Later documents suggest the exemption may have been extended more widely,[4] but under Philadelphus it is the privileged position of school teachers that is striking; the value of education, of Greek education, was thus recognized. The scale of this early literacy drive is now becoming clearer, as more of the third century tax documents in both Greek and Demotic are published. The texts recently edited in volume XIII of the Greek Rainer papyri, together with the Demotic texts of volume III of the Lille papyri from Ghôran, well illustrate the scale of education in the villages of the Faiyum. We may excerpt the following figures from the reign of Ptolemy III.

In Trikomia (Themistes meris) there were three registered teachers, all male, in a total adult (taxable) population of 331, that is one teacher to 110 adults. Of these 331 adults, 170 were male which means that, on the assumption that only boys received Greek formal education, there was one teacher to fifty-seven adult males (*CPR* XIII 1.10, 12 [254–44 B.C.]). From neighboring Lagis with a total adult population of 323, three teachers are registered of whom two were men. The density here is 1:161 overall or 1:82 males (*CPR* XIII 2.30 [254–44 B.C.]). From the village of Per-Hemer near Apias in the same division, two teachers (a man and his wife) were registered for salt-tax exemption. The density here was 1:398 overall or 1:218 males (*P. dem. Lille* III 99, verso, col. ii.15 [229/8 B.C.]). And for the whole area of which Per-Hemer formed part, with a total adult population of 10,876 there were twenty-four persons under the heading of teachers, fifteen of them men. The density here was 1:725 adults or 1:350 adult males (*P. dem. Lille* III 99, verso, col. iva.1–7 [229/8 B.C.]). What such figures may mean in terms of actual staff to student ratios is less easy to know. In the absence of information of certain basic facts — life expectancy rates, the length of elementary schooling, and indeed the ages between which this took place — it is difficult to be more explicit.

Since some villages had no teachers at all (Athenas Kome, for instance, with a total adult population of 153 [*CPR* XIII 11.11], or Lysimachis with only eighty [*CPR* XIII 2.4 (254–244 B.C.)]) this final density of 1:350 may perhaps be taken as a guide for the area as a whole. The Arsinoite nome of course was an area of quite intense Greek settlement, so how far this picture is representative is impossible to know. We lack comparable figures for the Delta or the Nile valley.[5]

Such a number or teachers is, I think, worthy of note. And if the contemporary school book, probably from the same area, can be brought into the discussion we may also have some idea of the content of this schooling (Guéraud and Jouguet 1938). Besides the Greek alphabet and numbering system, pupils learned lists of months, gods, and rivers (both Macedonian and from the world that Alexander had conquered) before being introduced to Homer, the tragedians and new comic writers, and finally the elegists of Alexandria. Pupils learned to read and write, to count and calculate with the new Greek denominations, and their education was also cultural, based on the Greek classics with more recent Alexandrian poetry added. Such a system of schooling was, in my view, the Ptolemaic answer to the needs of the new administration.

4. *P. dem. Lille* III 101.ii.7, *pastophoros* pays half rate; v.26–28 and vi.20 (244/3 B.C.), payments instead of the salt-tax made to temples; *P. Petrie* III 59b, *hiera ethne* exempt, perhaps from salt-tax.

5. From Upper Egypt it is mainly tax receipts on ostraca that have survived; Petrie 1907, p. 33, no. E1, from Shashotep may be a second century B.C. Demotic example from the valley of Middle Egypt.

I shall venture further. In these same tax documents there are listed two further privileged classes — the Hellenes and, in Demotic, the Medes, or Persians as they are called in Greek.[6] These two classes paid the salt-tax but, like teachers, they were not liable for the obol-tax which other men paid. Who were these Hellenes? Some, of course, were cleruchs, the Greek soldiers settled in the Egyptian countryside; others are specified as doctors, teachers, fullers, priests, and so on (e.g. *P. dem. Lille* III 99, verso [229/8 B.C.]; *SB* XII 10860). And from the summary figures of one composite record of five tax districts it appears that in 228 B.C. Hellenes here formed 16% of the total number recorded, 1,756 out of 10,876 (*P. dem. Lille* III 99, verso, iiia.8 and 17 [229/8 B.C.]. It is, of course, well known that the Faiyum, from where this document comes, was an area of high Greek settlement, but even so the percentage and number both seem very high for those of immigrant Greek origin.

Another Ghôran document, *P. dem. Lille* III 101 (244/3 B.C.), may suggest an explanation. This is a person-by-person list of tax payments which records most men paying both the salt-tax and the obol-tax (and, being in Demotic, the Egyptian system of calculation was used, with the one drachma salt-tax for men recorded as $\frac{1}{2}$ *kite*). Scattered among the Egyptian names and family groups are men with Greek names who pay only the salt-tax and not the obol-tax (*P. dem. Lille* III 101.ii.5, 26; iii.1, 7; iv.12, 13, 18, 29; v.5, 20). Some may be cleruchs and one at least has been identified as belonging to an Alexandrian family known from the Petrie wills;[7] others are otherwise unknown. But what is striking about these men is not that their fathers or wives are often Egyptian by name — that should cause no surprise — but that in two cases their Egyptian-named brothers, who are listed together with them and even recorded as native soldiers, pay the full rate of both the salt-tax and the obol-tax, while the brothers with Greek names pay only the salt-tax.[8] Well integrated in their village, as de Cenival noted in her edition of this text, these men with their Greek names apparently enjoyed a fiscal privilege, immunity from the obol-tax (see de Cenival 1984, p. 52). Perhaps indeed these individuals are numbered among the Hellenes of the village? The tentative suggestion I should like to make is that it was a Greek education which fitted a local villager for a career in the administration, and this in turn allowed him to change both his name and status.[9] It was a Greek education or maybe the job which followed which made him a 'Hellene,' and with the status of Hellene came exemption from the obol-tax. It was, on this hypothesis, through investment in education, with the combined inducement of status and tax break, that the Ptolemies were able to move over to an administration run mainly in Greek. Isocrates' earlier claim for Athens that community of culture, *paideusis*, was more important than common origin, *koine physis*, in the definition of a Hellene would thus in Hellenistic Egypt have become reality in a wider world (*Panegyricus* 50, 15.293).

6. E.g. Hellenes: *CPR* XIII 1.18; 2.5, 15, 32; 4.109; 11.13; *P. dem. Lille* III 99, verso, ii.11; iiia.11. Medes: *P. dem. Lille* III 99, verso, ii.12; va.1. Persians: *CPR* XIII 2.5, 32.

7. For Monimos son of Kleandros (*P. dem. Lille* III 101.iii.1) as related to Kleandros son of Monimos in *P. Petrie* III 1 (237/6 B.C.) see *Chapter 6* by W. Clarysse above.

8. *P. dem. Lille* III 101.iv.27–29, Peisikles is brother of Padiou, son of Nehemesise, a soldier; *P. dem. Lille* III 101.v.18–21, Diodoros is brother of Padiou, son of Paher, a soldier.

9. BGU VI 1213 (third century B.C.), record of a legal extract concerned with change of *patris* and *onomata*. For the somewhat similar recognition (on application to the Governor General) of educated Indonesians as 'Dutch' in the Dutch East Indies during the late nineteenth and early twentieth centuries, see Geertz 1983, p. 227; Hooker 1978, pp. 197–98, article 163 (5) of the Indische Staatsregeling.

CHAPTER 41

L'ARMÉE DE TERRE LAGIDE: REFLET D'UN MONDE MULTICULTUREL?

E. VAN'T DACK
Katholieke Universiteit Leuven / Koninklijke Academie van België

Il est superflu d'insister, croyons-nous, sur le caractère multiculturel — nous préférons ce terme-là à l'hybride polyculturel — de l'armée lagide. Pour s'en convaincre, il suffit de consulter l'ouvrage de M. Launey et en particulier les listes dressées par l'auteur. Ses *Recherches sur les armées hellénistiques* (1949–50) ont connu une réimpression avec une mise à jour de Garlan, Gauthier, et Orrieux (1987) en postface. Ceux-ci ont retouché autant que possible quelques conceptions périmées de l'auteur qui, influencé par l'atmosphère des années d'après-guerre, était inévitablement en quelque sorte prisonnier de son époque. "À un moment où l'émancipation des peuples colonisés ... pouvait encore être simplement considérée comme un effet limité et conjoncturel de la seconde guerre mondiale,"[1] Launey (1949–50, cf. p. 16, pp. 44–49, pp. 57–59) ne s'était pas trop attardé au rôle de l'Égypte et des autochtones dans l'effort militaire des Ptolémées. Cette lacune, si nous osons dire, a été largement comblée e.a. par notre propre maître Peremans, qui, dans sa monographie *Vreemdelingen en Egyptenaren in Vroeg-Ptolemaeïsch Egypte*, parue en 1937, avait lui aussi donné un aperçu hâtif de ce même secteur aux pp. 70–73, mais qui, dans une série d'articles, y a accordé ensuite toute l'attention requise.[2]

Si nous reprenons ce sujet à présent, c'est que peut-être certains aspects de l'enquête pourraient être mis en évidence de façon plus explicite.

Il y a, entre autres, le milieu dans lequel l'armée devait opérer. Il va de soi que la situation était très différente pour les militaires égyptiens selon qu'ils étaient envoyés à l'étranger, par exemple, dans une des possessions extérieures des Lagides, ou qu'ils se trouvaient dans la capitale, Alexandrie ἡ πρὸς Αἰγύπτῳ, voire à la cour, ou qu'ils étaient installés dans la chôra.

Commençons par les soldats lagides à l'étranger et plus particulièrement dans le monde grec, mais non en Nubie par exemple. Grâce à J. K. Winnicki on pourra dorénavant utiliser un nouveau critère pour détecter les Égyptiens dans ce secteur: l'allusion à un repatriement d'objets cultuels révélerait l'engagement d'autochtones dont le rôle dans le cadre de l'expédition reste difficile à préciser.[3] D'autre part, il nous semble dangereux de doter sans plus le titre de μάχιμος d'une connotation ethnique; il nous faut d'autres éléments avant de pouvoir classer ces μάχιμοι parmi les Égyptiens (Van't Dack 1988, p. 21, note 112; p. 67 avec la note 11).

1. Garlan, Gauthier, et Orrieux 1987, p. xxi d'après É. Will; cf. Bingen 1989c, pp. 473–77, surtout pp. 474–76.
2. Voir la bibliographie, avec les contributions de W. Peremans et d'autres, dans Van't Dack 1988, pp. 4–6, pp. 42–43. À la bibliographie on ajoutera e.a. les contributions de J. K. Winnicki mentionnées ici même pp. 327–28, 337.
3. "Militäroperationen" (à paraître A) et "Die von Persern," (à paraître B).

Ceci dit, parcourons les données disponibles, qui nous mènent depuis le début de l'époque hellénistique jusqu'à la fin de la dynastie lagide. En 312 av. J.-C., à Gaza, Ptolémée I se présenta avec 18.000 fantassins et 4000 cavaliers, ainsi qu'avec un Αἰγυπτίων πλῆθος; plusieurs de ceux-ci n'étaient sans doute pas armés mais plutôt destinés à d'autres tâches; il y avait pourtant aussi parmi eux un groupe, πλῆθος, καθωπλισμένον καὶ πρὸς μαχὴν χρήσιμον, armé et prêt à se battre (Diod. XIX 80.4); on peut rattacher la restitution de statues divines, mentionnée dans la "stèle des Satrapes," à ces mêmes événements (cf. note 3). Plus tard, vers 274 av. J.-C., la stèle de Pithom (Hêrôônpolis) situe une campagne de Ptolémée II Philadelphe en Syrie et encore une fois il est question du repatriement de statues divines (Winnicki 1990, pp. 157–67). Puis au début de la guerre de Chrémonidès, probablement au printemps de 264 av. J.-C.,[4] Patroklos n'ose se mesurer sur terre avec les troupes d'Antigonos Gonatas sans l'appui préalable des Spartiates, ses propres hommes n'étant qu' Αἰγυπτίους ... καὶ ναύτας (Paus. III 6.4–6); le décret de Rhamnous[5] démontre qu'au moins une partie de ceux-ci étaient considérés comme des [στρα]τ̣ιῶται. Ptolémée III Évergète, engagé dans la 3e guerre syrienne, est l'objet de louanges dans le monumentum Adulitanum[6] et la stèle de Canope,[7] pour avoir restitué des ἱερά ἀγάλματα aux temples. À la fin du 3e siècle, en 217 av. J.-C., à la bataille de Raphia, les Égyptiens représentaient moins d'un tiers sur un total d'environ 75.000 hommes; ils étaient actifs aussi bien dans la cavalerie que dans l'infanterie.[8]

Pour le 2e siècle av. J.-C., retenons seulement deux témoignages certains. Après 163 av. J.-C. une liste de noms — tous égyptiens sans exception — nous permet de conclure que nous avons affaire, en l'occurrence, à un contingent de soldats indigènes, envoyés par Ptolémée VI à Gortyne pour combattre l'adversaire, sans doute des Κνώσιοι,[9] aux côtés des troupes de la ville. Et à la fin de ce siècle, de 103 à 101 av. J.-C., se situe un conflit judéo-syro-égyptien, que nous avons étudié ailleurs et auquel des Égyptiens prirent part, enrôlés dans un corps expéditionnaire de Cléopâtre III et de Ptolémée X Alexandre I en territoire séleucide (Van't Dack 1989, cf. pp. 127–36); ce qui explique le caractère polyglotte du dossier dont nous disposons concernant cette "guerre de sceptres."

Dans ce dernier cas il s'agit d'un conflit dynastique opposant Ptolémée IX Sotèr II à Cléopâtre III et Ptolémée X Alexandre I. Depuis ce moment et jusqu'à l'arrivée des Romains, il ne faut plus s'attendre à des exploits lagides à l'étranger.

Bien sûr, il faudrait préciser davantage la situation concrète de ces troupes. Tous les militaires susmentionnés prennent apparemment part à une expédition éphémère; mais existe-t-il, parmi eux, aussi des troupes d'occupation à long terme? S'agit-il d'unités uniformes — comme apparemment les σύμμαχοι égyptiens de Gortyne — ou de corps mixtes — comme les troupes de Cléopâtre III et de son fils Ptolémée X Alexandre I?

Dans ce dernier cas, les autochtones ne sont pas seulement des simples militaires ou des gradés ou des officiers d'un grade inférieur ou encore des membres du personnel adjoint de l'administration, mais ils occupent parfois un rang très élevé (Van't Dack 1989, surtout pp. 131–34).

La présence de ces Égyptiens de la haute société dans l'armée n'est d'ailleurs pas une nouveauté, loin de là.

Passons à Alexandrie, qui ne fait pas partie de l'Égypte au sens strict du mot puisqu'elle est πρὸς Αἰγύπτῳ, mais qui se distingue déjà très nettement d'autres *poleis* du monde grec. C'est ce

4. Voir en dernier lieu Gabbert 1987, pp. 230–35.
5. Cf. Heinen 1972; texte pp. 152–54; cf. ligne 24. Van't Dack et Hauben 1978, pp. 87–89.
6. *OGIS* I 54 ligne 21.
7. *OGIS* I 56 lignes 10-11.
8. Voir en dernier lieu Winnicki 1989a, pp. 213–30, surtout p. 221, pp. 223–24.
9. Inscr. Cret. IV 195; cf. Bagnall 1973, pp. 124–27.

qu'en dit Polybe, qui visita la capitale dans la seconde moitié du 2e siècle av. J.-C. Il en esquisse l'ambiance dans un fragment de son livre XXXIV, fragment qui nous a été transmis par Strabon XVII 1.12 (C 797); en voici une traduction:[10]

> Lors de son séjour à Alexandrie, Polybe ressentit quelque dégoût pour l'état de choses existant alors dans cette cité. Il y avait, nous dit-il, trois catégories d'habitants: les Égyptiens indigènes, impulsifs et [inaptes??] à la vie civique; les mercenaires, formant une masse de gens brutaux et indociles — depuis longtemps, en effet, on entretenait des soldats étrangers, qui avaient appris à commander plutôt qu'à obéir, à cause de l'incapacité des rois; enfin, en troisième lieu, les Alexandrins, qui n'étaient pas, eux non plus et pour les mêmes raisons, doués de sens civique, mais qui valaient tout de même mieux que les précédents. En effet, bien qu'ils fussent d'origines très diverses, ils étaient d'ascendance grecque et n'avaient pas tout oublié des coutumes des Hellènes. Mais cette partie de la population avait été presque anéantie, en particulier par l'action de Ptolémée Évergète dit Physcon, sous le règne duquel Polybe visita Alexandrie, et qui, se voyant en butte à une opposition populaire, lança à plusieurs reprises ses mercenaires sur les foules et les fit décimer. Telle était dès lors la situation dans cette ville, le vers du poète apparut dès lors conforme à la réalité: 'Se rendre en Égypte est une expédition bien longue et bien pénible' (*Odyssée* IV 483).

Réduisant l'armée alexandrine à une masse de mercenaires, Polybe n'a certes voulu donner qu'une impression personnelle. Dans une parade (πομπή) de Ptolémée II Philadelphe, Kallixeinos de Rhodos signale 57.600 cavaliers et 23.200 fantassins avec leurs armements spécifiques à côté d'autres troupes difficiles à dénombrer (Athén., *Deipn.* V 202f–203a); plusieurs ont dû appartenir à des unités de mercenaires (Rice 1983, surtout pp. 123–26; Winnicki 1989a, p. 221; et Förtmeyer 1988, pp. 90–94). Examinons donc cette armée de plus près.

Il y a d'abord la cour royale. D'après Winnicki (1985, pp. 41–55, plus spécialement p. 42, p. 49 avec la note 41; 1989a, pp. 228–29), Ptolémée II Philadelphe aurait repris une tradition pharaonique en introduisant dans sa garde en 271/70 ou 270/69 av. J.-C. une unité de militaires égyptiens sous le commandement de leurs propres chefs. Le passage en question de la stèle de Mendès est toutefois interprété de façon différente par Derchain (1986, pp. 203–04). La traduction traditionnelle en est la suivante:

> Alors sa Majesté choisit (?) ses gardes parmi les beaux adolescents, parmi les enfants de militaires d'Égypte. Leurs chefs (furent choisis) parmi les enfants (d'Égypte) et Elle en fit ses gardes du corps.

Mais Ph. Derchain propose:

> Sa Majesté avait levé ses recrues, beaux jeunes hommes, parmi les enfants de l'armée d'Égypte, les premiers de celle-ci à être nés en Égypte, car ils étaient ses favoris.

La garde égyptienne disparaît ainsi et est remplacée par des recrues, apparemment des descendants de la clérouchie grecque. L'auteur défend sa thèse en soulignant: "Cette traduction tient compte du sens ordinaire de *mnfyt* dans les décrets trilingues, correspondant au démotique *mšꜥ* et au grec λαός, où l'on reconnaît l'armée, comprenant également les βασιλικοὶ γεωργοί, c'est-à-dire les anciens mercenaires macédoniens."

N'étant pas égyptologue, nous ne pouvons nous prononcer sur le fond du problème. Remarquons seulement que le titre démotique de *mr mšꜥ* peut être appliqué en effet à chaque stratège et non seulement aux chefs d'unités autochtones. D'autre part il nous semble que le mot *mnfyt* dans la stèle de Mendès est précisé par le vocable désignant le pays de l'Égypte; or, le mot grec λαός dans ce sens spécifiquement militaire ne se retrouve que dans un seul titre, celui de λαάρχης qui indique en principe les commandants des *machimoi*.

10. Polybe, *Histoire*. Texte traduit, présenté et annoté par Roussel 1970, p. 1149: fragment 14 du livre XXXIV.

De toute façon, c'est précisément ce titre de laarque que l'on retrouve dans une inscription grecque[11] du tout début du règne de Ptolémée V Épiphane avant son mariage avec Cléopâtre I (194/3 av. J.-C.). Il y désigne incontestablement les chefs d'une unité de la garde royale: [---]ôtês, le fils de Hôros, et Tearoôs, son frère, laarques et ἡγεμόνες τῶν περὶ αὐ⟨λ⟩ὴν ἐπιλέκτων μαχίμων.[12]

Mais quittons la cour et cherchons ailleurs. Dans la ville, on rencontre des *machimoi* et d'autres soldats, appartenant apparemment à des contingents mixtes de militaires de carrière. En effet, dans l'*UPZ* I 110 de 164 av. J.-C., on lit des formules telles que:

> οἱ παρε[φ]εδ[ρε]ύοντες ἐν 'Αλεξανδ[ρ]είαι τῶν | τ' ἐπιλέκτων καὶ τῶν (ἑπταρούρων) καὶ (πενταρούρων) μαχίμων καὶ | τῶν ἐπὶ τῶν φυλακίδων [τ]εταγμένων ναυκλη|ρομαχίμων: lignes 20–23
>
> τῶν παρεφε|δρευόντων ἐν 'Αλεξανδρείαι τῶν τε ἐπιλέκτων | καὶ τῶν (ἑπταρούρων) καὶ (πενταρούρων) μαχίμων καὶ τῶν ἄλλων τῶν |⟨ἀν⟩επιτηδείων: lignes 195–98
>
> οὐκ ὀλίους (*sic*) δὲ καὶ τῶν ἐν τῶι στρατιωτικῶι | φερομένων καὶ τὴν ἀναγκαίαν τροφὴν μόλις ἐχόν|των ἀπὸ τῶν ἐκ τοῦ βασιλικο[ῦ] τιθεμένων, ἐνίους δὲ | καὶ τῶν μαχίμων μᾶλλον δὲ τοὺς πλείστους: lignes 103–06
>
> μὴ μόνων (*sic*) – – – τοῖς μαχίμοις, ἀλλὰ καὶ το[ῖ]ς | ἄλλοις τοῖς στρατι[ε]υομένοις (*sic*) – – – καὶ τοῖς στρατηγοῖς | αὐτοῖς: lignes 174–76
>
> τῶν μὲ[ν] | ταλαιπώρων λαῶν καὶ τῶν μαχίμων καὶ τῶν ἄλλων | τῶν ἀδυνατούντων: lignes 131–33
>
> οἱ ἐν τῆι | πόλει μάχιμοι: lignes 198–99
>
> tous ceux-ci font partie τῶν ἐν τῆι πόλει (ligne 91), τῶν [ἐ]ν τῆι πόλει παρεφετρευόν|των (*sic*) (lignes 206–07)

Ce que ces contingents peuvent représenter dans des moments de crise interne, l'auteur du *de bello Alexandrino* nous l'apprend lorsqu'il décrit la levée de troupes qui s'opposeront à César:

> nam in omnes partes per quas fines Aegypti regnumque pertinet, legatos conquisitoresque dilectus habendi causa miserant magnumque numerum in oppidum telorum atque tormentorum convexerant et innumerabilem multitudinem adduxerant.[13]

Il y a certes quelque exagération dans ce récit. On ne voit pas très bien ce que les *omnes partes, per quas fines Aegypti regnumque pertinet*, représentent encore à cette date très tardive et dans ces circonstances en dehors de l'Égypte. Il faudra réduire aussi l'*innumerabilem numerum* à des proportions bien plus modestes. L'essentiel paraît assez net: les *legati conquisitoresque* ont mobilisé des catœques et des *machimoi* dans les clérouchies de la chôra; en même temps ils ont amené à la capitale des miliciens de carrière, déjà casernés dans des garnisons ou nouvellement enrôlés dans les mêmes lieux.

Bien souvent ces Égyptiens, envoyés à Alexandrie, ont dû y rester casernés pendant une assez longue période. Leur situation ne semble certes pas enviable à en juger d'après l'*UPZ* I 110.

Il ne faut pas uniquement tenir compte des militaires sans grade et de leur administration;[14] il y a incontestablement parmi les généraux de plus haut rang des représentants de la noblesse indigène et cela dès le début de l'époque lagide.[15]

11. *SB* V 8925 = *OGIS* II 731 = RÉG 84 (1971), pp. 342–45 no. 1; cf. Winnicki 1985, p. 52 avec note 55.
12. Pros. Ptol. II 2048 et 2050 (cf. VIII add.).
13. 2.1. Traduction de Andrieu, éd. 1954, p. 3: "En effet, ils avaient dépêché dans toutes les régions où s'étendent le territoire et le royaume d'Égypte des envoyés et des recruteurs pour faire des levées, avaient amassé dans la place un grand nombre de traits et de machines de jet et amené des troupes en quantité innombrable."
14. Cf. Pros. Ptol. II 2415 et VIII add.
15. Voir surtout Peremans 1977, pp. 175–85. Il ne nous revient pas de préciser la signification de titres hiéroglyphiques ou démotiques, ni de juger du caractère héréditaire et factice de certains de ces titres. Signalons seulement que l'on pourrait parfois douter de la datation de quelques cas.

Les sources nous font connaître, par exemple, un Dionysios Petosarapis qui souleva Alexandrie contre Philométor, ou un Paôs qui commanda les troupes envoyées en 131/30 av. J.-C. contre les "impies" d'Hermonthis (cf. Peremans 1972, pp. 67–76, surtout pp. 69–70). Celui-ci fut d'abord stratège de plusieurs nomes en Thébaïde, puis gouverneur de toute la Haute-Égypte.[16] Et l'un de ses successeurs dans cette dernière charge, Phommous, ne serait-il pas envoyé d'Alexandrie en Thébaïde pour revenir en Basse-Égypte à la fin de sa carrière?[17] Et que penser du général Petimouthês, originaire de Tell el-Balamoun, qui "atteignit le pays de Khor en compagnie de la reine" sans doute en 103 av. J.-C. et qui fit ériger sa statue dans le temple de Karnak (cf. Quaegebeur 1989, pp. 88–108)? On est en droit de supposer que ces généraux et hauts fonctionnaires aient été détachés d'Alexandrie; Platôn, par exemple, un des successeurs de Phommous, appartient manifestement à une famille alexandrine (Cf. Mooren et Van't Dack 1981, pp. 535–44).

Il n'est pas possible de présenter ici un aperçu plus détaillé. Et les rapports de cette couche de la population locale avec la royauté ou les immigrés du même niveau exigeraient une étude spéciale qui ne peut être entreprise dans le cadre de la présente communication.

Assez pour Alexandrie; entrons dans la chôra où la documentation devient plus abondante et nous permet d'aborder des problèmes que nous devions passer sous silence dans les pages précédentes. Prenons d'abord la clérouchie.

En général on la présente comme un milieu cloisonné. Les unités, dont les unes sont constituées par des immigrés et les autres ouvertes aux *machimoi*, semblent nettement séparées. Il faut toutefois tenir compte de certains facteurs, qui pourraient modifier quelque peu cette conception.

En premier lieu il y a les facteurs particuliers. Les clérouques/catœques, pour une large part descendants de militaires du premier Ptolémée (cf. Bagnall 1984, pp. 7–20), ne se privaient certes pas de mariages mixtes. Nous pensons à Esoêris, la compagne de l'Alexandrin Monimos, qui se situe dans un milieu clérouchique du Fayoum en plein troisième siècle (cf. Clarysse 1988a, pp. 137–40), ou à Neoptolemos, aussi dénommé Onnôphris sans doute par sa mère indigène Haünchis, quoique étant lui-même originaire d'un même milieu grec, à la fin du 3ᵉ ou au début du 2ᵉ siècle av. J.-C (1988b, pp. 7–10).

D'autres militaires, qui détiennent un kléros, résident sans doute à Alexandrie ou dans la métropole d'un nome, en tout cas dans un centre plus ou moins urbain; en tant que "habitually absentee landlords," ils louent leur tenure à une tierce personne qui souvent la sous-loue. Par contre, dès le 2ᵉ siècle av. J.-C., plusieurs clérouques sont γεωργοὶ αὐτοί de leur domaine; quelle que puisse être la signification précise de ce terme, il témoigne au moins d'une participation plus active dans l'exploitation de leur domaine.[18]

À côté des facteurs particuliers, il y a, bien sûr, les structures imposées par Alexandrie. Un papyrus du Memphite de l'an 273 av. J.-C. nous fait connaître un ἑκατονδεκάρουρος, un ἑβδομηκοντάρουρος, un ἑξηκοντάρουρος, des τεσσαρακοντάρουροι.[19] Certaines de ces catégories

16. Pros. Ptol. I 197 et VIII add.; cf. Mooren 1975, pp. 91–92, no. 054, p. 117, no. 0120; Idem 1977, p. 116.

17. Pros. Ptol. I 202 et VIII add.; cf. Mooren 1975, pp. 94–95, no. 058; Clarysse et Winnicki 1989b, pp. 73–74 comm. no. 6, ligne 10; Van't Dack 1989, p. 132.

18. Sur tous ces problèmes concernant la résidence des clérouques, la location ou la sous-location des kléroi, la participation active dans l'exploitation en tant que γεωργὸς αὐτός, cf. exempli gratia la documentation réunie par Übel 1968, passim. Voir encore Braunert 1964, pp. 38–40, p. 80, p. 85; Crawford 1971, pp. 76–77, pp. 84–85, pp. 147–54, tableaux I, II, III; Bingen 1973, pp. 215–22; Keenan et Shelton 1976, intr. pp. 10–12, p. 15; Bingen 1978b, pp. 74–80 (non vidimus); idem 1979, pp. 87–94; Brashear, BGU XIV, 1980, pp. 225–55; Bingen 1983, pp. 1–11.

19. *P. Cair. Zen.* I 59001. Pour les clérouques désignés par un nombre d'aroures, cf. provisoirement Pros. Ptol. IV pp. 57–89; mais voir déjà VIII 4188f.

pourraient être fictives par suite du système des σύγκληροι.[20] Plus tard, en ce qui concerne les cavaliers grecs, on a affaire surtout aux ἑκατοντάρουροι, puis aux ὀγδοηκοντάρουροι et aux ἑβδομηκοντάρουροι. Les hékatontaroures sont apparemment les premiers à faire partie d'une hipparchie numérotée. Quant aux ogdoèkontaroures, dont le titre en démotique vient d'être retrouvé par Vleeming (1983, pp. 97–99), il n'est pas exclu qu'à l'origine ils aient été des μισθόφοροι κληροῦχοι.[21] Les hebdomèkontaroures ont dû appartenir à une hipparchie à nom ethnique[22] avant d'être enrôlés — dès la première moitié du 2e siècle av. J.-C. (vers 170) — dans une hipparchie numérotée (cf. Daniel 1977, pp. 76–82 [P. Mich. inv. 3236 = *SB* XIV 12101]). Mais en quoi ces trois catégories se distinguaient-elles l'une de l'autre après l'introduction de chacune dans une hipparchie numérotée? Sans doute ne faut-il pas attacher trop d'importance à la superficie nominale d'une tenure qui souvent ne concorde pas avec la superficie réelle, reprise dans les cadastres antiques. Il est vrai que parfois on a affaire à des tenures dispersées, dont les parties se situent dans deux ou plusieurs villages et qui, prises dans leur ensemble, approchent de la valeur nominale. Mais s'agit-il vraiment d'un "split-holding" dans tous les cas où l'on constate une différence notoire entre la valeur, indiquée par un titre, et celle, enregistrée dans les cadastres?[23] Ces écarts pourraient révéler aussi un certain déclin, encore occasionnel et pas encore généralisé, du système clérouchique grec. En tout cas, on constate au moins un essai d'uniformisation technique et simplificatrice. En outre, une ordonnance de Ptolémée VI Philométor, dans sa 32e année de règne (150/49 av. J.-C.), précise que dorénavant les terres cultivées ne peuvent plus être affectées à la clérouchie. Les nouveaux venus doivent donc se contenter en principe d'une terre ἐν ὑπολόγῳ, normalement γῆ χέρσος.[24] La décision semble concerner uniquement les catœques grecs, les *machimoi* n'en seraient pas touchés.[25] Même si la superficie d'une nouvelle tenure correspondait à la valeur nominale d'antan, sa qualité ne serait plus comparable à celle d'une dotation antérieure; à elle seule, elle a dû abaisser le niveau social de maint nouveau catœque.

Passons aux τριακοντάρουροι, clérouques grecs qui à l'origine étaient tous fantassins. Dans le quatrième volume de la *Prosopographia Ptolemaica*, leur liste contient un assez grand nombre de Macédoniens τῶν οὔπω ὑφ'ἡγεμόνα[26] à Thôlthis dans l'Oxyrhynchite ou ailleurs (Héracléopolite, Arsinoïte) sous le règne d'Évergète I ou celui de Philopator. Une réorganisation se prépare-t-elle? Quoi qu'il en soit, bientôt on enregistre des μεταβεβηκότες εἰς τὴν κατοικίαν ἐκ τῶν (τριακονταρούρων) Φυλέως.[27] Cet officier éponyme Phyleus[28] était en fonction sous le règne de

20. En 273 av. J.-C. les σύγκληροι sont père et fils; plus tard on a affaire aussi à deux frères σύγκληροι; cf. Crawford 1971, p. 57, note 5, pp. 65–66.

21. Pros. Ptol. II 1902 et VIII add.

22. Pros. Ptol. II 2735-2746 et VIII add.

23. Sur ces problèmes, voir par exemple Crawford 1971, pp. 59–60, p. 62, p. 69, pp. 74–75, pp. 148–54, tableau III; Keenan et Shelton 1976, intr., p. 10, p. 15.

24. Voir par exemple Kießling 1938, pp. 213–29, surtout pp. 218–19; Préaux 1939a, pp. 469–70; Übel 1968, p. 173, note 3, p. 177, notes 1–2, p. 261, note 4; Crawford 1971, p. 58, pp. 63–64; *C. Ord. Ptol.*² 44; 53, lignes 36–48; 54, lignes 3–5; All. 49, 68, 69, 78; *C. Ord. Ptol.** All. 54*.

25. P. Tebt. I pp. 554–55; Crawford 1971, pp. 63–64.

26. Pros. Ptol. II 3261 et VIII add.; VIII 3453a; IV 8877 = II 3146; 8885 = II 3341 et VIII add.; 8887 = VIII 3426a; 8892a = VIII 3514a; 8900 = II 3550; 8901a = VIII 3574a; 8902 = II 3582 et VIII add.; en outre BGU XIV 2394, lignes 6–7; 2397, lignes 4–5, lignes 19–21; P. Hels. I 16, lignes 3–5 (Persês—163 av.J.-C.). On y ajoutera en dehors de Thôlthis et de l'Oxyrhynchite: IV 8888 = II 3452 et VIII add.; 8497 = 8906 = II 3633 et VIII add.; cf. Übel 1968, p. 359, p. 363, p. 370, p. 379, pp. 380–83. Nous ne signalons pas ici les οὔπω ὑφ' ἡγεμόνα qui ne portent pas explicitement le titre de triakontaroure.

27. Pros. Ptol. II 2632 = IV 8883 (cf. III 6611); II 2690 et VIII add. = IV 9509; aux références de la Pros. Ptol. on ajoutera: P. Tebt. IV 1095, lignes 13–14; 1096, lignes 8–9; 1103, ligne 65; 1108, lignes 8–9; 1109, lignes 18–20; 1110, lignes 49–50; 1113, lignes 1–4; 1114, lignes 24–26; 1115, lignes 5–7; 1117, lignes 11 et 13; 1120, lignes 42–43; cf. Übel 1968, pp. 172–73, nº 594 avec la note 4.

28. Pros. Ptol. II 2020 et VIII add.

Philopator et au début du règne d'Épiphane; sous celui-ci il y a eu un transfert εἰς τὴν κατοικίαν qui ne peut signifier qu'une promotion (*sic*) de l'infanterie à la cavalerie.[29] Ces triakontaroures μεταβεβηκότες ont-ils vu augmenter de façon substantielle la superficie de leur kléros, comme J. Lesquier l'a suggéré jadis sous forme d'hypothèse (1911, p. 179, note 6)? Même en admettant que les $18\frac{3}{8}$ aroures, attribuées dans Kerkéosiris à un descendant de ces μεταβεβηκότες, constituent un supplément à sa tenure de quelque 30 aroures dans un autre village, le montant total n'en resterait pas moins très inférieur aux valeurs nominales qui figurent dans la titulature des cavaliers-catœques. Ou faut-il plutôt supposer qu'il n'y a eu aucune compensation pour les nouvelles charges qui leur incombent dorénavant en tant que cavaliers? Dans cette hypothèse leur situation serait comparable à celle des τριακοντάρουροι χερσέφιπποι.

Ceux-ci ont été classés sous la rubrique réservée à la police. Présents à Kerkéosiris dès le règne de Philopator, ils semblent être "chargés de garder les endroits χέρσοι et probablement les limites du désert et de la terre cultivée contre les incursions des nomades."[30] Nous ne connaissons qu'un seul membre: Pantauchos qui appartenait aux (τριακονταρούρων) χερσεφίππων et à qui succéda son fils Menandros; le kléros en question comporte $34\frac{3}{32}$ aroures et dépasse donc légèrement la valeur nominale prévue.[31] À côté de ces χερσέφιπποι montés, les Lagides ont manifestement créé des unités de χερσάνιπποι à pied, que l'on retrouve déjà en plein 3e siècle. Dans ce secteur aussi nous n'avons que deux témoignages: Αἰσχίνας Θεσσαλὸς τῶν Ἀλκίππου χερσάνιππος πεντακοσία[ρχος τῶν ἐκ τῆς (?) Σύρων κώ]μης τοῦ Ἀρσινοίτου ainsi que Nikostratos, simple χερσάν̣ι̣ππος;[32] la titulature d'Aischinas nous fait penser aux structures de l'armée. En serait-il de même pour les χερσέφιπποι, dont la situation sociale serait proche de celle des μεταβεβηκότες εἰς τὴν κατοικίαν ἐκ τῶν (τριακονταρούρων) Φυλέως?

Ce n'est d'ailleurs pas seulement ce dernier transfert de l'infanterie à la cavalerie à l'intérieur de la milice grecque qui est en jeu. Il faut tenir compte en outre de la promotion (*sic*) de la police à la κατοικία. Nous pensons aux ephodes[33] ou aux phylacites[34] dont la tenure, agrandie en compensation du transfert, leur permet de dépasser les triakontaroures ou de se rapprocher de ceux-ci. Il y a aussi des *erêmophylakes* occupant 10 aroures à peine à l'entrée dans la κατοικία.[35] Il se pourrait même que ladite compensation n'ait été qu'un cadeau empoisonné: le transféré aurait consenti à prendre à charge un lot de terre de moindre qualité et à le rendre cultivable (cf. Crawford 1971, p. 69, note 6). Tous ces transferts ont d'ailleurs eu lieu après l'ordonnance de Philométor en 150/49 av. J.-C. concernant la qualité des terres réservées aux nouveaux catœques.

C'est précisément dans la catégorie de ces derniers transferts que le changement de statut s'accompagne parfois de l'adoption d'un nom grec.[36]

Parmi les ephodes transférés on retrouve Apollônios, le fils de Ptolemaios. Rien n'y trahirait le phénomène de la métonymie, si l'on ne connaissait pas Ptolemaios ὃς καὶ Petesouchos, fils

29. Cf. Crawford 1971, pp. 60–61.

30. Grenfell, Hunt, et Smyly, P. Tebt. I, 1902, pp. 550–51; Lesquier 1911, citation p. 263; Crawford 1971, p. 59.

31. Pros. Ptol. II 4828 = IV 8896; II 2676 = IV 9390 (faut-il vraiment classer Ménandros parmi les catœques?). Aux références dans la Pros. Ptol. on ajoutera: P. Tebt. IV 1109, lignes 10–11; 1110, lignes 39–40; 1114, lignes 12–13; 1115, lignes 178–79; 1116, ligne 91; 1118, lignes 148–49. Cf. aussi Crawford 1971, p. 59, p. 120, p. 148.

32. Aischinas: Pros. Ptol. II 2302 et VIII add. = IV 9069; l'officier éponyme Alkippos (Pros. Ptol. II 1830 et VIII add.) est déjà attesté en 252/51 av. J.-C.; Nikostratos: Pros. Ptol. VIII 4827b.

33. Crawford 1971, pp. 64–65, p. 66, pp. 67–69.

34. Ibid., p. 63, p. 69, note 1.

35. Pros. Ptol. II 3738 = 4835 et VIII add. = IV 9149; II 3756 = IV 9403; II 3761 et VIII add. = IV 9501; II 3764 = IV 9527; cf. Crawford 1971, p. 63, p. 65.

36. Sur les *prostagmata* royaux concernant le changement de nom et d'ethnique, voir *C. Ord. Ptol.*, All. 34 et 47.

d'Apollônios ὃς καὶ Haruôtês, Πέρσης τῆς ἐπιγονῆς, qui pourrait être son fils.[37] En serait-il de même dans le cas de Petrôn, le fils de Theôn, Πέρσης lui aussi? De toute façon, il est promu à la 5e hipparchie des hécatontaroures quoiqu'on ne sache rien de l'accroissement de sa tenure.[38]

Quant aux anciens phylacites, signalons surtout Nek⟨t⟩saphthis ou Nech⟨t⟩saphthis, le fils de Petosiris, doté de 10 aroures. Il est promu à la *katoikia* en recevant en surplus un lot de terre — χέρσος, désert, ou en tout cas ἄσπορος, non cultivé — de 15 aroures. Il reste jusqu'à un âge avancé γεωργὸς αὐτός, mais dorénavant il pourra se parer du titre de (ἑκατοντάρουρος). En même temps il se décide à prendre le nom de Marôn, fils de Dionysios, et l'ethnique Μακεδών.[39]

Le transfert des *erêmophylakes* à la *katoikia* ne semble pas toujours donner lieu à une métonymie. Ainsi Nektenibis, le fils d'Hôros, dont le kléros de dix aroures n'a apparemment pas été agrandi à l'occasion de sa promotion, n'a pas, pour autant que nous sachions, jugé utile de s'arroger un nom grec.[40]

Le phénomène de la "métonymie" grécisante a été mis en relief par Clarysse (1985, pp. 57–66). Selon lui l'emploi du nom dépend du caractère — grec ou non — de la fonction et en ce sens "the value of the onomastic criterion in establishing the ethnic origin of persons in government service would be seriously diminished. It certainly points to the Greek (or Egyptian) character of an office: if an Egyptian entered a Greek office he tended to adopt a Greek name and no doubt also tended to Hellenize in other ways" (p. 65).

Quant aux *machimoi* indigènes, déjà en 253 av. J.-C. ils opèrent sous le commandement d'un ἡγεμών, ce qui, d'après J. K. Winnicki, évoque un contexte militaire.[41] Plus tard les cavaliers du laarque Chomênis se rapprochent du niveau social de certains catœques puisqu'ils reçoivent un kléros de 20, voire de 30 aroures.[42] Les *machimoi* fantassins, dotés de 10, de 7 ou de 5 aroures,[43] restent figés dans leur position sociale. Ceux d'entre eux qui sont détachés à Alexandrie, se trouvent dans une situation lamentable, comme nous l'apprend l'*UPZ* I 110. Il faut, bien sûr, tenir compte également des Ἕλληνες μάχιμοι;[44] mais c'est là un autre problème. Faut-il donner au mot *machimos* le sens que certains auteurs anciens lui attribuent (cf. supra p. 339 avec la note 3)? Ou avons-nous plutôt affaire à des miliciens, provenant d'un milieu grec mais entrés dans la clérouchie

37. Pour Apollônios, fils de Ptolemaios: Pros. Ptol. II 2607 = IV 9129; pour le fils: Pros. Ptol. IV 9500 = 9939? Voir depuis lors: P. Tebt. IV 1108, lignes 35–36; 1110, lignes 80–82; 1113, lignes 34–36; 1114, lignes 55–57; 1115, lignes 37–39. Cf. Übel 1968, p. 178, no. 608; Crawford 1971, pp. 64–65, p. 135, pp. 150–51, p. 168.

38. Pros. Ptol. II 2682 et VIII add. = IV 8707; P. Tebt. IV 1110, ligne 132; 1114, ligne 104; 1115, lignes 180–81; 1117, ligne 48; 1118, lignes 90–91. Cf. Crawford 1971, p. 68, p. 121, p. 152, p. 167.

Pour Asklêpiadês, fils de Ptolemaios, promu — lui aussi — à la 5e hipparchie des hécatontaroures et détenteur de 24 aroures κλήρου (ἑκατονταρούρου), cf. Pros. Ptol. II 2617 et VIII add. = IV 8613; P. Tebt. IV 1110, lignes 80 et 83; 1113, lignes 34 et 37; 1114, lignes 55 et 58; 1115, lignes 37 et 40; 1116, ligne 65; 1118, lignes 131–32; 1147, lignes 190 et 193; Übel 1968, p. 178, no. 609; Crawford 1971, pp. 64–65.

39. Par exemple Pros. Ptol. II 2674 = 4692 et VIII add. = IV 8683; P. Tebt. IV 1108, lignes 45 et 48; 1110, lignes 133–34; 1114, lignes 106–07; 1115, lignes 80–81; 1118, lignes 106–07 et 114–15; 1120, ligne 123; 1144, ligne 13; 1147, lignes 189–90 et 195; cf. Übel 1968, p. 180, no. 616; Crawford 1971, p. 22, p. 63, p. 69, p. 79, p. 134, note 5, p. 135, p. 154, p. 165.

40. Pros. Ptol. II 3756 = IV 9403; P. Tebt. IV 1108, lignes 39–40; 1117, lignes 154–55; cf. Übel 1968, p. 179, no. 611; Crawford 1971, p. 65, pp. 150–51.

41. Pros. Ptol. II 4752 et VIII add.; cf. Winnicki 1985, p. 49, 1989a, p. 228.

42. Pour les tenures de 30 aroures, voir Pros. Ptol. II 2047; II 2725 = IV 8120. On y ajoutera les références P. Tebt. IV, p. 161 concernant I 84, ligne 78; 1103 (= 1110 verso), ligne 269; 1108, lignes 69–70; 1110, lignes 141–43; 1115, lignes 88–90; 1120, ligne 96; 1124, ligne 18; 1147 (= P. Tebt. I 98), lignes 10, 58–59 et 76.

43. Cf. P. Tebt. I 5, lignes 44–46; pour les *machimoi* dotés de 10 ou de 7 aroures; pour ceux dotés de 7 ou de 5 aroures, voir, par exemple, *UPZ* I 110, mentionné et cité plus haut, p. 342.

44. P. Tebt. I, p. 552 (sur les Ἕλληνες μάχιμοι).

égyptienne? En tout cas, les listes des μάχιμοι signalent çà et là quelques noms grecs de préférence parmi les cavaliers (Winnicki 1985, p. 52 avec la note 57).

De toute façon, ces changements et ces transferts, allant de pair avec un rapprochement des différents niveaux sociaux, ont dû favoriser à la longue la création d'une ambiance plus ou moins mixte dans certaines couches de la société. On pense au P. Moscou 123[45] et à *Ḥtj*, "le cavalier-clérouque parmi les catœques," peut-être un hécatontaroure; il garde son nom égyptien et s'exprime dans sa langue démotique quoique son testament ait pu contenir quelques éléments de droit grec. Au moins deux de ses fils, l'aîné et le puîné, destinés à succéder à leur père en tant qu'enfants d'un cavalier-clérouque parmi les catœques", le puîné portant un double nom grec et égyptien,[46] reprendront chacun $19\frac{1}{2}$ aroures du kléros après la mort de leur père. Ainsi ils entreront dans la même catégorie sociale que certains transférés de la police à la κατοικία ou les *machimoi*-cavaliers de Chomênis au Fayoum. Et pourtant, dans le cas de *Ḥtj*, on se trouve en Haute-Égypte, plus précisément à Panopolis.

Parlant de groupements mixtes, il faut accorder une attention particulière à la création par les Ptolémées d'une sorte de milice de carrière. Il s'agit de *misthophoroi* ou *taktomisthoi*, "hommes qui reçoivent une solde," sans attaches directes ni avec la clérouchie en tant que μισθοφόροι κληροῦχοι, ni avec les mercenaires enrôlés à l'étranger (ξενολογηθέντες); pour des raisons que nous ne devons pas développer à présent, ils sont enrôlés à l'intérieur du pays dès le règne de Philométor; des descendants d'anciens clérouques ou d'autres immigrés et des autochtones y marchent côte à côte. C'est ce secteur qui nous a fourni des archives ou des dossiers assez fournis qui nous permettent de suivre de plus près une personne, voire une famille, jusqu'au début du 1er siècle av. J.-C.

Pour la Thébaïde, à Pathyris,[47] on s'instruira dans les archives de Dryton, le fils de Pamphilos, et dans le dossier concernant un *Erbstreit*.[48] Pamphilos susmentionné, Crétois d'origine, doit avoir résidé en Égypte, puisque ses deux fils — Dryton[49] et son frère[50] — se trouvent dans la chôra égyptienne; tous deux sont devenus citoyens de Ptolémaïs Hermiou, capitale de la Haute-Égypte. C'est à la garnison de cette ville que Dryton fait son service; à un moment donné il est détaché à Diospolis ἡ μικρά.[51] Il a été promu au rang d'hipparque et porte de ce fait le titre aulique τῶν διαδόχων. Son frère serait cavalier misthophore. Esthladas, le fils de Dryton d'un premier mariage, Πτολεμαιεύς comme son père, a fait carrière, lui aussi, dans la cavalerie.[52] Puis Dryton a épousé en secondes noces Apollônia ἡ καὶ Senmônthis, Cyrénéenne d'origine lointaine et entourée de militaires de carrière dans sa propre famille. À en juger d'après l'emploi de noms doubles, son arrière-grand-père s'était déjà installé en Égypte; son grand-père[53] et son père[54] étaient *taktomisthoi*

45. Pros. Ptol. VIII 2712a. Cf. Clarysse 1985, p. 65 avec la bibliographie antérieure.
46. Cf. Bingen 1968, pp. 421–23, surtout p. 423: Hermôn ὃς καὶ *Twt*.
47. Voir en général Pestman 1963, pp. 10–53.
48. Pour la bibliographie concernant l'*Erbstreit* et Dryton, voir provisoirement et à titre d'exemple: Plaumann 1910, pp. 65–67; Gerhard 1911; Gradenwitz, Preisigke, Spiegelberg 1912; Montevecchi 1935, pp. 111–14; R. Calderini 1942, p. 17; Übel 1968, p. 27; Ritner 1984, pp. 171–87; Clarysse 1986, pp. 99–103; Vandorpe 1986; Lewis 1986, Chapter 6; Van't Dack 1988, p. 35; Scholl 1988, pp. 141–44.
49. Pros. Ptol. II 2206 et VIII add. = 2884 et VIII add. = IV 11343.
50. Ἑρμ[ά]φιλο[ς] Παμφίλου Φιλωτέρε[ιος] dans P. Grenf. I 12 ligne 22; restitution de W. Clarysse.
51. Cf. P. Amh. II 36 lignes 7–9: ἀπὸ τῶν ἐκ τοῦ ἐν Πτολεμαίδι | ὑπαίθρου νυνὶ δὲ παρεφεδρεύων | ἐν Διοσπόλει τῆι μικρᾶι. Sur παρεφεδρεύω et ἀποτάσσω, on lira Zucker 1937, p. 26–27. Pour la dispersion de détachements en provenance de cette garnison de Ptolémaïs Hermiou à travers la Thébaïde, on lira, par exemple, P. Grenf. I 42 = Wilcken 1912b, 447.
52. Pros. Ptol. II 2895 et VIII add. = IV 12236.
53. Pros. Ptol. II 2976 = II 4214 = IV 10713; lisez Hermokratês ὃς καὶ Panas.
54. Pros. Ptol. II 2977 = IV 10998; lisez Ptolemaios ὃς καὶ Pamenôs.

ou *misthophoroi*, deux termes qui sont rendus en démotique par le même titre et nous semblent plus ou moins synonymes; en outre sa tante avait épousé un fantassin.[55] Dès lors, rien d'étonnant à ce que deux filles de Dryton et d'Apollônia/Senmônthis aient épousé, l'une un misthophore,[56] l'autre un cavalier.[57] Une étude plus attentive de ces dossiers révélerait l'influence de l'entourage égyptien sur la famille d'Apollônia/Senmônthis; son mariage avec Dryton, dont la famille avait sans doute immigré plus tard que la sienne et qui faisait d'ailleurs son service à un échelon plus élevé, non dans l'infanterie mais dans la cavalerie, a pu quelque temps freiner l'évolution et promouvoir le recours à la langue grecque, mais la génération suivante emploie de nouveau le démotique.

Les dossiers de quelques notaires grecs, agoranomes, proviennent également de Pathyris et de la voisine Crocodilopolis. Ces gens ont apparemment vécu dans un milieu égyptien avant d'accéder à la fonction de notaire: leur double nom ou le nom égyptien de leur femme ou de parents et même leurs écrits en témoignent. Deux d'entre eux, Ammônios/Pakoibis et Hermias, étaient d'abord Πέρσαι τῶν μισθοφόρων ἱππέων, une carrière qui leur a permis sans doute de se familiariser davantage avec la langue grecque.[58] Les deux frères d'Hermias se sont d'ailleurs engagés, eux aussi, dans l'armée: Ptolemaios était [Π]έρσης τῶν μι[σθοφόρων) ἱπ(πέων)] et τακ[τ]όμι(σθος);[59] il serait intéressant d'étudier de plus près Nechoutês, dénommé aussi Eunous ou Eunomos ou vice versa, qu'il faut situer sans doute dans l'infanterie.[60]

À cette famille se rattache encore par alliance Hôros, dont le père Nechoutês avait épousé la tante d'Hermias. Ce Hôros mériterait également d'être étudié à fond dans son entourage; mais pour ce faire, il faudrait exploiter toutes les données d'un autre dossier bilingue, édité e.a. dans P. Adler.[61] Ce Πέρσης (τῆς ἐπιγονῆς) ou "Grec né en Égypte", homme d'Assouan, *ʿm* et serviteur d'Harsemtheus, est enrôlé dans la compagnie de Lochos comme le précédent Nechoutês/Eunous/ Eunomos. Il figure encore parmi les correspondants de soldats, ses compagnons sans doute, qui s'expriment tantôt en grec tantôt en démotique lorsqu'ils font campagne en Syrie et dans le Delta de 103 à 101 av. J.-C. Apparemment Hôros se trouve sous les ordres de Patês et de Pachratês; tous ces miliciens se considèrent comme φιλοβασιλισταί, fervents partisans de la royauté légitime à Alexandrie, ennemis des habitants impies d'Hermônthis.

On pourrait encore s'en référer à la famille de Peteharsemtheus, le fils de Panebkhounis,[62] dont au moins deux membres font partie de la force armée dans l'ὕπαιθρον de Crocodilopolis: Hôros, le fils de Pelaias,[63] et Panebkhounis, le père de Peteharsemtheus; Panebkhounis lui-même est Πέρσης τῆς ἐπιγονῆς ou Πέρσης τῶν προσγράφων.[64]

55. Pros. Ptol. II 3447 = IV 10778: Kallimêdês ὃς καὶ Patous, fils d'Apollônios ὃς καὶ Psemmônthês.

56. Pros. Ptol. II 4139.

57. Pros. Ptol. II 2889; lisez [Psenen]oupis au lieu d'[Eri]enoupis (Winnicki 1972, p. 350, note 61); ce mariage a été dissous.

58. Cf. Pestman 1978, pp. 203–10, arbre généalogique p. 208. Cf. Pros. Ptol. II 2535 et VIII add. = III 7650 et IX add. (on y ajoutera Messeri 1985, p. 79: P. Lond. III 686d, ligne 5); II 2545 et VIII add. = III 7689 et IX add. (on y ajoutera Messeri 1985, pp. 74–75: P. Lond. III 888a, ligne 14; 1989, p. 241: P. Brux. inv. E8441, ligne 12).

59. Pros. Ptol. II 2556 et VIII add.

60. Pros. Ptol. II 3925 et VIII add. = 4021 et VIII add. = 4180 et VIII add. = VIII 4021a. Cf. aussi I 286. On consultera à son sujet: Pestman 1965b, p. 48, note 10; 1981, pp. 295–315. Faut-il rattacher le cavalier Pelaias, fils de Patseous (Pros. Ptol. II 2933 et VIII add.), à cette famille?

61. Pros. Ptol. II 4145 et VIII add.; IV 11152. Cf. Pestman 1963, p. 30, note 2, pp. 51–53, no. 130; 1965, pp. 47–48, note 5; Clarysse et Winnicki 1989b, pp. 53–54, comm. pap. no. 3 ligne 4; cf. pp. 39–49, pap. no. 1.

62. Cf. Pestman 1965b, pp. 47–105; arbre généalogique p. 57 (avec quelques addenda, Van't Dack 1988, p. 5, note 30); Lewis 1986, Chapter 8; Bingen 1989a, pp. 235–44.

63. Pros. Ptol. II 4143 et surtout VIII add.; cf. Pestman 1963, p. 53, no. 132.

64. Pros. Ptol. II 4035 et VIII add. = IV 11572 et 12259; cf. Pestman 1963, pp. 38–39, no. 50.

En dehors de ces quelques familles, on connaît, bien sûr, des militaires de Pathyris-Crocodilopolis qui appliquent la métonymie à la manière de certains policiers μεταβεβηκότες εἰς τὴν κατοικίαν à Kerkéosiris.[65] Mais citons plutôt quelques exemples à d'autres endroits de la Haute-Égypte. Esaroêris ou Esoroêris, fils de Petosiris, ἀφωντεὺς ἄμισθος jadis kalasiris de *ʿfntj*,[66] caserné à Syène, ne retouche évidemment pas son nom, mais Neoptolemos, fils de Neoptolemos, Cyrénéen en garnison à la même Syène,[67] a épousé une dame qui se présente sous un double nom: Isias ἣ καὶ Sennêsis, fille de Patepnebteus, ἀφώντισσα.[68] Et ailleurs dans l'ancienne capitale de la Thébaïde, Diospolis Magna ou les environs, on retrouve Apollônios ὃς καὶ Psemmônthês (Psenmônthês), fils d'Hermias ὃς καὶ Petenephôtês, cavalier misthophore,[69] ou Ammônios ὃς καὶ Harpaêsis, fils de Patrôn ὃς καὶ Phibis, *Wynn* misthophore sous l'officier Eumenês, inscrit à la *rs.t* de *Rs-nf*.[70]

Outre le comportement de quelques familles ou individus, on aimerait connaître la composition des unités armées. Partant de certaines lettres écrites en démotique comme le P. Erbach (Spiegelberg 1905, pp. 44–47), où plusieurs auteurs et/ou adressés sont mentionnés explicitement, on a l'impression que tous les miliciens de ces troupes proviennent d'un milieu égyptien. On ne peut toutefois perdre de vue qu'il s'agit d'une correspondance entre amis issus d'un même environnement; on ne parvient malheureusement pas à identifier le toponyme *Sgntn*, où des militaires de la garnison de Djémé ont été détachés. À côté des papyrus, nous disposons d'inscriptions qui parfois contiennent plusieurs noms de militaires et qui illustrent de cette façon la composition de l'unité. Nous pensons, par exemple, aux *basilistai* qui se sont réunis ἐν Σήτει τῆι τοῦ Διονύσου νήσωι et qui honorent — au nom du roi, de la reine et de leurs enfants — τοῖς ἐπὶ τοῦ Καταράκτου δαίμοσιν présentés chaque fois sous un nom double;[71] au moins un sixième de ces *nomina* renvoie à un milieu égyptien. Une autre dédicace de Ptolémaïs Hermiou, la nouvelle capitale de la Haute-Égypte,[72] témoigne de la composition hétérogène d'une unité qui s'est transformée en association sous la présidence d'un hipparque ἐπ' ἀνδρῶν. Constituée de cavaliers, elle dédie un temple aux dieux locaux. À côté de noms perses, sémitiques et thraces, on y lit une majorité de noms grecs ou peut-être grécisés, mais aussi quelques noms nettement indigènes (cf. Peremans 1972, pp. 67–76, surtout p. 74); ces derniers militaires, apparemment d'origine égyptienne, n'ont pas encore cédé à la mode d'une métonymie grécisante, tandis que d'autres ont pu en profiter pour camoufler leur origine. À première vue on serait enclin de signaler aussi les listes imposantes d'*Apollôniatai*, cantonnés dans la garnison d'Hermoupolis Magna;[73] mais ceux-ci ou leurs unités

65. Par exemple: Pros. Ptol. II 2540 et VIII add. = IV 11257; cf. Pestman 1963, p. 31, no. 4; Pros. Ptol. II 2215 = 2549 = IV 12371; cf. Pestman 1963, p. 35, no. 27; Pros. Ptol. II 2561 = 3909; cf. Pestman 1963, p. 49, no. 116; Pros. Ptol. II 3997 et VIII add. = IV 10796; cf. Pestman 1963, p. 36, no. 34; Pros. Ptol. VIII 3844a. Au moins dans les trois premiers cas, il s'agit de Πέρσαι.

66. Pros. Ptol. II 3046 et VIII add.; dans BGU VI 1247, ligne 2 le même personnage est présenté comme Ἐσορ[ό]ηρις ὁ Πετοσε[ί]ριος τῆς ἐπιγονῆς. Pour d'autres *aphônteis* voir Pros. Ptol. II 3045 et VIII add.; 3049 et VIII add.; 4061 et VIII add.; VIII 3050b (avec la bibliographie); voir surtout Winnicki 1977, pp. 265–66 avec la note 38. On comparera avec des formules telles que: "homme d'Éléphantine (Winnicki 1986, pp. 21–22); "homme de Philae" (Pros. Ptol. VIII 4020a; IV 8260 = 10851, cf. Winnicki 1977, p. 266, note 39) ou "homme de Syène" (cf. supra Hôros, fils de Nechoutês; aussi Pros. Ptol. II 3048 et VIII add., cf. Winnicki 1986, p. 22, note 21).

67. Pros. Ptol. II 4018.

68. BGU VI 1248, ligne 3; 1249, ligne 2.

69. Pros. Ptol. II 2537 = 2956 et VIII add.

70. Pros. Ptol. II 3795 et VIII add. = IV 10630.

71. I. Th. Sy. 303; mais voir aussi J. Bingen 1991, pp. 103–07 et Heilporn 1990, p. 118.

72. *SB* III 6184 (138 av. J.-C.).

73. Voir Pros. Ptol. II, pp. 134–73 et VIII, pp. 182–84, avec p. 182, note 1: *SB* I 599 (fin 2e siècle av. J.-C.), 4206 (80/79 av. J.-C.), V 8066 (78 av. J.-C.); à ce sujet on lira surtout Zucker 1938, pp. 279–84.

sont désignés par les qualificatifs ξένος ou ξενικός qui pourraient souligner qu'ils se considèrent "als Ausländer," "als staatsrechtlich den Ptolemäern nicht untertänige Personen. Das würde bedeuten, daß sie nicht eine in Ägypten angesiedelte Gruppe oder Nachkommen einer solchen sind."[74]

À Hermoupolis nous avons déjà quitté la Thébaïde au sens strict du mot pour entrer en Moyenne-Égypte. Jetons-y un coup d'oeil.

À Tênis/Akôris du Môchitês, toparchie de l'Hermopolite, on a retrouvé les archives de Dionysios ὃς καὶ Plênis, le fils de Kephalas/Kephalos.[75] Βασιλικὸς γεωργός,[76] il entre dans l'armée comme son frère Paêsis ὃς καὶ Patês(?). Tous deux se font miliciens de carrière, mais alors que le frère a opté pour la cavalerie des misthophores,[77] Dionysios rejoint l'infanterie. Leur père appartenait d'ailleurs, lui aussi, aux ἐν τῶι Ἑρμοπολίτηι μισθοφόρων;[78] s'il exprime sa crainte ἀντ' ἐλ̣ευ̣θέρου δοῦ̣λος γενέσθαι,[79] il ne faut certes pas prendre ses mots au pied de la lettre. On peut ranger la famille parmi les gens aisés du village. Ce qui surprend surtout dans ce dossier, c'est un mélange constant de mercenaires et de clérouques-catœques des environs.[80]

La documentation papyrologique concernant les misthophores ne s'arrête certes pas à la frontière nord de l'Hermopolite. Dans d'autres nomes de la Moyenne-Égypte, et surtout au Fayoum, les références — même celles renvoyant à un militaire en campagne au nom égyptien — ne manquent pas. Faute d'archives détaillées concernant une personne ou une famille, il est toutefois difficile de savoir dans la plupart des cas s'il s'agit d'un misthophore au sens strict du mot ou d'un clérouque en service actif.[81]

Arrêtons-nous toutefois à Memphis, où l'on a retrouvé une inscription comparable à celles d'Hermoupolis Magna.[82] Cette ancienne capitale nous a fourni en outre et surtout le dossier de Ptolemaios, Μακεδὼν τῆς ἐπιγονῆς τῶν ἐκ τοῦ Ἡρακλεοπολίτου, mieux connu comme le reclus du Sérapéum ou plus précisément de l'Astartieion.[83] Apollônios, le plus jeune de ses frères,[84] était, lui aussi, ἐν κατοχῆι ἐν τῶι πρὸς Μέμφει μεγάλωι Σαραπιείωι. Il a joué un rôle important dans la constitution du dossier; au sujet de ses relations avec la population locale, sa connaissance de leur langue et d'autres caractéristiques, on lira l'exposé d'U. Wilcken. Depuis 157 il s'est engagé, en tant que Μακεδών, dans une σημέα de Dexilaos (Dexeilaos, Dexêlaos), notamment une ση[μέα] πρώτη ἣ τὸ τεταγμένον ἔχει ἐν Μέμφει. Il a été en service actif, du moins pendant quelque temps, et semble avoir entretenu des relations assez étroites avec la gendarmerie de l'Anoubieion.[85]

L'unité, dont Apollônios a fait partie, était e.a. constituée d'ἐπίγονοι.[86] Le père d'Apollônios — Glaukias — τῶν ἐν τῶι Ἡρακλεοπολίτηι συγγενῶν κατοίκων[87] était jadis détenteur d'un kléros

74. Cf. Zucker 1937, p. 27. Pour les noms gréco-égyptiens ou égyptiens, voir pp. 54–55.

75. Pros. Ptol. II 2544, 2553a, IV 8141. Voir l'examen approfondi de Boswinkel et Pestman 1982. Cf. Lewis 1983b, pp. 55–58; 1986, Chapter 8.

76. P. Rein. 18, lignes 2–4 = P.L. Bat. XXIIA 11; P. Rein. 19, lignes 1–2, ligne 6 = P.L. Bat. XXIIA 12.

77. Pros. Ptol. II 2553.

78. Pros. Ptol. II 2550 = V 14392.

79. P. Rein. 7, ligne 4 = P.L. Bat. XXIIA 9.

80. Cf. P.L. Bat. XXIIA intr. §4, pp. 34–55.

81. On lira les hésitations de Übel 1968, p. 71, note 7, p. 104, note 1, p. 120, note 5, p. 208, note 7.

82. *SB* I 681; le texte conservé ne dit toutefois pas explicitement qu'il s'agit de militaires. Voir au sujet de ce texte et ses parallélismes avec les inscriptions d'Hermoupolis Magna, Zucker 1937, pp. 34–49; cf. aussi Launey 1949–50, vol. II, pp. 1072–77.

83. Pros. Ptol. III 7334 et IX add.

84. Pros. Ptol. II 3820 et VIII add.; III 7324 et IX add.

85. *UPZ* I, pp. 113–16.

86. *UPZ* I 14, ligne 70.

87. Pros. Ptol. II 2577 et VIII add.

aux environs de Psychis (Psichis) du Coïte. D'après F. Übel, son fils aurait plutôt rejoint la milice de carrière.[88]

En est-il de même de Philippos, le fils de Sôgenês, στρατι[ώτ]ης ἐκ τῆς σημείας τοῦ Πυ..ρῶτος?[89] Nous le connaissons surtout comme ami intime de l'égyptienne Nephoris, la mère des jumelles du Sérapéum. Nous apprenons bien des détails sur la façon dont il maltraita le père des jumelles; mais sur sa position dans l'armée nous sommes mal informés. Tout aussi clairsemées sont les données concernant la situation militaire de Dêmêtrios, le fils de Sôsos, Κρῆς τῶν πρότερον Εὐμήλου τακτόμισθος, l'ami du reclus Ptolemaios.[90] Übel (1968, p. 122, note 4) voudrait le classer parmi les clérouques, mais il ajoute: "die Belege für ihn geben keinerlei Anhaltspunkte dafür, daß er ein Kleruche wäre." Comme on le constate, même en se basant sur le dossier de l'ἐγκάτοχος Ptolemaios, on est loin de recueillir autant d'informations que dans les archives bilingues provenant de contrées plus méridionales.

En ce qui concerne le Delta, nous avons déjà fait allusion à la présence de militaires, sans doute originaires des environs de Pathyris-Crocodilopolis, à Pélousion et à Mendès en 102 av. J.-C.[91] Plus à l'intérieur du pays on pourrait signaler des troupes, cantonnées à Naukratis, mais il s'agit ici d'une ville grecque et on a pu enrôler des ξένοι à l'étranger.[92] Revenons plutôt à l'*UPZ* I 110, que nous avons déjà cité en examinant la situation à Alexandrie.

Dôriôn, l'hypodiœcète responsable au moins pour l'ouest du Delta en 164 av. J.-C., reçoit une lettre du diœcète en chef concernant les παρεφεδρεύοντες ἐν Ἀλεξανδρείαι, parmi lesquels nous avons retrouvé des *machimoi* et des miliciens de carrière. Certains d'entre eux ont dû provenir du district relevant de la compétence de Dôriôn; toutefois, dans la dernière partie du texte, une lettre adressée à Theôn, épimélète τῶν κάτωι (*sic*) τόπων τοῦ Σαίτου (lignes 193–213), il n'est plus question que de la plainte des ἐν τῆι | πόλει μάχιμοι (lignes 198–99). La situation des misthophores n'y est pas comparable à celle de leurs collègues du Sud. Il est dommage que les sources ne nous révèlent même pas leur nom et ne nous permettent pas de présenter une prosopographie de quelque ampleur pour le Delta. A fortiori il nous manque l'information nécessaire pour élaborer des "case studies" pour cette partie de la chôra.

Ce sont pourtant les riches archives de personnes ou de familles qui nous révèlent des "split personalities" qui, selon la situation dans laquelle elles se trouvent, ont recours tantôt à la langue et aux coutumes indigènes, tantôt à la koinè grecque et aux usages des Hellènes. Il s'agit d'une assimilation occasionnelle, dictée souvent par les circonstances variables et concrètes de la vie quotidienne dans un milieu plus ou moins mixte qui tend à une symbiose de deux cultures différentes. Parfois on a sans doute affaire à une acculturation partielle mais plus constante. Ainsi on est encore loin d'une transculturation qui conduit à l'osmose de deux cultures différentes dans un nouvel ensemble de quelque envergure.

Mais sur quoi reposent ces conclusions? Il est vrai que la documentation est souvent analytique et certes fragmentaire; elle est, de plus, assez disparate selon que nous désirons nous informer sur le monde extérieur, y compris Alexandrie, sur la Moyenne-Égypte ou sur la Haute-Égypte. Nous voilà confrontés avec le problème épineux de la représentativité de nos sources. De fait, il s'agit d'un problème à double aspect. Il y a la valeur de la documentation pour l'analyse de l'armée en soi; il y a, en outre, la représentativité de l'armée pour la société dans son ensemble.

88. Voir la plainte contre le ὑπηρέτης Argeios, Pros. Ptol. II 2437 et VIII add., Übel 1968, p. 88, note 1, p. 279, no. 1178 avec les notes 3–9. D'autres *epigonoi* pourraient être εἰκοσιπεντάρουροι; cf. Pros. Ptol. IV, pp. 80–81; Übel 1968, p. 422, index 3a, s.v.

89. Pros. Ptol. II 4123.

90. Pros. Ptol. II 3872.

91. Collectanea Hellenistica, I, les papyrus nos. 4–6 et l'inscription no. 1.

92. Zaki Aly 1948, p. 79 = *SB* VIII 9747.

Jetons d'abord, à titre d'exemple, un bref coup d'oeil sur l'armée romaine d'Égypte de 30 av. J.-C. à 284 après J.-C. H. De Kuyffer y a consacré une thèse de doctorat à la Katholieke Universiteit Leuven en 1989. Compte tenu des effectifs sous les empereurs successifs et de la durée normale du service militaire, le total pour toute cette époque d'environ 300 ans est estimé à quelque 200.000 personnes. Or nous en connaissons 3130, officiers compris, donc à peu près 1,5%, ce qui dépasse le pourcentage habituel des enquêtes statistiques contemporaines. En outre les historiens des institutions romaines ont souligné à plusieurs reprises que la structure de l'armée est un décalque fidèle de la société romaine en général. L'étude de l'armée serait donc un domaine idéal pour démontrer la validité des recherches prosopographiques. Sans doute devra-t-on çà et là atténuer la portée des conclusions : non seulement les pertes nous semblent avoir été sous-estimées, mais la prosopographie nous informe surtout sur les militaires, nés en Égypte ou installés définitivement dans cette province, bien plus que sur les militaires de passage, ce qui doit déséquilibrer l'enquête sur certains points.

Néanmoins le chercheur se sentira plus à l'aise à l'époque romaine qu'à celle des Lagides. Personne n'oserait affirmer que les phénomènes d'une symbiose ou même d'une certaine acculturation dans les unités lagides reflètent une tendance générale, perceptible dans tous les secteurs sociaux et à chaque niveau. Loin de là. Laissons à d'autres, plus compétents en la matière dans sa totalité — la documentation hiéroglyphique, démotique et grecque à la fois ainsi que l'approche sociologique — de se prononcer sur ces questions globales mais délicates et confinons-nous prudemment dans les cadres militaires.

Nous n'oserions guère plus évaluer le nombre total des miliciens qui ont rejoint l'armée pendant les quelque 300 ans de la domination lagide. Trop d'éléments restent incalculables pour se risquer au jeu: les fluctuations des effectifs depuis Ptolémée I Sotèr jusqu'à Cléopâtre VII; la part d'un mercenariat mobile, avec des militaires enrôlés pour une seule campagne et quittant l'empire par la suite (cf. Lesquier 1911, pp. 17–18); la durée normale du service pour les autres, depuis l'âge de leur enrôlement jusqu'à leur mort. À quoi pourraient nous servir les trop rares et d'ailleurs discutables points de repère: les 250.000 *Kalasiries* et les 160.000 *Hermotybies* qu'Hérodote attribue à l'apogée de l'époque pharaonique (Hérodote II, 164–166; cf. Winnicki 1985, pp. 42–47), ou les 240.000 hommes de l'armée de terre de Ptolémée II Philadelphe qu'Appien (Chapitre 10) mentionne dans l'introduction à ses Ῥωμαικά, ou les quelque 75.000 soldats que Ptolémée IV Philopator oppose à Antiochos III à Raphia en 217 av. J.-C. (Polybe V 65, 79.2) et qui n'atteignent même pas le nombre de plus de 80.000 fantassins et cavaliers dans la πομπή de Philadelphe?[93]

Nous ne pouvons donc proposer un pourcentage raisonnable qui représenterait les cas connus par rapport au total présumé des effectifs pour toute l'époque ptolémaïque. De toute façon on s'attend à un total dépassant de loin celui de la période romaine.

Il n'en reste pas moins vrai que le nombre absolu des données ptolémaïques dépasse apparemment les 3130 cas de l'époque romaine. Le volume II de la *Prosopographia Ptolemaica*, consacré à l'armée de terre et à la police, contient 3159 numéros dont 459 seulement se rapportent à la police. Au volume IV, qui a trait à l'agriculture et à l'élevage, 1094 numéros sont réservés aux clérouques, mais il faut préciser qu'un certain nombre figure déjà au volume II. N'insistons pas sur les données concernant la flotte au volume V où l'on comptera, par exemple, quelque 40 navarques. Les officiers, les intendants et les militaires opérant à l'étranger sont réunis dans le volume VI où ils occupent 544 numéros. Et on n'oubliera certes pas les addenda — plus de 250 numéros — groupés dans le volume VIII. Résultat final: 4488 numéros au moins, y compris les références doubles du volume IV, mais hormis toute la documentation sur la police, de la flotte et de toutes les données dont le caractère militaire n'est pas établi par un titre explicite.

93. Athén., Deipn. V 202f–203a. Cf. supra p. 341

À côté de ces données prosopographiques, il y a les informations plus globalisantes fournies par des auteurs anciens et quelques papyrus comme *UPZ* I 110, sources que nous avons utilisées e.a. pour la description de l'armée à l'étranger et à Alexandrie.

Mais revenons à la prosopographie. A. E. Samuel (1989, Chapter III, pp. 35–49) a souligné combien nos connaissances se limitent somme toute à l'histoire de quelques familles ou personnes aisées. "To understand the bottom 70 or 80 percent of the population we must develop some creative means of using our evidence to learn something about them. We would like to know how much upward mobility existed, in fact, for people born into the peasant life. And we would like to know if, at this level, at least, the Greeks in Egypt merged with the vast mass of Egyptians, to bridge, at least at that level, the two solitudes in which the cultured carried on their separate lives" (p. 49).

Voici quatre remarques au sujet de cet avertissement. D'abord il est vrai que les dossiers plus fournis appartiennent à des familles ou à des personnes aisées que l'on peut ranger parmi les 10 à 20% de la population. Mais c'est ici qu'on peut se risquer à des "case studies."

En second lieu, nous avons l'impression qu'une prosopographie exhaustive, groupant sans exception tous les cas connus d'après leur fonction ou leur situation sociale, nous permet de pousser notre enquête au delà de la limite, tracée par A. E. Samuel, et d'étendre nos recherches à des secteurs du niveau inférieur. Les *machimoi* fantassins et certains transférés de la police se situent sans doute parmi les 70 ou 80% des appauvris. La documentation concernant chaque individu se fait plus clairsemée; mais aussi fragmentaire qu'elle soit, nous pouvons poser avec succès quelques questions fondamentales. Par quelle voie peut-on aboutir à une promotion sociale? Celle-ci conduit-elle à une sorte d'assimilation?

En troisième lieu, la combinaison des deux catégories de recherches — les "case studies" et la prosopographie exhaustive[94] — nous permettra d'évaluer en quelle mesure les résultats acquis peuvent être généralisés de part et d'autre. La confrontation de l'esquisse d'un milieu de catœques, dotés de 20 à 30 aroures au moins en Moyenne-Égypte au 2e siècle av. J.-C., d'une part et de l'image plus détaillée qui ressort des "case studies", entreprises à la même époque dans une région plus méridionale parmi les miliciens de carrière, d'autre part peut suggérer des parallélismes au sujet du niveau de vie ou des phénomènes d'acculturation.

Enfin, soulignons tout spécialement — à l'encontre des hellénistes d'antan qui croyaient pouvoir s'en tenir à la documentation grecque — qu'il est exclu d'aborder ces problèmes fondamentaux sans avoir recours à la fois aux sources hiéroglyphiques, démotiques et grecques. Quant aux égyptologues, le moment est venu de s'associer davantage aux efforts des hellénistes. C'est l'union qui fait la force. La 'Koninklijke Academie van België' y contribuera par l'édition d'archives bilingues de l'époque lagide.

94. Sur les différentes catégories de prosopographie, voir par exemple Van't Dack, dans *Proceedings of the Nineteenth International Congress of Papyrology*, Cairo, à paraître.

CHAPTER 42

THE TITHE OF THE SCRIBES (AND) REPRESENTATIVES*

S. P. VLEEMING
University of Leiden

I propose to deal here with the transfer tax known from the Greek texts as ἐγκύκλιον, usually translated as 'tax on sales.'[1] Perhaps the necessity of this uninspiring task may be admitted, if it is recalled that the last presentation of the Egyptian material was given by E. Revillout in 1892 — that is, now more than one century ago.

We have among the Egyptian texts documentation concerning the transfer tax in hieratic and Demotic which goes back into the seventh century B.C. I hope to have collected most of the citations of the transfer tax in the following pages. They consist of statements of the payment of the tax within sale contracts, listed here in §A. These range from the seventh to the third century B.C. Then we have actual tax receipts. Those of the third century feature the transfer tax of $\frac{1}{10}$, listed in §B; and those of the second century the transfer tax of $\frac{1}{20}$, listed in §C. Our §D, to conclude, contains two citations of the payment of the tax from the second century, its rate again at $\frac{1}{20}$.

(A) P. Choix 9 (635 B.C.) line 13: 'We have received from you these 3 *kite* of silver, of the Treasury of Harshef, in exchange for them (= the sale's object), as their money, … … [line 15:] besides the $\frac{1}{10}$ of the *xxxx*-scribe of the Domain of Amun: $\frac{1}{5}\,\frac{1}{10}$ *kite* of silver, total $3\,\frac{1}{5}\,\frac{1}{10}$ *kite* of silver.'

P. Choix 10 (620 B.C.) line 9: 'I have received from you these 5 *deben* of silver, of the Treasury of Harshef, in exchange for them (= the sale's object), as their [line 10:] money, besides the $\frac{1}{10}$ of the *xxxx*-scribe of the Domain of Amun: $\frac{1}{2}$ *deben* of silver, total $5\frac{1}{2}$ *deben* of silver, as their money.'

* I should like to thank Dr. W. J. Tait for correcting the worst defects of the English of my paper in Chicago, and more defects again afterwards in Huntingdon.

1. For the tax, see Préaux 1939a, p. 331ff., note 1, and the references given there. The exact translation of the tax seems to escape us, as reflected in F. Ll. Griffith's grumbling note: "'trafficking-tax' … or 'current tax' or 'ordinary tax', … a tax on sales … whatever its etymological meaning may be" (1901, p. 301, note *). Wilcken 1899, p. 184, had argued, possibly with good reasons, against the translations by 'current, ordinary', as well as 'yearly', which had been proposed previously, but his proposal to regard the word as reflecting the 'values in circulation' seems too modern to be true. The word apparently acquired a specialized meaning in Egypt, and as such the current translation by 'tax on sales' is practical. The word is to be found in Demotic transliteration once, see below, in the *Postscript*.

P. Br. Mus. Reich 10117 (± 540 B.C.) line 6: 'You have contented my heart with their money, besides the $\frac{1}{10}$ of the accounting(?) scribes[2] of the Temple of Amun in the district of Koptos.'

P. Choix 11 [= P. Tsenhor 10] (510 B.C.) line 3: 'You have contented my heart with its money, besides the $\frac{1}{10}$ of the representatives in Thebes, to give it to the God's Domain of Amun.'

P. Philad. 2 (314 B.C.) line 4: 'You have contented my heart with its money, besides the $\frac{1}{10}$ of the scribes (and) representatives in Thebes.'

P. Schreibertr. 15 (243 B.C.) line 6: 'I have received their price in money from you, it being complete and without remainder; my heart is contented therewith, besides the $\frac{1}{10}$ of the scribes (and) representatives in Thebes.'

Pap. Choix 9–11: Malinine 1953; P. BM Reich: Reich 1914; P. Tsenhor: Pestman (*Papyrus Tsenhor* [in press B]); P. Philad.: el-Amir 1959; P. Schreibertr.: Zauzich 1968.

(B) Pap. BM Glanv. 10537 and 10536 (284 and 278 B.C.): 'FN has brought such-and-such an amount for the tax of the house, which she had bought from NN,'

10537: 'before Xenanthos(?), the commissioner, the representative of the Chief of the Army.'[3]

10536: 'before Zenodoros, the commissioner.'

Scribe:

10537: 'Peteêsis, son of Psenkhonsis.'

10536: 'Sminis, son of Phibis, who receives the tax,[4] this representative of Phibis, son of Harnouphis.'

Pap. BM Glanv. 10529 (274 B.C.) and 10530–535 (281–277 B.C.): 'There is such-and-such an amount of money that FN has given' for 'the $\frac{1}{10}$ of the scribes (and) representatives in Thebes, on account of the house ....'

Scribe:

10529: 'The scribe of the land in Thebes, Amasis, son of *Ḏd-Ḫnsw-iw.f-ꜥnḫ*, the scribe of the phyle.'

10530–535: 'The scribe of the land in Thebes, Osoroêris, son of Spotous, the First Priest.'[5]

O. Berlin P. 890 (yr. 15 = 268/232? B.C.): 'NN [has brought] the tax of $\frac{1}{10}$ for this cow.'[6]

2. One is tempted to equate the abnormal hieratic title of Pap. Choix 9 and 10 with the early Demotic title occurring in P. BM Reich 10117. Malinine read the early Demotic title as *ḥsb-it*, 'accountant of grain' (1953, p. 70, note 16). Reading from the published photo, I concur in reading *ḥsb*, written notably in alphabetical manner, 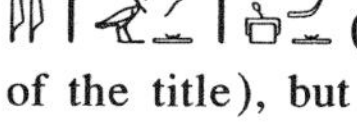 (as if the orthography was no longer available in Demotic, which suggests a proper Theban origin of the title), but I unfortunately fail to recognize which signs Malinine read as *it*, 'grain': to my mind the problematical sign at the end of *ḥsb* should be its determinative. Such a reading suggests an evolution in the shape of the title through the seventh and sixth centuries, but not necessarily an evolution in the office, *if* the titles are to be equated, a thing I should not be unwilling to accept.

3. The editor (Glanville 1939, p. 40) read *pꜣ rt(?) pꜣ šm*, "the agent(?) of the harvest," instead of our *pꜣ rd pꜣ ḥry-mšꜥ*.

4. Adopting the reading *nti šd n* proposed by the editor (Glanville 1939, p. 42, note 2 §2) and taking *pꜣy rd n Pꜣ-hb* as an apposition to this function description (cf. below, footnote 22).

5. Adopting the reading proposed by Hughes and Nims 1940, p. 261.

6. Supplementing [*in*], 'has brought,' after Pap. BM Glanville 10537–10536 and Louvre 2441, and adopting the reading *dni*, 'tax,' proposed by the editor (Zauzich 1986a, p. 131 §4).

Scribe: 'Phagônis son of Parêtis [who is] responsible for the grain revenue(s) (?) (*prosodos sitinon*?).'[7]

P. Louvre 2441 (> 227 B.C.): three rather damaged receipts similar to Pap. BM Glanville 10537–36?

[For unpublished Pap. Bruxelles 8255 and 8256, see footnotes 15–16.] Pap. BM Glanville: Glanville 1939; O. Berlin P. 890: Zauzich 1986a, p. 131; P. Louvre 2441: Revillout 1880, pp. 288–89.

(C) *Ét. Pap.* 8, p. 60 (yr. 5, IV *šmw* 14 = 176 B.C.): at the foot of a contract: 'NN has brought the tax of $\frac{1}{20}$ for this document written above in year 5, 4th month of the *šmw* season (Mesorê) (day) 14.'

Scribe: 'Harsiêsis son of Khestefnakht who is responsible for the $\frac{1}{20}$ in Jême in this year 5.'[8]

P. Berlin 3111 (yr. 6, II *ꜣḫ.t* 14 = 176 B.C.): at the foot of a contract: 'NN has brought the tax of $\frac{1}{20}$ for this document written above in year 6, 2nd month of the *ꜣḫ.t* season (Phaôphi) (day) 14.'

Signed: 'Psenamenôphis son of Snakhyti who is responsible for the $\frac{1}{20}$ [of year] 6.'[9]

P. BM Reich 10226 (yr. 20, III *pr.t* 18 = 185 B.C.): at the foot of a contract: 'FN has brought such-and-such an amount for the $\frac{1}{20}$ of [the] above document.'

Scribe: 'Phabis son of Kluj (= the Notary) who is responsible for the $\frac{1}{20}$, in year 20, 3rd month of the *pr.t* season (Phamenôth) (day) 18.'[10]

[See also the additional material indicated below, in the postscript.] *Ét. Pap.* 8, p. 60: el-Amir 1957, p. 60; P. Berlin: Spiegelberg 1902; P. BM Reich: Reich 1914.

(D) P. Berl. 3112 (175 B.C.) lines 15–16: note at the end of this copy of a contract: 'They paid its $\frac{1}{20}$ into the bank of Pharaoh[l.p.h.].'

P. Bibl. Nat. 218 (146 B.C.): note at the foot of a copy of a contract, referring to the original of *UPZ* II 175 *c*: 'They paid its $\frac{1}{20}$ into the bank of Thebes.'

P. Berlin: Spiegelberg 1902; P. Bibl. Nat. 218: Revillout 1880, pp. 62–84; *UPZ* II: Wilcken 1935.

If we confront this information with that of the Greek texts, it transpires that the Greek documentation seems to commence only in the middle of the third century, and that it is very meager indeed: it really starts to flow in the second century, notably in a long series of tax receipts at the foot of documents, which I have not listed here.[11]

7. Reading *ḥr* rather than *ḫr* in view of the regular idiom in §C (cf. below, footnote 8). The words 'grain revenue(s)' are written alphabetically *prshwts tysnn* (*sic*), and, I think plausibly, explained as *prosodos sitinon* by the editor.

8. The editor omitted to read a sign that may be read as *tꜣy*, 'this,' between 'Jême' and 'year.' This function finds its exact translation in G. Vitelli 1929, doc. 1014, line 5, ὁ πρὸς τῆι (εἰκοστῆι) τῶν Μεμ(νονείων), whereas the tax farmer is usually called ὁ πρὸς τῆι ὠνῆι; see Pestman, *Theban Choachytes* (in Press A, *loc. cit.* in footnote 11, below; see now also below, *Postscript*).

9. The signature may be an autograph, whereas the receipt itself seems to have been written by the hand of the Notary.

10. The scribe wrote confusingly the date of the payment instead of naming the year for which he farmed the tax as in the other instances of this expression.

11. See e.g. the texts listed in P. W. Pestman, *Theban Choachytes* (in press A, Chapter III, §9, tables 18–19).

Table 42.1. Comparison in the Rate of the Transfer Tax from the Seventh through the Second Centuries B.C.*

B.C.	*THEBES*		*B.C.*	*REVENUE LAWS*		*B.C.*	*MIDDLE EGYPT & FAIYUM*	
635	P. Choix 9	$\frac{1}{10}$						
620	P. Choix 10	$\frac{1}{10}$						
±540	P. BM Reich 10117	$\frac{1}{10}$						
510	P. Choix 11	$\frac{1}{10}$						
314	P. Philad. 2	$\frac{1}{10}$						
284–274	P. BM Glanv. 10529–10537	$\frac{1}{10}$						
243	P. Schreibertr. 15	$\frac{1}{10}$	259	Rev. Laws	$\frac{1}{20}$ (?)			
232?	O. Berlin P. 890	$\frac{1}{10}$				230/ 228	Gr. P. Hibeh I 70*a*, 70*b*, and 163	$\frac{1}{20}$
>227	P. Louvre 2441	$\frac{1}{10}$						
210	Gr. *SB* I 5729	$\pm\frac{1}{12}$						
209	Gr. P. Lond. III 1200	$\pm\frac{1}{12}$	205	*UPZ* I 112	$\frac{1}{10}$ (?)	209	Gr. P. Lond. VII 2189	$\pm\frac{1}{12}$
	Second Century B.C.:	$\frac{1}{20}$				201	Gr. P. Petrie III 57 *b*	$\frac{1}{20}$
±130	raised to:	$\frac{1}{10}$						

* The Demotic texts in the above table are those listed above in §§A–B. *SB* I: *Sammelbuch* I 1915; Gr. P. Lond. III: Kenyon and Bell 1907; Rev. Laws: Mahaffy 1896; *UPZ* I: Wilcken 1927; Gr. Pap. Hibeh I: Grenfell and Hunt 1906; Gr. P. Lond. VII: Skeat, ed., 1974; Gr. P. Petrie III: Mahaffy 1905.

Another thing one can glean from Table 42.1 is the fair amount of fluctuation in the rate of the tax, which amounts basically to this: that from its original $\frac{1}{10}$, or 10 percent, it was changed to $\frac{1}{20}$, or 5 percent, at about the turn of the third and second centuries B.C. I do intend to make this the major concern of my paper, but to arrive there in good order, we ought perhaps to turn to the earlier Demotic documentation first.

Looking over the texts in §A, above, one is struck by the long time span covered by these citations of the $\frac{1}{10}$ transfer tax, running apparently without a break from the middle of the seventh to the middle of the third century B.C. In the early period, all contracts are *sales* and concern *landed property*.[12] In the Ptolemaic period this was to be changed: the tax was then paid for various transactions, among which were donations, and also on a wider range of sale objects, as for example on the cow in the Berlin ostracon (§B). Its relative rarity in the contracts of the Ptolemaic period, when the tax has apparently been found only in two out of the numerous sale contracts collected in Prof. Zauzich's *Schreibertradition*,[13] may imply that the scribes forewent to mention the transfer tax, because separately made-out receipts similar to those of §B usually sufficed. The growing number of receipts of the tax written in Greek at the foot of contracts in the second century B.C. (see footnote 11), then, possibly reflects no more than a change in scribal practice. The new

12. Thus Pestman, *Papyrus Tsenhor* (in press B, Chapter II, doc. 10, note V), contrasting P. Choix 11 = Tsenhor 10 with P. Tsenhor 9 = unpublished P. Turin 2123, a donation of a building plot bordering on that acquired by P. Tsenhor 10 = Choix 11. The only text by which this could be tested, so far as I know, is P. Loeb 68, a sale of land, which is unfortunately too damaged in its middle portion to allow of any certain conclusion.

13. P. Philad. 2 (= P. Schreibertr. 2) and P. Schreibertr. 15; see above, §A.

practice of having the receipts at the foot of the contract does show plainly that a sale was not legally complete without acquittal of the transfer tax. As a consequence, in the second century Demotic receipts listed in §C, the tax was regarded as relating to the sale's contract, rather than to the sale's price as previously.

The attestations of the tax in §A connect the properly Egyptian institution with the Greek sales tax ἐγκύκλιον, and suggest that the Greeks never changed much in the organization of the collection of the tax, at least not in native eyes. In the early period, between 540 and 510 B.C., the 'representatives in Thebes' were made to replace scribes of the Temple of Amun. The reading of the title of Amun's scribes is, unfortunately, not certain, which is only balanced by the fact that we also do not know by exactly whose 'representatives' they had been replaced in the administration of the tax in 510 B.C. As the 'representatives' were most likely, in the final analysis, pharaoh's representatives, the change was plainly brought about to assure the civil authorities a better grip on the tax. Please note that P. Choix 11 piously added that the 'representatives' were 'to give it,' that is the transfer tax, 'to the God's Domain of Amun'; however, we cannot believe that they would have handed over all they received.[14] I intend to come back to this point shortly.

If we now turn to the early Ptolemaic period receipts published by Glanville (§B), it is to be noted that they represent two different formulas, one the ordinary 'this or that person has brought so and so much money,'[15] the other an apparently unknown formula, reading 'there is so and so much money that this or that person has given on account of the $\frac{1}{10}$.'[16] All the scribes have Egyptian names, but in the latter type of receipt, they are characterized as temple administrators by their titles: one is a scribe of the priestly phylae,[17] and the other even the first prophet, who happens to be known from hieroglyphic sources (see Quaegebeur 1974b, pp. 41f.). Their role in these receipts is that of *sẖ-ꜣsṯ* 'scribe of the land,' an otherwise unknown function in which *ꜣsṯ* was perhaps a conscious archaism (Glanville 1939, p. 41, note *d*).

In the receipts of the common type, one of the scribes is said to be the regular recipient of the tax, supposedly of the transfer tax.[18] It is interesting to note that this man is probably identical

14. See Pestman, *Papyrus Tsenhor* (in press B, *loc. cit.* in footnote 12, above).

15. Pap. BM Glanville 10537 and 10536. Cf. unpublished Demotic Pap. Bruxelles E. 8255 A (311 B.C.) and E. 8256 A–B as described by Quaegebeur 1979a, p. 45: "La première taxe (E. 8255 A), dont le montant est de 2,5 kite (les honoraires de 0,5 kite pour le scribe inclus), est payée à un fonctionnaire (*pꜣ sḥn*) égyptien qui s'appelle Nekhtharmaïs." p. 46: "les deux reçus de paiement de taxe sur la vente de tombes (E. 8256 A–B). Quant au formulaire et au montant (2,5 kite dont 0,5 pour la redaction du document), ils sont à comparer avec le premier reçu (E. 8255 A)."

16. Pap. BM Glanville 10529, 10530, and 10535. Cf. unpublished Demotic P. Bruxelles E. 8255 B (311 B.C.) as described by Quaegebeur 1979b, p. 726: "une quittance démotique de la taxe d'un dixième sur l'achat d'une maison .... Le paiement est effectué en présence de fonctionnaires financiers égyptiens et le reçu est signé par le premier prophète d'Amon," Spotous, probably the father of Osoroëris of Pap. BM Glanville 10530–10535; see Quaegebeur 1979a, p. 45, and also 1974b, pp. 41f.

17. The title is perhaps not securely read as *sẖ sꜣ(?)*, one expects *sẖ sꜣ.w* or *sẖ n pꜣ* IV *sꜣ.w*, 'scribe of the phylae,' or 'scribe of the 4 phylae.'

18. Sminis in P. BM Glanville 10536, line 3. I understand from Bogaert's recent article (1988, p. 137, note 112), that we cannot reckon with the presence of bankers at this early date, the more so as these scribes have Egyptian names, so they were supposedly exactly what the one scribe calls himself, 'recipient of the tax.' This was perhaps the same office as that first attested in P. Choix 11 of 510 B.C. (cf. footnote 12 above).

with a Notary known from a fair number of Demotic documents:[19] this points to the same mixture of activities as found in the second century texts of §C. More excitingly, in these texts the payments were made before two men with Greek names, both said to have been *sḥn*, 'commissioner,' a rather vague title. One of the two, however, was 'representative' of the *ḥry pꜣ mšꜥ*, 'Chief of the Army' (P. BM 10537, line 3). This title was described as a 'high military and court rank' (see Smith and Kuhrt 1982, p. 203), and so one is tempted to translate it as '*stratêgos*' here. The *stratêgos*, originally the highest military commander in a district, is known to have replaced the *nomarkhês*, 'governor of the district,' as head of the civil administration by about 230 B.C.; developments in the preceding decade leading up to this change have been noted (see J. D. Thomas 1978, p. 192, note 37), but our text dates to 284 B.C. If one is not prepared to view the *stratêgos* as encroaching upon the competence of the civil administration at such an early date, there may be any number of *ad hoc* explanations for the occurrence of the *stratêgos* in our text. I should think that the scribe of this text may have had nebulous ideas about the Greek administration, and just possibly he regarded the *stratêgos* as the highest local authority because of the position of the Greeks in the southern provinces which may have been different from that in the better documented Faiyum. For the purpose of my paper, however, the important thing is to note that there seem to have been two distinct collecting institutions concerned with the tax of 'the scribes (and) representatives in Thebes,'[20] the one derived from a temple, and the other from a state milieu. I hope to come back to this point shortly.

Central to every discussion of this piece of fiscal history is the fluctuation in the rate of the tax. From the seventh through the third centuries, the rate was apparently $\frac{1}{10}$ or ten percent. Through most of the second century, the ἐγκύκλιον was $\frac{1}{20}$, that is five percent.[21] For completeness' sake I might add that the ἐγκύκλιον was raised to $\frac{1}{10}$ in the last decades of the second century,[22] but for our purposes this is a secondary matter. From the above table 42.1, it is clear that in the last decades of the third century there was some vacillation between the third century rate of ten percent and the second century rate of five percent. Possibly Mlle. Préaux was correct in suggesting that the rate "varie non seulement selon les exigences du budget royal, mais selon la nature des mutations et des objets transmits. Il se pourrait aussi qu'il varie selon les régions, la législation des Lagides n'étant pas uniforme dans toute l'Égypte" (1939a, p. 333). This view may well explain any odd fact that resists harmonious interpretation, but the puzzling fact remains that the third century rate of ten percent was halved in the second century. Or, as Grenfell and Hunt put it in their comments on the Greek Hibeh papyri: "It is very unlikely that the Ptolemies lowered a rate which they found already

19. From 304–264 B.C.; see Clarysse 1981, p. 261, §7738, taken up from a suggestion by de Meulenaere 1959b, p. 249, note 2. A puzzle is created, at least for me, by Sminis' relation to the Phibis mentioned at the end of the text. De Meulenaere conjectured that Phibis was a nephew of Sminis, 'probably already aged' in 278 B.C. Differently from what he thought, however, I think the first editor of the text was mistaken in making Phibis also the representative of Phibis (translating, "the agent being Phib son of Harnufi," cf. above, footnote 4), for the text seems to make Sminis the representative of Phibis, who must have been most gratified to have had his notary uncle as assistant.

20. The nexus in this expression (§§A–B) is susceptible of various interpretations: 'the scribes of the representatives in Thebes' (genitive: thus Glanville 1939 p. 41), 'the lieutenant scribes in Thebes' (apposition: thus Reich 1936, p. 15, line 4 end, "scribes bailiffs"), and my 'the scribes (and) representatives' (coordination: thus el-Amir 1959, p. 11). The interpretation of *sẖ.w* as 'writings,' first proposed by Revillout (1880, p. 271), has to be rejected in view of the early parallel expressions in §A.

21. See Pestman, *Theban Choachytes* (in press A, Chapter III, §9), who studies the transfer tax in the second century B.C.

22. See Pestman, *Theban Choachytes* (in press A, Chapter III, §9, note 4): "probably between 137 and 131 B.C.," with reference to Pestman, *Theban Choachytes* (in press A, Chapter III, §8 *c*, note 7).

established; the tendency of their taxes was rather in the opposite direction."[23] The obvious answer would seem to be that the rate was indeed lowered, supposedly by Ptolemy V or VI, in response to the unrest in the country and the economic decline we assume to have resulted therefrom. This is in fact the position Revillout took (1892, p. 121). I should like to envisage another solution, however.

There are two Greek receipts from the Faiyum of 126 and 125 B.C., both of which relate to a single sale, for which the one certifies the ἐγκύκλιον tax payment, and the other the payment of a similar tax due to the Temple of Soukhos, which apparently had similar rights on the property traded.[24] The noteworthy thing is that the buyer had to pay the transfer tax to the state as well as to the temple, which apparently had equal sovereign rights concerning the property in question.

If we now think back to P. Choix 11, only four centuries older, which suggests a similar division, and to the early Ptolemaic period receipts of §B, also apparently deriving from twin administrations, a picture emerges in which the transfer tax of ten percent was shared by the state and the temple. At a certain point between the last of the early Ptolemaic period receipts (274 B.C.) and the earliest well established ἐγκύκλιον payment (230 B.C.), the part that went to the state was fixed at five percent. Not much later, the civil administration may have endeavored to raise the rate temporarily,[25] but it was soon dissuaded, and left it at the portion of $\frac{1}{20}$, or five percent, which it had determined previously.

The exact proportion of the division of the transfer tax between the temple and the state in the Saite and early Ptolemaic periods remains unfortunately obscure. In the early Ptolemaic period receipts (§B), it seems as though the state received a fixed sum of $2\frac{1}{2}$ *kite* (= 5 drachmas), but one does not know whether these were full or partial payments, whereas the temple received 'the $\frac{1}{10}$ of the scribes (and) representatives' (see above, footnote 16 and below, footnote 25). As the formula in the contracts (§A) refers only to this $\frac{1}{10}$, one is left to wonder whether the state's $2\frac{1}{2}$ *kite* was comprised therein, or perhaps simply ignored. The temple tax, in turn, frequently went unmentioned, or so I suppose, and it just may be that it was always levied at its rate of ten percent, from the early into the Roman period (see footnote 24), whereas the state tax grew from its early Ptolemaic fixed sum of $2\frac{1}{2}$ *kite*, via the five percent of the late third and most of the second centuries (see footnote 21), to the ten percent of the late second century B.C. (see footnote 22).

All this is a reconstruction, of course, but most of the facts seem to fit. The Greek Hibeh papyri apparently concerned only the state's part of the tax, or perhaps they concerned property that lay outside temple claims.[26] The rate of the tax in the Revenue Laws of 259 B.C. does now accord with the assumed 'half rate' of five percent of the period. That of ten percent in 205 B.C., however, is at

23. Grenfell and Hunt 1906, p. 220 (ad doc. 70 *a*). As none of the Demotic sources listed for the third century were known in reliable editions at the time of her writing, Préaux, being of a different generation from Grenfell and Hunt, did not reckon with Revillout's paper of 1892, and thus she had to admit that the Ptolemies did not immediately adopt the Egyptian rate of one-tenth due on transfers (1939a, p. 334): "Les Lagides n'ont pas adopté tout de suite, notons-le, le taux égyptien de la dîme due sur les mutations. Tout se passe comme s'ils ne s'étaient pas avisés tout d'abord des droits fiscaux que leur donnaient leurs droits souverains sur les immeubles de leurs sujets."

24. Pap. Tebt. II 280 and 281. They were found rolled up inside Demotic P. Cairo 30620, with which they apparently have nothing to do; thus Spiegelberg 1908a, p. 71, note 2. Spiegelberg 1903b, doc. 748 from the Faiyum (A.D. 48). See Wilcken 1899, p. 360, §152.

25. See Gr. Pap. *SB* I 5729, Lond. III 1200 and VII 2189, with their rate of $8\frac{3}{8}$ percent (cf. above, p. 348, after footnote 22). I think that Skeat (1959, pp. 77–78, §2), in his commentary on this last text, has correctly connected this rate with a tax operation started in about 209/208 B.C. in order to collect the tax on property 'in previous possession' (its proclamation is mentioned in both Pap. Lond. III 1200 and VII 2189). This rate might have had a punitive character, accordingly. Be this as it may, the Pap. Hibeh show that the tax on sales was not instituted at the time of these papyri as Skeat suggested.

26. I, nos. 70 *a*, 70 *b*, and 163, listed above, in table 42.1.

variance with our theory. These two rates are followed by question marks in the above Table 42.1, because the transfer tax and its rate were not expressly stated in these texts, but they were inferred by modern commentators to explain certain passages.[27] I think the simplest solution is to free ourselves of the illusion that the relevant passages from these texts concern the transfer tax: there is no difficulty in assuming that the function of the $\frac{1}{20}$ in the earlier and that of the $\frac{1}{10}$ in the later Revenue Laws was that of a premium pure and simple.[28]

Postscript. Professor Pestman points out to me that the subscriptions of *Catalogue* numbers 9, 41, and 42 (Andrews 1990) contain some more examples of the Demotic sales tax receipts listed above in §C; and, more interestingly, that the subscription of *Catalogue* number 18, of 209 B.C. (previously studied by Zauzich 1986b, pp. 161f.), mentions an official *nti ḥr pꜣ ꜣggryn n pꜣ tš n Pr-Ḥ.t-Ḥr*, 'who is in charge of the *enkyklion* in the nome of Pathyris,' not of the *aggareion*, 'requisitioning for traveling officials' or for the 'posting system,' as had been suggested by Zauzich 1986b, and Clarysse 1987a, p. 21, note 67, nor of the *archeion*, 'town hall,' as suggested by Andrews 1990, p. 57, note 22.

27. See Wilcken on p. 511 of his edition of *UPZ* I 112, referring to Bouché-Leclerq, who apparently invented the theory; it is adopted by Préaux 1939a, p. 332, note 4.

28. This explains why the text differentiates between the premium and the ἐγκύκλιον, which distinction Wilcken failed to grasp (1935, pp. 516f., note 5).

CHAPTER 43

DEMOTISCHE STELEN AUS TERENUTHIS*

J. K. WINNICKI
University of Warsaw

Jeder, der sich auch nur ein wenig für die Kultur des alten Ägyptens interessiert, kennt die Terenuthisstelen, publiziert in zahlreichen Werken über die ägyptische, griechische oder koptische Kunst und aufbewahrt in allen größeren Sammlungen der alten Kunst.[1] Die Stelen besitzen charakteristische Merkmale, dank denen sie leicht von anderen Objekten ähnlicher Art zu unterscheiden sind. Die meisten von ihnen stammen aus Terenuthis oder eigentlich aus dessen Nekropole Kom Abu Billu. Manche dieser Denkmäler wurden allerdings in den Nachbargebieten gefunden (Parlasca 1970, S. 178–79; Bingen 1987, S. 4). Alle enthalten Auskünfte über die Bevölkerung des südwestlichen Teiles des Deltas, über ihre Kultur und Sitten zur Zeit der Griechen und Römer. Ihre Bedeutung ist umso größer, als das Delta keine umfangreichere Menge von Denkmälern geliefert hat.[2]

In der griechisch-römischen Periode war Terenuthis eine am Wüstenrand gelegene Provinzortschaft, die zum Gau Prosopitis gehörte. Durch sie strömten aus dem Wadi Natrun Natrontransporte, die im weiteren auf ganz Ägypten verteilt wurden. Der vorbeifließende Rosettanilarm lieferte den dortigen Einwohnern Beschäftigung im Fischfangwesen und Flußtransport. Jahrhundertelang war die Ortschaft für ihren Kult von Hathor, der Herrin von Mefkat, bekannt. Ptolemaios I. baute ihr einen Tempel, dessen wenige zerstreute Blöcke heute in den Museen Europas und Amerikas aufbewahrt sind. Später trat der Kult der Schlangengöttin *Tꜣ-Rnn.t* in den Vordergrund, von der der von uns gebrauchte griechische Name Terenuthis und der des jetzigen Dorfes Tarranah stammen.[3]

Die Terenuthisstelen sind gekennzeichnet durch unregelmäßige Steinränder, was mit dem Umstand verbunden war, daß sie nicht freistehend aufgestellt, sondern in die Grabnischen eingebaut wurden, was die Unregelmäßigkeiten verhüllte (vgl. Hooper 1961, S. 2; Parlasca 1970, S. 176). Die in die Stelen gehauenen Reliefs stellen den Toten meistens als Oranten oder auf einer

* Den Organisatoren des Kongresses in Chicago und besonders Frau J. Johnson, sowie Herren E. Cruz-Uribe und L. Koenen möchte ich hiermit für ihre Unterstützung, die mir die Teilnahme an diesem Kongreß ermöglicht hat, und Herrn H. Heinen für das Korrigieren der deutschen Fassung, meinen herzlichen Dank aussprechen.

1. Vgl. die von J. Bingen 1987, S. 3, Anmerkung 1, angegebene Bibliographie.

2. Das griechische epigraphische Material aus dem Westdelta stellte A. Bernand 1970, zusammen. Für die hieroglyphischen Inschriften siehe Munro 1973, S. 171–72. Eine Liste der demotischen Texte lieferte Devauchelle bei Abd el-Al, Grenier, und Wagner 1985, S. 87.

3. Kees 1934, S. 718–19; Satzinger 1983, S. 243–45. Vgl. die Bemerkungen von Kramer 1985, S. 253–55; Griffiths, *LÄ* VI, Kol. 424.

Kline auf der linken Körperseite liegend mit einem Becher in der rechten Hand dar. Es sind Elemente aus den griechischen Grabvorstellungen. Manchmal wird der Tote in die Fassade eines griechischen Gebäudes eingeschrieben, dessen Säulen jedoch ägyptisch sind. Den Toten begleiten oft ein Schakal und ein Falke, die mit der ägyptischen Religion verbunden sind. Zusammenfassend können wir sagen, daß die Reliefs dieser Stelen sowohl aus den griechischen als auch aus den ägyptischen Grabvorstellungen stammende Elemente enthalten.[4]

Diese Denkmäler sind schwer zu datieren. Die Vorschläge der einzelnen Forscher, die die Zeitspanne zwischen dem 1. und dem 5. Jh.n.Chr. umfassen, zeigen, daß bis jetzt keine sicheren Datierungskriterien ausgearbeitet worden sind. Im Lichte der letzten Bemerkungen von Bingen (1987, S. 3–14) sind wohl die meisten Stelen in die Zeit des 1.–2. Jh.n.Chr. anzusetzen.

Über die Bevölkerung selbst können wir aus diesen Texten wenig ablesen. Selten enthalten die Inschriften mehr als den griechischen oder ägyptischen Namen des Toten, sein Lebensalter und das Datum seines Todes, wo das Regierungsjahr immer anonym ist. Die einzelnen Stelen nennen nur eine Person, oft ohne Vatersnamen, so daß wir über die Familienzusammensetzung nichts erfahren. Die einzigen verfügbaren Quellen darüber verdanken wir einer Katastrophe, die in Terenuthis oder dessen Umgebung am 11. Hathyr des 20. Regierungsjahres eines unbekannten Herrschers geschehen ist. Eine Reihe von Angaben läßt vermuten, daß diese am 8. November 179 stattgefunden hat, als viele Leute ums Leben gekommen sind. Die einzelnen Familien haben ihre Verwandten in ein gemeinsames Grab gelegt und ihre Namen auf einer Grabstele geschrieben. Auf diese Weise kennen wir die Namen von Mitgliedern von fünf Familien:

—Καρπ⟨ί⟩μη (50 Jahre alt) —Ἄρτεμις (47) —Ἰσιδώρα (8).

—Διονυσάριν (45) —Διδύμη (40) —Θεδώρα (19) —Ἀθᾶς (1)

—Νεμαισᾶς (60) —Ἡφαιστᾶς (40) —Ἀπολλώναριν (35) —Νεμεσάμμων (?).

—Εὐδαιμονίς (53) —Διοσκοροῦς (30) —Ἡράκλεια (30) —Πόσις (11) —Θέωνα (2).

—Θαυβάστις (56) —Ἡρακλῆς (7) —Ποταμίτης (3) —Ἥρων (1).[5]

Diese Familien sind nicht komplett. Es sind nur diejenigen Mitglieder, die der genannten Katastrophe erlegen sind. Es fällt dabei die Dominanz von Frauen und Kinder auf. Es herrschen auch griechische Namen vor.[6] Es ist schwer anzunehmen, obwohl nicht ganz auszuschließen, daß aus irgendwelchen Gründen nur Griechen Opfer dieser Katastrophe geworden sind. Wahrscheinlicher ist, daß die in den Stelen vertretene Gesellschaft in Wirklichkeit ethnisch differenziert war und wenigstens ein Teil der dort genannten Menschen neben den hier belegten griechischen auch ägyptische Namen führte. Der Gebrauch der griechischen Namen könnte damit zusammenhängen, daß die Texte der Stelen in ebendieser Sprache verfaßt waren.[7]

Der obige Schluß steht in innerer Beziehung mit einer anderen in den Stelen vorkommenden Erscheinung. Der ägyptische oder griechische Name auf der Stele steht in keinem Zusammenhang mit der Auswahl der auf dieser Stele ausgeführten Reliefelemente oder mit dem Gesamtcharakter der Darstellung. Möglicherweise können wir daraus schließen, daß diese Stelen eine gemischte

4. Der obige Überblick erhebt keinen Anspruch darauf, dieses Thema zu erschöpfen. Er zählt nur die häufigsten Elemente auf.

5. Diese Angaben stellte Bingen 1987, S. 6–14, zusammen.

6. Von den 20 im obigen Verzeichnis vorkommenden Namen ist nur Θαυβάστις evident ägyptisch und Ἀθᾶς unklar. Die Bezeichnung eines Mannes aus Prosopitis als Πετεῆσις ὁ καὶ Ἀθᾶς könnte darauf hinweisen, daß Ἀθᾶς griechisch ist. Vgl. Yoyotte 1955, S. 130.

7. Eine ähnliche Erscheinung beobachten wir zur Zeit der Ptolemäer. Vgl. z.B. Boswinkel und Pestman 1982, S. 3–8; Pestman 1978, S. 203–10.

griechisch-ägyptische Kultur dieser Gesellschaft wenigstens im Bereich der Grabvorstellungen widerspiegeln.

Die meisten Terenuthisstelen enthalten griechische Inschriften. Ein Teil von ihnen ist nicht beschriftet, obwohl die im Stein geschnittenen Linien zeigen, daß eine Inschrift geplant war, und ein roter Fleck auf der Stelle, wo die Inschrift gewöhnlich vorkommt, scheint darauf hinzuweisen, daß diese mit Ocker niedergeschrieben, aber später verwischt wurde.

Nur wenige Stelen enthalten demotische Inschriften. Unter den zahlreichen aus dem Antikenhandel stammenden Denkmälern ist keine in dieser Sprache beschriftet. Von 200 aus den Ausgrabungen der University of Michigan stammenden Stücken sind nur drei demotisch (Hooper 1961, Nr. 11, 17, und 45). Dieses Verhältnis der beiden Stelenarten ist für die aus den ägyptischen Ausgrabungen stammenden Stücke nicht festzustellen. Man nennt zwei Zahlen: 146 (el-Nassery und Wagner 1978, S. 234) und 450 (Hawwass 1979, S. 80) für alle aufgefundenen Stelen, aber die Inventarnummern (TS = Terenuthis Stelen ?) übersteigen die Zahl 2000 Exemplaren. Für die demotischen Stelen wird die Zahl von 40 Exemplaren angegeben (Hawwass 1979, S. 82). Von dieser Gruppe hat D. Devauchelle fünf Stelen herausgegeben TS 1069 (el-Nassery und Wagner 1978, S. 250, Nr. 36, Tafel 78)[8] und TS 226, 1067, 1107, und 1110 (Abd el-Al, Grenier, und Wagner 1985, Nr. 34, 35, 40, und 60) und ich konnte dank der Freundlichkeit von H. Riad, der mir Photos zur Verfügung gestellt hat, sechs weitere lesen. Diese möchte ich hier mitteilen [Leider habe ich von ägyptischen Kollegen die Maße der Steine nicht erhalten.]:

STELE I

TS 1661. (Pl. 43.1a)

Rechteckige Stele mit unregelmäßigen Rändern. Der linke Rand ist stark korrodiert, die linke Oberecke abgebrochen. Der Einschnitt in der rechten Oberecke macht den Eindruck, daß die Stele ursprünglich mit einem eingeschnittenen Bogen abgeschlossen war.

Dargestellt ist eine stehende männliche Gestalt mit Chiton und Mantel. Beide Arme sind betend erhoben, wobei die Handflächen nach vorne gewendet sind. Die Figur ist frontal wiedergegeben, doch die Füße sind in Schrittstellung nach rechts gewendet. An jeder Seite der Figur ist je ein hockender Schakal eingeritzt.

Darunter befinden sich zwei Linien. Über der oberen die Inschrift:

Pꜣ-šr-Ḥr(?) iw=f ir rnp.t 50 hrw[a] *ḥꜣ.t-sp 10 ibd 2 [...*[b] *sw ...]*

"Psenyris. Er lebte[c] fünfzig Jahre. Der Tag (seines Todes erfolgte) im 10. Regierungsjahr, 2. Monat der [...]-Jahreszeit,[d] [am ... Tag]."

a. Ähnliche Schreibung in TS 1736.

b. Nur der Wortanfang ist erhalten geblieben. *Pr.t* und *šmw* sind zwei alternative Lesungen.

c. Wörtlich: "Er machte 50 Jahre." Diese Wendung kommt auch auf der Stele Kairo 22074, 1 (Spiegelberg 1904, S. 67, Tafel XXI) vor. Sie bildet die abgekürzte Fassung der ausführlicheren Ausdrücke: *ir=f rnp.t ʿnḫ* × "Er lebte × Lebensjahre" (Stele Kairo 31103, 5; Spiegelberg 1904, S. 36–38); *iw=f mwt iw=f ir rnp.t* × "Er ist gestorben, als er × Jahre

8. Die Umschrift und Übersetzung dieser Stele (aber mit Inventarnummer TS 1609) gibt der Autor auch bei Abd el-Al, Grenier, und Wagner 1985, S. 87, an. Auf Grund der in *BIFAO* publizierten Tafel sind wohl die in der Stele genannten Namen als *ʿll sꜣ Wn-...* oder *Pꜣ-ll sꜣ Wn-...* zu lesen.

lebte" (Stele Kairo 31122a, 1; Spiegelberg 1904 S. 48, Tafel XI). Für ähnliche Wendungen siehe die Stele in University of Michigan (Ann Arbor; Spiegelberg 1928, S. 37, Tafel 10b) und Mumientäfelchen (vgl. Pestman 1965a, S. 50).

d. Mechir oder Payni.

STELE II

TS 1678. (Pl. 43.1b)

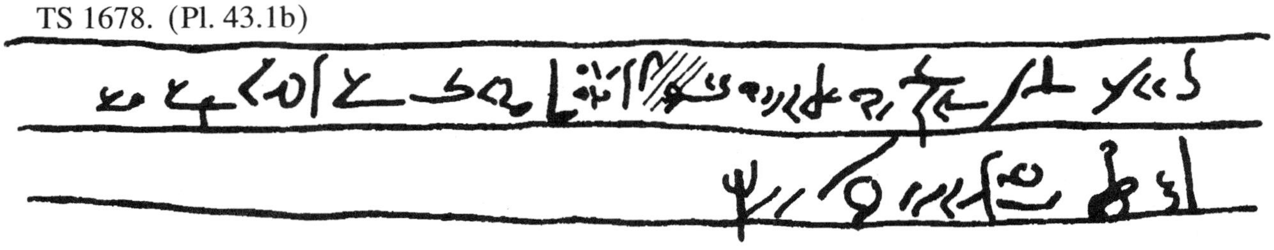

Rechteckige Stele mit unregelmäßigen Rändern.

Die Tote ist mit ausgestreckten Beinen auf einer Kline gelagert. In der Rechten hält sie einen zweihenkligen Becher, die Linke ist ohne Attribut. Der rechte Fuß der Verstorbenen, im Profil dargestellt, ist über den linken geschlagen, der nach vorne gerichtet ist. Das summarisch wiedergegebene, in der Mitte gescheitelte und nach hinten gekämmte Haar fällt beiderseits auf die Schulter. Auf dem Reliefgrund ist skizzenhaft ein hockender Schakal eingraviert. Die Kline enthält eine Matratze und zwei Kissen, alle mit Zickzackdekor verziert. Die Klinenbeine sind unverziert und verjüngen sich nach oben. Vor der Kline von links nach rechts sind ein Blumenstrauß oder eine Getreidegarbe,[9] eine Amphora in Ständer mit Schöpflöffel und ein Dreifußtisch mit zwei Bechern eingeritzt.

Darunter drei Linien, über den zwei oberen folgende Inschrift:

1. *Ḫ ʿlbrt* (oder: *Ḫ ʿlḏrt*) *sꜣ*[a] *Tꜣ-šr.t-pꜣ-[...]*[b] *iw=s ir rnp.t 48*
2. *ḥꜣ.t-sp 33 ẖwj*[c] *sw 20*

1. "*Ḫ ʿlbrt* (oder: *Ḫ ʿlḏrt*),[d] Tochter[e] der Senpa[...]. Sie lebte 48 Jahre.
2. 33. Regierungsjahr,[f] Sebastos, am 20. Tag."

a. Lies *ta*. Die Figur (Scheitel und langes Haar, vgl. Hooper 1961, S. 5; Abd el-Al, Grenier, und Wagner 1985, S. 58–59) und *iw=s* im weiteren Text zeigen, daß wir es mit einer Frau zu tun haben. *Sꜣ* "Sohn" ist daher unrichtig. Solche Fehler finden wir auch auf Mumientäfelchen. Vgl. z.B. F(orrer) 34 und 37 (Spiegelberg 1901, Tafeln 12 und 13); Leiden F 1949/4.2 (Pestman 1977, vol. I, Nr. 19; vgl. auch S. 116–17).

b. Die Oberfläche des Steines ist hier beschädigt.

c. Die ganze Zeile 2 enthält das Todesdatum. Nach dem Regierungsjahr finden wir jedoch weder einen üblichen Monatsnamen noch den der Jahreszeit. Die vorhandenen Zeichen sind wohl nur als *ẖwj* "heilig, ehrwürdig" zu lesen. (Für eine ähnliche Schreibweise vgl. Graff. Dakka 33, 1; Graff. Philae 273, 4; 317.) Das Wort kommt aber als Monatsname nur in dem Ausdruck *pꜣ ibd ntj ẖwj* "Monat, der heilig ist" = Sebastos = Thoth vor. Vgl. Mattha 1945, S. 220; Nur-el-Din 1974, S. 454. Das Sonnendeterminativ, das sonst in Zeitbegriffen erscheint, zeigt, daß hier der Monat gemeint ist.

9. Über den Charakter dieses Objekts sind sich die Forscher nicht einig. Es wird entweder wie in TS 2003 mit den knapp aneinander anliegenden Blumenstengeln oder Getreidehalmen dargestellt, oder wie oben, wo diese auseinander fallen. Es bleibt mir unklar, ob wir mit zwei verschiedenen Darstellungsweisen oder mit verschiedenen Objekten zu tun haben.

d. Die alphabetische Schreibweise und das Fremdlanddeterminativ weisen auf den Fremdnamen hin.

e. Normal kommt nach *sꜣ* oder *ta* der Vatersname vor, hier haben wir aber mit dem Anfang des Muttersnamens zu tun. Die Auslassung des Vatersnamens findet sich z.B. auch in dem Mumientäfelchen Louvre 610 und E 10396 (Baratte und Boyaval 1974, S. 181, Nr. 45 und S. 245, Nr. 232). Ähnliche Fälle beobachten wir in den Papyri, wo diese Benennung eines Mannes oder einer Frau mit ihrem Rechtsstatus verbunden war; in dieser Weise konnten Söhne und Töchter der römischen Bürger, besonders der Soldaten während ihres Militärdienstes, bezeichnet werden (vgl. Youtie 1975, S. 723–40, bes. 737–38). Es ist aber nicht sicher, ob diese Deutung sich auf Tote beziehen kann.

f. Wegen des hohen Regierungsjahres kommen hier wohl nur die Kaiser Augustus und Commodus in Frage, also die Jahre 3 oder 192 n.Chr. Die Herrschaft von Diokletian (316) scheint zu spät zu sein. Vgl. den allgemeinen Kommentar unten.

STELE III

TS 1706. (Pl. 43.1c)

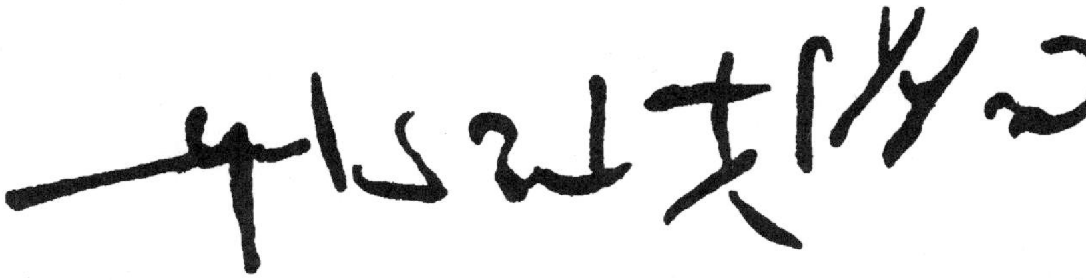

Rechteckige Stele mit unregelmäßigen Rändern. Der linke Rand ist glatt gesägt. Das Relief ist mit trapezoidaler oben bogenförmiger Umrahmung umgeben.

Dargestellt ist eine stehende Frau mit Chiton und Mantel. Beide Arme sind betend erhoben, wobei die Handflächen nach außen gewendet sind. Das Haar, nach hinten gekämmt, fällt auf die Schulter. Die Ohren sind sichtbar. Die Figur ist frontal wiedergegeben, die Füße jedoch in Schrittstellung nach rechts gewendet. An jeder Seite der Figur hockt je ein Schakal.

Darunter folgende Inschrift:

ꜣllw iw⸗s ir (rnp.t)[a] *17*

"*ꜣllw.*[b] Sie lebte 17 (Jahre)."

a. Für diese Wendung s. Kommentar zu TS 1661(c).

b. Der Name ist mit einem Fremdlanddeterminativ abgeschlossen. Ähnliche Formen *ꜣrl*, *ꜣllj* ohne dieses Determinativ sind als männliche Namen der römischen Kaiserheit bekannt (vgl. *Dem. Nb.* I, S. 29 und 36). Vgl. aber *Pꜣ-ꜣllw* mit diesem Determinativ (*Dem. Nb.* I, S. 155). Der Name bezeichnet hier eine Frau.

STELE IV

TS 1736. (Pl. 43.2a)

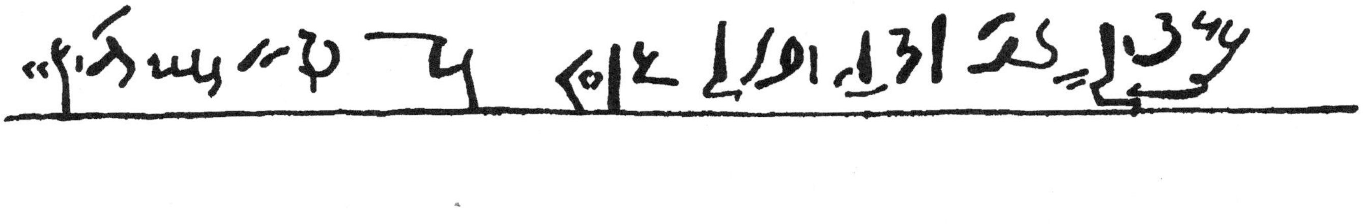

Die Stele verjüngt sich nach oben. Ihr Oberteil wurde zurückgeschnitten, so daß ein bogenförmiger Vorsprung entstanden ist.

Dargestellt ist eine stehende männliche Gestalt mit Chiton und Mantel. Beide Arme sind betend erhoben, wobei die Handflächen nach vorne gewendet sind. Die Figur ist frontal dargestellt, doch sind die Füße in Schrittstellung nach rechts gewendet. Links ist ein hockender Schakal und hinter ihm wohl eine stehende Mumie,[10] rechts ein Falke mit feinem Strich dargestellt.

Darunter sind zwei Linien geritzt. Über der oberen folgende Inschrift:

Pꜣ-ꜥḫm sꜣ Ḥr (mw.t⸗f)[a] *Tꜣ-šr(.t)-iḥj*[b] *rnp.t 7 hrw ibd 4 šmw sw 26*

"Pachomis, Sohn des Horos, (seine Mutter war) Senaies.[c] Sieben Jahre. Der Tag (seines Todes erfolgte) am 26. Mesore."

a. Der senkrechte Strich nach *Ḥr* bildet dessen Determinativ (vgl. TS 2025). Direkt danach beginnt der Muttersname. Es fehlt hier das übliche *mw.t⸗f* "seine Mutter."

b. Die männliche Form dieses Namens *Pꜣ-šr-iḥj* "Der Sohn des *iḥj* (des jugendlichen Horus)" notiert *Dem. Nb.* I, S. 227. Auf Grund der bilinguen Texten (BGU VI 1342; O. Edfu Inv. 2, Devauchelle und Wagner 1982, S. 99–100) weiß man, daß ihr griechisches Äquivalent Ψεναιῆς ist.

c. Die hier gebrauchte griechische Form ist von der obengenannten männlichen abzuleiten.

STELE V

TS 2003. (Pl. 43.2b)

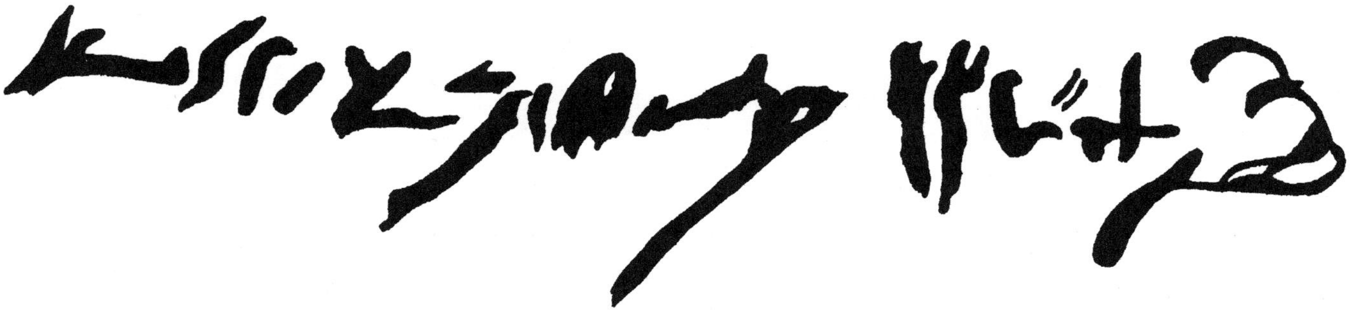

Rechteckige Stele mit unregelmäßigen Rändern. Relief und Inschrift sind von einer Umrahmung umgeben.

Dargestellt ist eine männliche Gestalt mit ausgestreckten Beinen, auf einer Kline gelagert. In der Rechten hält sie einen Becher, die Linke ist ohne Attribut. Der rechte Fuß ist im Profil über den linken von vorne sehr skizzenhaft dargestellt. Auf dem Reliefgrund ist ein liegender Schakal dargestellt. Auf der Kline liegen eine Matratze und zwei Kissen, alle mit schrägen Kannelen verziert. Die Klinenbeine sind gedrechselt. Vor der Kline von links nach rechts sind ein Blumenstrauß oder eine Getreidegarbe, ein Dreifußtisch und eine Amphora in einem Ständer dargestellt.

Darunter folgende Inschrift:

Wn-nfr iw⸗f ḫn rnp.t 40

"Onnophris. Er war 40 Jahre (alt)."[a]

a. Wörtlich: "Er war im 40. Jahr." Dies ist eine abgekürzte Form von *iw⸗f (iw⸗s) ḫn rnp.t (n) ꜥnḫ* × "Er (Sie) war im ×. Lebensjahr." Vgl. z.B. Mumientäfelchen Berlin 10628 (Möller 1913, Nr. 21). Siehe auch den ausführlicheren Ausdruck: *N. ir mwt iw⸗f (iw⸗s) ḫn*

10. Vgl. ähnliche Darstellung in TS 1049 (el-Nassery und Wagner 1978, S. 247, Nr. 28 und Tafel LXXVI).

rnp.t n ʿnḫ × "N. ist gestorben, als er (sie) im × Lebensjahr war" (vgl. z.B. Stele Kairo 31151, 2–3; Spiegelberg 1904, S. 60, Tafel XVIII); Mumientäfelchen Berlin 10630 (Möller 1913, Nr. 23). Über diese Wendungen siehe Spiegelberg 1901, S. 17; Möller 1913, S. 6.

STELE VI

TS 2025. (Pl. 43.2c)

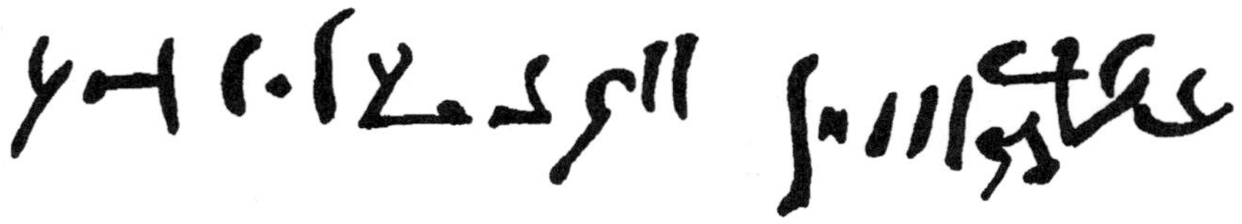

Stele mit unregelmäßigen Rändern. Der rechte Rand ist glatt gesägt. Das Relief und Inschrift sind von einer trapezoidalen Umrahmung umgeben.

Dargestellt ist eine stehende männliche Gestalt mit Chiton und Mantel. Beide Arme sind betend erhoben, wobei die Handflächen nach außen gewendet sind. Die Figur ist frontal wiedergegeben, die Füße sind in Schrittstellung nach rechts gewendet. An jeder Seite der Figur hockt ein Schakal.

Darunter folgende Inschrift:

Ḥr-tšj iw=f ir rnp.t 12

Ḥr-tšj.[a] Er lebte 12 Jahre."

a. Der Name ist bei *EDG*, S. 658, notiert.

Es bestehen keine Kennzeichen, die uns diese Denkmäler eindeutig datieren lassen. Eines von ihnen (TS 226) gibt aber als Todesdatum ihres Besitzers das 35. Regierungsjahr an, das sich nur auf die Herrschaft von Augustus, also auf das Jahr 5 n.Chr. beziehen kann. Eine der oben besprochenen Stelen (TS 1678) nennt das 33. Regierungsjahr. In diesem Fall ist das Datum nicht sicher, weil hier auch die Herrschaft von Commodus, also das Jahr 192 n.Chr. in Frage kommt. Das von Pestman (1967, S. 109) angefertigte chronologische Verzeichnis der demotischen Texte nennt eine griechisch-demotische Grabstele aus Theben aus dem 21. Regierungsjahr des Commodus (180/181),[11] aber sie ist die einzige datierte Stele aus einer so späten Periode. Dieser Umstand scheidet die so späte Datierung der Terenuthisstelen nicht aus, er kann aber darüber Zweifel erregen, weil die demotische Schrift bekanntlich seit dem 2. Jh.n.Chr. im Schwinden begriffen ist (Pestman 1967, S. 2–3). Da wir auf Grund der zugänglichen Fotos feststellen, daß die übrigen demotischen Terenuthisstelen weder im Charakter noch in der Ausführung von der aus der Zeit des Augustus abweichen, können wir mit großer Wahrscheinlichkeit annehmen, daß auch sie im 1. Jh.n.Chr. ausgeführt worden sind.

Diese Stelen enthalten dieselben Darstellungen und weisen dieselbe Werkstatt auf wie die griechischen Stelen. Ähnlich wie die griechischen Texte nennen die demotischen den Namen des Toten, gelegentlich den des Vaters oder der Mutter, sein Lebensalter und Todesdatum, wo das Regierungsjahr immer anonym ist. Es fällt auf, daß irgendwelche religiösen, aus den ägyptischen Grabstelen so gut bekannten Formeln und Darstellungen gänzlich fehlen.[12] Die Stelen mit demotischen Texten weisen keine näheren Beziehungen zu der ägyptischen Religion auf als die oben besprochenen Stelen mit griechischen Texten.

11. Es geht um die Stele Kairo 57057a (Spiegelberg 1932, S. 36–37, Tafel XVI; *SB* I 18).

12. Das Formular dieser Stelen erörtert Menu 1974, S. 69–70.

Die Ägypter bildeten sicherlich die Mehrzahl der Bevölkerung von Terenuthis. Die kleine Zahl der demotischen Stelen gibt deshalb zu denken. Sie ergibt sich nicht aus ihrer Herkunft aus dem ägyptischen, nicht genauer untersuchten Teil der Nekropole; ja, wir wissen nicht einmal, ob ein solch reinägyptischer Teil überhaupt bestanden hat. Vielmehr erlauben die identischen Darstellungen und die gemeinsame Provenienz der griechischen wie der demotischen Stelen aus der gleichen Werkstatt den Schluß, daß wir es mit einer einheitlichen Sozialgruppe zu tun haben. Die Ursachen der genannten Disproportion sind nicht in Terenuthis selbst zu suchen. Die Kenntnis des Griechischen gab während der Ptolemäerzeit und später manchen Schichten der ägyptischen Bevölkerung die Möglichkeit eines sozialen Aufstiegs. Wir beobachten auch eine Empfänglichkeit der Ägypter für die Hellenisierung, indem sie griechisch-ägyptische Doppelnamen annahmen. Eine andere Erscheinungsform desselben Prozesses war wohl der Gebrauch der griechischen Sprache auf den meisten Stelen. Es scheint nämlich, daß ihre Besitzer weder Griechisch sprechen, noch die auf den Grabsteinen angebrachten Namen gebrauchen mußten, zumindest nicht im Familien- oder Freundeskreis.

a

b

c

Demotische Stelen aus Terenuthis: (*a*) TS 1661; (*b*) TS 1678; (*c*) TS 1706.

a

b

c

Demotische Stelen aus Terenuthis: (*a*) TS 1736; (*b*) TS 2003; (*c*) TS 2025.

CHAPTER 44

EIN ZUG NACH NUBIEN UNTER AMASIS

KARL-THEODOR ZAUZICH
University of Würzburg

Unter dem Titel "Erwähnung eines Zuges nach Nubien unter Amasis in einem demotischen Text" hat Erichsen (1941, S. 56–61) ein kleines Papyrusfragment von 21 × 15 cm publiziert (P. Berlin 13615). Dieses hat trotz seines kurzen Textes eine erhebliche historische Bedeutung, weil es die einzige Quelle über eine sonst unbekannte Expedition nach Nubien im Jahre 529 v.Chr. ist (vgl. Kienitz 1953, S. 129f.). Zu diesem Fragment konnte ich vor etlichen Jahren zugehörige Stücke in der Papyrussammlung der Staatlichen Museen zu Berlin entdecken, die teils unter anderen Nummern inventarisiert waren, teils noch ohne Inventarnummern in Kisten lagerten. Nach kurzen Mitteilungen hierüber (Zauzich 1969, S. 46–47; Zauzich 1971, S. 40) konnte ich 1990 die Zusammensetzung der Fragmente abschließen, wobei mir die Papyrusrestauratorin der Sammlung, Frau Mirjam Krutzsch, in freundlicher Weise behilflich war und ein paar "joins" selbständig entdeckt hat. Dafür möchte ich ihr auch hier vielmals danken.

Nach der Zusammensetzung hat der Papyrus, der auch künftig unter der Nummer P. 13615 zitiert werden soll, eine Länge von rund 120 cm. An vielen Stellen ist die volle Höhe der Papyrusrolle mit 24,5 cm erhalten. Insgesamt umfaßt der Text jetzt neun Kolumnen, von denen sechs annähernd vollständig bewahrt sind.

Bei dem Symposion mit dem Titel "Life in a Multi-Cultural Society" in Chicago habe ich den gesamten Text in einer möglichst genauen Abzeichnung vorgelegt, den Aufbau des Textes demonstriert und einige ausgewählte Probleme diskutiert. Davon kann ich hier aus Platzgründen nur weniges wiederholen. Zugleich soll dies eine Vorschau auf die Publikation des Gesamttextes sein, die ich in baldiger Zukunft vorzulegen hoffe.

1. Durch die neuen Fragmente werden einige Korrekturen zu Erichsens oben genanntem Aufsatz möglich. Davon greife ich die Titel der an der Expedition beteiligten Personen heraus.

a) In Zeile 4a ist das von Erichsen ungelesene Wort nach mehreren anderen Belegen als *ṯꜣy-mtn* 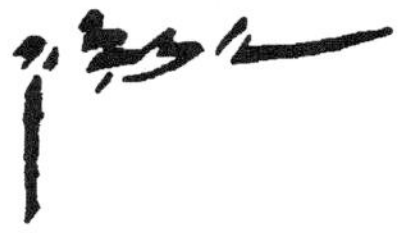 "Wegführer" (vgl. *mṯn Wb.* II,176 sowie ϪΙ ΜΟΕΙΤ *CD*, 188) zu erkennen. Er trägt ein Epitheton *rmt ḏm* ,[1] das ich mit einigem Zweifel als "Mann der Jungmannschaft" auffasse.

1. Hier abgezeichnet nach Kolumne II, 1. Vgl. *ḏꜣm* > ϪⲰΜ *Wb.* V,523. Die Übersetzung "Jungmannschaft" ist nur ein Notbehelf. In unserem Zusammenhang sollte *rmt ḏm*, wenn denn die Lesung stimmt, eher "Offizier" oder "Mann der Elitetruppe" o.ä. heißen. Gleiches Wort vielleicht im P. Rylands IX.19, 13.

b) Das von Erichsen in Z. 6b als *rmt qnqn* verstandene Wort ist nach anderen Stellen als  zu erkennen und m.E. als *swrt* zu lesen. Dieses Wort ist bereits aus den Papyri Louvre E 3333,3 und E 3334,1 bekannt (Ray 1977, S. 97ff.; Zauzich 1979, S. 122). Es ist dort der Titel eines für die Angelegenheiten des Ibis zuständigen Mannes. Im hier diskutierten Papyrus steht in Kolumne II,8 die Verbindung  *swrt n tꜣ ẖrpy*. Leider ist auch die Bedeutung von *ẖrpy* (*EDG*, 392) nicht sicher,[2] so daß die Berufsbezeichnung vorläufig nicht genau bestimmt werden kann. Ob *swrt* etwas mit dem "Träger" des *EDG*, S. 442 zu tun hat, ist ganz ungewiß.

c) Das von Erichsen in Z. 7b *mšʿ* gelesene Wort ist nach dem Vergleich mit anderen Stellen (z.B. Kolumne I,14b) eindeutig als *hyt*  "Matrose" (*EDG*, 269) zu bestimmen.

d) Schließlich bietet das in Z. 8b von Erichsen erkannte *rmt n pꜣ tꜣ nḥs* Probleme, da an einer Militärexpedition gegen Nubien eigentlich keine Nubier teilnehmen sollten. Das fragliche Wort kommt mehrfach in den neuen Fragmenten vor und läßt sich aus verschiedenen Stellen (Kolumne I,16b; Kolumne II,13 u.a.) so 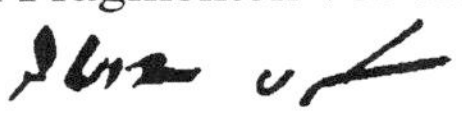 rekonstruieren. Eine Lesung *stm-mnṱ* erscheint mir danach zwingend. Das Wort ist jedoch völlig neu. Da es in unserem Text wiederholt nach anderen Ausländern wie *rmt H̱r* und *Išwr* erscheint, stelle ich zur Debatte, ob *stm-mnṱ* nicht eine unetymologische Schreibung für *st.tj(w)* "Asiat" (*Wb.* IV,348) und *mn.tj(w)* "Asiat" o.ä. (*Wb.* II,92) ist, also etwa *st(j) n mnṱ > stm-mnṱ*. Mehr als eine Vermutung kann dies freilich zur Zeit nicht sein.

2. An zweiter Stelle möchte ich ein Paar Worte zum Aufbau des Gesamttextes sagen. Die Aufzeichnungen waren ohne Zweifel dafür bestimmt, die Zahl und auch die Namen der Teilnehmer an der Expedition festzuhalten. Dabei wurde minutiös registriert, welche Personen zu den einzelnen Schiffen gehörten und welche an bestimmten Orten von Memphis bis Syene hinzugekommen oder abgegangen sind. In den ersten beiden Kolumnen erscheinen die Personen jedoch nur mit ihren Titeln, u.a. "Männer, die vor Pharao stehen" (*rmt iw=f ʿḥʿ m-bꜣḥ pr-ʿꜣ*), zu denen anscheinend auch ein "Schreiber des Lebenshauses" (*sẖ pr-ʿnḫ*) und ein Arzt (*swnw*) gehören. Einzig der "Wegführer" wird mit seinem Namen *Iʿḥ-ms sꜣ Wḏꜣ-ḥr-rsn* aufgeführt. Dieser muß ohne Zweifel ein wichtiger Mann gewesen sein, doch konnte ich ihn bisher nicht in anderen Quellen wiederfinden. Von Kolumne III an sind dann einzelne Schiffe[3] aufgelistet, die jeweils durch den Namen eines einzelnen Mannes näher bestimmt werden. Es folgen dann immer Listen mit Namen von Personen, die diesen Schiffen zugeordnet sind, wie z.B. 12 Schildträger (*rmt sbḫy*, Kolumne III, 11ff.) oder 10 Schildträger (Kolumne V, 2ff.), 14 Matrosen (*hyt*, Kolumne IV, 6ff.) oder 10 Matrosen (Kolumne V, 14ff.). Auch ein Lotse (*nfꜣ mw byn*) scheint zu jedem Schiff zu gehören, was bei einer Fahrt über den 1. Katarakt hinaus unumgänglich war.

2. Der zu heilende Körperteil(?) eines Kindes *ẖrpy.t* bei Reymond 1976, S. 86 und 144 hilft hier auch nicht weiter.

3. Schiff ist dabei eindeutig *rme* 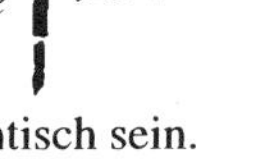 geschrieben (Kolumnen III, 1; V, 1; VII, 12), muß aber doch wohl trotzdem mit *rms* (*EDG*, 247) identisch sein.

Von großem Wert an diesen Listen sind die Personennamen, die zum Teil im demotischen Schrifttum neu sind. Als Beispiele hierfür seien erwähnt:

Wn-mtw=f-nḫt (Kolumne III, 14)[4] 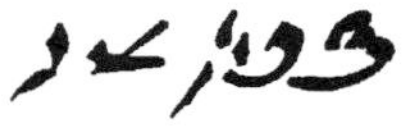

Nꜥ-n=f-bꜣst.t (Kolumne III, 18; vgl. V, 17)[5] 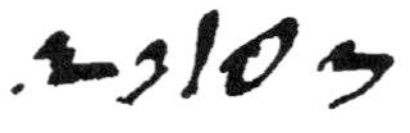

Ns-nꜣy=s (Kolumne IV, 10)[6] 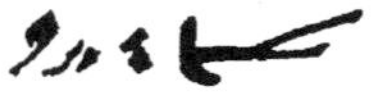

Daß sich unter den Namen auch Problemfälle befinden, wird niemanden überraschen. Dafür erwähne ich die beiden sicher miteinander vergleichbaren Namen in Kolumne IV, Zeile 12 und 15:

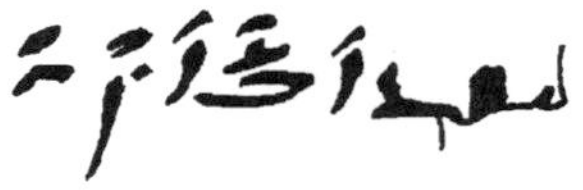 

Sollten dies womöglich entstellte Schreibungen für *Pꜣ-sbꜣ-ḫꜥ-n-nw.t* (Psusennes) sein (vgl. *PN* I 117.1 und Bonhême 1987, S. 73)?

3. An dritter Stelle meiner Ausführungen möchte ich kurz auf die Namen von 14 “Assyrern” (*Išwr*) zu sprechen kommen, die in den Kolumnen VI/VII einzeln aufgeführt werden. Diese Namen sind wahrscheinlich der interessanteste Teil des ganzen Textes und zugleich der schwierigste, weil die Bestimmung der den demotischen Transkriptionen zugrundeliegenden semitischen Namen vielfach problematisch sein dürfte.[7] Alle Namen sind, wie üblich, in der Form *A sꜣ B*, d.h. “A, Sohn des B” angegeben. Dabei lassen sich drei verschiedene Fälle unterschieden:

a) A und B sind fremde Namen

b) A ägyptischer Name, B fremder Name

c) A und B sind ägyptische Namen.

Da man davon wird ausgehen dürfen, daß ein “Assyrer” erst dann einen ägyptischen Namen erhielt, wenn er in Ägypten geboren wurde, kann man schließen, daß z.B. ein “Assyrer” namens *Wḏꜣ-ḥr-rsn*, Sohn des *Pꜣ-r.dy-wsir* (Kolumne VII, 3), mindestens in der 3. Generation in Ägypten ansässig war. Rechnen wir für eine Generation rund 25 Jahre, so kommen wir vom Datum unseres Textes 529 v.Chr. auf 604 v.Chr. zurück, d.h. in die zeitliche Nähe zum Untergang des assyrischen Reiches. Man kann daher mit aller gebotenen Vorsicht als Arbeitshypothese vorschlagen, daß die in unserem Papyrus erwähnten Assyrer Nachkommen von assyrischen Soldaten sind, die etwa zur Zeit der Feldzüge Nechos zum Euphrat oder nach seiner Niederlage gegen Nebukadnezar in den ägyptischen Dienst getreten sind.

4. Auch nicht bei *PN* I belegt, doch nach dem Muster *Wn-mdj=s-ḥs.t* (PN 78.28) gebildet.

5. Vgl. *Nꜥ-n=f-imn Dem. Nb.* I, 633 sowie *PN* I 182.17 und II, 366.

6. Der Name, der so keinen Sinn ergibt, ist gewiß eine unetymologische Schreibung für *Ns-nꜣ-is.t* (s. de Meulenaere 1962, S. 31ff.).

7. Ich werde hierfür die Hilfe anderer Kollegen erbitten, da meine eigene Kompetenz überschritten wird.

Die Bestimmung der fremden Namen steht, wie gesagt, in vielen Fällen noch aus. Dafür einige Beispiele:

Mškmt (Kolumne VI, 21)[8] 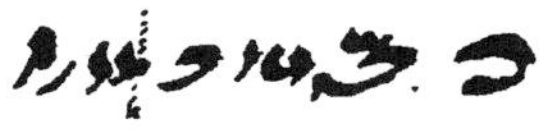

Mbkr (Kolumne VII, 1)[9] 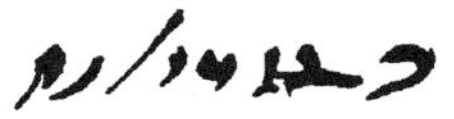

Šrtr (Kolumne VII, 2)[10] 

Bei der bekannten Großzügigkeit, mit der die Ägypter Ausländer unter manchmal wenig passenden Sammelbegriffen zusammengefaßt haben, muß natürlich nicht in jedem Fall wirklich ein assyrischer Name zugrundeliegen. So scheint ein *ʿyr* (Kolumne VI, 22)  doch wohl zum hebräischen Wort עַיִר "junger Esel" zu gehören,[11] und *ʿgbr* (Kolumne VII, 7)  könnte zu עַכְבָּר "Maus" oder besser עַכְבּוֹר gehören, was ebenfalls ein mehrfach im Alten Testament vorkommender Name (Septuaginta: Αχοβωρ u.ä.) ist, aber auch phönizisch belegt ist (Kornfeld 1978, S. 66).

Die vollständige Publikation dieses singulären Textes dürfte neben der historischen Information unsere Kenntnis über die Personennamen in der 26. Dynastie und über die seinerzeitigen Transkriptionsregeln für die demotische Wiedergabe fremder Namen ein gutes Stück voranbringen.

8. Zum eigentümlichen Fremddeterminativ s. Hughes 1984, S. 76–77.

9. Auch *Nbkr* ist möglich.

10. Sollte dies etwa *Šarru-dūri* "der König ist meine Schutzmauer" sein? Vgl. Kornfeld 1978, S. 75, s.v. *ŠRDR*.

11. Der Name עִירָא wurde von einem Priester Davids getragen (2. Sam. 20,26) und kommt auch sonst im Alten Testament vor.

LIST OF BIBLIOGRAPHIC ABBREVIATIONS*

AA	Archäologischer Anzeiger, Berlin
AAAHP	*Acta ad Archaeologiam et Artium Historiam Pertinentia*, Rome
AC	*L'Antiquité Classique*, Brussels
AcOr	*Acta Orientalia*. Ediderunt Societates Orientales Danica Norvegica Svecica (Le Monde Orientale), Copenhagen
Aegyptus	*Aegyptus. Rivista Italiana di Egittologia e Papirologia*, Milan
AfP	*Archiv für Papyrusforschung*, Leipzig and Berlin
AJSLL	*American Journal of Semitic Languages and Literatures*, Chicago
AJPh	*American Journal of Philology*, Baltimore
AMI	*Archäologische Mitteilungen aus Iran*, Berlin
ANRW	*Aufstieg und Niedergang der römischen Welt*, Berlin and New York
ArOr	*Archiv Orientální. Journal of the Czechoslovak Oriental Institute*, Prague
ASAE	*Annales du Service des Antiquités de l'Égypte*, Cairo
BASP	*Bulletin of the American Society of Papyrologists*, Chico, California
BASP Supp.	Bulletin of the American Society of Papyrologists, Supplement
BCH	*Bulletin de Correspondance Hellénique*, Athens and Paris
BdE	*Bibliothéque d'Étude*, Cairo
Berytus	*Berytus Archaeological Studies*, Copenhagen and Beirut
BES	*Bulletin of the Egyptological Seminar*, Brooklyn
BGU	Ägyptische Urkunden aus den Königlichen Museen zu Berlin — Griechischen Urkunden, Berlin
BICS	*Bulletin of the Institute of Classical Studies*, London
BIE	*Bulletin de l'Institut d'Égypt*, Cairo
BIFAO	*Bulletin de l'Institut Française d'Archéologie Orientale*, Cairo
BJRL	*Bulletin of the John Rylands Library*, Manchester
BL	*Berichtigungsliste der Griechischen Papyrusurkunden aus Ägypten*. 7 vols. Berlin and Leipzig: Walter de Gruyter and Leiden: E. J. Brill, 1922–86

* Please consult Oates et al. 1985 for a complete listing of standard abbreviations of Greek papyri and ostraca.

BLKon.	W. Clarysse, R. W. Daniel, F. A. J. Hoogendijk, and P. van Minnen, *Berichtigungsliste der Griechischen Papyrusurkunden aus Ägypten. Konkordanz und Supplement zu Band I–VII*. Louvain: Peeters, 1989
BSAE	The British School of Archaeology in Egypt, London
BSAEP	The British School of Archaeology in Egypt and The Egypt Research Account, Publications, London
BSEG	*Bulletin de la Société d'Égyptologie, Genève*, Geneva
BSFE	*Bulletin de la Société Française d'Égyptologie*, Paris
CASP	University of California Publications in Semitic Philology, Berkeley and Los Angeles
Cat. or *Catalogue*	*see* Carol A. R. Andrews 1990
CD	W. E. Crum, *A Coptic Dictionary*, 6 vols. Oxford: The Clarendon Press, 1929–34
CdE	*Chronique d'Égypte*, Brussels
CdK	*Cahiers de Karnak*, Paris
CDME	Raymond O. Faulkner, *A Concise Dictionary of Middle Egyptian*. Oxford: The Griffith Institute, 1962
CED	Jaroslav Černý, *Coptic Etymological Dictionary*. Cambridge: Cambridge University Press, 1976
CEML	*see* François Baratte and Bernard Boyaval 1974, 1975, 1976, and 1977
CGC	Catalogue Général des Antiquités égyptiennes du Musée du Caire
CJ	*The Classical Journal*, Gainesville, FL
Collectanea Hellenistica I	E. Van't Dack, W. Clarysse, G. Cohen, J. Quaegebeur, and J. K. Winnicki, *The Judean-Syrian-Egyptian Conflict of 103–101 B.C. A Multilingual Dossier Concerning a "War of Sceptres."* Brussels: Comité Klassieke Studies, Subcomité Hellenisme, Koninklijke Academie voor Wetenschappen, Letteren en Schone Kunsten van België, 1989
C. Ord. Ptol.	Marie-Thérèse Lenger, *Corpus des Ordannances des Ptolémées*. Académie royale de Belgique. Classe des Lettres. Memoires in 8°. 2e série, tome 57, fasc. 1. Brussels: Palais des Académies, 1964
C. Ord. Ptol.^{2}	Marie-Thérèse Lenger, *Corpus des Ordannances des Ptolémées*. Second Impression. Memoires de la Classe des lettres. Collection in-8°. 2e série, tome 64, fasc. 2. Brussels: Palais des Academies, 1980
*C. Ord. Ptol.**	Marie-Thérèse Lenger, *Corpus des Ordonnances des Ptolémées: Bilan des additions et corrections (1964–1988)*. Papyrologica Bruxellensia, vol. 24. Documenta et Opuscula, no. 11. Brussels : Fondation Égyptologique Reine Élisabeth, 1990
CPG I	Mariadele Manca Masciardi and Orsolina Montevecchi, *I contratto di biliatico*. Corpora Papyrorum Graecarum, vol. 1. Milan: n. p., 1984 [for CPG II, *see* Casarico 1985]

CPJ	Victor A. Tcherikover, Alexander Fuks, and Menahem Stern, *Corpus Papyrorum Judaicarum*. 3 vols. Cambridge, MA: Harvard University Press, 1957–64
CPR	Coprus Papyrorum Raineri, Vienna
CRAIBL	*Comptes Rendus des Séances de l'Académie des Inscriptions et Belles-Lettres*, Paris
CRIPEL	*Cahier de Recherches de l'Institut de Papyrologie et d'Égyptologie de Lille*, Lille
CW	*Classical World* (originally *Classical Weekly)*, New York
DELC	Werner Vycichl, *Dictionaire Étymologique de la Langue Copte*. Louvain: Peeters, 1984
Dem. Nb.	Erich Lüddeckens, *Demotisches Namenbuch*. 10 fascicles (to date). Wiesbaden: Dr. Ludwig Reichert Verlag, 1980–91
DG	Wilhelm Spiegelberg, *Demotische Grammatik*. Heidelberg: Carl Winters Universitätsbuchhandlung, 1925
DGT	Aristide Calderini, *Dizionario dei nomi geografici e topografici dell'Egitto greco-romano*, 5 vols. and 1 supplement. Cairo, Madrid, and Milan: Istituto Cisalpino - La Goliardica, 1935–88
DLE	Leonard H. Lesko, *A Dictionary of Late Egyptian*, 5 vols. Berkeley: B. C. Scribe Publications, 1982–90
EAO	Egyptian Antiquities Organization, Cairo
Edfu III	Émile Chassinat, *Le Temple d'Edfou*, volume 3. MMAF, vol. 20. Cairo: IFAO, 1928
Edfu V	Émile Chassinat, *Le Temple d'Edfou*, volume 5. MMAF, vol. 22. Cairo: IFAO, 1930
Edfu VII	Émile Chassinat, *Le Temple d'Edfou*, volume 7. MMAF, vol. 24. Cairo: IFAO, 1932
EDG	Wolja Erichsen, *Demotisches Glossar*. Kopenhagen: Ejnar Munksgaard, 1954
EDL I	Wolja Erichsen, *Demotische Lesestücke*, vol. 1 (in 3 parts). Leipzig: J. C. Hinrichs Verlag, 1937
EDL II	Wolja Erichsen, *Demotische Lesestücke*, vol. 2 (in 2 parts). Leipzig: J. C. Hinrichs Verlag, 1939
EdP	*Études de Papyrologie*, Cairo
EEF	Egypt Exploration Fund, London
EES	Egypt Exploration Society, London
EM	Excavation Memoirs of the Egypt Exploration Fund (Society), London
Enchoria	*Enchoria. Zeitschrift für Demotistik und Koptologie*, Wiesbaden
Eos	*Eos. Commentarii Societas Philologae Polonorum*, Warsaw
EpAn	*Epigraphica Anatolica. Zeitschrift für Epigraphik und historische Geographie Anatoliens*, Bonn

ER	*Egyptian Religion*, New York
EVO	*Egitto e Vicino Oriente*, Pisa
G-EL	Henry George Liddell, Robert Scott, and Sir Henry Stuart Jones, *A Greek-English Lexikon*, 2 vols. Cambridge: The Clarendon Press, 1940
GM	*Göttinger Miszellen*, Göttingen
GRM	Graeco-Roman Memoirs, London
HP I	Georg Möller, *Hieratische Paläographie. Die aegyptische Buchschrift in ihrer Entwicklung von der fünften Dynastie bis zur römischen Kaiserzeit. Erster Band: Bis zum beginn der achtzehnten Dynastie*. Leipzig: J. C. Hinrichs'sche Buchhandlung, 1909
HP II	Georg Möller, *Hieratische Paläographie. Die aegyptische Buchschrift in ihrer Entwicklung von der fünften Dynastie bis zur römischen Kaiserzeit. Zweiter Band: Von der Zeit Thutmosis' III bis zum Ende der einundzwanzigsten Dynastie*. Leipzig: J. C. Hinrichs'sche Buchhandlung, 1909
HP III	Georg Möller, *Hieratische Paläographie. Die aegyptische Buchschrift in ihrer Entwicklung von der fünften Dynastie bis zur römischen Kaiserzeit. Dritter Band: Von der zweiundzwanzigsten Dynastie bis zum dritten Jahrhundert nach Chr*. Leipzig: J. C. Hinrichs'sche Buchhandlung, 1912
ICS	*Illinois Classical Studies*, Urbana
IFAO	Institut Français d'Archéologie Orientale, Cairo
Inscr. Cret. IV	Margarita Guarducci, *Inscriptiones Creticae, Volume IV: Tituli Gortynii*. Rome: La Libreria dello Stato, 1950
I. Th. Sy.	André Bernand, *De Thèbes à Syène*. Paris: Editions du Centre National de la Recherche Scientifique, 1989
Iura	*Iura. Rivista Internazionale di Diritto Romano e Antico*, Naples
JA	*Journal Asiatique*, Paris
JARCE	*Journal of the American Research Center in Egypt*, New York
JD	Marcus Jastrow, *Hebrew–Aramaic–English Dictionary. A Dictionary of the Targumim, the Talmud Babli and Yerushalmi, and the Midrashic Literature*, 2 vols. New York and Berlin, 1926
JEA	*Journal of Egypian Archaeology*, London
JESHO	*Journal of the Economic and Social History of the Orient*, Leiden
JHS	*Journal of Hellenic Studies*, London
JJP	*Journal of Juristic Papyrology*, New York and Warsaw
JNES	*Journal of Near Eastern Studies*, Chicago
JRS	*Journal of Roman Studies*, London
JSS	*Journal of Semitic Studies*, Manchester
Kêmi	*Kêmi. Revue de Philologie et d'Archéologie Égyptiennes et Coptes*, Paris
KDG	Walter Till, *Koptische Dialektgrammatik*. Munich: C. H. Beck, 1931 (1st ed.), 1961 (2d ed.)

KG	Walter Till, *Koptische Grammatik.* Leipzig: Veb Verlag Enzyklopädie, 1961
KHwb	Wolfhart Westendorf, *Koptisches Handwörterbuch.* Heidelberg: Carl Winter Universitätsverlag, 1977
Klio	*Klio. Beiträge zur alten Geschichte*, Leipzig and Wiesbaden
KRI	K. A. Kitchen, *Ramesside Inscriptions: Historical and Biographical*, 8 vols. Oxford: B. H. Blackwell Ltd., 1975–90
Kush	*Kush. Journal of the Sudan Antiguities Service*, Khartoum
LÄ	Wolfgang Helck and Eberhard Otto, eds., *Lexikon der Ägyptologie*, 7 vols. Wiesbaden: Otto Harrassowitz, 1975–90
Man (NS)	*Man. The Journal of the Royal Anthropological Society of Great Britain and Ireland*, New Series, London
The Mariner's Mirror	*The Mariner's Mirror. The Journal of the Society for Nautical Research*, Greenwich, England
MBP	Münchener Beiträge zur Papyrusforschung und antiken Rechtsgeschichte, Munich
MDAIK	*Mitteilungen des Deutschen Archäologischen Instituts Abteilung Kairo*, Mainz am Rhein
MEFRA	*Mélanges de l'École Français de Rome, Antiquité*, Rome
MH I	The Epigraphic Survey, *Medinet Habu. Volume I: Earlier Historical Records of Ramses III*. OIP, vol. 8. Chicago: The University of Chicago Press, 1930
MH II	The Epigraphic Survey, *Medinet Habu. Volume II: Later Historical Records of Ramses III*. OIP, vol. 9. Chicago: The University of Chicago Press, 1932
MIFAO	Mémoires publiés par les Membres de l'Institut Français d'Archeologie Orientale, Cairo
MIO	*Mitteilungen des Instituts für Orientforschung*, Berlin
MMAF	Mémoires publiés par les Membres de la Mission Archéologique Français au Caire, Cairo
MMJ	*Metropolitan Museum Journal*, New York
Mnemosyne	*Mnemosyne. Bibliotheca Classica Batava, Series IV*, Leiden
MPER	Mitteilungen aus der Papyrussammlung der Österreichischen Nationalbibliothek (Papyrus Erzherzog Rainer), Neue Serie, Vienna
MRE	Monographies Reine Élisabeth, Brussels
MVG	*Mitteilungen der Vorderasiatischen Gesellschaft*, Leipzig
NAG	Adolf Erman, *Neuaegyptische Grammatik*. Leipzig: Verlag von Wilhelm Engelmann, 1933
Nb.	Friedrich Preisigke, *Namenbuch*. Heidelberg: Selbstverlag des Herausgebers, 1922
OA	Daniele Foraboschi, *Onomasticon Alterum Papyrologicum. Supplemento al Namenbuch di Friedrich Preisigke*. Testi e Documenti per lo Studio dell'Antichità, vol. 16 (Serie Papirologica, vol. 2). 4 vols. Milan: Istituto Editoriale Cisalpino, 1967–71

OCD	N. G. L. Hammond and H. H. Scullard, eds., *The Oxford Classical Dictionary*. 2d ed. Oxford: The Clarendon Press, 1970
ODN	Edda Bresciani, Sergio Pernigotti, and Maria C. Betrò, *Ostraka demotici da Narmuti*. Quaderni di Medinet Madi, vol. 1. Pisa: Guardini, 1983
OGIS	Wilhelm Dittenberger, *Orientis Graeci Inscriptiones Selectae*. 2 vols. Lipsiae: S. Hirzel, 1903–05
OINE	Oriental Institute Nubian Expedition, Chicago
OIP	Oriental Institute Publications, Chicago
OLA	Orientalia Lovaniensia Analecta, Louvain
OLP	*Orientalia Lovaniensia Periodica*, Louvain
OMM	Ostraca from Medinet Madi (Narmuthis)
OMRO	*Oudheidkundige Mededelingen uit het Rijksmusem van Oudheden te Leiden*, Leiden
Onoma	*Onoma. Bibliographic and Information Bulletin*, Louvain
ORANT	*Oriens Antiquus. Rivista del Centro per le Antichità e la Storia dell'Arte del Vicino Oriente*, Rome
Orientalia	*Orientalia. Commentarii Trimestres a Facultate Studiorum Orientis Antiqui Pontificii Instituti Biblici in Lucem Editi in Urbe*, Rome
PBA	*The Proceedings of the British Academy*, London
Phoenix (Toronto)	*Phoenix. Journal of the Classical Association of Canada*, Toronto
Phoenix (Leiden)	*Phoenix. Bulletin uitgegeven door het Vooraziatisch-Egyptisch Genootschap*, Leiden
PLB	Papyrologica Lugduno-Batava, Leiden
PMMA	Publications of the Metropolitan Museum of Art, New York
PN I	Hermann Ranke, *Die ägyptischen Personennamen. Band I: Verzeichnis der Namen*. Glückstadt: J. J. Augustin, 1935
PN II	Hermann Ranke, *Die ägyptischen Personennamen. Band II: Einleitung. Form und Inhalt der Namen. Geschichte der Namen. Vergleiche mit andren Namen. Nachträge und Zusätze zu Band I. Umschreibungslisten*. Glückstadt: J. J. Augustin, 1952
PN III	Hermann Ranke, *Die ägyptischen Personennamen. Band III: Verzeichnis der Bestandteile*. Glückstadt: J. J. Augustin, 1977
PSBA	*Proceedings of the Society of Biblical Archaeology*, London
PSI	Pubblicazioni della Società Italiana per la ricerca dei papiri greci e latini in Egitto. 15 vols., Florence
PUG	(= P. Univ. Giss.) H. Kling et al. *Mitteilungen aus der Papyrussammlung der Giessener Universitätsbibliotek*, 1924
RAPH	Recherches d'Archéologie, de Philologie et d'Histoire, Cairo
RB	*Revue Biblique*, Paris
RdE	*Revue d'Égyptologie*, Paris
RdL	*Revue du Louvre*, Paris

RdP	*Recherches de Papyrologie*, Paris
RdT	*Recueil de Travaux relatifs a la Philologie et a l'Archéologie Égyptiennes et Assyriennes*, Paris
RE	*Revue Égyptologique*, Paris
REG	*Revue des Études Grecques*, Paris
RIDA	*Revue Internationale des Droits de l'Antiquité*, Serie 3, Brussels
ROM	Royal Ontario Museum, Toronto
RSO	*Rivista degli Studi Orientali*, Rome
SAK	*Studien zur Altägyptischen Kultur*, Hamburg
SAKB	*Studien zur Altägyptischen Kultur Beihefte*, Hamburg
Sammelbuch or *SB*	Friedrich Preisigke et al., *Sammelbuch griechischer Urkunden aus Ägypten*, 14 vols. (to date), 1915–
SAOC	Studies in Ancient Oriental Civilization, Chicago
SASAE	Supplément aux Annales du Service des Antiquités de l'Égypt, Cairo
SCO	*Studi Classici e Orientali*, Pisa
SPAW	*Sitzungsberichte der preussichen Akademie der Wissenschaften*, Berlin
Sphinx	*Sphinx. Revue Critique. Embrassant le domaine entier de l'égyptologie*, Upsala
SSEAJ	*The Society for the Study of Egyptian Antiquities Journal*, Toronto
SYRIA	*SYRIA. Revue d'Art Oriental et d'Archéologie*, Paris
TAD A	B. Porten and A. Yardeni, *Textbook of Aramaic Documents from Ancient Egypt: Newly Copied, Edited and Translated into Hebrew and English*, Volume 1: *Letters*. Jerusalem: Department of the History of the Jewish People, The Hebrew University, 1986
TAD B	B. Porten and A. Yardeni, *Textbook of Aramaic Documents from Ancient Egypt: Newly Copied, Edited and Translated into Hebrew and English*, Volume 2: *Contracts*. Jerusalem: Department of the History of the Jewish People, The Hebrew University, 1989
TAD C	B. Porten and A. Yardeni, *Textbook of Aramaic Documents from Ancient Egypt: Newly Copied, Edited and Translated into Hebrew and English*, Volume 3: *Literature and Lists*. Jerusalem: Department of the History of the Jewish People, The Hebrew University, In Preparation
TAPA	*Transactions (and Proceedings) of the American Philological Association*, Lancaster, PA and Atlanta
TAVO	*Tübinger Atlas des Vorderen Orients*, Wiesbaden: Dr. Ludwig Reichert Verlag, 1991
Tryphon	*See* Biscottini 1966
Tyche	*Tyche. Beiträge zur Alten Geschichte, Papyrologie und Epigraphik*
UGAÄ	Untersuchungen zur Geschichte und Altertumskunde Ägyptens, Leipzig
Urk. I	Kurt Sethe, *Urkunden des Alten Reiches*. Urkunden des Ägyptischen Altertums, vol. 1. Leipzig: J. C. Hinrichs'sche Buchhandlung, 1903

Urk. II	Kurt Sethe, *Hieroglyphische Urkunden der griechisch-römischen Zeit.* Urkunden des Ägyptischen Altertums, vol. 2. Leipzig: J. C. Hinrichs'sche Buchhandlung, 1904
Urk. III	Heinrich Schäfer, *Urkunden der älteren Äthiopenkönige I.* Urkunden des Ägyptischen Altertums, vol. 3. Leipzig: J. C. Hinrichs'sche Buchhandlung, 1905
Urk. IV	Kurt Sethe and Wolfgang Helck, *Urkunden der 18. Dynastie.* Urkunden des Ägyptischen Altertums, vol. 4. Leipzig: J. C. Hinrichs'sche Buchhandlung, 1905–09
Urk. V	Hermann Grapow, *Religiöse Urkunden.* Urkunden des Ägyptischen Altertums, vol. 5. Leipzig: J. C. Hinrichs'sche Buchhandlung, 1915–17
Urk. VI	Siegfired Schott, *Urkunden mythologischen Inhalts nebst deutscher Übersetzung*. Urkunden des Ägyptischen Altertums, vol. 6. Leipzig: J. C. Hinrichs'sche Buchhandlung, 1929
Urk. VII	Kurt Sethe, *Historisch-Biographische Urkunden des Mittleren Reiches.* Urkunden des Ägyptischen Altertums, vol. 7. Leipzig: J. C. Hinrichs'sche Buchhandlung, 1935
Urk. VIII	Otto Firchow, *Thebanische Tempelinschriften aus griechisch-römischer Zeit.* Urkunden des Ägyptischen Altertums, vol. 8. Berlin: Akademie-Verlag, 1957
Wb.	Adolf Erman and Hermann Grapow, *Wörterbuch der Aegyptischen Sprache*, 7 vols. Leipzig: J. C. Hinrichs'sche Buchhandlung; Berlin: Akademie-Verlag, 1926–82
Wb. Beleg.	Adolf Erman and Hermann Grapow, *Wörterbuch der Aegyptischen Sprache. Die Belegstellen*, 5 vols. Leipzig: J. C. Hinrichs'sche Buchhandlung, 1935–53
W*Chres.*	*See* Wilcken 1912b
ZDMGS	Zeitschrift der Deutschen Morgenländischen Gesellschaft Supplement, Stuttgart
ZÄS	*Zeitschrift für ägyptische Sprache und Altertumskunde*, Leipzig and Berlin
ZPE	*Zeitschrift für Papyrologie und Epigraphik*, Bonn

BIBLIOGRAPHY

Abd el-Al, Abd el-Hafeez; Grenier, Jean-Claude; and Wagner, Guy

1985 *Stèles funéraires de Kom Abu Bellou.* Éditions Recherche sur les Civilisations, Memoire nº 55. Paris: Éditions Recherche sur les Civilisations.

Abd-El-Ghany, Mohamed E.

1989 "The Arabs in Ptolemaic and Roman Egypt through Papyri and Inscriptions," in *Egitto e storia antica dall' ellenismo all' età araba. Atti del Colloquio Internazionale, Bologna, 31 agosto – 2 settembre 1987*, edited by Lucia Criscuolo and Giovanni Geraci. Bologna: Cooperativa Libraria Universitaria Editrice, pp. 233–42.

Adams, William Y.

1977 *Nubia: Corridor to Africa.* London: Allen Lane.

Agel, Jerome and Glanze, Walter D.

1990 *Cleopatra's Nose, the Twinkie Defense, & 1500 Other Verbal Shortcuts in Popular Parlance.* New York: Prentice Hall Press.

Aldred, Cyril; Daumas, François; Desroches-Noblecourt, Christiane; and Leclant, Jean

1980 *L'Égypte du crépuscule de Tanis à Méroé 1070 av. J.-C. – IVe siècle apr. J.-C.* Le monde égyptien, Part 3: Les Pharaons. L'Univers des forms, vol. 28. Paris: Gallimard.

Alföldi-Rosenbaum, Elisabeth

1971 *Anamur Nekropolü: The Necropolis of Anemurium.* Türk Tarih Kurumu Yayinlarindan, Seri 6, no. 12. Ankara: Türk Tarih Kurumu Basımevi.

Allam, Schafik

1967 "Eine Abstandsurkunde aus der Zeit des Neuen Reiches," *JEA* 53: 47–50.

1973a *Hieratische Papyri und Ostraka aus der Ramessidenzeit.* Urkunden zum Rechtsleben im Alten Ägypten, vol. 1. Tübingen: Selbstverlag von des Herausgebers.

1973b *Das Verfahrensrecht in der altägyptischen Arbeitersiedlung von Deir el-Medinah.* Untersuchungen zum Rechsleben im Alten Ägypten, vol. 1. Tübingen: Selbstverlag von des Herausgebers.

1985 "Bemerkungen zur Abstandsschrift," *Enchoria* 13: 1–5.

1986 "Réflexions sur le <<Code légal>> d'Hermopolis dans l'Égypte ancienne," *CdE* 61: 50–75.

Allam, Schafik (*cont.*)

1990 "Women as Holders of Rights in Ancient Egypt (During the Late Period)," *JESHO* 33: 1–34.

1991 "Glossen zu einem schiedsrichterlichen Verfahren," *MDAIK* 47: 1–9.

Almagro, M. and Presedo, F.

1976 "The Most Recent Findings at Herakleopolis Magna," in *Abstracts of Papers. First International Congress of Egyptology. Cairo, October 2, 1976*, edited by Dietrich Wildung. Munich: Karl M. Lipp, pp. 3–5.

al-Maqrizi, Ahmad Ibn Ali

1853 *Kitâb Al-Mawâʾiẓ wal-Iʿtibâr bi-Dhikr al-Khitat wal-Âthâr*. Cairo.

Anderson, Graham, trans.

1989 "Xenophon of Ephesus: An Ephesian Tale," in *Collected Ancient Greek Novels*, edited by B. P. Reardon. Berkeley: The University of California Press, pp. 125–69.

Andrews, Carol A. R.

1988 "The Sale of Part of a Pathyrite Vineyard (P. BM 10071)," in *Pyramid Studies and other Essays Presented to I. E. S. Edwards*, edited by John Baines, T. G. H. James, Anthony Leahy, and A. F. Shore. Occasional Publications, no. 7. London: EES, pp. 193–99.

1990 *Catalogue of Demotic Papyri in the British Museum IV: Ptolemaic Legal Documents from the Theban Area*. London: British Museum Publications.

Andrieu, J., ed.

1954 *Le dialogue antique. Structure et presentation*. Collection d'Études Latines, Serie Scientifique, fascicle 29. Paris: Les Belles Lettres.

Apuleius

1965 *The Golden Ass*, translated by Jack Lindsay. Bloomington: Indiana University Press.

Arangio-Ruiz, Vincenzo

1930 *Persone e famiglia nel diritto dei papiri*. Pubblicazioni della Universita cattolica del Sacro cuore, Series 2: Scienze giuridiche, vol. 26. Milan: Societa Editrice "Vita e Pensiero."

Assmann, Jan

1985 "Gibt es eine 'Klassik' in der ägyptischen Literaturgeschichte? — Ein Beitrag zur Geistesgeschichte der Ramessidenzeit," in *XXII. Deutscher Orientalistentag vom 21. bis 25. März 1983 in Tübingen*, edited by Wolfgang Röllig. ZDMGS, vol. 6. Stuttgart: Franz Steiner Verlag Wiesbaden GmbH, pp. 35–52.

Avi-Yonah, Michael

1961 *Art in Roman Palestine*. Studi Semitici, vol. 5. Rome: Centro di Studi Semitici.

Badawy, Alexander

1978 *Coptic Art and Archaeology: The Art of the Christian Egyptians from the Late Antique to the Middle Ages*. Cambridge, MA: The MIT Press.

Bagnall, Roger S.

1973 "Three Notes on Ptolemaic Inscriptions," *ZPE* 11: 121–27.

1976 *The Administration of the Ptolemaic Possessions Outside Egypt*. Leiden: E. J. Brill.

1978 "Notes on Greek and Egyptian Ostraca," *Enchoria* 8: 143–50.

1981 "Egypt, the Ptolemies, and the Greek World," *BES* 3: 5–21.

1984 "The Origins of the Ptolemaic Cleruchs," *BASP* 21: 7–20.

1985 "The Camel, the Wagon, and the Donkey in the Later Roman Egypt," *BASP* 22: 1–6.

1988 "Greeks and Egyptians: Ethnicity, Status, and Culture," in *Cleopatra's Egypt: Age of the Ptolemies*, edited by R. S. Bianchi. Brooklyn: The Brooklyn Museum, pp. 21–27.

—— *Egypt in Late Antiquity*. Princeton: Princeton University Press, forthcoming (1993: Professor Bagnall's Symposium paper, "Language, Literacy, and Ethnicity in Late Roman Egypt," will make up elements of Chapter 7 of this book).

Bagnall, Roger S. and Samuel, Alan E.

1976 *Ostraka in the Royal Ontario Museum II*. American Studies in Papyrology, vol. 15. Toronto: Samuel Stevens Hakkert and Company.

Baines, John

1983 "Literacy and Ancient Egyptian Society," *Man (NS)* 18: 572–99.

1988 "Literacy, Social Organization, and the Archaeological Record: The Case of Early Egypt," in *State and Society: The Emergence and Development of Social Hierarcy and Political Centralization*, edited by John Gledhill, Barbara Bender, and Mogens Trolle Larsen. One World Archaeology, vol. 4. London: Unwin Hyman, pp. 192–214.

Balconi, Carla

1984 "Απογραφαί προβάτων καί αἰγῶν dell' età di Tiberio e Caligola," *Aegyptus* 64: 35–60.

Baratte, François and Boyaval, Bernard

1974 "Catalogue des étiquettes de momies du Musée du Louvre (C.E.M.L.) - textes grecs," *CRIPEL* 2: 155–264.

1975 "Catalogue des étiquettes de momies du Musée du Louvre (C.E.M.L.) - textes grecs - 2ème partie," *CRIPEL* 3: 151–261.

1976 "Catalogue des étiquettes de momies du Musée du Louvre (C.E.M.L.) - textes grecs - 3ème partie," *CRIPEL* 4: 173–254.

1977 "Catalogue des étiquettes de momies du Musée du Louvre (C.E.M.L.) - textes grecs - 4ème partie," *CRIPEL* 5: 237–339.

Bataille, André

1952 *Les memnonia. Recherches de papyrologie d'épigraphie grecques sur la nécropole de la Thèbes d'Égypte aux époques hellenistique et romaine*. RAPH, vol. 32. Cairo: IFAO.

Beaux, Nathalie

1988 "Étoile et étoile de mer: une tentative d'identification du signe ⋆," *RdE* 39: 197–204.

Beckwith, John

1963 *Coptic Sculpture 300–1300*. London: Alec Tiranti.

Beinlich, Horst

1990 "Spätzeitquellen zu den Gauen Unterägyptens," *GM* 117/118: 59–88.

Bell, H. I.

1943 "Comments on the Foregoing," *JEA* 29: 46–50.

1947 "The *Constitutio Antoniniana* and the Egyptian Poll Tax," *JRS* 37: 17–23.

Bellion, Madeleine

1987 *Égypte ancienne. Catalogue des manuscrits hiéroglyphiques et hiératiques et des dessin sur papyrus, cuir ou tissu publié ou signalés*. Paris: Madeleine Bellion.

Belon, Pierre

1970 *Voyage en Égypte de Pierre Belon du Mans, 1547*, edited by Serge Sauneron. Cairo: IFAO.

Bengston, Herman

1967 *Die Strategie in der hellenistischen Zeit: Ein Beitrag zum antiken Staatsrecht, Dritter Band*. MBP, vol. 36. Munich: C. H. Beck'sche Verlagsbuchhandlung.

Berger, Adolf

1911 *Die Strafklauseln in den Papyrusurkunden. Ein Beitrag zum gräko-ägyptischen Obligationenrecht*. Leipzig: B. G. Teubner.

Berger, Jacques-Edouard; Parlasca, Klaus; and Pintaudi, Rosario

1985 *El-Fayyum*. Milan: Franco Maria Ricci.

Bernand, André

1970 *Le delta égyptien d'après les textes grecs. Tome 1: Les confins libyques*. MIFAO, vol. 91. Cairo: IFAO.

Bernand, Etienne

1969 *Les inscriptions métriques d'Égypte gréco-romaine. Recherches sur la poésié épigrammatique des grecs en Égypte*. Annales Littéraires de l'Université de Besançon, vol. 98. Paris: Les Belles Lettres.

1975 *Recueil des inscriptions grecques du Fayoum, I: La "meris" d'Hérakleidès*. Leiden: E. J. Brill.

1979 "Épigraphie greque et histoire des cultes au Fayoum," in *Hommages à la mémoire de Serge Sauneron. Tome II: Égypte post-pharaonique*, edited by J. Vercoutter. BdE, vol. 82. Cairo: IFAO, pp. 57–76.

1981a *Recueil des inscriptions grecques du Fayoum. Tome II: La "meris" de Thémistos*. BdE, vol. 79. Cairo: IFAO.

1981b *Recueil des Inscriptions Grecques du Fayoum, Tome III: La "meris" de Polémôn*. BdE, vol. 80. Cairo: IFAO.

Betrò, M. Carmela

1984 "Due tavolette demotiche e il P. gr. Amherst II 31," *EVO* 7: 41–60.

Bevan, Edwyn Robert

1927 *A History of Egypt under the Ptolemaic Dynasty*. A History of Egypt, vol. 4, edited by W. M. Flinders Petrie. London: Methuen and Company.

1968 *The House of Ptolemy*. Chicago: Argonaut.

Bianchi, Robert S., ed.
1988 *Cleopatra's Egypt: Age of the Ptolemies*. Brooklyn: The Brooklyn Museum.

Biedermann, E.
1913 *Studien zur Ägyptische Verwaltungsgeschichte in ptolemäische-Römische Zeit*. Ph.D. dissertation, Berlin.

Bietak, Manfred
1988 "Zur Marine des Alten Reiches," in *Pyramid Studies and Other Essays Presented to I. E. S. Edwards*, edited by John Baines, T. G. H. James, Anthony Leahy, and A. F. Shore. London: EES, pp. 35–40.

Bilabel, Friedrich
1923 "Siglae," in *Paulys Real-Encyclopädie der classischen Altertumswissenschaft. Zweite Reihe [R–Z], Vierter Halband: Selinuntia – Sila*, edited by Wilhelm Kroll and Kurt Witte. Stuttgart: J. B. Metzlersche Verlagsbuchhandlung, cols. 2279–2315.

Bingen, Jean
1946 "Les colonnes 60–72 du P. Revenue Laws et l'aspect fiscal du monopole des huiles," *CdE* 21: 127–48.

1949 "Les papyrus de la Fondation Égyptologique Reine Élisabeth, XIII, " *CdE* 24: 306–12.

1968 Review of *Partage testamentaire d'une propriété familiale (Pap. Moscou n° 123)* by Michel Malinine. *CdE* 43: 421–23.

1970 "Grecs et egyptiens d'après PSI 502," in *Proceedings of the Twelfth International Congress of Papyrology*, edited by Deborah H. Samuel. American Studies in Papyrology, vol. 7. Toronto: A. M. Hakkert Ltd., pp. 35–40.

1973 "Présence grecque et milieu rural ptolémaïque," in *Problèmes de la terre en Grèce ancienne*, edited by M. I. Finley. Civilisations et Sociétés, Tome 33. Paris: Mouton & Co., pp. 215–22.

1978a *Le Papyrus Revenue Laws: tradition grecque et adaptation hellenistique*. Vortrage: Rheinisch-Westfalische Akademie der Wissenschaften: Geisteswissenschaften, G 231.

1978b "The Third-Century B.C. Land-leases from Tholthis," *ICS* 3: 74–80.

1979 "Kerkéosiris et ses grecs au IIe siècle avant notre ère," in *Actes du XVe congrès international de papyrologie, Tome IV: Papyrologie documentaire*, edited by Jean Bingen and Georges Nachtergael. Papyrologica Bruxellensia, vol. 19. Brussels: Fondation Égyptologique Reine Élisabeth, pp. 87–94

1983 "Les cavaliers catoeques de l'Héracléopolite au 1er siècle," in *Egypt and the Hellenistic World. Proceedings of the International Colloquium, Louvain — 24–26 May 1982*, edited by E. Van't Dack, P. von Dessel, and W. van Gucht. Studia Hellenistica, vol. 27. Louvain: Orientaliste, pp. 1–11.

1987 "La série *kappa* des stelès de Térénouthis," in *Studia Varia Bruxellensia ad Orbem Graeco-latinum Pertinentia*, edited by R. de Smet, H. Melaerts, and C. Saerens. Louvain: Peeters, pp. 3–14.

Bingen, Jean (*cont.*)

1989a "Vente de terre par Pétéharsemtheus (Pathyris, 100 av. J.-C.)," *CdE* 64: 235–44.

1989b "Épitaphes chrétiennes grecques d'Hermonthis," *CdE* 64: 365–67.

1989c "Rapport sur le XIXe congrès international de papyrologie," *Bulletin de la Classe des Lettres et des Sciences Morales et Politiques*, 5e série, tome 75. Brussels: Académie Royale de Belgique, pp. 473–77.

1991 *Pages d'épigraphie grecque: Attique-Égypte (1952–1982)*. Epigraphica Bruxellensia, vol. 1. Brussels: Epigraphica Bruxellensia.

Bingen, Jean and Clarysse, Willy

1989 *Elkab III. Les ostraca grecs (O. Elkab gr.)*. Brussels: Fondation Égyptologique Reine Élisabeth.

Biscottini, Maria Valentina

1966 "L'archivio di Tryphon, tessitore di Oxyrhynchos," *Aegyptus* 46: 60–90, 186–292.

Bleeker, Claas Jouco

1967 *Egyptian Festivals: Enactments of Religious Renewal*. Studies in the History of Religion, vol. 12. Leiden: E. J. Brill.

Boak, Arthur E. R.

1935 *Soknopaiou Nessos. The University of Michigan Excavations at Dimê in 1931–32*. The University of Michigan Humanistic Series, vol. 39. Ann Arbor: The University of Michigan Press.

Bodanis, David

1986 *The Secret House*. New York: Simon and Schuster, Inc.

Bogaert, Raymond

1988 "Liste chronologique des banquiers royaux thébains 255–84 avant J.-C.," *ZPE* 75: 115–38.

1989 "Listes de taxes et banques dans l'Égypte romaine," *ZPE* 79: 207–26.

Bonhême, Marie-Ange

1987 *Les noms royaux dans l'Égypte de la troisième période intermédiaire*. BdE, vol. 98. Cairo: IFAO.

Bonino, Marco

1978 "Lateen-rigged Medieval Ships. New Evidence from Wrecks in the Po Delta (Italy) and Notes on Pictorial and other Documents," *The International Journal of Nautical Archaeology and Underwater Exploration* 7: 9–28.

Bonneau, Danielle

1964 *La crue du Nil. Divinite egyptienne a travers mille aus d'histoire (332 av. –641 ap. J.-C.)*. Paris: Librairie C. Klincksieck.

1971 *Le fisc et le Nil. Incidence des irrégularités de la crue du Nil sur la fiscalité fancière dans l'Égypte greque et romaine*. Paris Editions Cujas.

1979a *Le egyptologie en 1979. Axes prioritaires de recherches, I*. Colloques internationaux du Centre de la Recherche Scientifique, no. 595. Paris: Editions du Centre National de la Recherche Scientifique.

1979b "Ptolémaïs Hormou dans la documentation papyrologique," *CdE* 54: 310–26.

Borchardt, Ludwig
1930 *Statuen und Statuetten von Königen und Privatleuten, vol. 3, Nos. 1–1294*. CGC, vol. 9. Berlin: Reichsdruckerei.

Boreux, Charles
1924 *Études de nautique égyptienne: L'Art de la navigation en Égypte jusqu'à la fin de l'ancien empire.* MIFAO, vol. 50. Cairo: IFAO.

Boswinkel, Ernst
1983 "Die Araber im Zenon-Archiv," in *Araber in Ägypten: Freundesgabe für Helene Loebenstein zum 65. Geburtstage.* Vienna: n. p., pp. 27–37.

Boswinkel, E. and Pestman, P. W.
1982 *Les archives privées de Dionysios, fils de Kephalas (P. L. Bat. 22). Textes grecs et démotiques.* 2 vols. PLB, vols 22A–B. Leiden: E. J. Brill.

Bothmer, Bernard V.
1987 "Ancestral Bust," in *Antiquities from the Collection of Christos G. Bastis*, edited by Emma Swann Hall. Mainz am Rhine: Verlag Philipp von Zabern, pp. 24–29.

1988 "Egyptian Antecedents of Roman Republican Verism," *Ritratto ufficiale e ritratto privato. Atti della II Conferenza Internazionale sul Ritratto Romano, Roma, 26–30 Settembre 1984*, edited by Nicola Bonacasa and Giovanni Rizza. Quaderni de la "ricerca scientifica," vol. 116. Rome: Consiglio Nazionale della Ricerche, pp. 47–65.

Bothmer, Bernard V.; de Meulenaere, Herman; and Müller, Hans Wolfgang
1960 *Egyptian Sculpture of the Late Period.* Brooklyn: The Brooklyn Museum.

Botti, Giuseppe
1900 *Ville d'Alexandrie (Égypte), catalogue des monuments exposés au Musée Gréco-romain d'Alexandrie.* Alexandria: The Graeco-Roman Museum.

Botti, Guiseppe
1956 "Papyri demotici dell'epoca imperiale da Tebtynis," in *Studi in onore di Aristide Calderini e Roberto Paribeni, Volume II: Studi di papyrologia e di antichità orientali.* Milan: Ceschina, pp. 75–86.

1959 *La Glorificazione di Sobk e del Fayyum in un papiro ieratico da Tebtunis.* Analecta Aegyptiaca, vol. 8. Copenhagen: Ejnaar Munksgaard.

Bouché-Leclercq, A.
1903 *Histoire des Lagides. Tome I: Les cinq premiers Ptolémées (323–181 avant J.-C.).* Paris: Ernest Leroux, Éditeur.

Bouriant, Urbain
1890 "Notes de voyage," *RdT* 13: 153–79.

Bowersock, G. W.
1983 *Roman Arabia.* Cambridge, MA: Harvard University Press.

1986 "Rostovtzeff in Madison," *The American Scholar* 55 (Summer): 391–400.

1990 *Hellenism in Late Antiquity.* Ann Arbor: The University of Michigan Press.

Bowman, Alan K.
1985 Review of *Genesi della provincia roma d'Egitto* by Giovanni Gerasi. *JRS* 75: 285–86.

Bowman, Alan K. (*cont.*)

1986 *Egypt After the Pharaohs. 332 BC–AD 642: from Alexander to the Arab Conquest.* London: British Museum Publications Limited.

Boyaval, Bernard

1973 "Papyrus ptolémaïques inédits de Ghôran et Magdôla," *CRIPEL* 1: 185–285.

1976 *Corpus des étiquettes de momies grecques*. Villeneuve-D'ascq: Université de Lille.

Boyd, Susan and Vikan, Gary

1981 *Question of Authenticity among the Arts of Byzantium: Catalogue of an Exhibition held at Dumbarton Oaks*. Dumbarton Oaks, Byzantine Collections Publications, no. 3. Washington, D.C.: Dumbarton Oaks.

Braemer, François

1984 "Un apport de l'Égypte à la narbonnaise dans la technique sculpturale," in *Alessandria e il mondo ellenistico-romano: Studi in onore di Achille Adriani*, edited by Giuseppina Barone, Elena Epifanio, Caterina Greco, and Antonella Mandruzatto. 3 vols. Studi e Materiali, Istituto di Archeologia, Università di Palermo, vols. 4–6. Rome: "L'Erma" di Bretschneider, pp. 421–29.

Brashear, William M.

1980 *Ptolemäische Urkunden aus Mumienkartonage*. Urkunden aus den Staatlichen Museen zu Berlin, Griechische Urkunden, Band 14. Berlin: Staatliche Museen Preussischer Kulturbesitz.

Braun, Martin

1938 *History and Romance in Graeco-Oriental Literature*. Oxford: Basil Blackwell.

Braunert, Horst

1956 "IΔIA: Studien zur Bevölkerungs geschichte de ptolemäischen Ägypten," *JJP* 9/10: 211–328.

1964 *Die Binnenwanderung. Studien zur Sozialgeschichte Aegyptens in der Ptolemäer- und Kaiserzeit*. Bonner historische Forschungen, Band 26. Bonn: Ludwig Röhrscheid Verlag.

Breasted, James H.

1905 *A History of Egypt*. New York: Charles Scribner's Sons.

Breccia, Evaristo

1932 *Le Musee Greco-Romain 1925–31*. Bergamo: Istituto Italiano d'Arti Grafiche.

1933 *Le Musee Greco-Romain 1931–32*. Bergamo: Istituto Italiano d'Arti Grafiche.

Brémond, Gabriel

1974 *Voyage en Égypte de Gabriel Brémond, 1643-1645*, edited by Georges Sanguin. Cairo: IFAO.

Bresciani, Edda

1960 "Due stele demotiche del Museo del Cairo," *SCO* 9: 119–26.

1963 "Testi demotici nella Collezione Michaelidis," *ORANT* 2: 1–26.

1964 *Der Kampf um der Panzer des Inaros (Papyrus Krall)*. MPER, vol. 8. Vienna: Georg Prachner Verlag.

1980 *Kom Madi 1977 e 1978. Le pitture murali del cenotafio di Alessandro Magno*. Serie archeologica, vol. 1. Pisa: Giardini.

1984 "Testi lessicali demotici inediti da Tebtuni presso l'Istituto Papirologico G. Vitelli di Firenze," in *Grammata Demotika. Festschrift für Erich Lüddeckens zum 15. Juni 1983*, edited by Heinz-Josef Thissen and Karl-Theodor Zauzich. Würzburg: Gisela Zauzich Verlag, pp. 1–9.

1990a *Letteratura e poesia dell'antico Egitto*. 2d ed. Turin: Giulio Einaudi.

1990b "La corazza di Inaro era fatta con la pelle del grifone del Mar Rosso," *EVO* 13: 103–07.

Bresciani, Edda and Pestman, P. W.

1965 *Papiri della Università degli studi di Milano (P. Mil. Vogliano)*. vol 3. Milan: Instituto Editoriale Cisalpino.

Bresciani, E. and Pintaudi, R.

1987 "Textes démotico-grecs et greco-démotiques des ostraca de Medinet Madi: un problème de bilinguisme," in *Aspects of Demotic Lexicography: Acts of the Second International Conference for Demotic Studies, Leiden, 19–21 September 1984*, edited by S. P. Vleeming. Studia Demotica 1. Louvain: Peeters, pp. 123–26.

Bresciani, Edda; Pernigotti, Sergio; and Betrò, Maria C.

1983 *Ostraka demotici da Narmuti I (nn 1–33)*. Quaderno di Medinet Madi, vol. 1. Pisa: Giardini.

Brewster, Ethel Hampson

1927 "A Weaver of Oxyrhynchus: Sketch of a Humble Life in Roman Egypt," *TAPA* 58: 132–54.

1931 "A Weaver's Life in Oxyrhynchus," in *Classical Studies in Honor of John C. Rolfe*, edited by George DePue Hadzsits. Philadelphia: University of Pennsylvania Press, pp. 19–45.

1935 "In Roman Egypt," *CW* 29: 25–29

Brugsch, H.

1871 "Ein Decret Ptolemaios' des Sohnes Lagi, des Satrapen," *ZÄS* 9: 1–13.

Brunner, Hellmut

1957 *Altägyptische Erziehung*. Wiesbaden: Otto Harrassowitz.

1966 *Grundzüge einer Geschichte der altägyptischen Literatur*. Darmstadt: Wissenschaftliche Buchgesellschaft.

Brunsch, Wolfgang

1977 Review of *Le Dieu Egyptien Shaï dans la Religion et l'Onomastique* by Jan Quaegebeur. *Enchoria* 7: 211–13.

1978 "Untersuchungen zu den griechischen Wiedergaben ägyptischer Personennamen," *Enchoria* 8: 1–142.

1984 "Index zu HEUSERs 'Personennamen der Kopten,'" *Enchoria* 12: 119–53.

1987–88 "Zwei demotische Texte aus Hamburg," *OrSu* 36–37: 5–9.

Bunnens, Guy

1985 "Le luxe phénicien d'après les inscriptions royales assyriennes," in *Phoenicia and its Neighbours*, edited by E. Gubel and E. Lipiński, Studia Phoenicia, vol. 3. Louvain: Uitgeverij Peeters, pp. 121–33.

Burkard, Günter

1977 *Textkritische Untersuchungen zu altägyptischen Weisheitslehren des alten und mittleren Reiches*. Ägyptologische Abhandlungen, Band 34. Wiesbaden: Otto Harrassowitz.

1980 "Bibliotheken im alten Ägypten," *Bibliothek, Forschung und Praxis* 4: 79–115.

Burton, Anne

1972 *Diodorus Siculus Book I: A Commentary*. Leiden: E. J. Brill.

Butin, J.-M. and Schwartz, J.

1985 "*Post Philonis Legationem*," *Revue d'histoire et de philosophie religieuse* 65: 127–29

Cadell, Helene

1966 *Papyrus de la Sorbonne*. Publications de la Faculte des Lettres et Sciences humaines de Paris. Serie "Textes et documents," Tome 10. Paris: Presses Universitaires de France.

Calderini, Aristide

1938 "Censimento topografico delle banche dell'Egitto greco-romano," *Aegyptus* 18: 244–78.

Calderini, Rita

1941 "Richerche sul doppio nome personale nell'Egitto greco-romano," *Aegyptus* 21: 221–60.

1942 "Richerche sul doppio nome personale nell'Egitto greco-romano," *Aegyptus* 22: 3–45.

Cannuyer, Christian

1988 Review of *Les Leçons de Silvanos (*NH VII, *4)* by Yvonne Janssens. *CdE* 63: 198–201.

1990 "Encore le naufrage du *Naufragé*," *BSEG* 14: 15–21.

Casanova, P.

1901 "Un texte arabe transcrit en caractères coptes," *BIFAO* 1: 1–20.

Casarico, Loisa

1983 "Papiri documentari dell'Università Cattolica di Milano: Frammento di ΔΙΕΚΒΟΛΗ," *Aegyptus* 63: 44–44.

1985 *Il controllo della popolazione nell'egitto romano: 1. Le denunce di morte*. CPG, vol. 2. Azzate: Tipolitografia Tibiletti s. n. c.

Casson, Lionel

1971 *Ships and Seamanship in the Ancient World.* Princeton: Princeton University Press.

Cauville, Sylvie

1983 *La théologie d'Osiris à Edfou*. BdE, vol. 91. Cairo: IFAO.

1987 *Essai sur la théologie du temple d'Horus a Edfou II: catalogue des divinités*. BdE, vol. 102. Cairo: IFAO.

Chappaz, Jean-Luc
1989 "Remarques sur un exercice scolaire," *BSEG* 13: 33–43.

Charles, Robert Henry
1916 *The Chronicle of John, Bishop of Nikiu*. London: Williams and Norgate.

Černý, Jaroslav and Gardiner, Alan H.
1957 *Hieratic Ostraca, Volume I*. Oxford: The Griffith Institute.

Cheshire, Wendy
1986 "Demotic Writings of 'Tebtynis,'" *Enchoria* 14: 31–42.

Chevereau, Pierre-Marie
1985 *Prosopographie des cadres militaires égyptiens de la basse époque. Carrières militaires et carrières sacerdotales en Égypte du XIe au IIe siècle avant J.-C.* Paris: Pierre-Marie Chevereau.

Christensen, Thorkild Fogh
1983 "Comments on the Stela AEIN 1037 (E 872; A 752) Ny Carlsberg Glyptotek, Copenhagen," *GM* 65: 7–24.

Clarysse, Willy
1974 "The nomarchs Abat [- -] and Aristarchos," *ZPE* 13: 84.

1978 "Notes on Some Graeco-demotic Surety Contracts," *Enchoria* 8: 5–8.

1980 "Philadelpheia and the Memphites in the Zenon Archive," in *Studies in Ptolemaic Memphis* by Dorothy J. Crawford, Jan Quaegebuer, and Willy Clarysse. Studia Hellenistica, vol. 24. Louvain: Katholieke Universiteit Louvain, pp. 91–122.

1981 *Addenda et corrigenda au Volume III (1956)*. Prosopographica Ptolemaica, vol. IX, edited by W. Peremans and E. Van't Dack. Studia Hellenistica, vol. 25. Louvain: Orientaliste.

1984 "A Roman Army Unit near Thebes," in *Atti del XVII congresso internazionale di papirologia*, vol. 3, Naples: Centro Internationale per lo Studio dei Papiri Ercolanesi, pp. 1021–26.

1985 "Greeks and Egyptians in the Ptolemaic Army and Administration," *Aegyptus* 65: 57–66.

1986 "Le mariage et le testament de Dryton en 150 avant J.C.," *CdE* 61: 99–103.

1987a "Greek Loan-words in Demotic," in *Aspects of Demotic Lexocography. Acts of the Second International Conference for Demotic Studies, Leiden, 19–21 September, 1984*, edited by S. P. Vleeming. Studia Demotica, vol. 1. Louvain: Peeters, pp. 9–33.

1987b "The Greek Versos of the *Cautionnements démotiques*," Paper presented at the Third International Congress for Demotic Studies, Cambridge.

1988a "Une famille alexandrine dans la chora," *CdE* 63: 137–40.

1988b "A Demotic Self-Dedication to Anubis," *Enchoria* 16: 7–10.

Clarysse, W. and Lanciers, E.

1989 "Currency and the Dating of Demotic and Greek Papyri from the Ptolemaic Period," *Ancient Society* 20: 117–32.

Clarysse, W. and Winnicki, J. K.

1989 "Documentary Papyri," in *The Judean-Syrian-Egyptian Conflict of 103–101 B.C. A Multilingual Dossier Concerning a "War of Sceptres,"* by E. Van't Dack, W. Clarysse, G. Cohen, J. Quaegebeur, and J. K. Winnicki. Collectanea Hellenistica I. Brussels: Comité Klassieke Studies, Subcomité Hellenisme, Koninklijke Academie voor Wetenschappen, Letteren en Schone Kunsten van België, pp. 37–81.

Coppin, Jean

1971 *Voyages en Égypte de Jean Coppin, 1638–1639, 1643–1646*, edited by Serge Sauneron. Cairo: IFAO.

Corcoran, Lorelei

1988 *Portrait Mummies from Roman Egypt*. Ph.D. diss., The University of Chicago.

Couroyer, B.

1954a Addition to "Review of *The Brooklyn Museum Papyri — New Documents of the Fifth Century B.C. from the Jewish Colony at Elephantine*, edited with a historical introduction by Emil G. Kraeling" by J. T. Milik. *RB* 61: 251–53

1954b "Termes égyptiens dans les papyrus araméns du Musée de Brooklyn," *RB* 61: 554–59.

Cowley, Arthur Ernest

1923 *Aramaic Papyri of the Fifth Century B.C.* Oxford: The Clarendon Press.

Crawford, Dorothy J.

1971 *Kerkeosiris. An Egyptian Village in the Ptolemaic Period.* Cambridge: Cambridge University Press.

Criscuolo, Lucia

1977 "I miriaruri nell'Egitto tolemaico: note sull'amministrazione dell'Arsinoite nell III secolo a.C.," *Aegyptus* 57: 109–22.

1978 "Ricerche sul *Komogrammateus* nell'Egitto tolemaico," *Aegyptus* 58: 3–101.

1981 "Miriaruri: nuove riflessioni," *Aegyptus* 61: 116–18.

1989 "La successione a Tolemeo Aulete ed i pretesi matrimoni di Cleopatra VII con i fratelli," in *Egitto e storia antica dall'ellenismo all'età araba. Atti del colloquio internazionale, Bologna, 31 agosto – 2 settembre 1987*, edited by Lucia Criscuolo and Giovanni Geraci. Bologna: Cooperativa Libraria Universitaria Editrice, pp. 325–39.

Crum, W. E.

1931 "Nouveau mot copte pour 'navire'," *BIFAO* 30: 453–55.

1939 "Coptic Documents in Greek Script," *PBA* 25: 3–25.

Cruz-Uribe, Eugene D.

1985 *Saite and Persian Demotic Cattle Documents. A Study in Legal Forms and Principles in Ancient Egypt.* Chico, CA: Scholars Press.

—— *The Archive of Tikas, Demotic Texts from Philadelphia in the Fayum* (in press).

Cumont, Franz
1933 "Deux monuments des cultes solaires," *SYRIA* 14: 381–95.

D'Abbadie, J. Vandier
1946 "À propos des bustes de laraires," *RdE* 5: 133–35.

Daniel, R. W.
1977 "Two Michigan Papyri," *ZPE* 24: 75–88.

Daressy, Georges
1901 *Ostraca.* 2 vols. CGC, vol. 23. Cairo: IFAO.

1911 "Un décret de l'an XXIII de Ptolémée Épiphane," *RdT* 33: 1–8.

1916 "Statue de Georges, prince de Tentyris," *ASAE* 16: 268–70.

1917 "Un second exemplaire du décret de l'an XXIII de Ptolémée Épiphane," *RdT* 38: 175–79.

Daris, Sergio
1984 "Toponimi della meris di Polemone," *Aegyptus* 64: 101–20.

Darnell, John C.
—— "The Location of *Ptolemais theron*," in the *Behrens Festschrift* (forthcoming).

Daumas, François
1952 *Les moyens d'expression du grec et de l'égyptien comparés dans les décrets de Canope et de Memphis.* SASAE, vol. 16. Cairo: IFAO.

Davidson, Hugh M. and Dubé, Pierre H.
1975 *A Concordance to Pascal's Pensées.* Ithaca: Cornell University Press.

Davies, Norman de Garis
1933 *The Tomb of Nefer-Ḥotep at Thebes.* 2 vols. PMMA, vol. 9. New York: The Metropolitan Museum of Art.

Debut, Janine
1986 "Les documents scolaires," *ZPE* 63: 251–78.

de Cenival, Françoise
1967 "Deux serments démotiques concernant des coptes de bétail," *Recherches de papyrologie, IV.* Publications de la Faculté des Lettres et Sciences Humaines de Paris-Sorbonne, Série "recherches," tome 36. Travaux de L'Institut de Papyrologie de Paris, Fascicule 5. Paris: Presses Universitaires de France, pp. 99–107.

1968 "Un document inédit relatif à l'exploitation de terres du Fayoum (P. dém. Lille, Inv. Sorb. 1186)," *RdE* 20: 37–51.

1972a *Les associations religieuses en Égypte d'après les documents démotiques.* BdE, vol. 46. Cairo: IFAO.

1972b "Un acte de renonciation consécutif à un partage de revenus liturgiques memphites (P. Louvre E 3266)," BIFAO 71: 11–65.

1973 *Cautionnements démotiques du début de l'époque ptolémaïque (P. dém Lille 34 à 96).* Paris: Éditions Klincksieck (= P. dém. Lille II).

1977 "Deux papyrus inédits de Lille avec une révision du P. dém. Lille 31," *Enchoria* 7: 1–49.

de Cenival, Françoise (*cont.*)

1978 "La deuxième partie du P. dém. Lille 18: déclaration de petit bétail (P. Inv. Sorbonne 1248)," *Enchoria* VIII.2: 1–3.

1980 "Compte de céréales de plusieurs villages du Fayoum. *P. dém Lille 110* (Inv. Sorbonne 205 à 213)," in *Institute française d'archéologie orientale du Caire, livre du centenaire, 1880–1980*, edited by Jean Vercoutter. MIFAO, vol. 104. Cairo: IFAO, pp. 193–203.

1984 *Papyrus démotiques de Lille*. Volume III. MIFAO, vol. 110. Cairo: IFAO.

1987 "Répertoire journalier d'un bureau de notaire de l'époque ptolémaique en démotique (P. dém. Lille 120)," *Enchoria* 15: 1–9.

1988 *Le mythe de l'oeil du soleil. Translitteration et traduction avec commentaire philologique*. Demotische Studien, Band 9. Sommerhausen: Gisela Zauzich Verlag.

de Meulenaere, Herman

1951 *Herodotos over de 26ste dynastie (II, 147–III, 15)*. Bibliotheque du Muséon, vol. 27. Louvain: Louvainse Universitaire Uitgaven.

1959a "Les strategès indigènes du nome tentyrite à la fin de l'époque ptolémaïque et au début l'occupation romaine," *RSO* 34: 1–25.

1959b "Prosopographica Ptolemaica," *CdE* 34: 244–49.

1962 "Recherches onomastiques," *Kêmi* 16: 28–37.

1963 "La famille royale des Nectanébo," *ZÄS* 90: 90–93.

1966a "La mère d'Imouthès," CdE 41: 40–49.

1966b *Le surnom égyptien à la basse époque*. Uitgaven van het Nederlands Historisch-Archaeologisch Instituut te İstanbul, vol. 19. Istanbul: Nederlands Historisch-Archaeologisch Instituut in het Nabije Oosten.

1967 "Prosopographica Ptolemaica. Troisième serie," *CdE* 42: 297–305.

1981 "Le surnom égyptien à la basse époque (addenda et corrigenda)," *OLP* 12: 127–34.

1987 "E pluribus una," *BIFAO* 87: 135–40.

Dentzer, Jean-Marie

1982 *Le motif du banquet couché dans la proche-orient et le monde grec du VIIè au IVè siècle avant J.-C.* Bibliothèque des Écoles Françaises d'Athènes et de Rome, fascicule 246è. Rome: École Française de Rome.

Derchain, Philippe

1986 "La garde 'égyptienne' de Ptolémée II," *ZPE* 65: 203–04.

1987 *Le dernier obelisque*. Brussels: Fondation Egyptologique Reine Elisabeth.

1988 Review of *Egyptian and Hermetic Doctrine* by Erik Iversen. *CdE* 63: 258.

1990 "L'auteur du papyrus Jumilhac," *RdE* 41: 9–30.

Desroches-Noblecourt, Christiane and Kuentz, Charles

1968 *Le petit temple d'Abou Simbel I: Étude archéologique et épigraphique, essai d'interpretation*. Cairo: Ministére de la Culture de la République Arabe Unie.

Devauchelle, Didier

1978 in "Nouvelles stèles de Kom Abu Bellou," by S. A. A. el-Nassery and G. Wagner, *BIFAO* 78: 231–58; *see* p. 250.

1983 *Ostraca démotiques du Musée du Louvre. Tome I: Reçus*. BdE, vol. 92. Cairo: IFAO.

1984 "Remarques sur les méthodes d'enseignement du démotique," in *Grammata Demotika. Festschrift für Erich Lüddeckens zum 15. Juni 1983*, edited by Heinz-Josef Thissen and Karl-Theodor Zauzich. Würzburg: Gisela Zauzich Verlag, pp. 47–59.

1987a "Le Papyrus démotique Louvre E 9416: Une vente de terrain," *BIFAO* 87: 161–65.

1987b "Cinq ostraca démotiques de Karnak," *CdK* 8: 137–42.

1988 "Le papyrus démotique du Musée de Figeac (Inv. E9): un prêt d'argent," *Cahiers du Musée Champollion* 1: 10–15.

Devauchelle, Didier and Wagner, Guy

1982 "Ostraca ptolémaïques bilingues d'Edfou," *ASAE* 68: 89–101.

1984 *Les graffites du Gebel Teir: Textes démotiques et grecs*. RAPH, vol. 22. Cairo: IFAO.

Diels, Hermann

1904 "*Laterculi Alexandrini* aus einem Papyrus Ptolemäischer Zeit," *Abhandlungen der Königlich preussischen Akademie der Wissenschaften, Philosophisch-Historische Klasse*. Berlin: Verlag der Königlich Akademie der Wissenschaft, pp. 1–16.

Donadoni, S.

1938 "Notizia sugli scavi della Missione Fiorentina ad Antinoe," *ASAE* 38: 493–501.

Doresse, Jean

1960 *Des hiéroglyphes à la croix: Ce que le passé pharaonique a légué au christianisme*. Uitgaven van het Nederlands Historisch-Archaeologisch Instituut te İstanbul, vol. 7. Istanbul: Nederlands Historisch-Archaeologisch Instituut het Nabije Oosten.

Douin, Georges

1922 *La flotte de Bonaparte sur les côtes d'Égypte*. Mémoires de la Société Royale de Géographie d'Égypte, vol. 3. Cairo: Institut Français d'Archéologie Orientale pour la Société Royale de Gógraphie d'Égypte.

Drewes, Peter

1970 *Die Bankdiagraphe in den gräko-ägyptischen Papyri*. Im Auftrag der Juristischen Fakultät der Universität Freiburg.

1974 "Die Bankdiagraphe in den gräko-ägyptischen Papyri," *JJP* 18: 95–155.

Drioton, Étienne

1942–3 "Les fêtes de Bouto," *BIE* 25: 1–19.

1944 "Les dédicaces de Ptolémée Évergète II sur le deuxiéme pylône de Karnak," *ASAE* 44: 111–62.

Driver, Godfrey Rolles

1954 *Aramaic Documents of the 5th Century B.C.* Oxford: The Clarendon Press.

DuBourguet, Pierre

1964 *L'Art copte.* Petits Guides des Grandes Musées, Nr. 19. Paris: Editions des Musées Nationaux.

Dunbabin, Katherine M. D.

1978 *The Mosaics of Roman North Africa. Studies in Iconography and Patronage.* Oxford: The Clarendon Press.

Dunham, Dows

1957 *The Royal Cemeteries of Kush IV: Royal Tombs at Meroë and Barkal.* Boston: The Museum of Fine Arts.

DuQuesne, Terence

1991 *A Coptic Initiatory Invocation (PGM IV 1–25).* Oxfordshire Communications in Egyptology, vol. 2. Thame Oxon: Darengo Publications.

Duthuit, Georges

1931 *La sculpture copte: statues, bas reliefs, masques.* Paris: G. van Oest.

Duttenhöfer, Ruth

1991 "P. Oxy. II 252 und 253," *ZPE* 86: 264–66.

Eddy, Samuel K.

1961 *The King is Dead. Studies in the Near Eastern Resistance to Hellenism 334–31 B.C.* Linclon: University of Nebraska Press.

Edgar, C. C.

1907 "A Portrait of a Schoolgirl," *Le Musée Égyptien* 2: 49–52.

Edgerton, William F., ed.

1937 *Medinet Habu Graffiti: Facsimiles.* OIP, vol. 36. Chicago: The University of Chicago Press.

Edgerton, William F. and Wilson, John A.

1936 *Historical Records of Ramses III: The Texts in Medinet Habu Volumes I and II.* SAOC, vol. 12. Chicago: The University of Chicago Press.

Edwards, I. E. S.

1960 *Oracular Amuletic Decrees of the Late New Kingdom.* Hieratic Papyri in the British Museum, Fourth Series. London: The Trustees of the British Museum.

Ehrenberg, Victor

1926 *Alexander und Ägypten.* Beihefte zum Alten Orient , vol. 7. Leipzig: J. C. Hinrichs'sche Buchhandlung.

el-Amir, Mustafa

1957 "A Demotic Papyrus from Pathyris," *Études de Papyrologie* 8: 59–67.

1959 *A Family Archive from Thebes.* Cairo: General Organisation for Government Printing Offices.

el-Nassery, S. A. A. and Wagner, G.

1978 "Nouvelles stèles de Kom Abu Bellou," *BIFAO* 78: 231–58.

Emery, W. B.

1965 "Preliminary Report on the Excavations at North Saqqâra, 1964–5," *JEA* 51: 3–8.

1966 "Preliminary Report on the Excavations at North Saqqâra, 1965–6," *JEA* 52: 3–8.

1967 "Preliminary Report on the Excavations at North Saqqâra, 1966–7," *JEA* 53: 141–45.

1968 "Editorial Foreword," *JEA* 54: 1–2.

1969 "Preliminary Report on the Excavations at North Saqqâra, 1968," *JEA* 55: 31–35.

1970 "Preliminary Report on the Excavations at North Saqqâra, 1968–9," *JEA* 56: 5–11.

1971 "Preliminary Report on the Excavations at North Saqqâra, 1969–70," *JEA* 57: 3–13.

Emery, W. B. and Smith, H. S.
1970 "Editorial Foreword," *JEA* 56: 1–3.

Ensslin, Wilhelm
1926 "Ein Prozessvergleich unter Klerikern von Jahre 481," *Rheinisches Museum für Philologie* 75: 422–46.

Erichsen, Wolja
1941 "Erwähnung eines Zuges nach Nubien unter Amasis in einem demotischen Text," *Klio* 34: 56–61.

1942 "Ein demotischer Prozeßvertrag," *ZÄS* 77: 92–100.

1948 *Eine ägyptische Schulübung in demotischer Schrift*. Kongelige Danske Videnskabernas Selskab, Historisk-filologiske Meddelelser, Bind 31, Nr. 4. Copenhagen: Ejnar Munksgaard.

Erman, Adolf and Wilcken, Ulrich
1900 "Die Naukratisstele," *ZÄS* 38: 127–33.

Farag, F. Rofail
1976–77 "Is There Any Justification for the Existence of Coptic Art? Two Recent Critical Opinions," *Kunst des Orients* XI, 1/2: 22–42.

Farber, J. Joel
1990 "Family Disputes in the Patermouthis Archive," *BASP* 27: 111–22.

Farid, Adel
1985 *Fünf demotische Stelen aus Berlin, Chicago, Durham, London und Oxford mit zwei demotischen Türinschriften aus Paris, mit einer Bibliographie der demotischen Inschriften*. Ph.D. dissertation, Julius-Maximilians-Universität zu Würzburg.

1989 "Eine Statue des Strategen Pakhom-Pa-Schu, des Sohnes des Pakhom-Remet-Behedet," *MDAIK* 45: 155–68.

Farid, Shafik
1973 "Preliminary Report on the Excavations of the Antiquities Department at Kôm Abû-Billo," *ASAE* 61: 21–26.

Faulkner, Raymond O.
1972 *The Book of the Dead*, vol. 1. New York: The Limited Editions Book Club.

Fazzini, Richard A. and Jasnow, Richard
1988 "Demotic Ostraca from the Mut Precinct in Karnak," *Enchoria* 16: 23–48.

Fecht, Gerhard
1972 *Der Vorwurf an Gott in den "Mahnworter des Ipu-Wer."* Heidelberg: Carl Winter Universitätsverlag.

Ferguson, John
1970 *The Religions of the Roman Empire*. Ithaca, NY: Cornell University Press.

Finnegan, Ruth H.
1988 *Literacy and Orality: Studies in the Technology of Communication*. Oxford: Blackwell.

Firth, C. M.
1915 *The Archaeological Survey of Nubia, Report for 1909–1910*. Cairo: Government Press.

Fischer, Henry G.
1973 "An Eleventh Dynasty Couple Holding the Sign of Life," *ZÄS* 100: 16–28.

Förtmeyer, Victoria
1988 "The Dating of the Pompe of Ptolemy II Philadelphus," *Historia* 37: 90–94.

Foraboschi, Daniele
1988 "Movimenti e tensioni sociali nell'Egitto romano," *ANRW* Part II, Volume 10.1: pp. 807–40.

Fornara, Charles W.
1971 *Herodotus: An Interpretive Essay*. Oxford: The Clarendon Press.

Fowden, Garth
1986 *The Egyptian Hermes: A Historical Approach to the Late Pagan Mind*. Cambridge: Cambridge University Press.

1987 "Nicagoras of Athens and the Latern Obelisk," *JHS* 107: 51–57.

Fraser, P. M.
1960 "Inscriptions from Ptolemaic Egypt," *Berytus* 13: 123–61.

1972 *Ptolemaic Alexandria*. 2 vols. Oxford: The Clarendon Press.

Fraser, P. M. and Roberts, C. H.
1949 "A New Letter of Apolonius," *CdE* 24: 289–94.

Friedman, Florence
1985 "On the Meaning of Some Anthropoid Busts from Deir el-Medina," *JEA* 71: 82–97.

Fuller, John F. C.
1954 *A Military History of the Western World, Volume I: From the Earliest Times to the Battle of Lepanto*. New York: Minerva Press.

Funk, Wolf-Peter
1976 "Ein doppelt überliefertes Stück spätägyptischer Weisheit," *ZÄS* 103: 8–21.

Gaballa, G. A.
1976 *Narrative in Egyptian Art*. Mainz am Rhein: Philipp von Zabern.

Gabbert, Janice J.
1987 "The Anarchic Dating of the Chremonidean War," *CJ* 82: 230–35.

Gallazzi, Claudio
1979 *Ostraka da Tebtynis della Università di Padova I*. Milan: Istituto Editoriale Cisalpino.

Gallo, Paolo
1989 "Ostraca demotici da Medinet Madi," *EVO* 12: 99–123.

Garbrecht, G.
1986 "Wasserspeicherung im Fayum (Moris-See), Legende oder Wirklichkeit," in *Vortrage der Tagung "Geschichtliche Wasserbauten in Agypten," Kairo, 10. bis 17. Februar 1986*, edited by G. Garbrecht. Braunschweig: Leichtweiss-Institut für Wasserbau der Technischen Universität Braunscheig, pp. 1–22.

Gardiner, Alan H.
1932 *Late-Egyptian Stories*. Bibliotheca Aegyptiaca, vol. 1. Brussels: Édition de la Fondation Égyptologique Reine Élisabeth.

1943 "The Name of Lake Moeris," *JEA* 29: 37–46.

1947 *Ancient Egyptian Onomastica*, 3 vols. Oxford: Oxford University Press.

1948 *The Wilbour Papyrus. Volume II: Commentary*. Brooklyn: The Brooklyn Museum.

1961 *Egypt of the Pharaohs*. Oxford: Oxford University Press.

Garlan, Y.; Gauthier, Ph.; and Orrieux, Cl.
1987 *Recherches sur les armés hellénistiques*. Reprint (of M. Launey 1949–50) with additions. Paris: De Boccard.

Gauthier, Henri
1975 *Dictionnaire des noms géographique contenus dans les texts hieroglyphiques*, III, Osnabruck: O. Zeller.

Gauthier, H. and Sottas, H.
1925 *Un décret trilingue en l'honneur de Ptolemée IV*. Cairo: IFAO.

Gayet, Albert
1902a *L'Art copte. Ecole d'Alexandrie, architecture monastique, sculpture, peinture, art sumptuaire*. Paris: Ernest Leroux.

1902b *L'Exploration des nécropoles gréco-byzantines d'Antinoë et les sarcophages de tombes pharaoniques de la ville antique*. Annales du Musée Guimet, vol. 30, part 2. Paris: Ernest Leroux.

Gazda, Elaine K.; Hessenbruch, Carolyn; Allen, Marti Lu; and Hutchinson, Valerie
1978 *Guardians of the Nile. Sculptures from Karanis in the Fayoum (c. 250 B.C. – A.D. 450)*. Ann Arbor: The Kelsey Museum of Archaeology.

Geertz, Clifford
1983 *Local Knowledge: Further Essays in Interpretive Anthropology*. New York: Basic Books.

Geraci, Giovanni
1971 "Ricerche sul proskynema," *Aegyptus* 51: 3–211.

1983 *Genesi della provincia romana d'Egitto*. Studi di Storia Antica, vol. 9. Bologna: Cooperativa Libraria Universitaria Editrice.

Gerhard, Gustav Adolf

1911 *Ein gräko-ägyptischer Erbstreit aus dem zweiten Jahrhundert vor Chr.* Sitzungsberichte der Heidelberger Akademie der Wissenschaften, Band 8. Heidelberg: C. Winter.

Gibson, John C. L.

1975 *Textbook of Syrian Semitic Inscriptions. Volume II: Aramaic Inscriptions, Including Inscriptions in the Dialect of Zenjirli.* Oxford: The Clarendon Press.

Glanville, Stephen R. K.

1939 *A Theban Archive of the Reign of Ptolemy I, Soter.* Catalogue of Demotic Papyri in the British Museum, vol. 1. London: The British Museum.

1955 *The Instructions of ʿOnchsheshonqy. (British Museum Papyrus 10508).* Catalogue of Demotic Papyri in the British Museum, vol. 2. London: The British Museum.

Goedicke, Hans

1963 "Ein geographisches Unicum," *ZÄS* 88: 83–97.

1985 "Comments on the Satrap Stele," *BES* 6: 33–54.

Götte, Karin

1985/86 *Die Weinopferszenen im Tempel von Edfu.* Magisterarbeit, Universität zu Koln.

1986 "Eine Individualcharacteristik ptolemäischer Herrscher anhand der Epitheta-Sequenzen beim Weinopfer," *RdE* 37: 63–80.

Göttlicher, Arvid

1978 *Materialien für ein Corpus der Schiffmodelle im Altertum.* Mainz am Rhein: Verlag Philipp von Zabern.

Golenischeff, W.

1890 "Stèle de Darius aux environs de Tell el-Maskhoûtah," *RdT* 13: 99–109.

Gomaà, Farouk; Müller-Wollermann, Renate; and Schenkel, Wolfgang

1991 *Mittelägypten zwischen Samalūṭ und dem Gabal Abū Ṣīr.* Beihefte zum Tübinger Atlas des Vorderen Orients, Reihe B (Geisteswissenschaften), Band 69. Wiesbaden: Dr. Ludwig Reichert Verlag.

Goody, Jack

1986 *The Logic of Writing and the Organisation of Society.* Cambridge: Cambridge University Press.

1987 *The Interface between the Written and the Oral.* Cambridge: Cambridge University Press.

Goudriaan, Koen

1988 *Ethnicity in Ptolemaic Egypt.* Dutch Monographs on Ancient History and Archaeology, vol. 5. Amsterdam: J. C. Gieben.

Goyon, Jean Claude

1969 "La statuette funéraire I. E. 84 de Lyon et le titre Säite ," *BIFAO* 67: 159–71.

Gradenwitz, O.; Preisigke, F.; and Spiegelberg, W.

1912 *Ein Erbstreit aus dem ptolemäischen Ägypten.* Schriften der Wissenschaftlichen Gesellschaft in Straßburg, Band 13. Strassburg: Karl J. Trübner.

Green, Michael
1983 "A private Archive of Coptic Letters and Documents from Teshlot," *OMRO* 64: 61–122.

Green, Peter
1989 *Classical Bearings*. London: Thames and Hudson.

Grelot, Pierre
1972 *Documents araméens d'Égypte*. Littératures Anciennes du Proche-Orient, vol. 5. Paris: Les Éditions du CERF.

Grenfell, Bernard P. and Hunt, Arthur S.
1899 *The Oxyrhynchus Papyri, Part II*. GRM, vol. 2. London: EEF.
1906 *The Hibeh Papyri, Part I*. GRM, vol. 7 London: EEF.

Grenfell, Bernard P.; Hunt, Arthur S.; and Goodspeed, Edgar J.
1907 *The Tebtunis Papyri, Part 2*. GRM, vol. 52. Oxford: Oxford University Press.

Grenfell, Bernard P.; Hunt, Arthur S.; and Hogarth, David G.
1900 *Fayûm Towns and their Papyri*. GRM, vol. 3. London: EES.

Grenfell, Bernard P.; Hunt, Arthur S.; and Smyly, J. Gilbart
1902 *The Tebtunis Papyri*. GRM, vol. 4. London: EEF.

Grenier, Jean-Claude
1977 *Anubis alexandrin et romain*. Études Preliminaires aux Religions Orientales dans l'Empire Romain, tome 57. Leiden: E. J. Brill.
1987 "Le protocole pharaonique des empereurs romains (analyse formelle et signification historique)," *RdE* 38: 81–104.
1988 "Notes sur l'Égypte romaine (I, 1–7)," *CdE* 63: 57–76.

Grenier, Jean-Claude and Coarelli, Filippo
1986 "La tombe d'Antinous à Rome," *MEFRA* 98: 217–53.

Griffith, F. Ll.
1890 "The Seasons 1887–8.—Minor Excavations," in *The City of Onias, the Antiquities of Tell el Yahûdîyeh, and the Mound of the Jew*, by Edouard Naville and F. Ll. Griffith. EM, vol. 7. London: Kegan Paul, Trench, Trübner & Co., pp. 60–74.
1900 *Stories of the High Priests of Memphis. The Sethon of Herodotus and the Demotic Tales of Khamuas*. 2 vols. Oxford: The Clarendon Press.
1901 "A Sale of Land in the Reign of Philopator," *PSBA* 23: 294–302.
1909 *Catalogue of the Demotic Papyri in the John Rylands Library, Manchester*. Volume I: *Atlas of Facsimiles*. Volume II: *Hand Copies of the Earlier Documents*. Volume III: *Key-List, Translations, Commentaries, and Indices*. Manchester: The University Press.
1935 *Catalogue of the Demotic Graffiti of the Dodecaschoenus*, volume I. Les Temples Immergés de la Nubie. Oxford: Oxford University Press.
1937 *Catalogue of the Demotic Graffiti of the Dodecaschoenus*, volume II. Les Temples Immergés de la Nubie. Oxford: Oxford University Press.

Griffith, F. Ll. and Petrie, W. M. F.
1889 *Two Hieroglyphic Papyri from Tanis*. EM, vol. 9. London: Trübner and Company.

Griffith, F. Ll. and Thompson, H.
1909 *The Demotic Magical Papyrus of London and Leiden*. 3 vols. London: H. Grevel and Company.

Griffith, Guy Thompson
1935 *The Mercenaries of the Hellenistic World*. Cambridge: Cambridge University Press.

Griffiths, J. Gwyn
1979 "Egyptian Nationalism in the Edfu Temple Texts," in *Glimpses of Ancient Egypt: Studies in Honour of H. W. Fairman*, edited by John Ruffle, G. A. Gaballa, and Kenneth A. Kitchen. Warminster: Aris and Philipps Ltd., pp. 174–79.

1982 "Eight Funerary Paintings with Judgement Scenes in the Swansea Wellcome Museum," *JEA* 68: 228–52.

Grimal, N.-C.
1981 *Quatres stèles napatéennes au musée du Caire, JE 48863–48866: textes et indices*. MIFAO, vol. 106. Cairo: IFAO.

Grimm, Alfred
1989 "Altägyptische Tempelliteratur. Zur Gliederung und Funktion der Bücherkataloge von Edfu und et-Tôd," *Akten des vierten Internationalen Ägyptologen Kongresses, München 1985. Band 3: Linguistik, Philologie, Religion*, edited by Sylvia Schoske. *SAKB*, Band 3. Hamburg: Helmut Buske Verlag, pp. 159–69.

Grimm, Günter
1974 *Die römischen Mumienmasken aus Ägypten*. Wiesbaden: Franz Steiner Verlag GmbH.

Grunert, Stefan
1981 *Thebanisches Kaufverträge des 3. und 2. Jahrhunderts v. u. Z.* Demotische Papyri aus dem Staatlichen Museen zu Berlin, vol 2. Berlin: Akademie-Verlag.

Guéraud, Octave and Jouguet, Pierre F. A.
1938 *Un livre d'écolier du IIIe siècle avant J.-C.* Société Royale Égyptienne de Papyrologie, Publications, Textes et Documents, no. 2. Cairo: IFAO.

Gutbub, Adolphe
1962 "Remarques sur les dieux du nome tanitique à la basse époque," *Kêmi* 16: 42–75.

Häge, Günther
1968 *Ehegüterrechtliche Verhältnisse in den griechischen Papyri Ägyptens bis Diocletian*. Graezistische Abhandlungen, Band 3. Cologne: Graz, Bohlau.

1970 "Die μὴ ἐλαττουμένου-Klausel in den griechischen Papyri Aegyptens," *Proceedings of the Twelfth International Congress of Papyrology, Ann Arbor, 13–17 August 1968*. American Studies in Papyrology, vol. 7. Toronto: Samuel Stevens Hakkert and Company, pp. 195–205.

Hässler, Manfred
1960 *Die Bedeutung der Kyria-Klausel in den Papyrusurkunden*. Berliner Juristische Abhandlungen, Band 3. Berlin: Duncker and Humblot.

Hajjar, Youssef

1977 *La triade d'Héliopolis-Baalbek: son culte et sa diffusion a travers les textes littéraires et les documents iconographiques et épigraphiques*, vols. 1–2. Études Préliminaires aux Religions Orientales dans L'Empire Romain, tome 59. Leiden: E. J. Brill.

Handoussa, Tohfa

1988 "A Late Egyptian Text written in different scripts," *MDAIK* 44: 111–15.

Hanson, Ann Ellis

1979 "Documents from Philadelphia Drawn from the Census Register," in *Actes du XVe congrès international de papyrologie, Tome II: Papyrus inédits*, edited by Jean Bingen and Georges Nachtergael. Papyrologica Bruxellensia, vol. 17. Brussels: Fondation Égyptologique Reine Élisabeth, pp. 60–74.

1980a "P. Princeton I 11 and P. Cornell 21v," *ZPE* 37: 241–48.

1980b "Juliopolis, Nicopolis, and the Roman Camp," *ZPE* 37: 249–54.

1984a "Caligulan Month-names at Philadelphia and Related Matters," in *Atti del XVII congresso internazionale di papirologia*, vol. 3, Naples: Centro Internationale per lo Studio dei Papiri Ercolanesi, pp. 1107–18.

1984b "The Archive of Isidoros of Psophthis and P. Ostorius Scapula, *Praefectus Aegypti*," *BASP* 21: 77–87.

1989a "Declarations of Sheep and Goats from the Oxyrhynchite Nome," *Aegyptus* 69: 61–69.

1989b "Village Officials at Philadelphia: a Model of Romanization in the Julio-Claudian Period," in *Egitto e storia antica dall'ellenismo all'età araba. Atti del colloquio internazionale, Bologna, 31 agosto – 2 settembre 1987*, edited by Lucia Criscuolo and Giovanni Geraci. Bologna: Cooperativa Libraria Universitaria Editrice, pp. 428–40.

1990 "*P. Princeton* I 13: Text and Context Revised," in *Miscellanea papyrologica in occasione del bicentenario dell'edfizione della charta Borgiana*, edited by Mario Capasso, Gabriella Messeri Savorelli, and Rosario Pintaudi. Florence: Edizioni Gonnelli, pp. 259–83.

Harrauer, Hermann

1987 *Griechische Texte IX: Neue Papyri zum Steuerwesen im 3. JH. v. Chr.* CPR, vol. 13. Vienna: Verlag Brüder Hollinek.

Harrauer, Hermann and Sijpesteijn, P. J.

1985 *Neue Texte aus dem antiken Unterricht*. MPER, vol. 15. Vienna: Verlag Brüder Hollinek.

Harrauer, Hermann and Vittmann, Günther

1985 "Papyrus Wien D 6934 — Fragment einer Urkunde über Hausverkauf aus Soknopaiu Nesos," *Enchoria* 13: 67–71.

Harris, J. R.

1973 "Nefertiti Rediviva," *AcOr* 35: 5–13.

1974 "Neferneferuaten Regnans," *AcOr* 36: 11–21.

Hasitzka, Monika R. M.
1987 *Koptische Texte*. 2 vols. CPR, vol. 12. Vienna: Verlag Brüder Hollinek.

Hauben, Hans
1972 "The Command Structure in Alexander's Mediterranean Fleets," *Ancient Society* 3: 55–65.

1975–76 "Antigonos' Invasion Plan for his Attack on Egypt in 306 B.C.," in *Miscellanea in honorem Josephi Vergote*, edited by P. Naster, H. de Meulenaere, and J. Quaegebeur. *OLP* 6/7: 267–71.

Hawwass, Zaki A.
1979 "Preliminary Report on the Excavations at Kôm Abou Bellou," *SAK* 7: 75–87.

Heeren, A. H. L.
1838 *Historical Researches into the Politics, Intercourse, and Trade of the Carthaginians, Ethiopians, and Egyptians*, vol. 2. Oxford: D. A. Talboys.

Heidorn, Lisa A.
1991 "The Saite and Persian Period Forts at Dorginarti," in *Egypt and Africa: Nubia from Prehistory to Islam*, edited by W. V. Davies. London: British Museum Press in association with EES, pp. 205–19.

Heilporn, Paul
1990 "La provenance de la dédicace *I. Th. Sy*. 302," *CdE* 65: 116–21.

Heinen, Heinz
1972 *Untersuchungen zur hellenistischen Geschichte des 3. Jahrhunderts v. Chr. Zur Geschichte der Zeit des Ptolemaios Keraunos und zum Chremonideischen Krieg*. Historia Einzelschriften, Heft 20. Wiesbaden: Franz Steiner Verlag GmbH.

1990 "Neue christliche Inschriften aus Hermonthis," *ZPE* 81: 270–73.

Helck, Wolfgang
1974 *Die altägyptischen Gaue*. Wiesbaden: Dr. Ludwig Reichert Verlag.

Helderman, J.
1988 "Van Jablonski/Te Water tot Vycichl. Bij Jozef Janssens's pleidooi voor een nieuwe 'Wiedemann'," *Phoenix* (Leiden) 34.2: 54–58.

Hengstl, Joachim
1991 "Bemerkungen zu Papyri und Ostraka," *ZPE* 86: 237–42.

Henne, Henri
1935 *Liste des strateges des nomes egyptiens a l'epoque greco-romaine*. Cairo: IFAO.

Hermann, Alfred
1963 "Die Deltastadt Terenuthis und ihre Göttin," *MDAIK* 5: 169–72.

Hermann, John J., Jr.
1988 "Roman Bronzes," in *The Gods Delight. The Human Figure in Classical Bronze*, edited by Arielle P. Kozloff and David Gordon Mitten. Cleveland: Cleveland Museum of Art, pp. 274–364.

Hess, J. J.
1897 "Demotica," *ZÄS* 35: 144–49.

Hinz, Walther
1975 "Darius und der Suezkanal," *AMI* 8: 115–21.

Hobson, Deborah W.

1984 "*PVINDOB. GR.* 24951 + 24556: New Evidence for Tax-Exempt Status in Roman Egypt," *Atti del XVII congresso internazionale di papirologia*, vol. 3. Naples: Centro Internazionale per lo Studio dei Papiri Ercolanesi, pp. 847–64.

Hofmann, Inge

1975 *Wege und Möglichkeiten eines indischen Einflusses auf die meroitische Kultur*. Studia Instituti Anthropos, vol. 23. St. Augustin bei Bonn: Anthropos-Institut.

Hooker, M. B.

1978 *A Concise Legal History of South-East Asia*. Oxford: The Clarendon Press.

Hooper, Finley A.

1961 *Funerary Stelae from Kom Abou Billou*. Kelsey Museum of Archaeology Studies, vol. 1. Ann Arbor: The Kelsey Museum of Archaeology.

Hopfner, Th.

1946 "Graezizierte, griechisch-ägyptische, bzw. ägyptisch-griechische und hybride theophore Personennamen aus griechischen Texten, Inschriften, Ostraka, Mumientäfelchen und dgl. und ihre religionsgeschichte Bedeutung," *ArOr* 15: 1–64.

Horak, Ulrike

1989 "Πινουτίων μουσικός und Βίκτωρ Τάραξ," *Tyche* 4: 101–07.

Hornblower, Jane

1981 *Hieronymus of Cardia*. Oxford Classical and Philosophical Monographs. Oxford: Oxford University Press.

Hughes, George R.

1951 "A Demotic Astrological Text," *JNES* 10: 256–64.

1952 *Saite Demotic Land Leases*. SAOC, vol. 28. Chicago: The University of Chicago Press.

1984 "The So-called Pherendates Correspondence," in *Grammata Demotika. Festschrift für Erich Lüddeckens zum 15. Juni 1983*, edited by Heinz-Josef Thissen and Karl-Theodor Zauzich. Würzburg: Gisela Zauzich Verlag, pp. 75–86.

Hughes, George R. and Nims, Charles F.

1940 "Some Observations on the British Museum Demotic Theban Archive," *AJSLL* 57: 244–61.

Husson, Geneviève

1982 "Ὑπό dans le grec d'Égypte et la préposition egyptienne *ḫr*," *ZPE* 46: 227–30.

1990 "Houses in Syene in the Patermouthis Archive," *BASP* 27: 123–36.

Huyse, Philip

—— "*Analecta Iranica* aus den demotischen Dokumenten von Nord-Saqqara," (forthcoming).

Iversen, Erik

1958 *Papyrus Carlsberg Nr. VII: Fragments of a Hieroglyphic Dictionary*. Historisk-filologiske Skrifter adgivet af Kongelige Danske Videnskabernas Selskab, Bind 3, nr. 2. Copenhagen: Ejnar Munksgaard.

1987 "Some Remarks on the *ḥꜣw-nbw.t*," *ZÄS* 114: 54–59.

Jacobson, Howard

1981 "Tacitus and the Phoenix," *Phoenix* (Toronto) 35: 260–61.

Jacoby, Felix

1958 *Die Fragmente der griechischen Historiker*, vol. 3C. Leiden: E. J. Brill.

James, T. G. H.

1962 *The Ḥeḳanakhte Papers and Other Early Middle Kingdom Documents*. PMMA, vol. 19. New York: The Metropolitan Museum of Art.

Jansen-Winkeln, Karl

1989 "Zur Schiffsliste aus Elephantine," *GM* 109: 31.

Jaritz, Horst

1980 *Elephantine III: Die Terrassen vor den Tempeln des Chnum und der Satet: Architektur und Deutung*. Archäologische Veröffentlichungen, Band 32. Mainz am Rhein: Verlag Philipp von Zabern.

1981 "Zum Heiligtum am Gebel Tingar," *MDAIK* 37: 241–46.

1982 "Stadt und Tempel von Elephantine, Neunter/Zehnter Grabungsbericht, Teil IV: Untersuchungen im Bereich des späten Chnumtempels," *MDAIK* 38: 306–29.

1990 "Stadt und Tempel von Elephantine, 17./18. Grabungsbericht, Teil IX.3: Brüstung der Chnumtempel-Terrasse," *MDAIK* 46: 248–49.

Jaritz, Horst and Bietak, Manfred

1977 "Zweierlei Pegeleichungen zum Messen der Nilfluthöhen im Alten Ägypten: Untersuchung zum neuentdeckten Nilometer des Chnum-Tempels von Elephantine (Strabon, XVIII I.48)," *MDAIK* 33: 47–62.

Jaritz, Horst and Laskowska-Kusztal, Ewa

1990 "Das Eingangstor zu einem Mandulisheiligtum in Ajuala/Unternubien," *MDAIK* 46: 157–84.

Jaritz, Horst; Maehler, Herwig; and Zauzich, Karl-Theodor

1979 "Inschriften und Graffiti von der Brüstung der Chnumtempel-Terrasse in Elephantine," *MDAIK* 35: 125–54.

Jensen, Herman Ludin

1950 *The Coptic Story of Cambyses' Invasion of Egypt: A Critical Analysis of its Literary Form and its Historical Purpose*. Oslo: Jacob Dybwad.

Johnson, J. de M.

1912 "A Botanical Papyrus with Illustrations," *Archiv für Geschichte der Naturwissenschaften und der Technik* 4: 403–08.

Johnson, Janet H.

1974 "The Demotic Chronicle as an Historical Source," *Enchoria* 4: 1–17.

1976 "The Dialect of the Demotic Magical Papyrus of London and Leiden," in *Studies in Honor of George R. Hughes, January 12, 1977*, edited by Edward F. Wente and Janet H. Johnson. SAOC, vol. 39. Chicago: The Oriental Institute, pp. 105–32.

1983 "The Demotic Chronicle as a Statement of a Theory of Kingship," *SSEAJ* 13: 61–72.

1984 "Is the Demotic Chronicle an Anti-Greek Tract?" *Grammata Demotika: Festschrift für Erich Lüddeckens zum 15. Juni 1983*, edited by H.-J.Thissen and K.-Th. Zauzich. Würzburg: Gisela Zauzich Verlag, pp. 107–24.

1986 "The Egyptian Priesthood in Ptolemaic Egypt," in *Egyptological Studies in Honor of Richard A. Parker*, edited by L. H. Lesko. Hanover, NH: Brown University Press, pp. 79–82.

1987 "Ptolemaic Bureaucracy from an Egyptian Point of View," in *The Organization of Power: Aspects of Bureaucracy in the Ancient Near East*, edited by McGuire Gibson and Robert D. Biggs. SAOC, vol. 46. Chicago: The Oriental Institute, pp. 141–49.

1990 "L'Egiziano," in *Storia della Linguistica. Volume 1*, edited by Guilio C. Lepschy. Bologna: Società editrice il Mulino, pp. 86–96.

Jones, Brian W. and Whitehorne, John E. G.

1983 *Register of Oxyrhynchites, 30 B.C. – A.D. 96*. American Studies in Papyrology, vol. 25. Chico, CA: Scholars Press.

Jones, Dilwyn

1988 *A Glossary of Ancient Egyptian Nautical Titles and Terms*. New York: Kegan Paul International.

Jouguet, Pierre

1901 "Fouilles du Fayoum: rapport sur les fouilles de Médinet-Mâʾdi et Médinet-Ghôran," *BCH* 35: 380–411.

1902 "Notice sur les fouilles de Médinet-Ghôran et de Médinet-en-Nahas," *Bulletin de l'Université de Lille et de l'Académie de Lille*. Juillet 1902.

1907–28 *Papyrus de Lille: Papyrus grecs*, vol. 1. Paris: Institut Papyrologique de l'Université de Lille.

Junge, Friedrich

1987 *Elephantine XI: Funde und Bauteile. 1.–7. Kampagne, 1969–1976*, Archäologisches Veröffenttlichungen, vol. 49. Mainz am Rhein: Philipp von Zabern.

Junker, Hermann

1941 "'Handlung' als Präfix in Zusammensetzungen," *ZÄS* 77: 3–7.

Kahl, Jochem

1991 "Von *h* bis *ḳ*. Indizien für eine 'alphabetische' Reihenfolge einkonsonantiger Lautwerte in spätzeitlichen Papyri," *GM* 122: 33–47.

Kákosy, Laszlo

1979 "Some Problems of Late-Egyptian Religion," in *Schriften zur Geschichte und Kultur des Alten Orients*, edited by Walter F. Reineke. Berlin: Akademie-Verlag, pp. 347–52.

Kaplony, Peter

1977 "Die Definition der schönen Literatur im alten Ägypten," in *Fragen an die altägyptischer Literatur und Geschichte Studien zum Gedenken an Eberhard Otto*, edited by Jan Assmann, Erika Feucht, and Reinhard Grieshammer. Wiesbaden: Dr. Ludwig Reichert Verlag, pp. 289–314.

Kaplony-Heckel, Ursula

1963 *Die demotischen Tempeleide.* 2 vols. Ägyptologische Abhandlung, Band 6. Wiesbaden: Otto Harrassowitz.

1966 "Demotische Texte aus Pathyris," *MDAIK* 21: 133–70.

1974 "Schüler und Schulwesen in der ägyptischen Spätzeit," *SAK* 1: 227–46.

1990 "Theben-West und Theben-Ost (31 demotische *r-rḫ=w* Ostraka aus dem British Museum," in *Studies in Egyptology Presented to Miriam Lichtheim*, edited by Sarah Israelit-Groll. 2 vols. Jerusalem: The Magnes Press, The Hebrew University, pp. 517–624.

Kaser, M.

1971 *Das römische Privatrecht*, 2nd ed., erster Abschnitt. Munich: C. H. Beck'sche Verlagsbuchhandlung.

1975 *Das römische Privatrecht*, 2nd ed., zweiter Abschnitt. Munich: C. H. Beck'sche Verlagsbuchhandlung.

Kasher, Aryeh

1985 *The Jews in Hellenistic and Roman Egypt: The Struggle for Equal Rights.* Texte und Studien zum antiken Judentum, vol. 7. Tübingen: J. C. B. Mohr.

Kasser, Rodolphe

1980 "Expression de l'aspiration ou de la non-aspiration à l'initiale des mots copto-grecs correspondant à des mots grecs commençant par (E) I-," *BSEG* 3: 15–21.

1988 "Graphèmes coptes jumeaux," *OLP* 19: 117–21.

Keenan, James G.

1990 "Evidence for the Byzantine Army in the Syene Papyri," *BASP* 27: 137–50.

Keenan, James G. and Shelton, John C.

1976 *The Tebtunis Papyri, Volume IV.* GRM, vol. 64. London: EES.

Kees, Herman

1934 "Terenuthis," *Paulys Real-Encyklopädie der classischen Altertumswissenschaft*, vol. 5A. Stuttgart: J. B. Metzler, cols. 718–19.

1956 *Der Götterglaube im Alten Ägypten.* (Zweite ergänzte Auflage). Berlin: Akademie-Verlag.

Keith-Bennett, Jean

1981 "Anthropoid Busts II: Not from Deir el-Medineh Alone," *BES* 3: 43–71.

Kenyon, Frederic G. and Bell, Harold I.

1907 *Greek Papyri in the British Museum. Volume III.* London: The British Museum.

Kienitz, Friedrich Karl

1953 *Die politische Geschichte Ägyptens vom 7. bis zum 4. Jahrhundert vor der Zeitwende.* Berlin: Akademie-Verlag.

Kießling, Emil

1938 "Streiflichter zur Katökenfrage," *Actes du Ve congrès international de papyrologie, Oxford, 30 août – 3 septembre 1937*, edited by Marcel Hombert. Brussels: Fondation Égyptologique Reine Élisabeth, pp. 213–29.

1970 "Zwei Papyrus urkunden aus der Giessener Sammlung," *Proceedings of the Twelfth International Congress of Papyrology, Ann Arbor, 13–17 August 1968*. American Studies in Papyrology, vol. 7. Toronto: Samuel Stevens Hakkert and Company, pp. 243–48.

Kiss, Zsolt

1984 *Studia nad Rzymskim Portetem Cesarskim w Egipcie* (*Études sur le portrait impérial romain en Égypte*). Prace Zakładu Archeologii Śródziemnomorskiej Polskiej Akademii Nauk. Warsaw: Państwowe Wydawnictwo Naukowe.

Kitchen, K. A.

1973 *The Third Intermediate Period in Egypt (1100–650 B.C.)*. Warminster: Aris and Phillips Ltd.

1986 *The Third Intermediate Period in Egypt (1100–650 B.C.)*. 2nd ed. Warminster: Aris and Phillips Ltd.

1988 "A Note on Asychis," in *Pyramid Studies and Other Essays Presented to I. E. S. Edwards*, edited by John Baines, T. G. H. James, Anthony Leahy, and A. F. Shore. London: EES, pp. 148–51.

Knudstad, James

1966 "Serra East and Dorginarti: A Preliminary Report on the 1963–64 Excavations of the University of Chicago Oriental Institute Sudan Expedition," *Kush* 14: 165–86.

Koenen, Ludwig

1988 "The Ptolemaic King as a Religious Figure," paper delivered at a conference on Hellenism at the University of California, Berkeley, (forthcoming).

Koenen, Ludwig and Henrichs, A.

1978 "Der Kölner Mani Kodex (P. Colon. inv. nr. 4780), Περὶ τῆϲ γέννηϲ τοῦ ϲώματοϲ αὐτοῦ, Edition der Seiten 72, 8–99, 9," *ZPE* 32: 87–199.

Köster, August

1923 *Das antike Seewesen*. Berlin: Schoetz and Parrhysius Verlags buchhandlung.

Kool, Pieter

1954 *De Phylakieten in Grieks-Romeins Egypte*. Amsterdam: Studentdrukkerij "Poortpers" n.v.

Kornfeld, Walter

1978 *Onomastica Aramaica aus Ägypten*. Sitzungsberichte der Österreichischen Akademie der Wissenschaften, Philosophisch-historische Klasse, Band 333. Vienna: Verlag der Österreichischen Akademie der Wissenschaften.

Kramer, Bärbel

1985 "232. Sklavenkauf," in *Kölner Papyri, Band 5*, edited by Michael Gronewald, Klaus Maresch, and Wolfgang Schäfer. Papyrologica Coloniensia, vol. 7. Opladen: Westdeutscher Verlag GmbH, pp. 253–79.

Krause, M.

1972 "Ein Fall friedensrichterlicher Tätigkeit im ersten Jahrzehnt des 7. Jahrhunderts in Oberägypten," *RdE* 24: 101–07.

Krebs, Walter

1965 "Einige Transportprobleme der antiken Schiffahrt," *Das Altertum* 11: 86–101.

Kreutz, Barbara M.

1976 "Ships, Shipping, and the Implications of Change in the Early Medieval Mediterranean," *Viator, Medieval and Renaissance Studies* 7: 79–109.

Kuentz, Charles

1920 "Autour d'une conception égyptienne méconnue: l'*Akhit* ou soi-disant horizon," *BIFAO* 17: 121–90.

Kurth, Dieter

1980 "Historischer Hintergrund in Ritualszenen am Beispiel Edfou III 241, 11–242, 2," *SAK* 8: 153–68.

Kutscher, Edward Yechezkel

1977 *Hebrew and Aramaic Studies*, edited by Zeev Ben-Ḥayyim, Aharon Dotan, and Gad Sarfatti. Jerusalem: The Magnes Press, The Hebrew University.

Kutzner, Edgar

1989 *Untersuchungen zur Stellung der Frau im römischen Oxyrhynchos*. Europäische Hochschulschriften. Reihe III: Geschichte und ihre Hilfswissenschaften, Band 392. Frankfurt am Main: P. Lang.

Lafuma, Louis

1951 *Blaise Pascal, pensées sur la religion et sur quelques autres sujets*. Paris: Éditions du Luxembourg.

Lambertz, Maximilian

1911 "Zur Doppelnamigkeit in Aegypten," in *XXVI. Jahresbericht über das K. K. Elisabeth-Gymnasium in Wien für das Schuljahr 1910/1911*, edited by Peter Maresch. Vienna: Selbstverlag der Anstalt, pp. 1–30.

Lammeyer, Joseph

1933 "Die 'audentia episcopalis' in Zivilsachen der Laien in römischen Kaiserrecht und in den Papyri," *Aegyptus* 13: 193–202.

Launey, Marcel

1949–50 *Recherches sur les armées hellénistiques.* 2 vols. Bibliotheque des Ecoles Françaises d'Athenes et de Rome. 1e ser. (in 8o), fascicle 169. Paris: E. de Boccard.

Leahy, Anthony

1988 "The Earliest Dated Monument of Amasis and the End of the Reign of Apries," *JEA* 74: 183–99.

Leblanc, Christian

1985 "Diodore, le tombeau d'Osymandyas et la statuaire du Ramesseum," in *Melanges Gamal Eddin Mokhtar*, vol. 2, edited by Paule Posener-Krieger. BdE, vol. 97. Cairo: IFAO, pp. 69–82.

Leclant, Jean

1971 "Fouilles et travaux en Égypte et au Soudan, 1969–1970: 6. Kôm Abou Billou," *Orientalia* 40: 227.

1972 "Fouilles et travaux en Égypte et au Soudan, 1970–1971: 4. Kôm Abou Billou," *Orientalia* 41: 251.

1973 "Fouilles et travaux en Égypte et au Soudan, 1971–1972: 4. Kôm Abou Billou," *Orientalia* 42: 394.

1974 "Fouilles et travaux en Égypte et au Soudan, 1972–1973: 6. Kôm Abou Billou," *Orientalia* 43: 173.

1975 "Fouilles et travaux en Égypte et au Soudan, 1973–1974: 3. Kôm Abou Billou," *Orientalia* 44: 201.

1976 "Fouilles et travaux en Égypte et au Soudan, 1974–1975: 9. Kôm Abou Billou," *Orientalia* 45: 278.

1977 "Fouilles et travaux en Égypte et au Soudan, 1975–1976: 5. Kôm Abou Billou," *Orientalia* 46: 235.

1978 "Fouilles et travaux en Égypte et au Soudan, 1976–1977: 6. Kôm Abou Billou," *Orientalia* 47: 269.

Leclercq, Henri

1963 "Note concernant les noms doubles en Égypte ptolémaïque," *Aegyptus* 43: 192–94.

1975/76 "Note de grammaire sur les doubles noms dans le Nouveau Testament grec," *OLP* 6/7: 361–72.

Lefebvre, Gustave

1923 *Le tombeau de Petosiris III: vocabulaire et planches*. Cairo: IFAO.

1955 *Grammaire de l'égyptien classique*. 2nd ed. BdE, vol. 12. Cairo: IFAO.

Legrain, Georges

1896a "Textes gravés sur le quai de Karnak," *ZÄS* 34: 111–18.

1896b "Les crues du Nil depuis Shoshenk Ier jusqu'à Psametik," *ZÄS* 34: 119–21.

Lemaire, André

1987 "Les phéniciens et le commerce entre la mer rouge et la mer méditerranée," in *Studia Phoenicia*, vol. 5: *Phoenicia and the East Mediterranean in the First Millennium B.C.*, edited by E. Lipiński, OLA, vol. 22. Louvain: Uitgeverij Peeters, pp. 49–60.

Lenger, Marie-Thérèse

1967 "Ordres administratifs et *prostagmata* dans l'Égypte ptolémaïque," *CdE* 42: 145–55.

Le Père, J. M.

1822 *Description de l'Égypte*. 2nd ed. Paris: Imprimerie Impériale.

Lesquier, Jean

1911 *Les institutions militaires de l'Égypte sous les Lagides*. Paris: Ernest Leroux, Éditeur.

Lewis, Naphtali

1945 "The Meaning of σὺν ἡμιολία and Kindred Expressions in Loan Contracts," *TAPA* 76: 126–39.

1983a *Life in Egypt under Roman Rule*. Oxford: The Clarendon Press.

1983b "Notationes Legentis," *BASP* 20: 55–58.

1986 *Greeks in Ptolemaic Egypt. Case Studies in the Social History of the Hellenistic World*. Oxford: Oxford University Press.

Lexa, František

1933 "La légende gnostique sur Pistis Sophia et le mythe ancien égyptien sur l'oeil de Rê," *ER* 1: 106–16.

Lichtheim, Miriam

1957 *Demotic Ostraca from Medinet Habu*. OIP, vol. 80. Chicago: The University of Chicago Press.

1976 "The Naucratis Stele Once Again," in *Studies in Honor of George R. Hughes*, edited by Edward F. Wente and Janet H. Johnson. SAOC, vol. 39. Chicago: The Oriental Institute, pp. 139–46.

1980 *Ancient Egyptian Literature, A Book of Readings. Volume 3: The Late Period*. Berkeley: The University of California Press.

1983 *Late Egyptian Wisdom Literature in the International Context: A Study of Demotic Instructions*. Orbis Biblicus et Orientalis, vol. 52. Göttingen: Vandenhoeck and Ruprecht.

Lillyquist, Christine

1988 "The Gold Bowl Naming General Djehuty: A Study of Objects and Early Egyptology," *MMJ* 23: 5–68.

Limme, Luc

1983 "Een laat-egyptische autobiografisch opschrift uit Heracleopolis (Stèle Napels 1035)," in *Schrijvend Verleden. Documenten uit het oude Nabije Oosten vertaald en Toegelicht*, edited by K. R. Veenhof. Leiden: Ex Oriente Lux, pp. 324–29.

Lloyd, Alan B.

1972a "Triremes and the Saïte Navy," *JEA* 58: 268–79.

1972b "The So-called Galleys of Necho," *JEA* 58: 307–08.

1975a "Were Necho's Triremes Phoenician?" *JHS* 95: 45–61.

1975b *Herodotus, Book II: Introduction*. Leiden: E. J. Brill.

1976 *Herodotus, Book II: Commentary 1–98*. Leiden: E. J. Brill.

1977 "Necho and the Red Sea, Some Considerations," *JEA* 63: 142–55.

1980 "M. Basch on Triremes: some observations," *JHS* 100: 195–98.

1988a *Herodotus, Book II: Commentary 99–182*. Leiden: E. J. Brill.

1988b "Herodotus' Account of Pharaonic History," *Historia* 37: 22–53.

Luckhard, Fritz

1914 *Das Privathaus im ptolemäischen und römischen Ägypten*. Giessen: Hof- und Universitätsdruckerei Otto Kindt.

Lüddeckens, Erich

1968 *Demotische und koptische Texte*. Papyrologica Coloniensia, vol. 2. Cologne: Westdeutscher Verlag.

1972 "Demotische und koptische Urkundeformeln," *Enchoria* 2: 21–31.

Luft, Ulrich

1976 *Beiträge zur Historisierung der Götterwelt und der Mythenschreibung*. Studia Aegyptiaca, vol. 4. Budapest: Ókori Keleti Történeti Tanszek, Eötvös Loránd Tudományegyetem.

MacCoull, Leslie S. B.

1990 "Christianity at Syene/Elephantine/Philae," *BASP* 27: 138–62.

MacMullen, Ramsay

1964 "Nationalism in Roman Egypt," *Aegyptus* 44: 179–99.

Maehler, Herwig

1970 "Griechische Inschriften aus Elephantine," *MDAIK* 26: 169–72.

1983a "Die griechische Schule im ptolemäischen Ägypten," in *Egypt and the Hellenistic World. Proceedings of the International Colloquim, Louvain — 24–26 May 1982*, edited by E. Van't Dack, P. von Dessel, and W. van Gucht. Studia Hellenistica, vol. 27. Louvain: Orientaliste, pp. 191–203.

1983b "Egypt under the last Ptolemies," *BICS* 30: 1–16.

Mahaffy, J. P.

1896 "Introduction," in *Revenue Laws of Ptolemy Philadelphus, Edited from a Greek Papyrus in the Bodleian Library, with a Translation, Commentary, and Appendices*, by Bernard P. Grenfell. Oxford: The Clarendon Press.

1899 *A History of Egypt. Volume IV: The Ptolemaic Dynasty*. New York: Charles Scribner's Sons.

1905 *The Flinders Petrie Papyri, with Transcription, Commentaries and Index. Volume III*. Cunningham Memoirs, vol. 11. Dublin: Royal Irish Academy.

Malaise, Michel

1966 "Sésostris, pharaon de légende et d'histoire," *CdE* 41: 244–72.

Malinine, Michel

1950 "Un prêt des céréals à l'époque de Darïus I," *Kemi* 11: 1–23.

1951 "Un jugement rendu à Thèbes sous la XXV[e] dynastie (Pap. Louvre E. 3228[c])," *RdE* 6: 157–78.

1953 *Choix de textes juridiques en hiératique "anormal" et en démotique (XXV[e]–XXVII[e] dynastie)*. Volume I. Paris: Librairie Ancienne Honoré Champion.

1961 "Taxes funéraires égyptiennes à l'époque gréco-romaine," *Melanges Mariette*, edited by Jean Sainte Fare Garnot. BdE, vol. 32. Cairo: IFAO.

1973 "Une affaire concernant un partage (P. Vienne D 12003 et D 12004)," *RdE* 25: 192–208.

1975 "Ventes de tombes à l'époque Saite" *RdE* 27: 164–74.

1983 *Choix de Textes juridiques en Hieratique Anormal et en Démotique*. Volume II. RAPH, vol. 18. Cairo: IFAO.

Malinine, M.; Posener, G.; and Vercoutter, J.

1968 *Catalogue des stèles du Sérapéum de Memphis*. 2 vols. Paris: Imprimerie Nationale.

Mariette, Auguste

1873 *Denderah. Description générale du grand temple de cette ville*, vol. 4. Paris: Librairie A. Franck, 109 (7)–110 (3).

Marrou, Henri-Irenée

1965 *Histoire de l'éducation dans l'antiquité*. 6th ed. Paris: Editions du Seuil.

Martin, Geoffrey Thorndike

1971 "Editorial Foreword," *JEA* 57: 1–2.

1973 "Excavations in the Sacred Animal Necropolis at North Saqqâra, 1971–2: Preliminary Report," *JEA* 59: 5–15.

1974 "Excavations in the Sacred Animal Necropolis at North Saqqâra, 1972–3: Preliminary Report," *JEA* 60: 15–29.

1979 *The Tomb of Hetepka and Other Reliefs and Inscriptions from the Sacred Animal Necropolis, North Saqqara, 1964–73*. Texts from Excavations, Fourth Memoir. Excavations at North Saqqara, Documentsry Series, vol. 2. London: EES.

1981 *The Sacred Animal Necropolis at North Saqqara*. EM, vol. 50. London: EES.

Maspero, Gaston

1911 *Les contes populaires de l'Égypte ancienne*. 4th ed. Paris: Libraire Orientale et Américaine.

Masson, Olivier and Yoyotte, Jean

1988 "Une inscription ionienne mentionnant Psammétique Ier," *EpAn* 11: 171–80.

Mattha, Girgis

1945 *Demotic Ostraca from the Collections at Oxford, Paris, Berlin, Vienna and Cairo*. Publications de la Société Fouad I de Papyrologie. Textes et Documents, vol. 6. Cairo: IFAO.

Mattha, Girgis and Hughes, George

1975 *The Demotic Legal Code of Hermopolis West*. BdE, vol. 45. Cairo: IFAO.

Mayser, Edwin

1970 *Grammatik der griechischen Papyri aus der Ptolemäerzeit. Band 1: Laut- und Wortlehre, Teil 1: Einleitung und Lautlehre*. 2nd ed., edited by Hans Schmoll. Berlin: De Gruyter.

Méautis, G.

1918 *Hermoupolis-la-grande*. Lausanne: Imprimerie la Concorde.

Meeks, Dimitri

1972 *Le grand texte des donations au temple d'Edfou*. BdE, vol. 59. Cairo: IFAO.

1979 *Année lexicographique*, vol. 3. Paris: Dimitri Meeks.

Megally, Tawfik

1989 "Ancient Egyptians Pioneered Today's T-Shirt," *ARCE Newsletter* 147: 25 (reprinted from the *Egyptian Gazette*, November 12, 1989).

Meiggs, Russell

1982 *Trees and Timber in the Ancient Mediterranean World*. Oxford: The Clarendon Press.

Mendels, D.

1990 "The Polemical Character of Manetho's *Aegyptiaca*," in *Purposes of History: Studies in Greek Historiography from the 4th to the 2nd Centuries B.C.*, edited by H. Verdin, G. Schepens, and E. De Keyser. Studia Hellenistica, vol. 30. Louvain: Katholieke Universiteit Leuven, pp. 91–110.

Menu, Bernadette

1974 "Une stèle démotique inédite," *RdE* 26: 66–72.

1981 "Deux ostraca démotiques inédits (O. D. Cortegianni n° 1 et 2)," *CRIPEL* 6: 215–24.

Mertens, Jan and Tassier, Emmanuel

1988 "Proposal for a Bibliography and Description of Demotic Literary Texts," *GM* 101: 49–55.

Merzagora, Maria

1929 "La navigazione in Egitto nell'età greco-romana," *Aegyptus* 10: 105–48.

Messeri, Gabriella

1985 "Grammenti di documenti agoranomici tolemaici della British Library," in *Papyrology*, edited by Naphtali Lewis. Yale Classical Studies, vol. 28. Cambridge: Cambridge University Press.

Milik, J. T.

1954 Review of *The Brooklyn Museum Papyri — New Documents of the Fifth Century B.C. from the Jewish Colony at Elephantine*, edited with a historical introduction by Emil G. Kraeling. *RB* 61: 247–51.

Milne, J. G.

1913 *Theban Ostraca. Part III: Greek Texts*, edited by Alan H. Gardiner, Herbert Thompson, and J. G. Milne. University of Toronto Studies. Toronto: The University of Toronto Library.

Mitteis, Ludwig

1912a *Grundzüge und Chrestomathie der Papyruskunde. Zweiter Band: Juristischer Teil, Erste Hälfte: Grundzüge*. Leipzig and Berlin: B. G. Teubner.

1912b *Grundzüge und Chrestomathie der Papyruskunde. Zweiter Band: Juristischer Teil, Zweite Hälfte: Chrestomathie*. Leipzig and Berlin: B. G. Teubner.

Modrzejewski, Józef

1952 "Private arbitration in the Law of Greco-Roman Egypt," *JJP* 6: 239–56.

Möller, Georg

1913 *Demotische Texte aus den königlichen Museen zu Berlin. Erster Band: Mumienschilder*. Leipzig: J. C. Hinrichs'sche Buchhandlung.

1920 "Zu Herodots ägyptischen Geschichte," *ZÄS* 56: 76–79.

Mokhtar, Mohamed Gamal el-Din

1983 *Ihnâsya el-Medina (Hierakleopolis Magna). Its Importance and its Role in Pharaonic History*. BdE, vol. 40. Cairo: IFAO.

Moll, Friedrich

1929 *Das Schiff in der bildenden Kunst von Altertum bis zum ausgang des Mittelalters*. Bonn: Kurt Schroeder Verlag.

Momigliano, Arnaldo

1975 *Alien Wisdom, the Limits of Hellenization.* Cambridge: Cambridge University Press.

Montevecchi, Orsolina

1935 "Richerche di sociologia nei documenti dell'Egitto greco-romano, I: I testamenti," *Aegyptus* 15: 67–121.

1970 "Nerone a una polis e ai 6475," *Aegyptus* 50: 5–33.

Montserrat, Dominic

1991 "Mallocouria and Therapeuteria: Rituals of Transition in a Mixed Society," *BASP* 28: 43–49.

Mooren, Leon

1975 *The Aulic Titulature in Ptolemaic Egypt. Introduction and Prosopography.* Verhandelingen van de Koninklijke Academie voor Wetenschappen, Letteren en Schone Kunsten van België, Klasse der Letteren; Jaarg. 37, Nr. 78. Brussels: Paleis der Academien.

1977 *La hiérarchie de cour ptolémaïque: contribution a l'etude des institutions et des classes dirigeantes a l'epoque hellenistique.* Studia Hellenistica, vol. 23. Louvain: Universitas Catholica Lovaniensis.

1984 "On the Jurisdiction of the Nome Strategoi in Ptolemaic Egypt," in *Atti del XVII congresso internazionale di papirologia*, vol. 3. Naples: Centro Internationale per lo Studio dei Papiri Ercolanesi, pp. 1217–25.

Mooren, L. and Swinnen, W.

1975 *Prosopographia Ptolemaica VIII: addenda et corrigenda aux volumes I (1950) et II (1952).* Studia Hellenistica, vol. 21. Louvain: Universitas Catholica Lovaniensis.

Mooren, L. and Van't Dack, E.

1981 "Le stratège Platon et sa famille," *AC* 50: 535–44.

Morris, Royce L. B. and Oates, John F.

1985 "An Official Report," *BASP* 22: 243–47.

Morrison, John S. and Williams, Roderick T.

1968 *Greek Oared Ships.* Cambridge: Cambridge University Press.

Morschauser, Scott

1985 "Observations on the Speeches of Ramesses II in the Literary Record of the Battle of Kadesh," in *Perspectives on the Battle of Kadesh*, edited by Hans Goedicke. Baltimore: Halgo, Inc., pp. 123–206.

Müller, Christa

1975 "Stadt und Tempel von Elephantine, Fünfter Grabungsbericht. VIII. Drei Stelenfragmente," *MDAIK* 31: 80–84.

Müller, Dieter

1961 *Ägypten und die griechischen Isis-Aretologien.* Abhandlungen der Sächsischen Akademie der Wissenschaften zu Leipzig, Philologische-historische Klasse, Band 53, Heft 1. Munich: Akademie-Verlag.

Muffs, Yochanan

1968 *Studies in the Aramaic Legal Papyri from Elephantine.* Leiden: E. J. Brill.

Munro, Peter

1973 *Die spätägyptischen Totenstelen*. Ägyptologische Forschungen, Heft 25. Glückstadt: Verlag J. J. Augustin.

Murray, Gilbert

1911 *The Story of Nefrekepta*. Oxford: Oxford University Press.

Murray, Oswyn

1970 "Hecataeus of Abdera and Pharaonic Kingship," *JEA* 56: 141–71.

1980 *Early Greece*. Atlantic Highlands, NJ: Humanities Press Inc.

Mussies, G.

1983 Review of *Textes grecs, démotiques et bilingues (P. L. Bat. 19)* by E. Boswinkel and P. W. Pestman. *Mnemosyne* 36: 224–28.

Muszynski, Michel

1980 "Dédicace à Anubis pour Apollônios et Zênôn," in *Greek and Demotic Texts in the Zenon Archive*, edited by P. W. Pestman, 2 vols. PLB, vol. 20. Leiden: E. J. Brill, pp. 274–75.

Nachtergael, Georges

1985 "Les terres cuites 'du Fayoum' dans les maisons de l'Égypte romaine," *CdE* 60: 223–39.

1989 "Le chameau, l'âne et le mulet en Égypte gréco-romaine," *CdE* 64: 287–336.

Naguib, Saphinaz-Amal

1982 "Deux 'surintendants de la flotte royale' à Oslo," *BSEG* 6: 69–75.

Naville, Edouard

1891 *The Season's Work at Ahnas and Beni Hasan*. Special Extra Report of the Egypt Exploration Fund. London: EES.

1894 *Ahnas-el-Medina (Heracleopolis Magna) with Chapters on Mendes, the Nome Thoth, and Leontopolis*. Excavation Memoir. London: EES.

1898 *The Temple of Deir el Bahari. Part III: Plates LVI.–LXXXVI. End of Northern Half and Southern Half of the Middle Platform*. EM, vol. 16. London: EES.

Nelson, Carroll A.

1979 *Status Declarations in Roman Egypt*. American Studies in Papyrology, vol. 19. Amsterdam: Adolf M. Hakkert.

Neugebauer, O.

1943 "Demotic Horoscopes," *JAOS* 63: 115–27.

Neugebauer, O. and Parker, Richard A.

1968 "Two Demotic Horoscopes," *JEA* 54: 231–35.

Nims, Charles F.

1947 "Additional Demotic Evidence on the *ḥōnĕ* of Mi-wēr," *JEA* 33: 92.

1948 "The Term *HP*, 'Law, Right'," *JNES* 7: 249–60.

Nock, A. D.

1929 "Greek Magical Papyri," *JEA* 15: 219–35.

Nur-el-Din, Mohamed A.-H.

1974 *The Demotic Ostraca in the National Museum of Antiquities at Leiden*. Collections of the National Museum of Antiquities at Leiden, vol. 1. Leiden: E. J. Brill.

1987 "Some Demotic School Exercises," *ASAE* 71: 199–204.

Oates, John F.; Bagnall, Roger S.; Willis, Willam H.; and Worp, K. A.

1985 *Checklist of Editions of Greek Papyri and Ostraca*. 3rd ed. BASP Supp., no. 4. Atlanta: Scholars Press.

Obsomer, Claude

1989 *Les campagnes de Sésostris dans Hérodote*. Brussels: Connaissance de l'Égypte ancienne.

Omar, Sayed

1988 "Zwei Kopfsteuerquittungen aus dem Archiv des Soterichos (*PKairo* SR 3732/20, 21)," *Proceedings of the XVIII International Congress of Papyrology, Athens, 25–31 May 1986*, vol. II, edited by Basil G. Mandilaras. Athens: Greek Papyrological Society, pp. 287–91.

1991 "Neue Kopfssteuerquittungen aus dem Archiv des Soterichos," *ZPE* 86: 215–29.

Orlandi, T.

1984 "La traduzioni dal greco e lo sviluppo della letteratura copta," in *Graeco-coptica. Griechen und Kopten im byzantinischen Ägypten*, edited by Peter Nagel. Wissenschaftliche Beiträge / Martin-Luther-Universitat Halle-Wittenberg, 1984/48. Halle (Salle): Martin-Luther-Universitat Halle-Wittenberg, pp. 181–203.

Orrieux, Claude

1985 *Zénon de Caunos, parépidèmos, et le destin grec*. Paris: Belles Lettres.

Osing, Jurgen

1976 *Die Nominalbildung des Ägyptischen*. Mainz am Rhein: Philipp von Zabern.

1987 *Der spätägyptische Papyrus BM 10108*. Ägyptologische Abhandlungen, Band 33. Wiesbaden: Otto Harrassowitz.

Osing, J.; Moursi, M.; Arnold, D.; Neugebauer, O.; Parker, R. A.; Pingree, D.; and Nur-el-Din, M. A.

1982 *Denkmäler der Oase Dachla: Aus dem Nachlass von Ahmed Fakhry*. Archäologische Veröffentlichungen, vol. 28. Mainz am Rhein: Verlag Philipp von Zabern.

Otto, Walter

1934 *Zur Geschichte der Zeit des 6. Ptolemäers*. Munich: Verlag der Bayerischen Akademie der Wissenschaften.

Pack, Roger Ambrose

1965 *The Greek and Latin Literary Texts from Greco-Roman Egypt*. Ann Arbor: The University of Michigan Press.

Parker, Richard A.

1959 *A Vienna Demotic Papyrus on Eclipse and Lunar Omnia*. Brown Egyptological Studies, vol. 2. Providence, RI: Brown University Press.

1972 *Demotic Mathematical Papyri*. Providence, RI: Brown University Press.

1984 "A Horoscope Text in Triplicate," in *Grammata Demotika. Festschrift für Erich Lüddeckens zum 15. Juni 1983*, edited by Heinz-Josef Thissen and Karl-Theodor Zauzich. Würzburg: Gisela Zauzich Verlag, pp. 141–43.

Parlasca, Klaus

1966 *Mumienporträts und Verwwandte Denkmäler*. Wiesbaden: Franz Steiner Verlag GmbH.

1969 *Ritratti di mummie*. Repertorio d'Arte dell'Egitto Greco-romano, Series B, vol. 1, edited by Achille Adriani. Palermo: Banco di Sicilia, Fondazione Mormino.

1970 "Zur Stellung der Terenuthis-Stelen — Eine Gruppe römischer Grabreliefs aus Ägypten in Berlin," *MDAIK* 26: 173–98.

Parrott, D. M., ed.

1979 *Nag Hammadi Codices V,2–5 and VI with Papyrus Berolinensis 8502, 1 and 4*. Nag Hammadi Studies, vol. 11. Leiden: E. J. Brill.

Paton, W. R., trans.

1975 *Polybius. The Histories*. 6 vols. Cambridge, MA: Harvard University Press.

Perdu, Olivier

1985 "Le monument de Samtoutefnakht à Naples [première partie]," *RdE* 36: 89–113.

Peremans, W.

1937 *Vreemdelingen en Egyptenaren in Vroeg-Ptolemaeïsch Egypte*. Louvain: Universitaire Stichting van België.

1972 "Egyptiens et étrangers dans l'armée de terre et dans la police de l'Égypte ptolemaïque," *Ancient Society* 3: 67–76.

1977 "Un groupe d'officiers dans l'armée des Lagides," *Ancient Society* 8: 175–85.

1981 "Les mariages mixtes dans l'Égypte des Lagides," in *Scritti in onore di Orsolina Montevecchi*, edited by Edda Bresciani, Giovanni Geraci, Sergio Pernigotti, and Giancarlo Susini. Bologna: Cooperativa Libraria Universitaria Editrice, pp. 273–81.

Peremans, W. and Van't Dack, Edmond

1950 *Prosopographia Ptolemaica. I: L'adminstration civile et financière*. Studia Hellenistica, vol. 6. Louvain: Presses Universitaires.

1953 *Prosopographica*. Studia Hellenistica, vol. 9. Louvain: Presses Universitaires.

Pernigotti, Sergio

1985 "I papiri copti dell'Università Cattolica di Milano. I," *Aegyptus* 65: 67–105.

Pestman, Pieter Willem

1961 *Marriage and Matrimonial Property in Ancient Egypt*. PLB, vol. 9. Leiden: E. J. Brill.

1963 "A proposito dei documenti di Pathyris," *Aegyptus* 43: 10–53.

1965a "Der demotische Tekst der Mumientäfelchen aus Amsterdam," *OMRO* 46: 44–51.

1965b "Les archives privées de Pathyris à l'époque ptolémaïque. La famille de Pétéharsemtheus, fils de Panebkhounis" in *Studia Papyrologica Varia*, edited by E. Boswinkel, P. W. Pestman, and P. J. Sijpesteijn. PLB, vol. 14. Leiden: E. J. Brill, pp. 47–105.

Pestman, Pieter Willem (*cont.*)

1967 *Chronologie égyptienne d'après les textes démotiques (332 av. J.-C. – 453 ap. J.-C.)*. PLB, vol. 15. Leiden: E. J. Brill.

1971 "Loans Bearing No Interest?" *JJP* 16–17: 7–29.

1977 *Recueil de textes démotiques et bilingues*. 3 vols. Leiden: E. J. Brill.

1978 "L'Agoranomie: un avant-poste de l'administration grecque enlevé par les égyptiens?" in *Das Ptolemäische Ägypten. Akten des internationalen Symposions 27.–29. September 1976 in Berlin*, edited by Herwig Maehler and Volker Michael Strocka. Mainz am Rhein: Verlag Philipp von Zabern, pp. 203–10.

1981 "Nahomensis, una donna d'affari di Pathyris. L'archivio bilingue di Pelaias, figlio di Eunus," in *Scritti in onore di Orsolina Montevecchi*, edited by Edda Bresciani, Giovanni Geraci, Sergio Pernigotti, and Giancarlo Susini. Bologna: Cooperativa Libraria Universitaria Editrice, pp. 295–315.

1983 "L'origine et l'extension d'un manuel de droit égyptien. Quelques réflexions à propos du soi-disant Code de Hermoupolis," *JESHO* 26: 14–21.

1985 "Registration of Demotic Contracts in Egypt. P. Par. 65. 2nd Cent. B.C.," in *Satura Roberto Feenstra: sexagesimum quintum annum aetatis complenti ab alumnis collegis amicis oblata*, edited by J. A. Ankum, J. E. Spruit, and F. B. J. Wubbe. Fribourg, Switzerland: Editions Universitaires, pp. 17–25.

1989 "Egizi sotto dominazioni straniere," in *Egitto e storia antica dall'ellenismo all'età araba. Atti del colloquio internazionale, Bologna, 31 agosto – 2 settembre 1987*, edited by Lucia Criscuolo and Giovanni Geraci. Bologna: Cooperativa Libraria Universitaria Editrice, pp. 137–58.

1990 *The New Papyrological Primer*. 5th ed. Leiden: E. J. Brill.

—— A *The Archive of the Theban Choachytes ... Survey. Part B: Studies* (in press).

—— B *Les papyrus démotiques de Tsenhor*. Studia Demotica, vol. 4 (in press).

Pestman, P. W., ed.

1985 *Vreemdelingen in het land van Pharao*. Zutphen: Terra.

Pestman, P. W.; Clarysse, W.; Korver, M.; Muszynski, M.; Schutgens, A.; Tait, W. J.; and Winnicki, J. K.

1981 *A Guide to the Zenon Archive* (*P. L. Bat.* 21). Papyrologica Ludduno-Batava, vol. 21A–B. Leiden: E. J. Brill.

Petrie, W. M. Flinders

1885 *Tanis. Part 1, 1883–4*. EM, vol. 2. London: EEF.

1888 *Tanis II, Nebesheh (Am) and Defenneh*. EM, vol. 5. London: EEF.

1889 *Hawara, Biahmu and Arsinoe*. London: Field and Tuer, The Leadenhall Press.

1905a *Ehnasya 1904*. EM, vol. 26. London: EES.

1905b *Roman Ehnasya 1904*. Special Extra Report of the Egypt Exploration Fund. London: EES.

1906 *Hyksos and Israelite Cities*. BSAEP, vol. 12. London: BSAE.

1907 *Gizeh and Rifeh*. BSAEP, vol. 13. London: BSAE.

1911 *Roman Portraits and Memphis IV*. BSAEP, vol. 20. London: BSAE.

1925 *Tombs of the Courtiers and Oxyrhynkhos*. BSAEP, vol. 37. London: BSAE.

Petrie, W. M. Flinders and Bruntun, Guy
1924 *Sedment I*. BSAEP, vol. 34. London: BSAE.

Petrie, W. M. Flinders and Griffith, F. Ll.
1888 *Tanis Part II, 1886*. London: Trübner and Co.

Philipp, Hanna
1972 *Terrakotten aus Ägypten im Ägyptischen Museum Berlin*. Berlin: Gebr. Mann Verlag.

Piankoff, Alexandre
1930 *Le "coeur" dans les textes égyptiens depuis l'ancien jusqu'à la fin du nouvel empire*. Paris: Librairie Orientaliste Paul Geuthner.

Piankoff, Alexandre and Rambova, N.
1957 *Mythological Papyri. Part I: Texts*. Bollingen Series XL, no. 6. New York: Pantheon Books Inc.

Pierce, Richard Holton
1972 *Three Demotic Papyri in the Brooklyn Museum. A Contribution to the Study of Contracts and their Instruments in Ptolemaic Egypt*. Symbolae Osloenses, fasc. supplet. 24. Oslo: Universitetsforlaget.

Plaumann, Gerhard
1910 *Ptolemais in Oberägypten. Ein Beitrag zur Geschichte des Hellenismus in Ägypten*. Leipziger historische Abhandlungen, Heft 8. Leipzig: Quelle & Meyer.

Pomeroy, Sarah B.
1984 *Women in Hellenistic Egypt: From Alexander to Cleopatra*. New York: Schocken Books.

1989 "Plenary Lecture," American Research Center in Egypt, Annual Convention, Philadelphia, April 21.

Poo, Mu-chou
1984 *The Offering of Wine in Ancient Egypt*. Ph.D. dissertation, The Johns Hopkins University.

Popper, William
1951 *The Cairo Nilometer*. CASP, vol. 12. Berkeley and Los Angeles: The University of California Press.

Porten, Bezalel
1968 *Archives from Elephantine. The Life of an Ancient Jewish Military Colony*. Berkeley: The University of California Press.

1986 *Select Aramaic Papyri from Ancient Egypt*. Jerusalem: Institute for the Study of Aramaic Papyri.

Porten, Bezalel and Szubin, H. Z.
1982 "'Abandoned Property' in Elephantine: A New Interpretation of Kraeling 3," *JNES* 41: 123–31.

Porten, Bezalel and Zauzich, Karl-Theodor

—— *Hor bar Punesh, eine Erzählung in aramäischer und demotischer Überlieferung.* Demotische Studien, Band 11. Sommerhausen: Gisela Zauzich Verlag (in press).

Posener, Georges

1936 *La premiere domination perse en Égypte*. BdE, vol. 11. Cairo: IFAO.

1953 "On the Tale of the Doomed Prince," *JEA* 39: 107.

1965 "Sur l'orientation et l'ordre des points cardinaux chez les Égyptiens," in *Göttinger Vorträge vom ägyptologischen Kolloquium der Akademie am 25. und 26. August 1964*, edited by Siegfried Schott. Göttingen: Vanderhoeck and Ruprecht, pp. 69–78.

1986 *Le papyrus Vandier*. Bibliotheque Generale, tome 7. Cairo: IFAO.

Préaux, Claire

1935 *Les ostraca grecs de la collection Charles-Edwin Wilbour au Musée de Brooklyn.* New York: The Brooklyn Museum.

1939a *L'Économie royale des Lagide*. Brussels: Fondation Égyptologique Reine Élisabeth.

1939b *Les ostraca grecs de la Collection Charles-Edwin Wilbour au Musée de Brooklyn.* Brussels: Fondation Égyptologique Reine Élisabeth.

1956 "La stabilité de l'Égypte aux deux premiers siècles de notre ère," *CdE* 31: 311–31.

1978 *Le monde hellénistique*. Nouvelle Clio, L'Historie et ses Problèmes, vol. 6. Paris: Presses Universitaires de France.

Preisendanz, Karl

1973 *Papyri Graecae Magicae. Die griechischen Zauberpapyri*. 2 vols. 2nd ed. Stuttgart: B. G. Teubner.

Preisigke, Friedrich

1910 *Girowesen im griechischen Ägypten, enthaltend Kornigiro, Geldgiro, Girobanknotariat mit Einschluß des Archivwesens: ein Beitrag zur Geschichte des Verwaltungsdienstes im Altertum.* Straßburg: Schlesier and Schweikhardt.

1925 *Wörterbuch der griechischen Papyrusurkunden, I. Band: A–K.* Berlin: Selbstverlag der Reben. Zu beziehen durch Frl. Grete Preisigke.

1927 *Wörterbuch der griechischen Papyrusurkunden, II. Band: Λ–Ω.* Berlin: Selbstverlag der Reben. Zu beziehen durch Frl. Grete Preisigke.

1931 *Wörterbuch der griechischen Papyrusurkunden, III. Band: Besondere Wörterliste.* Berlin: Selbstverlag der Reben. Zu beziehen durch Frl. Grete Preisigke.

Preisigke, Friedrich and Spiegelberg, Wilhelm

1914 *Die Prinz-Joachim Ostraka: Griechische und demotische Beisetzungsurkunden für Ibis- und Falkenmumien aus Ombos*. Schriften der Wissenschaftlichen Gesellschaft in Straßburg, Heft 19. Straßburg: Karl J. Trübner.

1915 *Ägyptische und griechische Inschriften und Graffiti aus den Steinbrüchen des Gebel Silsile (Ober ägypten).* Straßburg: Verlag von Karl J. Trübner.

Presedo Velo, F. J.
1976 "The Herakleopolis Magna Findings (1976)," in *Abstracts of Papers. First International Congress of Egyptology. Cairo, October 2, 1976*, edited by Dietrich Wildung. Munich: Karl M. Lipp, pp. 94–96.

Priese, Karl-Heinz
1977 "Eine verschollene Bauinschrift des fruhmeroitischen Konigs Aktisanes (?) vom Gebel Barkal," in *Ägypten und Kusch* (Festschrift Fritz Hintze), edited by Erika Endesfelder, Karl-Heinz Priese, Walter-Friedrich Reineke, and Steffen Wenig. Berlin: Akademie-Verlag, pp. 343–67.

Pryor, John H.
1984 "Naval Architecture of Crusader Transport Ships, Part III," *The Mariner's Mirror* 70: 363–86.

Quaegebeur, Jan
1969 "Een nieuwe onderzoeksmethode naar de oud-egyptische dialekten," in *Handelingen van het XXVIIe Vlaams Filologencongres 8–10 April 1969*, edited by J. Van Haver. Brussels: n.p., pp. 162–66.

1971a "Le nom propre Tsonesontis," *CdE* 46: 158–72.

1971b "Ptolémée II en adoration devant Arsinoé II divinisée," *BIFAO* 69: 191–217.

1973 "Considérations sur le nom propre égyptien Teëphthaphônukhos," *OLP* 4: 85–100.

1974a "The Study of Egyptian Proper Names in Greek Transcription. Problems and Perspectives," *Onoma* 18: 403–20.

1974b "Prêtres et cultes thébains à la lumière de documents égyptiens et grecs," *BSFE* 70–71: 37–55.

1975 *Le dieu égyptien Shaï dans la religion et l'onomastique*. OLA, vol. 2, Louvain: Louvain University Press.

1975/76 "Les appellations grecques des temples de Karnak," *OLP* 6/7: 463–78.

1978 "Mummy Labels: an Orientation," in *Textes grecs, démotiques et bilingues*, edited by E. Boswinkel and P. W. Pestman. PLB, vol. 19. Louvain: E. J. Brill, pp. 232–59.

1979a "De nouvelles archives de famille thebains à l'aube de l'époque ptolémaïque," in *Actes du XVe congrès international de papyrologie, Tome IV: papyrologie documentaire*, edited by Jean Bingen and Georges Nachtergael. Papyrologica Bruxellensia, vol. 19. Brussels: Fondation Égyptologique Reine Élisabeth, pp. 40–48.

1979b "Documents égyptiens et rôle économique du clergé en Égypte hellénistique," in *State and Temple Economy in the Ancient Near East II*, edited by Edward Lipiński. OLA, vol. 6. Louvain: Department Oriëntalistiek, pp. 707–29.

1980 "The Genealogy of the Memphite High Priest Family in the Hellenistic Period," in *Studies on Ptolemaic Memphis*, edited by Dorothy J. Crawford, Jan Quaegebeur, and Willy Clarysse. Studia Hellenistica, vol. 24. Louvain: n.p., pp. 43–89.

Quaegebeur, Jan (*cont.*)

1981 "Demotic and Greek Ostraca Excavated at Elkab," in *Proceedings of the Sixteenth International Congress of Papyrology, New York, 24–31 July 1980*, edited by Roger S. Bagnall, Gerald M. Brown, Ann E. Hanson, and Ludwig Koenen. American Studies in Papyrology, vol. 23. Chico, CA: Scholars Press, pp. 527–36.

1982 "De la préhistoire de l'écriture copte," *OLP* 13: 125–36.

1983a "Cultes égyptiens et grecs en Égypte hellénistique. L'exploitation des sources," in *Egypt and the Hellenistic World, Proceedings of the International Colloquium Louvain — 24–26 May 1982*, edited by E. Van't Dack, P. Van Dessel, and W. Van Gucht. Studia Hellenistica, vol. 27. Louvain: Orientaliste, pp. 303–24.

1983b "De l'origine égyptienne du griffon Némésis," in *Visages du destin dans les mythologies. Mélanges Jacqueline Duchemin. Actes de collogue de Chantilly 1er–2 mai*, edited by François Jouan. Centre de Recherches Mythologiques de l'Université de Paris, vol. 10. Paris: Société d'Édition "*Le Belles Lettres*," pp. 41–54.

1983c "Eseremphis. Une Isis de haute époque en vogue dans l'Égypte gréco-romaine," in *Das römisch-byzantinische Ägypten. Akten des internationalen Symposions 26.–30. September 1978 in Trier*, edited by Günter Grimm, Heinz Heinen, and Erich Winter. Aegyptiaca Treverensia, Band 2. Mainz am Rhein: Verlag Philipp von Zabern, pp. 67–75.

1984 "Papyrologie grecque et religion égyptienne. Projet d'un répertoire explicatif," in *Atti del XVII congresso internazionale di papirologia*, vol. 1, Naples: Centro Internationale per lo Studio dei Papiri Ercolanesi, pp. 107–11.

1986 "Osservazioni sul titolare di un libro dei morti conservato ad Assisi," *ORANT* 25: 69–80.

1987 "Une statue égyptienne représentant Héraclès-Melqart?," in *Phoenicia and the East Mediterranean in the First Millennium B.C*, edited by E. Lipiński. Studia Phoenicia, vol. 5. OLA, vol. 22. Louvain: Peeters, pp. 157–66.

1988 "Cleopatra VII and the Cults of the Ptolemaic Queens," in *Cleopatra's Egypt: Age of the Ptolemies*, edited by Robert S. Bianchi. Brooklyn: The Brooklyn Museum, pp. 41–54.

1989 "La statue du général Pétimouthês, Turin, Museo Egizio cat. 3062 + Karnak, Karakol n° 258," in *The Judean-Syrian-Egyptian Conflict of 103–101 B.C. A Multilingual Dossier Concerning a "War of Sceptres,"* by E. Van't Dack, W. Clarysse, G. Cohen, J. Quaegebeur, and J. K. Winnicki. Collectanea Hellenistica, vol. I. Brussels: Comité Klassieke Studies, Subcomité Hellenisme, Koninklijke Academie voor Wetenschappen, Letteren en Schone Kunsten van België, pp. 88–108.

1991 "Les quatre dieux Min," in *Religion und Philosophie im alten Ägypten. Festgabe für Philippe Derchain zu seinem 65. Geburtstag am 24. Juli 1991*, edited by Ursula Verhoeven and Erhart Graefe. OLA, vol. 39. Louvain: Peeters, pp. 253–68.

—— A "Cléopâtre VIII et le temple de Dendera" (forthcoming).

—— B "The Demotic and Greek Ostraca from Elkab," in *Acts of the Nineteenth Congress of Papyrology, Cairo, 1989*, edited by Jean Bingen (forthcoming).

Quaegebeur, Jan, Clarisse, Willy, and van Maele, Beatrijs
1985 "Athêna, Nêith and Thoêris in Greek Documents," *ZPE* 60: 217–32.

Rabinowitz, Jacob J.
1956 *Jewish Law: Its Influence on the Development of Legal Institutions*. New York: Bloch Publishing Company.

Raschke, Manfred G.
1974 "The Office of Agoranomos in Ptolemaic and Roman Egypt," *Akten des XIII internationalen Papyrologenkongresses, Marburg/Lahn 2. bis 6. August 1971*, edited by E. Kießling and H. A. Rupprecht. MBP, Heft 66. Munich: Verlag C. H. Beck, pp. 349–56.

1976 "An Official Letter to an Agoranomus: *P. Oxy*. I 170," *BASP* 13: 17–29.

Ray, John D.
1972 "Two Inscribed Objects in the Fitzwilliam Museum, Cambridge," *JEA* 58: 247–53.

1976 *The Archive of Ḥor*. Texts from Excavations, Second Memoir. Oxford: EES.

1977 "The Complaint of Herieu," *RdE* 29: 97–116.

Reardon, B. P., ed.
1989 "An Ephesian Tale," in *Collected Ancient Greek Novels*. Berkeley: The University of California Press.

Reekmans, Tony
1948 "Monetary History and the Dating of Ptolemaic Papyri," in Studia Hellenistica, vol. 5. Louvain: Universitas Catholica Lovaniensis, pp. 15–43.

1949 "Economic and Social Repercussions of the Ptolemaic Copper Inflation," *CdE* 24: 324–42.

Reekmans, T. and Van't Dack, E.
1952 "A Bodleian Archive on Corn Transport," *CdE* 53: 149–95.

Reich, Nathaniel
1914 *Papyri Juristischen Inhalts in hieratischer und demotischer Schrift aus dem British Museum*. Vienna: Kaiserlichen Akademie der Wissenschaften.

1924 "A Grammatical Exercise of an Egyptian Schoolboy," *JEA* 10: 285–88.

1936 "Barter for Annuity and Perpetual Provision of the Body (Papyrus University Museum, Philadelphia, 873; Jar 1; 29–86–508 = Document 1)," *Mizraim* 3: 9–17.

Remondon, R.
1952 "Ostraca provenant de fouilles françaises de Deir el-Médina et de Karnak," *BIFAO* 50: 1–15.

Revillout, Eugène
1880 *Chrestomathie démotique*. Paris: F. Vieweg, Libraire-Éditeur.

1885 "Le tribunal égyptien de Thèbes," *RE* 3: 9–16.

1892 "Un papyrus bilingue du temps de Philopator. Part II," *PSBA* 14: 12032.

Reymond, E. A. E.
1965–66 "Studies in Late Egyptian Documents Preserved in the John Rylands Library. II. Dimê and its Papyri: An Introduction," *BJRL* 48: 433–66.

Reymond, E. A. E. (*cont.*)

1966–67 "Studies in Late Egyptian Documents Preserved in the John Rylands Library. III. Dimê and its Papyri: Demotic Contracts of the 1st Century A.D.," *BJRL* 49: 464–96.

1973 *Embalmers' Archive from Hawara*. Catalogue of Demotic Papyri in the Ashmolean Museum, vol. 1. Oxford: The Griffith Institute.

1976 From the Contents of the Libraries of the Suchos Temples in the Fayyum. Part I: A Medical Book from Crocodilopolis, P. Vindob. D. 6257. MPER, vol. 10. Vienna: Verlag Brüder Hollinek.

1983 "Demotic Literary Works of Graeco-Roman Date in the Rainer Collection of Papyri in Vienna," in *Festschrift zum 100-jährigen Bestehen der Papyrussammlung der Österreichischen Nationalbibliothek: Papyrus Erzherzog Rainer (P. Rainer Cent.)*, edited by Josef Zessner-Spitzenberg. 2 vols. Vienna: Verlag Brüder Hollinek, pp. 42–60.

Rice, E. E.

1983 *The Grand Procession of Ptolemy Philadelphus*. Oxford Classical and Philosophical Monographs. Oxford: Oxford University Press.

Ricketts, Linda M.

1980 *The Administration of Ptolemaic Egypt under Cleopatra VII*. Ph.D. dissertation, The University of Minnesota. Ann Arbor: University Microfilms.

1982/83 "The Epistrategos Kallimachos and a Koptite Inscription: SB V 8036 Reconsidered," *Ancient Society* 13/14: 161–65.

1984 "Remarks on the Herakleopolite Papyri." Paper delivered at the American Research Center in Egypt Annual Meeting, Cleveland.

1989 "The Last Ptolemaic Co-Regency," in *ARCE Annual Meeting, Philadelphia, April 21–23, 1989: Program and Abstracts*, p. 46.

1990 "A Dual Queenship in the Reign of Berenice IV," *BASP* 27: 49–60.

Ritner, Robert K.

1980 "Kababash and the Satrap Stele — A Grammatical Rejoinder," *ZÄS* 107: 135–37.

1984 "A Property Transfer from the Erbstreit Archives," in *Grammata Demotika: Festschrift für Erich Lüddeckens zum 15. Juni 1983*, edited by H.-J. Thissen and K.-Th. Zauzich. Würzburg: Gisela Zauzich Verlag, pp. 171–87.

1989 Review of *Herophilus: The Art of Medicine in Early Alexandria* by Heinrich von Staden. *Newsletter of the Society for Ancient Medicine and Pharmacy* 17: 39–40.

—— "Egyptian Magical Practice under the Roman Empire: The Demotic Spells and their Religious Context," *ANRW*, Part II, Volume 18.5 (forthcoming).

Roccati, Alessandro

1987 "Ricerche sulla scrittura egizia. II. L'alfabeto e la scrittura egizia," *ORANT* 26: 81–83.

1988 "Postille all 'bilingue' sulla statua di Dario a Susa," in *Bilinguismo e biculturalismo nel mondo antico: Atti del colloquio interdisciplinare tenuto a Pisa il 28 e 29 settembre 1987*, edited by Enrico Campanile, Giorgio R. Cardona, and Romano Lazzeroni. Testi Linguistici, vol. 13. Pisa: Giardini, pp. 145–50.

1989 "Varietà linguistica e registro umile nella letteratura egizia tarda," in *Atti del Sodalizio Glottologico Milanese XXVIII*, edited by Istituto di Glottologia, Università di Milano. Milan: Paideia Editrice, Brescia, pp. 49–56.

Ronchi, Giulia

1975 *Lexicon theonymon rerumque sacrarum et divinarum ad Aegyptum pertinentium quae in papyris ostracis titulis Graecis Latinisque in Aegypto repertis laudantur*, vol. III. Testi e Documenti per lo Studio dell'Antichita, vol. 45. Milan: Istituto Editoriale Cisalpino "La Goliardica."

1977 *Lexicon theonymon rerumque sacrarum et divinarum ad Aegyptum pertinentium quae in papyris ostracis titulis Graecis Latinisque in Aegypto repertis laudantur*, vol. V. Testi e Documenti per lo Studio dell'Antichita, vol. 45. Milan: Istituto Editoriale Cisalpino "La Goliardica."

Roquet, Gérard

1973 "Vieux-français et copte: contacts lexicaux," *BIFAO* 73: 1–25.

Rostovtzeff, Michael

1920 "The Foundations of Social and Economic Life in Egypt in Hellenistic Times," *JEA* 6: 161–78.

1922 *A Large Estate in Egypt in the Third Century B.C. A Study in Economic History*. University of Wisconsin Studies in the Social Sciences and History, vol. 6. Madison: The University of Wisconsin Press.

1926 *The Social and Economic History of the Roman Empire*. Oxford: The Clarendon Press.

1940 "Πλῖα Θαλάσσια on the Nile, in *Études dédiées à la mémoire d'André M. Andréadès*, edited by K. Varvaressos et al. Athens: Imprimerie Pyrsos S. A., pp. 367–76.

1941 *The Social and Economic History of the Hellenistic World*, volume 1. Oxford: The Clarendon Press.

1953 *A Social and Economic History of the Hellenistic World*. Revised Edition. 3 vols. Oxford: The Clarendon Press.

Roussel, D., trans.

1970 *Histoire de Polybe. Texte traduit, presente, et annote*. Bibliotheque de la Pleiade, no. 219. Paris: Éditions Gallimard.

Rübsam, Winfried J. B.

1974 *Götter und Kulte in Faijum während der griechisch-römisch-byzantinischen Zeit*. Bonn: Rudolf Habelt Verlag GmbH.

Rupprecht, Hans Albert

1967 *Untersuchungen zum Darlehen im Recht der graeco-aegyptischen Papyri der Ptolemärezeit*. MBP, Heft 51. Munich: Verlag C. H. Beck.

1971 *Studien zur Quittung im recht der graeco-ägyptischen Papyri*. MBP, Heft 57. Munich: Verlag C. H. Beck.

Russmann, Edna R. and Finn, David

1989 *Egyptian Sculpture: Cairo and Luxor*. Austin: The University of Texas Press.

Saddington, D. B.

1975 "Race relations in the Early Roman Empire," *ANRW* Part II, Volume 3.1: pp. 112–37.

Säve-Söderbergh, Torgny

1946 *The Navy of the Eighteenth Dynasty*. Uppsala Universitets, Årsskrift, no. 6. Uppsala: A.-B. Lundequistska Bokhandeln.

Saleh, Mohamed and Sourouzian, Hourig

1987 *Official Catalogue. The Egyptian Museum Cairo.* Cairo: EAO.

Salmi, Mario

1945 "I dipinti paleocristiani di Antinoe," in *Scritti dedicati alla memoria di Ippolito Rosellini nel primo centenario della morte*, edited by Mario Salmi. Florence: Felice Le Monnier, pp. 157–69.

Samuel, Alan Edouard

1966 "The Internal Organization of the Nomarch's Bureau in the Third Century B.C.," in *Essays in Honor of C. Bradford Welles*, edited by Alan E. Samuel. American Studies in Papyrology, vol. 1. New Haven: American Society of Papyrologists, pp. 213–29.

1983 *From Athens to Alexandria: Hellenism and Social Goals in Ptolemaic Egypt.* Studia Hellenistica, vol. 26. Louvain: Orientaliste.

1989 *The Shifting Sands of History: Interpretations of Ptolemaic History*. Publications of the Association of Ancient Historians, vol. 2. Lanham, MD: University Press of America.

Samuel, Deborah H.

1977 "New Editions of Two Vienna Papyri," *BASP* 14: 123–43.

1981 "Greeks and Romans at Socnopaiou Nesos," *Proceedings of the Sixteenth International Congress of Papyrology, New York, 24–31 July 1980*, edited by Roger S. Bagnall, Gerald M. Brown, Ann E. Hanson, and Ludwig Koenen. American Studies in Papyrology, vol. 23. Chico, CA: Scholars Press, pp. 389–403.

Satzinger, Helmut

1983 "Zum Namen der Göttin Thermouthis," *ORANT* 22: 233–45.

1984 "Die altkoptischen Texte als Zeugnisse der Beziehungenzwischen Ägyptern und Griechen," in *Graeco-coptica. Griechen und Kopten im byzantinischen Ägypten*, edited by Peter Nagel. Wissenschaftliche Beiträge / Martin-Luther-Universitat Halle-Wittenberg, 1984/48. Halle (Salle): Martin-Luther-Universitat Halle-Wittenberg, pp. 137–46.

Sauneron, Serge

1960 "Une document égyptien relatif à la divinasation de la reine Arsinoé II," *BIFAO* 60: 83–110.

1963 *Le temple d'Esna, textes nos. 194–398*. Esna, vol. 3. Cairo: IFAO.

1980 *The Priests of Ancient Egypt*, translated by Ann Morrissett. Reprint. New York: Grove Press, Inc.

1982 *L'écriture figurative dans les textes d'Esna*. Esna, vol. 7. Cairo: IFAO.

1983 *La porte ptolémaique de l'enceinte de Mout à Karnak.* MIFAO 107. Cairo: IFAO.

Sayce, A. H.
1891 "Inscriptions grecques d'Égypte," *REG* 4: 46–57.

Schäfer, Heinrich
1931 "Armenisches Holz in altägyptischen Wegnereien. Die ägyptisches Konigsstandarte in Kadesch am Orontes." *SPAW* 25: 730–42.

Schiller, A. Arthur
1927 "A Coptic Dialysis," in *Tijdschrift voor Rechtsgeschiedenis*, vol. 7, edited by L. J. van Apeldoorn et al. Haarlem: H. D. Tjeenk Willink and zoon, pp. 432–53.

1931 "Coptic Law," *The Juridical Review* 43: 211–40.

1932 *Ten Coptic Legal Texts*. PMMA, vol. 2. New York: The Metropolitan Museum of Art.

1935 "Koptisches Recht," in *Kritische Vierteljahresschrift für Gesetzgebung und Rechtswissenschaft*, vol. 63, edited by A. Onross, W. Kisch, E. Mezger, E. Riezler, and L. Wenger. Munich, Berlin, and Leipzig: J. Schweitzer Verlag, pp. 18–46.

1953 "A Family Archive from Jeme," in *Studi in onore di Vincenzo Arangio-Ruiz*, vol. 4. Naples: Editore Jovene, pp. 327–75.

1957 "Coptic Documents. A Monograph on the Law of Coptic Documents and a Survey of Coptic Legal Studies, 1938–1956," in *Zeitschrift für vergleichende Rechtswissenschaft, einschließlich der ethnologischen Rechtsforschung*, vol. 60, edited by Leonhard Adam. Stuttgart: Ferdinand Enke Verlag, pp. 190–211.

1961 "The Budge Coptic Papyrus of Columbia University and Related Greek Papyri of the British Museum," in *Actes du Xe congrès international des papyrologues*, edited by Józef Wolski. Warsaw: Zakład Narodowy Imienia Ossolińskich, pp. 193–200.

1964 "The Interrelation of Coptic and Greek Papyri; P Bu and P BM Inv. Nos. 2017 and 2018," in *Studien zur Papyrologie und antiken Wirtschaftsgeschichte. Friedrich Oertel zum achtzigsten Geburtstag gewidmet*, edited by Horst Braunert. Bonn: Rudolf Habelt Verlag, pp. 107–19.

1968 "The Budge Papyrus of Columbia University," *JARCE* 7: 79–118.

1971a "The Courts are no More," in *Studi in onore di Edoardo Volterra*, vol. 1, edited by Luigi Aru et al. Milan: Casa Editrice Dott. A. Guiffrè, pp. 496–502.

1971b "Introduction," in *Koptische Rechtsurkunden des achten Jahrhunderts aus Djême (Theben)*, by W. Crum and G. Steindorff, 2d ed. Leipzig: Zentralantiquariat, pp. 1–12.

Schneider, Rudolf
1985 "Index zu den bisher publizierten Demotica in *Orientalia Suecana* (*OrSu*) 2–30," *Enchoria* 13: 163–71.

Schönborn, Hans-Bernhard
1976 *Die Pastophoren im Kult der ägyptischen Götter*. Beiträge zur klassischen Philologie, Heft 80. Meisenheim am Glan: Verlag Anton Hain.

Scholl, Reinhold
1988 "Drytons Tod," *CdE* 63: 141–44.

Schott, Siegfried

1954 *Die Deutung der Geheimnisse des Rituals für die Abwehr des Bösen.* Wiesbaden: F. Steiner Verlag GmbH.

1990 *Bücher und Bibliotheken im Alten Ägypten. Verzeichnis der Buch- und Spruchtitel und der Termini technici.* Wiesbaden: Otto Harrassowitz.

Schubart, Wilhelm and Schäfer, Diedrich

1933 *Spätptolemäische Papyri aus amtlichen Büros des Herakleopolites.* BGU, Vol. 8. Berlin: Wiedmannsche Buchhandlung.

Schwartz, Jacques

1961 *Les archives de Sarapion et de ses fils. Une exploitation agricole aux environs d'Hermoupolis Magna.* BdE, vol. 29. Cairo: IFAO.

Segal, J. B.

1983 *Aramaic Texts from North Saqqara with Some Fragments in Phoenician.* Texts from Excavations, Sixth Memoir. Excavations at North Saqqara, Documentary Series, vol. 4. London: EES.

Seibert, Jakob

1969 *Untersuchungen zur Geschichte Ptolemaios' I.* MBP, vol. 56. Munich: C. H. Beck'sche Verlagsbuchhandlung.

Seider, Richard

1938 *Der Nomarches. Beiträge zur Ptolemäischen Verwaltungsgeschichte.* Quellen und Studien zur Geschichte und Kultur des Altertums und Mittelalters. Reihe D: Untersuchungen und Mitteilungen, Heft 8. Heidelberg: F. Bilabel.

Seidl, Erwin

1929 *Der Eid im Ptolemäischen Recht.* Munich: Buchdruckerei F. Straub.

1962 *Ptolemäische Rechtsgeschichte*, 2d ed. Ägyptologische Forschungen, vol. 22. Glückstadt: J. J. Augustin.

1964 "Altägyptisches Recht," in *Orientalisches Recht.* Handbuch der Orientalistik, Erster Abteilung Der Nahe und der mittlere Osten, Dritter Band. Leiden/Cologne: E. J. Brill, pp. 1–48.

1968 "Der Prozeß Chrateanch gegen Tefhape im Jahre 170 v. Chr.," *Zeitschrift für vergleichende Rechtswissenschaft, einschließlich der ethnologischen Rechtsforschung*, vol. 69. Stuttgart: Ferdinand Enke Verlag, pp. 96–117.

1973 *Rechtsgeschichte Ägyptens als römischer Provinz. Die Behauptung des ägyptischen Rechts neben dem römischen.* Sankt Augustin: Verlag Hans Richarz.

Seidl, Erwin and Stricker, B. H.

1937 "Studien zu Papyrus BM e. g. 10591," *Zeitschrift der Savigny-Stiftung für Rechtsgeschichte (romanistische Abteilung)* 57: 272–308.

Sethe, Kurt

1906 "Eine ägyptische Expedition nach dem Libanon im 15. Jahrhunderts v. Chr.," *SPAW* 15: 356–63.

1916 *Von Zahlen und Zahlworten bei den alten Ägyptern und was fur andere volker und sprachen daraus su lemen ist. Ein beitrag zur geschichte von rechenkunst und sprache*. Schriften der Wissenschaftlichen Gesellschaft Straßburg, Heft 25. Straßburg: K. J. Trubner.

1917 "Der Name der Phönizier bei Griechen und Ägyptern," in *Orientalistische Studien. Fritz Hommel zum Sechzigsten Geburtstag am 31. Juli 1914*, vol. 1. *MVG*, vol. 2. Leipzig: J. C. Hinrichs'sche Buchhandlung, pp. 305–32.

1928 *Dramatische Texte zu altägyptischen Mysterienspielen*. UGAÄ, vol. 10. Leipzig: J. C. Hinrichs'sche Buchhandlung.

Sethe, K. and Partsch, J.

1920 *Demotische Urkunden zum ägyptischen Bürgschaftsrechte vorzüglich der Ptolemäerzeit*. Leipzig: B. G. Teubner.

Severin, Hans-Georg

1981 "Gli scavi eseguiti ad Ahnas, Bahnasa, Bawit e Saqqara: storia delle interpretazioni e nuovi risultati" in *XXVII corso di cultura sull'arte Ravennate e Bizantina*. Ravenna: Edizione del Girasole, pp. 315–36.

Shelton, John C.

1976 "Zum Steuersatz bei der frühptolemäischen ἁλική," *ZPE* 20: 35–39.

1978 Review of *Michigan Papyri (P. Mich. XII)*. *BASP* 15: 283–86.

1988a "*ʿrt(.t)* = λειτουργικόν," *Enchoria* 16: 137.

1988b *Greek Ostraca in the Ashmolean Museum from Oxyrhynchus and Other Sites*. Papyrologica Florentina, vol. 17. Florence: Edizioni Gonnelli.

Shisha-Halevi, Ariel

1989 "Papyrus Vandier *recto*: An early Demotic Literary Text?" *JAOS* 109: 421–35.

Shore, A. F.

1979 "Votive Objects from Dendera of the Graeco-Roman Period," in *Glimpses of Ancient Egypt: Studies in Honor of H. W. Fairman*, edited John Ruffle, G. A. Gaballa, and Kenneth A. Kitchen. Warminster: Aris and Philipps Ltd., pp. 138–60.

Sijpesteijn, P. J.

1979 "Three Papyri from the Michigan Collection," *ZPE* 33: 244–53.

1987 *Customs Duties in Graeco-Roman Egypt*. Studia Amstelodamensia ad Epigraphicam ius Antiquum et Papyrologicam Pertinentia, vol. 17. Zutphen: Terra Publishing Company.

Simon, Dieter

1971 "Zur Zivilgerichtsbarkeit im spätbyzantinischen Ägypten," *RIDA* 18: 623–58.

1974 "Zur Zivilgerichtsbarkeit im spätbyzantinischen Ägypten," in *Akten des XIII. internationalen Papyrologenkongresses Marburg/Lahr, 2.–6. August 1971*, edited by Emil Kießling and Hans-Albert Rupprecht. MBP, heft 66. Munich: C. H. Beck'sche Verlagsbuchhandlung, p. 389.

Skaist, Aaron

1983 "The *Clasula Salvatoria* in the Elephantine and Neo-Assyrian Documents," in *Arameans, Aramaic and the Aramaic Literary Tradition*, edited by Michael Sokoloff. Ramat-Gan: Bar-Ilan University Press, pp. 31–41.

Skeat, T. C.
1959 "A Receipt for *ENKYKLION*," *JEA* 45: 75–78.
1960 "Notes on Ptolemaic Chronology, I. 'The Last Year Which is Also the First'," *JEA* 46: 91–94.

Skeat, T. C., ed.
1974 *Greek Papyri in the British Museum VII: The Zenon Archive*. London: The British Museum.

Smelik, K. A. D.
1979 "The Cult of the Ibis in the Graeco-Roman Period. With Special Attention to the Data from the Papyri," in *Studies in Hellenistic Religions*. Études preliminaires aux religions orientales dans l'empire romaine, vol. 78, edited by M. J. Vermaseren. Leiden: E. J. Brill, pp. 225–43.

Smith, H. S.
1958 "Another Witness-Copy Document from the Fayyūm," *JEA* 44: 86–96.
1972 "Dates of the Obsequies of the Mothers of Apis," *RdE* 24: 176–87.
1974a *A Visit to Ancient Egypt: Life at Memphis & Saqqara (c. 500–30 BC)*. Warminster: Aris & Phillips Limited.
1974b "The Archives of the Sacred Animal Necropolis at North Saqqâra. A Progress Report," *JEA* 60: 256–68.
1976 "Preliminary Report on Excavations in the Sacred Animal Necropolis, Season 1974–1975," *JEA* 62: 14–17.

Smith, H. S. and Jeffreys, D. G.
1977 "The Sacred Animal Necropolis, North Saqqâra: 1975/6," *JEA* 63: 20–28.

Smith, H. S. and Kuhrt, A.
1982 "A Letter to a Foreign General," *JEA* 68: 199–209.

Smith, H. S. and Tait, W. J.
1981 "15. Demotic Letter," in *Papyri Greek & Egyptian, Edited by Various Hands in Honour of Eric Gardner Turner on the Occasion of his Seventieth Birthday*, edited by P. J. Parsons and J. R. Rea. GRM, vol. 68. London: EES, pp. 75–79.
1983 *Saqqara Demotic Papyri I (P. Dem. Saq. I)*. Texts from Excavations, Seventh Memoir. Excavations at North Saqqara, Documentary Series, vol. 5. Oxford: EES.
1984 "A Proposal to Undertake Tax-Administration for a District Official," *Enchoria* 12: 43–49.

Smith, Mark
1977 "A New Version of a Well-known Egyptian Hymn," *Enchoria* 7: 115–49.
1987 *The Mortuary Texts of Papyrus BM 10507, Catalogue of Demotic Papyri in the British Museum*, vol. 3. London: The Trustees of the British Museum.
1988 "Four Demotic Ostraca in the Collection of the Ashmolean Museum," *Enchoria* 16: 77–88.
1991 "Did Psammetichus I Die Abroad?" *OLP* 22: 101–09.

Sottas, Henri

1921 *Papyrus démotiques de Lille*. Paris: Libraire Paul Geuthner.

Spalinger, Anthony J.

1977a "Egypt and Babylonia: A Survey (620 B.C. – 550 B.C.)," *SAK* 5: 221–44.

1977b "On the Bentresh Stela and Related Problems," *SSEAJ* 8: 11–18.

1978a "The Reign of King Chabbash: An Interpretation," *ZÄS* 105: 142–54.

1978b "The Concept of the Monarchy during the Saite Epoch — An Essay of Synthesis," *Orientalia* 47: 12–36.

1979a "The Civil War Between Amasis and Apries and the Babylonian Attack Against Egypt," in *Acts of the 1st International Congress of Egyptologists*, edited by Walter F. Reineke. Schriften zur Geschichte und Kultur des Alten Orients, vol. 14. Berlin: Akademie-Verlag, pp. 593–604.

1979b "The Military Background of the Campaign of Piye (Piankhy)," *SAK* 7: 273–302.

Spiegelberg, Wilhelm

1901 *Aegyptische und Griechische Eigennamen aus Mumienetiketten der römischen Kaiserzeit*. Demotische Studien, vol. 1. Leipzig: J. C. Hinrichs'sche Buchhandlung.

1902 *Demotische Papyrus aus de Königlichen Museen zu Berlin*. Leipzig: Giesecke und Devrient

1903a "Das na der Ortsbezeichnung," *Sphinx* 6: 86–88.

1903b *Griechische Urkunden, Band III*. Ägyptische Urkunden, Königliche Museen zu Berlin. Berlin: Weidmann.

1904 *Die demotischen Denkmäler, I: Die demotischen Inschriften*. CGC, vol. 73. Leipzig: W. Drugulin.

1905 "Papyrus Erbach. Ein demotisches Brieffragment," *ZÄS* 42: 43–60.

1908a *Die demotischen Denkmäler, II: Die demotischen Papyri*. CGC, vol. 74. Straßburg: Buchdruckerei M. Dumont Schauberg.

1908b "Demotische Miscellen," *RdT* 30: 144–59.

1910 *Der Sagenkreis des Königs Petubastis*. 2 vols. Demotische Studien, vol. 3. Leipzig: J. C. Hinrichs'sche Buchhandlung.

1911 "Aus der Straßburger Sammlung demotischer Ostraka," *ZÄS* 49: 34–41.

1912a "Zwei Kalksteinplatten mit demotischen Texten," *ZÄS* 50: 32–36.

1912b "Denkstein einer Kultgenossenschaft in Dender aus der Zeit des Augustus," *ZÄS* 50: 36–39.

1912c *Demotische Texte auf Krügen*. Demotische Studien, vol. 5. Leipzig: J. C. Hinrichs'sche Buchhandlung.

1913 "Zu den beiden demotischen Kalksteinplatten," *ZÄS* 51: 137–38.

1914a "Eine Urkunde über die Eröffnung eines Steinbruchs unter Ptolemaios XIII," *ZÄS* 51: 65–75.

Spiegelberg, Wilhelm (*cont.*)

1914b Die sogenannte Demotische Chronik des Pap. 215 der Bibliothèque Nationale zu Paris. Demotische Studien, vol. 7. Leipzig: J. C. Hinrichs'sche Buchhandlung.

1918a "Der ägyptische Possessivartikel," *ZÄS* 54: 104–10.

1918b "Das Heiligtum der zwei Brüder in Oxyrhynchus," *ZÄS* 54: 140.

1922a *Der demotische Text der Priesterdekrete von Kanopus und Memphis (Rosettana) mit den hieroglyphischen und griechischen Fassungen und deutscher Ubersetzung nebst demotischen Glossar*. Heidelberg: Im Selbstverlag des Verfassers.

1922b "Der Stratege Pamenches (mit einem Anhang über die bisher aus ägyptischen Texten bekannt gewordenen Strategen)," *ZÄS* 57: 88–92.

1925 "Zu den griechischen Übersetzungen ägyptischer Eigennamen," in *Ägyptologische Mitteilungen*. Sitzungsberichte der Bayerischen Akademie der Wissenschaften, Philosophisch-philologische und historische Klasse, Jahrgang 1925, 2. Abhandlung. Munich: Verlag der Bayerischen Akademie der Wissenschaften, pp. 6–8.

1927 "Die Falkenbezeichnung des Verstorbenen in der Spätzeit," *ZÄS* 62: 27–34.

1928 *Demotica II*. Sitzungsberichte der Bayerischen Akademie der Wissenschaften, Philosophisch-philologische und historische Klasse, Jahrgang 1928, Nr. 2. Abhandlung. Munich: Verlag der Bayerischen Akademie der Wissenschaften, pp. 3–57.

1930 "Eine neue Erwähnung eines Aufstandes in Oberägypten in der Ptolemäerzeit," *ZÄS* 65: 53–57.

1931 *Die demotischen Papyri Loeb*. Munich: C. H. Beck'sche Verlagsbuchhandlung.

1932 *Die demotischen Denkmäler, III: Demotische Inschriften und Papyri*. CGC, vol. 76. Berlin: Reichsdruckerei.

Springer, Ernst

1885 "Die Sicherungsklauseln der koptischen Rechtsurkunden," *ZÄS* 23: 132–44.

Steinwenter, Artur

1920 *Studien zu den koptischen Rechtsurkunde aus Oberägypten*. Studien zur Palaeographie und Papyruskunde, vol. 19. Leipzig: Verlag H. Haessel.

1929–30 "Zur Lehre von der episcopalis audentia," *Byzantinische Zeitschrift* 30: 660–68.

1935 "Das byzantinische Dialysis-Formular," in *Studi in memoria di Aldo Albertoni*, vol. 1, edited by Pietro Ciapessoni. Padua: Casa Editrice Dott. Antonio Milani, pp. 71–94.

1951 "Zum Problem der Kontinuität zwischen antiken und mittelalterlichen Rechtsordnungen," *Iura* 2: 15–43.

1955 *Das Recht der koptischen Urkunden*. Handbuch der Altertumswissenschaft, vol. 10. Munich: C. H. Beck'sche Verlagsbuchhandlung.

1956 "Die Stellung der Bischöfe in der byzantinischen Verwaltung Ägyptens," in *Studi in onore di Pietro de Francisci*, vol. 1. Milan: Dott. Antonio Giuffrè, pp. 77–99.

Steuer, Robert O.
1948 "*wḫdw* Aetiological Principle of Pyaemia in Ancient Egyptian Medicine," *Supplement to the Bulletin of the History of Medicine*, no. 10. Baltimore: The Johns Hopkins University Press.

Steuer, Robert O. and Saunders, J. B. de C. M.
1959 *Ancient Egyptian and Cnidian Medicine*. Berkeley and Los Angeles: The University of California Press.

Stewart, H. F.
1965 *Pascal's Pensées*. New York: Pantheon Books.

Stricker, B. H.
1959 "Graeco-Agyptische private sculptuur," *OMRO* 40: 1–16.

Strong, Donald
1976 *Roman Art*. The Pelican History of Art, vol. 39. Baltimore: Penguin Books.

Strzygowski, Josef
1904 *Koptische Kunst. Catalogue générale des antiquités égyptiennes du Musée du Caire, Nos. 7001–7394 et 8742–9200*. CGC, vol. 12. Vienna: A. Holzhausen.

Swiggers, Pierre and Wouters, Alfons
1990 "Langues, situations linguistiques et reflexions sur le langage dans l'antiquité," in *Le langage dans l'antiquité*, edited by Pierre Swiggers and Alfons Wouters. La Pensée Linguistique, tome 3. Louvain: Leuven University Press, pp. 10–46.

Tait, John Gavin
1930 *Greek Ostraca in the Bodleian Library at Oxford and Various Other Collections. Volume I*. GRM, vol. 21. London: EES.

Tait, W. J.
1976 "The Fable of Sight and Hearing in the Demotic *Kufi* Text," *AcOr* 37: 27–44.

1977 *Papyri from Tebtunis in Egyptian and in Greek (P. Tebt. Tait)*. Texts from Excavations, Third Memoir. London: EES.

1982 Review of *Das ptolemäische Ägypten: Akten des internationalen Symposions* edited by Herwig Maehler and Volker Michael Strocka. *BiOr* 39: 78–87.

1984 "A Demotic List of Temple and Court Occupations: P. Carlsberg 23," in *Grammata Demotika. Festschrift für Erich Lüddeckens zum 15. Juni 1983*, edited by Heinz-Josef Thissen and Karl-Theodor Zauzich. Würzburg: Gisela Zauzich Verlag, pp. 211–33.

Taylor, John H.
1988 "Tanis Under the Greeks and Romans," in *Gold of the Pharaohs. Catalogue of the Exhibition of Treasures from Tanis. City of Edinburgh Art Centre 2 February – 30 April 1988*, edited by Herbert Coutts. Edinburgh: City of Edinburgh Museums and Art Galliers, pp. 90–97.

Tcherikover, Victor
1937 "Palestine under the Ptolemies (A Contribution to the Study of the Zenon Papyri)," *Mizraim* 4–5: 9–90.

1950 "Syntaxis and Laographia," *JJP* 4: 179–207.

Thieme, Marjolein and Pestman, P. W.

1978 "Cloth from the Mummy of Hierax," in *Textes grecs, démotiques et bilingues*, edited by E. Boswinkel and P. W. Pestman. PLB, vol. 19. Louvain: E. J. Brill, pp. 134–36.

Thissen, Heinz-Joseph

1977 "Zur Familie des Strategen Monkores," *ZPE* 27: 181–91.

1980 "Chronologie der frühdemotischen Papyri," *Enchoria* 10: 105–25.

1984 *Die Lehre des Anchscheschonqi (P. BM 10508). Einleitung, Übersetzung, Indices.* Papyrologische Texte und Abhandlung, Band 32. Bonn: Habelt.

1986 "Demotische Urkunden," in *Griechische und Demotische Papyri der Universitäts-bibliothek Freiburg*, edited by Robert W. Daniel, Michael Gronewald, and Heinz-Joseph Thissen. Mitteilung aus der Freiburger Papyrussammlung, vol. 4. Papyrologische Texte und Abhandlung, Band 38. Bonn: Dr. Rudolf Habelt GmbH, pp. 79–97.

1989 "Der verkommene Harfenspieler," *ZPE* 77: 227–40.

Thomas, J. David

1970 "Unedited Merton Papyri. I," *JEA* 56: 172–78.

1975a "A Re-edition of *P. Oxy.* II 320," *ZPE* 16: 309–14.

1975b *The Epistrategus of Ptolemaic and Roman Egypt, Part I: The Ptolemaic Epistrategus*. Papyrologica Coloniensia, vol. 6. Opladen: Westdeutscher Verlag.

1978 "Aspects of the Ptolemaic Civil Service: The Dioiketes and the Nomarch," in *Das ptolemäische Ägypten. Akten des internationalen Symposions 27.–29. September 1976 in Berlin*, edited by Herwig Maehler and Volker Michael Strocka. Mainz am Rhein: Verlag Philipp von Zabern, pp. 187–94.

Thomas, Thelma K.

1989 "An Introduction to the Sculpture of Late Roman and Early Byzantine Egypt," in *Beyond the Pharaohs: Egypt and the Copts in the 2nd to 7th Centuries A.D*, edited by Florence D. Friedman. Providence, RI: Museum of Art, Rhode Island School of Design, pp. 54–64.

1990 *Niche Decorations form the Tombs of Byzantine Egypt (Heracleopolis Magna and Oxyrhynchus, A.D. 300–600): Visions of the Afterlife*. Ph.D. dissertation, New York University.

Thompson Crawford, Dorothy J.

1984 "The Idumaeans of Memphis and the Ptolemaic *Politeumata*," in *Atti del XVII congresso internazionale di papirologia*, vol. 3, Naples: Centro Internationale per lo Studio dei Papiri Ercolanesi, pp. 1069–75.

Thompson, David L.

1978–79 "A Painted Triptych from Roman Egypt," *The J. Paul Getty Museum Journal* 6–7: 185–92.

1982 *Mummy Portraits in the J. Paul Getty Museum.* Malibu: The J. Paul Getty Museum.

Thompson, Dorothy J.

1988 *Memphis under the Ptolemies.* Princeton: Princeton University Press.

—— "Literacy in Early Ptolemaic Egypt," in *Proceedings of the Nineteenth International Congress of Papyrology*, edited by Jean Bingen (forthcoming).

Thompson, Sir Herbert

1913 *Theban Ostraca. Part III: Demotic Texts*, edited by Alan H. Gardiner, Herbert Thompson, and J. G. Milne. University of Toronto Studies. Toronto: The University of Toronto Library.

1934 *A Family Archive from Siut*, 2 vols. Oxford: Oxford University Press.

1940 "Two Demotic Self-Dedications," *JEA* 26: 68–78.

1965 "Self-Dedications," in *Actes du Ve congrés international de papyrology, Oxford, 30 août – 3 septembre 1937*. Brussels: Fondation Égyptologique Reine Élisabeth, pp. 497–504.

Thür, Gerhard and Pieler, Peter E.

1978 "Gerichtsbarkeit," in *Reallexikon für Antike und Christentum. Sachwörterbuch zur Auseinandersetzung des Christentums mit der antiken Welt. Band X: Genesis – Gigant*, edited by Theodor Klauser, Carsten Colpe, Ernst Dassman, Albrecht Dihle, Bernhard Kötting, Wolfgang Speyer, and Jan Hendrik Waszink. Stuttgart: Anton Hiersmann, cols. 360–492.

Till, Walter Curt

1955 *Die Gnostischen Schriften des Koptischen Papyrus Berolinensis 8502*. Texte und Untersuchungen zur Geschichte der altchristlichen Literatur, Band 60. Berlin: Akademie-Verlag.

Torp, Hjalmar

1969 "Leda Christiana: The Problem of the Interpretation of Coptic Sculpture with Mythological Motifs," *AAAHP* 4: 101–12.

Trigger, Bruce G.

1965 *History and Settlement in Lower Nubia*. Yale University Publications in Anthropology, no. 69. New Haven: Department of Anthropology, Yale University.

Tsiparis, Christos

1979 *Ostraca Lundensia. Ostraca aus der Sammlung des Instituts für Altertumskunde an der Universität zu Lund*. Lund: Tryckbaren.

Turner, Eric Gardner

1974 "A Commander-in-Chief's Order from Saqqâra," *JEA* 60: 239–42.

Übel, Fritz

1966 "Die frühptolemäische Salzsteuer," in *Atti dell'XI congresso internationale di papirologia, Milano, 2–8 settembre 1965*, edited by Aristide Claderini, Ignazio Cazzaniga, Silvio Curto, Orsolina Montevecchi, and Mariangela Vandoni. Milan: Istituto Lombardo di Scienze e Lettere, pp. 325–68.

1968 *Die Kleruchen Ägyptens unter den ersten sechs Ptolemäern*. Abhandlungen der Deutschen Akademie der Wissenschaften zu Berlin, Klasse für Sprachen, Literatur und Kunst, Jahrgang 1968, Nr. 3. Berlin: Akademie-Verlag.

1969 "Ostraka aus frühptolemäischer Zeit," *AfP* 19: 62–73.

Vaggi, Giuseppina
1937 "Siria e Siri nei documenti dell'egitto greco-romano," *Aegyptus* 17: 29–51.

Vanderlip, Vera Fredericka
1972 *The Four Greek Hymns of Isidorus and the Cult of Isis*. American Studies in Papyrology, vol. 12. Toronto: A. M. Hakkert Ltd.

Vandersleyen, Claude
1971 *Les guerres d'Amosis*. MRE, vol. I. Brussels: Fondation Égyptologique Reine Élisabeth.

van de Walle, Baudouin
1948 *La transmission des textes littéraires égyptiens*. Brussels: Fondation Égyptologique Reine Élisabeth.

Vandoni, Mariangela
1975 "Dall'archivio del tessitore Trifone," *Proceedings of the XIV International Congress of Papyrologists, Oxford 24–31 July 1974*, edited by P. J. Parsons, J. R. Rea, and E. G. Turner. GRM, no. 61. London: EES, pp. 331–36.

Vandorpe, Katelijn
1986 *Het "Erbstreit"-archief. Een tweetalig archief uit Pathyris (2e eeuw v.Chr.).* Ph.D. dissertation, Katholieke Universiteit Leuven.

van Maele, Beatrijs
1982 *De Egyptische naam "De twee broers" in Griekse transcriptie* (unpublished study).

van Minnen, Peter
1986 "A Change of Names in Roman Egypt after A.D. 202? A Note on P. Amst. I 72," *ZPE* 62: 87–92.

Van't Dack, Edmond
1948 "La toparchie dans l'Égypte ptolémaïque," *CdE* 23: 147–61.

1949 "Recherches sur l'administration du nome dans la Thébaïde au temps des Lagides," *Aegyptus* 29: 3–44.

1951 "Recherches sur les institutions de village en Égypte ptolémaïque," in *Ptolemaica*, edited by L. Cerfaux and W. Peremans. Studia Hellenistica, vol. 7. Louvain: Orientaliste, pp. 5–38.

1976 "Sur l'évolution des institutions militaires Lagides," in *Armées et fiscalité dans le monde antique. Actes du colloque national, Paris, 14–16 Octobre 1976*. Colloques Nationaux du Centre National de la Recherche Scientifique, no. 936. Paris: Éditions du Centre National de la Recherche Scientifique, pp. 77–105.

1988 *Ptolemaica Selecta. Études sur l'armée et l'administration lagides*. Studia Hellenistica, vol. 29. Louvain: Universitas Catholica Lovaniensis.

1989 "Les armées en cause," in *The Judean-Syrian-Egyptian Conflict of 103–101 B.C.: A Multilingual Dossier Concerning a "War of Sceptres,"* by E. Van't Dack, W. Clarysse, G. Cohen, J. Quaegebeur, and J. K. Winnicki. Collectanea Hellenistica I. Brussels: Comité Klassieke Studies, Subcomité Hellenisme, Koninklijke Academie voor Wetenschappen, Letteren en Schone Kunsten van België, pp. 127–36.

—— "Prosopographia Ptolemaica. Sa place dans le système prosopographique, problèmes de méthode," in *Proceedings of the Nineteenth International Congress of Papyrology*, edited by Jean Bingen (forthcoming).

Van't Dack, Edmond and Hauben, Hans

1978 "L'apport égyptien à l'armée navale Lagide," in *Das ptolemäische Ägypten. Akten des internationalen Symposions 27.–29. September 1976 in Berlin*, edited by Herwig Maehler and Volker Michael Strocka. Mainz am Rhein: Verlag Philipp von Zabern, pp. 59–94.

Ventre Pacha

1896 "Crues modernes et crues anciennes du Nil," *ZÄS* 34: 95–107.

Vercoutter, J.

1949 "Les haou-nebout ()," *BIFAO* 48: 107–209.

Vergote, Jozef

1954 *Les noms propres du P. Bruxelles Inv. E. 7616: essai d'interprétation*. PLB, vol. 7. Leiden: E. J. Brill.

1960 *De oplossing van een gewichtig probleem: de vocalisatie van de Egyptische werkwoordsvormen*. Mededelingen van de Koninklijke Vlaamse Academie voor Wetenschappen, Letteren en Schone Kunsten van België. Klasse der Letteren Jaargang 22, 1960, Nr. 7. Brussels: Koninklijke Vlaamse Academie voor Wetenschappen.

1962 "Le roi Moiris-Marēs," *ZÄS* 87: 66–76.

1973 *Grammaire copte. Tome 1a. Introduction, phonétique et phonologie, morphologie synthématique (structure des sémantèmes. Partie synchronique)*. Louvain: Éditions Peeters.

Vernus, Pascal

1986 *Le surnom au moyen empire: répertoire, procedes d'expression et structures de la double identité du début de la XIIe dynastie à la fin de la XVIIe dynastie.* Studia Pohl, vol. 13. Rome: Biblical Institute Press.

1990 "Entre néo-égyptien et démotique: la langue utilisée dans la traduction du rituel de repousser l'agressif (études sur la diglossie I)," *RdE* 41: 153–208.

Viereck, Paul

1928 *Philadelphiea. Die Gründung einer hellenistischen Militärkolonie in Ägypten.* Morgenland. Darstellung aus Geschichte und Kultur des Orients, heft 16. Leipzig: J. C. Hinrichs'sche Buchhandlung.

Vila, André

1980 *La nécropole de Missiminia I: Les sépultures napatéennes*. La prospection archéologique de la vallée du Nil au sud de la cataracte de Dal (Nubie Soudanaise), vol. 12. Paris: Centre National de la Recherche Scientifique.

Vitelli, Girolamo, ed.

1929 *Papiri greci e latini*, Volume IX. Florence: Società Italiana per la Ricerca dei Papiri Greci e Latini in Egitto.

Vleeming, Sven P.

1983 "Two Underground Greek Concepts in Demotic P.B.M. 10597," *CdE* 58: 97–99.

Vleeming, Sven P. (*cont.*)

1984 "The Village Scribes of Pathyris," in *Atti del XVII congresso internazionale di papirologia*, vol. 3, Naples: Centro Internationale per lo Studio dei Papiri Ercolanesi, pp. 1053–56.

1987 "Two Greek-Demotic Notes," *Enchoria* 15: 155–62.

1980 "The Sale of a Slave in the Time of the Pharaoh Py," *OMRO* 61: 1–17.

Vogliano, Achille

1939 "Madinet Madi. Fouilles de l'Université Royale de Milan," *CdE* 14: 87–89.

Vogliano, Achille; Cinotti, Amalia; and Colombo, Anna Maria

1953 "Papyrologica," in *Studi in onore di Vincenzo Arangio-Ruiz nel XLV anno del suo insegnamento*, vol. 2. Naples: Editore Jovene, pp. 497–526.

Volten, Aksel

1951 "The Papyrus-Collection of the Egyptological Institute of Copenhagen," *ArOr* 19: 70–74.

1952 "An 'Alphabetical' Dictionary and Grammar in Demotic," *ArOr* 20: 496–508.

1956 "Der demotische Petubastisroman und seine Beziehung zur griechischen Literatur," in *Akten des VIII. internationalen Kongresses für Papyrologie Wien 1955*, edited by Hans Gerstinger. MPER, vol. 5. Vienna: Georg Prachner Verlag, pp. 147–52.

1962 *Ägypter und Amazonen: eine demotische Erzahlung des Inaros-Petubastis-Kreises aus zwei Papyri der Österreichischen Nationalbibliothek, (Pap. Dem. Vindob. 6165 und 6165A)*. MPER, vol. 6. Vienna: Georg Prachner Verlag.

von Beckerath, Jürgen

1966 "The Nile Records at Karnak and their Importance for the History of the Libyan Period (Dynasties XXII and XXIII)," *JARCE* 5: 43–55.

von Bissing, Friedrich W.

1901 *Der Bericht des Diodor uber die Pyramiden (Bibl. I 63.2–64)*. Berlin: Verlag von Alexander Duncker.

1914 *Denkmäler ägyptischer Sculptur*, 2 vols. Munich: F. Bruckmann A.-G.

1950 "Tombeaux d'époque romain à Akhmîm," *ASAE* 50: 547–84.

von Staden, Heinrich

1989 *Herophilos: The Art of Medicine in Early Alexandria*. Cambridge: Cambridge University Press.

Walbank, Frank W.

1979 "Egypt in Polybius," in *Glimpses of Ancient Egypt: Studies in Honour of H. W. Fairman*, edited John Ruffle, G. A. Gaballa, and Kenneth A. Kitchen. Warminster: Aris and Philipps Ltd., pp. 180–89.

Wallace, Samuel LeRoy

1938a *Taxation in Roman Egypt*. Princeton University Studies in Papyrology. Princeton: Princeton University Press.

1938b "Census and Poll Tax in Ptolemaic Egypt," *AJPh* 59: 418–42.

Wallet-Lebrun, Christiane
1985 "A propos d'*WB3*: note lexicographique," *GM* 85: 67–88.

Wångstedt, Sten V.
1957 "Aus der demotischen Ostrakonsammlung zu Uppsala II," *OrSu* 6: 9–20.

1968 "Demotische Steuerquittungen nebst Texten andersartigen Inhalts," *OrSu* 16: 22–56.

1969 "Demotische Ostraka aus ptölemaisch-römischer Zeit," *OrSu* 18: 69–100.

1971–72 "Demotische Steuerquittungen aus ptolemäisch-römischer Zeit," *OrSu* 19–20: 23–53.

1974–75 "Demotische Bescheinigung über Begräbnissteuer," *OrSu* 23–24: 7–43.

1984 "Ein demotischer Denkstein aus Dendera," in *Grammata Demotika: Festschrift für Erich Lüddeckens zum 15. Juni 1983*, edited by Heinz-Josef Thissen and Karl-Theodor Zauzich. Würzburg: Gisela Zauzich Verlag, pp. 271–73.

Weiss, Egon
1908 "Communio pro diviso und pro indiviso in den Papyri," *AfP* 4: 330–65.

Wenig, Steffen
1967 "Bemerkungen zur Chronologie des Reiches von Meroe," *MIO* 13: 1–44.

Wente, Edward F.
1971 "Mysticism in Pharaonic Egypt?," *JNES* 41: 161–79.

1973 "The Quarrel of Apophis and Seknenre," in *The Literature of Ancient Egypt*, edited by William Kelly Simpson. New Haven: Yale University Press, pp. 77–80.

Wessel, Klaus
1963 *Koptische Kunst. Die Spätantike in Ägypten.* Recklinghausen: Verlag Aurel Bongers.

Wessel, Klaus, ed.
1964 *Christentum am Nil. Internationale Arbeitstagung zur Austellung "Koptische Kunst," Essen, Villa Hügel, 23.–25. Juli 1963.* Recklinghausen: Verlag Aurel Bongers.

Wessely, Carl
1904 *Topographie des Faijûm (Arsinoites Nomus) in griechischer Zeit.* Vienna: C. Gerold's sohn.

Wessetsky, Vilmos
1977 "An der Grenze von Literatur und Geschichte," in *Fragen an die altägyptischer Literatur und Geschichte Studien zum Gedenken an Eberhard Otto*, edited by Jan Assmann, Erika Feucht, and Reinhard Grieshammer. Wiesbaden: Dr. Ludwig Reichert Verlag, pp. 499–502.

West, Stephanie
1969 "The Greek Version of the Legend of Tefnut," *JEA* 55: 161–83.

Whitehorne, John E. G.
1984 "Tryphon's Second Marriage (*P Oxy.* II 267)," in *Atti del XVII congresso internationale di papirologia*, vol. 3. Naples: Centro Internationale per lo Studio dei Papiri Ercolanesi, pp. 1267–74.

Wilcken, Ulrich

1899 *Griechische Ostraka aus Aegypten und Nubien. Ein Beitrag zur antiken Wirtschaftsgeschichte*. 2 vols. Leipzig and Berlin: Giesecke and Devrient.

1903 "Die Berliner Papyrusgrabungen in Herakleopolis Magna im Winter 1898/9," *AfP* 2: 294–336.

1908 "Aus der Straßburger Sammlung," *AfP* 4: 115–47.

1912a *Grundzüge und Chrestomathie der Papyruskunde. Erster Band: Historischer Teil, Erste Hälfte: Grundzüge*. Leipzig and Berlin: B. G. Teubner.

1912b *Grundzüge und Chrestomathie der Papyruskunde. Erster Band: Historischer Teil, Zweite Hälfte: Chrestomathie*. Leipzig and Berlin: B. G. Teubner.

1913 "Ein Gymnasium in Omboi," *AfP* 5: 410–16.

1925 "Zur Trierarchie im Lagidenreich," in *Raccolta di scritti in onore di Giacomo Lumbroso (1844–1925)*, edited by Pietro Bonfanto et al. Pubblicazioni Scientifiche di Aegyptus, vol. 3. Milan: Aegyptus, pp. 93–99.

1927 *Urkunden der Ptolemäerzeit (Ältere Funde), Erster Band*. Berlin and Leipzig: Walter de Gruyter and Company.

1935 *Urkunden der Ptolemäerzeit (Ältere Funde), Zweiter Band*. Berlin and Leipzig: Walter de Gruyter and Company.

Wildung, Dietrich

1977 *Imhotep und Amenhotep. Gotterwerdung im alten Ägypten*. Münchner Ägyptologische Studien, vol. 36. Munich: Deutscher Kunstverlag.

Wilfong, Terry

1990 "The Archive of a Family of Moneylenders from Jême," *BASP* 27: 163–81.

Wilkinson, Alex

1971 *Ancient Egytpian Jewelry*. London: Methuen and Co. Ltd.

Williams, Bruce B.

1990 *Excavations Between Abu Simbel and the Sudan Frontier, Part 7: Twenty-fifth Dynasty and Napatan Remains at Qustul: Cemeteries W and V*. OINE, vol. 7. Chicago: The Oriental Institute.

Williams, Ronald J.

1977 "Some Fragmentary Demotic Wisdom Texts," in *Studies in Honor of George R. Hughes, January 12, 1977*, edited by Janet H. Johnson and Edward F. Wente. SAOC, vol. 39. Chicago: The Oriental Institute, pp. 263–71.

1981 "The Sages of Ancient Egypt in the Light of Recent Scholarship," *JAOS* 101: 1–19.

Winnicki, Jan K.

1972 "Ein ptolemäischer Offizier in Thebais," *Eos* 60: 343–53.

1977 "Die Kalasirier der spätdynastischen und der ptolemäischen Zeit," *Historia* 26: 257–68.

1985 "Die Ägypter und das Ptolemäerheer," *Aegyptus* 65: 41–55.

1986 "Zwei Studien über die Kalasirier," *OLP* 17: 17–32.

1989a "Das ptolemäische und hellenistische Heerwesen," in *Egitto e storia antica dall'ellenismo all'età araba. Atti del colloquio internazionale, Bologna, 31 agosto – 2 settembre 1987*, edited by Lucia Criscuolo and Giovanni Geraci. Bologna: Cooperativa Libraria Universitaria Editrice, pp. 213–30.

1989b "Militäroperationen von Ptolemaios I. und Seleukos I. in Syrien in den Jahren 312–311 v.Chr. (I)," *Ancient Society* 20: 55–92.

1990 "Bericht von einem Feldzug des Ptolemaios Philadelphos in der Pithom-Stele," *JJP* 20: 157–67.

—— A "Militäroperationen von Ptolemaios I. und Seleukos I. in Syrien in den Jahren 312–311 v.Chr. (II)," *Ancient Society* 22 (forthcoming).

—— B "Die von Persern entführten Götterbilder," *ZPE* (forthcoming).

Winter, Erich

1981 "The Temple of Dendur and its Religious Significance," in the Supplement to *Les temples immergés de la Nubie: The Temple of Dendur*, edited by A. M. Blackman. (Reprint of 1911 Original) Cairo: Dar el-Maaref, pp. 373–82.

1991 "Hieroglyphen," in *Reallexikon für Antike und Christentum. Sachwörterbuch zur Auseinandersetzung des Christentums mit der antiken Welt. Band XV: Hibernia – Hoffnung*, edited by Ernest Dassmann, Carsten Colpe, Albrecht Dihle, Josef Engemann, Bernhard Kötting, Wolfgang Speyer, and Klaus Thraede. Stuttgart: Anton Hiersmann, cols. 83–103.

Wipszycka, Ewa W.

1988 "La christianisation de l'Égypte aux IVe–VIe siècles. Aspects sociaux et etniques," *Aegyptus* 68: 117–65.

Wolff, Hans Julius

1939 *Written and Unwritten Marriages in Hellenistic and Postclassical Roman Law*. Philological Monographs, no. 9. Haverford, PA: American Philological Association.

1970 *Das Justizwesen der Ptolemäer*. 2nd ed. MBP, vol. 44. Munich: C. H. Beck'sche Verlagsbuchhandlung.

1978 *Das Recht der griechischen Papyri Ägyptens in der Zeit der Ptolemäer und des Prinzipats*, 2 vols. Handbuch der Altertumswissenschaft, Abteilung 10: Rechtsgeschichte des Altertums, Teil 5, Band 2. Munich: C. H. Beck'sche Verlagsbuchhandlung.

Wouters, Alfons

1979 *The Grammatical Papyri from Graeco-Roman Egypt. Contributions to the Study of the "Ars Grammatica" in Antiquity*. Verhandelingen van de Koninklijke Academie voor Wetenschappen, Letteren en Kunsten, Klasse der Letteren, Jaargang 41, 1979, Nr. 92. Brussels: Paleis der Academien.

Wulff, Oskar Konstantin

1918 *Altchristliche und byzantinische Kunst I: Die altchrisliche Kunst*. Berlin-Neubabelsberg: Akademische Verlagsgesellschaft Athenaion m.b.h.

Yaron, Reuven

1958 "Aramaic Marriage Contracts from Elephantine," *JSS* 3: 1–39.

Yaron, Reuven (*cont.*)

1961 Introduction to the Law of the Aramaic Papyri. Oxford: The Clarendon Press.

Youtie, Herbert C.

1970 "Callimachus in the Tax Rolls," in *Proceedings of the XII International Congress of Papyrology*, edited by Deborah H. Samuel. American Studies in Papyrology, vol. 7. Toronto: A. M. Hakkert, Ltd., pp. 545–51.

1973 *Scriptiunculae, Volume II*. Amsterdam: A. M. Hakkert.

1975 "ΑΠΑΤΟΡΕΣ: Law vs. Custom in Roman Egypt," in *Le monde grec: pensée, litterature, histoire, documents: hommages a Claire Préaux*, edited by Jean Bingen, Guy Cambier, and Georges Nachtergael. Brussels: Éditions de l'Université de Bruxelles, pp. 723–40.

1976 "Paniskos and his Wife's Name," *ZPE* 21: 193–96.

1981 *Scriptiunculae posteriores*, vol. I. Bonn: Habelt.

Yoyotte, Jean

1955 "Une étude sur l'anthroponymie gréco-égyptienne du nome Prosôpite," *BIFAO* 55: 125–40.

1958 "Notes de toponymie egyptienne," *MDAIK* 16: 414–30.

1962a "Études géographiques II: les localités méridionales de la region memphite et le 'Pehou d'Héracléopolis'," *RdE* 14: 75–111.

1962b "Processions géographiques mentionnant le Fayoum et ses localités," *BIFAO* 61: 79–138.

1969 "Bakhtis — religion égyptienne ey culture grecque à Edfou," *Religions en Égypte hellénistique et romaine. Colloque de Strasbourg 16–18 mai 1967*, edited by Ph. Derchain. Paris: Presses Universitaires de France, pp. 127–41.

1972a "La localisation de Ouenkhem," *BIFAO* 71: 1–10.

1972b "Les inscriptions hiéroglyphiques. Darius et l'Égypte," *JA* 260: 253–66.

1989 "Le nom égyptien du 'ministre de l'économie' de Saïs à Méroé," *CRAIBL* 1989: 73–90.

Zaghloul, El-Hussein Omar M.

1985 *Frühdemotische Urkunden aus Hermupolis*. Bulletin of the Center of Papyrological Studies, vol. 2. Cairo: Center of Papyrological Studies of Ain Shams University.

Zaki Aly

1948 "A Dedicatory Stele from Naucratis," *EdP* 7: 73–92.

Zalateo, Giorgio

1961 "Papiri scolastici," *Aegyptus* 41: 160–235.

Zandee, Jan

1981 "'Die Lehre des Silvanus' und drei andere Schriften von Nag Hammadi (*Nag Hammadi-Codices* VII, 4 und II, 6; II, 7; VI, 3)," *MDAIK* 37: 515–31.

Zauzich, Karl-Theodor

1968 *Die Ägyptische Schreibertradition in Aufbau, Sprache und Schrift der demotischen Kaufvertäge aus Ptolemäischer Zeit*. 2 vols. Ägyptologische Abhandlungen, Band 19. Wiesbaden: Otto Harrassowitz.

1969 "Neue demotische Papyri in Berlin," in *XVII. deutscher Orientalistentag vom 21. bis 27. Juli 1968 in Würzburg*, edited by Wolfgang Voigt. *ZDMGS*, vol. 1. Wiesbaden: Franz Steiner Verlag GmbH, pp. 41–47.

1971 *Ägyptische Handschriften, Teil II*. Verzeichnis der orientalischen Handschriften in Deutschland, Band XIX, Nr. 2. Wiesbaden: Franz Steiner Verlag GmbH.

1974 "Spätdemotische Papyrusurkunden III," *Enchoria* 4: 71–82.

1976a "Demotische Fragmente zum Ahiqar-Roman," in *Folia Rara: Wolfgang Voigt LXV. Diem Natalem Celebranti*, edited by Herbert Franke, Walther Heissig, and Wolfgang Treue. Verzeichnis der orientalischen Handschriften in Deutschland, Supplementband 19. Wiesbaden: Franz Steiner Verlag GmbH, pp. 180–85.

1976b "Der Schreiber der Weissagung des Lammes," *Enchoria* 6: 127–28.

1977 "Spätdemotische Papyrusurkunden IV," *Enchoria* 7: 151–80.

1978 *Papyri von der Insel Elephantine*. Demotische Papyri aus den Staatlichen Museen zu Berlin, Lieferung 1. Berlin: Akademie-Verlag.

1979 "Einige Bemerkungen zu den demot. Papyri Louvre E. 3333 und E. 3334," *Enchoria* 9: 121–24.

1980 "Einige Bemerkungen zu der demotischen Bronzetafel von Dendera," *Enchoria* 10: 189–90.

1983 "Das Lamm des Bokchoris," in *Festschrift zum 100- jährigen Bestehen der Papyrussammlung der Österreichischen Nationalbibliothek: Papyrus Erzherzog Rainer (P. Rainer Cent.)*, edited by Josef Zessner-Spitzenberg. 2 vols. Vienna: Verlag Brüder Hollinek, pp. 165–74.

1986a "150 Jahre Enforschung demotischer Ostraka," *Enchoria* 14: 129–34.

1986b "Der Alexanderpriester des Jahres 210/9 v. Chr.," *Enchoria* 14: 161–62.

1987a "Eine Statueninschrift aus Soknopaiu Nesos," *Enchoria* 15: 215–17.

1987b "Das topographische Onomastikon im P. Kairo 31169," *GM* 99: 83–91.

1990 "Eine dennoch sinnvolle demotische Schülerübung," *Enchoria* 17: 163–66.

Ziegler, Christiane

1979 "Deux étoffes funéraires égyptiennes," *RdL* 4: 251–57.

Ziegler, Karl-Heinz

1971 *Das private Schiedsgericht im antiken römischen Recht*. MBP, vol. 58. Munich: C. H. Beck'sche Verlagsbuchhandlung.

Zilliacus, Henrik

1940 "Griechische Papyruskunden des VII. Jahrhunderts n. Chr.," *Eranos. Acta Philologica Suecana* 38: 79–107.

Zivie-Coche, Christiane M.

1987 "Les travaux de Panemerit et de Pikhaâs à Tanis," in *Cahiers de Tanis I*, edited by Philippe Brissaud. Éditions Recherche sur les Civilisations, vol. 75. Paris: Éditions Recherche sur les Civilisations, 177–88.

Zucker, Friedrich

1910 "Aegypten," *AA* n.s.: 244–56.

1937 *Doppelinschrift spätptolemäischer Zeit aus der Garnison von Hermopolis Magna*. Abhandlungen der Preussische Akademie der Wissenschaften, Philosophisch-Historische Klasse, Jahrgang 1937, Nr. 6. Berlin: Akademie der Wissenschaften.

1938 "Nachträge zur 'Doppelinschrift spätptolemäischer Zeit aus der Garnison von Hermopolis Magna'," *Aegyptus* 18: 279–84.

GENERAL INDEX

Monimos, 52, 326, 331

Monkores, 279

Mons Claudianus, 213

Mons Porphyrites, 213

Mont(h), 250–51, 266, 268
    Mnṯ, 250

Montesouphis, 110

mortgage, 1

mr, 65

mr-ꜣḥ.w Pꜣ(-nꜥ-ỉḥy/Pꜣ(-n)-sy(?) sꜣ ꜣrṯkš, 298

mr ḫꜣs.t, 250

mr-mšꜥ, 107–08, 295, 329–30
    mr-mšꜥ wr, 108

mr šn, 250

mšꜥ, 69, 121, 329, 362

mšꜥ=sn, 75

Mškmt, 364

Ms-wr, 166, 171

mṯn, 361

mtw=k s n ṯꜣy(n) pꜣ hrw r-ḥry šꜥ ḏt, 263

mtw=k s.t, 260
    mtw=k s, 260

mtw=(y) tỉ.t n=k, 262

mtw ḏd pꜣ ỉḳd, 14

mummy cartonnage, 149, 151, 237

Musta, 52

Mut, 79–81, 88, 208, 278

mutatis mutandis, 195

m wꜣḏ-wr, 82

mw.t=f, 356

myriaroure, 152–53

mysterium, 228

"Mythus vom Sonnenauge" (= Kufi), 305–06, 308

Mytrḫꜣ (?), 296, 299

nꜣ ꜥ(.wy).w, 245

nꜣ ꜥ(.wy).w mḥ.ṯ(w), 244

nꜣ ꜥ(.wy).w mḥ.ṯw, 245

nꜣ ḥḏ.w ỉ-ỉr ỉw, 238, 240

nꜣ ḥn.w … ḫr mṯk, 264

nꜣj(w), 127
    njw.t, 127–28

nꜣ Mdy.w, 295

nꜣ mr.w, 11

nꜣ wpti.w, 7

nꜣ wpṯy.w, 296

nꜣ Wy[nn.w], 296

Nꜥ-n=f-bꜣst.t, 363
    Nꜥ-n=f-imn, 363

Nabaireh, 68–69, 72–73, 80, 88

names, 22–23
    compound, 224
    Coptic, 213
    Demotic-derived, 224
    Egytpian, 133, 137, 140–44
    Greek, 51, 133–34, 136–37, 140–44
    Greek-Egyptian double names, 53–55
    rendering foreign names in Demotic script, 363
    Roman, 135, 140–44, 212f.
    royal names, 47–49
    theophoric, 240

Napatan kingdom, 147

Narmer, 18

Narmuthis, 119–24, 126–29; *see also* Medinet Madi
    Nꜣj-Rnn.t, 127
    Niw.t-Rnmwtj.t, 119, 127
    Niw.t-Rnmwt.t, 120

narratio, 2, 5

Natakamani, 17

Natho, 127
    Nꜣj-tꜣ-ḥwt, 127

Naukratis, 77, 82, 127, 133, 339
    Nꜣ(j)-Krṯ, 127
    dmḏ Krḏ, 127

Naunakhte, 7

INDEX OF GREEK WORDS AND PHRASES

ἐπὶ τοῦ ἐν Παθύρει ἀρχείου, 12
ἐπῷ ἀνδρῶν, 337
ερεῶν, 250
Ἑρμ[ά]φιλο[ς] Παμφίλου Φιλωτέρε[ος], 335
Ἑρμίου, 211
Ἑρμογένουϲ, 184
Ἑρμοπολίτηι, 338
Ἐσορ[ό]ηρις, 337
Ἑστία, 266
ἐϲτραγευμένοι, 135
ἐϲτρατευμένοι, 135
Εὐδαιμονίς, 352
Εὐδαίμων, 266
Εὐμενοῦς, 209
Εὐμήλου, 339
ζωνοφόροι, 162
ἡγεμόνες τῶν περὶ αὐΐλόὴν ἐπιλέκτων μαχίμων, 330
ἡγεμών, 334
ἡ μικρά, 335
ἡπητής, 42
ἡ πρὸς Αἰγύπτῳ, 327
Ἥρα, 266
Ἥραι, 209–10
Ἡράκλεια, 352
Ἡρακλεοπολίτου, 338
Ἡρακλῆς, 352
Ἡρακλ(ῆϲ) (ὁμοίωϲ) Ἶβιϲ, 137
Ἥραϲ, 192
Ἡρᾶτοϲ, 193
Ἥρων, 121, 352
Ἥρωνος, 266
ἡ τοῦ δεῖνος νομαρχία, 150
Ἡφαιστᾶς, 352
Θαήϲιοϲ, 193, 200
Θαῆϲιϲ, 192
θάλασσα, 73, 82
Θαυβάστις, 352
Θεαδέλφια, 54
Θεδώρα, 352
Θεμειτις, 271
Θερμουθέωνος, 245
Θερμούθιον, 189
Θέωνα, 352
Θέωνοϲ, 141, 145
Θηβάρχης, 246
Θοώνιοϲ, 200
ἰατρικόν, 53
ἰατρός, 42
ἰβιοβοσκοί, 126
Ἰβιών εἰκοσιπενταρούρων, 126
ἰδιόγραφοϲ ϲυνγραφή, 195
ἰδιόγραφοϲ ϲυγγραφή, 196
ἱερά ἀγάλματα, 328
Ἱέραξ, 266
ἱερεῖς, 159
Ἱππάρχωι, 152
Ἱπποδρόμου, 188
ἱπποκόμος, 42
Ἰϲάκι Ἰουδαίωι, 141–42
Ἶσει, 209
Ἰσιδώρα, 352
Ἰώϲηποϲ, 137
Καίσαρος, 41, 212
καὶ τῶι μ(υρι)αρού(ρωι) καὶ, 152
καὶ τῶι χ[.]κ, 152
Καλακάνθη, 271
Καλλικράτου, 209
Καρπ(ί)μη, 352
καρπῶναι, 137
κατ' ἄνδρα, 42

INDEX OF COPTIC WORDS

INDEX OF HEBREW WORDS

INDEX OF AUTHORS CITED

INDEX OF PAPYRI, OSTRACA, AND OBJECTS

PAPYRI

OSTRACA

OBJECTS

KEY TO THE OBJECTS INDEX

BO	=	Bowl	MI	=	Mirror
BU	=	Bust	MT	=	Mummy Tag
BZ	=	Bronze	NA	=	Naos
CA	=	Cartonnage	PA	=	Palette
CI	=	Coffin Inscription	PG	=	Pictorial Graffito
CO	=	Codex	PR	=	Parchment or Paper
FI	=	Figure; Figurine	PT	=	Painting
GO	=	Gold	SH	=	Shroud
GR	=	Graffito	SL	=	Stele; Stele Fragment
HS	=	Headstone (for burial)	ST	=	Statue
IN	=	Inscription	TA	=	Tablet
LD	=	Leather Document	TC	=	Terracotta

DATE DUE
